THE UNAUTHORISED AGENT

The focus of this book, the legal situation created when an agent acts without authority, is one of the most important issues in agency law. The analysis is divided into three sections: apparent authority, ratification and the liability of the *falsus procurator*. Adopting a unique comparative perspective, the contributions are drawn from many different legal systems, providing the opportunity for analysis of the European common law/civil law divide. The analysis extends beyond Europe, however, taking into account the mixed legal system of South Africa, as well as the United States. Finally, there is a useful consideration of the Principles of European Contract Law and the UNIDROIT Principles of International Commercial Contracts 2004. This book will be an invaluable guide for those interested in the study of comparative law, international practitioners and those interested in the harmonisation of European Private Law.

DANNY BUSCH is an attorney-at-law with De Brauw Blackstone Westbroek, Amsterdam, and a Senior Research Fellow in the Business & Law Research Centre, University of Nijmegen.

LAURA J. MACGREGOR is a Senior Lecturer and Director of the Edinburgh Centre for Commercial Law at the Law School, Edinburgh University.

THE UNAUTHORISED AGENT

Perspectives from European
and Comparative Law

Edited by

DANNY BUSCH

AND

LAURA J. MACGREGOR

CAMBRIDGE
UNIVERSITY PRESS

CAMBRIDGE UNIVERSITY PRESS
Cambridge, New York, Melbourne, Madrid, Cape Town, Singapore, São Paulo, Delhi

Cambridge University Press
The Edinburgh Building, Cambridge CB2 8RU, UK

Published in the United States of America by Cambridge University Press, New York

www.cambridge.org
Information on this title: www.cambridge.org/9780521863889

First published 2009

Printed in the United Kingdom at the University Press, Cambridge

A catalogue record for this publication is available from the British Library

ISBN 978-0-521-86388-9 hardback

TABLE OF CONTENTS

LIST OF CONTRIBUTORS

ANA B. BAIDE, LLB, BA(HONS) Barrister and Solicitor of the High Court of New Zealand, Solicitor, Russell McVeagh

DR DANNY BUSCH M. JUR. (OXON) Attorney-at-law, De Brauw Blackstone Westbroek, Amsterdam
Senior Research Fellow, Business & Law Research Centre, University of Nijmegen

PROFESSOR DEBORAH A. DEMOTT David F. Cavers Professor of Law, Duke University School of Law

LAURA J. MACGREGOR Senior Lecturer in Commercial Law
Director, Edinburgh Centre for Commercial Law, University of Edinburgh

PROFESSOR FRANCIS REYNOLDS, QC (HON.), DCL, FBA Honorary Bencher of Inner Temple
Professor of Law Emeritus in the University of Oxford
Emeritus Fellow of Worcester College Oxford

DR SÉVERINE SAINTIER Senior Lecturer, Sheffield University

DR ILSE SAMOY Postdoctoral Fellow of the Research Foundation – Flanders K. U. Leuven

PROFESSOR DR IUR MARTIN SCHMIDT-KESSEL European Legal Studies Institute, University of Osnabrück, Dean of the Osnabrück Law Faculty

PROFESSOR TAN CHENG-HAN Dean, Faculty of Law, National University of Singapore

DAVID YUILL Attorney, Bowman Gilfillan, Inc., Johannesburg

FOREWORD

If A, purporting to act as the agent of a principal (P), makes a contract with a third party (TP) on behalf of P but without the authority of P, what are the legal consequences for TP, and P, and A? That is the problem lying at the heart of this book.

Needless to say, the answer depends on the facts and on the legal system within which the questions are asked. It may matter whether P has put forward A as his agent, or whether he has ratified A's unauthorised conduct. It may be relevant whether A is himself liable. These are the specific issues the authors have chosen to address.

This is a model comparative study, for two reasons in particular. First, the editors have cast their net widely, embracing four civilian legal systems (those of France, Belgium, Germany and the Netherlands), two common law systems (England and the United States), two mixed legal systems (Scotland and South Africa) and two international legal models (The Principles of European Contract Law and the UNIDROIT Principles of International Commercial Contracts). The breadth of this coverage makes for an unusually illuminating comparison. But, secondly, the editors and the authors have co-operated to concentrate on the topics chosen for attention, giving an intensity of focus which would be lost if the authors had embarked on more general expositions of the law of agency under the various systems considered.

This interesting and valuable book will, I hope, influence the analysis and development of the law in this significant commercial area, both by legislators and judges.

Tom Bingham
House of Lords
3 July 2008

PREFACE

The idea for this book was conceived in a café in the beautiful surroundings of Trento, Italy. The editors had come to the city to participate in a European project, the Common Core of European Private Law. They discovered a common interest in the law of agency, and began to discuss the possibility of publishing a comparative book. It was therefore in those magnificent surroundings, and in an atmosphere of discussion of the harmonisation of European private law, that the idea for the book took shape.

Several years later, our project has come to fruition. We would like to thank, above all, the contributors of the national chapters, not only for their excellent chapters, but also for their patience in the face of the challenges which comparative projects of this type tend to face. Co-ordinating different chapters on a number of legal systems is not an easy task. Thanks must also go to Finola O'Sullivan of Cambridge University Press for her patience and support throughout the project.

We would also like to express our sincere thanks to Professor Francis Reynolds. Not only did he provide an invaluable chapter bridging the gap between the English common law and the US Restatement (Third) on Agency, but he also acted as an 'honorary editor,' commenting on each of the national chapters. The book would indeed have been a different one without his input.

Danny Busch would also like to thank his firm, De Brauw Blackstone Westbroek, for their cooperation and, in particular, for providing him with sabbatical leave in order to work on this book.

Several of our academic colleagues deserve particular mention. Professors Arthur Hartkamp, Ewoud Hondius, Hector MacQueen and Kenneth Reid have given much of their time over the years to help us to develop our ideas. We are also grateful for the excellent editorial assistance from Andrew

Wilson and Mathias Wröbel. Finally, we would like to thank Marjolein and Denis for their patience, particularly when discussion of agency matters threatened to ruin an otherwise beautiful dinner in Amsterdam or Edinburgh.

Danny Busch
Laura Macgregor

ABBREVIATIONS

A 2d	Atlantic Reporter, Second Series
AC	Law Reports, Appeal Cases
AD	Appellate Division Reports
AJDA	*Actualité Juridique de Droit Administratif*
AJT	*Algemeen Juridisch Tijdschrift*
All ER	All England Reports
Am J Comp L	American Journal of Comparative Law
App Cas	Law Reports, Appeal Cases, House of Lords
Arr Cass	*Arresten van het Hof van Cassatie*
Arr R v St	*Arresten van de Raad van State*
Aust Bar Rev	Australian Bar Review
Bank Fin R	*Bank en Financieel Recht*
BCC	Belgian Civil Code (*Belgisch Burgerlijk Wetboek*)
BCLC	British Company Law Cases
BGB	German Civil Code (*Bürgerliches Gesetzbuch*)
BGHZ	*Entscheidungen des Bundesgerichtshofes in Zivilsachen*
Bull Civ	*Bulletin des arrêts des Chambres civiles de la Cour de cassation* (a selection of the decisions of the various civil chambers of the *Cour de cassation* which are reported in four different sections, designated by the appropriate Roman numeral)
Bull Com	*Bulletin des arrêts de la Chambre commerciale de la Cour de cassation* (a selection of the decision of the commercial chamber of the *Cour de cassation*)
Bull d'Aix	*Revue Juridique du Sud Est*: legal periodical published by the University of Aix-Marseille
Bull Joly	*Bulletin mensuel d'information des sociétés* (legal periodical)

Bull Soc	*Bulletin des arrêts de la Chambre sociale de la Cour de cassation* (a selection of the decision of the social chamber of the *Cour de cassation*)
CA	*Cour d'Appel* (Court of Appeal)
Cal Rptr 2d	California Reporter, Second Series
Camp	Campbell's Nisi Prius Reports
Cass Ass Plén	*Assemblé plénière de la Cour de Cassation* (Plenary session of the Court of Cassation)
Cass Ch Mixtes	*Chambres Mixtes de la Cour de Cassation* (hearing in more than one chamber of the Court of Cassation)
Cass Civ 1ère	*Première Chambre Civile de la Cour de Cassation* (first civil chamber of the Court of Cassation)
Cass Civ 2ème	*Deuxième Chambre Civile de la Cour de Cassation* (second civil chamber of the Court of Cassation)
Cass Civ 3ème	*Troisième Chambre Civil de la Cour de Cassation* (third civil chamber of the Court of Cassation)
Cass Com	*Chambre Commerciale de la Cour de Cassation* (commercial chamber of the Court of Cassation)
Cass Req	*Chambre des Requêtes* (one of the chambers of the Supreme Court, abolished in 1947)
Cass Soc	*Chambre Sociale de la Cour de Cassation* (social chamber of the Court of Cassation)
CB (NS)	Common Bench (New Series)
CC	*Code Civil* (French Civil Code)
Ch	Chancery Division
Ch D	Chancery Division
Ch Req	*Chambre des requestes*
CLP	Current Legal Problems
CLR	Commonwealth Law Reports
Colum L Rev	Columbia Law Review
Comm Code	*Code de Commerce* (French Commercial Code)
CP	Law Reports, Common Pleas
CPD	Cape Provincial Division Reports
CSOH	Court of Session, Outer House
Ct App	US Court of Appeals

D	*Recueil Dalloz* or *Dalloz Sirey* (this legal periodical is divided into different sections: 'Chron' refers to the *Chronique*; 'J' to Jurisprudence; 'Somm' or 'SC' to the *Sommaires Commentés* and 'IR' to the Informations Rapides)
D	Dunlop's Session Cases
D Aff	*Dalloz Affaires*, a new strand of the *Dalloz* periodical which concentrates on business-related law
DC Cir	United States Court of Appeal for the District of Columbia Circuit
DCC	Dutch Civil Code (*Burgerlijk Wetboek*)
DCFR	Draft Common Frame of Reference
De Verz	*Tijdschrift voor Verzekeringen*
DH	*Recueil hebdomadaire Dalloz* (1924–1940)
Dist Ct	District Court
DP	*Recueil Dalloz périodique* (legal periodical, prior to its amalgamation with Sirey in 1965 to form Dalloz Sirey ('D'))
E & B	Ellis & Blackburn's Queen's Bench Reports
Edin L R	Edinburgh Law Review
EWCA (Civ)	England and Wales Court of Appeal (Civil Division)
EWHC	England and Wales High Court
Exch	Exchequer Reports
F	Fraser's Session Cases
F 3d	Federal Reporter, Third Series
fasc.	*fascicule*
FC	Faculty Collection, Court of Session
Gaz Pal	*Gazette du Palais* (chiefly law reports)
GP	*Gazette de Palais* (chiefly law reports)
Harv L Rev	Harvard Law Review
HGB	German Commercial Code (*Handelsgesetzbuch*)
HR	*Hoge Raad der Nederlanden* (Dutch Supreme Court)
Hume	Hume's Decisions, Court of Session
ICR	Industrial Cases Reports
JBL	Journal of Business Law
J Cl Dalloz	*Juris-Classeur Dalloz*

JCP	*Juris Classeur Périodique – Semaine Juridique*
JCP E	*Juris Classeur Périodique – Semaine Juridique, édition Entreprise*
JCP G	*Juris Classeur Périodique – Semaine Juridique, édition Générale*
JLMB	*Revue de jurisprudence de Liège, Mons et Bruxelles*
JOR	*Jurisprudentie Onderneming & Recht* (a law report)
JR	Juridical Review
JT	*Journal des tribunaux*
LJCP	Law Journal Reports, Common Pleas New Series
Lloyd's Rep	Lloyd's Reports
LPA	*Les Petites Affiches* (legal periodical)
LQR	Law Quarterly Review
LRCP	Law Reports, Common Pleas
LR HL	Law Reports, House of Lords
M	Macpherson's Session Cases
MDR	*Monatsschrift für deutsches Recht*
Mor	Morison's Dictionary of Decisions, Court of Session
M & W	Meeson & Welsby's Exchequer Reports
NbBW	*Nieuwsbrief BW* (a law journal)
Neb L Rev	Nebraska Law Review
NE 2d	North Eastern Reporter, Second Series
NJ	*Nederlandse Jurisprudentie* (a law report)
NJ Super Ct	New Jersey Superior Court
NjW	*Nieuw Juridisch Weekblad*
NJW	*Neue Juristische Wochenschrift*
NJW-RR	*Neue Juristische Wochenschrift, Rechtsprechungsreport Zivilrecht*
NTBR	*Nederlands Tijdschrift voor Burerlijk Recht* (a law journal)
NTHR	*Nederlands Tijdschrift voor Handelsrecht* (a law journal)
NYS 2d	New York Supplement, Second Series
OJ	Official Journal of the European Union
Okla City U L Rev	Oklahoma City University Law Review
O P D	Orange Free State Provincial Division Reports

Pand B	*Pandectes belges*
Pas	*Pasicrisie*
P & B	*Tijdschrift voor Procesrecht en Bewijsrecht*
PECL	Principles of European Contract Law
PNLR	Professional Negligence and Liability Law Reports
QB/QBD	Queen's Bench
R	Rettie's Session Cases
R C J B	*Revue critique de la jurisprudence belge*
Rec gén enr not	*Recueil général de l'enregistrement et du notariat*
Req	*Chambre des requêtes de la Cour de Cassation*
Rev dr int comp	*Revue de droit international et de droit comparé*
Rev Loyers	*Revue des Loyers* (legal periodical)
Rev not b	*Revue du notariat belge*
Rev Soc	*Revue des sociétés* (legal periodical)
Rev trim dr civ	*Revue trimesterielle de droit civil*
RGAT	*Recueil général des assurances terrestres* (chiefly law reports)
RGE	*Reichsgericht-Rechtsprechung, amtliche Sammlung*
RGZ	*Entscheidungen des Reichsgerichts in Zivilsachen*
RJDA	*Revue de Jurisprudence de droit des affaires*
RPS	*Revue pratique des sociétés*
RTD Civ	*Revue Trimestrielle de Droit Civil*
RTD Com	*Revue Trimestrielle de Droit Commercial*
Rutgers LJ	Rutgers Law Journal
RW	*Rechtskundig Weekblad*
S	*Sirey* (legal periodical, prior to its amalgamation with Recueil Dalloz in 1965 to form Dalloz Sirey ('D'))
SA	*Société Anonyme*
S A	South African Law Reports
SALJ	South African Law Journal
SAL Rev	South African Law Review
SARL	*Société à Responsabilité Limitée*
S C	Session Cases
SC (HL)	Session Cases, House of Lords
SE 2d	South Eastern Reports, Second edition
Sh Ct Rep	Sheriff Court Reports
Sing JLS	Singapore Journal of Legal Studies

SLR	Singapore Law Reports
SLR	Scottish Law Reporter
SLT	Scots Law Times
SLT (Sh Ct)	Scots Law Times, Sheriff Court Reports
So 2d	Southern Reporter, Second Series
Stellenbosch L Rev	Stellenbosch Law Review
SWA	Reports of the High Court of South West Africa
SW 2d	SouthWestern Reporter, Second Series
TBBR	*Tijdschrift voor Belgisch Burgerlijk Recht*
TBH	*Tijdschrift voor Belgisch Handelsrecht*
THRHR	*Tydskrif vir Hedendaagse Romeins-Hollands Reg*
TLR	Times Law Reports
TPD	Transvaal Provincial Division Decisions
TPR	*Tijdschrift voor Privaatrecht*
TRV	*Tijdschrift voor rechtspersoon en vennootschap*
T Vred	*Tijdschrift voor de Vrederechters*
UAC	Geneva Convention on Agency in the International Sale of Goods
UNIDROIT	*Institut International pour L'Unification du Droit Privé*
UP	UNIDROIT Principles of International Commercial Contracts 2004
US	United States Supreme Court Reports
UTLJ	University of Toronto Law Journal
Vand L Rev	Vanderbilt Law Review
Verkeersrecht	*Verkeersrecht* (a law report)
Wash & Lee L R	Washington and Lee Law Review
WL	Westlaw Transcripts
WLR	Weekly Law Reports
WPNR	*Weekblad voor Privaatrecht, Notariaat en Registratie* (a law journal)
W & S	Wilson and Shaw's House of Lords Cases
ZHR	*Zeitschrift für das gesamte Handelsrecht und Wirtschaftsrecht*

TABLE OF CASES

Chapter 1 (Introduction)

Chapter 2 (France)

Chapter 3 (Belgium)

Chapter 4 (Germany)

Chapter 5 (The Netherlands)

Chapter 6 (England)

Chapter 7 (US)

Chapter 8 (The American Restatements and other common law countries)

Chapter 9 (Scotland)

Chapter 10 (South Africa)

NB A full list of cases cited in the Comparative Chapters (Chapters 13 and 14) is not provided here. The cases noted below are those cited in the Comparative Chapters which have not been cited in any other chapter in the book.

Chapter 14 (Comparative conclusions)

Introduction

DANNY BUSCH AND LAURA MACGREGOR

Table of contents

I The subject matter of this book: unauthorised agency

This book explores the legal problems caused by agents who act in an unauthorised manner. This general idea is broken down into three central issues in the analysis which follows: apparent authority, ratification and the liability of the *falsus procurator*. Each of these individual ideas will be expanded upon below. For the moment, the question which may arise is why this particular area has been selected as worthy of analysis. Agency law is a much under-researched area, and there are undoubtedly many other aspects equally deserving of attention. We would argue that the problems caused by unauthorised agents illustrate a central tension in agency law: the tension between the use of the concept of contract as the primary tool for the analysis of the legal relationships involved and the tri-partite nature of those relationships (involving principal, agent and the principal's contracting party known as the 'third party'). In other words, a legal concept formed with bi-partite relationships in mind is applied to more complex tri-partite legal relationships.

The major problem inherent in the use of a contractual analysis is that it brings with it a significant role for the concept of consent. Where two parties are involved in a contractual relationship, they will normally reach *consensus in idem* in a direct manner. Where three parties are involved, consent is achieved in a more indirect way. The situation has been rationalised by explaining that the principal consents in advance to all the agent's acts carried out on his behalf.[1] The principal's consent exists in the 'background' during the agent's negotiations, and can be referred to later in order to create the *consensus in idem* required for the formation of a contract between principal and third party.

It is perhaps helpful to consider the practical implications of the role of consent in agency. Consent is provided when the principal gives to the agent authority to act on his behalf. That authority is, of course, not unlimited. By granting authority to the agent, the principal identifies the specific activities which the agent is able to carry out on his behalf, and, by implication, those which lie beyond the scope of the agent's power. It seems, however, to be an unavoidable fact of commercial life that agents regularly act beyond the confines of their authority. Often, this is due to fraudulent intentions on the part of the agent, but this may not be the case. The agent may take a 'calculated risk' that the principal will view the prospective contract favourably. His prediction may not, however, turn out to be accurate. Fluctuations in market prices occurring since the date on which the agent purported to conclude a contract on his principal's behalf may have rendered the contract unattractive to the principal. Because the agent has stepped beyond the boundaries of his authority, one can no longer utilise the principal's 'lurking' consent. *Consensus in idem* is not present, and, as a general rule, no contract is formed. The third party who is unaware of the agent's lack of authority is disappointed. The anticipated contract does not exist.

It seems clear that to adhere too rigidly to this general rule would be unacceptable in principle. It seems almost unarguable that, of the three actors involved in agency situations, third parties are the most deserving of the law's protection. They may have little choice but to transact using an agent: the issue may not be one which is open for

---

[1] See the useful discussion of the role of consent in the context of agency relationships in G. McMeel, 'The Philosophical Foundations of the Law of Agency' (2000) 116 *LQR* 387.

negotiation. But the major factor pointing in favour of third party protection is the 'information asymmetry' which exists: the third party is unable to access the information necessary in order for him to determine whether the agent is indeed properly authorised. That information is available only to the principal and the agent. The third party may struggle to understand the opaque hierarchy of the principal's business, and the powers of those working therein. Enquiries from the third party may go unanswered, or be answered incorrectly.[2] Even if it is possible for the third party to access this information, one could question whether it is efficient for him to do so. Each transaction will involve a different third party, and each of those third parties would have to carry out similar time-consuming checks on the agent's authority. It would be cheaper and simpler to require the principal to increase supervision of the agent to minimise the risk of agents acting in an unauthorised manner.

Whilst there is an undoubted need for third party protection, strict liability is not the answer. It could lead to an unmanageable amount of liability on the part of the principal, and eventually to a downturn in the use of agents generally. It might also fail to deal adequately with situations where the third party acts in bad faith. Judging from case-law, this is a common problem, particularly where third parties collude with fraudulent agents.[3] The third party's conduct and knowledge are clearly significant factors which may rule out liability on the part of the principal.

The solution to this problem lies, we would suggest, in the application of a judicial discretion. It could be tailored to the circumstances of the case, and be applied bearing in mind the policy factors discussed above. The central issue in this project has been the analysis of the extent of third party protection existing in the legal systems studied. Those protections have been compared in order to ascertain whether a common approach exists. That common approach has then been assessed, and suggestions have been made as to what, in our view, would constitute an 'ideal' approach.

---

[2] For a good illustration of this point, see *British Bank of the Middle East* v. *Sun Life Assurance Company of Canada (UK) Ltd* [1983] 2 Lloyd's Rep 9, discussed by J. Collier in his article, 'Actual and Ostensible Authority of an Agent: A Straightforward Question and Answer' (1984) 43 *CLJ* 26.

[3] See, e.g., the conduct taking place in the leading English case of *Armagas Ltd* v. *Mundogas SA, The Ocean Frost* [1986] AC 717 or the Scottish case of *International Sponge Importers* v. *Watt and Sons* 1911 SC (HL) 57.

II The three aspects of unauthorised agency: apparent authority, ratification and the liablity of the *falsus procurator*

Having set out our general aim, we can now descend to a more particular level. As stated at the beginning of this Introduction, the general topic has been split into three particular concepts: apparent authority, ratification and the liability of the *falsus procurator*. The first of these, apparent authority (adopting, for the moment the common law term), becomes relevant where a principal, whether actively or passively, leads a third party to believe that his agent is authorised when this is not, in fact, the case. At a later stage, the principal seeks to deny the appearance of authority, and therefore the existence of any contractual tie with the third party. Although the national forms of apparent authority differ, they all share the same general effect: the principal is prevented from relying on the agent's lack of authority. The third party therefore has a claim against the principal for protection of his expectation interest. This constitutes, however, only a limited degree of protection. It exists only where it can be proved that the principal is 'at fault' in the creation of the erroneous impression. Where fault cannot be proved, for example, because the third party relied on the agent's representations of authority, the third party has no claim against the principal. The results of this rather limited approach appear to have been unsatisfactory. In many of the legal systems analysed here, one can find attempts to extend the principal's liability. One of the most interesting issues arising from this comparison is the identification of different methods used by each legal system in order to extend liability on the part of the principal.

The second of the three central concepts, ratification, poses similar, if perhaps less serious, concerns. Again, the agent purports to enter into a contract on behalf of his principal whilst possessing insufficient authority. In contrast to apparent authority cases where the principal rejects the contractual tie, ratification enables him to validate an otherwise non-binding contract. The consent of the principal is present, albeit that it is provided at a late stage. Ratification poses fewer problems also because it tends to operate in the third party's favour: it validates a contract which the third party, all along, has considered to be binding. Importantly, however, the principal cannot be forced into ratifying. This statement must be qualified given that, in some of the systems analysed, the third party has important powers which can be used to force the principal to confirm whether or not he intends to ratify within a reasonable time.[4]

A particularly difficult issue in this context is the case of the third party who intends to be bound, but, having discovered the agent's original lack of authority, seeks to withdraw unilaterally from the 'contract'. The problem arises in part due to the retrospective effect of ratification, an idea shared by all the legal systems studied. Effective ratification creates a valid contractual nexus between principal and third party backdated to the moment when the agent purported to act on the principal's behalf. To give to ratification its full retrospective effect is to deny the third party the right to withdraw, even if he purports to do so prior to the principal's act of ratification.

The clash of interests between the principal and third party in this situation is a difficult one to resolve. The starting position is, we would suggest, the backdrop of the third party's information asymmetry. Because the third party is initially disadvantaged, cogent arguments are required in order to prevent him withdrawing from what is not a valid contract at the time of withdrawal. Nevertheless, there are arguments against a right to withdraw. The third party could be accused of 'playing the market': rejecting a contractual relationship which has, with the passage of time, become unattractive. There is no extra factor such as undue influence which would justify his withdrawal. The right to withdraw, in general, threatens one of the major functions of contract law. Contracts allow parties to assess future risks at the moment of formation and thus to achieve certainty through their agreement. It is also necessary to consider parties situated outside the immediate tri-partite situation. Others, so-called 'fourth parties', may be equally unaware of the agent's lack of authority, yet equally reliant on the validity of the principal/third party contract. To 'unravel' that contract could send ripples out into the commercial world, upsetting contractual relationships and, potentially, transfers of ownership of property. Such consequences clearly ought to be avoided. The attitude of a particular legal system to the third party's right to withdraw is a particularly significant issue. It acts as a 'barometer,' measuring the extent of third party protection within that particular legal system.

Thus far, the discussion has been limited to the choice of principal or third party as the most appropriate bearer of losses. It may seem unusual to omit the agent, usually the most blameworthy party, from this

---

[4] See Chapter 4 (Germany), V 3 (§ 177(2) BGB); Chapter 5 (The Netherlands), V 4 (b) (Art. 3:69(4) DCC); Chapter 12 (UP), VI 4 (b) (Art. 2.2.9(2) UP).

discussion. With the third of the three central concepts we can turn our attention to the agent. All of the systems studied recognise an action which can be raised by the disappointed third party against the agent. It is curious, however, to note its lack of importance, particularly in English and Scots law. It seems to be seldom used, and, as a result, its rationale has not been clearly worked out. It is not clear why this action should have such a low profile. It may simply be a reflection of the fact that the principal tends to be in a stronger position financially, and is therefore, in the third party's eyes, a more attractive target than the agent. Alternatively, the agent may simply have disappeared.

This action is generally discussed under the heading of 'the liability of the *falsus procurator*' in continental Europe and 'breach of warranty of authority' in the common law and mixed legal systems. With this concept we move into new territory. No actual contract exists between third party and agent. A legal system must therefore 'construct' a legal basis for the action. The legal systems studied here have tended to favour the use of either an implied unilateral undertaking or an implied contract. Both of these solutions are, in effect, legal fictions and therefore relatively unsatisfactory. As is illustrated below, some legal systems have explored the possibility of a legal basis within tort law. This third concept is the final, and perhaps the most unusual, of the three central concepts studied in this book.

Although we have now set out the ambit of our enquiry, it will be clear that it is not entirely comprehensive. We have not considered the implications of unauthorised agency for the principal/agent relationship. This omission can now be explained. Our central aim was to assess the extent of third party protection in each of the legal systems studied. This being the case, the external, and not the internal, aspect of agency forms the major focus of the book. As a result, the remedies open to the principal against the misbehaving agent are generally not analysed in the chapters that follow, although they may be touched upon in passing. To include this aspect within our enquiry would undoubtedly have proved interesting, providing a more comprehensive picture of the law in this area. We decided to exclude this angle entirely in order to constrain an already extensive subject matter within manageable bounds.

III Direct, not indirect, agency

For common law lawyers and those from mixed legal systems, the distinction between direct and indirect agency is not a familiar one. In continental Europe, whether an agency situation is classed as direct or indirect depends upon whether or not the agent discloses when he concludes the contract on the principal's behalf that he is acting in the name of the principal. If he does so, this is direct representation, the effect of which is the formation of a contract between principal and third party. Where the agent acts in his own name, but still on behalf of the principal in the sense that the transaction is ultimately at the risk, and for the benefit, of the principal, this is indirect representation. The effect in this latter case is the formation of a contract between agent and third party. This outcome applies in indirect representation even where the third party is aware that the agent is acting on behalf of (though not in the name of) a principal. While indirect agency is in widespread usage in continental Europe, it is virtually unknown in the UK.[5]

The concept of unauthorised agency is usually only associated with unauthorised direct agency. The same is true for apparent authority and ratification. Although it is possible to apply these concepts to (certain cases of) indirect agency,[6] the focus of this book is direct rather than indirect agency. This decision was motivated by two main factors. Importantly, again we did not want the project to extend beyond manageable boundaries. Additionally, direct agency, as the method of dealing present in the common law, the civil law and the mixed legal systems, constitutes the obvious area for comparison.

IV The aim of this book: the search for common European rules

Our principal aim in producing this book is to identify common approaches, or the 'common core' of the rules with respect to unauthorised agency.[7] In addition, we highlight the areas where, in our view, the solution adopted by the common core is unsatisfactory, bearing in mind our principal concern, already expressed, of third party protection. To the extent that the common core is lacking, we suggest what would be a

---

[5] See H. L. E. Verhagen, 'Agency and representation', in J. M. Smits, *Elgar Encyclopaedia of Comparative Law* (Cheltenham/Northampton: Edward Elgar, 2006), pp. 47–48; D. Busch, 'Indirect Representation and the Lando Principles: An Analysis of Some Problem Areas from the Perspective of English Law' (1999) 7 *ERPL* 319.

[6] See, on 'unauthorised indirect representation', 'apparent authority for indirect representation' and 'ratification of unauthorised indirect representation', D. Busch, *Indirect Representation in European Contract Law* (The Hague: Kluwer Law International, 2005), pp. 232–7.

[7] To borrow the terminology from the Trento Common Core of European Private Law Project referred to in our Preface.

welcome approach. In setting out this 'common core' we are pursuing different aims. The first relates to the development of a common contract law for Europe. With the much-awaited publication of a Common Frame of Reference, Europe stands at a pivotal point in the harmonisation process.[8] It is thus timely that this book is available as a resource to those involved in the development of agency rules at European level.

Furthermore, we would certainly hope that, by studying the approach of another legal system, readers will be encouraged to develop their own legal systems in new ways, be it in their capacity as legislators, judges or legal practitioners or as academics. In making this point we recognise that those seeking to reform the law should not lose sight of the doctrinal foundations of their own systems, remembering the words of the late Professor Bill Wilson that 'a legal system which has no doctrinal foundation must drift'.[9] As a result, we imagine that civil lawyers will be most interested in the chapters describing other civilian systems, and *mutatis mutandis* the chapters on the common law and mixed legal systems. Nevertheless, it would not be surprising, as we emerge into a new phase of harmonisation of European contract law, to see examples of borrowing from beyond the same legal family.[10]

Thus we aim to identify common European rules, and create a body of work which will enable different legal systems to learn from one another. A further aim is that which relates to the inclusion of mixed legal systems within our project. This aim is best explored in the discussion below where we set out the reasons which motivated our choice of the legal systems taking part in this project.

V The legal systems studied

Within this book the reader will find chapters on unauthorised agency in France, Belgium, Germany, the Netherlands, England, the United States,

---

[8] The Draft Common Frame of Reference ('DCFR') is intended to act as a '"toolbox" or handbook for the EU legislator, to be used when revising existing and preparing new legislation in the area of contract law': see European Parliament resolution of 12 December 2007 on European Contract Law, B6-0513/2007. It is not intended to be binding in nature. The DCFR was delivered to the Commission on 28 December 2007.

[9] W. A. Wilson, 'The Importance of Analysis', in D. Carey Miller and D. W. Meyers, *Comparative and Historical Essays in Scots Law: A Tribute to Professor Sir Thomas Smith* (Edinburgh: Butterworths and Law Society of Scotland, 1992), p. 162 at 171.

[10] See generally on the aims and functions of comparative law: K. Zweigert and H. Kötz, *Introduction to Comparative Law* (trans. T. Weir), 3rd edn (Oxford: Oxford University Press, 1998), pp. 13–31.

Scotland, South Africa, the Principles of European Contract Law[11] and the UNIDROIT Principles of International Commercial Contracts 2004.[12] At first sight this may seem to be a strange and random grouping. Our principal aim was, as stated above, the search for common European rules. It was therefore important to include major European systems such as France and Germany. The Netherlands provided the opportunity to analyse a relatively modern, sometimes innovative, civil code. Belgian law often, but not always, followed the lead provided by French law. The PECL, as a highly influential contract 'code', undoubtedly merited a place in our project, given that they form the basis of development of a Common Frame of Reference for Europe. The inclusion of the major common law system within Europe, England, completed our European picture.

We have included two legal systems which are 'mixed' in the sense that, in those systems, an initial and strong civil law base has been overlaid with English influence.[13] They are Scotland and South Africa. Their inclusion allows us to enquire whether systems which stand between Europe's two great legal traditions might have some distinctive contribution to make to the problems of unauthorised agency.

A body of literature exists in which the usefulness to comparative law of mixed legal systems is discussed. At times, expansive and possibly exaggerated claims have been made on this point. For example, in 1924 Henri Lévy-Ullman stated:

> Scots law as it stands gives us a picture of what will be, some day ... the law of the civilised nations, namely, a combination between the Anglo-Saxon system and the continental system.[14]

A similar view is expressed by Zweigert and Kötz in their leading text on comparative law.[15] MacQueen too, for similar reasons, has suggested that Scots law could help inform the development of the PECL.[16] Whilst some continue to emphasise the contribution to comparative law made

---

[11] Referred to below as 'PECL'.   [12] Referred to below as 'UNIDROIT Principles'.

[13] See on mixed legal systems, *inter alia*, J. du Plessis 'Comparative Law and the Study of Mixed Legal Systems', in M. Reimann and R. Zimmermann (eds.), *The Oxford Handbook of Comparative Law* (Oxford: Oxford University Press, 2006), pp. 477–512; J. du Plessis, 'The Promises and Pitfalls of Mixed Legal Systems: The South African and Scottish Experiences' (1998) *Stell LR* 338 at 339; and N. R. Whitty, 'The Civilian Tradition and Debates on Scots Law' (1996) *TSAR* 227 and 442 at 457.

[14] Henri Lévy-Ullman (trans. F. P. Walton), 'The Law of Scotland' (1925) *JR* 370 at 390.

[15] Zweigert and Kötz, *Introduction to Comparative Law*, p. 204.

[16] H. MacQueen, 'Scots and English Law: The Case of Contract' (1998) *CLP* 204.

by mixed legal systems such as Scotland,[17] others doubt that mixed legal systems can indeed select the best from the competing solutions offered by the civil law and the common law.[18] Whilst we would not seek to argue that Scots law offers 'the best' solution, we would indeed suggest that the experience of Scots law proves that the enterprise of mixing of this type is at least possible.

Some might challenge our inclusion of these mixed legal systems in the project on different grounds. Agency is sometimes classed as part of commercial law and sometimes part of contract law. Only contract law, and not commercial law, is truly 'mixed' in Scots and South African law.[19] Those who classify agency law as part of commercial law would argue that there is nothing to be gained from its analysis here. The point of reference ought to be the dominant influence, English law. We do not agree. In our view such rigid distinctions cannot be made. As Niall Whitty has pointed out, '… no clear division exists between commercial law and large swathes of property and obligations'.[20] Agency law is a concept which crosses the boundaries between contract and commercial law. It is also relevant to note that solutions used in agency law problems often depend upon more general private law concepts, for example, ratification or personal bar. Those concepts have a wide ambit, much wider than the law of agency alone. They may have a civilian rather than a common law flavour. When applied in an agency context, the influence of the civil law arrives 'through the back door'. For all these reasons, we would argue that one cannot categorise agency law as part of commercial law and thus the product of common law influences alone.

Whilst not wishing to anticipate the conclusions on mixed legal systems made in our final chapter, what we can say is that the analysis of the mixed legal systems in this project has been useful. South African law in particular has developed solutions, some of which stem from the civil law and some from the common law. Scots law, based in a small country with a limited case-law, has not progressed as far as South

---

[17] See the work of J. M. Smits, particularly in *The Contribution of Mixed Legal Systems to European Private Law* (Antwerp: Intersentia, 2001); and *The Making of European Private Law: Towards a Ius Commune Europaeum as a Mixed Legal System* (trans. N Kornet) (Antwerp: Intersentia, 2002).

[18] See the discussion of the competing arguments in du Plessis, 'The Promises and Pitfalls', p. 338.

[19] K. G. C. Reid, 'The Idea of Mixed Legal Systems' (2003) 78 *Tul LR* 5 at 25; see also Whitty, 'The Civilian tradition', pp. 444 and 448–52.

[20] Whitty, 'The Civilian Tradition', p. 449.

African law. In many cases there is simply no solution to a particular problem. It remains to be seen whether the solutions finally adopted in Scots law are motivated by a desire to create a more rational legal system, or by non-legal factors, such as the desire for uniformity either with England or with continental Europe. We have come to the particular conclusion that mixed legal systems have much to learn from one another.[21] A solution adopted in South African law may prove workable in Scots law.

Before this discussion of mixed legal systems draws to a close, we should make the perhaps obvious point that the two 'codes' analysed in this book are themselves examples of 'mixed legal systems'. The PECL and the UNIDROIT Principles are the product of collaboration between civilian and common lawyers. Parts of these codes may indeed embody the 'best' rule chosen from the civil law and the common law. This argument should not be pushed too far, however. In projects of this type, outcomes may be determined by the strength of the personalities of the actors involved, or even possibly by 'horse-trading' between different contributors. Arguably, Scots law is a mixed system which is 'organic' in nature. By contrast, the PECL and the UNIDROIT Principles are codes created by committee.

Leaving to one side the question of the success of the solutions found in these 'codes', one can at least provide evidence of their 'mixed' nature. In the PECL agency provisions, the influence of the civil law is visible in the field of apparent authority. The PECL do not adopt the classic 'estoppel' version of the concept found in common law systems. Rather, they favour a type of 'deemed authority'[22] similar to that found in Dutch and Belgian law. In those systems, apparent authority involves the creation of a contract binding both third party and principal. The influence of the common law, too, is visible in the PECL, particularly in the provisions on 'indirect representation'.[23] Usage of this term in the PECL is something of a misnomer: it is not used to refer to the institution of indirect representation generally present in civil law countries and commented on at III above. The PECL provisions aim, rather, to create direct rights between a third party and principal where the intermediary (agent) has not acted in the name of his principal. The decision to include these

---

[21] See the arguments on this point raised by du Plessis, 'The Promises and Pitfalls' or Reid, 'The Idea of Mixed Legal Systems'.
[22] Art 3:201(3) PECL, and Comment D.   [23] PECL, Chapter 3, section 3.

provisions and the content thereof was clearly influenced by the common law concept of the undisclosed principal.[24]

To summarise, in selecting the legal systems to participate in this project, our dominant motive was indeed to identify the 'common core' of European agency law. A further motive was to view agency law through the different lenses of the common law, the civil law and mixtures of the same.

We have mentioned only one common law system thus far: England. A balanced comparison clearly required the participation of more common law systems. We were very pleased to secure the participation of two of the leading agency lawyers from the common law world. Firstly, Deborah de Mott, the Reporter to the *Restatement (Third) of Agency*, agreed to submit a chapter on the *Restatement*. There we find a valuable discussion of a new and innovative common law system of unauthorised agency. Secondly, we were equally pleased that Francis Reynolds was willing to contribute a chapter which would form a 'bridge' between the English and American chapters.[25]

VI Methodology

It was important to us as editors to provide the contributors of the national chapters with flexibility in the preparation of their chapters. The instructions they received were brief; limited, in fact, to a short outline of the three central aspects of unauthorised agency. They were provided with a style structure (including section headings) modelled on the Dutch chapter. We did not, however, seek to impose that structure, nor did we impose uniformity of approach in general. We considered it important to allow the contributors to emphasise the principles and remedies which are important in their own legal systems. At times, one of the national chapters may discuss an issue not covered in the other chapters. We were happy to include such features, provided that they

---

[24] For a general discussion of these provisions and comparison with English law, see Busch, 'Indirect Representation and the Lando Principles'. For a recent English perspective on undisclosed agency, see C.-H. Tan, 'Undisclosed Principals and Contract' (2004) 120 *LQR* 480.

[25] As regards the problem of selection of legal systems, see, *inter alia*: Zweigert and Kötz, *Introduction to Comparative Law*, pp. 36–40; D. Kokkini-Iatridou *et al.*, *Een inleiding tot het rechtsvergelijkende onderzoek* (Deventer: Kluwer 1988), pp. 137–42; A. E. Oderkerk, *De preliminaire fase van het rechtsvergelijkend onderzoek* (Nijmegen: Ars Aequi Libri, 1999), pp. 47–60.

covered material which was relevant. We saw it as the duty of the editors to draw on the national material to create the overall picture in our comparative evaluation. As long as each chapter provided us with the main ingredients, uniformity of approach in the national chapters themselves was simply not necessary.

In this book we have used the so-called successive comparative law method, according to which raw material from national legal systems is analysed first, followed by the comparative evaluation.[26] This being the case, the book is split, roughly, into two parts: part one contains chapters on the national legal systems,[27] and part two a comparative evaluation and comparative conclusions. In our view, especially in view of the fact that no fewer than ten legal systems are taken into account, this method is the best way of ensuring that the research is clearly organised and can be easily consulted and checked.

VII Structure of the book

Part one of the book is structured according to legal families, i.e. into three sections comprising first the civil law family, secondly the common law family and thirdly the mixed legal systems.

The civilian section opens with an analysis of French law (Chapter 2). This is immediately followed by a legal system influenced by French law: Belgian law (Chapter 3). German law, another highly influential civilian system, is analysed next (Chapter 4). The final chapter in this section concerns Dutch law, a relatively modern and sometimes innovative legal system (Chapter 5).

The common law family is analysed next. It begins with a chapter on English law (Chapter 6), followed by a chapter on the *Restatement (Third) of Agency* (Chapter 7). It concludes with a chapter on the *Restatement (Third) of Agency* from the viewpoint of an English lawyer (Chapter 8). In our discussions this final chapter was referred to as a 'bridge', and we think that this description expresses its purpose well. The chapter identifies the parts of US law where English influence is evident and those in which new solutions have been developed. It bridges the gap between the original source, English law, and modern US law.

---

[26] On this subject, see Kokkini-Iatridou *et al.*, *Een inleiding tot het rechtsvergelijkende onderzoek* (Deventer: Kluwer, 1988) pp. 187–8.

[27] The exception being Chapter 8 on the *Restatement (Third) of Agency* from the viewpoint of an English lawyer, which is in fact comparative in nature.

The analysis then moves to the mixed legal systems: Scots law (Chapter 9) and South African law (Chapter 10). This is followed immediately by the 'codes' which, as we have argued, are themselves mixed in nature: the PECL (Chapter 11) and the UNIDROIT Principles (Chapter 12).

In the second part of the book our comparative evaluation is divided into two sections: Chapter 13 contains the comparative analysis and Chapter 14 the overall comparative conclusions.

VIII Use of the personal pronoun

The use of personal pronouns is, as ever, a controversial issue. We decided not to use the cumbersome 'he or she' throughout this book. The use of 'he' should not, however, be taken as a gender-biased approach to the law in this area. Indeed, this book is perhaps rare, having achieved close to an equivalence in the gender balance of the contributors.

PART 1

The civilian legal systems

Unauthorised agency in French law

SÉVERINE SAINTIER

Table of contents

I Introduction

Under the French rules regulating agency relationships, the essence of the 'internal relationship' is the power of representation that the agent has.[1] In fact, the French civil code defines the *mandat* or *procuration* as 'a transaction by which a person gives to another the authority to do something for the principal and in his name'.[2] The main effect of this representation is that the principal alone will be bound by any acts entered into by the agent within his authority, in the name and on behalf of the principal.

The French Civil Code therefore defines the internal relationship solely by reference to the concept of representation. This is a restrictive approach, since the principal will only be bound when he consents to the agent's acting on his behalf within the limits of the authority defined by the mandate. This is confirmed by the fact that the civil code expressly stipulates that the agent cannot act beyond the authority granted by the principal in the mandate.[3] The text further adds that the principal can only be bound to perform the undertakings contracted by the agent in accordance with the authority granted (Art. 1998-1 CC).[4] For undertakings contracted by the agent outside the authority granted by the mandate, the principal will only be bound if he has ratified them expressly or impliedly (Art. 1998-2 CC).[5]

From the above, it can be seen that French law sees the mechanism of representation solely as a means of facilitating the legal life of the

---

[1] *Civ 14-4-1886, DP* 1886, 1, 221, where the court held: 'the essential characteristic of this contract is the power given to the agent to represent the principal.'

[2] Translation obtained from the French official website: www.legifrance.gouv.fr. Art. 1984-1 CC: 'le mandat ou procuration est un acte par lequel une personne donne à une autre le pouvoir de faire quelque chose pour le mandant et en son nom.'

[3] Art. 1989 CC.

[4] Translation obtained from the French official website: www.legifrance.gouv.fr.: 'Le mandant est tenu d'exécuter les engagements contractés par le mandaire conformément au pouvoir qu'il lui a été donné.'

[5] Translation obtained as above: 'Il n'est tenu que de ce qui a pu être fait au delà, qu'autant qu'il l'a ratifié, expressément ou tacitement.'

principal,[6] since he cannot be bound unwillingly. In the light of the logic behind the mechanisms of the representation, this restrictive approach towards the agency relationship makes sense. In fact, when the agent acts outside his authority or even in the absence of any authority, the mechanisms of representation dictate that the principal is not bound[7] since, technically, the agent acts without his consent. The principal can only be bound if he so chooses through ratification.

The rules in the French Civil Code fail adequately to deal with all the facets of the tri-partite nature of the agency relationship. More importantly, they fail to take into consideration the interests of third parties who alone bear the risk of the agent acting outside his authority or even acting without authority. Precisely because the agency relationship is a triangular relationship, there is a need to balance the interests of the principal with those of the third party.[8] This need has been recognised by the French courts,[9] which, over the years, have created rules to supplement the civil code.

---

[6] C. W. Chen, *Apparence et représentation en droit positif français* (Paris: LGDJ, 2000), para. 1, p. 1.

[7] *Ibid.*, para. 4, p. 3.

[8] See J. Huet, *Traité de droit civil: les principaux contrats spéciaux*, 2nd edn. (Paris: LGDJ, 2001), p. 1140, para. 31201.

[9] Although French law has no formal doctrine of binding precedent, the decisions of the various Courts of Appeal (35) and of the Supreme Court, the Cour de Cassation, have strong persuasive effect. The decisions of the Courts of Appeal are referred to merely by the particular name of the court in question and the date the case was heard, i.e. *CA Riom, 10-6-1992*.

The Cour de Cassation is composed of six chambers (three for civil affairs, one for commercial affairs, one for social and employment affairs and one for criminal cases). The question of law raised in a given dispute will therefore dictate which chamber will be competent. The way the cases are referenced indicates which chamber heard the case and the date of the hearing: *Cass Civ 1ère* (followed by the date) for the first civil chamber; *Cass Civ 2ème* for the second civil chamber; *Cass Civ 3ème* for the third civil chamber; *Cass Com* for the commercial chamber, *Cass Soc* for the social chamber and *Cass Crim* for the criminal chamber.

When a legal dispute raises more than one question of law, the matter is heard by several chambers of the Cour de Cassation, referred to as Chambres Mixtes. The reference is as follows: *Ch Mixtes* followed by the date of the case. When a case raises a point of law which is of crucial importance (*question de principe*), the Cour de Cassation will sit in its most formal session, the plenary session. The reference will be *Ass Plén*.

The main role of the Cour de Cassation is to check that the law and procedure have been correctly interpreted and applied. The court therefore does not judge on the facts. The Cour de Cassation can confirm the earlier decision (*rejet du pourvoi*, dismissal of the appeal) or annul it (*cassation*). When the decision is annuled, the case is remanded to another Court of Appeal, which decision may again be appealed to the Cour de Cassation. In this case, the Court will hear the case in its plenary session; it may, again, confirm an earlier decision or quash it and remand the case to yet another Court of Appeal. In the latter case, the determination of the plenary session on points of law is binding.

As a result, aside from the paradigm case scenario defined within the French Civil Code, an 'agent' can be deemed by law to have power to bind the 'principal' without the latter's consent and, in some situations, without there being any agency relationship at all. This occurs in two circumstances, namely: (a) when the principal chooses to ratify an unauthorised transaction entered into by the agent; and (b) when the conditions of the theory of apparent authority or *mandat apparent* are present.

The French rules which supplement the civil code will be reviewed in three main parts. First, the doctrine of *mandat apparent* will be considered, including its origin, how and why it came to be created and how it is applied by the French courts. Then, ratification will be considered, its conditions of application and its effects on the 'internal' and 'external' agency relationships. Thirdly, the liability of the *falsus procurator* will be discussed. However, in keeping with the format of the book, two further specific topics will be covered: the fate of those dealing with a company yet to be incorporated and the more specific issue of acting for someone yet to be named.

II The doctrine of *mandat apparent*[10]

As previously mentioned, the rules regulating the agency relationships within the French Civil Code are based on the concept of representation. Those rules also act in the principal's favour. The rules of the civil code are therefore inadequate, since they do not cover all the legal consequences of the agency concept, and this therefore jeopardises the very essence of agency itself.[11] The balance needs to be redressed in order to meet the needs of third parties including the fact that, in commercial transactions, one must act quickly. To proceed quickly, one must be sure, without having to conduct lengthy searches, of the validity of the acts done by an agent.[12] Such are the needs of third parties and this is where

---

[10] Interestingly, in both French and English law, the respective names of *mandat apparent* and 'apparent authority' have been criticised for similar reasons. In both countries, the criticism relates to the fact that the name implies a mandate when there is none. For French law, this view is supported by the fact that the effects of *mandat apparent* are those which relate to the representation only and not those involving the normal rights and obligations of the parties. See R. de Quenaudon, 'Le mandat', *Jurisc Dalloz*, fasc. 20, p. 42, para. 60. For English law see R. Bradgate and F. White, *Commercial Law*, 8th edn (Blackstone: London, 2001), p. 44, para. 4.2.

[11] Arguably, if agency becomes less attractive to third parties, they will cease dealing with agents and the concept will disappear.

[12] J. Calais-Auloy, D 1963, J 277.

the doctrine of *mandat apparent* fits in: if, in good faith, a third party mistakenly believes that the person he contracted with was an agent who had authority to bind his principal, the latter can be bound by this appearance of authority providing that certain conditions are complied with.[13]

Mandat apparent is therefore a significant tool created by the French courts as an attempt to re-establish a balance between the conflicting interests of the principal and those of the third party. The origin of *mandat apparent* as new source of obligation for the principal will be considered first before moving on to its scope and conditions of application.

1 The birth of the doctrine of mandat apparent

The doctrine of *mandat apparent* is a specific application of the wider doctrine of *l'apparence*, whereby the French courts will attach legal consequences to a person's erroneous perception of reality. This notion of *l'apparence*, which can now be found in a large number of areas in French law,[14] was first created in order to protect the interests of third parties who act in good faith as well as reinforcing the sanctity of contracts.[15]

Interestingly, the civil code itself recognises *l'apparence* in relation to the mandate, albeit very restrictively. This occurs in the context of validation of transactions concluded when the agent[16] or the third party[17] acts in

---

[13] The reverse situation is not clear, i.e. whether the principal himself can invoke the doctrine of *mandat apparent* against the third party.

[14] See, e.g., Art. 1240 CC, which stipulates that payment in good faith to the person who bears the credit note (the *créance*) will be valid even though that person is not the real creditor, etc. For an interesting application of *l'apparence* in the formation of a contract, see *CA Riom, 10-6-1992, RJDA* 1992, no. 893 at 732, *RTD Civ* 1993, 343, where a party who had terminated negotiations was found liable for damages to the other on the basis of *l'apparence*: the Court of Appeal found that the behaviour had caused the other party legitimately to believe that the parties were about to enter into a contract. For a complete review of the notion of *l'apparence*, see J. Guestin, *Traité de droit civil: Introduction générale* (Paris: LGDJ, 1994), pp. 828–63. See also M. Boudot, 'Apparence' (2003) *Repértoire de droit civil* 1–15.

[15] Boudot, 'Apparence', para. 23.

[16] Art. 2008 CC: 'si le mandataire ignore la mort du mandant ou l'une des autres causes qui font cesser le mandat, ce qu'il a fait dans cette ignorance est valide.' Where an agent has no knowledge of the death of the principal or of one of the other causes which make an agency come to an end, what he has done in that ignorance is valid. Translation obtained from the French government website: www.legifrance.gouv.fr.

[17] Art. 2005 CC: 'la révocation notifiée au seul mandataire ne peut être opposée aux tiers qui ont traité dans l'ignorance de cette révocation, sauf au mandant son recours contre le mandataire.' A revocation of which only the agent has been given notice is not effective

ignorance of revocation of the mandate by the principal.[18] However, the civil code will only protect third parties in such circumstances if they have acted in good faith.[19]

It is said that the law, by giving legal consequences to the mistaken belief of a third party as to the reality of a given situation, plays a curative[20] or corrective[21] role, tempering the strict mechanisms of the civil code. This is certainly true of the doctrine of *mandat apparent*, which the French courts originally created in order to protect third parties who, in good faith, contracted with directors of a company who had acted in breach of their authority granted in the company's statutes. This was so because it was thought inopportune constantly to ask third parties to check the extent of powers of company directors.[22] However, following reform of French company law in 1966,[23] the doctrine of *mandat apparent* is now enshrined in the French commercial code and applies to all types of companies.[24]

In the light of this legislative intervention, it was feared that the doctrine of *l'apparence* would slowly disappear from mandate. This fear proved unfounded initially since, for some time, case-law in this area grew to such an extent that *mandat apparent* became the largest application of the theory of *l'apparence*. Some explain this growth by the fact that it is necessary to maintain the security of transactions.[25] However, more recently, its application has grown more rare and *mandat apparent* tends now to be applied as a last resort.[26] This might be due to some drawbacks in the doctrine, as will be seen later. However, even

---

against third parties who have dealt without knowing of that revocation, except for the remedy of the principal against the agent. See also *Cass Civ 3ème, 10-1-1984*, Bull Civ 1984, III, no. 7.

[18] The principal bears the burden of proving that the third party was aware of the fact that the agency has ended: *Cass Com 17-6-1997*, RJDA 1997, no. 1341.

[19] Art. 2009 CC.   [20] Guestin, *Traité de droit civil*, p. 829.

[21] M. Boudot speaks of *l'apparence* as 'corrective justice': Boudot, 'Apparence', para. 8.

[22] P. Malaurie, L. Aynès and P. Y. Gautier, *Cours de droit civil: Les Contrats spéciaux*, 14th edn (Paris: Cujas, 2002), p. 371, para. 579.

[23] Statute no. 66-357 of 24-7-1966. The present French company law derives from the Civil Code of 1804 and the Commercial Code of 1807. However, by 1966, following the successive additions and modifications made to the codes since the nineteenth century, the legislation had become out of date and rather inconsistent. Modernisation was effected by the Law of 24 July 1966 and the Decree of 23 March 1967. For more information on the historical evolution of French company law, see J. Le Gall, *French Company Law* (London: Oyez Publishing, 1974).

[24] For more detail, see A. Danis-Fatôme, *Apparence et contrat* (Paris: LGDJ, 2004), pp. 137–43.

[25] See Malaurie, Aynès and Gautier, *Contrats spéciaux*, p. 371, para. 579.

[26] *Ibid.* See also Ph. Le Tourneau, 'Mandat' (2000) *Répertoire de droit civil*, para. 175.

though the 'golden age of l'apparence is gone, l'apparence has not disappeared yet'.[27]

For some time, the doctrine of *mandat apparent* did not have an independent existence, but relied rather on the mechanisms of the law of tort for its legal basis.[28] Under this basis in the law of tort, the third party could only rely on *mandat apparent* and hold the principal liable provided two conditions were fulfilled, namely: (a) by proving that the principal was at fault,[29] that he had participated in the creation of the appearence of authority of the agent that the third party had believed in and relied upon it; and (b) that he had acted in good faith.[30] Good faith as a requirement was very easily proven.[31] The latter condition operated to ensure that the third party was indeed worthy of protection; if the third party knew that the agent had acted beyond his authority, then, regardless of the fault of the principal, he could not rely on *mandat apparent* to bind the principal. Today, the element of good faith, although not expressly required by the French courts is, nevertheless, still present in the French courts' assessment of the legitimacy of the belief (this matter is explored further below).[32]

To base the principal's liability on fault is the best possible solution. It protects the third party who is the victim of an illusion and reinforces the sanctity of contracts. More importantly, it also explains how the principal can be liable for acts to which he did not consent.[33] In other words, when the actions of the principal have participated in the creation of the appearance of authority, it seems justifiable to hold him liable. Over the years, the actions of the principal which have been found by the courts to

---

[27] Boudot, 'Apparence', p. 2, para. 1. For a similar view, see Le Tourneau, 'Mandat', who cites as an example *Cass Civ 1ère, 6-1-1994, Mlle Paris* v. *Epoux Salgado, Gaz Pal* 1994, 1, 108; *Bull Civ* 1994, I, no. 1, where the third party could rely on the existence of an apparent mandate created by an estate agent even though the law relating to estate agents requires the authority of the agent to be in writing.

[28] Its legal basis was Art. 1382 CC, which stipulates that whoever causes damage to a third party through his fault, imprudence or negligence must compensate the victim of that damage (author's translation). 'Tout fait quelconque de l'homme qui cause à autrui un dommage, oblige celui par la faute duquel il est arrivé à le réparer.'

[29] *Civ 30-12-1935, DH* 1936, 81.

[30] *Cass Req 26-1-1903, DP* 1904, 1, 391.

[31] Good faith is presumed in French law. It is a presumption which can be rebutted by showing, by any means, that the third party knew of the reality of the situation: *Cass Civ 3ème, 18-7-1995*, no. 93-17278, as cited in Boudot, 'Apparence', para. 126.

[32] See II 2 below.

[33] Such are the recurring themes behind the corrective notion of *mandat apparent*. Boudot, 'Apparence', para. 24.

constitute fault have been wide and varied. Some cases look at the manner in which the principal has drafted the agency contract. If it is drafted in very general[34] or obscure[35] terms, or when the principal gives the agent a free hand,[36] the principal is liable since such terms can lead the third party to believe that the agent has particular powers when that is not, in fact, the case. Similarly, the principal who secretly reduces the agent's authority will be liable.[37] Other cases concentrate on the principal's imprudence in, for instance, allowing the agent to imitate his signature,[38] allowing one employee to use the name of the company for his own personal use, or for failing to criticise the agent who had, several times before, acted in breach of his authority.[39] A wide number of issues can be understood as constituting imprudence on the part of the principal as the following case illustrates:[40] the owner of a shop had asked someone he did not know to look after his shop in his absence and, in particular, had asked him to receive delivery of various goods. The owner also allowed the person in question to use the shop's commercial stamp. That person used the stamp to order goods from a third party. He sold these goods and disappeared with the proceeds. When the supplier of the goods in question requested payment from the principal, the latter was found liable on the basis of apparent authority, created by his imprudence in entrusting his shop to someone he did not know.

The obvious problem of using tort as the legal basis of the principal's liability is that, when the principal is not to blame, the third party is left unprotected. Recognising the need to protect the interests of third parties acting in good faith, the French courts sought to widen the liability of principals through the subterfuge of finding the principal liable simply for choosing the wrong agent[41] or for giving the agent the means to deceive a third party.[42] Such attempts were, however, seen as artificial[43]

---

[34] *CA Paris, 25-3-1892, DP* 1892, 2, 263. [35] *CA Montpellier, 4-5-1949, D* 1949, *Somm* 46.
[36] The French legal expression is a '*blanc seing*'. *Req 13-2-1883, DP* 1884, 1, 80.
[37] *Req 14-6-1875, S* 1875, 1, 368. [38] *Req 20-2-1922, DP* 1922, 1, 201, note Savatier.
[39] *Cass Com 3-3-1953, Bull Civ* 1953, III, no. 62. [40] *CA Paris 5-12-1953, D* 1954, J 315.
[41] *Req 14-6-1875, S* 1875, 1, 368.
[42] In *Cass Com 8-12-1959, Bull Civ* 1959, I, no. 434: where an insurance company which gave the director of one of its branches abroad some letter-headed paper was found to be at fault when the director used this paper to act in breach of authority.
[43] J. Calais-Auloy, *D* 1963, J 278. See an interesting decision where the Supreme Court indicated that the principal could be found vicariously liable, as occurs in the relationship between master and servant under Art. 1384-5 CC in *Req 8-5-1840*, JCP 1941, II, 1610. However, this is not a satisfactory solution, given that the agent is not in a similar position of subordination. This jurisprudence was never applied again.

and the courts were criticised for trying to find fault in the principal's behaviour at all costs.[44]

This unsatisfactory situation dramatically changed in 1962, with the case of *Banque Canadienne Nationale*,[45] when the French Supreme Court, in its most formal setting,[46] abandoned the notion of fault[47] as the legal basis for *mandat apparent* and the doctrine finally gained legal autonomy. In this case, the director of a bank[48] set up as a limited liability company[49] had signed a contract with a third party whereby the bank would act as a guarantor to the value of FF 700,000. When the third party asked the bank to honour its guarantee, the bank denied any liability. It argued that the director had no authority to bind the bank. The statutes of the bank expressly required the signature of two agents who had been given specific power to act in this way. Relying on the well-established basis of *mandat apparent* in the law of tort, the bank argued that because they had committed no fault, nor had they been negligent or even imprudent, they could not be bound by the appearance of authority that the third party believed the director to have.

The Supreme Court rejected such a plea and held that:

> The principal can be liable on the basis of the *mandat apparent*, even in the absence of fault on the part of the principal, provided that the belief of the third party as to the extent of the powers of the agent is legitimate. Such belief is legitimate when the circumstances were such that the third party was allowed not to check the exact limit of this power.[50]

With this decision, the doctrine of the *mandat apparent* finally emerged as an independent doctrine, and the source of the principal's liability,

---

[44] G. Cornu, *RTD Civ* 1963, 573.

[45] *Cass Ass Plén 13-12-1962, Banque Canadienne Nationale*, D 1963, J 277, note Calais-Auloy.

[46] Following a division amongst the judges of the first civil chamber of the Cour de Cassation as to whether apparent authority could exist even without the principal's fault, the President of the said chamber called the court to sit in its plenary session in order to give a definite answer. See P. Esmein (1963) *JCP* II, 13104. As mentioned above, the decision of the plenary session is final (see n. 9).

[47] It is, however, clear that if the conditions for liability in tort are present, such basis can and will be used: *Cass Civ 1ère, 15-10-1974*, D 1975, *Somm* 13.

[48] In French, Président Directeur Général.   [49] In French, Société Anonyme, or SA.

[50] Author's translation. The French version is: 'Attendu que le mandant peut être engagé sur le fondement du mandat apparent, même en l'absence d'une faute susceptible de lui être reprochée, si la croyance du tiers à l'étendue des pouvoirs du mandataire est légitime, ce caractère supposant que les circonstances autorisaient le tiers à ne pas verifier les limites exactes de ce pouvoir.'

based on the legitimate belief of the third party in the authority of the agent.[51] All that is required on the part of the third party is proof that he legitimately believed that the agent had authority to bind his principal.

Given that this notion of the third party's *legitimate belief*[52] is the sole condition required for the *mandat apparent* to apply, it is possible now to explore both its meaning and content.

2 The sole condition of application of the doctrine of mandat apparent: *the legitimate belief of the third party that the agent has authority to act*

The 1962 case of *Banque Canadienne Nationale* is a crucial decision. By replacing the requirement of principal's fault with the notion of legitimate belief, it significantly reinforces the protection of third parties[53] and gives the *mandat apparent* its long-awaited autonomy. All that the third party is required to do is to establish that his belief in the appearance of authority of the agent is legitimate. Unfortunately, however, the court has failed to define a legitimate belief. It simply states that the belief is legitimate when the 'circumstances are such that the third party was allowed not to check the exact limit of his power'. This is a serious omission, as the notion was, until this case, unknown in French law.

Following this case, over a period of a few years, the civil chambers of the Cour de Cassation failed to apply the doubtful notion of the legitimate belief. Instead, it required the victim to establish that he had made a 'common mistake',[54] a requirement which already existed for cases of apparent ownership. This is, however, problematic, given that a common mistake is very difficult to prove.[55] Consequently, the results of this

---

[51] It must be noted that the notion of a legitimate belief had already been used by the Cour de Cassation, although never in such a formal setting: *Ch Req 4-5-1936* and *Ch Req 11-5-1936*, H. Capitant (ed.), *Les Grands Arrêts de la Jurisprudence Civile*, 10th edn (Paris: Dalloz, 1997), p. 788.

[52] The fact that this source of obligation can merely be the legitimate belief of a third party is criticised as failing to constitute a proper legal basis; in other words, it seeks to bind the principal to something to which he did not consent. It is now accepted that this legitimate belief creates a quasi-contract between the principal and the third party. Boudot, 'Apparence', p. 7, paras. 51–53.

[53] Some say that the result of this case means that 'en fait de mandat, croyance légitime vaut titre'. Malaurie, Aynès and Gautier, *Contrats spéciaux*, p. 371, para. 580.

[54] In French, *erreur commune*.

[55] Common mistake was described by Professor Calais-Auloy as a mistake that is 'humanly impossible not to make'. See his note in *D 1966, J 449*.

approach were harsh on the third party,[56] as the 1965 decision of *Epoux Perrais* v. *Veuve Morrand et autres*[57] illustrates. In this instance, Mr and Mrs Perrais were farmers who were working on land belonging to Mrs Vachon. The couple wished to buy a portion of that land and in April 1958, in the presence of the notary usually employed by Mrs Vachon, Mr Perrais signed a contract of sale. Mrs Vachon refused to sell the land in question arguing that her notary, in this instance, had no authority to act. Mr and Mrs Perrais therefore sued Mrs Vachon for breach, arguing that she was bound on the basis of apparent authority. They pointed to the fact that a contract had been signed in the presence of the notary, whom the couple knew to be the notary that Mrs Vachon usually employed. This, they argued, led to a legitimate belief that he had authority to act for Mrs Vachon to sell the portion of land in question. There was therefore no need for Mr and Mrs Perrais to check whether the notary, in fact, possessed full authority.

The Court of Appeal and the Cour de Cassation rejected their plea and held that *mandat apparent* can only be created when the third party proves that he made a common mistake, which has to be both 'likely and excusable'. The Cour de Cassation then added that, in the present circumstances, the fact that Mr Perrais knew that the notary was the one that Mrs Vachon usually used, was insufficient to establish his mistake as a common mistake.

Some have explained the reluctance of the civil chamber of the Cour de Cassation, in this case, to apply the notion of legitimate belief by reference to its desire to control the manner in which the lower courts apply the concept.[58] To others, the court's approach can be explained by reference to the fact that acts of disposition require a greater degree of caution on the part of the third party. A mistake in such circumstances will be considered more strictly by the courts.[59]

The reluctance on the part of the first civil chamber to apply the notion of legitimate belief ended in 1969, when the first civil chamber of the

---

[56] The strictness is all the more apparent in later cases where the courts took into consideration the fact that the agent was a professional agent such as a notary. In such cases it was accepted that the third party's belief in the appearance of authority was legitimate. See nn. 103, 104 and 105 below for further details.

[57] *Cass Civ 1ère, 30-11-1965*, D 1966, J 449, note Calais-Auloy.

[58] The assessment of the legitimacy of the third party's belief was, at first, thought to be purely a question of fact. Since the Cour de Cassation can only review issues of law and not fact, it could not therefore control it: R. Lindon in his note on *Cass Com 28-2-1966*, *JCP* 1967, II, 15217.

[59] J. Calais-Auloy, D 1966, J 449.

Supreme Court in *SCI Les Genévriers et autres* v. *Bonnin et autre*[60] and *Consorts Kenicq* v. *Martin*[61] (the first and third of three cases heard on the same day)[62] reasserted the *ratio* of *Banque Nationale Canadienne*[63] by stating that:

> If one person can be bound on the basis of apparent authority, this is so on condition that the belief of the third party that the supposed agent has authority to act is legitimate; such a belief is legitimate when the circumstances are such that the third party was justified in not checking the power in question.[64]

Apart from the fact that this constitutes a clear return to the legitimate belief of the third party as the legal basis for *mandat apparent*, the outcome of this case significantly widens the *ratio* of *Banque Nationale Canadienne* by applying the doctrine of *mandat apparent* to situations where the agent has no authority to act whatsoever.[65] Whereas in *Banque Nationale Canadienne* the court stipulated that 'circumstances were such the third party was authorised not to check *the exact limit of the power in question*', the Court, in the first and third decisions of 1969 stipulated that 'circumstances are such that the third party was authorised *not to check the power in question*'.

---

[60] *Cass Civ 1ère, 29-4-1969, 1ère espèce, JCP G* 1969, II, 15972; *RTD Civ* 1969, 804.

[61] *Cass Civ 1ère, 29-4-1969, 3ème espèce, JCP G* 1969, II, 15972.

[62] The second decision is that of *Riou* v. *SA La Cuiller en Bois*. In spite of the repetition of the ratio almost to the letter, the 1969 decisions divided academics on the issue of the conditions necessary in order for *mandat apparent* to be effective. Some authors thought that, in addition to the legitimacy of the belief, the 1969 decisions added the condition that the third party must act in good faith. Others only saw one condition, that of the legitimacy of the belief. Professor de Quenaudon argues that closer attention must be paid to the wording of the decision, which indicates that the belief must be legitimate: see de Quenaudon, 'Le mandat', fasc. 20, p. 46, para. 67.

[63] It has been suggested that there was a return to the notion of legitimate mistake in a decision which took place three years previously: *Cass Com 29-3-1966, RTD Civ* 1968, 169; *JCP* 1967, II, 15310. See also *Cass Civ 1ère 13-6-1967, JCP* 1967, II, 15317.

[64] Author's translation. The French version is as follows: 'si une personne peut être engagée sur le fondement d'un mandat apparent, c'est à la condition que la croyance du tiers aux pouvoirs du prétendu mandataire soit légitime, ce caractère supposant que les circonstances autorisaient le tiers à ne pas vérifier lesdits pouvoirs.'

[65] The 1969 ratio was confirmed in *Cass Com 29-4-1970; Cass Com 4-10-1975*. It has been suggested that the courts are more demanding in relation to the burden of proof where the agent has no authority whatsoever. See de Quenaudon, 'Le mandat', fasc. 20, p. 45, paras. 65–66. As a result, there is disagreement as to whether the doctrine really applies to both situations. See Huet, *Contrats spéciaux*, § 31208 and de Quenaudon, 'Le mandat', fasc. 20, p. 42, para. 61.

The facts of the third decision can now be reviewed briefly (*Consorts Kenicq* v. *Martin*). In this case, the Supreme Court widened the scope of the doctrine of *mandat apparent* to situations where there was no agency at all. In this case, Mr Martin was the tenant of a flat in a building co-owned by Mr and Mrs Kenicq and Mr and Mrs Kenicq-Léger. A dispute arose between Mr Martin and the landlord, Mr Kenicq, in relation to work to be undertaken in the flat that Mr Martin was renting. Negotiations ensued between Mr Martin and the co-owners. In order to end the negotiations, Mrs Kenicq alone agreed in writing that they would pay for the work requested by Mr Martin. This document was sent to Mr Martin through his counsel. When Mr Martin tried to enforce the promise, Mr Kenicq refused on the ground that Mrs Kenicq was not party to the negotiations and therefore had no power to make such a promise on behalf of the others. Mr Martin raised proceedings. He argued that Mrs Kenicq's presence during the negotiations and her status as wife of one of the co-owners gave rise to a legitimate expectation that she had authority to make such a promise in writing.

At first instance and on appeal, the courts found in favour of Mr Martin on the basis of apparent authority. The Supreme Court, however, quashed the decision of the Court of Appeal on the basis that it had not specified the circumstances that absolved Mr Martin from the duty to check whether Mrs Kenicq could act as agent at all. As such, therefore, the decision lacked a proper legal basis.

The 1969 decisions did indeed widen the concept of *mandat apparent*, to the extent that the 'principal' will find himself bound by a contract which is not necessarily in his best interests.[66] This wide application of the doctrine has attracted both criticism and praise. Some authors have criticised the court for going too far, arguing that the application of *mandat apparent* stretches the principle of representation beyond acceptable bounds. Others have justified the attitude of the court on equitable principles and contractual sanctity.[67] Interestingly, even though the 1969 decisions of *Consorts Kenicq* v. *Martin*[68] and *SCI Les Genévriers et autres* v. *Bonnin et autres*[69] widened the ratio of the case of *Banque Nationale Canadienne*, in none of these cases was the third party's belief found to be legitimate.

---

[66] *Cass Com 21-3-1995, D 1995, IR 139.*   [67] Huet, *Contrats spéciaux*, § 31217, p. 1151.
[68] *Cass Civ 1ère, 29-4-1969, 3ème espèce, JCP G 1969, II, 15972.*
[69] *Cass Civ 1ère, 29-4-1969, 2ème espèce, JCP G 1969, II, 15972.*

The 1962 case of *Banque Nationale Canadienne* and the 1969 decisions of *Consorts Kenicq v. Martin*[70] are undeniably important. However, even after these decisions, exactly what constituted a 'legitimate belief' remained subject to doubt. The court failed to identify the types of 'circumstances' which absolve the third party from the duty of checking the powers and/or the extent of the authority of the agent.

The resultant approach does, of course, give to judges a certain degree of flexibility. The situation is nevertheless regrettable because it renders the theory of *mandat apparent* difficult to apply[71] and undermines certainty. The burden of proving the legitimacy of the belief relating to authority and/or the existence of mandate lies on the person[72] wishing to rely on *mandat apparent*. The lack of detail is therefore regrettable, since it undermines the position of those it seeks to protect.

The lower courts have the power to ascertain the legitimacy of the belief, although this power is controlled by the Supreme Court. The two aspects must be looked at in turn in order to assess the criteria which apply to the legitimacy of the belief.

(a) The manner in which the lower courts assess the legitimacy of the belief of the third party

In most circumstances, the belief will relate to a factual situation. In rare circumstances, however, a belief which relates to the law will be relevant.[73] There is no restriction as to the type of acts undertaken by the agent to which *mandat apparent* can apply.[74] This wide protection of the

---

[70] *Cass Civ 1ère, 29-4-1969, 3ème espèce, JCP* G 1969, II, 15972.

[71] Malaurie, Aynès and Gautier, *Contrats spéciaux*, p. 372, para. 582.

[72] *Cass Civ 1ère, 13-11-1980, D* 1981, J 541. Whilst in most scenarios such a person will be the third party, there are a few examples where it will be the principal. See *CA Versailles 9-3-1982, Rev Loyers* 1983, 204, where the landlords tried, unsuccessfully, to claim that the person whose name appeared on the tenancy agreement was bound as principal of the person who had used her identity in order to get the tenancy. See also *Cass Civ 3ème, 12-2-1986, Rev Loyers* 1986, 131: no *mandat apparent* for the renewal of a tenancy agreement signed by one spouse when the business (*fonds de commerce*) belonged to two spouses. The landlady's argument that the signature of one spouse bound both spouses, the signing spouse being the agent of the other was unsuccessful. She had been told that signature of such a contract necessitated both signatures. However, in such situations, the courts apply a strict approach to the question of the legitimacy of the belief of the principal, especially if he is a professional (the matter is explored further below at II 2(a)(i)).

[73] *Cass Civ 7-8-1883, DP* 1884, 1, 5 In this case couples were married by a civil officer who did not have the requisite authority to do so. Although this involved ignorance of the law, this factor could not be used against the couples married in this way.

[74] Boudot, 'Apparence', p. 10, para. 80.

third party is counterbalanced by the fact that he has to prove that his belief is legitimate, i.e. that his failure to check the agent's power or extent of his authority was justified in the circumstances.

Although there is no clear indication of what those 'circumstances' are, it is possible to divide them into two categories: those which relate to the parties within the triangular agency relationship; and those which do not.[75]

(i) Circumstances relating to the agent, principal or third party

Circumstances relating to the victim of the apparent authority   The personality of the victim of apparent authority is of crucial importance to the courts, since it is the legitimacy of his belief that the courts assess.[76] In fact, it has even been said that the way in which the French courts assess legitimacy depends to a great extent on whether the third party requires protection.[77] This view can be supported by case-law and can, in part, be explained by the notion of good faith.

As mentioned earlier, prior to the decision of *Banque Canadienne Nationale* in 1962, a third party would only be protected by the doctrine of *mandat apparent* provided that the principal was at fault and that he, himself, had acted in good faith. Following the above-mentioned decision, the good faith of the third party is clearly not a condition of the application of the *mandat apparent*. Good faith is, arguably, nevertheless still present in the way the French courts analyse the legitimacy of the belief of the victim.[78] Some even suggest that good faith is inherent in the 'legitimacy' of the belief.[79] A third party who knows of the limit and/or lack of authority of the agent cannot claim to have legitimately believed in the appearance of authority. This would constitute acting in bad faith.[80] It is possible, therefore, to argue that good faith continues to play an important role.[81]

---

[75] This classification is borrowed loosely from Danis-Fatôme, *Apparence et Contrat*, pp. 145–68.

[76] See *ibid.*, p. 145.

[77] Huet, *Contrats spéciaux*, p. 1153, § 31219. See also Guestin, *Traité de droit civil*, p. 855, para. 864.

[78] Some even argue that, for *mandat apparent* to apply, two conditions must be satisfied, namely (a) that the belief must be legitimate and (b) that the mistaken party must be acting in good faith. See Huet, *Contrats spéciaux*, p. 1153, § 31219.

[79] Le Tourneau, 'Mandat', para. 183.   [80] Esmein, *JCP* 1963, II, 13105.

[81] *Cass Civ 1ère, 12-11-1998, Cne de Moulin* v. *Mme Henriques et autre*, D 1999, IR 39.

In the light of the above, when assessing the legitimacy of the third party's belief, the courts pay close attention to his status.[82] In particular, the courts will consider whether the victim is educated[83] or not;[84] and whether the victim is employed or not. Such circumstances are significant to the task of ascertaining whether the third party was more likely to fall victim to the appearance of authority. However, the mere fact that the third party is in employment does not automatically mean that the belief cannot be legitimate. The courts will also look at the type of work that the third party does and the amount of responsibility that the job entails. Looking at the case-law, it seems that the less responsibility the job requires, the more likely the courts will be to find that the belief of the third party is legitimate, as is illustrated by the case of *Melle Paris* v. *Epoux Salgado*.[85]

In this case an estate agent was in charge of selling a flat, but, in contravention of a statutory requirement, did not have authority in writing.[86] Nevertheless, he had, on behalf of the owner, signed an agreement to sell to the defendants. The buyers later sought to hold the owner liable on the basis of apparent authority. The court held that the couple's belief in the agent's authority was legitimate. The court took into consideration, amongst other factors, the fact that the husband was an ironmonger and his wife was unemployed. They stated that, under such circumstances, the belief that the agent had authority to sell the flat was legitimate and that they did not have to ask to see the contract of mandate. In another case, the court noted that, since the third party was a teacher, his belief that the agent had authority to act could not be legitimate.[87] In a further example, the court even took into consideration the fact that the husband of the victim was working in the legal

---

[82] *CA Lyon 26-11-1970, SCI Les Genévriers* v. *Coinde et autre, D* 1971, *Somm* 69, where the Court of Appeal held that in order to analyse the legitimacy of the third party's belief, one had to take into consideration, amongst other things, the personality of the third party.

[83] In *CA Riom 28-7-1938, Gaz Pal* 1938, 2, 674, the court held that the belief in apparent authority was an 'inadmissible mistake for a man of such a level of education'.

[84] *Cass Civ 3ème, 4-3-1971, Bull Civ* 1971, III, no. 160, where it was held that an old woman with very little education and very modest means could reasonably believe the *appearance* of authority that had been created. Similarly, in *Cass Civ 3ème, 27-11-1969, Bull Civ* 1969, III, no. 771: the third party was a person with no real education. The third party's belief that the agent was acting within his authority was found to be legitimate.

[85] *Cass Civ 1ère, 6-1-1994, Bull Civ* 1994, I, no. 1 at 1; *D* 1994, *SC* 208.

[86] Statute 70–9 of 2-6-1970.

[87] *CA Aix en Provence, 12-9-1985, Bull d'Aix* 1985, p. 42, no. 128.

profession in order to find that her belief in the appearance of authority was not legitimate.[88]

In addition to taking into account the third party's social status, the courts also make a clear distinction between professionals and non-professionals, the latter's erroneous belief in apparent authority being more likely to be excused and therefore legitimate.[89] It is said that the reason why the courts are stricter on third parties who are professionals is because their experience in business is such that it should make them more cautious.[90] This seems clear in the case of *Mme Mc Kelvey* v. *Banque Régionale de l'Ouest*.[91] In this case, a father gave certain bonds to the bank as security when his daughter applied for a loan. When the bank came to rely on such bonds, the daughter denied that the father had authority. The bank sought to retain the father's bonds on the basis of apparent authority. The court held that there was no apparent authority, since the bank, as a professional body, should have known that for such transactions, mandate must be expressly agreed in writing, which was not the case on the facts.

The courts seem particularly strict with a third party who is a professional when the position he holds is such that he should be aware of certain customs, as the following two decisions illustrate.

In *SCI Les Genévriers et autre* v. *Bonnin et autre*,[92] the two defendants (Bonnin and Coinde) had contracted with the managing director of a building society, specialising in the sale and administration of real estate (SCI Les Genévriers), to buy a portion of the company's real estate. The company, however, refused to sell as agreed on the basis that the director had no authority to sell since the statutes of the building society expressly limited the powers of its director to the administration and not the sale of its real estate. Bonnin and Coinde raised legal proceedings against the building society arguing that it was bound by the acts of its director on the basis of *mandat apparent*. Bonnin and Coinde argued that they were not required to check the statutes of the building society, since they could

---

[88] *Cass Civ 3ème, 28-5-1997, Juridisque Lamy*, case no. 865.

[89] Danis-Fatôme, *Apparence et contrat*, para. 219, p. 146. The author remarks that the distinction between professionals and non-professionals is problematic, because the courts can have a strange conception of exactly what a non professional is. See, e.g., *Cass Com 16-1-1990, RTD Com* 1990, 270, where the court considered that a small mutual insurance company which had no litigation department was a consumer.

[90] Malaurie, Aynès and Gautier, *Contrats spéciaux*, nos. 582 and 583.

[91] *CA Versailles, 24-6-1988, D* 1988, *IR* 241.

[92] *Cass Civ 1ère, 29-4-1969, 1ère espèce, JCP G* 1969, II, 15972.

assume that the director of a building society specialising in the sale and administration of real estate had power to sell parts of such real estate and their belief that the director had authority was therefore legitimate. The Court of Appeal agreed.

The first chamber of the Supreme Court, however, quashed the decision of the Court of Appeal on the ground that the belief of the defendants that the director of the building society had the power to sell was not legitimate. The court held that since Bonnin and Coinde were professionals and one of them was himself a managing director of a company, they could not assume that the director had power to sell real estate simply because he was the director of a building society without checking the statutes of the company. The belief might have been legitimate had it related to non-professionals, but not to professionals.

In *Riou v. Société Anonyme La Cuiller en Bois*,[93] Riou, a businessman, had lent FF 22,500 to a restaurant business, which was set up as a limited company. Riou had conducted the negotiations for the loan with Dame Sée, who appeared to be the director of the company, and was the person who had signed an acknowledgement of the debt on behalf of the restaurant business. When Riou asked the defendant company to reimburse the said sum, the latter refused, arguing that Dame Sée was a simple employee and had therefore no authority to borrow money on their behalf. Riou therefore raised an action, claiming that the restaurant was bound on the basis of *mandat apparent*. Riou claimed that his belief that Dame Sée was the director was legitimate since she had signed the acknowledgement of the debt as 'Dame Sée, acting as director, with authority', which gave him the impression that she had authority to do so. The Cour de Cassation confirmed the decision of the Court of Appeal that Riou's belief that Dame Sée had authority to act was not legitimate. This was on the grounds that he was a businessman, and as such, he should have known that the conditions in which the loan had been agreed were 'in total contrast to the normal commercial customs in this area of business'. The Court held that Riou was therefore taking a risk by not following the normal customs and his belief could therefore not be legitimate.

These two decisions show that a professional has a duty to be vigilant. The courts are stricter in their analysis of the legitimacy of the belief insofar as it applies to such persons. Some even suggest that the courts are more likely to doubt the good faith of a professional compared to a

---

[93] *Cass Civ 1ère, 29-4-1969, 2ème espèce, ibid.*

non-professional.[94] The more recent decision of *Commune de Matoury* v. *Société Unimat*,[95] however, casts doubt on this view. In this case, in September 1993, the mayor of a town had signed, without the required authority from the municipal council, two contracts for the hire of certain office supplies. Despite the lack of authority, the municipal council nevertheless paid the monthly instalments due under the contract for a year and then stopped. The supplier sued the town for breach of contract and claimed damages. The municipal council argued that they did not owe anything; the contract signed by the mayor was null and void. This was on the basis that he did not have authority, not having obtained the required authority of the municipal council before signing the contract. The supplier, however, argued that the town was bound on the basis of apparent authority. The court accepted their plea on the ground that, even in the absence of approval of the municipal council, the behaviour of the latter was such that it had created an appearance of authority. The court stated that, since the municipal council is in charge of the budget of the town, the council could not be unaware of the existence of the two contracts in question since it had paid the monthly instalments. Since the council had not questioned the existence of such contracts, such behaviour expressly authorised the mayor to sign such contracts. The supplier's belief that the mayor had authority to act was therefore legitimate.

Even though the status of the third party is of paramount importance in the exercise of analysing whether that person is more likely to fall victim to the appearance or not, there are nevertheless circumstances where even a non-professional's belief in the appearance of authority will not be found to be legitimate. Thus, a person can be under a duty to check the power of the agent and, if he fails to discharge this duty, he will not be protected. A good illustration of this point is a case in which the agent purported to represent a church.[96] In this case, a priest had approached the defendants and offered to sell them a piece of land. The priest, however, had no authority to do so, since the piece of land in fact belonged to one of the plaintiffs, Le Cyste SA, a commercial company, which was under the control of the church. The latter claimed, therefore, not to be contractually bound. The defendants, however, claimed that there was a contract on the basis of apparent authority. The Court of Appeal of Bastia rejected their plea on the ground that, seven years

---

[94] G. Cornu, *RTD Civ* 1969, 804–6.   [95] *Cass Civ 1ère, 28-6-2005, AJDA* 2005, 2124.
[96] *CA Bastia 20-12-1985 SARL d'Etudes et de Réalisations Immobilières Sériomo; Ass Le Cyste et Ass diocésaine du diocèse d'Ajaccio* v. *Consorts Orazzi, D* 1987, J, 363.

earlier, the defendants had bought a portion of a land adjacent to the one in dispute and therefore knew that the land in question belonged to the plaintiff. In consequence, the defendants could not legitimately believe that the priest had apparent authority to bind the company. Similarly, the court will reject a plea of apparent authority when the third party who contracts with an agent who is unauthorised actually knows the real agent of the principal.[97]

If the belief of the third party that the agent has power to act is due to the third party's own negligence, then the third party cannot rely on the appearance of authority. In such cases a simple investigation of the circumstances would have disclosed the reality. For instance, the third party should not remain passive if, after having observed that the contract he was about to sign stated that no agent had been appointed, he deals with an agent.[98] Similarly, there will be no legitimate belief when a few elementary precautions would have allowed the third party to avoid being mistaken as to the reality.[99] This would also be the case where the presence of certain anomalies should have raised the suspicion of the third party,[100] or even when the circumstances surrounding the formation of the contract are themselves suspicious. An example of this idea occurred in a case where the victim of a fraud tried to rely on the doctrine of apparent authority in order to bind an insurance company.[101] In July 1982, the victim enquired from the senior cash clerk of an insurance company about setting up a contract of capitalisation. The victim wanted to pay in cash (a mode allowed by statute for bearer bonds). The senior cash clerk arranged the transaction and, in December of the same year, the victim handed to the clerk the sum of FF 399,000 in two instalments. This took place in a café outside the insurance company buildings. The senior clerk gave the victim a receipt on letter-headed paper of the insurance company for each of the instalments. Unbeknown to the victim, the cash clerk had been dismissed two months earlier and he

---

[97] *TC Le Havre, 2-7-1962, GP* 1963, unreported, cited in Danis-Fatôme, *Apparence et contrat*, para. 238, p. 161.

[98] *Cass Civ 1ère, 15-10-1991, Bull Civ* 1991, I, no. 272.

[99] *CA Lyon 9-10-1963, D* 1964, 402.

[100] *Cass Civ 1ère, 6-7-1976, JCP* 1978, II, 45. In this case a third party's belief was found not to be legitimate. The belief related to the fact that a husband was the agent for his wife. The third party was, however, aware that the couple had been involved in divorce proceedings for years. A contract in terms of which the third party had rented a farm was therefore held null and void. It has been remarked that it is now very difficult to establish apparent authority between husband and wife. See G. Cornu, *RTD Civ* 1977, 570.

[101] *Cass Civ 1ère, 4-3-1997, RJDA* 1997, no. 902.

disappeared with the victim's money. When the victim raised the issue of apparent authority before the Court of Appeal of Versailles, the court accepted his plea on the ground that the manner in which the victim handed over the money was not suspicious since the victim had every reason to believe that the cash clerk was still employed by the insurance company. This was particularly so given that the clerk had provided a receipt for the money on letter-headed paper. The Cour de Cassation, however, quashed the decision of the Court of Appeal on the ground that the circumstances were such that the victim should have checked the authority of the alleged agent. The victim's belief was held not to be legitimate in the circumstances. Finally, it probably goes without saying that the third party cannot rely on apparent authority when he knows that the agent does not have authority to act.[102]

Circumstances relating to the 'agent'   A court will also take into account the circumstances relating to the agent, and, in particular, whether they could lead the third party to believe that the agent has authority. Relevant circumstances include the status of the agent and the way he behaves towards the third party.

The status of the agent can induce the third party to believe that the agent has authority to act. This can lead the victim to decide not to check whether the agent is authorised. This is particularly likely to be true where the agent is a professional who inspires particular confidence, such as a barrister,[103] a solicitor[104] or a notary.[105] The status of the

---

[102]   *CA Versailles, 16-1-2004, RG* 01/06298 unreported. In this case the third party claimed that an art expert had apparent authority to sell a painting, even though the expert had told the third party that the owner of the painting had not yet given his unconditional assent to the sale.

[103]   *CA Lyon, 8-1-1986 Epoux P* v. *Soc R, D* 1987, SC 66. In this case, the lawyer of the plaintiff had written to the lawyer of the defendant in order to settle a dispute out of court. The letter started as follows: 'I am the usual counsel of Mr P.' The letter went on to explain the terms of the settlement. When the plaintiff refused to pay the money as agreed in the settlement on the ground that his lawyer had no authority, the defendant argued that the plaintiff was bound on the basis of apparent authority. The court held that the manner in which the offer of settlement was formulated, i.e. the fact that the barrister of the plaintiff had mentioned that he was his 'usual counsel', was such that the defendant could legitimately believe that he had authority to settle on behalf of his client. There was therefore no need for him to check the extent of his power and the plaintiff was therefore bound by the terms of the settlement.

[104]   *CA Paris, 1-4-1936, Gaz Pal* 1936, 2, 165.

[105]   *Cass Civ 3ème 5-6-2002, Bull Civ* 2002, III, no. 131; *Cass Civ 3ème, 4-10-2000, SCI Megève* v. *SAFER Rhone-Alpes et autre, Bull Civ* 2000, III, no. 160, where a party had

agent is also relevant when the agent, because of his profession, is perceived to have general powers, since it gives the impression that he will be able to bind the principal in all circumstances.[106] An example of such an agent is the insurance agent who represents only one insurance company.[107]

However, on its own, the third party's perception that certain powers are associated with a given profession is not always sufficient. The courts may also look at the nature of the powers involved. If the powers used by the agent are powers which are usual for that kind of profession, then the third party's belief that there is authority and/or mandate will be considered to be legitimate. There will be no need to check the existence and/or extent of the agent's powers. However, if the powers are not usual for the kind of profession that the agent is in, then the belief will not be legitimate. As a result, the third party will be subject to the duty to check the agent's powers, as the case of *Veuve Vigournoux* v. *Margot*[108] illustrates. In this case, the court held that the third party could not legitimately believe that the notary empowered to receive money due under the contract for a life annuity[109] would also have the power to cancel a termination clause in case of late payment. Such a power would have been manifestly much wider than the power the notary had been granted under the mandate.

The fact that an agent has special authority in any given case can lead the third party to believe that the agent has a similar degree of authority in a related situation. There are many illustrations of this point, particularly in the case of estate agents; for instance, an estate agent who has power to conclude a lease can lead the third party to believe that he also has power to modify the terms of the lease.[110] Similarly, an estate agent who has authority to renew a lease can lead the third party to believe that he also has authority to collect the rent.[111] Finally, an estate agent who

---

relied upon the act of a notary to believe that the notary had authority to act on behalf of his client. There was a legitimate belief and the sale of the land at the price and conditions defined by the notary was valid. Because of the act, there was no need for SAFER to check that the notary had power as such power is inherent within such a position. This decision can be contrasted with the 1965 decision where the court used the notion of common mistake, see n. 56 above.

[106] Danis-Fatôme, *Apparence et Contrat*, p. 149, para. 222.

[107] In France they are know as *agents généraux d'assurance*: general insurance agents.

[108] *Cass Civ 3ème, 15-6-1976, D 1976, IR 272* .   [109] In French, *rente viagère*.

[110] *Cass Soc 20-6-1962, Bull Soc IV, No 577, p. 157.*

[111] *Cass Civ 3ème, 13-10-1958, Bull Civ 1958, III, no. 341 at 287.*

has authority to sign the lease also has authority to terminate it.[112] This idea is not, however, unlimited.[113]

The courts also take into consideration the way the agent behaves towards the third party. The fact that the agent introduces himself to the third party as the agent of the principal may legitimise the belief of the third party that he is indeed the agent.[114] Relevant issues include the fact that the agent signs a contract of sale agreement as an agent,[115] or that he has drafted an insurance contract and that he has sent a certificate of insurance which is valid until the insurance policy is established.[116] Another example is a case in which a couple reserved a flat with a person they believed was the agent. They had no concerns about his authority because he had always been the only person the couple had negotiated with. It was held that they could indeed rely on that agent's apparent authority.[117] A further example is the case of *Compagnie Gan Incendie* v. *Mme de Campos*,[118] where an insurance broker was found to be the agent of an insurance company on the basis that, on the various documents he had sent to the defendant, the logo and insignia of the plaintiff's insurance company appeared in large, bold letters.

Circumstances relating to the principal   Ever since the seminal decision of *Banque Nationale Canadienne* in 1962, fault on the part of the principal is no longer a requirement for apparent authority.[119] Yet some argue that the principal's fault can still be taken into consideration

---

[112] *CA Paris, 10-3-1992*, unreported, cited in J. Monéger, 'Baux commerciaux et théorie de l'apparence' (1993) I *Juris-Classeur périodique: édition notariale et immobililière* 103 at 109.

[113] In *Cass Civ 1ère, 2-10-1974*, D 1974, IR 239, JCP 1975, II, 17860, the court held that simply because the agent had power to negotiate the sale did not mean that the agent had power to receive the sale proceeds.

[114] *Cass Civ 1ère, 6-1-1955*, JCP 1955, II, 8731, note Besson.

[115] *Cass Civ 1ère, 6-1-1994*, Mlle Paris v. Epoux Salgado, Bull Civ 1994, I, no. 1 at 1, D 1994, SC 208, note Delebecque; RTD Com 1994, p. 548, no. 12, note Bouloc.

[116] *Cass Civ 1ère, 9-5-1978*, Bull Civ 1978, I, no. 182 at 68.

[117] *Cass Civ 3ème, 8-11-1968*, Bull Civ 1968, III, no. 455 at 347. For a similar outcome, see *Cass Civ 1ère, 3-6-1998*, RTD Civ 1998, no. 1, 668, note Mestre, where a third party was arguing that the principal was bound on the basis of apparent authority on the ground that he had a telephone conversation with the agent and the latter had sent him some brochures with prices.

[118] *CA Versailles 19-9-1997*, no. 97–802 (unreported).

[119] *Cass Ass Plén 13-12-1962, Banque Canadienne Nationale*, D 1963, J 277, note Calais-Auloy.

by the courts, if that fault has created or contributed to the third party's erroneous belief that the agent had authority to act.[120]

The manner in which the courts assess the principal's role in the creation of the appearance tends to operate against the principal, as is illustrated by the case of *Rouquette* v. *Fermatec SA*.[121] In this case, a railway station building was left without any surveillance. A rogue went into the building and used the phone and telex to order goods from a third party. The goods were duly dispatched to the rogue, who took delivery of the goods and then disappeared without paying for them. The third party invoiced the station manager, who refused to pay for them. The court, however, held that the station manager was liable on the basis of *mandat apparent*. The court held that the belief of the third party was legitimate. It was relevant to this decision that the rogue was able to use the premises and the telex in order to place the order for the goods. This being the case, there could be no doubt in the third party's mind that he had authority to do so. The court added that the station manager 'was no stranger to the circumstances created and was therefore bound to pay for the goods even though such goods had been ordered without his consent and without his authority'.

A similar result was reached in a more recent case[122] where the court held that a banker who holds a promissory note in good faith is not required to check either the signature or the extent of the power of the person who signed it. The court added that a company was bound by the signature of its agent unless the company could prove that it had not played any part in the creation of the appearance of authority towards the bank.[123]

The courts also rely on the behaviour of the principal in order to reject the legitimacy of the third party's belief. As a result, the fact that the principal negotiated the contract terms and price with the third party was held by the court[124] to be an issue which was relevant to their rejection of the existence of that apparent authority. The principal's involvement

---

[120] Danis-Fatôme, *Apparence et contrat*, p. 153, para. 225.
[121] *Cass Com 12-5-1987, D* 1987, IR 134.
[122] *Cass Com 9-3-1999 Caisse Mutuelle de Dépôts et de Prêts d'Hagondage* v. *Société de Construction et de Bâtiments et industrie, RJDA* 1999, no. 464; *D* 1999, IR 94; *D* 1999, *Aff* 831, *LPA*, no. 73 of 13-4-1999, p. 11; *RJDA* 1999, no. 464.
[123] The court stated: 'sauf à elle d'établir être étrangère dans la formation de cette apparence de mandat.'
[124] *Cass Civ 1ère, 15-10-1991, JCP* 1991, IV, 438.

meant that the third party was subject to a duty to check whether the agent had authority to act.

(ii) Circumstances external to agent, principal and third party

Urgency can constitute a relevant 'circumstance' leading to a finding that the third party's belief in *mandat apparent* is legitimate. This has been found to be the case even where the third party failed to check the powers of the agent.[125] This explains why the courts accept *mandat apparent* more readily in commercial transactions where trust and speed of the transaction are of paramount importance.[126]

The nature of the contract entered into is also considered carefully. If the contract involves large sums of money, the courts usually require a greater degree of vigilance from the third party and it will therefore be more difficult for that party to prove the legitimacy of his belief.[127] This is especially the case if the third party is a professional.[128] Similarly, it has been remarked that the court is less likely to accept the legitimacy of the third party's belief when the contract involves an act of disposition compared to an act of administration.[129] On the other hand, if the third party orders goods which are of little financial value, the courts are more likely to find the belief to be legitimate.[130]

If, in a particular area of commerce, it is not customary to check the powers of an agent, the courts are more likely to find that *mandat*

---

[125] *Cass Civ 1ère, 11-10-1972, Bull Civ* 1972, I, no. 201, where urgency during a presidential campaign was such that the printing company did not check the powers of the member of the committee of support (*comité de soutien*) of a presidential candidate.

[126] Guestin, *Traité de droit civil*, p. 856, para. 864.

[127] *Cass Civ 1ère, 13-10-1998, Juridisque Lamy*, case no. 1545, where the court rejected the plea of the third party after emphasising the nature of the contract involved (a sale of a real estate) and the fact that the sums involved were very high.

[128] See, e.g., *Cass Com 20-10-1998*, D 1999, *Aff* 28, where a credit financial backer (*crédit-bailleur*) was not entitled to rely on apparent authority to bind a bank to the acts of a credit-taker (*crédit-preneur*). In this instance, the sums at stake were huge and the court held that the immatriculation number of the credit-taker was false and he was not a client of the bank the financial backer was dealing with. The third party should have been put on guard because of the sums involved.

[129] J. Huet, *Droit civil: Les contrats spéciaux civils et commerciaux*, 5th edn (Paris: Montchrestien, 2001) p. 449, no. 703.

[130] *Cass Com 8-7-1981, Bull Civ* 1981, IV, no. 315 for the purchase of some hams by an employee of a company. The circumstances which made the third party's belief that the agent had authority legitimate were that the employee had large powers of representation and the value of the goods was reasonably small. See also *TI Nîmes, 29-6-1982*, D 1983, J 13, where the tribunal found that a child who had bought goods of small value through a mail catalogue was an 'agent' of his parents, who were consequently bound.

apparent exists. This is the case for a variety of professionals such as estate agents,[131] notaries[132] or publicity agents.[133]

(b) The control of the Supreme Court over the legitimacy of the belief

The Supreme Court controls the reasoning of the lower courts, ensuring that it is applied in a consistent manner. Some have criticised this level of control, arguing that it intrudes into consideration of the facts, over which, traditionally, the Supreme Court has no jurisdiction. However, this level of control is justified by the need for consistency.[134] The court's supervisory power can be split into three headings: the material elements of the appearance of authority; its intensity; and the coherence of the reasoning.[135] Each of these elements will now be considered.

Under the first heading, the Supreme Court ensures that the reasoning of the lower courts is sufficiently precise. The decision will be quashed if the lower courts have failed to explain precisely what are the elements allowing the third party to argue that his belief was legitimate, as was the case in the aforementioned decision of *SCI Les Genévriers et autre* v. *Bonnin et autre*.[136]

Under the second heading, the court may check whether the appearance would have caused a reasonable man to be legitimately mistaken.

Finally, under the third heading, the *Cour de Cassation* may check whether the reasoning of the lower court is logical and consistent. If it is not, then the decision will be quashed. This occurred in the case already referred to involving an insurance scam.[137] It will be recalled that, in that

---

[131] *CA Aix en Provence, 25-9-1984, JCP* G 1984, IV, 215: it is not the custom for a potential tenant to require the estate agent to show him the agency agreement he has with the landlord in order to check the agent's extent of authority. See also *Cass Civ 1ère, 6-1-1994, RJDA* 1994, no. 802; *Bull Civ* 1994, I, no. 1 at 1, *D* 1994, *SC* 208 where an estate agent had bound the apparent principal in the sale of his house even though the sale had not been carried out in conformity with the Statute 70-9 of 2-1-1970. This lack of conformity could be legitimately ignored by the third party as it is not usual for a third party to enquire whether an estate agent has authority to sell or not.

[132] *Cass Civ 3ème, 2-10-1974, JCP* G 1976, II, 18247.

[133] *Cass Civ 1ère, 11-2-1997, Bull Civ* 1997, I, no. 52. A third party's belief that the department of Gers was the principal of a publicity agent was found to be legitimate. This was on the strength of the agent's statements that his company was acting on behalf of the principal and a contract between them showing that the agent had power to send the bill for the rent of publicity space directly to the department of the Gers.

[134] Guestin, *Traité de droit civil*, p. 857, para. 865.

[135] Classification adopted from Boudot, 'Apparence', p. 17, paras. 146–8.

[136] See n. 92 above and associated text.   [137] *Cass Civ 1ère, 4-3-1997, RJDA* 1997, no. 902.

case, a third party had tried to rely on apparent authority to bind an insurance company. The third party had handed over cash to an ex-cashier of the insurance company in a café outside the company building. On the one hand, the court of appeal had held that the plaintiff could legitimately believe that the ex-chief cashier could be regarded as the agent of the insurance company. On the other, the Court of Appeal stated that the circumstances in which the party had handed over the cash were such that the third party was at fault. This fault negated the fact that the mistake was legitimate.

The discussion above has illustrated the fact that the rules in this area are uncertain. This is indeed regrettable, although some argue that this is a normal consequence of a system created to correct rules of law. Such corrections apply only as and when necessary.[138]

III Ratification

As previously mentioned, the general position in the French Civil Code is that the principal cannot be bound by acts which the agent has carried out in breach of his authority. This restrictive position exists because of the strict mechanisms of representation. When the agent acts outside his mandate, he has no power to act on behalf of and in the name of the principal. The agent therefore does not represent the principal and cannot, in consequence, create a binding obligation on his behalf. This principle, although strictly adhered to by the French courts,[139] is nevertheless subject to exceptions, one of which is that the principal may choose to be bound by ratifying the unauthorised acts of the agent.

Even though ratification is expressly permitted by the civil code, it is defined restrictively. The principal can only ratify acts carried out by the

---

[138] Guestin, *Traité de droit civil*, p. 857, para. 865.

[139] *Ch Req 30-12-1931, DH* 1932, 65, where the director of a bank, in breach of his authority, granted one of the bank's clients (a company) credit facilities which were disproportionate to the power of the company to repay them. Relying on the rule of the civil code whereby the principal is only bound by the acts of the agent carried out in accordance with the powers granted within the mandate, the bank argued that they were not bound by the transaction and the court accepted their plea. See also *Cass Civ 3ème, 12-4-1976, JCP* 1976, II, 18840: the owners of a flat asked an estate agent to find a potential buyer for their property and to give them the name of this potential buyer. In breach of his authority, the estate agent sold the property to a third party. The couple successfully resisted the sale to the third party on the ground that the estate agent had only been given the power to introduce a potential customer and had breached his mandate by selling the property to the third party.

agent in breach of his authority (Art. 1998-2 CC). However, the French
courts have interpreted this article widely, allowing the principal to ratify
a much wider variety of acts, ranging from acts carried out by the agent in
excess of power, acts where the agent has no power whatsoever, or
situations in which the agent has continued to act after the contract of
mandate has been revoked. This wide interpretation does not raise any
real difficulty since, as it has been remarked,[140] in none of these three
situations is the agent authorised. The law does not treat the 'agent' as
agent, but rather as the manager of the principal's affairs.[141] The 'agent's'
acts can be adopted by the 'principal' through ratification.

This idea was extended in 1980 in the case of *Cauvin* v. *Sté Librairie
Flammarion*,[142] where the Supreme Court found ratification to be possible even where the 'agent' who had acted outside his authority had also
purported to act in his own name. In 1957 the defendant had published a
book on insects written by Mr Cauvin. In 1962, following poor sales, the
parties agreed to end their relationship. In December 1972, the defendant
contacted the plaintiff to inform him that they had entered into a
publishing contract with Sterling, an American publishing company,
for the publication of an English version of the plaintiff's book. The
plaintiff noticed mistakes in the text and requested the defendant to delay
publication pending correction of the mistakes. No such delay took
place, and the plaintiff raised an action, arguing that the publishing
contract should be set aside on the basis that the defendant had breached
its authority by allowing publication of an English version of the book.
The plaintiff also claimed damages. The Court of Appeal held that the
publishing contract had been ratified and was therefore valid, although it
additionally awarded the claim for damages. On appeal to the Supreme
Court, the plaintiff argued that ratification could not have occurred since
the defendant, in breach of its authority, had also purported to act in its

---

[140] de Quenaudon, 'Le mandat', fasc. 20, p. 31, para. 40.

[141] In French, *le gérant d'affaires*. The relationship between the *gérant* and the owner is a
quasi-contractual one called a *gestion d'affaires*. It is regulated by Art. 1372 CC, which
stipulates that: 'where one voluntarily manages another's business, whether the owner is
aware of the management, or whether he is not, he who manages contracts a tacit
undertaking to continue the management which he has embarked on, and to complete it
until the owner is in a position to look after it himself; he must also take charge of all the
continuations of that business. He is then subject to all the obligations which would
result from an express authority which the owner might have confided to him.'
Translation from www.legifrance.gouv.fr.

[142] *Cass Civ 1ère, 28-4-1980, Bull Civ* 1980, I, no. 129 at 105; *RTD Civ* 1981, 408.

own name. The Supreme Court, however, held that this did not prevent ratification by the plaintiff.

This decision has received equal amounts of praise and criticism. Those who argue in its favour rely on the adage *ubi lex non distinguit*, whereby the civil code does not make a distinction as to how the agent acted. They further argue that, provided the principal shows a clear willingness to ratify, the status of the person who carried out the act is irrelevant.[143] The opponents of the decision argue that it goes too far, mainly on the basis that the agent acted in his own name. It should follow, therefore, that there is no representation. They further argue that the condition that there must be representation is implied in the text of Art. 1998-2 CC. Ratification is, therefore, ruled out.[144]

As with the doctrine of apparent authority, the burden of proof of ratification falls on the party who wishes to rely on it.[145] The conditions that must be satisfied in order for a plea of ratification to be successful will now be analysed. A review of the effect of ratification will follow, which will encompass not only the relationship between the agent and the principal but also that between the principal and the third party.

1 Form and conditions of ratification

Ratification is a unilateral act carried out by the principal. The civil code stipulates that ratification can be express or implied (Art. 1998-2 CC). In spite of this apparent absence of formality, the case of *d'Hauterive* v. *Perdrigeon*[146] nevertheless suggests that the process of ratification must follow similar requirements as apply to the process of confirmation defined in Art. 1338 CC.[147] In this case, the defendant, in breach of his authority, had completed a financial operation on the stock market. When the defendant informed the plaintiff of his actions, the latter did not object and in fact later accepted in writing that the action was valid. However, the plaintiff later sued the defendant for breach of authority claiming that ratification was not valid, having failed to fulfil the

---

[143] For more details, see de Quenaudon, 'Le mandat', fasc. 20, p. 35, para. 49.

[144] *Ibid.* [145] *CA Poitiers, 19-4-1967, D 1968, SC 9.*

[146] *Cass Req 13-6-1883, D 1884, 184.*

[147] Art 1338-1CC stipulates that: 'An instrument of confirmation or ratification of an obligation against which legislation allows an action for annulment or rescission is valid only where are found therein the gist of that obligation, mention of the ground of the action for rescission, and the intention to cure the defect upon which that action is based.' Translation from www.legifrance.gouv.fr.

conditions defined in Art. 1338 CC. The Supreme Court rejected this plea, stating that ratification of an unauthorised act is regulated by Art. 1998 CC and not Art. 1338 CC. Consequently, ratification could result 'from any act, fact, or circumstance'. This decision therefore reinforced the position reached a few years earlier when the court stated that there was 'no prescribed form of ratification'.[148]

The only exception to this general rule is that where the act to be ratified is subject to a formality, the ratifying act is subject to the same formality.[149]

This lack of formality is understandable if one considers that the central issue requiring to be proved in ratification is the principal's consent.[150] Consequently, ratification will be valid on the cumulative conditions (a) that the 'act, fact or circumstance' show 'on the principal's part, a clear willingness to ratify';[151] and (b) that the principal knows of all the acts carried out by the agent which either lie outside his authority or exist in circumstances where the agent had no authority whatso-ever.[152] Judges at a lower level can verify whether these two conditions have been fulfilled,[153] given that, in essence, they involve a factual enquiry. The conditions are cumulative but interlinked, since a principal cannot display a clear wish to ratify if he is not aware of the existence of the agent's act. This point is illustrated by the case of *Veuve Taconet* v. *Mage*.[154] In this case, the plaintiff's financial affairs were managed by a notary. In May 1930, in breach of his authority, the notary sold to the defendant some hypothecary claims[155] belonging to the plaintiff. Two months later, in July 1930, the notary wrote to the plaintiff asking her to provide him with a mandate to sell some of her claims by signing a pre-prepared form. The notary did not, however, provide the plaintiff with full details of what had been sold to the defendant. The plaintiff signed the form as requested and sent it back to the notary. The Court of Appeal held that this amounted to ratification of the contract of sale entered into in May 1930 and the plaintiff was therefore bound to the defendant. The decision was, however, quashed by the Supreme Court, which held that the mere fact that the plaintiff signed the blank form

---

[148] *Cass Req 11-11-1879, DP 1880, 1, 421. Cass Req 6-12-1893, DP 1893, 1, 352.*
[149] *Civ 13-12-1875, DP 1875, 1, 97.*
[150] de Quenaudon, 'Le mandat', fasc. 20, p. 32, para. 42.
[151] *Cass Req 6-12-1893, DP 1893, 1, 352.*
[152] *Cass Req 27-7-1863, DP 1863, 1, 460.*
[153] *Cass Civ 1ère, 6-2-1996, Bull Civ 1996, I, no. 66.*
[154] *Cass Civ 30-12-1935, D 1936, 81.*   [155] In French, *créances hypothécaires.*

could not amount to ratification. This was because, on the date that the form had been signed, she was unaware of the notary's acts which had taken place two months previously. She could not therefore consent to the agent's act.

It is usually not difficult to prove that the principal has consented to ratify. In particular this may be proved where the principal willingly performs the contractual obligations concluded on his behalf by the agent. This point is illustrated by a case in which a wife promised to the director of a company that she would buy shares in the company on her husband's behalf. She did not, however, have authority to do so. When her husband paid the price of the shares to the director of the company, the court held that this amounted to ratification.[156] The principal's desire to ratify was established by his subsequent actions.[157]

Problems arise, however, when the principal neither specifically objects to the 'unauthorised' act, nor yet expressly ratifies it. The French courts have held that the principal has ratified where he fails to show his disapproval of the act.[158] An illustration of this is *George Blanche* v. *Boutonnet et autres*,[159] where the plaintiff and defendant inherited a house. Neither party lived in the house, although the defendant was in charge of management of it. In this capacity, the defendant entered into a contract with a third party, a Mrs Dufour, who agreed initially to rent, but eventually to buy, the house. Payments of rent were sent each month to the plaintiff's bank account. However, when Mrs Dufour sought to enforce the agreement for the sale of the house, the plaintiff refused, arguing that he was not bound by such a contract. He argued that he was not even aware of its existence and could not, therefore, have ratified it. The court disagreed, finding that the plaintiff could not claim to be unaware of the contract since he had received rental payments each month without objection. His silence amounted to tacit ratification and, consequently, he was bound.

In cases where silence on the part of the principal is involved, the courts must take particular care to ensure that the second condition of ratification is fulfilled, in other words that the principal is aware of the transactions entered into. This was made clear in the case of *Lerestif des Tertres* v. *Thomas*,[160] when the court stated: 'if the silence of the

---

[156] *Civ 7-4-1851, DP 1851, 1, 92.*   [157] *CA Pau 16-3-1892, S 1893, 2, 125.*

[158] *Req 6-2-1893, DP 1893, 1, 352.*

[159] *Cass Req 9-6-1931, S 1931, 1, 312.* It is to be noted that this case expressly refers to *gestion d'affaires* and not mandate.

[160] *Cass Civ 27-7-1863, D 1863, 457.*

principal … can, in certain circumstances be regarded as a tacit ratification of acts done in his name, it is on the condition that the principal was
aware of such acts.' Silence alone cannot bind the principal.[161] The
assessment of the knowledge of the principal is, once again, a question
of fact, as the case of *de la Châteigneraie* v. *Commune de Marsillargues*
illustrates.[162] In this case the defendant, the council of a small town,
wanted to acquire a small portion of the plaintiff's land in order to build a
canal to bring water to the town. The defendant wrote to Mr Poilon, who
was in charge of the plaintiff's affairs. Mr Poilon agreed to the defendant's proposal. Some time after the work had started, the plaintiff
contended that she was not bound by the agreement since Mr Poilon
had no authority to act on her behalf. She further argued that, since she
had not ratified the agreement, she was not bound. The Court rejected
her plea. Ratification had occurred through silence: since the plaintiff
knew of Mr Poilon's letter agreeing to the defendant's request and had
failed to object to it, this amounted to ratification.[163] It has been suggested that there are similarities between ratification through silence and
apparent authority, given that both are used by the courts to protect the
third party.[164]

Two further conditions are necessary in order for ratification to be
valid: the principal must have capacity to ratify;[165] and the act itself must
be capable of being ratified (i.e. ratification must occur within a certain
time limit). This is especially important if such a limit has been defined
by the third party as occurred in a case in 1934.[166] In this case, the third
party made an offer to an agent to buy goods, stipulating that this offer
had to be accepted within a certain time limit. The agent had no authority
to accept, but nevertheless did so within the agreed time limit. The
principal attempted to ratify but the ratification came after the expiry
of the time limit. The court held that the ratification was not valid, since
the consent of the third party had lapsed.

---

[161] See, e.g., the case of *Veuve Taconet* v. *Mage*, n. 154 above and associated text.
[162] *Cass Req 4-6-1872, S 1872, 1, 295.*
[163] See also *Cass Civ 3ème, 2-5-1978, Austin* v. *Epoux Barley et autres, Bull Civ 1978*, III,
no. 173, where the Supreme Court confirmed the decision of the Court of Appeal, which
held that silence had amounted to ratification. In the fifteen years prior to his death, the
'principal' had neither criticised nor contested any of the acts done by the 'agent'. He
had received the full price for the sale of the group of flats and therefore his estate was
bound by it.
[164] Huet, *Contrats spéciaux*, ch. 3, p. 1150, para. 31214.
[165] Le Tourneau, 'Mandat', para. 368.   [166] *Cass Civ 18-4-1934, Gaz Pal 1934, 1, 970.*

The third party need not be made aware of ratification by the principal for it to be valid. It has been suggested that this is justifiable on the basis that the third party consents to the act when he contracts with the agent.[167]

2 The effects of ratification

Following the adage that 'ratification amounts to mandate',[168] it will have an impact both on the 'internal' and the 'external' relationship. These relationships can be considered separately.

(a) Internal relationship

Considering first the relationship between principal and agent, ratification has the same effect between the parties as would be the case had a proper mandate been granted. Thus, the agent has a right to be paid for his services. More importantly, ratification retroactively validates acts performed by the agent.[169] The principal cannot therefore sue the agent for breach of authority or delay in the administration of his affairs.[170] Thus some have argued that ratification is the renunciation by the principal of the right to criticise his agent.[171] The principal may, however, expressly reserve the right to do so in the act of ratification.[172] The principal can 'tailor' the act of ratification according to his needs, for example, limiting the effect of the ratification to his dealings with third parties only. In this way it does not affect his rights *vis-à-vis* the agent.[173]

(b) External relationship

Considering now the external relationship, ratification binds the principal to the third party on the terms agreed to by the unauthorised agent. Because ratification applies not only to cases in which the agent acts outside the authority but also to cases where the 'agent' has no authority at all, in most situations, ratification will be beneficial to third parties.

---

[167] However, others say that the third party does not enter into a contract with the agent, since the latter does not want to be personally bound. The correct analysis is therefore as follows: the third party makes an offer; following the rules of creation of contracts *in absentia*, this offer is then accepted when the principal ratifies. de Quenaudon, 'Le mandat', fasc. 20, p. 35, para. 50.

[168] Adage used in *Cass Civ 14-1-1868*, S 1868, 1, 136.

[169] *Cass Req 14-3-1860, DP* 1860, 1, 258.   [170] *Cass Civ 9-5-1853, DP* 1853, 1, 293.

[171] M. Storck, as cited in de Quenaudon, 'Le mandat', fasc. 20, para. 52.

[172] *Cass Civ 9-5-1853, DP* 1853, 1, 293.   [173] *Cass Req 28-3-1855, DP* 1855, 1, 165.

The principal will be required to perform the act as agreed by the 'agent'. In fact, it is more common for third parties to seek to rely on ratification. However, because ratification has retroactive effect, the principal can also rely on ratification to require performance from the third party. The case of *Société Tastevin et Co.*[174] is a rare illustration of this. In this case, the third party asked the agent of the company Société Tastevin et Co. to buy shares in the company. The agent did so, in breach of his authority. The director of the company purported to ratify and the third party became a sleeping partner.[175] However, after the third party had subscribed for shares, but before ratification, the company went into liquidation. When required to pay FF 10,000, the third party claimed that he was not bound, because the agent had acted in breach of his authority. The court disagreed and held that, since ratification had retroactive effect, the third party was bound from the time the agent had accepted his offer and was consequently obliged to pay.

Finally, retroactivity does not apply to 'pure third parties', i.e. third parties who are total strangers to the agency relationship. As a result, if such third parties have acquired rights, those rights cannot be affected by ratification.[176]

Thus far, this chapter has illustrated the manner in which a principal can be bound to a third party in circumstances in which he did not originally consent to be bound. This has been achieved through the use of apparent authority and ratification. These rules are present in order to protect the interests of third parties. Yet the agent has breached his contract of mandate and can be found liable for such breach. In the following section, the agent's liability to the principal and to the third party is considered.

IV The liability of the *falsus procurator*

The term *falsus procurator* applies equally to a person who pretends to third parties to be acting for a principal, i.e. for *mandat apparent*, and also to the agent who merely acts in breach of his authority. In the former case there is no mandate, and in the latter mandate is present. The latter situation is covered by the civil code, which contains clear rules. The former is, however, subject to doubt and, as a result, the two situations

---

[174] *Cass Req 14-3-1860, DP 1860, 1, 258.*   [175] In French, *associé commanditaire.*
[176] de Quenaudon, 'Le mandat', fasc. 20, paras. 56–8.

must be clearly distinguished. For ease of reference in this section the *falsus procurator* will be referred to as the agent.

The liability of the agent towards the third party is dealt with by Art. 1997 CC. This article stipulates that, where an agent has informed the third party of the real extent of his authority, that agent cannot be bound by transactions entered into beyond his authority unless he gives to the third party a personal undertaking to that effect.[177] Much therefore depends on the knowledge of the third party. It is also important to assess whether the agent makes a promise to the third party.

When a third party enters into a contract with an agent in the knowledge that the agent is acting in breach of his authority and failing to obtain a personal commitment from the agent, the third party will have no action against the agent for breach of authority. In such cases the third party bears the risk of contracting with the agent knowing the lack of his power. This acceptance of risk breaks the chain of causation.[178]

When the third party obtains a personal undertaking from the agent, the latter's liability will depend on the nature and extent of his undertaking. Usually, this undertaking constitutes a promise that the principal will ratify the act. This is referred to in French law as a *promesse de porte-fort*. In the absence of ratification by the principal, the agent is contractually liable for damages for his breach[179] (in which case damages will be assessed according to the rules within the civil code).[180] He is not, however, liable to perform the contract. This will only be the case if the

---

[177] In French, Art. 1997 CC reads as follows: 'Le mandataire qui a donné à la partie avec laquelle il contracte en cette qualité une suffisante connaissance de ses pouvoirs n'est tenu d'aucune garantie par ce qui a été fait au delà, s'il ne s'y est personnellement soumis.'

[178] Le Tourneau, 'Mandat', para. 339. The matter is dealt with by the courts with great clarity: see *Cass Civ 9-7-1872, DP 1872*, 1, 404, where the court held that the third party could not claim anything from the agent, since his loss was self-inflicted because the third party knew of the limitation of the agent's power. See also *Cass Civ 1ère, 16-6-1954, Bull Civ* I, no. 200, where even though the third party did not know of the limitation of the power, no liability arose. It was held that he ought to have known.

[179] *Cass Com 25-1-1994, D 1994, SC 211.*

[180] The rules relating to the assessment of contractual damages are defined by Art. 1149-1152 CC. Art. 1149 CC stipulates that, as a general rule, the party in breach is liable for the loss suffered and the profits he has been deprived of, i.e. the expectation interest. This only covers foreseeable or foreseen loss if the breach is not intentional (Art. 1150 CC). The limit is extended in case of an intentional breach, but even in such a situation, the contract breaker is only liable for immediate and direct consequences of the breach (Art. 1151 CC). It is, however, to be noted that there is very little case-law on the assessment of damages, since such a task is within the sovereign power of assessment of the *juges du fond* (first instance judges).

agent promised that the principal would perform the transaction (the agent is then a *del credere* agent).[181]

Reading Art 1997 CC *a contrario*, it is thought[182] that if the agent has not made the extent of his authority clear to the third party, the agent is liable for acts done in excess of that authority. The agent is at fault in failing to disclose the extent of his authority, and will consequently be liable for losses caused to the third party. The third party may himself have acted in a negligent manner. In such cases it has been suggested that liability may be apportioned between agent and third party.[183] The legal basis of this liability is the law of tort.[184] The agent is liable not only to the third party but also to any other person who has a direct interest in the proper performance of the contract.[185] The agent may be subject to an award of compensation *in natura*. The agent will thus be bound to perform the act in question unless performance is impossible because the contract was of a personal nature. Interestingly, however, in relation to bills of exchange[186] and in the statute for cheques,[187] the agent will be liable to perform the obligation on the principal's behalf.

The agent can also be contractually liable to the third party where, in breach of his authority, he purports to act in his own name and not in that of the principal.[188] In this situation the third party has no action against the principal.

---

[181] *Cass Req 19-1-1832, S 1832, 1, 677.*

[182] Huet, Contrats spéciaux, ch. 3, p. 1169, para. 31239. For a similar opinion, see de Quenadon, 'Le mandat', fasc. 20, para. 93.

[183] Le Tourneau, 'Mandat', para. 343.

[184] Tort rules are defined by Art. 1382-1386 CC. Liability will arise when there is a fault, a loss and a clear link between both. French law distinguishes between *préjudice* (loss which is susceptible to compensation) and *réparation* (quantification of damages). Compensation can be in kind (*en nature*) or by an equivalent sum (*par équivalent*), i.e. damages. Although the rules relating to the latter are based upon the principle that the victim must receive compensation for the entire loss suffered (*réparation intégrale*), it is nevertheless difficult to define which interest is protected, i.e. reliance or expectation. Assessing how much compensation is due is a question of fact and therefore within the sovereign power of the *juges du fond*. For more detail, see J. Bell, S. Boyron and S. Whittaker, *Principles of French Law*, 2nd edn (Oxford: Oxford University Press, 2008), pp. 415–17.

[185] *Cass Civ 1ère, 11-4-1995, Bull Civ I 1995, no. 171, D 1995, SC 231.*

[186] Art. L 511-5 al 3 code com stipulates that when someone adds his name to a bill of exchange on behalf of someone else without power to do so, that person will be bound in the same way as the 'principal' would have been had he acted with authority. If this person has paid, he has the same rights that the supposed principal would have had. The same applies for the agent has exceeded his authority.

[187] Art. 11 of the *decret-loi* of 30-10-1935 uses the same formula as above for the cheque.

[188] *Cass Civ 3ème, 17-10-1972, Bull Civ 1972, III, no. 528.*

The more pressing question, perhaps, is whether the agent can be found liable on the basis of the *mandat apparent* towards the third party. It seems that this question must be answered in the negative, since it is clear that the sole effect of *mandat apparent* is to bind the principal to the third party.[189] Although there is little case-law on this issue, it has nevertheless been argued[190] that the rules defined above, in terms of which an agent who fails to inform the third party of the extent of his authority is liable in tort to third parties (and to any other person having a direct interest in the proper performance of the contract[191]) additionally apply to the apparent agent as *falsus procurator*. However, in such a situation, the liability of the agent is based on tort,[192] and not on *mandat apparent*. This is because, through his behaviour, he has caused the third party to hold an incorrect belief as to the extent or existence of his authority.[193] Following the general principle that compensation for losses caused in tort can be *in natura*,[194] the apparent agent can be found liable to perform the apparent contract entered into with the third party (unless it is impossible for him to do so because the contract is of a personal nature). There is, however, an exception to this rule in that the apparent agent of a spouse cannot be held liable to perform the contract entered into.[195] The contract is null and void in order to protect the 'principal' spouse.

The third party therefore has a choice. He can choose to sue the principal, holding him liable on the contract by invoking the doctrine of apparent authority. He can instead choose to sue the false agent in tort provided that the relevant conditions apply.

V Acting for a company yet to be incorporated

Under French company law, once a company's statutes are signed, the company exists. However, following EU harmonisation on the

---

[189] *Cass Com 21-3-1995 Société Thalassa Shipping et autre v. Société Béninoise d'entreprises maritimes et autres, Bull Com* IV 1995, no. 101, pp. 89–90.

[190] Le Tourneau, 'Mandat', para. 343.

[191] *Cass Civ 1ère, 11-4-1995, Bull Civ* I 1995, no. 171, *D* 1995, SC 231.

[192] The basis of liability in the law of tort was reiterated in *CA Versailles, 30-11-1982 Rev Loyers* 1985, 133.

[193] *CA Dijon, 19-5-1931, DH* 1931, 405; *Civ 1ère, 3-5-1955, Bull Civ* I, no. 181.

[194] Le Tourneau, 'Mandat', para. 344.

[195] *Cass Civ 1ère 24-3-1981, Bull Civ* I no. 99; *JCP* 1982, II, 19746, note Le Guidec; *RTDCiv* 1981 854, note Durry; *Cass Civ 1ère 11-1-1983, Bull Civ* I, no. 14; *Cass Civ 1ère 28-3-1984, JCP* 1985 II 20430, note Henry.

subject,[196] the company does not acquire legal personality until it is fully registered. It is generally useful for certain contracts to be entered into even before registration occurs (for example, those relating to the opening of bank accounts or the hiring of employees). Since the company does not have legal personality, it cannot enter into such contracts. It is consequently necessary for someone, either the promoters of the company[197] or the company's directors, to 'lend their personality' to the company and act on its behalf during this period. In such a situation, the law is clear: whoever acts in the name of a company yet to be incorporated will be liable for such acts, unless the company, once fully registered, adopts them.[198] It is therefore possible to analyse the mechanism through which this is possible.

1 The duly registered company adopts the contracts

There are three methods which can be used by the duly registered company to adopt the contracts entered into on its behalf before registration. First, the simplest method is for the registered company to adopt the contracts through signature of the statutes. A precise account of all contracts entered into on behalf of the unincorporated company can be

---

[196] First Council Directive 68/151/EEC of 9 March 1968 on coordination of safeguards which, for the protection of the interests of members and others, are required by member states of companies within the meaning of the second paragraph of Art. 58 of the Treaty, with a view to making such safeguards equivalent throughout the Community, OJ 1968 No. L65, 14 March 1968, pp. 8–12. Before this, under French law, a company acquired legal personality as soon as the '*contrat de société*' was signed. For details, see M. Cozian, A. Viandier and F. Barbaux-Deboissy, *Droit des sociétés*, 17th edn (Paris: Litec, 2004), p. 87.

[197] In French, *les fondateurs*.

[198] Historically, the present French law of commercial companies derives from the civil code of 1804 and the commercial code of 1807. As a consequence, the above-mentioned rules can be found both in the civil code and the commercial code. Art. 1843 CC stipulates: 'Persons who have acted on behalf of a firm in the making before registration are liable for the obligations arising from the acts so performed, jointly and severally where the firm is a merchant, jointly in other cases. A firm regularly registered may take upon itself the undertakings entered into, which are then deemed to have been contracted by it as from the outset.' The corresponding article in the commercial code, Art. L 210-6 al 2 code com, stipulates: 'Persons who have acted in the name of a company in formation before it has acquired enjoyment of legal personality shall be held jointly and indefinitely liable for the acts thus accomplished unless the company, after having been formed and registered in due form, takes over its obligations thus entered into. These obligations shall then be deemed to have been entered into from the start by the company.' Both translations obtained from the French official website: www.legifrance.gouv.fr.

presented to the members[199] before they sign the company's statutes. By signing the statutes, the members effectively ratify such contracts.

Secondly, it is possible for the members to decide, prior to the signature of the company's statutes, to provide authority[200] to one or more of them to enter into contracts on behalf of the unincorporated company. In such a case, following the normal rules of representation, such acts will be automatically adopted by the company once it is fully registered, provided that such contracts are entered into by someone with authority to do so. The authority must explicitly define which contracts the person has authority to enter into. It is therefore not sufficient for the director[201] to rely on a clause within the company's statutes to the effect that 'all contracts entered into by the director within the objects[202] of the unincorporated company will be adopted by the company as soon as it is duly registered'. This does not enable the director to avoid personal liability.[203] It is therefore not possible for the company to adopt the contract on the basis of implied authority or on the basis of a mandate of a general nature. The burden of proof that a person has authority to act on behalf of an unincorporated company is on the person relying on it.[204]

Thirdly, the registered company can adopt the contracts entered into on its behalf by a decision reached by a majority of the members. Such a decision must be express and cannot be implied from the mere performance of an act by the company, as the following decision illustrates. In a case heard by the first civil chamber,[205] a member of an unincorporated company, later appointed director, had, for the benefit and on behalf of the unincorporated company, obtained a loan from a bank. After repaying the first instalments on the loan, the company was unable to repay the remaining sums due. The bank called on the guarantors of the company to pay, on the ground that repayment by the company of the first instalments constituted an implicit ratification by the company of the loan entered into by the members. The Cour de Cassation quashed the decision of the Court of Appeal.

---

[199] In French, *un associé*.

[200] Authority may have been granted in the statutes themselves or in a separate contract.

[201] In French, *le gérant*.

[202] In French, *l'objet social*. The form of the company will depend on the objects of the company. Certain forms of companies (limited companies, such as the SARL) can be formed in order to pursue any object or to carry out any activities, whether civil or commercial in character.

[203] *Cass Com, 21-7-1987, Rev Soc, 1987, 590.*   [204] *Cass Com 3-4-1973, Rev Soc, 1974, 90.*

[205] *Cass Civ 1ère, 2-10-2002, Bull Joly 2002, p. 1335; JCP E 2003, I, 627; D 2002, 2807.*

2 The conditions of the adoption of the contracts by the company

Two conditions can be noted here: those relating to the company itself and those relating to the contracts entered into.

In relation to the company, the central condition is registration. If the company is not registered, it cannot acquire legal personality. In such cases, the person who has entered into the contract will be personally liable. However, if this person was given authority to act by the members, either through an agency contract or through the statutes, then normal agency rules will apply and the company will be liable for all the acts entered into by the agent within his authority.[206] French law imposes no specific time limit within which a company must be registered.[207] However, in order to protect third parties from delays in company registration, they can rely on the concept of a company created in fact.[208] This means that although the company is not registered, it nevertheless exists in the eyes of the law and has therefore acquired legal personality because of its activity. The company in question is therefore liable for the acts entered into for the unincorporated company. This mechanism is advantageous to the third party because it leads to liability on the part of all directors, even those who did not personally enter into the contracts on behalf of the company.[209]

The conditions relating to contracts entered into on behalf of the company are threefold. First, the contract must be a legally binding contract. The company cannot therefore be liable for a tort committed such as unfair competition.[210] In the same vein, negotiations entered into by a director cannot be adopted since they are not binding.[211] Secondly, the contract must be entered into in the interests of the company, not those of the person who enters into the contract. Thirdly, the contract must be entered into in the name of the unincorporated company. The third party must be aware of the nature of the contract and that there may be a substitution of parties once the company is fully registered and adopts the contract.

---

[206] Although there appears to be no case-law on this issue, arguably, the rules of the apparent authority would also apply here.

[207] D. Vidal, *Droit des sociétés*, 4th edn (Paris: LGDJ, 2003), p. 153, para. 321.

[208] In French, *société créée de fait*.

[209] Vidal, *Droit des sociétés*, p. 153, para. 322.

[210] *CA Paris, 24-2-1977, JCP* G 1978, II, 18957, where some senior employees resigned from a company in order to create their own company and in doing so convinced some other employees to resign too in order to work for them.

[211] *CA Orléans, 22-2-1978, JCP* 1989, II, 19403.

3 The consequences of the adoption of the contract by the company

Following Art. 1843 CC, the adoption of the contract by the company is retroactive: the company is liable for the contract *ab initio* and the person who entered into the contract is released from any further contractual obligations. There is therefore a substitution of contractual parties.[212] However, the person who contracted with the third party will remain personally liable if the company was fraudulently created for the sole purpose of allowing him to avoid his liability to the third party.[213]

In order for the adoption of the contract by the company to be valid, the consent of the third party is not necessary. The contract may, of course, not always be in the interests of the third party.[214] He may wish to preserve his right to sue the member who entered into the contract on behalf of the company. That member may act as guarantor of the company, in which case, he remains liable in cases of default by the company.[215]

Finally, it is important to mention that when the company fails to confirm whether or not it is adopting the contract, the third party cannot force the company to do so. Where this is the case, his only action is against the person who entered into the contract. As already noted, if the company is not, in fact, registered, the third party will be able to rely on the mechanism of a company created in fact.

VI Acting for a party yet to be named

In French law, the mechanism of representation is at the heart of an agency relationship. However, it is not the sole condition of existence of an agency relationship. There can be representation without an agency relationship, as is the case when representation is imposed by law.[216] It is also possible to have an agency relationship without representation, as is the case with the '*déclaration de command*' and '*convention de prête-nom*'.[217] Such mechanisms have no link with the notion of apparent authority in the way it is understood in the common law.

---

[212] *Cass Com 10-10-1984, Bull Civ* IV, p. 214, para. 261.

[213] *CA Paris 22-11-1988, RTD Com* 1989, 241.

[214] Following Art. 1843 CC, the liability of persons who have contracted on behalf of the unincorporated company is joint. If the unincorporated company is a limited company, liability will therefore be reduced.

[215] This was the case in *Cass Civ 1ère, 26-4-2000, LPA*, 20-2-2001, note Bruggeman.

[216] Art. 389-3 CC for the representation of minors, Art. 219-1CC for the representation between spouses.

[217] M. L. Izorche, 'A propos du contrat sans représentation' *D* 1999, *Chron*, 369–373.

Both mechanisms have a secret or clandestine element[218] since, in the former, the identity of the 'principal' is not revealed to the third party from the outset and, in the latter, the third party is not even aware of the existence of the 'principal'.

The '*déclaration de command*' is used mainly in contracts for the sale of real estate, although it is not restricted to such contracts. The mechanism works as follows: the buyer or '*commandé*' may reveal to the seller, once the contract of sale has been entered into, that a third party, the '*command*', is the real purchaser since the *commandé* was only acting to the *command*'s order. The *command* is therefore substituted for the *commandé*. This doctrine is strictly applied, since the *command* must reveal himself within 24 hours of the conclusion of the contract of sale.[219] Otherwise, the *commandé* becomes the owner of the goods and the contract becomes a *convention de prête-nom*.[220] *Déclarations de command* are used, generally, for fiscal purposes,[221] because there is only one '*mutation*' between the seller and the *command* and not two (one between the seller and the *commandé* and then another one between the *commandé* and the *command*). This mechanism seems to be rarely used.[222]

The *convention de prête nom* is a type of simulation because an agency contract exists whereby the principal gives authority to the agent to act, but asks the agent not to reveal to the third party that he is acting on behalf of the principal. This explains the name of this concept – the agent lends his name to the principal. This *convention de prête nom* is very close to the English concept of undisclosed agency and has similar effects since the agent is personally liable for the acts he has entered into in his name with third parties. Those third parties will therefore be able to choose whether to act against the agent[223] or against the principal once he is revealed.

---

[218] Some even suggest that there is an element of 'disloyalty' involved: G. Flattet, *Les contrats pour le compte d'autrui: essai critique sur les contrats conclus par un intermédiaire en droit français* (Toulouse: F. Boisseau, 1950), no. 210.

[219] Art. 686 al 2, *code général des impôts* (tax code).

[220] Huet, *Contrats spéciaux*, no. 11504.

[221] P. Didier and Y. Lequette, *De la représentation en droit privé* (Paris: LGDJ, 2000), p. 71, para. 108. Some even say that the sole reason for its creation is fiscal: Flattet, *Les contrats pour le compte d'autrui*, no. 210.

[222] Didier and Lequette, *De la représentation*, p. 72, para. 108.

[223] *Cass Com 26-4-1982*, D 1986, 233, note Rambure.

VII Conclusion

This chapter has illustrated the manner in which the French courts have sought to redress the limitations of the civil code in protecting third parties' interests when the agent acts either in breach of his authority or with no authority whatsoever. In such situations, the third party's interests will only be protected in two instances, namely, if (a) the principal chooses to ratify the transactions in question or (b) the doctrine of *mandat apparent* applies. If neither of these options apply, the third party's only other solution is to seek to hold the agent personally liable for the transactions and claim compensation.

Holding the principal liable under the transaction is considered to be the best solution. This is because it protects third parties' interests at the same time as upholding the sanctity of contract. As such, ratification is a useful method of protection of the third party's interest. This is particularly so since the French courts have interpreted the principle of the civil code widely, so that it applies not only where the agent acts in breach of the authority defined in the mandate but also to those where a purported 'agent' acts for a 'principal'. Ratification also has the double advantage of being an informal act (express or implied), and has retroactive effect. However, ratification is only possible where the principal clearly consents to the transaction with the third party. As such, it tends to be limited to situations where the principal himself has an interest in being bound by the unauthorised act of the agent. The protective nature of ratification is therefore limited because it does not depend solely on the wishes of the third party. Similarly, the third party's ability to hold the agent liable seems to be an act of last resort, which will apply only when other avenues have failed. Moreover, since case-law in this area is very limited, the rules are under-developed. Academic writing in this area is also very sparse. This solution is therefore even less practically useful than ratification.

The third party will also be able to hold the principal liable for the acts of the agent through the doctrine of *mandat apparent*. This notion, which was created by the French courts specifically to protect third parties, has two main advantages. First, it has the same wide scope of application as ratification, since it covers both situations where the agent acts in breach of his authority and those where the third party believes a person to be the 'agent' of a 'principal' when this is not the case. Secondly, unlike ratification, it does not depend on the wishes of the principal. Finally, the doctrine of *mandat apparent* is easily invoked because the third party need only establish his *legitimate belief* in the appearance of authority and/or representation of the agent. Yet we have seen that this last advantage is something of a double-edged sword. On the one hand, use of the third party's *legitimate belief* is preferable to use of the principal's fault. This is because it widens the liability of the principal to situations in which he is not to blame. On the other hand, the notion of *legitimate belief* has never been clearly defined by the French courts, which have held that the belief will be legitimate when 'circumstances' are such that the third party is 'allowed not to check the authority and/or existence of the mandate of the agent'.[224]

There are advantages in this ambiguity: the concept is sufficiently to allow the French courts to apply it according to the needs of given situations. As such, the notion does fulfil the aim for which it was created: to give the courts the power to redress the rigours of the civil code towards third parties.[225] Even though this discretion is subject to the control of the Supreme Court, it nevertheless creates uncertainty. This, in turn, undermines its application and therefore the protective purpose of the doctrine. This uncertainty might very well explain the lack of use of the notion in recent times.

---

[224] *Ass Plén 13-12-1962, D 1962,* J 277 and *Cass Civ, 1ère, 29-4-1969, D 1970,* J 23.
[225] Le Tourneau, 'Mandat', para. 178.

3

Unauthorised agency in Belgian law

ILSE SAMOY

Table of contents

I Introduction

Representation is a legal mechanism that enables a person (the agent) to perform a legal act with a third person (the third party) on behalf of another person (the principal) and by which the legal effects of the act are imputed to the principal. As will be expanded upon below, the mechanism of representation is subject to two conditions: the agent must possess authority to represent, and the agent and the third party must act with the will to represent (*contemplatio domini*). When the first condition is not met, there is unauthorised agency.

The Belgian Civil Code ('BCC') does not contain general rules on representation. Rather, the BCC contains only specific applications of representation, in particular the contract of mandate (a contract whereby one party (the principal) grants authority to represent to another party (the mandatory) and instructs him to conclude a legal act on his behalf). Rules on the conditions and effects of representation are therefore integrated by the legislator in the rules on mandate, namely in Arts. 1997 and 1998 BCC. Moreover, these articles are said to be incomplete and badly edited.[1] The editors of the BCC considered the contract of mandate to be a small and unimportant contract to which only a few articles could be devoted.

In this chapter the general rules applicable in cases of unauthorised agency will be considered first (II). Attention will then be turned to the exceptions to this general rule: the doctrine of the apparent mandate (III) and ratification by the principal (IV). Finally, the analysis will focus upon the liability of the unauthorised agent (V), the consequences of acting in the name of a principal yet to be named (VI), and acting in the name of a company yet to be incorporated (VII). The chapter ends by considering the provisions of Belgian law which recognise the possibility of a personal commitment by the agent (VIII).

II The general rules on unauthorised agency

1 Notion of unauthorised agency

As mentioned above, the mechanism of representation is subject to two conditions. First, the agent must possess authority to represent, being authority granted by the principal to conclude a legal act the consequences of which will affect the property of the principal.[2] When this first condition is not met there is unauthorised agency.

Authority to represent can be granted as a matter of law (e.g. the representation of a minor by his parents), as the consequence of a judicial

---

[1] H. De Page, *Traité élémentaire de droit civil Belge*, vol. V (Brussels: Bruylant, 1975), p. 434.
[2] H. De Page, *Traité élémentaire de droit civil Belge*, vol. I (Brussels: Bruylant, 1961), p. 45; W. Van Gerven, *Bewindsbevoegdheid* (Brussels: Bruylant, 1962), pp. 186–7.

decision (e.g. the appointment of a trustee in bankruptcy) or by agreement (e.g. contract of mandate).[3] This threefold distinction reflects the traditional distinction between legal, judicial and contractual representation.

Moreover, the agent must act within the limits of the granted authority. To determine the extent of this authority to represent, a distinction is made between a *general* and a *special* authority. The first refers to all assets of the principal, whereas the second relates to a specific (set of) asset(s). In order to establish *which acts* a general or special agent may conclude in relation to the entrusted assets, a further distinction is made between representation *in general terms*, which only comprises so-called acts of management, and *an explicit authority to represent*, which permits acts of disposal.[4]

For reasons of completeness, the second condition for representation is also mentioned here, even though it is not immediately relevant for the topic of unauthorised agency. The agent and the third party must act with a will to represent (*contemplatio domini*). Both parties must intend that the agreement be concluded on behalf of a person other than the one acting and intend that the other person be directly bound by the legal effects of the agreement. The agent expresses its will to represent by acting on behalf of the principal. The third party can only be motivated by that will if he knows that the person with whom he is dealing acts as an agent. Therefore, it is necessary for the agent to express to the third party that he is acting in the capacity of agent in the name of the principal. This explains why this condition is often referred to as the condition of 'knowability'. At the same time, it follows from dealing in the name of and on behalf of another person that the agent himself intends to act in a representative capacity.

The agent is a person who can conclude legal acts for himself. A person concluding a legal act is presumed to act in his own name and on his own behalf. For that reason, a person wishing to act on behalf of another person has to give notice to the third party of the fact that he does not want to be personally bound. The latter also needs to know who his counterparty is, so that he is able to take into account that person's attributes and solvency.

---

[3] W. Van Gerven and S. Covemaeker, *Verbintenissenrecht* (Leuven: Acco, 2006), p. 159.

[4] De Page, *Traité*, vol. V, pp. 388–97; B. Tilleman, 'Lastgeving', in *Algemene Praktische Rechtsverzameling* (Deurne: Kluwer, 1997), pp. 143 and 151; P. Wéry, 'Droit des contrats, Le mandat', in *Répertoire Notarial* (Brussels: Larcier, 2000), pp. 88–97.

2 Effects of unauthorised agency

When the agent acts without authority or exceeds the limits of his authority, as a general rule neither the principal nor the agent is bound by the legal act.[5]

As regards the principal, this rule is laid down in Art. 1998 BCC, para. 2: the principal is not bound by acts performed by the agent outside the limits of the granted authority.[6] As such, an employer is not bound by a notice of dismissal given within a specific notice period by an agent of the employer to an employee without respecting the limits of his authority to represent. As long as the notice has not been ratified by the employer, the dismissal will not have the legal consequences stipulated in the law of 3 July 1978 on labour agreements.[7] Equally, a client will not be bound by the refusal of an inheritance by his attorney when the latter has not been instructed to carry out this act.[8]

This rule rests on the principle of the autonomy of the will. In cases of authorised agency, the principal expresses his will to be bound by the legal act by granting to the agent authority to represent. In cases of unauthorised agency, the principal's will to be bound is absent for lack of granted authority.[9]

As regards the agent, the general rule is laid down in Art. 1997 BCC: the agent who has given sufficient notice of (the scope of) his authority to the third party is not liable for acts performed outside the limits of his authority. Again, this rule rests on the principle of the autonomy of the will. The agent, by acting in the name of and on behalf of the principal,

---

[5] De Page, *Traité*, vol. V, pp. 440–1 and 446–7; P.-A. Foriers and F. Glansdorff, *Contrats spéciaux*, vols. I and III (Brussels: Brussels University Press, 2000), pp. 630–1; J. H. Herbots, S. Stijns, E. Degroote *et al.*, 'Overzicht van rechtspraak (1995–1998): Bijzondere Overeenkomsten' *TPR* 2002, 767; A. Kluyskens, *Beginselen van burgerlijk recht*, vol. IV, *De contracten* (Antwerp: Standaard, 1952), p. 645; C. Paulus and R. Boes, 'Lastgeving', in *Algemene Praktische Rechtsverzameling* (Gent: Story-Scientia, 1978), p. 137; I. Samoy, *Middellijke vertegenwoordiging. Vertegenwoordiging herbekeken vanuit het optreden in eigen naam voor andermans rekening* (Antwerp and Oxford: Intersentia, 2005), p. 84; Tilleman, 'Lastgeving', pp. 193 ff; Wéry, *Le mandat*, pp. 241 and 251.

[6] This rule applies not only to contracts but also to unilateral legal acts. See: Cass. 6 November 1995, *Arr Cass* 1995, 971 and *Pas.* 1995, I, 1002 and Art. 1239 BCC (a payment made to a third person who is not authorised to receive the payment does not liberate the debtor). See also Wéry, *Le mandat*, p. 241.

[7] Cass. 13 January 2003, *Pas* 2003, I, 112.   [8] Brussels 12 March 2003, *JT* 2003, 582.

[9] De Page, *Traité*, vol. V, pp. 440–1; Foriers and Glansdorff, *Contrats spéciaux*, vol. III, p. 630; Kluyskens, *Beginselen*, vol. IV, p. 645; Paulus and Boes, 'Lastgeving', p. 137; Tilleman, 'Lastgeving', p. 196.

expresses his will to bind the principal and not to bind himself through the legal act.[10]

These general rules on unauthorised agency can be subject to exceptions. On the one hand, the *principal* will nevertheless be bound in cases where the third party successfully invokes the doctrine of apparent mandate[11] or where the principal ratifies the unauthorised act.[12] The first exception is created by case-law, the other has its basis in statute law. On the other hand, the *agent* can be held liable in damages (based on tort law) if he fails to give sufficient notice of (the scope of) his authority to the third party. Additionally, he will be bound (on a contractual basis) if he makes a 'personal commitment to the legal act' (Art. 1997 BCC, *in fine*), a concept which is explained in more detail below.

III Apparent authority

1 Notion

The first exception to the general rule of Art. 1998 BCC, para. 2, is the doctrine of apparent mandate. This doctrine protects the third party who has acted with an apparently authorised agent. It holds the principal bound towards the third party in respect of the acts performed by the unauthorised agent in cases where the third party could reasonably believe in the existence of a contract of mandate.[13]

This theory of apparent mandate is frequently applied in the context of the banker–customer relationship where an agent or employee of the

---

[10] *Ibid.* See, e.g., Bergen 24 June 1981, *Pas* 1981, II, 125; Comm. Brussels 1 December 1932, *TBH* 1932, 222; Comm. Brussels 10 December 1930, *TBH* 1930, 474.

[11] *Leer van het schijnmandaat/théorie de l'apparence.* The meaning of the term 'apparent mandate' will be explained under III.

[12] *Bekrachtiging/ratification.*

[13] De Page, *Traité*, vol. V, p. 443; Foriers and Glansdorff, *Contrats spéciaux*, vol. III, p. 633; Herbots *et al.*, *Overzicht van rechtspraak*, pp. 770–9; Kluyskens, *Beginselen*, vol. IV, p. 646; Paulus and Boes, 'Lastgeving', pp. 141–4; Samoy, *Middellijke vertegenwoordiging*, p. 87; Tilleman, 'Lastgeving', pp. 223–49; Wéry, 'Le mandat', pp. 246–50. As is illustrated later in this chapter (see III 5, below), the doctrine of the apparent mandate protects the third party. He is not obliged to invoke the protection offered by apparent mandate. He has the choice either to uphold the appearances (performance by an authorised agent) or to choose the reality (performance by an unauthorised agent). Therefore, the apparent principal and the apparent agent cannot invoke the appearances towards the third party against his will. Only the principal is bound towards the third party by application of the doctrine of apparent mandate, not the third party towards the principal. Once the third party chooses to invoke the doctrine of apparent mandate, he will of course be bound by the legal act performed by the agent.

bank has intervened. There are many judgments in which a bank has been ordered to reimburse its clients who, through the intervention of an independent agent or an employee of the bank, entrusted assets to the bank. Apparent mandate becomes relevant where clients lose their money because the agent or employee vanishes. The classic argument which tends to be raised by banks is that the agent is independent and not an employee, so that the bank is not liable as an employer. However, when the facts suggest that an appearance of authority was created in terms of which the agent worked in the name of and on behalf of the bank and was part of the latter's personnel, and when the client could legitimately believe that his money was placed with the bank, the theory of apparent mandate will be applied. The concrete circumstances which may contribute to the appearance and to the legitimate belief are, for instance, the public display of the bank's name, logo or trademark in the agent's dealings with the client, a reference in the phone directory to the agent of the bank and the use of letter-heads with the bank's logo.

2 Legal basis

The Belgian Civil Code does not contain general provisions governing the doctrine of apparent mandate. Rather, Arts. 2005 and 2009 BCC (part of the chapter on the grounds of termination of a contract of mandate) state that the revocation of authority to represent is not immediately effective towards third parties. The revocation can only be invoked towards third parties after they have been notified of the revocation.[14]

Until the Court of Cassation decided what could be described as a 'mile-stone decision' on 20 June 1988 (see the next paragraph), the Court had followed De Page and traditional opinion that the doctrine of apparent mandate rests on an application of the rules on tort law (Arts. 1382–1383 BCC). For the doctrine to apply, the apparent existence of (sufficient) authority and the third party's faith in the existence of the apparent agent's authority must be caused by *a fault imputable to the apparent principal*.[15] The principal is held liable for having created a misleading appearance towards a third party who himself was acting in good faith. Reparation in kind (*in natura*) of the damage that the third

---

[14] Wéry, 'Le mandat', p. 272.
[15] Cass. 13 January 1972, *Arr Cass* 1972, 473 and *Pas* 1972, 472; Cass. 30 May 1979, *Pas* 1979, 1123 and *Arr Cass* 1978–79, 1145. See: De Page, *Traité*, vol. V, 1975, no. 448.

party would suffer if the appearances were not upheld results in the principal being held bound by the unauthorised legal act.

The mile-stone decision of the Court of Cassation[16] (dated 20 June 1988)[17] constituted, in effect, a revolution in the Court's case law. It clarified the fact that the legal basis of the doctrine of apparent mandate is not the concept of fault and the rules on torts. It is, rather, an application of the doctrine of appearances.[18] The Court of Cassation held in particular that the doctrine applies not only in cases where the apparent principal has created the appearances through his fault, but also in cases where – in the absence of fault – the third party legitimately believed in the (scope of the) agent's authority to represent.

The facts leading to the decision of the Court of Cassation are as follows. Some 800 people worked for a specific company. As a consequence of a strike of the workers, the majority of whom were members of the socialist workers' union, the company found themselves in a very difficult situation. If the strike continued, the company would face insolvency. The company sued a certain Mr X, who was the secretary-general of the local department of the socialist workers' union, together with two active union members, Mr A and Mr B, for injunctive relief. Mr X was not an employee of the company, but A and B were. The legal action aimed to terminate the company lock-out with immediate effect.

The case was heard before the Court of Appeal, which ordered X, A and B to cease obstructing the entrance of the company. The Court furthermore ordered Mr X, in his capacity as an agent of the socialist workers' union, to organise a meeting of the company workers at which the members would vote on the continuation of the strike.

X, A and B challenged the decision of the Court of Appeal before the Court of Cassation. They argued that the socialist workers' union was sued in the person of Mr X, whereas the socialist workers' union had no legal personality and could not be brought before a court, unless all of its members were sued in person (a so-called 'association-in-fact'). One or more agents can be authorised to act in the name of the members of the

---

[16] Hof van cassatie/Cour de cassation.

[17] Cass. 20 June 1988, *Pas* 1988, 1258 (summary), *Arr Cass* 1987–88, 1365, *JT* 1989, 547, obs. P.-A. Forriers, *RCJB* 1991, 45, obs. R. Kruithof, *RW* 1989–90, 1425, obs. A. Van Oevelen, *TRV* 1989, 540, obs. P. Callens and S. Stijns. See for an overview of the copious case-law, following this mile-stone decision: P.-A. Foriers and R. Jafferali, 'Le mandat (1991 à 2004)', in F. Glansdorff, *Actualités de quelques contrats spéciaux* (Brussels: Bruylant, 2005), pp. 91–2.

[18] *Schijnleer* or *vertrouwensleer*; *théorie de l'apparence* or *théorie de la confiance légitime*.

association. In the case at hand, it was impossible to ascertain whether such an authority had been granted to Mr X, as the socialist workers' union had no written regulations to that effect. The question to be answered by the Court was whether, in the absence of proof of the existence of a contract of mandate (granting authority to represent) between Mr X and the members of the socialist workers' union, the latter could be brought before a court in the person of Mr X. The Court of Appeal held that an apparent mandate existed. The circumstances leading to its finding included: all letters to the company in the context of the social negotiations were printed on the letter-head of the local chapter of the socialist workers' union and were signed by Mr X; in relation to the strike, Mr X wrote the company a letter in which he presented himself as the negotiator authorised by the socialist workers' union to follow up the social conflict until its solution; by means of a registered letter, the company answered X in his capacity as agent of the union and neither X himself nor the socialist workers' union raised any objection to this course of action.

The claimants before the Court of Cassation based their case on the classic tort-based theory of apparent mandate, arguing that the Court of Appeal had misapplied the legal concept of tort. X apparently acted as an authorised agent of the socialist workers' union. They argued that the Court of Appeal had unjustly inferred from that fact that the members had created an appearance of authority vested in X to represent the union in the social conflict. They also argued that the members were at fault in doing so.

The Court of Cassation did not follow this reasoning. It did not apply the tort-based concept of apparent mandate. Instead, it underlined the fact that the doctrine of apparent mandate applies, not only in cases where the apparent principal has, through his own fault, created the appearances by fault, but also in cases where, in the absence of fault, the third party legitimately believed in the (scope of the) agent's authority to represent.

There is a remarkable resemblance between this court decision of 20 June 1988 and the decision of the French Court of Cassation, decided nearly 28 years earlier, on 13 December 1962.[19] It is clear that the French decision was a source of inspiration for the Belgian decision.

---

[19] Cass. (France) 13 December 1962, *D* 1963, 277, obs. J. Calais-Auloy and *JCP* 1963, II, no. 13105, obs. P. Esmein.

3 Scope

The doctrine of apparent mandate can be applied in a wide variety of cases. It may be applied in cases where the principal has granted his agent no authority whatsoever, where the agent has exceeded his authority, or where the authority has been terminated. It can also be applied in cases where the wording of the procuration is unclear or ambiguous or where the procuration is void.[20]

The theory of apparent mandate can also apply when the execution of the performance of representation leads to the commission of a tortious or even criminal act.[21] The apparent principal can, in other words, also be bound by the consequences of a criminal offence committed by the agent. The case which led to the decision of the Court of Cassation of 20 January 2000 offers a striking illustration of this point (see also below, III 4(d)).[22] An independent agent of Argenta Spaarbank had been given savings by a couple. It had been agreed that he would make a deposit on a savings bank book to be opened to that effect. Although the Argenta agent delivered a receipt to the couple in the name of Argenta, he used the money for his own benefit. Before the Court of Appeal, Argenta was considered an apparent principal and was ordered to pay back the sums to the clients, given that, in the circumstances of the case, the parties could legitimately have believed that their money was under deposit with Argenta. The obligation to repay the sums arose from the apparent mandate of the agent.

This decision was challenged before the Court of Cassation. Argenta argued that a mandate can only apply to legal acts. When the damage is caused by a delict, the principal cannot be bound by the act because the delict necessarily falls outside the limits of the agent's authority to represent. However, the Court of Cassation reasoned that the extent to which the principal is bound is not influenced by the fact that the apparent agent behaved in an illegitimate manner in the execution of his mandate, even though such behaviour would constitute a criminal act.

---

[20] Wéry, 'Le mandat', p. 247.
[21] Cass. 20 January 2000, *RW* 2001–02 (summary), 501, obs. (mistake *RW* 2001–02, 792), *TBH* 2000, 483, obs. P.-A. Foriers and *RGDC* 2001, 407; Bergen 22 March 2004, *JT* 2004, 658; Brussels 7 December 2004, *RPS* 2004, 360, obs.; Brussels 7 May 2003, *RW* 2005–06, 1426; S. Stijns, 'Het algemeen regime van de verbintenis', in S. Stijns and H. Vandenberghe (eds.), *Verbintenissenrecht, Themis* (Bruges: Die Keure, 2000–01), pp. 18–20.
[22] Cass. 20 January 2000 (see n. 21).

Finally, the doctrine of apparent authority can also be applied if the principal is a legal person. Frequently, agreements will be concluded by an employee on behalf of his company. Often, it is discovered later that this employee was not authorised to represent the company and the company disputes that it is legally bound. Here also, the theory of apparent mandate can offer a solution to the third party. The latter is also subject to standards of reasonable behaviour. An illustration of this idea can be found in a case in which an employee entered into an agreement for the lease of a fax machine on behalf of his employer. The employee appeared not to be authorised to contract on behalf of his employer and thus the question which arose was whether the theory of apparent mandate applied. The court found that the conditions were not fulfilled. Based on the facts of the case, it could not be shown that there was an impression or appearance of authority to represent: the contract was not drafted in the company's office and was not printed on the company's letter-head, the usual stamp was not used (although the form used required this explicitly), the company did not pay an advance and not one of the documents used stemmed from the company. It was not proven that the company had, by any act or omission, caused the appearance. It followed, therefore, that the alleged appearance was not imputable to the company. Finally, it is a requirement that the third party did not know and should not have known that the appearance did not meet the reality. This condition was not fulfilled. The contract drafted by the lessor was not fully filled out. Although this ought to have raised the suspicions of the lessor, it did not do so. In sum, the lessor fell short of his 'duty to examine'.[23]

The existence of an apparent mandate was, however, accepted in a different case. A supervisor of the factory of an employer signed an invoice for works, confirming that the works had been properly executed. Some days later, the employer, a limited liability company in the form of a BVBA, disputed the invoice. This argument was not accepted either at first instance or before the court of appeal. This was because the acceptance of the work by the employee was imputable to the BVBA on the basis of the theory of apparent mandate.[24]

---

[23] Brussels 18 April 1996, *AJT* 1996–97, 353, obs. B. Cattoir.
[24] J. P. Grâce-Hollogne, 20 October 1995, *TRV* 1998, 112 and confirmed in appeal: Comm. Luik 25 April 1997, *TRV* 1998, 113, obs. J. Vananroye.

4 Conditions

(a) General

Legal doctrine and case-law specify the conditions which must be met in order to invoke succesfully the doctrine of apparent mandate: (1) an appearance of (sufficient) authority to represent;[25] (2) a legitimate faith or belief of the third party in the existence of (sufficient) authority to represent;[26] (3) the imputability of the apparent authority to the principal,[27] and (4) a (risk of) damage for the third party.[28] Only in those cases where these conditions are fulfilled can one justify placing the third party's interests over the agent's and the principal's.[29] A few authors, following Verougstraete, correctly mention a fifth condition: the legislator may not (expressly or impliedly) have excluded or limited the application of the doctrine of beliefs. Specific rules have priority over the application of the doctrine of beliefs (the principle of subsidiarity).

The existence of the first two conditions is confirmed in both case-law and legal doctrine. The third condition of imputability to the apparent principal has been the subject of fierce debate, settled in 2000 by a decision of the Court of Cassation (see below, III 4(d)). The fourth condition, the requirement for the third party to prove a (risk of) damage, remains under discussion. The fifth condition has received little consideration in either jurisprudence or case-law. Each of these conditions is examined below.

(b) An appearance of (sufficient) authority to represent

The appearance of (sufficient) authority forms the so-called 'objective' or 'material' component: there has to be an apparent situation (the existence of (sufficient) authority), deviating from the reality (absence

---

[25] *Schijn van vertegenwoordigingsbevoegdheid/apparence de pouvoir de représentation.*

[26] *Rechtmatig vertrouwen/confiance légitime.*

[27] *Toerekenbaarheid/imputabilité.*

[28] *Dreigende of geleden schade/risque de dommage ou dommage réel.* P.-A. Foriers, 'L'apparence, source autonome d'obligations, ou application du principe général de l'exécution de bonne foi', *JT* 1989, 543–4; R. Kruithof, 'Overzicht van rechtspraak', *TPR* 1994, 225–7; R. Kruithof, 'La théorie de l'apparence dans une nouvelle phase' (obs. to Cass. 20 June 1988), *RCJB* 1991, 68–73; S. Stijns and P. Callens, 'Over tijdelijke vennootschappen en (schijn-)vertegenwoordiging', *TRV* 1989, 73; W. Van Gerven, 'Algemeen deel', in *Beginselen van Belgisch Privaatrecht*, I (Antwerp: Story-Scientia, 1987), p. 227; A. Van Oevelen, 'De juridische grondslag en de toepassingsvoorwaarden van de verbondenheid van de lastgever bij een schijnmandaat', *RW* 1989–90, 1429–30; I. Verougstraete, 'Wil en vertrouwen bij het totstandkomen van overeenkomsten', *TPR* 1990, 1193.

[29] Van Gerven, 'Algemeen deel', pp. 227, 229.

or insufficiency of authority), but nevertheless seen as reality by the observer.[30]

For instance, a buyer of immovable property cannot claim the application of the theory of apparent mandate against a notary public who intervenes in the procedure, if the buyer's offer is drafted in such terms that it is clear that he was aware that the notary public had no authority to conclude the contract.[31] On the other hand, a bank raised the issue of apparent authority where an independent agent represented the bank in the course of all financial transactions. The bank had allowed all such transactions to take place in offices which appeared to belong to the bank.[32]

(c) The legitimate faith or belief of the third party in the existence of (sufficient) authority to represent

The third party must have a legitimate belief: he must be in good faith. This legitimate belief represents the so-called 'subjective', 'psychological' or 'intellectual' component. There is a legitimate belief when the third party believes that the appearance corresponds to reality. This belief must exist at the moment of performing the legal act. The belief is 'legitimate' when the third party does not know (subjective element) nor should he know (objective element) that the appearance does not correspond to reality.[33] Whether the third party acted in the same way as a reasonable person would have done in the same circumstances is an issue for the judge to determine. In a recent review of case-law, Foriers and Jafferali enumerate the elements taken into account by the judge: in particular, the importance and the nature of the legal act, the third party's qualifications and professional abilities, the principal's qualifications and the fact that the apparent agent has performed legal acts in the past with the third party in the name of the principal.[34] As the 'victim's' mistake should be excusable (i.e. a reasonable person in similar circumstances would have made the same mistake) and his belief legitimate, he is

---

[30] Kruithof, 'Overzicht van rechtspraak', *TPR* 1994, 225; Kruithof, 'La théorie de l'apparence', p. 68.

[31] Civ. Brussels 13 April 2000, *Rev not b* 2000, 491.

[32] Bergen 22 March 2004, *JT* 2004, 658.

[33] Kruithof, 'La théorie de l'apparence', p. 71; Van Gerven, 'Algemeen deel', p. 229; Van Oevelen, 'De juridische grondslag', p. 1430; M. Van Quickenborne, 'Le fondement de l'inopposabilité des contre-lettres' *RCJB* 1975, 268, in particular n. 22.

[34] Foriers and Jafferali, 'Le mandat (1991 à 2004)', pp. 92–4.

charged with a 'reasonable duty to investigate', the importance of which depends on the circumstances of the case.

In one case, the belief of a woman concerning an insurance company technical advisor's authority to represent was considered legitimate. Works were performed to the roof of her house and she obtained the appointment of an expert through injunctive relief. During a meeting between the expert, the woman, the contractor and the technical advisor of the insurer, a settlement was signed. Later, the insurance company disputed the authority of the technical advisor to sign the deed of settlement. They were, however, unsuccessful because of the woman's legitimate belief.[35]

In a further case, a prospective lessee's belief in the authority of the head of an office was held to be legitimate where he possessed keys to access the building, drafted the description of the state of the building and received from the lessee the warranty and payment of the first month's rent.[36]

The belief was held not to be legitimate, however, where an independent bank agent used documents which did not conform to requirements, promised an abnormally high interest rate and did not withhold taxes due.[37]

Finally, the holder of a diploma at law was unable to appeal to the theory of apparent mandate when he bought an apartment from an assistant of a notary public who was not authorised to act for those purposes. The fact that the intermediary in this case was an assistant of the notary public did not mean that the prospective buyer was freed from the duty to adopt the usual precautionary measures to check the agent's authority.[38]

(d) The imputability of the apparent authority to the principal

The requirement of the imputability of the appearance to the apparent principal was, for a long period of time, a controversial issue in Belgian law. The quoted decision of the Court of Cassation (dated 20 June 1988: see above, III 2) clarified that the doctrine of apparent mandate applies, not only where the apparent principal has committed a fault, but also where the third party can prove a legitimate belief. This decision marked

---

[35] Brussels 9 January 1998, *JLMB* 1998, 1827.
[36] Civ. Hoei 5 April 2000, *T Vred* 2001, 67, obs.
[37] Brussels 29 September 2004, *Bank Fin R* 2005, 340, obs. H. Van Acker.
[38] Brussels 23 October 2003, *Rev not b* 2004, 260.

the abandonment of the fault requirement as the legal basis of the doctrine of appearances, but gave rise to another question. Is the requirement of the third party's legitimate belief in the existence of an appearance sufficient to apply the doctrine of apparent mandate or is it necessary to prove additionally that the appearance is in a certain way 'imputable' to the apparent principal? In other words, does one have to prove that the appearance results from an action (whether or not involving fault) or an omission (again, whether or not involving fault) of the principal? The decision of 20 June 1988 failed to answer this question.

Because of the doubt which surrounded this question, not surprisingly, debate in legal doctrine was animated.[39] Those who opposed a separate condition of imputability argued that the presence of objective circumstances referring to the apparent principal's person (the so-called requirement of imputability) did not constitute a separate requirement. For those authors the requirement was met automatically when the other two conditions were fulfilled, namely the existence of an apparent situation and the legitimacy of the third party's belief.[40]

Meanwhile, however, the famous decision of the Court of Cassation (dated 20 January 2000) discussed above settled the debate.[41]

In a second decision (dated 25 June 2004), the Court of Cassation confirmed the decision in *Argenta Spaarbank* and, for the first time, provided a definition of 'imputability'.

The facts of that case were as follows. The claimant before the Court of Cassation had entrusted a person, X, with several sums of money. This person had represented himself as an independent credit broker for the company Alcredima, and promised to invest the money. The claimants were (wrongly) convinced that X acted as an agent of the company Alcredima and this belief was legitimate. It transpired that X had acted

---

[39] *In favour of* a separate requirement of imputability: H. Boonen, 'De rechtsschijn', *RW* 1950–51, 307; E. Dirix, *Obligatoire verhoudingen tussen contractanten en derden* (Antwerp: Kluwer, 1984), p. 24; Foriers and Glansdorff, *Contrats spéciaux*, p. 634; Kruithof, 'Overzicht van rechtspraak', pp. 225–6, no. 38; Kruithof, 'La théorie de l'apparence dans une nouvelle phase', p. 69; Van Gerven, 'Algemeen deel', p. 227 ff; Van Oevelen, 'De juridische grondslag', pp. 1429–30. *Against* a separate requirement of imputability: Stijns and Callens, 'Over tijdelijke vennootschappen en (schijn-) vertegenwoordiging', pp. 74–76; P. Van Ommeslaghe, 'L'apparence comme source autonome d'obligation et le droit belge' (1983) *Rev Dr Int Comp* 154, 158.

[40] See the authors taking the position against a separate requirement of imputability in the previous footnote.

[41] Cass. 20 January 2000, *RW* 2001–02 (summary), 501, obs. (mistake *RW* 2001–02, 792), *TBH* 2000, 483, obs. P.-A. Foriers and *RGDC* 2001, 407.

in a fraudulent manner by using the money for his own benefit. The claimants sought reimbursement from Alcredima. The Court of Appeal dismissed their claim because it considered that the appearance of an authority to represent was not imputable to Alcredima.

This decision was challenged before the Court of Cassation. The latter considered that a person can be bound on the basis of an apparent mandate, if the appearance is imputable to him. This meant that he had voluntarily contributed by his conduct, even faultless, to create an appearance or had tacitly permitted the appearance to exist. In the case at hand, the Court of Appeal had deduced from two witness declarations and other documents that X had obtained two booklets with transaction accounts through theft in the offices of Alcredima and had used them for fraudulent purposes. Alcredima itself was not aware of the theft of these forms. X was not allowed to use the forms, since he had neither the authority to represent nor was he empowered to receive moneys on behalf of Alcredima or to invest the same. The role of X was to bring parties together to conclude loans and to buy banknotes. Neither the name nor the logo of Alcredima was displayed at the building where X's offices were situated. Also it was accepted that even the strictest control system could not prevent the theft of booklets containing official forms. Therefore, Alcredima, even though it was aware that two such booklets were missing, could not do anything to prevent the use thereof. The appearance raised by the claimants had arisen against the will of Alcredima, which was not in a position to avoid it. It was also relevant that the claimants had not questioned why they failed to receive any official documents from Alcredima for a period of years. The Court of Cassation concluded that the Court of Appeal was justified in deciding that the claimants could not appeal to the theory of apparent mandate.[42]

The definition of imputability in the Court of Cassation's decision dated 25 June 2004 is influenced by the definition proposed by Foriers. Foriers adds that 'voluntary' means that a person acts without being forced to do so and while he is or should be aware of the situation. The definition therefore seeks to rule out situations in which the apparent principal is totally uninvolved with the appearances raised against his will, while he was not in a position to remedy the situation.[43] In other

---

[42] Cass. 25 June 2004, *RGDC* 2004, 457.

[43] P.-A. Foriers, 'Aspects de la représentation en matière contractuelle', in *Les Obligations Contractuelles* (Brussels: Jeune Barreau Edn, 2000), p. 252.

words, the apparent principal must have contributed to the creation of the appearance or must at least have tolerated it.[44]

Numerous illustrations of the condition of imputability can be found in case-law. An employer who failed to dispute an order placed by a former employee and failed to respond to an official notice to pay was held to have tolerated the appearance.[45] When moneys placed in a bank account were transferred to another account with the use of a false transaction form and without the holder of the first account having authorised this transfer, it was held not to be sufficient to state that the falsified form had all the characteristics of a real form. It must additionally be shown that this appearance was imputable to the account holder.[46] In a situation where a person bound himself contractually to pay the costs of his brother-in-law's stay in a home for the elderly, the widower of that person could not be sued for payment of these costs on the basis of apparent mandate. The appearance was not imputable to the person who would suffer the consequences of it.[47]

(e) A (risk of) damage for the third party

The final remaining condition is the requirement that the third party prove a (risk of) damage. The traditional view, based on Art. 1382 BCC and the rules on tort law, is that the separate requirement to prove damage is beyond doubt.[48] Indeed, Art. 1382 BCC demands proof of fault, damage and causality. More recent prevailing opinion, no longer based on Art. 1382 BCC but on the third party's legitimate belief, is less certain on this issue.

Some authors continue to stipulate that the third party must prove that he would suffer damage if appearances were not upheld.[49] To give priority to the third party's interest (invoking the appearance) over the interest of the person who creates the appearance (invoking reality) in the name of legal certainty can only be justified if the third party must

---

[44] Kruithof, 'La théorie de l'apparence dans une nouvelle phase', p. 71.

[45] J. P. Westerlo, 15 February 2002, *RW* 2004–05, 677 (mistake *RW* 2004–05, 960).

[46] Brussels 5 March 2005, *Bank Fin R* 2006, 82.

[47] Labour Court Oudenaarde 2 September 2002, *RW* 2003–04, 594.

[48] Foriers, 'L'apparence, source autonome d'obligations', p. 543; Kruithof, 'Overzicht van rechtspraak', p. 227; Kruithof, 'La théorie de l'apparence dans une nouvelle phase', p. 68, n. 88.

[49] Foriers and Jafferali, 'Le mandat (1991 à 2004)', p. 97; Foriers, 'L'apparence, source autonome d'obligations', p. 543; Van Oevelen, 'De juridische grondslag', p. 1430; Verougstaete, 'Wil en vertrouwen bij het totstandkomen van overeenkomsten', p. 1193.

be protected against an actual or potential risk of damage.[50] For other authors, on the contrary, it is no longer necessary to prove damage as a separate requirement. The person invoking the appearance must demonstrate an interest but that interest is, in itself, sufficient.[51]

The more modern view is indeed persuasive. By analogy with Dutch law, it can be argued that a separate condition of damage is unnecessary: it is sufficient that the third party proves a legitimate interest. Proving this legitimate interest requires the third party to prove that he acted based on his belief, i.e. he has concluded a legal act or has omitted to do so based on his belief.[52]

(f) The principle of subsidiarity

Only a few authors mention a fifth condition: the legislator may not (expressly or impliedly) have excluded or limited the application of the doctrine of beliefs. Specific rules have priority over the application of the doctrine of beliefs (the principle of subsidiarity).[53] As this is a condition for the theory of beliefs in general, it must also be relevant to the specific case of an apparent mandate.

This condition is illustrated by the following example: Art. 848 of the Judicial Code excludes the application of the theory of apparent mandate in cases of procedural acts which may be the subject of a procedure of denial of authority to represent before the court, the so-called 'mandate ad litem'.[54] When an attorney-at-law is instructed to begin legal proceeding in the name of his client or the defence of the client's interest, then he acts as an agent. Article 440, of the Judicial Code, para. 2, explicitly states:

---

[50] P.-A. Foriers, 'L'apparence, source autonome d'obligations', *JT* 1989, 543–4; Van Oevelen, 'De juridische grondslag', p. 1430; Verougstraete, 'Wil en vertrouwen bij het totstandkomen van overeenkomsten', p. 1193.

[51] Kruithof, 'La théorie de l'apparence dans une nouvelle phase', p. 68, n. 88; Wéry, *Le mandat*, p. 249.

[52] I. Samoy, 'De gevolgen van gesimuleerde rechtshandelingen', in J. Smits and S. Stijns (eds.), *Inhoud en werking van de overeenkomst naar Belgisch en Nederlands recht* (Antwerpen-Groningen: Intersentia, 2005), pp. 268–9; S. Stijns and I. Samoy, 'La confiance légitime en droit privé des contrats', in E. Dirix, Y.-H. Leleu (eds.), *Rapports belges au congrès de l'académie internationale de droit comparé à Utrecht* (Brussels: Bruylant, 2006), pp. 277–8.

[53] Verougstraete, 'Wil en vertrouwen bij het totstandkomen van overeenkomsten', p. 1193. Followed by: Stijns and Samoy, 'La confiance légitime en droit privé des contrats', p. 278; C. Verbruggen, 'La théorie de l'apparence: quelques acquis et beaucoup d'incertitudes', in *Mélanges offerts à Pierre Van Ommeslaghe* (Brussels: Bruylant, 2000), pp. 10, 14 and 20.

[54] B. Lambrecht and I. Samoy, 'Schijn van berusting en ontkentenis van proceshandeling' (obs. to Brussels 10 June 2002), *P&B* 2002, 307–12.

the attorney appears before the court as the agent of the party without having to prove his authority to represent, except in those cases where the law requires a special authority to represent.[55] On the basis of this rule, an attorney is presumed to be entrusted with the necessary authority to represent his client in a number of procedural acts.[56]

In this part of the Judicial Code, the legislator displays great confidence in the members of the bar. Nevertheless, in order to protect the interests of the client, Art. 848 foresees the possibility of the avoidance of procedural acts. This procedure allows certain procedural acts performed by the attorney to be declared void where these acts were performed in the name of a person who has not (even tacitly) provided instructions, nor allowed, nor confirmed them.

In jurisprudence and in case-law the question has arisen whether there is room for the application of the theory of apparent mandate in the context of these rules of the Judicial Code. An illustration is offered by the case of an attorney who represented two sisters in their claim in a liability case. The sisters' claim was dismissed. The attorney subsequently wrote to his opponent, informing him that the sisters accepted the judgment. Later, however, the sisters filed for an appeal and at the same time wished to apply Art. 848 of the Judicial Code in order to have the acceptance of the judgment by their attorney declared void. The Court of Appeal first stated that the attorney was not provided with the requisite special authority to represent. Next, the Court examined whether the acceptance, as it was notified by the attorney, was imputable to the sisters on the grounds of the theory of apparent mandate.[57]

The Court found that there was no case of apparent mandate because the condition of imputability was not fulfilled. A note which followed this Court decision posed the broader question of whether Art. 848 of the Judicial Code excluded any application of the theory of apparent mandate completely in such a situation. The question was answered affirmatively: the rules on avoidance of procedural acts take precedence over the theory of apparent mandate and thus lead to its inapplicability in such situations.[58]

---

[55] For the concept of special authority to represent, see II 1 above.

[56] Herbots et al., 'Overzicht van rechtspraak', 734, no. 884.

[57] Brussels 10 June 2002, P&B 2002, 307–312, obs. B. Lambrecht and I. Samoy.

[58] See also D. Depuyt, 'Artikel 848 Ger.W.', in P. Depuydt, J. Laenens, D. Lindemans and S. Raes, Gerechtelijk recht. Commentaar van rechtspraak en rechtsleer (Antwerp: Kluwer Rechtswetenschappen, 2005), p. 137. Contra: F. Van Liempt, 'Hoever reikt het mandaat

The procedure of avoidance of procedural acts gives the judge the ability to declare such an act void and without consequences. This is because the act was performed by a person, for example an attorney-at-law, who does not possess the necessary authority or has exceeded the limits of his existing authority.[59] The consequence of the application of the theory of apparent mandate is that, in order to protect the interests of a third party, the appearances are taken for reality.[60] In spite of the fact that a person does not possess the authority to represent or has exceeded the limits of his authority, he is nevertheless considered as an agent with (sufficient) authority.

The consistent application of the theory of apparent mandate in the context of Art. 848 of the Judicial Code leads to the following result: a judge who is confronted with a claim for avoidance of a procedural act and who considers that the conditions for the application of the theory of apparent mandate are fulfilled, will necessarily have to dismiss the claim. He will be bound to conclude that the attorney did possess (sufficient) authority to represent. The acceptance of the application in general would make the procedure for the avoidance of a procedural act meaningless.

5 Effects

If the doctrine of the apparent mandate applies, the third party is entitled to take appearances as, in effect, reality. The principal is unable to plead that he is not bound by the contract concluded with the third party because of the agent's lack of authority. Despite the fact that the agent acted without authority, the principal is both liable and entitled under the contract concluded with the third party.[61] A legal claim, for example, submitted against the general secretary of a trade union without legal personality, is permitted when the secretary has apparent authority to represent *ad litem*, granted by all the members of the trade union.[62] Likewise, the request to renew a commercial lease agreement, addressed to the apparent agent of the renter is valid.[63]

---

ad litem van een advocaat in het kader van een gerechtelijke vereffening-verdeling?', in W. Pintens and J. Du Mongh (eds.), *Patrimonium 2006* (Antwerp: Intersentia, 2006), pp. 373–4.

[59] Depuyt, 'Artikel 848 Ger.W.', p. 137.   [60] Van Gerven, 'Algemeen deel', p. 500.

[61] Bergen 18 January 1994, *TBH* 1995, 163; S. Stijns, D. Van Gerven and P. Wéry, 'Chronique de jurisprudence (1985–1995). Les obligations: les sources', *JT* 1996, 696; Tilleman, 'Lastgeving', p. 248; Wéry, 'Le mandat', p. 250.

[62] Cass. 20 June 1988, quoted in n. 17.   [63] Civ. Hasselt 25 June 1990, *TBBR* 1991, 83.

The doctrine of apparent mandate only creates rights *in favour of* the third party. The apparent principal and the apparent agent cannot invoke the appearances *against* the third party. In other words, neither the principal nor the agent can plead that the third party is bound by the contract concluded with the apparent agent, if this is against the third party's will. This fact proves that the protection emanating from the theory of beliefs is only relative: the protected party (i.e. the third party) can choose to waive its application. He can choose whether or not to rely on appearances.[64]

If the third party opts to rely on the theory of apparent mandate, he will, of course, be bound by the contract concluded with the agent.

IV Ratification

1 Notion

The second exception to the general rule that an unauthorised agent is unable to bind his principal is the principal's ability to ratify the unauthorised legal act. By ratifying, the principal grants to the agent *a posteriori* authority to represent and approves the legal act performed by the agent with the third party.[65] The possibility of ratification is explicitly stipulated in Art. 1998 BCC, para. 2 *in fine*: the principal is bound by a contract concluded in excess of the agent's authority only if he ratifies it expressly or implicitly.[66] Ratification is express if given in a clear and unambiguous manner. An express ratification can be enacted in writing or orally. An implied ratification arises as an inference from the circumstances; for example, the principal pays the costs of the performed legal act or executes the legal act.[67] In both cases an intention to ratify must be certain.[68]

---

[64] Foriers and Jafferali, 'Le mandat (1991 à 2004)', p. 92; R. Kruithof, H. Bocken, F. De Ly and B. De Temmerman, 'Overzicht van rechtspraak (1981–1992). Verbintenissen', *TPR* 1994, 227; Wéry, *Le mandat*, 250.

[65] P.-A. Foriers, 'Le droit commun des intermédiaires commerciaux: courtiers, commissionnaires, agents', in B. Glansdorff (ed.), *Les intermédiaires commerciaux* (Brussels: Editions du Jeune Barreau de Bruxelles, 1990), p. 79; Wéry, 'Le mandat', 243.

[66] De Page, *Traité*, V, 1975, 442–3; Foriers and Glansdorff, *Contrats spéciaux*, III, pp. 631–3; Herbots *et al.*, 'Overzicht van rechtspraak', p. 768; Kluyskens, *Beginselen*, pp. 645–6; Paulus and Boes, 'Lastgeving', pp. 139–40; Samoy, *Middellijke vertegenwoordiging*, p. 85; Tilleman, 'Lastgeving', pp. 203–22; Wéry, 'Le mandat', pp. 243–6.

[67] De Page, *Traité*, V, 1975, p. 442; Kluyskens, *Beginselen*, p. 645.

[68] See e.g. Brussels 10 May 1999, *RPS* 1999, 245, obs. W. Derijcke.

An example of ratification from case-law is a situation in which ratification was inferred from the co-signature by the principal of an agreement which the agent had concluded by exceeding the limits of his authority to represent.[69] The owner of an apartment had instructed a real estate agency to rent the apartment. The contract of mandate did not explicitly mention that the lease would include a garage. The lease agreement on the contrary did mention the garage, and that agreement was co-signed by the lessors. Subsequently, the garage was not made available to the lessees and the latter requested the contract to be terminated due to non-performance by the lessors. The lessor refused, explaining that the agent was not authorised to lease the garage in addition to the apartment. The judge, however, considered that the lessors, by co-signing the agreement, confirmed the lease of the garage.

In another case a notary public was entrusted with the liquidation and distribution of an inheritance. The inheritance comprised, *inter alia*, a co-owned parcel of land. The notary public (as an agent for the co-owners) offered the parcel of land for sale to a neighbouring owner for a certain price. This offer was accepted. Subsequently, one of the co-owners decided that he did not agree with the price. It transpired that the land was not situated in a forest area, but in a residential area, in which it would be possible for houses to be constructed. Because of this fact, the land was considerably more valuable than the agreed price. The co-owner did not consider himself bound by the acts performed by the notary public because the notary public acted as an unauthorised agent.

The judge in the case came to the conclusion that no authority to represent (based on a contract of mandate) could be proven. Next he examined whether the acts of the notary public had been ratified. He considered that ratification can be tacit and can be deduced from acts which, from the perspective of those performing them, point with certainty to the intention to ratify the legal act. The court considered it to be relevant that all co-owners were informed of the neighbouring owner's acceptance of the offer to sell for a certain price made by the notary public. When subsequently all co-owners signed a written contract of mandate to authorise the notary public to represent them, knowing that the parcel of land had already been sold, the facts of the case could not be interpreted in any way other than as a tacit but certain intention to ratify the concluded contract of sale.[70]

---

[69] J. P. Leuven 10 March 1998, *TBBR* 1998, 159.
[70] Civ. Hasselt 2 April 2001, *RW* 2004–05, 751.

2 Scope

In spite of the wording of Art. 1998 BCC, ratification is possible not only when an agent exceeds his authority, but also when he had no authority at all or in cases where the legal act has been performed within a null and void contract of mandate.[71] The rules regarding ratification may also apply if the principal is a legal person.

Ratification of legal acts performed by an unauthorised agent (Art. 1998 BCC) should not be confused with a 'ratification' or (better) confirmation[72] of invalid legal acts (Art. 1338 BCC). As was shown above, *ratification* of a legal act performed by an unauthorised agent is the unilateral legal act whereby the principal expressly or implicitly grants *a posteriori* authority to represent to the agent and approves the legal act performed by the agent with the third party. A *confirmation* of an invalid legal act, on the other hand, can be defined as the unilateral legal act whereby a party expressly or implicitly waives the right to claim nullity of the legal act concerned. A party, for example, who can invoke the nullity of a sales contract on the basis of mistake, can renounce the nullity and confirm the contract. Article 1338 BCC stipulates the conditions under which such a confirmation can take place. These conditions do not apply in cases in which a principal ratifies a legal act performed by an unauthorised agent.[73]

3 Effects

(a) Retroactive effect

In the relationship between the principal and the agent, ratification has retroactive effect: the legal act performed by the unauthorised agent has the same effect as if it had been performed by an authorised agent (*ratihabitio mandato comparatur*).[74] Unless the principal makes an express reservation of his rights in this respect, he will be taken to have waived any claim against the agent based on his unauthorised acting.

---

[71] Tilleman, 'Lastgeving', p. 203; Wéry, 'Le mandat', p. 243.

[72] *Bevestiging/confirmation*.

[73] Cass. 15 January 1857, *Pas* 1857, I, 78, obs.; De Page, *Traité*, V, 1975, p. 442; Wéry, 'Le mandat', p. 244.

[74] Cass. 21 September 1987, *Arr Cass* 1987–88, 84, *Pas*. 1988, I, 77, *RW* 1988–89, 1325, obs. and *Rec gén enr not* 1992, 182; De Page, *Traité*, V, 1975, pp. 442–3; Foriers and Jafferali, 'Le mandat (1991 à 2004)', p. 98; Foriers and Glansdorff, *Contrats spéciaux*, p. 632; Kluyskens, *Beginselen*, p. 646; Wéry, 'Le mandat', pp. 245–6.

In the relationship between the principal and the third party with whom the legal act was performed, ratification also has retroactive effect. By ratifying a contract of sale, for instance, the contract is considered to have been concluded on the date the unauthorised agent signed the contract on behalf of the principal.[75] The principal and the third party are mutually bound by the performed legal act. The third party can no longer hold the agent liable in damages based on his unauthorised acting.

(b) Rights granted to fourth parties prior to ratification are respected

In the relationship between the principal and fourth parties (i.e. parties other than the principal, the agent and the third party), ratification – as a general rule – also has retroactive effect. Nevertheless, rights granted to fourth parties after the time of conclusion of the contract and before ratification are respected.[76]

(c) Position of acts which themselves could not have been effectively carried out at the time of ratification

An exception to the retroactive effect of ratification towards the third party exists where, at the time of ratification, the relevant legal act could no longer be performed validly.[77]

The principal, for instance, cannot ratify a legal act if at the time of ratification the time limit within which the legal act was to be performed has expired. Acts which are subject to a time limit must be ratified prior to the expiry of the relevant time. This rule applies, for example, in the case of the dismissal (based on urgent grounds) of an employee within the legal time limit of three working days after the employer had notice of the facts leading to the urgent grounds. Ratification of a dismissal carried out by an unauthorised agent of the employer must take place before the expiry of the time limit of three days.[78]

Equally, the principal cannot effectively ratify if, at the time of ratification, the limitation period has already expired. Case-law offers one (old) illustration. A person wanted to instigate a criminal prosecution by

---

[75] Cass. 15 December 1932, *Pas* 1933, I, 53.
[76] Cass. 6 February 1953, *Pas* 1953, I, 436 and *RPS* 1953, 224, concl. H. De Termicourt, obs. P. D.; De Page, *Traité*, V, 1975, pp. 442–3; Foriers and Glansdorff, *Contrats spéciaux*, p. 632; Kluyskens, *Beginselen*, p. 646; Wéry, 'Le mandat', p. 246.
[77] Tilleman, 'Lastgeving', p. 219.
[78] Labour Court Brussels 11 September 1984, *RW* 1984–85, 2408.

making (prior to the expiration of the limitation term) a complaint based on a breach of hunting law. It transpired that the person who made the complaint was not authorised to do so, but his act was ratified after the expiration of the limitation term. Ratification took place too late, and the accused was therefore acquitted.[79]

Finally, in procedural law, the principal cannot ratify the act of the unauthorised agent who raises an appeal if, at the time of ratification, the term for appeal has already expired.[80]

4 Act of ratification: requirements

(a) A unilateral legal act

Ratification is a unilateral legal act. The third party's consent to ratification is not required: he is treated as having given his (irrevocable) consent to the result at the moment of conclusion of the contract with the agent.[81]

(b) No time limit

Ratification is not subject to a time limit. However, the third party may not be held in a situation of uncertainty for too long. A long period of silence on the part of the principal is considered to be an implied ratification. Moreover, a principal who expresses his refusal too late commits a fault towards the third party and can be held liable in damages.[82]

(c) No formal requirements

As a general rule, ratification is not subject to formal requirements. However, where a particular formality is required for the act granting authority to the agent, the same formality applies to the ratification.[83]

(d) Capacity

Ratification can be carried out by the principal himself, his heirs or his agent. For ratification to be valid, however, it is necessary that

---

[79] Brussels 4 February 1875, *Pas* 1875, II, 76.
[80] Comm. Gent 11 December 1987, *TRV* 1988, 376; State Council 29 May 1990, *Arr RvS* 1990, no. 35201.
[81] Wéry, 'Le mandat', p. 243.
[82] R. Demogue, *Traité des obligations en général*, vol. I (Paris: Librairie Arthur Rousseau, 1923), p. 208.
[83] Brussels 23 December 1999, *JT* 2000, 310; Wéry, 'Le mandat', p. 244.

the person who ratifies would himself be able to perform the unauthorised act.[84]

V Liability of the unauthorised agent

1 Notion

In the absence of the application of the doctrine of apparent mandate or
ratification, the principal will not be bound by the legal act carried out by
his unauthorised agent. In such cases, it is important to ascertain whether
the third party can claim from the unauthorised agent. As already mentioned (II 2), according to Art. 1997 BCC, the agent, who has given sufficient
notice of (the scope of) his authority to the third party, is not liable for acts
performed outside the limits of his authority. A contrario, the agent who has
given insufficient notice of (the scope of) his authority to the third party can
be held liable in damages. Whether the agent has provided sufficient notice
is an issue for the court.[85]

2 Legal basis

The agent's liability is based on a warranty duty: the person who acts as
an agent warrants the existence and the extent of his authority to
represent towards the third party. In cases of insufficient notice, the
agent commits a fault and can be held liable in damages towards the
third party.[86] The burden of proof of insufficient notice rests on the third
party, as fault cannot be presumed.[87]

The majority view is that Art. 1997 BCC is a specific application of the
general tort provision of Art. 1382 BCC. The agent who gives insufficient
notice of the existence and the extent of his authority to represent
commits an extra-contractual fault, as no valid contract has been concluded. This means that the unauthorised agent can be held liable in
damages towards the third party based on tort.[88] The minority view is
that the basis of liability of the unauthorised agent is contractual, and

---

[84] Paulus and Boes, Lastgeving, p. 139.
[85] Brussels 7 November 1999, RPS 2000, 345; Comm. Hasselt 22 July 1999, RW 2001–02,
1476; Foriers and Jafferali, 'Le mandat (1991 à 2004)', p. 87; Tilleman, 'Lastgeving',
p. 194; Wéry, 'Le mandat', p. 251.
[86] De Page, Traité, V, 1975, pp. 440–1 and 446–7; Foriers and Glansdorff, Contrats
spéciaux, pp. 630–1; Kluyskens, Beginselen, p. 646; Paulus and Boes, 'Lastgeving',
pp. 137–8; Wéry, 'Le mandat', pp. 251–2.
[87] De Page, Traité, V, 1975, p. 446.   [88] Tilleman, Lastgeving, p. 199; Wéry, 'Le mandat', p. 252.

is founded upon an implied warranty contract.[89] The agent, by acting as agent of a certain person, enters into a contract himself with the third party in terms of which the agent guarantees his authority to represent.[90]

Is the conduct of the third party relevant to the assessment of the unauthorised agent's liability? As a specific application of the general tort provision of Art. 1382 BCC, the agent can only be held liable in damages towards the third party if three conditions are fulfilled: (1) fault; (2) damages; and (3) a causal nexus. The general rules on tort law apply to the fulfilment of these three conditions. When the third party knows, or ought to have known, that authority was lacking, one may conclude that the agent gave sufficient notice and therefore did not commit a fault. One may also conclude that the conduct of the third party, knowing the lack of authority, constitutes fault, resulting in a partial breach of the causal nexus and in the sharing of liability between agent and third party.[91]

3 Scope

In spite of the wording of Art. 1997 BCC, the stipulated rule applies not only when an agent exceeds his authority but also *a fortiori* where the agent had no authority at all.[92]

4 Effects

According to the majority opinion, the unauthorised agent found liable can only be ordered to pay damages to the third party. He is not bound by the contract concluded in the name of and on behalf of the principal.[93]

According to the general rules on extra-contractual liability, a victim of an extra-contractual fault can only claim reliance or so called negative damages. However, in the field of pre-contractual liability case-law is

---

[89] Comm. Brussels 6 November 1928, *TBH* 1928, 318; F. Laurent, *Principes de droit civil français*, 33 parts (Brussels: Bruylant, 1878) XXVII, 1848, no. 49, p. 50.

[90] Tilleman, 'Lastgeving', p. 200.

[91] See on the effects of a fault of the victim on the tort liability: Van Gerven and Covemaeker, *Verbintenissenrecht*, pp. 432–3.

[92] Brussels 8 June 1978, *TBH* 1979, 145, obs.; De Page, *Traité*, V, 1975, p. 437, 446; Wéry, 'Le mandat', p. 251.

[93] Bergen 24 June 1981, *Pas.* 1981, II, 125; De Page, *Traité*, V, 1975, p. 446; Tilleman, 'Lastgeving', p. 200.

moving towards recognition of expectation or positive damages. If two parties are negotiating a contract and one party ends the negotiations and is at fault in doing so, he can be liable in positive damages, i.e. he must, through a damages award, place the other party in the same financial position he would have been in if the contract had been concluded. Although jurisprudence is rather cautious about this development, case-law is beginning to accept positive damages in cases where the negotiating parties reached the so-called 'point of no return'. This development is linked to the recognition of the doctrine of appearances as an autonomous source of obligations: at a certain point of the negotiations, there is a legitimate belief that the contract will be concluded and the parties lose the freedom to break off the negotiations.[94] This same reasoning could be applied to cases of unauthorised agency. One could argue that the unauthorised agent is liable to pay expectation damages to the third party, if the third party legitimately believes that the agent is sufficiently authorised.

Moreover, some authors argue that the judge, at the request of the third party, may also award compensation for damage suffered through reparation *in natura*, i.e. the agent himself is bound by the contract concluded in the name of and on behalf of the principal.[95] If Art. 1997 BCC is seen as a specific application of the general tort provision of Art. 1382 BCC, the possibility of reparation *in natura* must be taken into consideration. In practice, the third party will often prefer to receive damages. Reparation *in natura* may, of course, be impossible. Often the third party who wanted to conclude a contract with the principal is not interested in a contract with the agent. Reparation *in natura* may be impossible in cases where the contract implies a transfer of property by the principal.[96] The agent cannot dispose of other people's property.

Although the judge does not use the words 'reparation *in natura*', some authors have argued that a judgment of the Civil Court of Brussels (5 March 1998) is an example of the same. In this case, through lack of authority to represent, the unauthorised agent is said to have rented the material on his own behalf.[97] In another case, an unauthorised agent was

---

[94] S. Stijns, *Leerboek verbintenissenrecht* (Bruges: Die Keure, 2005), p. 139.
[95] Foriers and Jafferali, 'Le mandat (1991 à 2004)', p. 87; Van Gerven, 'Algemeen deel', p. 509.
[96] Wéry, 'Le mandat', pp. 252–3.   [97] Civ. Brussels 5 January 1998, *JLMB* 1998, 1835.

ordered to pay an invoice concerning an order made in the name of a non-existent principal.[98]

VI Acting in the name of a principal yet to be named: the '*Commandverklaring/Déclaration de command*' clause

1 Notion

An agent may contract in the name of a principal yet to be named. This agent leaves open the question of whether he will act for a principal or on his own account. In Belgian law the contractual clause which permits this to occur is known as the '*Commandverklaring/Déclaration de command*' or 'clause of declaration of command'. Such a clause can be included in different types of agreement such as a lease or a contract for works. Nevertheless, this concept is used most often, indeed almost exclusively, in the context of sale.

The clause of declaration of command is defined as an explicit clause which can be included in a contract of sale, whereby the buyer (apparent buyer or 'commandant') retains the right to designate, within a specific time period after formation of the contract, another person (the real buyer or 'command'), who is to replace him as the direct contractual party of the seller.

In such a case, the commandant can act as an authorised agent on the instructions of a principal who has granted him authority to represent in order to conclude a sale incorporating a clause of declaration of command. It is also possible for the commandant to act unilaterally, as an unauthorised agent, without prior instruction from a principal. The consequences of the two hypotheses are examined below.

2 Legal basis

The Civil Code does not contain any legal basis for the use of the clause of declaration of command. Nevertheless, the concept is generally recognised in case law and in jurisprudence. Moreover, several specific legal stipulations, especially in tax law, confirm its existence. The main reason why parties choose to use this concept is, in fact, the favourable fiscal regime. The use of a clause which fulfils the relevant fiscal conditions of

---

[98] Brussels 8 June 1978, *TBH* 1979, 145, obs.

validity leads to a presumption that only one contract is involved, not two consecutive sales contracts which would otherwise result in payment of double the tax liability.

3 Conditions

(a) General

A declaration of command is subject to a number of conditions for its validity, some of which stem from the civil law, and some from tax law. The conditions stemming from tax legislation serve only to avoid tax fraud. As already stated, a sale incorporating a declaration of command leads to only one contract of sale, and one amount of relevant tax liability. In order to avoid abuse of this rule, the legislator considered it necessary to enact a number of conditions, found in Art. 159, 1° of the Code for Registration duties. Because the non-fulfilment of these fiscal conditions has no effect on the civil status of the declaration of command, these will not be discussed in detail here. The only consequence is that the fiscal administration consider there to be two contracts of sale and thus two times the relevant tax liability.

(b) Agreement of the buyer/explicit clause in the contract of sale

The seller (as third party) must agree in explicit terms to include a clause of declaration of command in the contract. This explicit consent is required because the declaration of command forms an exception to the general rule of the law of obligations that one is presumed to bind only one's self and one's heirs and not a third person. One cannot confront the seller with a different buyer from the one with whom he had consented to deal. He has the right to refuse to deal with a buyer who is a 'stranger' and whose reputation and creditworthiness is unknown to him.

(c) Period

The declaration of command must take place within a certain period of time. In principle, this period is determined freely by the parties to the contract of sale. They can do so explicitly or tacitly. When no time period is mentioned in the contract, the declaration of command will be considered invalid and the buyer will be considered the real buyer. Should he designate a third party afterwards, the transfer of property of the goods to the party will only take place on the basis of a separate agreement and not on the basis of the original contract of sale.

(d) The acceptance of the declaration of command has to be unconditional

The declaration of command by the commandant and the acceptance by the command must be unconditional. Use of this clause must not involve a change to the object, the price or other terms of the original contract of sale. This follows logically because, otherwise, there can no longer be a single transfer of property in terms of which the command simply takes the place of the commandant. In cases where the terms have been modified, this will necessarily amount to a new contract of sale.

4 Effects

(a) General

Several distinctions are relevant to a declaration of command. First, a classical distinction is made between the consequences of the contract of sale prior to the designation of a command and after the designation. A further relevant distinction is whether the declaration of command happens timeously or occurs too late. Finally, the consequences of a declaration of command must be discussed separately from the perspective of the law of obligations and from that of the law of goods. Moreover, different treatment is necessary depending upon whether the commandant (as authorised agent) acts in the name of the command or on his own initiative (as unauthorised agent).

(b) Consequences prior to the designation of a command

From the outset, the legal status of the sale with a declaration of command is that of a contract between the seller and the commandant. Until the designation of a command and the acceptance by the latter, the party making the declaration of command is personally bound by the sale. Should the designation of a command not follow, or should the period for such designation lapse, this situation will continue. The sale is concluded between the seller and the commandant, regardless of whether the commandant acts as an authorised or unauthorised agent.[99]

---

[99] Civ. Charleroi 10 August 1886, *Pas* 1887, III, 286, obs.; H. De Page and A. Meinertzhagen-Limpens, *Traité élémentaire de droit civile belge*, vol. IV, *Les Principaux Contrats* (Brussels: Bruylant, 1997), p. 410; M.-P. Dumont, *L'opération de commission* (Paris: Litec, 2000), p. 322; L. Limpens, *La vente en droit belge* (Brussels: Bruylant, 1960), p. 341; W. Van Gerven, *Bewindsbevoegdheid* (Brussels: Bruylant, 1962), p. 169.

In terms of the law of goods, the contract of sale with a declaration of command leads to an immediate transfer of title from the property of the seller to the property of the commandant. Until the declaration of command and the acceptance by the command, the commandant is considered to be the owner of the goods concerned.[100] It will, for instance, become part of the commandant's inheritance should the commandant die during this period.[101] If no command is designated, the commandant will remain the owner of the goods without interruption.

Should the commandant merely act as an (authorised or unauthorised) agent of an as yet undesignated command, then he cannot be bound personally in the period preceding designation.[102] The rules relating to the sale with declaration of command deviate from this principle. The commandant is immediately held personally liable through the contract of sale. This rule is one which is based on case-law.[103] The rule points to the fact that the commandant is presumed to have concluded the sale in his own name and on his own behalf under the condition subsequent (or resolutive condition) of a valid declaration of command and an acceptance by the command.[104]

(c) Consequences of a declaration of command which is in time

If the commandant validly designates a command and if the latter accepts, then – from the perspective of the law of obligations – the contract of sale will be considered to have been concluded retroactively between the command and the seller. The seller and the command are considered to be the immediate and direct parties to the contract. There is only one contract of sale.[105]

---

[100] Brussels 17 June 1954, *RW* 1954–55, 92, under c).

[101] *Pand. b.*, v° *Command (Déclaration de)*, no. 48.

[102] *Pand. b.*, v° *Command (Déclaration de)*, no. 4 *ter*; Van Gerven, *Bewindsbevoegdheid*, p. 169.

[103] C. Cauffman, 'The Principles of European Contract Law', *TPR* 2001, 1254.

[104] Storck, *Juris-classeurs civils*, v° *art. 1119 C.civ.*, fasc. 7–1, 1992, no. 76. See also: Cass. 18 February 1932, *Pas* 1932, I, 75.

[105] Cass. 18 February 1955, *Pas* 1955, I, 655 and *RW* 1955–56, 138 (the seller cannot argue that he is not bound by an obligation to indemnify the command on the grounds that the command did not deal with him but with the commandant); Cass. 6 December 1951, *Pas* 1952, I, 179 (the commandant is not held to the clauses of the contract, in particular the clause which states the road is co-owned between the owners of several parcels of land); De Page and Meinertzhagen-Limpens, *Traité*, IV, p. 409; Kluyskens, *Beginselen*, p. 63; Limpens, *La vente en droit belge*, p. 340.

In terms of the law of goods, designation of the command leads to a direct and sole transfer of property from the estate of the seller to the estate of the command. The command is presumed to have directly obtained property from the seller himself from the moment of the original contract of sale. The commandant is not considered owner at any stage: no double transfer of property takes place.[106]

The legal basis for this arrangement lies in the concept of representation.[107] The commandant concludes the contract of sale as an (authorised or unauthorised) agent in the name of and on behalf of the command, under the condition precedent (or suspensive condition) of the designation of the command. Taken together with the above conclusion that the commandant also concludes the contract of sale in his own name and on his own behalf (under the condition subsequent of the declaration of command), it is possible to conclude that the commandant enters into the contract in a double capacity and under a condition which is both subsequent and precedent. He enters into the agreement in his own name and on his own behalf under the condition subsequent of the declaration of command and also as the (authorised or unauthorised) agent in the name of and on behalf of the command under the condition precedent of the declaration of command. If the commandant acted as an unauthorised agent, the acceptance of the command constitutes ratification after an unauthorised representation. If the commandant acted as an authorised agent, the acceptance by the command is considered to be confirmation of the consent to the sale which was previously given. Consent is comprised in the authority to represent which has already been granted.

In principle the commandant disappears from the legal relation which results from the sale. On the one hand, he cannot derive any rights from the sale. He cannot appeal to the capacity of seller *vis-à-vis* the command.[108] On the other hand, the sale does not result in obligations which bind the commandant. For instance, he cannot be held liable to pay the

[106] Cass. 18 February 1955, *Pas* 1955, I, 655 and *RW* 1955–56, 138; Cass. 6 December 1951, *Pas* 1952, I, 179; Cass. 18 February 1932, *Pas* 1932, I, 74; Brussels 17 June 1954, *RW* 1954–55, 91; Luik 26 June 1843, *Pas* 1845, II, 30 and *BJ* 1845, 950; Tilleman, 'Lastgeving', p. 36.

[107] Paulus and Boes, 'Lastgeving', p. 25.

[108] Luik 26 June 1843, *Pas* 1845 or 1847, II, 119 (the commandant cannot claim the resolution of a sale contract against the command based on non-payment of the price); Limpens, *La vente en droit belge*, p. 341.

price[109] or to indemnify the seller.[110] In principle, the commandant does not have to warrant the solvency of the command towards the seller, nor proper performance of the sale by the command.[111] The seller has explicitly consented to the possibility of the declaration of command at the moment of conclusion of the sale and in doing so has agreed to accept the risk involved in knowing neither the identity nor the creditworthiness of the potential command.[112]

(d) Consequences of a late declaration of command

It has already been stated that, at the moment of expiration of the period for a declaration of command, the contract of sale is considered to be concluded between the commandant and the seller. Where a command is designated after the expiry of this period, a new and second agreement will be concluded between the commandant and the command.[113] From the perspective of the laws of goods, there will be a second transfer of property from the property of the commandant to the property of the command.[114]

VII Acting in the name of a company yet to be incorporated

The First Directive for the Harmonisation of Company Law obliged the member states of the European Union to introduce rules for the protection of third parties in the context of actions carried out in the name of a company prior to its incorporation. In Belgium, the rules on a company yet to be incorporated can be found in Art. 60 of the Company Code. According to this article, the promoters of a company who conclude a contract in the name of and on behalf of a company yet to be formed are personally bound by the contract if the company is not formed afterwards and if the contract is not ratified.[115]

On the one hand, a promoter acts as an unauthorised agent in the name of and on behalf of such a company. He is, of course, unauthorised,

---

[109] Cass. (France) 16 December 1874, *D* 1875, I, 131.

[110] Cass. 18 February 1955, *Pas* 1955, I, 655 and *RW* 1955–56, 138.

[111] *Pand. b.*, v° *Command (Déclaration de)*, no. 59.

[112] G. Baudry-Lacantinerie *Traité théorique et pratique de droit civil*, XIX (Paris: Larose and Tenin, 1908), p. 173.

[113] Limpens, *La vente en droit belge*, p. 336; *Pand. b.*, v° *Command (Déclaration de)*, nos. 25 and 26.

[114] P. Petel, *Le contrat de mandat* (Paris: Dalloz, 1994), p. 16.

[115] See on this topic: S. Gilcart, *La société en formation, Une étude du mécanisme sui generis de l'article 60 du Code des sociétés* (Mechelen: Wolters Kluwer Belgium, 2004), p. 544.

because the only party that can grant him authority does not yet exist. Through the application of the general rules on unauthorised agency, it can be seen that neither the company yet to be formed nor the promoter is bound by the contract (as long as the company is not formed, nor the contract ratified). If the promoter is nevertheless, according to Art. 60 of the Company Code, personally bound by the contract, this must be explained by the fact that the promoter is supposed to act in his own name and on his own behalf, under the condition subsequent of ratification by the company to be formed.[116]

VIII A personal commitment by the agent

1 Notion

Finally, an unauthorised agent can be bound personally if he has made a personal commitment towards the third party as *'porte fort/sterkmaker'* or as debtor or party to the performed legal act. This possibility arises because of the terms of Art. 1997 BCC, *in fine*, which stipulates that the agent who has given sufficient notice of (the scope of) his authority to the third party is not liable for acts performed outside the limits of his authority *unless he has accepted that he will be personally bound.*[117]

In principle, this provision is relevant to situations where the agent is unable to provide the third party with sufficient certainty on the extent of his authority. He therefore promises as *porte fort* that the principal will ratify the performed legal act.[118] The concept of *porte fort* can be defined as a contract or a contractual clause by which a person (the *porte fort* or promisor) undertakes an obligation[119] towards another person (the promisee) to persuade a third person to undertake an obligation. In case of non-performance (i.e. where it transpires that the third person (here,

---

[116] Samoy, *Middellijke vertegenwoordiging*, pp. 9–10.

[117] De Page, *Traité*, V, 1975, p. 441, 446–7; Laurent, *Principes*, p. 48; Samoy, *Middellijke vertegenwoordiging*, pp. 79–82; Wéry, 'Le mandat', pp. 253–4.

[118] De Page, *Traité*, pp. 441, 446–7; Gilcart, *La société en formation*, p. 216; Laurent, *Principes*, p. 48; Tilleman, 'Lastgeving', p. 194; Wéry, 'Le mandat', pp. 253–4.

[119] The obligation undertaken by the *porte fort* is a 'result-obligation'. In Belgian law, a distinction is made between an obligation of effort and an obligation of result. An obligation of result is an obligation which obliges the debtor to achieve a specific result: the burden of proof in case of non-performance lies with the debtor. An obligation of effort (or means) is an obligation which binds the debtor to make the necessary efforts in order to achieve a result. Such efforts must be made but the result is not warranted: the burden of proof in case of non-performance lies with the creditor.

the principal) refuses to undertake the promised obligation), the promisor is liable to the third party in damages, without being personally bound to perform the promised obligation.

In this particular situation, an agent who cannot provide sufficient evidence of his authority promises to the third party that he will persuade the principal – even in cases where he is acting as an unauthorised agent – to ratify the performed legal act.[120] If the agent acted as an unauthorised agent and fails to persuade the principal to ratify the performed act, the agent is liable in damages to the third party. The agent cannot claim to perform the principal's obligation himself.

Although less frequent in practice and irrelevant for the topic of unauthorised agency, it is also possible for the agent to undertake a personal commitment as debtor of the performed act in addition to the principal, outside the hypothesis of unauthorised agency.[121] The third party can ask for such a personal commitment where he has more confidence in the agent's status and creditworthiness than in that of the principal. This can be the case, for example, when the principal is located in another country or is unknown to the third party.[122] If the agent agrees to undertake such a personal commitment, the third party will have two main debtors (the principal and the agent) and two main claims.[123]

In some cases, the law stipulates a personal commitment of the agent. A customs agent, for example, is bound personally, together with the principal, in case of an incorrect or incomplete customs declaration.[124]

Finally, the unauthorised agent can combine acting in the name of and on behalf of the principal with acting in his own name and on his own behalf, mostly under the condition subsequent of ratification by the principal. In some cases, the law supposes or obliges the unauthorised agent to have acted in his own name and on his own behalf. According to Art. 60 of the Company Code, for example, promoters who conclude a contract in the name of and on behalf of a company yet to be formed are personally bound by the contract, if the company is not formed later and if the contract is not ratified (see IV, above). The law on bills of exchange and cheques offers another example. According to Art. 8 of the Co-ordinated Statutes on Bills of Exchange and Promissory notes, the

---

[120] On the outcome should the agent fail to persuade the principal, see VIII 2 below.

[121] De Page, *Traité*, V, 1975, p. 447; Laurent, *Principes*, p. 49; Wéry, 'Le mandat', p. 253.

[122] Comm. Brussels 1 April 1922, *TBH* 1922, 193.   [123] Laurent, *Principes*, p. 49.

[124] Antwerp 25 October 2004, *NjW* 2005, 591; Foriers and Jafferali, 'Le mandat (1991 à 2004)', p. 84.

unauthorised agent who signs a bill of exchange is personally bound by the bill of exchange towards third persons in good faith. According to Art. 11 of the Cheque Statute of 1 March 1961, the same rule applies to the unauthorised agent who signs a cheque.[125] Finally, as explained above, in the context of a sale with declaration of command, the commandant combines his capacity as an (authorised or unauthorised) agent of the principal with dealing in his own name and on his own behalf (see VI, above).

2 Effects

The unauthorised agent who subscribed an obligation as *porte fort* is liberated as soon as the principal has ratified the performed act. The *porte fort* obligation is limited to the promised act of ratification. The *porte fort* is not liable in case of non-performance of the ratified legal act by the principal, nor in cases of insolvency. The agent cannot claim to perform the principal's obligations himself.[126]

An illustration of the concept of *porte fort* is provided in the context of a 'lease operation'. In Belgian law, a lease operation is analysed as a combination of two separate agreements: a sale contract between the seller and the lease company and a lease contract between the lease company and the lessee. To prepare a lease operation, the lessee will first negotiate the sale contract with the seller. Because reaching agreement with the lease company can take some time, in most cases the lessee immediately signs the order form (as unauthorised agent) in the name and on behalf of the lease company. At the same time, the lessee promises as *porte fort* that the lease company (the principal) will in any event ratify the contract of sale. If the lease company ratifies the contract of sale, the lessee is liberated as *porte fort*.

If the agent fails to convince the principal to ratify the performed legal act, the unauthorised agent is liable on a contractual basis and – according to Art. 1120 BCC – bound to indemnify the third party.[127]

---

[125] See Tilleman, 'Lastgeving', pp. 196–8.

[126] Brussels 15 November 1967, *Pas* 1968, II, 100; Gent 14 November 1930, *Pas*. 1931, II, 52; Civ Gent 1 June 1965, *RW* 1965–66, 1213; Civ. Brussels 18 April 1888, *Pas* 1888, III, 266; Civ. Antwerp 14 August 1873, *Pas* 1874, III, 57; De Page, *Traité*, II, 1964, pp. 708–9; Van Gerven and Covemaeker, *Verbintenissenrecht*, p. 231.

[127] Brussels 15 November 1967, *Pas* 1968, II, 101; De Page, *Traité*, II, 1964, 705, 708, 714–15; Laurent, *Principes*, p. 616; Van Gerven and Covemaeker, *Verbintenissenrecht*, p. 231; Wéry, 'Le mandat', p. 254.

The *porte fort* can only be liable in damages because performance *in natura* of his obligation (i.e. forcing the principal to ratify the legal act) is impossible. Therefore, the only possibility is equivalent performance. To return to the illustration of the lease contract, if the lease company does not ratify the sale contract, the lessee is not personally bound by the sale contract. He can only be liable in damages to the seller.

The unauthorised agent does not become bound by the act performed in the name of and on behalf of the principal.[128] There are nevertheless examples in legal doctrine and case-law where the *porte fort* performs the legal act himself because of non-ratification by the principal. The explanation is that reparation *in natura* by the *porte fort* is sometimes possible in cases of non-performance by him. In general, performance by equivalent takes place by a payment of a sum of money, i.e. a pecuniary equivalent. Legal doctrine recognises, however, the possibility of reparation *in natura*, i.e. a non-pecuniary equivalent.[129] Applied to the concept of *porte fort* and unauthorised agency, reparation *in natura* will result in performance of the legal act by the unauthorised agent. The damage suffered by the third party corresponds to the advantages the legal act would have brought to the third party and the best way to indemnify this damage is the performance of the legal act itself by the unauthorised agent.

Again (see V 4), although reparation *in natura* is possible in theory, in practice it might face insurmountable obstacles. On the one hand, it will be excluded when the legal act can only be performed by the principal himself. This is the case when the legal act implies a transfer of property or when the person to perform the legal act has been chosen for reasons relating to his own skill or talent (*intuitu personae*). Making a work of art, for example, requires specific talents.[130] On the other hand, the third party's decision to call on a *porte fort* to perform his function as

---

[128] De Page, *Traité*, II, 1964, p. 705; E. Dirix, B. Tilleman and P. Van Orshoven, *De Valks juridisch woordenboek* (Antwerp: Intersentia, 2001), p. 299; B. Tilleman, 'Sterkmaking', in *Ad amicissimum amici scripsimus, Vriendenboek Raf Verstegen* (Bruges: Die Keure, 2004), p. 292; Van Gerven and Covemaeker, *Verbintenissenrecht*, p. 231.

[129] P. Wéry, *L'exécution forcée en nature des obligations contractuelles non pécuniaires* (Brussels: Kluwer, 1993), in particular p. 147.

[130] Gilcart, *La société en formation*, p. 219; B. Tilleman, 'Volmacht en sterkmaking bij oprichting van vennootschappen', in A. Benoit-Moury, O. Caprasse, N. Thirion and B. Tilleman (eds.), *De oprichting van vennootschappen en de opstartfase van de ondernemingen* (Brussels, Die Keure, 2003), p. 332.

guarantor does not necessarily mean that the third party wants the *porte fort* to perform the legal act guaranteed.[131]

In a case decided by the Cantonal Judge (Justice of the Peace)[132] of Antwerp, for example, an unauthorised agent/*porte fort* concluded a rental contract on behalf of a company. The unauthorised legal act was not ratified by the company and the *porte fort* claimed the rented office space for his own use. The Cantonal Judge refused this claim because one cannot force a creditor (the third party) to accept a debtor (the agent) other than the one to whom he agreed to be bound (the principal).[133]

---

[131] De Page, *Traité*, II, 1964, p. 715; Laurent, *Principes*, pp. 621–2; Tilleman, 'Volmacht en sterkmaking bij oprichting van vennootschappen', p. 332.

[132] *Vrederechter/Juge de Paix.*

[133] J. P. Antwerp 7 November 1984, *RW* 1986–87, 2323, obs.

4

Unauthorised agency in German law

MARTIN SCHMIDT-KESSEL AND ANA BAIDE

Table of contents

I Introduction

Agency is a legal device which enables an effective division of tasks within an economic system.[1] Under German law, agency[2] is understood as a concept which is separated from the underlying relationship, which in most cases is a contract to provide a service[3] or a mandate contract.[4] Agency takes place when one person, the agent, performs a legal act in the name of another, the principal.[5] The most common legal act an agent would perform in the name of the principal is the conclusion of a contract with the third party.

Unauthorised agency (*Vertretung ohne Vertretungsmacht*) takes place when the legal act performed by the agent is not authorised by the principal whether there is an underlying contractual or other relationship or not. Consequently, questions as to the validity and enforceablity of contracts concluded with third parties will come to light. German law provides a comprehensive mechanism for dealing with issues arising out of acts of agents lacking authority. There are different situations in which an unauthorised agency may take place, such as when the agent has no authority or when he merely exceeds his authority. The main difficulty with unauthorised agency lies in the lack of control on the part of the principal. It is this lack of control which carries with it questions of liability, and/or extent of liability, of either the agent or the principal.

1 Functions of agency in German law

The crux of the law of agency lies in the regulation of the relationship between the principal, the agent and the third party by maintaining a balance between the principal's authority, the agent's actions and the

---

[1] K.-H. Schramm, in F. J. Säcker (ed.), *Münchener Kommentar zum Bürgerlichen Gesetzbuch*, Vol. I §§ 1–240, 5th edn (München: Beck-Verlag, 2006), § 164, no. 68. Similarly, K. Larenz and M. Wolf, *Allgemeiner Teil des Bürgerlichen Rechts*, 9th edn (München: Beck-Verlag, 2007), § 46, no. 2. Cf. M. Löwisch and D. Neumann, *Allgemeiner Teil des BGB*, 7th edn (München: Beck-Verlag, 2004), no. 195: 'Erweiterung der Privatautonomie in persönlicher Hinsicht.'

[2] *Stellvertretung.* As we separate agency from the underlying contract, it is simply a legal phenomenon not a relationship: *Stellvertretung* takes place.

[3] *Dienstvertrag.*   [4] *Auftrag.*

[5] This follows from §164(1) BGB, which may be translated as: 'A declaration of intent which a person makes in the name of a principal within the scope of his authority takes effect directly in favour of and against the principal. It makes no difference whether the declaration is made expressly in the name of the principal, or whether it may be gathered from the circumstances that it is to be made in his name.' (Translation by juris GmbH.)

third party's reliance. The key elements constituting the law of agency are: (1) the link between the principal and the agent; (2) the extent of control of the agent by the principal; (3) the comprehension and/or the reliance of the third party; (4) the responsibility of the principal; (5) the responsibility of the agent; and (6) the extent of the independence of the agent.

In the majority of cases, the connection between the principal and the agent's legal act (e.g. a contract with a third party) is clear from the outset. It contains the key elements required in order to legitimately[6] attribute the agent's acts to the principal, namely the legal act of the agent and the clearly made out fact that the agent is acting, and is allowed to act, in the name of the principal. However, cases will arise where such legitimacy will be called into question. In practical terms, the most important situation, and the one under scrutiny here, is that of an agent who acted in a manner which was not permitted in relation to the principal.

2 General principles of the German law of agency

The three general principles of German law of agency are: (1) the representation principle (*Repräsentationsprinzip*); (2) the principle of disclosure of agency (*Offenkundigkeitsprinzip*); and (3) the principle of independence of authority (*Abstraktheit der Vertretungsmacht*).

The representation principle refers to the idea that the agent 'represents' the principal as opposed to the view that the agent is an organ of the principal. The agent is the only person acting in a legal sense and this act is then attributed to the principal because the agent 'makes him present' by his (i.e. the agent's) own legal act(s). Any contract with a third party thus depends on the declaration of the agent, while only the consequences of such a legal transaction will reach the principal.[7] This declaration must be valid as a declaration of the agent: for example, the mistakes of the agent make the contract avoidable, while mistakes of the principal do not matter at all.[8] The only more general exception to

---

[6] As to legitimacy, see W. Flume, *Allgemeiner Teil des Bürgerlichen Rechts – Das Rechtsgeschäft*, Vol. II (Berlin: Springer Verlag, 1965), § 45 II, 1; Schramm, *Münchener Kommentar zum BGB*, § 164, no. 68.

[7] R. Bork, *Allgemeiner Teil des Bürgerlichen Gesetzbuchs*, 2nd edn (Tübingen: Mohr Siebeck-Verlag, 2006), no. 1343; Larenz and Wolf, *Allgemeiner Teil des Bürgerlichen Rechts*, § 46, nos. 1 and 6; D. Leipold, BGB I: *Einführung und allgemeiner Teil: ein Lehrbuch mit Fällen und Kontrollfragen*, 4th edn (Tübingen: Mohr Siebeck-Verlag, 2007), no. 667.

[8] E. Schilken in *J. von Staudingers Kommentar zum Bürgerlichen Gesetzbuch*, Vol. 1, *Allgemeiner Teil*, 13th edn (Berlin: Sellier – de Gruyter, 2004), Preface to §§ 164 *et seq.*, no. 32. Compare nos. 10–15 for the historical background.

that principle is the case of the principal's erroneous direction followed by the agent.[9]

The principle of disclosure of agency requires that the agent disclose to the third party that he is in fact acting as an agent and that he will not be party to the contract.[10] The declaration by the agent must therefore be made in the name of a principal. German law does not, however, require that the principal be identified at the outset:[11] in a case the Reichsgericht decided in 1933, the parties concluded a contract for the sale of immovable property by notarial deed. The persons acting for the buyer declared, before the notary, that they would name the buyer later on. The court held that the contract became valid after nomination of the buyer and ratification by him.[12] In cases of this kind the disclosure associates the declaration of the agent with the principal.[13] But basically the declaration of the agent is to be attributed to the principal only when there is either a clear authority at the time of such a declaration or where the principal ratifies it retrospectively. The agent in these cases acts as a direct agent, but this is rarely spelled out explicitly.

The principle of the independence of authority separates the necessary authority of the agent from a contractual relationship between them and the principal.[14] This independence – the *Abstraktheit der Vertretungsmacht* – aims to protect the reliance of third parties, which often are not aware of the internal affairs between the principal and the agent.[15] Therefore,

---

[9] See § 166(2) BGB, which may be translated as: 'When the power of representation (authority) is conferred by legal transaction, if the agent has acted in compliance with specific instructions given by the principal, the latter may not rely on the lack of knowledge of the agent about circumstances known to him. The same rule applies to circumstances which the principal ought to have known, insofar as the imputed knowledge is equivalent to knowledge.' (Translation by juris GmbH.)

[10] Bork, *Allgemeiner Teil des BGB*, no. 1378; Larenz and Wolf, *Allgemeiner Teil des Bürgerlichen Rechts*, § 46, no. 19; Leipold, *BGB I: Einführung und allgemeiner Teil*, no. 667; Schramm, *Münchener Kommentar zum BGB*, § 164, no. 14.

[11] Larenz and Wolf, *Allgemeiner Teil des Bürgerlichen Rechts*, § 46, no. 40.

[12] RGZ 140, 335, 338. The court held, further, that nomination and ratification needed not to meet the form requirements for the sale of immovable property under the former § 313 BGB which today is § 311b(1) BGB (notarial deed).

[13] Schramm, *Münchener Kommentar zum BGB*, § 164, no. 15.

[14] Bork, *Allgemeiner Teil des BGB*, no. 1487 et seq.

[15] Larenz and Wolf, *Allgemeiner Teil des Bürgerlichen Rechts*, §46 no., 135 et seq.; Schramm, *Münchener Kommentar zum BGB*, §164, nos. 74 and 97. This principle was developed by Laband in his famous article: P. Laband, 'Die Stellvertretung bei dem Abschluß von Rechtsgeschäften nach dem allgemeinen Deutschen Handelsgesetzbuch' (1866) 10 *ZHR* 183. Compare Schilken, *Staudinger*, Preface to §§164 et seq., nos. 12–14 for the historical background.

an invalid or void underlying contract between principal and agent does not prevent the agent's authority from raising legal consequences between the principal and a third party. On the other hand, the lack of authority for reason of an invalidity of the declaration of authority may lead to a breach of the underlying contract by the principal but leaves the validity of that contract untouched. In Germany the idea of *Abstraktheit* is mostly expressed by simply stating that § 139 BGB does not apply.[16] For example, the underlying contract may be void for lack of form while the authority remains valid and vice versa. The same holds true for the declaration of ratification which is likewise independent from such a contractual relationship.

II Overview: unauthorised agency and its consequences: §§ 177–180 BGB

The German law distinguishes between two cases of representation, namely the representation in the process of conclusion of a contract[17] and the representation in the field of unilateral legal transactions.[18]

1 Representation in the process of the conclusion of a contract[19]

In cases where an unauthorised agent concludes a contract with a third party, such a contract will not be automatically void, rather it would depend on the ratification by the principal. According to §§ 177(2) and 178 BGB, the third party may then choose either to request clarification by the principal (in which case the principal has two weeks within which to ratify the contract, failing which the contract becomes void),[20] or to revoke the contract at any time before the principal ratifies it.[21]

---

[16] See Schilken, *Staudinger*, Preface to §§164 *et seq.*, no. 33. §139 BGB translated reads: 'If a part of a legal transaction is void, the entire legal transaction is void, unless it may be assumed that it would have been entered into even if the void part had been omitted.' (Translation by juris GmbH.)

[17] §§ 177–179 BGB.   [18] § 180 BGB.

[19] The official title of §177 BGB reads 'Vertragsschluss durch Vertreter ohne Vertretungsmacht'.

[20] § 177(2) BGB, which may be translated as: 'If the other party demands that the principal declares whether or not he ratifies the contract, the declaration may only be made to such person; a ratification or a refusal to ratify declared to the agent before the demand is without effect. The ratification may only be declared before the expiry of two weeks after receipt of the demand; if it is not declared, it is deemed to have been refused.' (Translation by juris GmbH.)

[21] § 178 BGB, which may be translated as: 'Until ratification of the contract, the other party is entitled to revoke it, unless he knew of the lack of authority on conclusion of the contract. The revocation may also be declared to the agent.' (Translation by juris GmbH.)

For details as to the declaration of ratification, the *Genehmigung*, see V below.

The agent will be liable for any contract concluded while acting without authority, and should the principal refuse to ratify the contract, under § 179(1) BGB the third party can choose between specific performance[22] and damages, which include performance interest.[23] In cases where the agent is unaware of having acted without authorisation, the compensation available to the third party is restricted to reliance interest.[24] Further, § 179(3) BGB provides for two exclusions of liability of the agent in cases where the third party knew or should have known that the agent acted without authority, and in cases where the agent lacked legal capacity (e.g. where the agent is a minor).[25] As to the liability of the *falsus procurator*, see VI below.

2 Representation in the field of unilateral legal transactions[26]

The general rule contained in § 180 BGB, first sentence, provides that unilateral declarations by an agent who acts without authority will be void. Thereby, to give two examples, a notice to terminate a contract for breach or a notice to bring a contract which involves a continuous or permanent performance (*Dauerschuldverhältnis*) to an end by an *ordentliche Kündigung* is as a rule void if declared by an agent who acts without authority. This rule applies without any exception to all declarations which to become valid need not be made to a third party (*nichtempfangsbedürftige Willenserklärung*). For example, it is impossible to have a valid public offer of a reward under § 657 BGB (*Auslobung*) by an agent acting without authority.

---

[22] *Erfüllung.*

[23] The paragraph reads in English: 'A person who has entered into a contract as an agent is, if he has not furnished proof of his authority, bound to the other party at his choice either to perform the contract or to pay damages to him, if the principal refuses to ratify the contract.' (Translation by juris GmbH.)

[24] §179(2) BGB, which may be translated as: 'If the agent was not aware of his lack of authority, he is bound to make compensation only for the damage which the other party has suffered by his relying on the authority; not, however, beyond the value of the interest which the other party has in the validity of the contract.' (Translation by juris GmbH.)

[25] The paragraph reads in English: 'The agent is not liable, if the other party knew or ought to have known of the lack of authority. The agent is also not liable if he had limited capacity to contract, unless he acted with the consent of his legal representative.' (Translation by juris GmbH.)

[26] The official title of §180 BGB reads 'Einseitiges Rechtsgeschäft'.

However, an exception to this general rule is provided by § 180 BGB, second sentence, in cases where such a unilateral declaration must be made to a third party (*empfangsbedürftige Willenserklärung*) and the third party agrees to the agent acting without authority, or is seen to be agreeing should he show no objection.[27] In this exceptional case, the rules on the conclusion of a contract by an unauthorised agent, i.e. §§ 177–179 BGB, apply. It is therefore possible to ratify, for example, a notice to terminate a contract given by an agent who acts without authority if the other party to the contract did not reject the notice for lack of authority. For that second alternative of § 180 BGB, second sentence, to be applied, the third party only needs to know that the agent acts on behalf of the principal; knowledge of the lack of authority is not necessary. This alternative from a functional perspective therefore reverses in part the roles of rule and exception, namely for *empfangsbedürftige Willenserklärungen*.

3 Applicability of the rules for unauthorised agency

The above rules will apply in a number of different situations, some of which come within the scope of §§ 177–180 BGB, and others to which these sections apply by way of analogy. The first group consists of: (a) where the agent has no authority at all;[28] and (b) where the agent has an authority but does not act within its scope[29] (conflicts of interest, which are dealt with by § 181 BGB,[30] belong to this category). The second group to which §§ 177–180 apply by way of analogy consists of: (a) where

---

[27] §180 BGB, which may be translated as: 'Agency without authority is not permitted for a unilateral legal transaction. However, if the person with whom such a legal transaction was to be entered into did not object to the authority claimed by the agent on entering into the legal transaction or if he agreed that the agent may act without authority, the provisions on contracts apply with the necessary modifications. The same applies if a unilateral legal transaction is entered into with an unauthorised agent with his consent.' (Translation by juris GmbH.)

[28] This also covers cases where the authority has come to an end before the contract was concluded by the agent, see Schramm, *Münchener Kommentar zum BGB*, § 177, no. 11.

[29] Larenz and Wolf, *Allgemeiner Teil des Bürgerlichen Rechts*, § 49, no. 1; Schramm, *Münchener Kommentar zum BGB*, § 177, no. 10.

[30] § 181 BGB may be translated as: 'An agent may not without permission enter into a legal transaction in the name of the principal with himself in his own name or as an agent of a third party, unless the legal transaction solely consists in the fulfilment of an obligation.' (Translation by juris GmbH.)

the agent acts under the name of the principal;[31] (b) where the principal is not named;[32] and (c) where the principal does not exist.[33]

There is an ongoing discussion on the best method of dealing with the cases of abuse of authority.[34] The cases of abuse of authority normally arise where the authority of the agent is broader than his mandate under the contract with the principal. Abuse of authority is therefore a consequence of the principle that the agent's authority is independent from the underlying contract.[35] Because of that principle basically the declarations of the agent on behalf of the principal are therefore valid.[36] Abuse of authority applies mainly to cases where the third party is perfectly aware of the difference between authority and mandate of the agent,[37] but this must not always be the case. For example, in a case decided by the *Bundesgerichtshof* in 1988,[38] the principal provided the agent in a notarial deed with an authority, which enabled the agent to represent the principal 'against public authorities and private individuals in every aspect'. The agent was to sell immovable property of the principal but concluded a contract with an estate broker, who then sold the property and claimed his fees from the principal. The brokerage contract comprised a distribution of risks which was very unfavourable for the principal and therefore it was clearly covered by the authority of the agent but not by the mandate contract between the agent and the principal. The conclusion of the brokerage contract was qualified as a breach of the mandate contract. Because the agent and the broker where closely interrelated, the court drew from the facts the conclusion that the broker was aware, or at least could not have been unaware, of that breach and therefore asked the Appellate Court to reconsider a judgment which awarded the broker his fees.

---

[31] Bork, *Allgemeiner Teil des BGB*, no. 1410; Larenz and Wolf, *Allgemeiner Teil des Bürgerlichen Rechts*, § 46, no. 57; Schramm, *Münchener Kommentar zum BGB*, § 164, nos. 39; § 177, no. 6; and § 179, no. 10.

[32] But in this case there is only a liability under § 179 BGB applied by way of analogy (Larenz and Wolf, *Allgemeiner Teil des Bürgerlichen Rechts*, § 46, no. 40); without a principal named, there is no room for a ratification under § 177 BGB.

[33] Larenz and Wolf, *Allgemeiner Teil des Bürgerlichen Rechts*, § 49, no. 35; Schramm, *Münchener Kommentar zum BGB*, § 179, no. 11.

[34] Schilken, *Staudinger*, § 167, nos. 100–5.

[35] Larenz and Wolf, *Allgemeiner Teil des Bürgerlichen Rechts*, § 46, no. 139.

[36] Larenz and Wolf, *Allgemeiner Teil des Bürgerlichen Rechts*, § 46, no. 139.

[37] See Schramm, *Münchener Kommentar zum BGB*, § 164, no. 108 *et seq.*, citing further authorities.

[38] BGH NJW 1988, 3012.

For the rare cases in which such an abuse is of a relevant nature, there is some discussion as to the consequences: one opinion is that in such cases the agent has no authority.[39] Thus these situations are covered by §§ 177–180 BGB. The prevailing view, however, is that the declaration of the agent is void, either under § 138 BGB (transactions *contra bonos mores*) in cases where there is a collusion between the agent and the third party,[40] or in all other cases as a consequence of the general exception of abuse of rights, which is based on § 242 BGB (the good faith principle).[41] This prevailing opinion would normally lead to the result that the agent's declaration is void and the principal is therefore not bound by it. However, the courts and most legal scholars avoid such a result by applying §§ 177–180 BGB by way of analogy.[42] The consequence of this application is that the contract, although void under § 138 BGB, may nevertheless be ratified by the principal. The approach of the prevailing opinion seems to include a superfluous loop way compared to the idea of applying simply §§ 177–180. The advantage of that loop lies in the greater flexibility of the prerequisites of abuse of authority under § 138 BGB compared to absence of authority under § 177.

III Cases of constructive authority

The German civil code does not provide a general rule of constructive authority nor is there a general doctrine of constructive authority developed by courts or legal writers. Occasionally, such a general concept is seen in the doctrine of *Vertrauenshaftung* (liability for reliance),[43] which was mainly formulated by Professor Claus-Wilhelm Canaris.[44] But this doctrine was neither adopted completely by the German courts nor does it provide an adequate explanation for the cases where reliance does not lead to a liability for reliance interest but to one under which the

---

[39] Schilken, *Staudinger*, § 167, no. 103.
[40] RGZ 130,131,142; Larenz and Wolf, *Allgemeiner Teil des Bürgerlichen Rechts*, § 46, no. 143; Leipold, *BGB I: Einführung und allgemeiner Teil*, no. 722.
[41] Larenz and Wolf, *Allgemeiner Teil des Bürgerlichen Rechts*, § 46, no. 141; Leipold, *BGB I: Einführung und allgemeiner Teil*, no. 722; see BGH NJW 1990, 384, 385.
[42] BGHZ 141, 357, 364; Larenz and Wolf, *Allgemeiner Teil des Bürgerlichen Rechts*, § 46, no. 141; Schramm, *Münchener Kommentar zum BGB*, § 164, no. 111.
[43] Bork, *Allgemeiner Teil des BGB*, no. 1538 *et seq*; Larenz and Wolf, *Allgemeiner Teil des Bürgerlichen Rechts*, § 48, nos. 1 *et seq*. and 20 *et seq*.; Schramm, *Münchener Kommentar zum BGB*, § 167, no. 45.
[44] C.-W. Canaris, *Die Vertrauenshaftung im deutschen Privatrecht* (München: Beck-Verlag, 1971), especially pp. 32 *et seq*. and pp. 134 *et seq*.

performance interest is protected.[45] The several cases of constructive authority are not and cannot therefore be explained by the said doctrine. Even so, the element which all cases of constructive authority have in common is the third party's lack of awareness.

1 Prolongation of an authority which has ended

There are three types of constructive authority which are dealt with by the German Civil Code. All of them concern situations where an authority of an agent comes to an end but there is a need for an ongoing protection of certain third parties. The first is contained in § 169 BGB, the second in §§ 170 and 171 BGB and the third is the case of authority in writing, under § 172 BGB.

(a) Authority ends as a consequence of the termination of the underlying contract: § 169 BGB

Where the authority of the agent ends as a consequence of the termination of the underlying contract, §169 applies.[46] The reason for the termination of authority then is contained in the first sentence of § 168.[47] The contracts covered by these rules are the mandate in the sense of § 662 and the partnership under § 705 and the subsequent articles. Should these contracts come to an end, either a fiction of the continuation of the contract or the management duties under the partnership contract would exist under §§ 674 and 729.[48] The fiction of

---

[45] T. Lobinger, *Rechtsgeschäftliche Verpflichtung und autonome Bindung* (Tübingen: Mohr Siebeck-Verlag, 1999), pp. 237 *et seq.*

[46] § 169 BGB may be translated as: 'Insofar as a terminated authority of an authorised representative or a managing partner is deemed to continue in accordance with sections 674 and 729, it is not effective in favour of a third party who, at the time when a legal transaction is entered into, knows or ought to know of the expiry.' (Translation by juris GmbH.)

[47] The sentence may be translated as: 'The expiry of the authority depends on the legal relationship on which its conferment was based. The authority is revocable also if the legal relationship is continued, unless a different intention appears from this relationship.' (Translation by juris GmbH.)

[48] The articles may be translated as: 'If the mandate lapses any other way than by revocation, then it is still deemed to continue for the benefit of the mandatee until the mandatee becomes aware of the lapse or must be aware of it.' (§ 674 BGB) and 'If the partnership is dissolved, then the authority of a partner to manage is likewise deemed to continue in existence to his benefit until he becomes aware of the dissolution or must have become aware of it. The same applies to the authority of a partner leaving the partnership to manage when the partnership is carried on or for its loss in any other way.' (§ 729 BGB). (Translations by juris GmbH.)

continuation means that the mandate or management competencies are deemed to be continuing until the agent knows or should know of the termination of the contract. Such fiction of continuation and therewith the protection of both agent[49] and third party is transposed into the realm of agency via § 168, which allows for the continuation of the agent's authority until his knowledge of the termination. However, an authority such as this is only a constructive authority because it has no effect in favour of the third party who knows or should have known of the lack of authority, as is made clear by § 169.

(b) Declaration or notice of the authority to the third party: §§ 170 and 171 BGB

Sections 170 and 171 BGB deal with situations where the third party was in some way informed by the principal of the existence of authority. In the case of § 170 the authority itself, the so-called *Außenvollmacht*, is declared to the third party.[50] Under this provision a principal's revocation of the agent's authority originally declared to the third party will only become effective if there is a notice of such a termination made to that third party. The rule in § 171 applies where the declaration of the authority made to the agent was notified to the third party or the public. The agent will thus act with authority until the notice is revoked in the same manner as it was given.[51] In both cases the agent is only acting under a constructive authority. This follows from § 173 BGB where, once the third party knows or should know of the termination of the real authority, the constructive authority will come to an end.[52]

---

[49] See Larenz and Wolf, *Allgemeiner Teil des Bürgerlichen Rechts*, § 48, no. 19.

[50] Cf. Larenz and Wolf, *Allgemeiner Teil des Bürgerlichen Rechts*, § 48, no. 16. The article may be translated as: 'If authority is conferred by declaration to a third party, it remains in force in relation to this third party until he is notified by the principal of the expiry thereof.' (Translations by juris GmbH.)

[51] See the translation by juris GmbH: '(1) If a person has announced by separate notification to a third party or by public notice that he has granted authority to another, the latter, on the basis of this announcement, is authorised to represent the person to the particular third party in the former case, and any third party in the latter case.
(2) The authority remains effective until the notice is revoked in the same manner in which it was made.'

[52] The article may be translated as: 'The provisions of section 170, section 171(2) and section 172(2) do not apply, if the third party knows or ought to know of the termination of the authority when the legal transaction is entered into.' (Translation by juris GmbH.)

(c) Authority in writing: § 172 BGB

Where an authority in writing exists and comes to an end internally, i.e. between the principal and the agent, it will remain in force against every third party pursuant to § 172(2) BGB,[53] until the document containing the authority is returned to the principal under § 175 BGB or declared invalid under § 176 BGB. This is also a case of a constructive authority, since it comes to an end pursuant to § 173 where the third party knows or should know that the real authority has come to an end.

2 The authority of employees in stores and warehouses: § 56 HGB[54]

Under § 56 HGB: 'one who is employed in a store or warehouse open to the public is considered authorised to sell and receive anything which is customary for such a business or warehouse.' This provision does not apply to all contracts concluded by an employee, but is restricted to contracts which are typical for the type of commercial activity such an employee is involved in, in his shop or warehouse. The authority 'to receive' does not mean that an employee may organise the supply of goods (to his shop or warehouse). Receiving is limited to receiving money and similar counter-performances under the contract with the customers.

Section 54(3) HGB applies by analogy, therefore the constructive authority of an employee under § 56 is regarded as invalid against a third party who at the time of the conclusion of the contract knew or should have known of the lack of authority.

3 Trade Register

In the realm of commercial law, the authority of agents in the more significant roles has to be registered in the Trade Register. The two categories of agents required to be registered are: (1) director of a company (§ 39 GmbHG (Limited Companies Act) and § 81 AktG (Companies Limited by Shares Act)); and (2) the holder of a procuration (§ 53 HGB).

Procuration (*procura*) is a commercial law concept pertaining to the authority of an agent and his representation. The authority of a holder of

---

[53] The paragraph may be translated as: 'The authority remains effective until the power of attorney is returned to the principal or declared invalid.' (Translation by juris GmbH.)

[54] *Handelsgesetzbuch* – German Commercial Code.

procuration is a rather broad one. Only in rare cases can it be restricted, for example to one of the several branches of the particular company. The holder of a procuration has authority to conclude any kind of contract. The only exception is a contract for the disposition of immovable property, for which additional authority is required.

Since the registration in itself is not a prerequisite for the existence of the authority, it is common for differences between the register, the relevant publications and the real authority of an agent to exist. In such instances the agent may be authorised to act under a constructive authority. The general rule is that the third party can rely on the true facts without being bound by the faulty registration and/or publication or lack thereof. Where the agent has authority the principal will be bound irrespective of the content of the register and/or publication. However, where a constructive authority can be inferred from the content of the register and/or the publication, yet the agent does not possess authority, the third party is entitled to opt for the application of the rules on unauthorised agents (§ 177 and the subsequent articles), or for the protection given by the mechanisms of the register, i.e. of §§ 15(1) and (3) HGB.[55]

(a) The negative effect of the register: § 15(1) HGB

Section 15(1) HGB deals with the so-called negative effect of the register (*negative Publizität des Handelsregisters*). Under this provision: 'for so long as a fact requiring registration in the Trade Register is not restricted and published, it cannot be held against a third party by the one to whom the entry pertains unless the third party knew of such fact.' The most common situation when a constructive authority will be derived from this provision is when an existing and registered authority comes to an end, yet this termination is not subsequently registered and/or published.[56] The provision further applies to authorities which have come to an end without subsequent registration and/or publication, but were also not registered in the first place.[57] Some discussion exists as to the effects of a previous faulty registration under § 15(1) HGB, where the protection of a third party's reliance in the faulty register could come into

---

[55] As to the Community law aspects to this topic, see M. Schmidt-Kessel, *Handelsrecht – Unternehmensrecht*, in M. Schulze and R. Zuleeg, *Europarecht* (Baden-Baden: Nomos-Verlag, 2006), pp. 679 *et seq.*, nos. 25–78.

[56] Leipold, *BGB I: Einführung und allgemeiner Teil*, no. 731.

[57] P. Krebs, in C. Schmidt (ed.), *Münchener Kommentar zum Handelsgesetzbuch*, Vol. 1, 2nd edn (München: Beck-Verlag, 2005), § 15, no. 35.

play.[58] In any case, however, where the third party knows of the fact which should have been registered, i.e. in our case the presence or absence of the authority or termination of such authority, § 15(1) offers no protection.

(b) Section 15(3) HGB: the positive effect

The cases of the agent's lack of authority which are regulated by § 15(3) HGB have in common the fact that a disclosure of an authority took place where no such authority existed in the first place. Section 15(3) states: 'Where the fact was published incorrectly, a third party may claim reliance on the fact published *vis-à-vis* the one to whom the entry pertained unless he knew it to be incorrect.' If the fact referred to in this section is the authority of a director of a company or a holder of a procuration, then the provision provides those persons with a constructive authority. This rule is first applicable in situations where the content of the register is correct but the publication is not. However, the constructive authority also exists where there is no registration, where the content of the register and the publication contain the same error(s), or where there are different errors in the register and the publication.[59]

Another problem that is subject to debate is the situation in which the fact to be disclosed is correct, i.e. the authority is published correctly (or not published at all), yet the content of the register is erroneous. Some authors argue that § 15(3) HGB should be applied to such cases by way of analogy.[60] The prevailing view, however, rejects the analogy for historical reasons, since the possibility of giving § 15(3) wider scope was already discussed during the legislative drafting process, and subsequently rejected.

There is no constructive authority where the third party has knowledge of the fact and subsequent registration and/or publication errors.

4 Duldungsvollmacht – *authority granted by toleration of agent's actions*

Alongside the cases of constructive authority provided for in the Civil and Commercial Codes, German courts and legal scholars have

---

[58] Krebs, *Münchener Kommentar zum HGB*, § 15, no. 37.
[59] Krebs, *Münchener Kommentar zum HGB*, § 15, no. 88.
[60] A. Baumbach and K. J. Hopt, *Handelsgesetzbuch: HGB*, 33rd edn. (München: Beck-Verlag, 2008), § 15, no. 18.

developed a broader concept of constructive liability for situations where the principal had knowledge of the agent's actions but did not interfere. This concept is called *Duldungsvollmacht* (literally authority by toleration or acquiescence).

(a) Historical background

The concept of *Duldungsvollmacht* appeared in the nineteenth century.[61] The courts at that time held that in cases of reliance of the third party, where such reliance was caused by the principal, an authority would exist. From this reasoning two separate lines of thinking developed, one leading to the concept of apparent authority[62] and the other to *Duldungsvollmacht*. The distinguishing factor between these two concepts rests with the knowledge of the principal: where the principal has no knowledge of the agent's actions only apparent authority can exist.[63] *Dulden*, i.e. toleration of the agent's actions, presupposes knowledge of these actions, while causing the mere appearance of an existing authority may be due to lack of care of the principal.

(b) Scope and application

The general test for *Duldungsvollmacht*, while differing slightly from case to case but remaining substantially the same, was most recently formulated by the *XI Zivilsenat* of the BGH:

> A *Duldungsvollmacht* only takes place if the principal tolerates knowingly – and normally for an extended period of time – that another person without an authority given to them acted as an agent, and that the third party understands, and may by good faith understand, that that other person is authorised as an agent.[64]

In that case an authority established by the principal was held void for being contrary to public policy.[65] The third party argued that he was protected under the rules of *Duldungsvollmacht* but the two documents with which the principal had provided the agent were held to be insufficient to produce a *Dulden*, because they by themselves do not constitute an activity of the agent to be known and tolerated by the principal. If the

---

[61] See RGE 1, 149, 152.   [62] See sub. IV.

[63] Larenz and Wolf, *Allgemeiner Teil des Bürgerlichen Rechts*, § 48, nos. 22 and 25.

[64] BGH NJW 2004, 2745, 2746–47.

[65] The contract between principal and agent and the authority were held to contravene Art. 1, § 1 of the Legal Advice Act, which largely proscribes professional legal advice by non-lawyers.

agent had used the documents several times and the principal, knowing about this fact, had not objected, the result would have been the opposite.

Duldungsvollmacht works as an effective authority of the agent. The knowledge of the third party of the lack of authority creates no separate barrier to this type of constructive authority. However, the knowledge excluding the constructive authority is inherent in the aforementioned test for *Duldungsvollmacht*: a third party which knows or should know of the lack of authority may not 'by good faith understand, that that other person is authorised as an agent'.[66]

(c) Nature of the authority

There is much discussion on the nature of this kind of authority. One view considers that the basis of *Duldungsvollmacht* are the rules of legal protection of reliance, i.e. the doctrine of *Vertrauenshaftung*.[67] The contrary opinion views *Duldungsvollmacht* as constructive authority.[68] This discussion only has relevance for the issue whether the principal can avoid the authority under the provisions for mistake (§§ 119 ff. and §§ 142 ff). If *Duldungsvollmacht* was merely based on a reliance protection principle, avoidance would not be possible, since provisions for avoidance only apply to declarations and not to protection of reliance rules. Therefore, the second view is the correct one, as it is better suited to interact with the general rules relating to the conclusion of a contract. Under these rules the aforementioned tests would always lead to a declaration. In the case of avoidance of authority by the principal, the reliance interest of the third party is protected by § 122 BGB, which gives the third party a damages claim against the principal.

5 *Summary*

The common thread linking all the above cases of constructive authority may be derived from the correct interpretation of the principle of *Duldungsvollmacht*. In all the cases of constructive authority the third party is in a position reasonably to infer, from the information related to them by the principal, that a valid authority does exist. Such information

---

[66] BGH NJW 2004, 2745, 2746–7.
[67] See BGH NJW 1997, 312, 314; BGH NJW 2003, 2092; Bork, *Allgemeiner Teil des BGB*, no. 1550; Leipold, *BGB I: Einführung und allgemeiner Teil*, no. 733.
[68] Flume § 49, 3; Löwisch and Neumann, *Allgemeiner Teil des BGB*, no. 227.

may be taken as either a declaration of authority or at least as the notice of the authority given to the agent.

This general interpretation of the principles of constructive authority, when applied to § 15(3) HGB, provides the basis for the nexus between the false register and the behaviour of the principal. However, if such an unwritten requirement is not present, the register will replace those facts from which an actual declaration of authority will be derived in other situations. Constructive authority is therefore not an instrument of reliance protection.

IV Apparent authority

The early cases dealing with the protection of third party reliance have also inspired a second line of argument and cases which have led to the development of the concept of apparent authority (*Anscheinsvollmacht*).

1 The classical principle of apparent authority

The principle of apparent authority applies to situations where the principal had no knowledge of the agent's actions, but could have obtained such knowledge had he used due care. In these situations the agent is said to have acted under apparent authority, or *Anscheinsvollmacht*.[69] The test for apparent authority is that of a reasonable person in the shoes of the third party who would have reasonably inferred that the agent was acting with authority.[70] Such a reasonable inference of the third party ought to be directly caused by the principal's words and/or actions.[71]

The nature of *Anscheinsvollmacht* is subject to much debate. Two main lines of argument exist: the first equates apparent authority with the concept of constructive authority;[72] and the second advocates that *Anscheinsvollmacht* only protects the reliance of the third party and therefore gives a claim for damages for the reliance interest.[73] The second position is the correct one, since under the general principles of German

---

[69] Schramm, *Münchener Kommentar zum BGB*, §167, nos. 54 and 59 *et seq.*

[70] Larenz and Wolf, *Allgemeiner Teil des Bürgerlichen Rechts*, § 48, no. 25.

[71] Larenz and Wolf, *Allgemeiner Teil des Bürgerlichen Rechts*, § 48, no. 26.

[72] Bork, *Allgemeiner Teil des BGB*, no. 1565; Schramm, *Münchener Kommentar zum BGB*, § 167, no. 56. Cf. Leipold, *BGB I: Einführung und allgemeiner Teil*, no. 735 (*Gewohnheitsrecht* – customary law).

[73] BGHZ 30, 391, 398 *et seq.*; BGHZ 65, 13, 15; Flume § 49, 4; Schilken, *Staudinger*, § 167, no. 31.

private law the protection of the performance interest – be it by way of damages or by specific performance – needs to be legitimated by a statutory provision or by the legal acts of the parties. Neither of these two prerequisites is fulfilled; there is no rule in the Civil Code dealing with the questions of *Anscheinsvollmacht*, nor is there any possibility to draw an analogy from the several statutory provisions which were dealt with previously. In the view of both the Civil and the Commercial Code, constructive authority, with the consequence of a protection of the performance interest, is only given where it follows from the behaviour of the principal or where that behaviour is replaced by the rules of a registered authority.

2 Apparent authority and the principle of culpa in contrahendo

The rules of apparent authority form a part of a more general concept of pre-contractual liability which is regulated in § 311(2) BGB, the concept of *culpa in contrahendo*.[74] Under this concept the parties by commencement of contract negotiations or by similar business contacts establish a pre- and extra-contractual relationship with duties for both parties. These duties mainly oblige each party to take account of the rights, legally protected interests and other interests of the other party. This concept, *inter alia*, includes the protection of reasonable reliance of one party caused by the conduct of the other. The concept of *culpa in contrahendo* was originally developed by case-law. It was codified in the said provision by the Law of Obligations Modernisation Act 2002 (*Schuldrechtsmodernisierungsgesetz*). The breach of a duty flowing from the pre-contractual relationship now results in a fault liability for damages under § 280.[75]

The consequences of this codification of the general principles of *culpa in contrahendo* for the rules on apparent authority are not quite clear at present. The major textbooks do not argue this point and there is no other reliable authority. The correct view is that the classical order of prerequisites of *Anscheinsvollmacht* ought to be revised.

---

[74] Cf. Schramm, *Münchener Kommentar zum BGB*, § 177, no. 50 *et seq.*

[75] Paragraph (1) of this provision may be translated as: 'If the obligor breaches a duty under the obligation, the obligee may demand compensation for damage caused thereby. This does not apply if the obligor is not responsible for the breach of duty.' (Translations by juris GmbH.)

The first prerequisite is the establishment of a pre-contractual relationship between the principal and the third party. The major issue with regard to this requirement is establishing how and under which circumstances one can attribute the agent's behaviour to the principal in such a way that the pre-contractual relationship is not only established between the third party and the agent (on which see VI, below), but also between the principal and the third party. Several writers have suggested importing the rules of vicarious liability from contract and tort law[76] and applying them to this situation. However, applying these provisions poses a dogmatical difficulty: these provisions are intended to deal with the consequences of the fault principle in cases where it is not the principal himself who acts without due care but his servants or agents. However, in the situation of apparent authority, the provisions would not be applied to the standard of liability as they were originally meant to be applied, but to the creation of a duty subsequently breached by the principal.[77] Nevertheless, at least §§ 31 and 278 are not restricted to the original idea of steering the standard of principal's liability and often take part in the establishment of duties of a principal.[78]

By applying these provisions to the present situation the relationship between the principal and the agent becomes a decisive factor. Where there is a continuing, contractually organised, relationship between them, this relationship in itself provides a reason for attributing the behaviour of the agent to the principal since the principal is seen as employing the agent so as to fulfil the principal's duties. In the rare cases where there was originally no such relationship the situation under

---

[76] §§ 31, 278, 831 BGB. The main parts of these articles may be translated as: 'The association is liable for the damage to a third party that the board, a member of the board or another constitutionally appointed representative causes through an act committed by it or him in carrying out his duties, where the act gives rise to a liability in damages.' (§ 31 BGB); 'The obligor is liable for the fault of his legal representative, and of persons whom he employs to perform his obligation, to the same extent as for his own fault.' (§ 278, first sentence BGB); and 'Anyone using another person to perform a task is liable for the damage that the other has inflicted contrary to law on a third party when carrying out assistance. Liability in damages does not apply if the principal, when selecting the party deployed and, provided he was to procure supplies or equipment or to manage the business activity, observes the diligence required in business in procurement or management or if the damage would still have occurred with the application of such diligence.' (§ 831(1) BGB). (Translations by juris GmbH.)

[77] Schilken, *Staudinger*, §164, no. 41.

[78] See, e.g., BGB § 434(2) first sentence; see further, M. Schmidt-Kessel, in H. Prütting, G. Weinreich and G. Wegen, *BGB: Kommentar*, 2nd edn (Neuwied: Luchterhand-Verlag, 2007), § 278, no. 4.

§ 311(2) BGB, i.e. the pre-contractual relationship between the principal and the third party, would not normally come into existence by actions of the agent. It is possible, however, subsequently to establish such a relationship should the principal tolerate the behaviour of the agent. This subsequent tolerance would lead to a constructive authority of the agent, not only the liability for the reliance interest.

The pre-contractual relationship includes the duty not to be represented by agents without authority.[79] In other words, the principal is obliged to ensure congruence between the apparent and actual status of his agent's authority. Breaching that duty renders the principal liable for damage which the third party has sustained by relying on the apparent authority. The exception that the principal acted without fault under § 280(1) second sentence, will remain without effect in the present case, due to his lack of care, or the lack of care of the agent, which merely establish the pre-contractual relationship. In these cases there is always present a lack of care establishing the relationship which excludes the no-fault defence right from the outset.

The codification of the principle of *culpa in contrahendo* therefore leads to a reformulation of the rules on apparent authority. The former prerequisite of causation of the third party's reliance by the acts of the principal is now to be replaced by the general standards of attribution of liability for servants and agents.

V Ratification by the principal

1 General principles of ratification

Once an unauthorised agent concludes a contract with a third party, such a contract will be controlled by the German legal principle of *schwebende Unwirksamkeit*.[80] This principle seeks to explain the existing relationship between the parties. It stipulates that the contract is neither void nor enforceable, rather it is 'floating' and awaiting either ratification or refusal by the principal or revocation by the third party. This kind of relationship consequently gives options to both the principal and the third party. The choices open to the principal are either to ratify the contract or decline to do so, and the choices open to the third party

---

[79] § 311(2) BGB.
[80] See Larenz and Wolf, *Allgemeiner Teil des Bürgerlichen Rechts*, § 49, no. 4 *et seq.*; Schramm, *Münchener Kommentar zum BGB*, § 177, no. 15 *et seq.*

are either to withdraw,[81] or to commence the clarification process with the principal.[82] The role of the agent during this period is a passive one; he must merely await notification by either the principal or the third party of their respective decisions.

2 Declaration of ratification

The declaration of ratification should be made by the principal, and is commonly made to the third party. The principal may be represented by an agent (or by the agent who concluded the contract in the first place without authority). The declaration made by an agent on behalf of a principal is valid only if it is authorised. Ratification may also be declared by an heir or any legal successor (e.g. a company succeeding under the company/merger laws or in cases of assignment where the 'floating' state of the contract is also assigned).

The principal (or the authorised agent making the declaration in the name of the principal) has a choice to decide to whom to declare the ratification. Commonly, he will make the declaration to the third party. However, as follows from *argumentum e contrario*[83] ratification may be declared to the agent as well. Such a declaration is weaker than the declaration to the third party because it may be nullified under § 177(2) BGB if the third party begins the process to clarify the situation as laid out in this provision.[84] In the course of that procedure, ratification may only be declared to the third party.

(a) Form of the declaration of ratification

There is no prescribed requirement for the form of a declaration of ratification.[85] This rule also applies in cases where the declaration of

---

[81] § 178 BGB. The article may be translated as: 'Until ratification of the contract, the other party is entitled to revoke it, unless he knew of the lack of authority on conclusion of the contract. The revocation may also be declared to the agent.' (Translation by juris GmbH.)

[82] § 177 BGB. The translation of this article offered by juris GmbH reads as follows: '(1) If a person enters into a contract in the name of another without authority, the validity of the contract to the benefit or detriment of the principal depends on his ratification.

(2) If the other party demands that the principal declares whether or not he ratifies the contract, the declaration may only be made to such person; a ratification or a refusal to ratify declared to the agent before the demand is without effect. The ratification may only be declared before the expiry of two weeks after receipt of the demand; if it is not declared, it is deemed to have been refused.'

[83] Based on § 177(2), first sentence BGB.

[84] Schramm, *Münchener Kommentar zum BGB*, § 177, no. 21.   [85] § 182(2) BGB.

authority would have had to meet a specific requirement of prescribed form.[86] The ratification does not need to be explicit. The minimum requirement is that the principal is in agreement with the contract, and an implication from the behaviour and/or words of the principal to that effect is sufficient. An implicit ratification thus presupposes that the principal has sufficient knowledge of the lack of authority as well as his intention to give effect to the contract.[87] The courts have made an exception to this rule in the general category of cases dealing with mayors of local districts who act without authority. In such cases the local government laws and regulations will deal with the requirements of prescribed form for ratification declarations.[88]

There are certain cases dealing with commercial contracts in which the courts have held that mere passivity could provide a basis for an implication of ratification where parties to business transactions would ordinarily expect an explicit objection. In a case which was decided by the *Reichsgericht* in 1921,[89] the claimant asked for damages for non-performance of a contract of sale of goods. The respondent argued that no contract had been concluded because his agent acted without authority. The claimant, after the telephone conversation with the agent, had sent a letter, *inter alia*, noticing the content of the contract which remained unanswered by the respondent. The court held that, in the field of commerce, silence may suffice to establish ratification under § 177 BGB. The claimant, however, lost because he had, in the afore-mentioned letter, asked for an explicit confirmation by the respondent.

(b) The effects of the declaration of ratification

Once ratified, the contract comes into force retrospectively[90] as if the agent had acted with authority in the first place. Therefore, other questions related to the validity of the contract, for example mistake, are not solved by the ratification and may still lead to voidness or avoidance.[91] Where, on the other hand, the ratification is refused, the contract is held to be void from the outset.[92]

---

[86] BGH NJW 1994, 1344, 1345 *et seq.* (citing earlier authorities).
[87] BGH NJW 2002, 2325, 2327.
[88] See Schramm, *Münchener Kommentar zum BGB*, § 177, no. 40.
[89] RGZ 103, 95, 98.   [90] § 184(1) BGB.
[91] Schramm, *Münchener Kommentar zum BGB*, § 177, no. 44.
[92] Larenz and Wolf, *Allgemeiner Teil des Bürgerlichen Rechts*, § 49, no. 9; Schramm, *Münchener Kommentar zum BGB*, § 177, nos. 22 and 48.

3 Options for the third party

During the interim period while awaiting the principal's decision as to the ratification the third party has two avenues open to it.

The first avenue is contained in § 178 BGB and allows the third party to withdraw his consent at any time prior to the ratification. The third party has the free choice to declare his withdrawal to either the principal or to the agent (§ 178, second sentence). Such a declaration of revocation renders the contract void. However, if the third party knew of the lack of authority this avenue will be closed to them,[93] leaving only open the possibility to commence the clarification procedure pursuant to § 177(2) BGB.

The procedure pursuant to § 177(2) BGB is the second avenue open to a party without knowledge of the lack of authority. The clarification procedure may be commenced by demanding that the principal declare whether or not he ratifies the contract. The effect of such a demand will be that the principal will only be allowed to make the declaration of ratification to that third party. The demand will have a further retroactive effect in that it will nullify any previous declarations made by the principal to the agent. From the time of the third party's demand, the principal shall only have two weeks within which to ratify the contract. Should the principal fail to ratify the contract before the expiration of the two weeks, he shall be seen as having refused to do so: § 177(2), second sentence. A later declaration of ratification remains without effect.[94]

4 Special rules applying to unilateral transactions

The general rule contained in the first sentence of § 180 BGB provides that unilateral legal transactions by an unauthorised agent are void. It follows that, in these cases, ratification is not an available option for the principal. While the first sentence of § 180 BGB applies mainly in the rare cases where no receipt of the agent's declaration to the third party would have been necessary, the second sentence of § 180 BGB from a functional point of view is the more common rule.[95] It provides two broad categories of exceptions to the general rule in the first sentence.

---

[93] Schramm, *Münchener Kommentar zum BGB*, § 178, no. 3.

[94] Larenz and Wolf, *Allgemeiner Teil des Bürgerlichen Rechts*, § 49, no. 13.

[95] The provision may be translated as: 'Agency without authority is not permitted for a unilateral legal transaction. However, if the person with whom such a legal transaction was to be entered into did not object to the authority claimed by the agent on entering

These exceptions are the cases of agreement by the third party and of silence by the third party.

The first category covers the cases where the third party agrees to the fact that the declaration which constitutes the unilateral transaction is made without authority. The second category covers those cases where the agent, either explicitly or implicitly claims to have authority, and the third party does not object or query that authority. This provision is in line with § 174 BGB, giving the third party the right to reject a unilateral transaction of the agent where no document proving the authority is attached to the declaration.[96] The second case under the second sentence of § 180 therefore comes close to the case of agreement, since the third party is seen to have waived his protection under § 174. In the case both of agreement and of silence the first consequence is the possibility of ratification by the principal under § 177 BGB.

VI Liability of the *falsus procurator*

Section 179 BGB establishes a liability without fault of the agent who is lacking authority.[97] This liability is based on the guarantee by the agent stating the existence of his authority to act. The agent therefore bears the risk of acquiring a valid authority as well as proving its existence.[98]

---

into the legal transaction or if he agreed that the agent may act without authority, the provisions on contracts apply with the necessary modifications. The same applies if a unilateral legal transaction is entered into with an unauthorised agent with his consent.' (Translation by juris GmbH.)

[96] See Larenz and Wolf, *Allgemeiner Teil des Bürgerlichen Rechts*, § 49, nos. 15 and 16. § 174 BGB may be translated as: 'A unilateral legal transaction which an authorised representative enters into with another is ineffective if the authorised representative does not produce a power of attorney and the other rejects the legal transaction for this reason without undue delay. Rejection is barred if the principal notified the other of the authorisation.' (Translation by juris GmbH.)

[97] The article may be translated as: '(1) A person who has entered into a contract as an agent is, if he has not furnished proof of his authority, bound to the other party at his choice either to perform the contract or to pay damages to him, if the principal refuses to ratify the contract.

(2) If the agent was not aware of his lack of authority, he is bound to make compensation only for the damage which the other party has suffered by his relying on the authority; not, however, beyond the value of the interest which the other party has in the validity of the contract.

(3) The agent is not liable, if the other party knew or ought to have known of the lack of authority. The agent is also not liable if he had limited capacity to contract, unless he acted with the consent of his legal representative.' (Translation by juris GmbH.)

[98] Schramm, *Münchener Kommentar zum BGB*, § 179, no. 20.

1 Prerequisites for liability

For an agent to be liable, there need to exist the following prerequisites: (a) lack of authority (including apparent and/or constructive authority); (b) existence of a contract which but for the lack of authority would have been enforceable and carried out; and (c) absence of ratification by the principal. In the case where there exists a contract, which but for the lack of authority would have been enforceable and carried out, and the third party decides to revoke the contract pursuant to § 178 BGB,[99] the agent will not be liable under § 179 BGB.[100]

An open question exists with regard to § 311(2) BGB as to whether the third party can still obtain the reliance interest measure in damages under the aforementioned principle of *culpa in contrahendo* even if he revokes the contract under §178 BGB.[101] On the one hand, there is – at least after codification of the principle of *culpa in contrahendo* – an argument that there is a general pre-contractual duty of the principal not to frustrate a third party's reliance which is to be attributed to the principal. On the other hand, it could be argued that the rules in § 179 BGB are conclusive for the liability of the *falsus procurator* and that § 311(2) is overturned by the *lex specialis* on agency. It would then follow that the option under § 178 BGB includes no damages claim for the third party.

There are differing views as to the existence of liability in cases of insolvent principals, the predominant one being that under § 179(1) BGB no liability arises. The reasoning for such a view is that there is no reason to protect the third party more than he would otherwise be protected under a valid contract.[102]

2 Consequences of the liability

(a) Specific performance

The third party has a right to choose between damages or specific performance of the contract as against the agent. Specific performance does not mean there was a valid contract between the agent and the third party. The agent does not become a party to the contract but only

[99] For a translation of §178 see n. 21, above.
[100] Schramm, *Münchener Kommentar zum BGB*, §179, no. 21.
[101] Cf. Larenz and Wolf, *Allgemeiner Teil des Bürgerlichen Rechts*, § 49, no. 25. For the principle of *culpa in contrahendo*, see IV 2, above.
[102] OLG Hamm MDR 1993, 515; Flume, § 47(3)(b); Schilken, *Staudinger*, § 179, no. 15.

to a relationship established by law,[103] which carries with it certain consequences.

Unless the third party chooses specific performance, the agent has no right to perform the contract.[104] The agent is not bound by an arbitration clause.[105] However, if the other party chooses the performance of the contract, then the agent has all the same rights as if the contract were concluded between the agent and the third party. For example, the agent may claim that his duty to deliver the goods is a concurrent condition of payment of the price under § 320 BGB.[106] The agent being in the position of the buyer has all the remedies which apply in the case of defective goods, i.e. all the remedies mentioned in § 437 BGB at least.

In the case of non-performance by the agent, the general rules of liability for non-performance will apply.[107] Damages will then depend on the general fault principle.[108] Then there is no liability by a way of guarantee.[109]

(b) Damages

The alternative for the third party is to choose damages. The damages include the whole performance interest. He is restricted to monetary compensation. The other party cannot claim compensation *in natura* under § 249 BGB.[110] By choosing the claim for damages, the third party loses his right to specific performance.

3 Restriction of liability under § 179(2) BGB

The liability of an agent who is unaware of the fact that he lacks authority is restricted by § 179(2) BGB, which provides that in such situations the agent only need compensate the reliance interest, i.e. 'the damage which the other party has sustained relying upon the authority'.[111] The amount of damages is also limited to the amount of the possible performance interest, i.e. 'beyond the value of the interest which the other party has in

[103] Larenz and Wolf, *Allgemeiner Teil des Bürgerlichen Rechts*, § 49, no. 19; Schramm, *Münchener Kommentar zum BGB*, § 179, no. 32.
[104] BAG NJW 2003, 2054.   [105] BGHZ, 68, 356, 360–362.
[106] Larenz and Wolf, *Allgemeiner Teil des Bürgerlichen Rechts*, § 49, no. 20.
[107] §§ 280–292 and §§ 323–326 BGB.
[108] Contained in the second sentence of § 280(1) and in § 276 BGB.
[109] Under § 179(1) BGB.
[110] Larenz and Wolf, *Allgemeiner Teil des Bürgerlichen Rechts*, § 49, no. 21.
[111] § 179(2) BGB.

the validity of the contract'.[112] The burden of proof is on the agent to show that at the time he acted he had no knowledge of the lack authority by the principal.

There are two exceptions to the restriction of liability by § 179(2) contained in Art. 8 *Wechselgesetz* (Bills of Exchange Act) and Art. 11 *Scheckgesetz* (Cheques Act). These provisions were introduced in compliance with the respective Geneva Conventions seeking to unify this area of law. Under these provisions the agent, whether unaware of the lack of authority or not, is liable for the obligations under a bill of exchange or a cheque.

4 Exclusions of liability

Two main exclusions of liability exist in German law of agency. The first applies where the third party knew, or should have known, of the lack of authority.[113] The second applies to persons without legal capacity or with restricted legal capacity that have acted as agents. Persons without legal capacity cannot act as agents (e.g. a minor under seven years of age). Since the rules of the law of agency do not apply to persons without legal capacity, he cannot be liable. In principle, liability in tort is also excluded;[114] however, § 829 BGB gives judges the discretion to award compensation for equitable reasons. Persons with restricted legal capacity can act as agents. Such a person will be liable where he acted with the consent of his legal representatives. He will not be liable if he comes within the exception contained in the second sentence of § 179(3) BGB.

5 Liability in unilateral transactions

A point of distinction ought to be made between the cases that fall within the first sentence of § 180 BGB (cases of void contracts) and those that fall within the second sentence of § 180 and § 179 BGB (cases of liability).

In the cases falling within the first sentence of § 180 BGB, there is no liability under the specific rules of agency law.[115] However, there may exist a pre-contractual liability under § 280 and § 311(2) BGB, which represent the concept of *culpa in contrahendo*, or a liability in tort.[116] As the agent is not meant to become a party to the contract, liability

---

[112] § 179(2) BGB. [113] First sentence of § 179(3) BGB.
[114] §§ 827–828 BGB. [115] Schilken, *Staudinger*, § 180, no. 3.
[116] Larenz and Wolf, *Allgemeiner Teil des Bürgerlichen Rechts*, § 49, no. 17.

normally cannot arise under § 311(2) BGB but only under the more restrictive prerequisites of § 311(3) BGB – the pre-contractual liability of third parties.[117] The liability under § 311(3) presupposes a special type of reliance of the third party on the agent. It requires that all elements which constitute reliance and trust be satisfied, and thus applies only in rare cases.[118] The third party may also be liable in tort law. However, under the German law of tort pure economic loss normally cannot be recovered, therefore such liability would arise mainly in the cases of intentional torts such as fraud.

In the cases falling within the second sentence of § 180, § 179 applies. The agent may basically be liable under the rules of agency law. In the cases where the third party agrees to an agent acting without authority (case of agreement), this opens the way to § 177 and the subsequent articles, and therefore the applicability of § 179, but it merely becomes an academic question: § 179 is concurrently excluded since the third party knew of the lack of authority of the agent (§ 179(3), first sentence). In the case of silence, where the third party does not inquire as to the authority of the agent, § 179 applies. Because of the specific legal nature of most unilateral transactions specific performance will, however, not be available in most cases,[119] but, for example, in the case of an *Auslobung* (public offer of a reward) under § 657 BGB and the subsequent articles, the promised reward may be claimed from the agent *in natura*.

VII Agent's liability in the case of constructive or apparent authority

The questions of the co-existence of the agent's liability and other consequences of the acts by an agent without authority are not greatly discussed in German law.[120] The lack of discussion is mainly due to the predetermined conditions of liability contained in § 179 BGB. This provision presupposes that the agent acted without any authority and that his declarations were not ratified by the principal.[121] As in the

---

[117] Leipold, *BGB I: Einführung und allgemeiner Teil*, no. 749; Schramm, *Münchener Kommentar zum BGB*, § 164, no. 11. Please note that in the wording of § 311(3), the 'third party' would refer to the agent and not to the third party contracting with the principal in terms of agency law.
[118] Leipold, *BGB I: Einführung und allgemeiner Teil*, no. 749.
[119] More restrictive: Schilken, *Staudinger*, § 180, no. 6: no specific performance at all.
[120] But see Larenz and Wolf, *Allgemeiner Teil des Bürgerlichen Rechts*, § 48, no. 33.
[121] Schilken, *Staudinger*, § 179, no. 8.

cases of constructive authority, the agent acted under the authority in a legal sense and his liability under § 179 is therefore excluded.[122] Only the constructive authority under § 15(1) and (3) HGB gives the third party an option not to rely on it but to invoke the liability of the agent under § 179;[123] but that difference follows from the peculiarity of a constructive authority deriving from a faulty register. Where the declaration is subsequently ratified, liability under § 179 is likewise excluded. However, cases do arise where the need for the ratification delays the performance of the contract. The liability is then covered by the general rules of pre-contractual liability (§§ 280 and 311(2) BGB).[124]

In the cases of apparent authority the nature of that *Anscheinsvollmacht* is the determining factor. The prevailing view considers it a case of constructive authority and therefore § 179 cannot apply. However, as the cases of *Anscheinsvollmacht* are to be seen as cases of pre-contractual liability of the principal in which – even though constructive authority takes place – § 179 does apply, creating a claim against the agent. So long as his liabilities overlap the principal and the agent are liable as joint debtors, which normally means that the principal has a recourse against the agent under § 426 BGB or, as the case may be, under a contract between them.

VIII Special cases of defective authority

In addition to the common cases of agents acting without authority there exist in the field of law of representation special cases to which not all of the aforementioned rules apply, or to which unique rules apply. The first group of special cases is that of a principal who does not exist since he is not named by the agent (1), or because they are a company yet to be incorporated (2). The second group deals with particular kinds of lack of authority, mainly the conflict of interest (3). In the third group, minors, as a peculiar kind of agent, are of the specific interest (4).

1 Principal to be named

In German law, for a valid representation by an agent, it is not required that the agent name the principal at the time of the conclusion of the

---

[122] BGHZ 61, 59, 69; Schramm, *Münchener Kommentar zum BGB*, § 167, no. 75 and § 179, no. 29.
[123] See Larenz and Wolf, *Allgemeiner Teil des Bürgerlichen Rechts*, § 48, no. 33.
[124] OLG Hamm NJW 1994, 666.

contract.[125] If the agent does not name the principal after the conclusion of the contract, the rules which involve the acts of a principal will not apply. First, there would be no possibility of ratifying the contract. Secondly, no basis for establishing a constructive or an apparent authority would exist. The only remaining question would therefore be whether the agent is liable under § 179,[126] and, as far as unilateral legal transactions are concerned, under § 180 BGB.[127] There remain two problems with the application of § 179 to such cases. The first is the requirement that the principal deny the ratification. The second is the exclusion of liability due to the knowledge of the third party under §179(3), first sentence. The best way of dealing with the first issue is to apply § 179 by way of analogy. In the case of § 179(3) application by way of analogy is the only viable option. Nonetheless, the need for this argument sheds light on the imprecision of § 179 for this purpose. Eventually, the issue is not one of an agent acting without authority but of the more general concept of a pre-contractual liability where a person promises a valid contract with a third party and hence faces liability for his performance interest, be it in damages, or be it as a claim for specific performance. The case of the unnamed principal should therefore be dealt with under the special rule of *culpa in contrahendo* of a third party under § 311(3) BGB explained in VI 5, above.[128]

2 Company not yet incorporated and other non-existing principals

In the case of companies not yet incorporated and other non-existing principals, the rules on agents without authority apply by way of analogy, subject to exceptions. If a principal comes into existence after the agent has acted on his behalf, he may – at least in theory – ratify the agent's acts under § 177 BGB. The same holds true for § 179 BGB, which will apply even in the case where the principal never comes into existence. Nevertheless, this type of principal will not be liable under the rules of constructive or apparent authority. This is true not only for the cases where the principal never comes into existence, but equally so in the case where he does, since at the time of the agent's acts there would exist no reason for reliance by a third party, or for the attribution of the wrongful behaviour to the principal.

---

[125] Schilken, *Staudinger*, Preface to §§ 164 *et seq.*, no. 35.
[126] See, for the prevailing opinion, Schramm, *Münchener Kommentar zum BGB*, § 179, no. 15.
[127] BGH NJW 1995, 1739, 1742 *et seq.*   [128] Cf. BGHZ 129, 136, 149 *et seq.*

(a) Ratification by a company incorporated later on

Section 177 BGB applies by way of analogy to the case of companies not yet incorporated as opposed to those which never come into or are no longer in existence.[129] However, from a practical point of view the most common case of a non-existent principal is dealt with under the special rules of company law. Article 7 of the first EC directive for the harmonisation of company law[130] deals with the idea of the company 'assuming the obligations' arising from the agent's actions. The German transposition of that provision differs according to the type of the company.

The *GmbH-Gesetz* (Limited Companies Act) does not deal with the question of the GmbH assuming the respective obligations. There is therefore a clear gap in the transposition of the directive. This gap is filled by a judge-made rule which provides that the company coming into existence automatically becomes the debtor.[131] It follows from that automatic assumption that there is no need for ratification under § 177(1) BGB. Therefore, there is no room for the application of §§ 177(2) and 178 BGB.

For the *Aktiengesellschaft* (public limited company), and for the *Kommanditgesellschaft auf Aktien* (partnership limited by shares), § 41(2) *Aktiengesetz* (Public Limited Companies Act) understands 'assuming' in the technical sense of § 414 BGB and the following articles.[132] The provision lays down an exception to the general rule that the creditor has at least to ratify the assumption of the debt.[133] The debt to be assumed is the liability of the agent, and the assumption takes place by an agreement between the agent and the company which has come into existence. Besides this statutory rule, the courts have adopted the aforementioned judge-made rule of the law of the GmbH for the *Aktiengesellschaft*.[134] Section 41(2) of the *Aktiengesetz* is therefore only of limited practical relevance. It follows from these two rules that no unilateral ratification in the sense of § 177(1) BGB takes place and the

---

[129] Schramm, *Münchener Kommentar zum BGB*, § 177, no. 7.

[130] The First Council Directive 68/151/EEC of 9 March 1968 on coordination of safeguards which, for the protection of the interests of members and others, are required by member states of companies within the meaning of the second paragraph of Art. 58 of the Treaty, with a view to making such safeguards equivalent throughout the Community, *OJ* No. L65, 14 March 1968, pp. 8–12.

[131] BGHZ 80, 129, 143; BGHZ 80, 182 *et seq.* As to some exceptions see M. Lutter, P. Hommelhoff and W. Bayer, *GmbH Gesetz: Kommentar*, 16th edn (Köln: Otto Schmidt-Verlag, 2004) § 11, no. 26.

[132] A. Pentz, in W. Bayer (ed.), *Münchener Kommentar zum Aktiengesetz*, Vol. 1, 2nd edn (München: Beck-Verlag/Verlag Franz Vahlen, 2000), § 41, no. 154.

[133] § 415 BGB.   [134] Pentz, *Münchener Kommentar AktG*, § 41, nos. 154, 105 *et seq.*

third party does not have the option of invoking the procedure of § 177(2) BGB. Section 178 is regularly excluded due to the knowledge of the third party. The third party's right to withdraw from the contract is further excluded by the special rule of § 41(2) *Aktiengesetz*.

There are only a few further cases in which § 177 may apply to a not yet existing principal. The first case is that of an agent acting for a company (in the sense of Art. 7 of the first EC directive). This scenario involves the process for establishing a company which has not yet begun; for example, the contract between the shareholders has not been concluded. In this case Art. 7 of the first EC company law directive does not apply, nor do § 41(2) *Aktiengesetz* and § 11(2) *GmbH-Gesetz*. Section 177 BGB may also be applicable to those companies to which the EC directive does not apply, for example the private partnership, the *Offene Handelsgesellschaft* (general partnership), or *Kommanditgesellschaft* (limited partnership).[135]

(b) Liability of the agent

Section 179 BGB has a broader scope of application in this field than § 177, since it applies (by way of analogy) even to those cases in which the principal never comes into existence.[136] Applying § 179 by way of analogy to the present case scenario avoids the need for regular requirement of the denial of ratification. However, the consequences of § 179 remain unchanged; the third party may opt for specific performance, or claim damages for the performance interest. In the cases of § 179 (2), the bona fide agent without authority, the third party is restricted to damages for the reliance interest.

Like the rules of ratification, German law provides for some special rules on the liability of the agent. First, in the line of Art. 7 of the first EC company directive, there are separate provisions for the liability of an agent acting for a company yet to be incorporated. For these cases § 41(1) *Aktiengesetz*, second sentence, and § 11(2) *GmbH-Gesetz* establish a liability of all persons acting in the name of the future company. In practice, this liability only takes place where the incorporation of the company fails later on. Where the company comes into existence, it

---

[135] BGHZ 63, 45 (GmbH & Co KG); Schramm, *Münchener Kommentar zum BGB*, §177, no. 7.

[136] BGH NJW 1954, 145 (deceased principal); BGHZ 105, 283, 285 (*Bauherrengemeinschaft –* house builders partnership); AG Hamburg NJW-RR 1996, 1060 (limited company deleted from the register).

assumes the obligations created by the acts of the agent, and thereby relieves the agent of his liability.[137] The same is true in the case of § 54 BGB, second sentence, for the agent of an association which lacks legal personality at the time.[138]

Other special rules are to be found in Arts. 7 and 8 of the *Wechselgesetz* (Bills of Exchange Act) and Arts. 10 and 11 of the *Scheckgesetz* (Cheques Act). These provisions are all transpositions of the uniform acts which have been established by the Geneva Conventions of 1930. Article 7 *Wechselgesetz* and Art. 10 *Scheckgesetz* lay down that persons who sign the respective instruments with a signature of a fictitious person are liable as if he signed for himself. Article 8 *Wechselgesetz* and Art. 11 *Scheckgesetz* add to that an exception to § 179(2) holding the person who signed liable even in the case where he had no knowledge that he had no authority.[139]

3 Agent in a conflict of interest

Where the agent lacks authority due to a conflict of interest under § 181 BGB,[140] the general rules apply. The principal may ratify under § 177 BGB and if he does not the agent will be liable under § 179 BGB.[141] The rules of the conflict of interest are self-evident in that normally no constructive or apparent authority may be established.

Cases of constructive authority may well appear where the principal has provided the agent with authority to conclude contracts in the cases dealt with under the scope of § 181 BGB. Such an exception must be registered under the rules of the first company law directive.[142] Section 15 HGB, therefore, also applies to these cases. Where an authority of the agent to act in cases of § 181 BGB is registered and published, but does not exist, a third party – but not the agent themselves – may be protected by a constructive authority under the aforementioned rules of § 15(1) and (3) HGB.

---

[137] § 41(2) *Aktiengesetz*, read together with § 414 *et seq.* BGB; and the authorities cited in section b, above.

[138] OLG Düsseldorf MDR 1984, 489.   [139] Cf. BGHZ 61, 59.

[140] The article may be translated as: 'An agent may not without permission enter into a legal transaction in the name of the principal with himself in his own name or as an agent of a third party, unless the legal transaction solely consists in the fulfilment of an obligation.' (Translation by juris GmbH.)

[141] Schramm, *Münchener Kommentar zum BGB*, § 181, no. 41.

[142] Case 32/74, *Friedrich Haaga GmbH* [1974] ECR 1201.

4 Minors as agents

In German law, minors who have reached the age of seven may act as agents.[143] This provision includes minors acting as agents without authority.[144] Therefore, all the rules pertaining to agents without authority, and discussed above, apply. The only exception relates to the liability of the minors. The liability is excluded by § 179(3) BGB, second sentence, unless the minor had acted with the consent of his legal representative. In the latter case the minor is liable as if he were fully competent.

IX Concluding remarks

Looking at the German law of unauthorised agency as it stands today, one can see a remarkable borderline between the rules of ratification and liability of the agent on the one hand and the different and less coherent rules and principles dealing with the realm of constructive and apparent authority.

The civil code itself contains in §§ 177–180 BGB a set of coherent rules on ratification and the agent's liability. In the cases covered by the wording of these provisions there is basically no need for an amendment on the basis of general concepts of the law of obligations. In practice, however, §§ 177–180 have a much wider scope of application, because courts and legal writers are used to applying them by way of analogy.

Neither the German Civil Code nor the Commercial Code contains such a set of coherent rules for cases of constructive and apparent authority. Besides some jigsaw pieces in both codes, courts and legal writers developed the concepts of *Duldungsvollmacht* and *Anscheinsvollmacht*, both of them in a way connected to the more general concepts, on the one hand, of reliance protection under the general liability for *culpa in contrahendo* and, on the other hand, interpretation of parties' declarations and behaviour. But of all these rules, concepts and principles only the *Anscheinsvollmacht* can be explained in terms of reliance protection. After the *Schuldrechtsmodernisierungsgesetz* 2002 the whole topic should be dealt with therefore under the auspices of § 280 and § 311(2) and (3) BGB codifying the concept of *culpa in contrahendo*.

No sustainable general concept was developed, however, for the cases of constructive authority of the agent. *Duldungsvollmacht* only covers cases of the principal who is too tolerant against the agent. The ideas of

---

[143] § 165 BGB.   [144] Schilken, *Staudinger*, § 165, no. 4.

Vertrauenshaftung or *Rechtsscheinhaftung* cannot explain the protection of the performance interest of the third party. However, most of the aforementioned provisions as well as the concept of *Duldungsvollmacht* may be explained well by the interpretation of the behaviour and the declarations of the principal. The two ways in which a constructive authority can be derived from a faulty company register under § 15 HGB may basically be analysed in the same way; from the perspective of the third party. There is, however, a need for the further argument that in these cases there is not a real hypothetical understanding of that third party but a legal fiction of the respective hypothetical understanding of a reasonable person.

Unauthorised agency in Dutch law

DANNY BUSCH

Table of contents

I Introduction

Under Dutch law, unauthorised agency arises when a person (the 'agent') concludes a contract with a third party in the name of someone else (the 'principal') without (sufficient) authority.[1] The general effect is that neither the principal nor the third party is bound or entitled under a contract so concluded. This rule is not applied in cases where the third party successfully invokes the doctrine of apparent authority or where the principal subsequently ratifies the unauthorised act. Furthermore, in the case of unauthorised agency the third party may hold the unauthorised agent (the *falsus procurator*) liable for the damage which he has suffered as a consequence of the agent's lack of authority.

In this chapter, in part II, I first examine the distinction between direct and indirect agency. In part III, I devote some attention to the nature and general effect of unauthorised agency. I then turn to the main exceptions to the general effect of unauthorised agency: apparent authority (part IV) and ratification (part V). Part VI follows with some comments on the liability of the *falsus procurator* and part VII with a treatment of the interrelationship between apparent authority, ratification and the liability of the *falsus procurator*. Parts VIII and IX each elaborate on a special case which can be associated with unauthorised agency, namely acting in the name of a principal yet to be named and acting in the name of a company yet to be incorporated. Part X ends this chapter with some concluding observations.

---

[1] It should be noted that agency is also possible with respect to legal acts other than the conclusion of contracts. However, in the remainder of this chapter, for the sake of convenience, I will generally focus on the example of a contract. It should also be noted that in this chapter English translations of provisions of the Dutch Civil Code (*Burgerlijk Wetboek*, often referred to below as 'DCC') are largely, but not entirely, based on the translation provided by P. P. C. Haanappel and E. Mackaay, *New Netherlands Civil Code: Patrimonial Law (Property, Obligations and Special Contracts)* (The Hague/London/New York: Kluwer Law International, 1990); and the revised CD-ROM edition thereof (published by Kluwer Law International in 1999). It should finally be mentioned that Books 3, Patrimonial law in general (*Vermogensrecht in het algemeen*), 5, Real rights (*Zakelijke rechten*), 6, General part of the law of obligations (*Algemeen gedeelte van het verbinte-nissenrecht*) and parts of Book 7, Special contracts (*Bijzondere contracten*) of the Dutch Civil Code entered into force on 1 January 1992. The work on the new Dutch Civil Code started as early as 1947, the year in which Eduard Maurits Meijers, Professor of Private Law in Leiden, was appointed to draft a new Civil Code. See, on the re-codification process, E. O. H. P. Florijn, *Ontstaan en ontwikkeling van het nieuwe Burgerlijk Wetboek* (Maastricht: Universitaire Pers Maastricht, 1994) (with a summary in English).

II Direct and indirect agency

In common with most other civil law jurisdictions, Dutch law applies a distinction between direct and indirect agency.

Direct agency exists if two requirements are fulfilled. (1) It is necessary that the agent should have (sufficient) authority to bind the principal directly at the time of the conclusion of the contract with the third party. This may be a consequence of an authority granted by the principal to his agent (consensual agency, *volmacht*), but it may also result from statute or from a court ruling. (2) At the time of the conclusion of the contract with the third party, it is necessary that the agent acts 'in the name of' the principal: the agent should act as direct agent at the time of the conclusion of the contract in a manner reasonably apparent to the third party.

The legal consequence of direct agency is that a contract concluded by the agent with the third party is 'imputed' to the principal. This means that the principal (in place of the agent) becomes 'party' to the contract with the third party.[2]

Indirect agency exists if the following two requirements are fulfilled. (1) It is necessary that the agent should have (sufficient) authority to conclude a contract in his own name, but for the account and at the risk of the principal. As with authority for direct agency, authority for indirect agency may arise from the will of the principal, from statute or from a court ruling. (2) It is necessary that the agent at the time of the conclusion of the contract with the third party acts as indirect agent. In other words, he must act in his own name, but for the account and at

---

[2] With respect to agency pursuant to the will of the principal (*volmacht*, consensual agency) this is explicitly provided in Art. 3:66(1) DCC: 'A principal is bound by a legal act performed in his name by an agent acting within the limits of his authority.' However, pursuant to the linking provision of Art. 3:78 DCC, *inter alia*, Art. 3:66(1) DCC may in principle be applied outside the context of consensual ageny (e.g. in the context of authority pursuant to a statutory provision or judicial order or in the context of representation by a body of a legal person). Furthermore, pursuant to the linking provision of Art. 3:79 DCC, *inter alia*, Art. 3:66(1) DCC can in principle be applied to areas of the law other than patrimonial law, such as family law, procedural law and public law. See, on direct agency, S. C. J. J. Kortmann, *Mr. C. Asser's Handleiding tot de beoefening van het Nederlands burgerlijk recht, Vertegenwoordiging en rechtspersoon, De vertegenwoordiging*, 8th edn (Deventer: Kluwer, 2004), nos. 5, 17; J. Hijma, C. C. van Dam, W. A. M. van Schendel and W. L. Valk, *Rechtshandeling en Overeenkomst* (Studiereeks Burgerlijk Recht deel 3), 5th edn (Deventer: Kluwer, 2007), nos. 81, 87 ('Bloembergen/Van Schendel'); A. C. van Schaick, *Volmacht* (Monografieën Nieuw BW: B-serie; 5) (Deventer: Kluwer, 1999), nos. 2, 5–7, 39, 70; D. Busch, *Indirect Representation in European Contract Law* (The Hague: Kluwer Law International, 2005), pp. 7–10.

the risk of the principal. That he must act in his own name means that the agent should, at the time of the conclusion of the contract, make it known to the third party, in a manner that the third party can reasonably be expected to understand, that he is acting as the counterparty of the third party. That the agent at the time of the conclusion of the contract must not only act in his own name, but must also act for the account and at the risk of the principal, means that the principal receives the benefits and bears the burdens arising from the contract with the third party. Although (as stated above) it is necessary that, at the time of the conclusion of the contract, it is reasonably apparent to the third party that the agent acts in his own name, it is not necessary at that time that it should be reasonably apparent to the third party that the agent acts for the account and at the risk of the principal.

The primary legal effect of indirect agency is that the consequences of a contract concluded by the agent affect the agent himself. Unlike the case of direct agency, a contract concluded by the agent is therefore not 'imputed' to the principal. This means that the agent himself (and not the principal) is party to the contract with the third party. This accords with the fact that the agent acted in his own name and not in the name of the principal. However, in view of the fact that the transaction is concluded for the account and at the risk of the principal, indirect agency secondarily also takes account of the position of the principal. First, a third party who fails in the performance of his obligations is bound not only to compensate the agent for his own damage but also to reimburse damage which the principal has suffered in consequence of the failure (Art. 7:419 DCC).[3] Second, the third party and the principal may sue each other directly if a 'fault' occurs in the course of the legal relationship between the principal, the agent and the third party, for instance due to the bankruptcy of the agent (Arts. 7:420–421 DCC).[4]

---

[3] Art. 7:419 DCC reads as follows: 'If a mandatary in his own name has concluded a contract with a third party who does not perform his obligations, the third party is obliged also, within the limits of what otherwise results from the law relating to the obligation to pay damages, to pay the mandatary damages for loss suffered by the mandator.'

[4] Art. 7:420 DCC reads as follows: '(1) If a mandatary who in his own name concludes a contract with a third party, does not perform his obligations with respect to the mandator, becomes bankrupt or if a debt management (natural persons) scheme has been declared applicable to him, the mandator is entitled to have the transferable rights of the mandatary against the third party transferred to him by means of a written declaration to the third party and the mandator, except to the extent that these rights belong to the mandatary in his mutual relationship with the mandator. (2) The mandator is similarly

III Unauthorised agency

The concept of unauthorised agency is usually only associated with unauthorised direct agency. The same is true for the concepts of apparent authority and ratification. Although it is possible to apply these concepts to (certain cases of) indirect agency,[5] the focus of this chapter is on direct rather than indirect agency. In the remainder of this chapter 'direct agency' is simply referred to as 'agency'.

Unauthorised agency arises in a wide variety of cases. It arises when the agent concludes a contract in the name of the principal, but has no authority at all, when he exceeds his authority or when the agent's authority has ended at the time of the conclusion of the contract. Unauthorised agency may also arise when the agent's authority has been nullified (*vernietigd*) with retroactive effect (effect *ex tunc*). Nullification of the agent's authority with retroactive effect is, for example, possible if it was granted due to an error (*dwaling*) or under threat (*bedreiging*).[6]

The general effect of unauthorised agency is that neither the principal nor the third party is bound or entitled under the contract concluded by the unauthorised agent. The contract (or other legal act performed by an

entitled in case the third party does not perform his obligations with respect to the mandatary, unless the latter satisfies the mandator as if the third party had performed his obligations. (3) In the cases mentioned in paragraph (1) and (2) of this provision, the mandatary is on request obliged to communicate the name of the third party to the mandator.' Art. 7:421 DCC reads as follows: '(1) If a mandatary who in his own name concludes a contract with a third party, does not perform his obligations with respect to the third party, becomes bankrupt or if a debt management (natural persons) scheme has been declared applicable to him, the third party is entitled, after a written notification to the mandatary and the mandator, to exercise against the mandator those rights resulting from the contract, to the extent that the mandator is correspondingly obliged towards the mandatary at the time of notification. (2) In the cases mentioned in paragraph (1) of this provision, the mandatary is on request obliged to communicate the name of the mandator to the third party.' Arts. 7:419–421 DCC apply directly only when indirect agency arises pursuant to a contract of mandate (*lastgeving*). However, the linking provision of Art. 7:424(1) DCC provides that, *inter alia*, these provisions may be applied by way of analogy to *contracts* other than mandate. In the literature it is often said that Arts. 7:419–421 DCC can be regarded as general provisions on indirect agency, with the effect that they even apply, for instance, in the case that indirect agency arises not pursuant to a contract of mandate or other contract, but from statute. See, on indirect agency, Kortmann, *Vertegenwoordiging*, nos. 19, 102–15; Bloembergen/Van Schendel, *Rechtshandeling*, nos. 119–123; W. C. L. van der Grinten, *Lastgeving* (Monografieën Nieuw BW: B-serie; 81) (Deventer: Kluwer, 1999), nos. 30, 39–47, 59–60; Busch, *Indirect Representation*, pp. 10–72.

[5] See on 'unauthorised indirect representation', 'apparent authority for indirect representation' and 'ratification of unauthorised indirect representation', Busch, *Indirect Representation*, pp. 232–7.

[6] Cf. Van Schaick, *Volmacht*, no. 42.

unauthorised agent) is considered invalid.[7] This rule protects the autonomy of the principal because it prevents him from being bound and
entitled against his will.

IV Apparent authority

1 General

It seems fair to allow an exception to the general rule that neither the
principal nor the third party is bound or entitled in cases of unauthorised
agency where the third party reasonably believes that the agent was
authorised to conclude the contract concerned and where such beliefs
can be traced back to acts or conduct of the principal or to other factors
which lie within the principal's sphere of risk. This is the focus of attention
of the doctrine of apparent authority and it can therefore be said that
it rests upon the principle of the protection of reasonable beliefs. This
principle also plays an important role in the interpretation of legal acts
(such as contracts) in general (see Arts. 3:35 and 3:36 DCC).[8]

The doctrine of apparent authority exists for the benefit of the third
party. Therefore, the third party is *entitled* and not *obliged* to invoke it if

---

[7] Thus explicitly the parliamentary history of Book 3, *Vermogensrecht in het algemeen*
(Patrimonial law in general), W. H. M. Reehuis and E. E. Slob (eds.), *Invoering Boeken 3, 5
en 6, Parlementaire Geschiedenis van het nieuwe Burgerlijk Wetboek, Boek 3, Vermogensrecht
in het algemeen* (Deventer: Kluwer, 1990) (henceforth *Parliamentary History Book 3, Part II*),
pp. 1181, 1183–4. Similarly, the following legal authors: Kortmann, *Vertegenwoordiging*,
no. 83; Bloembergen/Van Schendel, *Rechtshandeling*, no. 108; A. S. Hartkamp, 'Bekrachtiging
van nietige rechtshandelingen in het nieuwe burgerlijk wetboek', in P. Abas, N. J. P. Giltay
Veth, Y. Scholten and G. J. Wolffensperger (eds.), *Non sine causa: opstellen aangeboden
aan Prof. Mr. G. J. Scholten ter gelegenheid van zijn afscheid als hoogleraar aan de
Universiteit van Amsterdam* (Zwolle: Tjeenk Willink, 1979), p. 131. But see the different
view of Van Schaick, *Volmacht*, no. 42, who argues that unauthorised legal acts are valid
but do not bind the principal unless the third party successfully invokes the doctrine of
apparent authority or unless the principal subsequently ratifies the unauthorised act.

[8] Cf. Kortmann, *Vertegenwoordiging*, no. 37; Bloembergen/Van Schendel, *Rechtshandeling*,
no. 104; HR 9 October 1998, NJ 1999, 581, with annotation by PvS (*Hartman v. Bakker*),
consideration 3.4.1. Art. 3:35 DCC reads as follows: 'The absence of intention in a
declaration cannot be invoked against a person who has interpreted another's declaration
or conduct, in conformity with the sense which he could reasonably attribute to it in the
circumstances, as a declaration of a particular tenor made to him by that other person.'
Art. 3:36 DCC states the following: 'A third party who under the circumstances reasonably bases an assumption as to the creation, existence or extinction of a legal relationship
on a declaration or conduct of another, and has acted reasonably on the basis of the
accuracy of that assumption, cannot have invoked against him the inaccuracy of that
assumption by the other person.'

he does not wish to do so.[9] However, in cases where it is clear that the principal wishes to uphold the contract concluded by the unauthorised agent, it will often be contrary to reasonableness and fairness (*redelijk-heid en billijkheid*) for the third party to take the position that the principal did not in fact grant his agent (sufficient) authority.[10]

It should be noted that the doctrine of apparent authority only addresses the question of whether the *third party* reasonably believes that there was sufficient authority. The question whether the *agent* reasonably believes that his principal granted him sufficient authority is a different question and is to be determined by reference to the general provisions on the legal acts of Arts. 3:33 and 3:35 DCC.[11] According to Art. 3:35 DCC (applied to the legal act of granting authority), if agent A reasonably assumes that his principal, P, has granted him authority of a certain kind, whereas in reality P did *not* intend to do so, A is never-theless entitled to assume that P indeed granted such authority to him. *If* A assumes this, the authority is regarded as real, also as against third parties. Therefore, if A subsequently concludes a contract in the name of P with third party, T, within the limits of the authority which A reasonably assumes he has, P and T are bound to each other not on the basis of an application of the doctrine of apparent authority, but on the basis of real authority.[12] It should be noted that A is only *entitled* and not *obliged* to assume that P granted him authority.[13] However, in cases where it is clear that P is willing to accept that A was entitled to believe that P granted him authority, it will often be contrary to reasonableness and fairness (*redelijkheid en billijkheid*) for A to take

---

[9] See C. J. Van Zeben, J. W. du Pon and M. M. Olthof (eds.), *Parlementaire Geschiedenis van het nieuwe Burgerlijk Wetboek, Boek 3, Vermogensrecht in het algemeen* (Deventer: Kluwer, 1981) (henceforth *Parliamentary History Book 3, Part I*), p. 176; *Parliamentary History Book 3, Part II*, p. 1184; B. W. M. Nieskens-Isphording and A. E. M. van der Putt-Lauwers, *Derdenbescherming* (Monografieën Nieuw BW. A-serie; 22), 3rd edn (Deventer: Kluwer, 2002), no. 6; Van Schaick, *Volmacht*, no. 51.

[10] Cf. Kortmann, *Vertegenwoordiging*, no. 85; Nieskens-Isphording and Van der Putt-Lauwers, *Derdenbescherming*, no. 6.

[11] Art. 3:33 DCC provides that: 'A legal act requires an intention to produce legal effects, which intention has manifested itself by a declaration.' See, for the text of Art. 3:35 DCC, n. 8 above.

[12] Cf. Kortmann, *Vertegenwoordiging*, nos. 32 and 37; Van Schaick, *Volmacht*, no. 51; H. C. F. Schoordijk, *Vermogensrecht in het algemeen naar Boek 3 van het nieuwe BW (titel 1t/m 5, titel 11)* (Deventer: Kluwer, 1986), p. 205.

[13] See, in relation to Art. 3:35 DCC in general, *Parliamentary History Book 3, Part I*, p. 176; *Parliamentary History Book 3, Part II*, p. 1184.

the position that P did not in fact intend to grant him sufficient authority (Art. 3:35 DCC).[14]

2 Legal basis

Art. 3:61(2) DCC explicitly deals with apparent authority. It reads as follows:

> Where a legal act has been performed[15] in the name of another person, the third party who, on the basis of a declaration or conduct of that other person, has assumed and in the given circumstances could reasonably assume the existence of sufficient authority, may not have invoked against him the inaccuracy of this assumption.

3 Scope

Article 3:61(2) DCC on apparent authority is included in Title 3 (Consensual agency, *Volmacht*) of Book 3 (Patrimonial law in general, *Vermogensrecht in het algemeen*) of the Dutch Civil Code.

In view of the fact that Art. 3:61(2) DCC on apparent authority is included in the title dealing with consensual agency, it applies directly only in the context of agency pursuant to the apparent will of the principal (*schijnvolmacht*, apparent consensual agency). Pursuant to the linking provision of Art. 3:78 DCC, some of the provisions on consensual agency may in principle be applied outside the context of consensual agency (e.g. in the context of authority pursuant to a statutory provision or judicial order or in the context of representation by a body of a legal person), but this linking provision does not mention Art. 3:61(2) DCC on apparent consensual agency. However (notwithstanding the fact that the linking provision of Art. 3:78 DCC does not mention Art. 3:61(2) DCC), Art. 3:61(2) DCC can be applied by way of analogy in cases other than apparent consensual agency as well. For example, Art. 3:61(2) DCC can sometimes be applied in the context of unauthorised representation by a body of a legal person.[16]

---

[14] See, in relation to Art. 3:35 DCC in general, A. S. Hartkamp and C. H. Sieburgh, *Mr. C. Asser's Handleiding tot de beoefening van het Nederlands burgerlijk recht, Verbintenissenrecht, Algemene leer der overeenkomsten*, 12th edn (Deventer: Kluwer 2005), no. 113; cf. Nieskens-Isphording and Van der Putt-Lauwers, *Derdenbescherming*, no. 6b.

[15] Typically, the conclusion of a contract.

[16] On the subject of analogous application of Art. 3:61(2) DCC in the context of unauthorised representation by a body of a legal person, see J. M. M. Maeijer, *Mr. C. Asser's Handleiding tot de beoefening van het Nederlands burgerlijk recht, Vertegenwoordiging en rechtspersoon,*

Furthermore, in view of the fact that Art. 3:61(2) DCC is included in the book dealing with patrimonial law in general, it applies directly only to the performance of legal acts (such as the conclusion of contracts) in patrimonial law. However, pursuant to the (very general and openly formulated) linking provision of Art. 3:79 DCC, *inter alia*, Art. 3:61(2) DCC can in principle be applied to areas of the law other than patrimonial law, such as family law, procedural law and public law.[17]

In the Netherlands, the authority of certain agents is registered in the (publicly accessible) Trade Register (*handelsregister*). This may be the case, for example, because there exists a legal duty to do so or because it is customary. For these situations Art. 3:61(3) DCC supplements Art. 3:61(2) DCC on apparent authority by providing that: 'where an agent's authority which has been made public in accordance with law or usage contains restrictions that are so unusual that the third party could not be expected to have anticipated their inclusion in the agent's authority, they cannot be invoked against the third party unless he has actual knowledge of them.' The rationale of this provision is to avoid the third party being required to consult the Trade Register for every ordinary transaction.[18]

Of more practical relevance is the rule that registration in the Trade Register of an agent's authority with restrictions that are *not* unusual does not imply that there can be no apparent authority.[19] See, for example,

---

De rechtspersoon, 8th edn (Deventer: Tjeenk Willink, 1997), nos. 101–2 (with further references). See also H. J. de Kluiver, 'Bekrachtiging van rechtshandelingen en besluiten. Over Art. 3:58 BW als vangnet en trampoline', in S. C. J. J. Kortmann, N. E. D. Faber and J. A. M. Strens-Meulemeester (eds.), *Vertegenwoordiging en tussenpersoon* (Serie Ondernemeing en Recht deel 17) (Deventer: Tjeenk Willink, 1999), pp. 76–7; E. E. G. Gepken-Jager, *Vertegenwoordiging bij NV en BV: Een rechtsvergelijkend onderzoek naar de uitvoering van artikel 9 eerste EG-richtlijn inzake het vennootschapsrecht* (Uitgave vanwege het Instituut voor Ondernemingsrecht Rijksuniversiteit Groningen no. 34) (Deventer: Kluwer, 2000), nos. 163–4. See generally on Art. 3:78 DCC: Kortmann, *Vertegenwoordiging*, no. 18; Bloembergen/Van Schendel, *Rechtshandeling*, no. 86; Van Schaick, *Volmacht*, nos. 71–2.

[17] See generally on Art. 3:79 DCC: Kortmann, *Vertegenwoordiging*, no. 18; Bloembergen/ Van Schendel, *Rechtshandeling*, no. 86; Van Schaick, *Volmacht*, no. 73.

[18] See *Parliamentary History Book 3, Part II*, p. 1180. A similar provision to Art. 3:61(3) DCC can be found in Art. 6:238(1), opening words, and under (b) DCC, which relates to unusual restrictions on the agent's authority in standard conditions of consumer contracts: 'In a [consumer contract], the fact that: … (b) the general terms and conditions contain limitations upon the agent's authority which are so unusual that the third party, in the absence of the stipulation, could not have expected them, unless he knew of them … cannot be invoked against the third party.' See on Art. 3:61(3) DCC and Art. 6:238(1), opening words, and under (b) DCC: Kortmann, *Vertegenwoordiging*, no. 49; Bloembergen/Van Schendel, *Rechtshandeling*, no. 107; Van Schaick, *Volmacht*, no. 53.

[19] Kortmann, *Vertegenwoordiging*, no. 49; Bloembergen/Van Schendel, *Rechtshandeling*, no. 107. Cf. Van Schaick, *Volmacht*, no. 53.

Nacap v. Kurstjens.[20] The Trade Register showed that the authority of the manager was limited to legal acts not exceeding a value of 100,000 Dutch Guilders. The third party (Kurstjens) was nevertheless entitled to assume on the basis of apparent authority (Art. 3:61(2) DCC) that the manager had sufficient authority to bind its employer (Nacap) for more than 100,000 Dutch Guilders.

Article 3:76(1) DCC[21] deals with apparent authority in the special case that an agent continues to conclude contracts in the name of his principal despite the fact that his authority has ended. Article 3:76(1) DCC is a *lex specialis* in relation to the general provision on apparent authority (Art. 3:61(2) DCC). It follows from Art. 3:76(1) DCC that the third party who has *actual* knowledge of either the termination itself or the terminating event will not be able to consider the agent as still being authorised.[22]

Furthermore, it follows from Art. 3:76(1) DCC that, generally, the agent's lack of authority cannot be invoked by the principal where the third party has no actual knowledge of the termination itself or the terminating event. In other words, generally the third party does not have the duty to investigate whether the agent's authority has ended. However, in certain situations the legislature considered it appropriate that the principal can invoke the termination of the agent's authority against the third party even though the third party has no actual knowledge of the termination itself or the terminating event. Article 3:76(1)(a)–(d) DCC provides an exhaustive list of situations in which the termination of the agent's authority can be invoked against the third party without actual knowledge. Subsection (a) concerns cases where the third party

---

[20] HR 23 October 1998, NJ 1999, 582, with annotation by PvS; JOR 1999/113, with annotation by S. C. J. J. Kortmann.

[21] Art. 3:76(1) DCC reads as follows: 'An event which has terminated the agent's authority may only be invoked against the third party who had no knowledge of the termination of the authority nor of the terminating event in the following circumstances:

(a) the termination of the agent's authority or the event which has terminated it has been communicated to the third party or has been made public in a manner which, by virtue of law or common opinion, justifies that the principal can invoke the termination of the authority against the third party;

(b) if the death of the principal was generally known;

(c) if the appointment or employment that gave rise to the agent's authority has been terminated in a fashion apparent to third persons;

(d) if the third party has obtained knowledge of the authority solely by means of a declaration of the agent.'

[22] Cf. Kortmann, *Vertegenwoordiging*, no. 60; Bloembergen/Van Schendel, *Rechtshandeling*, no. 116; Van Schaick, *Volmacht*, no. 54.

shall be deemed to have received a communication, although the communication actually failed to reach him (see Art. 3:37(3), second sentence, DCC).[23] It also concerns cases where the termination has been made public, but where the third party did not notice the publication of the termination of the agent's authority. Subsection (b) concerns the case where the death of the principal is generally known (e.g. the death of a famous person whose death has been extensively publicised and/or broadcast). Subsection (c) concerns the situation where the appointment or employment that gave rise to the agent's authority has been terminated in a fashion apparent to third parties. Finally, subsection (d) concerns the case where the third party exclusively relied on the agent's statement that he was so authorised. In such a case, the termination of this authority may always be invoked by the principal against the third party.[24]

As in the case of the general provision regarding apparent authority (Art. 3:61(2) DCC), the third party is *entitled* to invoke Art. 3:76(1) DCC, but he is not *obliged* to do so.[25] However, it will often be contrary to reasonableness and fairness (*redelijkheid en billijkheid*) if third party T rejects the protection of Art. 3:76(1) DCC and instead argues that the agent's authority has terminated, whereas P is perfectly willing to accept that T reasonably believed that the authority had not terminated.[26]

In view of the fact that Art. 3:76 DCC is (like Art. 3:61(2) DCC on apparent authority) included in the title dealing with consensual agency,

---

[23] Art. 3:37(3) DCC reads as follows: 'A declaration made to a specifically determined person, in order to be effective, must have reached that person. *Nevertheless, even a declaration which has not reached the person to whom it was made, or has not reached him in time, does have effect if this situation results from his own act, from the act of persons for whom he is responsible, or from the circumstances, which are personal to him and justify that he suffer the consequences.*' (emphasis added.)

[24] See Kortmann, *Vertegenwoordiging*, nos. 60–2; Bloembergen/Van Schendel, *Rechtshandeling*, no. 116; Van Schaick, *Volmacht*, no. 54.

[25] See *Parliamentary History Book 3, Part II*, Boek 3, pp. 1184–5 in conjunction with *Parliamentary History Book 3, Part I*, p. 176; Van Schaick, *Volmacht*, no. 54.

[26] A similar point of view can be found in the literature in relation to apparent authority (Art. 3:61(2) DCC), apparent ratification (Art. 3:69 in conjunction with Art. 3:35 DCC) and legal acts in general (Art. 3:35 DCC): Kortmann, *Vertegenwoordiging*, nos. 85, 86; C. E. du Perron, *Overeenkomst en derden* (Deventer: Kluwer, 1999), no. 9; Asser-Hartkamp/Sieburgh, *Algemene leer der overeenkomsten*, no. 113. See IV 1, above, and V 1, below. Pursuant to Art. 3:76(2) DCC, an agent who continues to act in the name of the principal in the circumstances described in Art. 3:76(1) DCC is liable to pay damages to the third party who did not know of the termination of the agent's authority. See further VI 3, below.

it directly only applies to the termination of consensual agency. However (notwithstanding the fact that the linking provision of Art. 3:78 DCC does not mention Art. 3:76 DCC), Art. 3:76(1) DCC can be applied by way of analogy in cases other than consensual agency.[27]

Furthermore, in view of the fact that Art. 3:76 DCC (like Art. 3:61(2) DCC) is included in the book dealing with patrimonial law in general, it directly only applies to the performance of legal acts (such as the conclusion of contracts) in patrimonial law. However, pursuant to the linking provision of Art. 3:79 DCC, *inter alia*, Art. 3:76 DCC can in principle be applied to areas of the law other than patrimonial law, such as family law, procedural law and public law.[28]

4 Effect

If unauthorised agent A concludes a contract in the name of principal P with third party T and T successfully invokes the doctrine of apparent authority, P cannot plead that he is not bound and entitled under the contract concluded with T because of A's lack of authority. In other words, as soon as T successfully invokes apparent authority and despite the fact that A was not sufficiently authorised, P and T are both bound and entitled under the contract concluded by A.[29]

In view of the fact that the doctrine of apparent authority exists for the benefit of T, T is *entitled* to invoke it but not *obliged* to do so if he does not wish to. However, in cases where it is clear that P wishes to uphold the contract concluded by A, it will often be contrary to reasonableness and fairness (*redelijkheid en billijkheid*) for T to take the position that P did not in fact grant A (sufficient) authority.[30]

5 Requirements

Article 3:61(2) DCC sets out the requirements which have to be met in order successfully to invoke the doctrine of apparent authority:

---

[27] See generally on Art. 3:78 DCC: Kortmann, *Vertegenwoordiging*, no. 18; Bloembergen/ Van Schendel, *Rechtshandeling*, no. 86; Van Schaick, *Volmacht*, nos. 71–2.

[28] See generally on Art. 3:79 DCC: Kortmann, *Vertegenwoordiging*, no. 18; Bloembergen/ Van Schendel, *Rechtshandeling*, no. 86; Van Schaick, *Volmacht*, no. 73.

[29] Cf. Kortmann, *Vertegenwoordiging*, no. 37; Bloembergen/Van Schendel, *Rechtshandeling*, no. 101.

[30] See IV 1, above.

(a) a declaration or conduct by the principal;

(b) the third party in the given circumstances could reasonably presume the existence of sufficient authority;

(c) the third party has presumed the existence of sufficient authority.

These three requirements will now be discussed in more detail.

(a) Declaration or conduct of the principal, supplemented by risk principle

Declaration or conduct of the principal

As explained above, apparent authority rests upon the principle of the protection of reasonable beliefs. According to the wording of Art. 3:61(2) DCC, a reasonable belief of (sufficient) authority must have been created by the principal of his own doing, i.e. by means of his declaration or conduct. It is not required that the principal is in some way at fault.[31] Conduct of the principal may also consist of inaction in cases where the principal had a duty to inform the third party that the agent had insufficient authority.

See, for an example, *Molukse Evangelische Kerk* v. *Clijnk*,[32] where the contracting authority (*Molukse Evangelische Kerk*, a church) was considered bound by legal acts performed by the architect in his (the church's) name with building contractor Clijnk. The inaction of the church consisted of the fact that it had left the renovation entirely up to the architect and did nothing to inform building contractor Clijnk, of the limits that it had imposed on the architect's authority. The Dutch Supreme Court (*Hoge Raad*) ruled that the church was deemed to have been aware of the duration and the fundamental character of the renovation activities and that, from the start of the renovation, the Church had been aware that the costs of the renovation would be more than the amount for which it had granted authority. An example that proves that conduct of the principal may also consist of inaction in cases where the principal had a duty to inform the third party that the agent lacked sufficient authority can also be found in *Kuipers* v. *Wijnveen*.[33]

---

[31] See *Parliamentary History Book 3, Part II*, p. 1181; Bloembergen/Van Schendel, *Rechtshandeling*, no. 101.

[32] HR 1 March 1968, NJ 1968, 246, with annotation by GJS, on which see Kortmann, *Vertegenwoordiging*, no. 38; Bloembergen/Van Schendel, *Rechtshandeling*, no. 103; Van Schaick, *Volmacht*, no. 51. See also *Parliamentary History Book 3, Part II*, p. 267.

[33] HR 12 January 2001, NJ 2001, 157.

The appearance of authority must exist at the time of the performance of the legal act concerned.[34] However, this does not mean that circumstances taking place *after* the performance of the legal act cannot be taken into account. Later circumstances may, after all, provide indications of whether or not there was an appearance of authority at the time of the performance of a legal act.[35] This is explicitly stated by the Dutch Supreme Court in *Kuipers* v. *Wijnveen*:

> The appearance of authority may ... depending on the other circumstances of the case, also consist of inaction, whereby it is not relevant whether part of the circumstances on which the appearance of authority rests, has taken place after the conclusion of the contract.[36]

Risk principle

In accordance with the wording of the apparent authority provision of Art. 3:61(2) DCC quoted above, a reasonable belief of (sufficient) authority must have been created by the principal of his own doing. However, since 1970, this 'of the principal's own doing' principle has been criticised by various writers, starting with Schoordijk, who was – interestingly enough – inspired by the Anglo-American doctrine of apparent authority.[37] Although there are differences of detail, these writers advocate replacing or supplementing the 'of the principal's own doing' idea by the risk principle. According to the latter principle, the third party is protected not only where the impression has been created by the principal but also where it is due to other circumstances that come within the ambit of the risks borne by the principal.[38]

Equally, it is possible to identify a trend in the decisions of the Dutch Supreme Court towards more emphasis on who should bear the risk for giving the impression of power of representation, and less emphasis on

---

[34] HR 26 September 2003, NJ 2004, 460, with annotation by JBMV; JOR 2004/32, with annotation by SCJJK (*Regiopolitie Gelderland-Zuid* v. *Hovax*).

[35] Cf. Kortmann, *Vertegenwoordiging*, no. 41; Bloembergen/Van Schendel, *Rechtshandeling*, no. 103.

[36] HR 12 January 2001, NJ 2001, 157, consideration 3.4.

[37] H. C. F. Schoordijk, 'Het leerstuk van de opgewekte schijn van volmacht en de Engels-Amerikaansrechtelijke leer van de "apparent authority"', in *Honderd jaar rechtsleven. De Nederlandse Juristen-Vereniging 1870–1970* (Zwolle: Tjeenk Willink, 1970), pp. 1–24; reprinted in J. M. van Dunné, J. H. Nieuwenhuis and J. B. M. Vranken (eds.), *Verspreid werk van Prof. Mr. H. C. F. Schoordijk* (Deventer: Kluwer 1991), pp. 197–221.

[38] Cf. Kortmann, *Vertegenwoordiging*, nos. 38–43, with many further references.

the 'of the principal's own doing' idea, particularly in cases where the principal is a legal person.[39]

The landmark case in this respect is *Felix* v. *Aruba*.[40] Mr Felix entered into negotiations with the airport manager of the international airport in Aruba regarding the transport of crew and passengers of light aircraft. In anticipation of a formal licence, Felix handled arrangements for light aircraft between March and December 1986. However, in November 1986 the Minister of Transport and Communication decided that, in future, the transport of crew and passengers would be conducted exclusively by Air Aruba NV, and Felix was forced to close his business. Felix filed a claim both for reliance expenses and expectation damages (loss of profit). He argued that he had been dealing with light aircraft from March 1986 onwards at the request of the Aruban government. During negotiations the airport manager had led him to believe that he would be able to continue to do so. The government was therefore in breach of contract. In reply, the government argued that the airport manager was not authorised to bind it. The Dutch Supreme Court held that, in the case of negotiations between a government functionary and a third party who incorrectly assumes that the functionary is authorised to bind the government, such an incorrect assumption might sometimes be the government's responsibility. This would occur where an authorised body led the third party to believe that the functionary was authorised to bind the government, but other factors might tend towards the same result, such as: (1) the position of the functionary within the government organisation and his declarations or conduct; (2) the circumstance that the organisation or division of authorities is non-transparent for third parties due to lack of clarity, complexity or inaccessibility of the relevant regulations; and (3) an omission on the part of the government to warn the third party that the functionary is not authorised.

---

[39] HR 4 June 1976, NJ 1977, 336, with annotation by BW (*Liberty II*); HR 27 January 1984, NJ 1984, 545, with annotation by G (*WGO* v. *Koma*); HR 24 April 1992, NJ 1993, 190, with annotation by HJS (*Kuyt* v. *MEAS*); HR 27 November 1992, NJ 1993, 287, with annotation by PvS (*Felix* v. *Aruba*); HR 19 November 1993, NJ 1994, 622, with annotation by JCS and PvS (*COVA*); HR 9 October 1998, NJ 1999, 581, with annotation by PvS (*Hartman* v. *Bakker*); HR 23 October 1998, NJ 1999, 582, with annotation by PvS, also printed in JOR 1999/113, with annotation by S. C. J. J. Kortmann (*Nacap* v. *Kurstjens*). But see HR 24 December 1993, NJ 1994, 303 (*Credit Lyonnais Bank* v. *T*); HR 12 January 2001, NJ 2001, 157 (*Kuijpers* v. *Wijnveen*), which stipulated the requirement that it should be the doing of the principal.

[40] HR 27 November 1992, NJ 1993, 287, with annotation by PvS (*Felix* v. *Aruba*).

Felix v. *Aruba* shows that the declarations or conduct of the principal[41] are not the only relevant factors leading to liability on the part of the principal. Other circumstances also lie within his sphere of risk, such as the non-transparent structure of the company and the position of the agent within the organisation. The case involved unauthorised representation of a government authority, but there seems to be no good reason why the reasoning should not also apply to unauthorised representation of private persons.[42]

In any event, in *Hartman* v. *Bakker*,[43] a case involving unauthorised representation of a private person, it was accepted that the function of a representative within the organisation of the principal can lead to an appearance of authority which may be successfully invoked by the third party where the representative concludes a contract in the principal's name which appears to be in line with his appointment.[44]

In yet another case, *Kuyt* v. *MEAS*[45] (discussed in more detail in (b), below), it was stated that a person to whom a bailiff offers a settlement may, in general, assume that the bailiff has sufficient authority to do so. Not surprisingly, some writers have argued that in cases where the appearance of authority derives from the function of the agent within the organisation of the principal, it is also arguable that the principal in such cases has granted the agent implied authority. In that approach, the authority is treated as real authority and not just as the appearance thereof.[46]

(b) The third party in the given circumstances could reasonably presume the existence of sufficient authority

The requirement that the third party in the given circumstances could reasonably presume the existence of sufficient authority is of a normative nature. Whether or not the third party's presumption was justified should be judged against the background of the principle of reasonableness and

---

[41] Including inaction where the principal had a duty to act, see (3) above. That inaction of the principal can lead to apparent authority is not new. See e.g. HR 1 March 1968, NJ 1968, 246, with annotation by GJS (*Molukse Evangelische Kerk* v. *Clijnk*), discussed above.

[42] Cf. P. van Schilfgaarde in his annotation no. 2 to *Felix* v. *Aruba*, 1993 NJ 287.

[43] HR 9 October 1998, 1999 NJ 581.

[44] See A. L. H. Ernes, 'Schijn van volmacht op grond van functie?' (1999) 6346 *WPNR* 143.

[45] HR 24 April 1992, NJ 1993, 190, with annotation by HJS.

[46] Cf. the observations in IV 1, above. See Kortmann, *Vertegenwoordiging*, nos. 36, 39, 48; T. F. E. Tjong Tjin Tai, 'Driemaal schijnvolmacht' (2001) *NbBW* 70; A. L. H. Ernes, 'Aanstellingsvolmacht, schijn van volmachtverlening en "usual authority"' (2004) *NTBR* 167.

fairness (*redelijkheid en billijkheid*) of Art. 6:2 DCC[47] and with reference to Art. 3:11 DCC.[48] The latter provision states the following:

> Where good faith of a person is required to produce legal effect, such person is not acting in good faith if he knew the facts or the law to which his good faith must relate or if, in the given circumstances, he should know them. Impossibility to inquire does not prevent the person, who had good reasons to be in doubt, from being considered as someone who should know the facts or the law.

Applied to the case of apparent authority, the situations referred to in Art. 3:11 DCC can be described as follows. The first type of case is where the third party *knows* that the agent exceeded his authority whereas, in more abstract terms, the appearance of authority exists. In such case, the third party in the given circumstances could *not* reasonably presume the existence of a sufficient authority. An example is the case where the agent stays within the limits of his written authority, but the third party knows that the principal has, in the meantime, limited the agent's authority.[49]

The second type of case is where, under the given circumstances, reasonableness and fairness result in a duty to investigate whether the person with whom he was dealing had sufficient authority, for example, by asking the principal. The words 'in the given circumstances' denote that much depends on the circumstances of the case.[50]

An example of a case where the third party in the given circumstances could *not* reasonably presume that the agent had sufficient authority is *Kuyt* v. *MEAS*.[51] In June 1989 Mr Kuyt had been ordered by the District Court to vacate the house which he rented from MEAS because he had not paid his rent for quite some time. An application for an interim ruling to suspend the execution of this decision was rejected in October 1989. Some weeks later, a bailiff (in charge of the eviction but not aware of the rejection of the interim ruling to suspend the execution) concluded a contract with Kuyt in the name of MEAS which, *inter alia*, stipulated that Kuyt had the

---

[47] Art. 6:2(1) DCC reads as follows: 'A creditor and a debtor must, as between themselves, act in accordance with the requirements of reasonableness and fairness.'

[48] Cf. Bloembergen/Van Schendel, *Rechtshandeling*, no. 102; Van Schaick, *Volmacht*, no. 52. See, on duties to inform and duties to investigate in the law of obligations in general, J. B. M. Vranken, *Mededelings-, informatie- en onderzoeksplichten in het verbintenissenrecht* (Zwolle: Tjeenk Willink, 1989).

[49] Kortmann, *Vertegenwoordiging*, no. 37. Cf. HR 16 March 1928, NJ 1928, 712 (*Russian uniforms*).

[50] Cf. Bloembergen/Van Schendel, *Rechtshandeling*, no. 102.

[51] HR 24 April 1992, NJ 1993, 190, with annotation by HJS.

right to stay in his house for at least six more months against payment of some 8,000 Dutch Guilders. The bailiff concluded this contract without any authority and without the knowledge of MEAS. When the bailiff again, some weeks later, initiated eviction proceedings, Kuyt for a second time applied for an interim ruling, this time with reference to the contract concluded with MEAS through the intermediary of the bailiff. The Dutch Supreme Court ruled that – also in view of the function of the bailiff in relation to the execution of decisions to evict – a person to whom a bailiff offers a settlement of the kind at hand may *in general* assume that the bailiff has sufficient authority to do so. However, in special circumstances such assumption may not be justified. According to the Dutch Supreme Court, the decision of the Court of Appeal that such special circumstances had arisen was in accordance with the law and therefore Kuyt's claim was rejected.

An example of a case where the third party in the given circumstances *was* entitled to assume that the agent had sufficient authority is *GWK Bank NV* v. *Cadform BV*.[52] Cadform BV (Cadform) conducted an enterprise engaged in the (coordination of the) supply of graphic arts products to its customers. With a view thereto, it placed orders with third parties. These orders were supplied directly to Cadform's customers. Cadform billed its customers for the amount it owed to the third parties plus a commission for the services it rendered *vis-à-vis* its customers. GWK Bank had been a customer of Cadform for about ten years. In the years 1996 and 1997, Cadform had taken orders from one J (who worked in the purchase department of GWK Bank and with whom Cadform had previously dealt) to buy certain products (printed matter) from a company named F and with the instructions that: (1) F would deliver the printed matter directly to GWK Bank; (2) the purchase price owed to F would be billed to Cadform; and (3) GWK Bank would be billed by Cadform for the amount Cadform owed to F plus a commission for the services rendered by Cadform. It was also the task of Cadform to pay F's invoices. GWK Bank had paid a sum of some 200,000 Dutch Guilders on the invoices from Cadform in relation to the products bought from F. It later turned out that the transactions with F were simulated. F, a friend of J's, had sent bills to Cadform but had not delivered anything to GWK Bank. F obtained payment from Cadform. J in his turn effected payment to Cadform. After the fraud perpetrated by J and F had been discovered, GWK Bank tried to recover the amounts paid from Cadform. Cadform had refused to repay these amounts. Against this background, GWK

---

[52] HR 4 October 2002, NJ 2002, 578.

Bank issued a writ against Cadform and claimed the repayment of the sum of some 200,000 Dutch Guilders plus interest and costs. Primarily, GWK Bank based its claim on undue payment (*onverschuldigde betaling*) because the sales contracts as referred to in Cadform's invoices were never concluded and the products referred to therein were never delivered. Cadform put forward as a defence that: (1) the fraud perpetrated by J was not apparent to Cadform; (2) for many years J had acted for GWK Bank; (3) it never became apparent that J only had a restricted authority to conduct business with Cadform in the name of GWK Bank; and (4) the orders at issue fitted in with the varied pattern of business conducted between J and Cadform. The Dutch Supreme Court stated, first, that there was no disagreement between the parties that J had, in fact, no authority to conclude the contracts with Cadform, because the contracts were used within the framework of J's fraudulent intention to make GWK Bank pay for goods that were, in fact, never delivered. However, in the view of the Dutch Supreme Court this did not alter the fact that if Cadform (1) had presumed and (2) in the given circumstances could reasonably presume the existence of a sufficient authority, GWK Bank was not entitled to invoke J's lack of authority. The Dutch Supreme Court affirmed the Court of Appeal's decision that Cadform was entitled to assume that J had sufficient authority, with the result that the payments were not undue.

(c) The third party has presumed the existence of sufficient authority

The requirement that the third party has presumed the existence of sufficient authority is of a factual nature: it depends on an interpretation of the facts. The third party who in the given circumstances could reasonably presume the existence of a sufficient authority (see directly above) does not have to prove that he, in fact, presumed the existence of sufficient authority. This would be otherwise if the principal makes it plausible that the third party did *not* presume the existence of sufficient authority. This rule of evidence follows from *Regiopolitie Gelderland-Zuid* v. *Hovax*.[53]

---

[53] HR 26 September 2003, NJ 2004, 460, with annotation by JBMV; JOR 2004/32, with annotation by SCJJK. Cf. Kortmann, *Vertegenwoordiging*, no. 37; Bloembergen/Van Schendel, *Rechtshandeling*, no. 102, n. 44. According to P. van Schilfgaarde, the requirement that the third party has in fact presumed the existence of sufficient authority is superfluous. In his view, the requirement that the third party in the given circumstances could reasonably presume the existence of a sufficient authority would be sufficient. See his article 'Vertegenwoordiging' (1974) 5280 *WPNR* 669; (1974) 5281 *WPNR* 693; reprinted in *Peter van Schilfgaarde Select. Een bloemlezing uit zijn werk* (Uitgaven vanwege het Instituut voor Ondernemingsrecht, Rijksuniversiteit Groningen, nr. 35)

V Ratification

1 General

As previously explained, if an unauthorised agent concludes a contract in the name of the principal, the general rule is that the contract so concluded is invalid and neither the principal nor the third party is bound or entitled. This general rule protects the autonomy of the principal because it prevents him from being bound and entitled against his will. However, the principal's autonomy is not violated if he has no objection to the contract concluded by his unauthorised agent and thus it seems practical that he should be able to ratify it.

Ratification (like the granting of authority) is a legal act, which means that the provisions of Title 3.2 (*Rechtshandelingen*, 'legal acts'; Arts. 3:32–3:59 DCC) apply. Whether there is ratification should be determined by reference to Arts. 3:33 and 3:35 DCC, which prescribe the establishment of legal acts in general. As a starting point, this means that the intention to ratify should be expressed *vis-à-vis* the third party (Art. 3:33 DCC). However, if a certain act or (absence of) conduct of principal P is reasonably understood by third party T as expressing the intention to ratify, whereas in reality there is no such intention, this may be treated by T as constituting ratification (Art. 3:35 DCC).[54] It should be noted that T is only *entitled* and not *obliged* to treat such appearance of ratification as constituting a valid ratification.[55] However, in cases where it is clear that P wishes to uphold the ratification, it will often be contrary to reasonableness and fairness (*redelijkheid en billijkheid*) for T to take the position that P did not, in fact, intend to ratify.[56]

2 Legal basis

The possibility of ratification (*bekrachtiging*) is expressed in Art. 3:69(1) DCC:

> A legal act[57] entered into by a person acting, without the authority to do so, as agent in the name of another, may be ratified by the latter and the legal act

---

(Deventer Kluwer, 2000), pp. 39–70; see also his annotation to HR 9 October 1998, NJ 1999, 581 (*Hartman* v. *Bakker*).

[54] Cf. Kortmann, *Vertegenwoordiging*, no. 84. See, for an example of appearance of ratification, HR 15 January 1999, NJ 1999, 574 (*Amrosan Establishment* v. *Mickey Groen*). See for the text of Arts. 3:33 and 3:35 DCC, n. 11 and n. 8, above, respectively.

[55] See, in relation to 3:35 DCC in general, *Parliamentary History Book 3, Part I*, p. 176; *Parliamentary History Book 3, Part II*, p. 1184.

[56] Cf. Kortmann, *Vertegenwoordiging*, no. 86, in conjunction with no. 85.

[57] Typically a contract.

will then have the same effect as if it had been performed pursuant to a sufficient authority.

3 Scope

Article 3:69 DCC on ratification is included in Title 3 (Consensual agency, *Volmacht*) of Book 3 (Patrimonial law in general, *Vermogensrecht in het algemeen*) of the Dutch Civil Code.

In view of the fact that Art. 3:69 DCC, on ratification, is included in the title dealing with consensual agency, it applies directly only in the context of consensual agency. However, pursuant to the linking provision of Art. 3:78 DCC, *inter alia*, Art. 3:69 DCC on ratification may in principle be applied outside the context of consensual agency (e.g. in the context of authority pursuant to a statutory provision or judicial order or in the context of representation by a body of a legal person).[58] Via that route, the doctrine of ratification can, for example, be applied to unauthorised representation by a body of a legal person.[59]

Furthermore, in view of the fact that Art. 3:69 DCC is included in the book dealing with patrimonial law in general, it directly only applies to the performance of legal acts (such as the conclusion of contracts) in patrimonial law. However, pursuant to the linking provision of Art. 3:79 DCC, *inter alia*, Art. 3:69 DCC can in principle be applied to areas of the law other than patrimonial law, such as family law, procedural law and public law.[60]

4 Position of the third party and other directly interested persons prior to ratification

(a) The third party in good faith may withdraw from the transaction unilaterally prior to ratification

Under the former Dutch Civil Code, the Dutch Supreme Court had decided that the third party in cases of unauthorised agency for his part was bound and that he could not withdraw from the transaction

---

[58] Cf. Kortmann, *Vertegenwoordiging*, nos. 91, 85. See generally on Art. 3:78 DCC: Kortmann, *Vertegenwoordiging*, no. 18; Bloembergen/Van Schendel, *Rechtshandeling*, no. 86; Van Schaick, *Volmacht*, no. 71.

[59] On the subject of analogous application of Art. 3:69 DCC in the context of unauthorised representation by a body of a legal person, see De Kluiver, 'Bekrachtiging', pp. 76–7. See generally on Art. 3:78 DCC: Kortmann, *Vertegenwoordiging*, no. 18; Bloembergen/Van Schendel, *Rechtshandeling*, no. 86; Van Schaick, *Volmacht*, nos. 71–2.

[60] See generally on Art. 3:79 DCC: Kortmann, *Vertegenwoordiging*, no. 18; Bloembergen/Van Schendel, *Rechtshandeling*, no. 86; Van Schaick, *Volmacht*, no. 73.

unilaterally.[61] There are certainly arguments for this position. The third party was willing to conclude the transaction so why should the law allow him to withdraw from the transaction? It may therefore be argued that the agent's lack of authority is an issue between the agent and the principal.[62]

Initially, the drafters of the current Dutch Civil Code had chosen a fundamentally different solution, based on the argument that a third party who on good grounds had assumed that he had concluded an unconditional and valid contract, should not have to accept a contract of which the validity and binding force is uncertain. Therefore, as long as there had been no ratification, the third party could communicate that he considered the relevant transaction as invalid and he could thus withdraw from it unilaterally.[63]

However, in the final version of Art. 3:69(3) DCC the legislature has tried to weigh the legitimate interests of the third party against those of the principal:

> Ratification has no effect, if at the time it is done, the third party has already communicated that he considers the relevant legal act[64] to be invalid for want of authority, unless the third party understood or under the circumstances should have understood, at the time of his acting, that insufficient authority had been granted.

The first part of Art. 3:69(3) DCC enables the third party to reject the unauthorised transaction and conclude another contract to satisfy his needs. This clearly serves the third party's legitimate interest to obtain certainty as soon as possible. The second part of Art. 3:69(3) DCC limits the third party's ability to withdraw unilaterally from the transaction, because he may not do so to the extent that at the time of the conclusion of the unauthorised transaction he already knew or should have known that the agent was insufficiently authorised. Thus, the second part of Art. 3:69(3) DCC is favourable to the principal.

The words 'at the time of his acting' denote the fact that one must distinguish between legal acts in which the third party is actively involved and legal acts in which the third party is only involved in a passive sense. There is, for example, no 'acting' on the side of the third party if the

---

[61] HR 30 April 1948, NJ 1949, 253, with annotation by DJV (*Smit* v. *Amsterdamse Huizenhandel*).

[62] See Bloembergen/Van Schendel, *Rechtshandeling*, no. 109.

[63] See *Parliamentary History Book 3, Part I*, p. 278.   [64] Typically a contract.

unauthorised agent terminates or nullifies a contract: the role of the third party is merely a passive one. In such cases, the third party may *also* reject the legal act concerned if he, at the time of the termination or nullification, understood or should have understood that no sufficient authority had been granted. In contrast, if the involvement of the third party is an active one – in particular in the case of the conclusion of a contract – the third party may *only* reject the contract if he, at the time of the conclusion of the contract, did not understand and under the circumstances could not have understood that insufficient authority had been granted.[65]

The rule that the third party may, in principle, withdraw from the transaction unilaterally has been criticised in the legal literature.[66] It is said that this rule leaves room for quibbling by the third party: he may reject the contract concerned merely because he has the opportunity to conclude a transaction elsewhere on more favourable terms. However, it has also been argued that the potential for such behaviour should not be overestimated. Strictly speaking, it may be argued, the third party's rejection is only permitted for 'want of authority'. Arguably, a rejection may therefore not take place merely because the third party wants to conclude a more favourable contract elsewhere. If such is the reason for rejecting the unauthorised contract, it may be argued that the rejection is null and void.[67]

The rule that the third party may, in principle, withdraw unilaterally has also been supported with the argument that in practice it happens too often that a party is unable to obtain certainty as to its legal position. According to that view, the last part of Art. 3:69(3) DCC sufficiently takes into account the principal's interests.[68] This is a welcome approach.

(b) A directly interested person can set a reasonable time for ratification

Article 3:69(4) DCC also tends to produce certainty for the third party. To the extent relevant here, it provides that a 'directly interested person' can

---

[65] Cf. *Parliamentary History Book 3, Part II*, pp. 281, 1182–3, 1187; Kortmann, *Vertegenwoordiging*, no. 85; Van Schaick, *Volmacht*, no. 45.

[66] See Kortmann, *Vertegenwoordiging*, no. 85; De Kluiver, 'Bekrachtiging', p. 74; Schoordijk, *Vermogensrecht*, p. 218–19.

[67] See Van Schaick, *Volmacht*, no. 45. It is also conceivable that this could lead to a refusal of the power to reject on the basis of reasonableness and fairness (*redelijkheid en billijkheid*), abuse of right (*misbruik van bevoegdheid*) or possibly to liability in damages towards the principal. See De Kluiver, 'Bekrachtiging', p. 74.

[68] See Van Schaick, *Volmacht*, no. 45.

determine a reasonable period for ratification by the supposed principal. 'Directly interested person' includes not only the third party, but also certain others, e.g. someone who purchased the principal's property from the third party. If ratification does not take place within a reasonable period, the power to ratify expires and the legal act concerned is *not* binding.[69]

Strictly speaking, Art. 3:69(4) DCC can only be applied in cases where it is *clear* to the third party that there is unauthorised agency. However, it seems fair to assume that this provision can be applied by way of analogy to cases where it is *unclear* whether there is unauthorised agency. The third party could then determine a reasonable period for the principal to declare whether he considers himself bound to the legal act performed by the agent.[70]

(c) Third party may refuse partial ratification

Third party T does not have to accept a partial or conditional ratification (Art. 3:69(4) DCC, second sentence). However, in the legal literature it has been argued that in certain circumstances T may be *obliged* to accept a partial or conditional ratification because of a duty to mitigate damage.[71] This seems a fair approach because even if the third party accepts a partial or conditional ratification, the unauthorised agent remains liable on the basis of Art. 3:70 DCC[72] (or in appropriate cases Art. 6:162 DCC) to the extent that the third party – notwithstanding a partial or conditional ratification by the principal – has suffered damage as a consequence of the unauthorised agency.

(d) Request for proof in writing of existence of the agent's authority

The rules outlined in (a), (b) and (c) above are not the only concepts which tend to produce legal certainty for the third party. Article 3:71 DCC also provides the third party with certainty in case there is doubt as to whether the agent has sufficient authority: a party may reject a declaration made by an agent as invalid, if he has forthwith asked the agent for proof of his authority and if he does not receive without delay

---

[69] See *Parliamentary History Book 3, Part I*, p. 281; Kortmann, *Vertegenwoordiging*, no. 90; Bloembergen/Van Schendel, *Rechtshandeling*, no. 109; Van Schaick, *Volmacht*, no. 46.
[70] See Kortmann, *Vertegenwoordiging*, no. 90.   [71] Van Schaick, *Volmacht*, no. 43.
[72] See, for an example of a conditional ratification combined with a liability of the *falsus procurator*, HR 28 March 1997, NJ 1997 (*Wisman* v. *Trijber*) (payment of 30,001 Dutch Guilders in exchange for a ratification), discussed in VI 4, below.

proof in writing of the agent's authority nor confirmation thereof by the principal (Art. 3:71(1) DCC). However, proof of the agent's authority cannot be required if: (1) the principal has informed the third party of the agent's authority; (2) it has been made public in a manner determined by law or by usage; or (3) if it results from an appointment known to the third party (Art. 3:71(2) DCC).[73]

In view of the fact that Art. 3:71 DCC is (like Art. 3:69 DCC on ratification) included in the title dealing with consensual agency, it applies directly only in the context of consensual agency. However, pursuant to the linking provision of Art. 3:78 DCC, *inter alia*, Art. 3:71 DCC may in principle be applied outside the context of consensual agency (e.g. in the context of authority pursuant to a statutory provision or judicial order and representation by a body of a legal person). In the legal literature it has been argued that the manner in which the agent can make it plausible that he has sufficient authority should depend on the nature of the agency relationship.[74]

Furthermore, in view of the fact that Art. 3:71 DCC is (again, like Art. 3:69 DCC on ratification) included in the book dealing with patrimonial law in general, it applies directly only to the performance of legal acts (such as the conclusion of contracts) in patrimonial law. However, pursuant to the linking provision of Art. 3:79 DCC, *inter alia*, Art. 3:71 DCC can in principle be applied to areas of the law other than patrimonial law, such as family law, procedural law and public law.[75]

5 Effect of ratification

(a) Retroactive effect

Ratification has retroactive effect, i.e. the legal act performed by the unauthorised agent has the same effect as if it had been performed by an authorised agent (see Art. 3:69(1) DCC).[76]

---

[73] See Kortmann, *Vertegenwoordiging*, no. 51; Bloembergen/Van Schendel, *Rechtshandeling*, no. 106; Van Schaick, *Volmacht*, no. 18.

[74] Cf. Kortmann, *Vertegenwoordiging*, no. 51; See generally on Art. 3:78 DCC: Kortmann, *Vertegenwoordiging*, no. 18; Bloembergen/Van Schendel, *Rechtshandeling*, no. 86; Van Schaick, *Volmacht*, no. 71.

[75] See generally on Art. 3:79 DCC: Kortmann, *Vertegenwoordiging*, no. 18; Bloembergen/Van Schendel, *Rechtshandeling*, no. 86; Van Schaick, *Volmacht*, no. 73.

[76] Cited in V 2, above. See *Parliamentary History Book 3, Part I*, p. 278. See also Kortmann, *Vertegenwoordiging*, no. 89; Bloembergen/Van Schendel, *Rechtshandeling*, no. 108; Van Schaick, *Volmacht*, no. 43.

(b) Rights granted to fourth parties prior to ratification are respected

Rights granted by the principal to 'fourth parties' (i.e. parties other than the principal, the agent and the third party) before ratification are respected (Art. 3:69(5) DCC). For example, an unauthorised agent A grants a right of pledge on a claim to third party T1 on a claim belonging to principal P. Thereafter, P grants a right of pledge on the same claim to third party T2 and subsequently ratifies the grant of pledge to T1. The right of pledge of T2 takes priority above the right of pledge of T1.[77]

(c) Position of acts which themselves could not have been effectively carried out at the time of ratification

During the debate of Art. 3:69 DCC in the Dutch Parliament, there was considerable discussion on whether ratification should have the desired effect if at the time of ratification the relevant legal act could no longer be performed validly. Some of the questions raised were: can the principal interrupt the limitation period if at the time of ratification the limitation period has already expired?; may the principal ratify the termination of a contract if at the time of ratification the term for termination has already expired?; or, in procedural law, may the principal ratify the unauthorised agent's taking a case on appeal, if at the time of ratification the term for appeal has already expired?

In the end, this possibility was accepted on the grounds that: (1) rights of 'fourth parties' (i.e. parties other than the principal, the agent and the third party) are sufficiently protected by Art. 3:69(5) DCC, which provides that rights granted by the principal to 'fourth parties' before ratification are respected; (2) the third party may, in principle, prevent ratification by rejecting the legal act concerned prior to ratification (Art. 3:69(3) DCC); and (3) the rule accords with Art. 15(6) of the Geneva Convention on Agency in the International Sale of Goods ('UAC').[78]

---

[77] See *Parliamentary History Book 3, Part I*, p. 278. See on Art. 3:69(5) DCC: Kortmann, *Vertegenwoordiging*, no. 89; Van Schaick, *Volmacht*, no. 43; Bloembergen/Van Schendel, *Rechtshandeling*, no. 109. Example taken from Kortmann, *Vertegenwoordiging*, no. 89.

[78] See *Parliamentary History Book 3, Part I*, p. 281; Kortmann, *Vertegenwoordiging*, no. 88; Van Schaick, *Volmacht*, no. 43. See further on Art. 3:69(3) and (5) DCC, sections V 4(a) and V 5(b), above, respectively. At the time of the debate on Art. 3:69 DCC in the Dutch Parliament, there was only a draft convention available, in which the relevant provision was to be found in Art. 28(3) UAC instead of in Art. 15(6) UAC. Art. 15(6) UAC states that: '[r]atification is effective notwithstanding that the act itself could not have been effectively carried out at the time of ratification.'

6 Act of ratification: requirements

Under Dutch law, there are few requirements to which the act of ratification is subject.

(a) No specific time limit

Apart from the general limitation period of twenty years (Art. 3:306 DCC), ratification is not subject to a specific time limit.[79] However, a directly interested person may set a reasonable time for ratification (Art. 3:69(4) DCC).[80]

(b) No particular form required

Since ratification (like the granting of an authority) is considered to be a legal act, it follows from Art. 3:37(1) DCC (concerning legal acts in general) that ratification can be enacted in any form, for example in writing or orally. However, where a particular formality is required for the granting of an authority to perform a legal act, the same formality applies to the ratification (Art. 3:69(2) DCC).

It also follows from Art. 3:37(1) DCC that ratification may be inferred from conduct, including the absence thereof. Ratification may also be apparent (Art. 3:35 DCC).[81] In practice, the line between ratification by conduct and apparent ratification is difficult to draw. (Apparent) ratification by conduct may, for example, arise where the principal pays the invoices relating to a contract concluded by an unauthorised agent.[82] (Apparent) ratification by absence of conduct arises where the principal remains silent when, in fact, he had a duty to inform the third party that he would not ratify the unauthorised act.[83]

---

[79] Art. 3:306 DCC reads as follows: 'Unless otherwise provided for by law, rights of action are prescribed on the expiry of twenty years.' Cf. Van Schaick, *Volmacht*, no. 43.

[80] See V 4(b), above.   [81] See V 1, above.

[82] See HR 20 May 1988, NJ 1988, 781 (*Smeets* v. *Kuyper*), on which see Busch, *Indirect Representation*, pp. 31–2. See, for other examples of (apparent) ratification by means of conduct: HR 12 March 1965, NJ 1965, 177, with annotation by GJS (*Zürich Versicherungsgesellschaft* v. *Eerste Rotterdamsche Maatschappij van Verzekering NV*); HR 15 January 1999, NJ 1999, 574 (*Amrosan Establishment* v. *Mickey Groen*). Compare also HR 11 April 1997, NJ 1997, 583, with annotation by Ma; JOR 1997/64, with annotation by H. J. de Kluiver (*Rabobank* v. *Hemmen*).

[83] See HR 13 January 1989, NJ 1989, 320 (*Gemeente Vianen* v. *Niemans Onroerend Goed BV*). See, on the form of ratification generally: Kortmann, *Vertegenwoordiging*, nos. 86 and 87; Bloembergen/Van Schendel, *Rechtshandeling*, no. 108; Van Schaick, *Volmacht*, no. 44.

As representation is possible in relation to legal acts in general, ratification may also be enacted through an authorised representative. This needs to be clearly distinguished from cases where the principal acts in such a manner that the reasonable impression arises on the side of the third party that the agent is authorised to ratify, where in fact he is not so authorised: that is a case of apparent authority in respect of ratification. I am not aware of any cases where such apparent authority in respect of ratification has been alleged, but it is perfectly conceivable.[84]

(c) Act of ratification must have been expressed *vis-à-vis* the third party

Authority can be granted by means of a notice addressed either to the agent or to the third party. Since ratification is not to be regarded as the subsequent granting of an authority (the act of ratification merely retroactively turns the invalid legal act performed by the unauthorised agent into a valid legal act), it is generally held that, in order to be effective, the act of ratification has to have reached the third party (Art. 3:37(3) DCC). Stated otherwise in the words of the Dutch Supreme Court, the act of ratification must have been expressed *vis-à-vis* the third party.[85]

(d) Capacity

For a valid ratification it is necessary that the principal would himself be able to perform the unauthorised act. Therefore, someone without legal capacity (a *handelingsonbekwame*), for example a minor, will not be able to ratify the unauthorised acts performed by his statutory representative.[86]

VI Liability of the *falsus procurator*

1 General

If neither the doctrine of apparent authority nor the doctrine of ratification applies, neither the principal nor the third party is bound or entitled

---

[84] Cf. Attorney-General Hartkamp (as he then was) in n. 3 of his conclusion regarding HR 15 January 1999, NJ 1999, 574 (*Amrosan Establishment* v. *Mickey Groen*).

[85] See Kortmann, *Vertegenwoordiging*, no. 84; Bloembergen/Van Schendel, *Rechtshandeling*, no. 108; Van Schaick, *Volmacht*, no. 43. See consideration 3 of HR 15 January 1999, NJ 1999, 574 (*Amrosan Establishment* v. *Mickey Groen*) in conjunction with no. 17 of the opinion of Advocate-General Hartkamp (as he then was); HR 27 June 1975, NJ 1976, 62 (*J Aldersma c.s.* v. *Bouwbedrijf de Wit BV*).

[86] See Kortmann, *Vertegenwoordiging*, no. 91.

under the contract (or other legal act) concluded by the unauthorised agent. In such cases, the third party can generally hold the unauthorised agent (the *falsus procurator*) liable for the damage which he has suffered as a consequence of the agent's lack of authority. This is only otherwise if: (1) the third party knew or should have known at the time of the conclusion of the contract (or the performance of another legal act) that the agent lacked sufficient authority; and (2) at the time of the conclusion of the contract (or the performance of another legal act) the agent fully disclosed the content of his insufficient authority to the third party. It can therefore be said that the doctrine of the liability of the *falsus procurator* aims to protect the reasonable beliefs of the third party.

During the debate in the Dutch Parliament, the Minister of Justice stated that the agent's liability is based on an implied warranty of authority entered into by the agent personally, i.e. on a unilateral legal act.[87] The practical relevance of the basis of the agent's liability becomes apparent in cases in which the agent lacks the capacity to perform legal acts (such as the conclusion of contracts), for instance because he is a minor. Where the agent's liability is the direct result of the operation of law, the agent will be unconditionally liable, whereas when one assumes that his liability is based on an implied warranty of authority, it may be annulled, for example on the basis of the agent's incapacity because he is a minor.[88]

According to some legal writers, the reasoning of the Minister of Justice is incorrect or at least artificial. According to these authors, it is preferable to consider the implied warranty of authority of the agent as an obligation arising by operation of law. However, according to these authors, the agent who is incapable of performing legal acts (for example a minor) should only be held liable if he acted tortiously. It should be noted that the mere fact that an agent acts without authority is in itself insufficient to establish a tort.[89]

2 Legal basis

Article 3:70 DCC specifically addresses the position of the *falsus procurator*. The provision reads as follows:

---

[87] See *Parliamentary History Book 3, Part I*, p. 283; see also Van Schaick, *Volmacht*, no. 47.

[88] See Art. 3:32(2) DCC: 'A legal act of an incapable person may be annulled. A unilateral legal act of an incapable person, however, is null where it is not addressed to one or more specifically determined persons.'

[89] See Kortmann, *Vertegenwoordiging*, no. 93; Bloembergen/Van Schendel, *Rechtshandeling*, no. 114. See further VI 3, below, *in fine*.

He who acts as agent warrants to the third party the existence and the extent of his authority, unless the third party knows or should have known that sufficient authority is lacking, or unless the agent has fully communicated the content of his authority to the third party.

3 Scope

Article 3:70 DCC on the position of the *falsus procurator* is included in Title 3 (Consensual agency, *Volmacht*) of Book 3 (Patrimonial law in general, *Vermogensrecht in het algemeen*) of the Dutch Civil Code.

In view of the fact that Art. 3:70 DCC is included in the title dealing with consensual agency, this provision directly only applies in the context of consensual agency. However, pursuant to the linking provision of Art. 3:78 DCC, *inter alia*, Art. 3:70 DCC on the position of the *falsus procurator* may in principle be applied outside the context of consensual agency (e.g. in the context of authority pursuant to a statutory provision or judicial order or in the context of representation by a body of a legal person).[90] Via that route, Art. 3:70 DCC can, for example, be applied to unauthorised representation by a body of a legal person.[91]

Furthermore, in view of the fact that Art. 3:70 DCC is included in the book dealing with patrimonial law in general, it applies directly only to the performance of legal acts (such as the conclusion of contracts) in patrimonial law. However, pursuant to the linking provision of Art. 3:79 DCC, *inter alia*, Art. 3:70 DCC can in principle be applied to areas of the law other than patrimonial law, such as family law, procedural law and public law.[92]

Article 3:76(2) DCC[93] deals with the liability of the unauthorised agent when an agent continues to conclude contracts in the name of

---

[90] Cf. Kortmann, *Vertegenwoordiging*, no. 98; Van Schaick, *Volmacht*, no. 71.

[91] See, for a recent example HR 28 March 1997, NJ 1997, 454 (*Wisman* v. *Trijber*), discussed in VI 4, below. On the subject of analogous application of Art. 3:70 DCC in the context of unauthorised representation by a body of a legal person, see De Kluiver, 'Bekrachtiging', p. 78. See generally on Art. 3:78 DCC: Kortmann, *Vertegenwoordiging*, no. 18; Bloembergen/Van Schendel, *Rechtshandeling*, no. 86; Van Schaick, *Volmacht*, nos. 71–2.

[92] See generally on Art. 3:79 DCC: Kortmann, *Vertegenwoordiging*, no. 18; Bloembergen/ Van Schendel, *Rechtshandeling*, no. 86; Van Schaick, *Volmacht*, no. 73.

[93] Art. 3:76(2) DCC reads as follows: 'An agent who continues to act in the name of the principal in the circumstances described in the preceding paragraph is liable to pay damages to the third party who did not know of the termination of the authority. The agent is not liable if he did not know nor ought to have known that his authority had terminated.'

his principal despite the fact that his authority has ended. Article 3:76(2) DCC is a *lex specialis* of Art. 3:70 DCC. It provides that an agent who continues to act in the name of the principal in the circumstances described in Art. 3:76(1) DCC[94] is liable in damages to the third party who had no *actual* knowledge of the termination of the agent's authority. In other words, the third party in such cases has no duty to investigate. The agent is not liable if the agent did not know nor should have known that his authority had been terminated.

Article 3:76(2) DCC differs from Art. 3:70 DCC. First, it differs to the disadvantage of the *falsus procurator*, because under Art. 3:76(2) DCC he is also liable in the case that it can be argued that the third party (had no actual knowledge, but) should have known of the agent's lack of authority. Second, it differs to the advantage of the *falsus procurator* in that he is not liable if he neither knew nor should have known that his authority had ended.[95]

In view of the fact that Art. 3:76(2) DCC is (like Art. 3:70 DCC) included in the title dealing with consensual agency, it applies directly only in the context of consensual agency. The linking provision of Art. 3:78 DCC does *not* state (as is the case with Art. 3:70 DCC) that Art. 3:76(2) DCC may in principle be applied outside the context of consensual agency (e.g. in the context of authority pursuant to a statutory provision or judicial order or in the context of representation by a body of a legal person).[96] However, it is nevertheless conceivable that Art. 3:76(2) can be applied by way of analogy in appropriate cases.

Furthermore, in view of the fact that Art. 3:76(2) DCC is (like Art. 3:69 DCC on ratification) included in the book dealing with patrimonial law in general, it directly only applies to the performance of legal acts (such

---

[94] The circumstances described in Art. 3:76(1) DCC can be summarised as follows: (1) cases where the third party shall be deemed to have received a communication, although the communication actually failed to reach him, and cases where the termination has been made public, but where the third party did not notice the publication of the termination of the agent's authority; (2) cases where the death of the principal is generally known (e.g. the death of a famous person whose death has been extensively publicised and/or broadcast); (3) situations where the appointment or employment that gave rise to the agent's authority has been terminated in a fashion apparent to third parties; (4) cases where the third party exclusively relied on the agent's statement that he was so authorised. In such case, the termination of this authority may always be invoked by the principal against the third party. See further IV 3, above.

[95] See *Parliamentary History Book 3, Part I*, p. 301. Cf. Kortmann, *Vertegenwoordiging*, no. 95; Bloembergen/Van Schendel, *Rechtshandeling*, no. 114; Van Schaick, *Volmacht*, no. 55.

[96] Cf. Kortmann, *Vertegenwoordiging*, no. 98. See generally on Art. 3:78 DCC: Kortmann, *ibid.*, no. 18; Bloembergen/Van Schendel, *Rechtshandeling*, no. 86; Van Schaick, *Volmacht*, no. 71.

as the conclusion of contracts) in patrimonial law. However, pursuant to the linking provision of Art. 3:79 DCC, *inter alia*, Art. 3:76(2) DCC can in principle be applied to areas of the law other than patrimonial law, such as family law, procedural law and public law.[97]

Depending on the circumstances, it may also be possible for the third party to found his action on tort (*onrechtmatige daad*; Art. 6:162 DCC[98]). In *Reisbureau De Globe* v. *Provincie Groningen*[99] the Dutch Supreme Court accepted this possibility, in particular when the agent acted as if he were the principal's authorised agent, while he knew or should have known that sufficient authority was lacking. The mere fact that the agent acted without authority is not sufficient for liability in tort.[100]

Finally, it should be noted that where a contractual relationship exists between the principal and the agent (e.g. a contract of employment (*arbeidsovereenkomst*) or a contract of mandate (*lastgeving*)), the principal may be vicariously liable for any torts committed by the agent (Arts. 6:170 and 6:171 DCC).[101]

4 Effect

The effect of Art. 3:70 DCC is not that the unauthorised agent himself becomes bound by the contract which he has purported to conclude in the name of the principal.[102] The unauthorised agent is merely liable

---

[97] See generally on Art. 3:79 DCC: Kortmann, *Vertegenwoordiging*, no. 18; Bloembergen/ Van Schendel, *Rechtshandeling*, no. 86; Van Schaick, *Volmacht*, no. 73.

[98] Art. 6:162 DCC reads as follows: '1. A person who commits an unlawful act against another which is attributable to him, must repair the damage suffered by the other in consequence thereof. 2. Except where there are grounds for justification, the following are deemed unlawful: the violation of a right and an act or omission breaching a duty imposed by law or a rule of unwritten law pertaining to proper social conduct. 3. A wrongdoer is responsible for the commission of an unlawful act if it is due to his fault or to a cause for which he is accountable in law or pursuant to generally accepted principles.'

[99] HR 31 January 1997, NJ 1998, 704, with annotation by CJHB; JOR 1997/47 with annotation by S. C. J. J. Kortmann.

[100] Kortmann, *Vertegenwoordiging*, no. 99; Bloembergen/Van Schendel, *Rechtshandeling*, no. 115a; Van Schaick, *Volmacht*, no. 49.

[101] Kortmann, *Vertegenwoordiging*, no. 99; Bloembergen/Van Schendel, *Rechtshandeling*, no. 115a; Van Schaick, *Volmacht*, no. 49; De Kluiver, 'Bekrachtiging', p. 79 (in relation to legal persons).

[102] But in exceptional cases the unauthorised agent *does* become bound. See, e.g., Art. 107 of the Dutch Commercial Code (*Wetboek van Koophandel*), which provides that the unauthorised agent himself is bound to a bill of exchange. Another example is Art. 8:262(2) DCC, in which it is provided that the captain of a ship binds himself where he

towards the third party for expectation damages (*positief contractsbelang*). Accordingly, the third party must be placed in the same financial position which he would have been in had the agent been sufficiently authorised.[103] It may be argued that the judge, at the request of the third party, may also award him compensation for his damage *in natura*, which can amount to specific performance. The Dutch Supreme Court has accepted this possibility in relation to tort law.[104] However, in most cases the facts of the case will not be suitable for this.[105]

The extent of the liability of the *falsus procurator* played a central part in the case *Wisman v. Trijber*.[106] In September 1990 Trijber bought half of the shares in International Litho Corporation BV ('ILC') from Renger Beheer BV ('RB') for a price of one Dutch Guilder. RB had been represented by Wisman, one of its managing directors, who was not authorised to represent RB on his own because he was only authorised to do so when acting jointly with the other managing director of RB. RB was only prepared to ratify the contract conditionally and in March 1991 Trijber and RB reached an agreement whereby Trijber bound himself to pay an amount of 30,001 Dutch Guilders in exchange for a ratification by RB. After Trijber had paid the amount, he sued Wisman for damages and claimed the additional amount of 30,000 Dutch Guilders as compensation for the damage he had suffered. The District Court rejected the claim and Trijber went up on appeal. The Court of Appeal accepted the claim. It ruled that it followed from the fact that Wisman had represented RB *vis-à-vis* Trijber without sufficient authority, that Wisman – who warranted his authority – was liable for the damage which Trijber had suffered as a consequence of Wisman's lack of authority. This damage consisted of the difference between the purchase price which Trijber

---

exceeds his authority. See further R. Zwitser, 'De aansprakelijkheid van de onbevoegde vertegenwoordiger naar Burgerlijk recht en Handelsrecht' (1999) *NTBR* 199, 202–4. See also VIII, below, regarding acting in the name of a principal yet to be named, and IX 4, below, regarding acting in the name of a company yet to be incorporated.

[103] See *Parliamentary History Book 3, Part I*, p. 283; HR 28 March 1997, NJ 1997 (*Wisman v. Trijber*); Kortmann, *Vertegenwoordiging*, no. 97; Bloembergen/Van Schendel, *Rechtshandeling*, no. 115; Van Schaick, *Volmacht*, no. 48.

[104] HR 17 November 1967, NJ 1968, 42 (*Pos v. Van den Bosch*). See also Art. 6:103 DCC: 'Reparation of damage is paid in money. Nevertheless, the judge may award reparation in a form other than the payment of a sum of money. Where such judgment is not executed within a reasonable period, the victim regains the right to demand reparation in money.'

[105] Cf. Kortmann, *Vertegenwoordiging*, no. 97; Bloembergen/Van Schendel, *Rechtshandeling*, no. 115.

[106] HR 28 March 1997, NJ 1997, 454.

agreed upon with Wisman (one Dutch Guilder) and the amount which
Trijber ultimately paid (30,001 Dutch Guilders), i.e. a total of 30,000
Dutch Guilders. Wisman appealed the decision to the Dutch Supreme
Court. The Dutch Supreme Court upheld the decision of the Court of
Appeal and ruled that it had rightly assumed that someone who concludes
a contract in the name of someone else warrants that he has sufficient
authority and that, if such authority is in fact lacking, the unauthorised
agent is obliged to compensate the third party for the damage he has
suffered as a consequence thereof. This damage includes the profit which
he would have received from the contract had it been valid.

5 Requirements

There are only a few requirements to which the liability of the
unauthorised agent is subject.

(a) Bad faith of the unauthorised agent not required

In order for the unauthorised agent to be liable towards the third party, it
is not required that the agent is in some way at fault. In cases where the
unauthorised agent did not know and could not reasonably have known
that he had insufficient authority, he can be held liable on the basis of
Art. 3:70 DCC.[107]

This is not the case if the agent continues to act in the name of the
principal despite the fact that his authority has ended in the circumstances described in Art. 3:76(1) DCC.[108] In the cases described there, the
agent is not liable in damages to the third party if the agent whose
authority has ended did not know and could not have known that his
authority had terminated (Art. 3:76(2) DCC).[109]

---

[107] Kortmann, *Vertegenwoordiging*, no. 92; Bloembergen/Van Schendel, *Rechtshandeling*, no. 114; Van Schaick, *Volmacht*, no. 47.

[108] The circumstances described in Art. 3:76(1) DCC can be summarised as follows: (1) cases where the third party shall be deemed to have received a communication, although the communication actually failed to reach him, and cases where the termina-tion has been made public, but where the third party did not notice the publication of the termination of the agent's authority. (2) cases where the death of the principal is generally known (e.g. the death of a famous person whose death has been extensively publicised and/or broadcast); (3) cases where the appointment or employment that gave rise to the agent's authority has been terminated in a fashion apparent to third parties; (4) cases where the third party exclusively relied on the agent's statement that he was so authorised. In such cases, the termination of this authority may always be invoked by the principal against the third party. See further IV 3, above.

[109] See VI 3, above.

Furthermore, in order for the unauthorised agent to be liable in damages on the basis of tort (Art. 6:162 DCC), it seems that it is required that he knows or should have known that sufficient authority was lacking. In any event, the mere fact that the agent acted without authority is not sufficient for liability in tort law.[110]

(b) Good faith of the third party required

The third party cannot claim damages on the basis of Art. 3:70 DCC if he knows or should know that sufficient authority is lacking or if the unauthorised agent has fully communicated the content of the authority to the third party (Art. 3:70 DCC, *in fine*).[111] The same rule probably applies if the third party wants to claim damages on the basis of the general tort provision of Art. 6:162 DCC.

The position is slightly different if the agent continues to act in the name of the principal despite the fact that his authority has ended in the circumstances described in Art. 3:76(1) DCC.[112] In the cases described there, the third party can also claim damages from the unauthorised agent if it can be argued that the third party should have known that the authority has ended, as long as he has no actual knowledge (Art. 3:76(2) DCC).[113] In other words, the third party in such cases has no duty to investigate.[114]

---

[110] Cf. HR 31 January 1997, NJ 1998, 704 (*Reisbureau De Globe* v. *Provincie Groningen*); JOR 1997/47 with annotation by S. C. J. J. Kortmann; Kortmann, *Vertegenwoordiging*, no. 99; Bloembergen/Van Schendel, *Rechtshandeling*, no. 115a; Van Schaick, *Volmacht*, no. 49.

[111] Cited in VI 2, above. Kortmann, *Vertegenwoordiging*, no. 94; Bloembergen/Van Schendel, *Rechtshandeling*, no. 114; Van Schaick, *Volmacht*, no. 50.

[112] The circumstances described in Art. 3:76(1) DCC can be summarised as follows: (1) cases where the third party shall be deemed to have received a communication, although the communication actually failed to reach him, and cases where the termination has been made public, but where the third party did not notice the publication of the termination of the agent's authority; (2) cases where the death of the principal is generally known (e.g. the death of a famous person whose death has been extensively publicised and/or broadcast); (3) cases where the appointment or employment that gave rise to the agent's authority has been terminated in a fashion apparent to third parties; (4) cases where the third party exclusively relied on the agent's statement that he was so authorised. In such cases, the termination of this authority may always be invoked by the principal against the third party. See further IV 3, above.

[113] See on Art. 3:76(2): VI 3, above.

[114] See *Parliamentary History, Book 3, Part I*, p. 300. Cf. Kortmann, *Vertegenwoordiging*, no. 60; Bloembergen/Van Schendel, *Rechtshandeling*, no. 114; Van Schaick, *Volmacht*, no. 55.

(c) Damage, causation, burden of proof

In order for the unauthorised agent to be liable, the third party must have suffered damage as a consequence of the agent's lack of authority in order to claim damages. The Dutch Supreme Court has ruled that the false agent is required to prove that the contract would *not* have been duly performed had the agent been duly authorised.[115]

VII The interrelationship between apparent authority, ratification and the liability of the *falsus procurator*

1 General

Now that I have dealt at some length with apparent authority, ratification and the liability of the *falsus procurator*, I will turn to consider the relationship between the three doctrines. Are they mutually exclusive or is it conceivable that they coincide in certain cases?

2 Apparent authority and ratification

In Dutch law, the doctrines of apparent authority and (apparent) ratification may coincide. This became apparent in the case of *Kuijpers* v. *Wijnveen*,[116] where in relation to both doctrines the Court of Appeal took into account circumstances which took place *after* the conclusion of the contract (in particular, not reacting to a confirmation of an order). According to the Dutch Supreme Court, the Court of Appeal was allowed to do so and the complaint that it did not distinguish between circumstances which could constitute grounds for apparent authority and those which could constitute (apparent) ratification was rejected:

> In many cases such a clear distinction cannot be made in practice and therefore the same circumstances may be taken into account in relation to both matters.[117]

---

[115] See HR 20 February 2004, NJ 2004, 254 (*Vreeswijk* v. *Van Heeckeren van Kill*); HR 8 October 2004, NJ 2006, 478, with annotation by Jac Hijma (*Arnold van de Kamp Makelaardij BV* v. *F. van der Veer Beleggingen BV*). Cf. Kortmann, *Vertegenwoordiging*, no. 93a; A. L. H. Ernes, 'De positie van de tussenpersoon jegens een derde: instaan voor bestaan en omvang van een volmacht' (2005) *NTHR* 73–80.

[116] HR 12 January 2001, NJ 2001, 157.

[117] *Ibid.*, considerations 3.4 and 3.6. See for the quotation consideration 3.6.

In other words: sometimes a third party will be able to invoke both apparent authority and (apparent) ratification on the basis of the same facts. It is submitted that the flexible, undogmatic approach adopted by the Dutch Supreme Court is to be welcomed because dogmatic distinctions should not hinder legal practice.[118] Furthermore, this approach is in line with the manner in which contracts are generally interpreted in the Netherlands. The Dutch Supreme Court has ruled many times that in order to ascertain the contents of a contract, the judge may also take into account circumstances taking place *after* the conclusion of the contract: e.g. the manner in which a contract is performed may be a relevant indication for what was actually contracted for.[119] It is also in line with the manner in which it is to be established whether someone has acted in the name of someone else or in his own name when concluding a contract, because circumstances which have taken place *after* the conclusion of the contract may also be taken into account (e.g. to whom is the invoice directed?).[120]

3 Apparent authority and liability of the falsus procurator

The doctrine of apparent authority and the liability of the *falsus procurator* are mutually exclusive; either there is a valid contract because third party T successfully invokes the doctrine of apparent authority, in which case T cannot successfully sue agent A for damages on the basis of Art. 3:70 DCC, or vice versa.

Since the doctrine of apparent authority exists for the benefit of the third party, he is *entitled* to invoke it but not *obliged* to do so if he does not wish to.[121] Therefore, third party T is generally entitled *not* to invoke

---

[118] In a similar vein: Bloembergen/Van Schendel, *Rechtshandeling*, no. 108.

[119] See, e.g.: HR 20 May 1994, NJ 1994, 574 (*NV Nederlandse Gasunie v. De Gemeente Anloo*); HR 3 March 1995, NJ 1995, 451 (*Erik van Rossum Makelaardij in Onroerende Zaken BV v. Van Erp*); HR 26 October 2001, JOR 2001, 275 (*Wm. H. Müller & Co. Nederland BV et al. v. Shipdock Amsterdam BV*). Cf. Asser-Hartkamp/Sieburgh, *Algemene leer der overeenkomsten*, no. 280; D. Busch, 'Uitleg van overeenkomsten' (2002) *NTBR* 410.

[120] See, in particular: HR 3 December 1971, NJ 1972, 117, with annotation by GJS (*Vermeesch v. Van Werven's Aannemingsbedrijf*); HR 20 May 1988, NJ 1988, 781 (*Smeets v. Kuyper*); HR 29 January 1993, NJ 1994, 172, with annotation by PvS (*Vermobo v. Van Rijswijk*); HR 10 January 1997, NJ 1998, 544, with annotation by CJHB (*Praktijkwaarnemer*). See Busch, *Indirect Representation*, pp. 30–2.

[121] See *Parliamentary History Book 3, Part I*, p. 176; *Parliamentary History Book 3*, Part II, p. 1184; Nieskens-Isphording and Van der Putt-Lauwers, *Derdenbescherming*, no. 6; Van Schaick, *Volmacht*, no. 51.

the doctrine of apparent authority and instead turn to agent A on the
basis of Art. 3:70 DCC (this may, for instance, be beneficial for T if P has
gone bankrupt). It is submitted that this may be different in cases where
it is *clear* that principal P wants to uphold the unauthorised contract,
because in such cases it will often be contrary to reasonableness and
fairness (*redelijkheid en billijkheid*) for the third party to take the position that P did not, in fact, grant A (sufficient) authority.[122] However, in
many cases it will *not* be clear that P is willing to uphold the contract,
which means that in most cases T will indeed be entitled to turn to A on
the basis of Art. 3:70 DCC.

4 Ratification and liability of the falsus procurator

If third party T withdraws from the transaction before ratification takes
place (Art. 3:69(3) DCC), agent A remains liable in damages on the basis
of Art. 3:70 DCC[123] or – in appropriate cases – on the basis of the general
tort provision of Art. 6:162 DCC.

After ratification, A will generally be freed from his liability pursuant
to Art. 3:70[124] or Art. 6:162 DCC. The reason is that, as a consequence of
the retroactive effect of ratification, T will not normally have suffered any
damage. This may be different in (at least) the following situations,
however.

In the first place, if the principal has granted rights to 'fourth parties'
(i.e. parties other than the principal, the agent and the third party) prior
to a ratification, these rights are respected (Art. 3:69(5) DCC). Therefore,
if the third party suffers damage as a consequence thereof, A remains
liable on the basis of Art. 3:70 DCC. For example, an unauthorised agent
A grants a right of pledge to third party T1 over a claim belonging to
principal P. Thereafter, P grants a right of pledge over the same claim to
third party T2 and subsequently ratifies the grant of pledge to T1. The
right of pledge of T2 takes priority above the right of pledge of T1.[125] If
T1 suffers any damage because his right of pledge ranks second instead of

---

[122] Cf. Kortmann, *Vertegenwoordiging*, no. 85.
[123] Van Schaick, *Volmacht*, no. 45; Cf. A. L. H. Ernes, *Onbevoegde vertegenwoordiging*
     (Deventer: Kluwer, 2000), pp. 204–5.
[124] Van Schaick, *Volmacht*, no. 43.
[125] Example taken from Kortmann, *Vertegenwoordiging*, no. 89, who does not use it in
     order to illustrate the possibility of a liability on the basis of Art. 3:70 DCC in spite of a
     ratification but merely as an example in which Art. 3:69(5) DCC can be applied.

first, A can be held liable on the basis of Art. 3:70 DCC or – in appropriate cases – Art. 6:162 DCC.

In the second place, third party T can reject a partial or conditional ratification (Art. 3:69(4) DCC), in which case agent A remains liable. As previously mentioned (see V 4(c), above), in the legal literature it is argued that, in certain circumstances, T may be *obliged* to accept a partial or conditional ratification because of his duty to mitigate damage.[126] This seems a fair approach because even if T accepts a partial or conditional ratification, the *falsus procurator* remains liable on the basis of Art. 3:70 DCC[127] (or in appropriate cases Art. 6:162 DCC) to the extent that the third party – notwithstanding a partial or conditional ratification by the principal – has suffered damage as a consequence of the unauthorised agency.

VIII Acting in the name of a principal yet to be named

A situation may occur in which an agent contracts in the name of a principal yet to be named. It is generally said that in such cases the agent leaves it open whether he will act for a principal or for himself. This situation is described in Art. 3:67 DCC. This provision obliges an agent who acts in the name of a principal yet to be named to disclose the identity of the principal within a reasonable period specified by law, contract, usage or, in the absence thereof, within a reasonable period (Art. 3:67(1) DCC). If he does not disclose the name of the principal in good time, he will be deemed to have entered into the contract for himself, unless the contract produces a different outcome (Art. 3:67(2) DCC).[128]

Where the identity of the principal is to be revealed later and the agent does not disclose the identity of the principal within a reasonable time, a situation *may* exist in which the agent still does not have a principal at the time when the contract is concluded. In such cases there is

---

[126] Van Schaick, *Volmacht*, no. 43.

[127] See, for an example of a conditional ratification combined with a liability of the *falsus procurator*, HR 28 March 1997, NJ 1997 (*Wisman* v. *Trijber*) (payment of 30,001 Dutch Guilders in exchange for a ratification), discussed in VI 4, above.

[128] On the subject of Art. 3:67 DCC, see Kortmann, *Vertegenwoordiging*, nos. 78 and 79; Bloembergen/Van Schendel, *Rechtshandeling*, no. 113; Van Schaick, *Volmacht*, nos. 32–5; Schoordijk, *Vermogensrecht*, pp. 215–17. See also HR 26 May 2000, NJ 2000, 442; AA (2000), 783–787, with annotation by S. C. J. J. Kortmann; JOR 2000/188 (*Weld-Equip* v. *Van de Pest*), in which it was provided that disclosure of the name of the principal within the meaning of Art. 3:67 DCC occurs only where disclosure is without reservation and the third party thus knows for certain the identity of the counterparty.

unauthorised agency. Exceptionally, in such cases of unauthorised agency, the third party can regard the agent as his contractual counterparty. This does not constitute a serious breach of the principle of autonomy. The third party is prepared to contract with a principal whose identity is not known to him at the time of the conclusion of the contract and is therefore evidently unconcerned about the identity of his contractual counterparty. There can, therefore, be no objection to the law providing that the agent is the counterparty in such cases.[129]

Art. 3:67 DCC is included in Title 3 (Consensual agency, *Volmacht*) of Book 3 (Patrimonial law in general, *Vermogensrecht in het algemeen*) of the Dutch Civil Code. In view of the fact that Art. 3:67 DCC is included in the title dealing with consensual agency, it applies directly only in the context of consensual agency. However, pursuant to the linking provision of Art. 3:78 DCC, Art. 3:67 DCC may in principle be applied outside the context of consensual agency (e.g. in the context of authority pursuant to a statutory provision or judicial order or in the context of representation by a body of a legal person).[130] Furthermore, in view of the fact that Art. 3:67 DCC is included in the book dealing with patrimonial law in general, it directly only applies to the performance of legal acts (such as the conclusion of contracts) in patrimonial law. However, according to Art. 3:79 DCC, *inter alia*, Art. 3:67 DCC can in principle be applied to areas of the law other than patrimonial law, such as family law, procedural law and public law.[131]

IX Acting in the name of a company yet to be incorporated

1 General

Article 7 of the First Directive for the Harmonisation of Company Law[132] obliged the member states of the European Union to introduce rules for the protection of third parties in the case of performance of legal acts

---

[129] See Busch, *Indirect Representation*, p. 21.

[130] See generally on Art. 3:78 DCC: Kortmann, *Vertegenwoordiging*, no. 18; Bloembergen/ Van Schendel, *Rechtshandeling*, no. 86; Van Schaick, *Volmacht*, no. 71.

[131] See generally on Art. 3:79 DCC: Kortmann, *Vertegenwoordiging*, no. 18; Bloembergen/ Van Schendel, *Rechtshandeling*, no. 86; Van Schaick, *Volmacht*, no. 73.

[132] First Council Directive 68/151/EEC of 9 March 1968 on coordination of safeguards which, for the protection of the interests of members and others, are required by member states of companies within the meaning of the second paragraph of Article 58 of the Treaty, with a view to making such safeguards equivalent throughout the Community, OJ 1968 No. L65, 14 March 1968, pp. 8–12.

(such as the conclusion of contracts) in the name of a company prior to its incorporation. In the Netherlands, this provision has been implemented in Art. 2:93 DCC (for *naamloze vennootschappen* or NVs, public limited liability companies) and Art. 2:203 DCC (for *besloten vennootschappen* or BVs, private limited liability companies). Articles 2:93 and 2:203 DCC can be regarded as a specific application of unauthorised agency.[133]

In section 2, below, I discuss the relationship between Arts. 2:93 and 2:203 DCC on the one hand and the doctrine of apparent authority on the other. I then turn, in sections 3 and 4, to the special rules which Arts. 2:93 and 2:203 DCC provide with respect to ratification and the liability of the *falsus procurator*. After that, I will examine, in section 5, the relationship between Arts. 2:93 and 2:203 DCC, on the one hand, and Art. 3:67 DCC with respect to acting in the name of a principal yet to be named, on the other. Finally, in section 6, I treat the question of whether the general provisions on unauthorised agency can be applied in cases which are similar (but not identical) to the case of acting in the name of a company yet to be incorporated.

2 Apparent authority

When someone acts in the name of a 'company yet to be incorporated', the third party usually knows (or at least *should* know) that the principal does not yet exist and that the agent is therefore unauthorised. This means that in most cases there cannot be an appearance of authority. In view of this, when an agent concludes a contract (or performs another legal act) in the name of a company yet to be incorporated, the third party will usually not be able successfully to invoke (an analogous application of) Art. 3:61(2) DCC on apparent authority.

3 Ratification

A company is, as a general rule, only bound by legal acts performed in its name prior to its incorporation if, after its incorporation, it expressly or

---

[133] See e.g. Advocate-General Hartkamp (as he then was) in his conclusion no. 8 to HR 24 January 1997, NJ 1997, 399, with annotation by Ma (*Stichting Diva*). Cf. also, *inter alia*, Hartkamp, 'Bekrachtiging', p. 132; H. C. F. Schoordijk, *Het handelen ten behoeve van de vennootschap in oprichting* (Ars Notariatus nr. 47) (Amsterdam: Stichting tot Bevordering der Notariële Wetenschap, 1990), nos. 18–25.

implicitly ratifies such legal acts (Arts. 2:93(1) and 2:203(1) DCC).[134] Articles 2:93(1) and 2:203(1) DCC can be regarded as a *lex specialis* in relation to Art. 3:69 DCC on ratification.[135]

4 *Liability of the* falsus procurator

Persons who perform a legal act in the name of a company yet to be incorporated shall – unless the contrary is expressly stipulated in respect of such legal act – be bound jointly and severally thereby until the company has ratified such legal act after its incorporation (Arts. 2:93(2) and 2:203(2) DCC).

Articles 2:93(2) and 2:203(2) DCC can be regarded as a *lex specialis* in relation to Art. 3:70 DCC on the position on the *falsus procurator*. There are important differences between Arts. 2:93(2) and 2:203(2) DCC, on the one hand, and Art. 3:70 DCC, on the other. First, in the cases covered by Art. 3:70 DCC, the third party can generally only claim damages from the unauthorised agent, whereas in the cases covered by Arts. 2:93(2) and 2:203(2) DCC, the third party may not only claim damages, but also claim specific performance from the unauthorised agent.[136] Second, a

---

[134] There are exceptions to this general rule. Pursuant to Arts. 2:93(4) and 2:203(4) DCC, the incorporators may bind the company in the deed of incorporation without any ratification being necessary by: (1) the issue of shares; (2) the acceptance of payments thereon; (3) the appointment of managing directors and members of the supervisory board; (4) the performance of any legal acts referred to in Arts. 2:94(1) and 2:204(1) DCC. Arts. 2:94(1) and 2:204(1) DCC mention legal acts: (a) pertaining to the subscription for shares whereby special obligations are imposed upon the (public or private) limited liability company (Arts. 2:94(1)(a)/2:204(1)(a) DCC); (b) pertaining to the acquisition of shares on a basis other than that on which a participation in the public limited liability company is offered to the public (Art. 2:94(1)(b) DCC); (c) purporting to confer an advantage on an incorporator of a (public or private) limited liability company or on a third person involved with the incorporation (Arts. 2:94(1)(c)/2:204(1)(b) DCC); (d) pertaining to a non-cash contribution (Arts. 2:94(1)(d)/2:204(1)(c) DCC). If an incorporator has not exercised sufficient care in respect of the legal acts mentioned under (1) – (4) (inclusive) above, however, Arts. 2:9 (regarding liability of managing directors towards the (public or private) limited liability company) and 2:138/2:248 (regarding liability of managing directors and shadow directors (*feitelijk beleidsbepalers*) towards the bankrupt estate of the (public or private) limited liability company) shall apply, *mutatis mutandis* (Arts. 2:93(4)/2:203(4) DCC).

[135] Cf. M. S. Koppert-Van Beek, *Handelen namens een op te richten vennootschap* (Deventer: Kluwer, 2003), p. 57.

[136] Cf. Koppert-Van Beek, *Handelen*, pp. 37–8. It is usually held that as soon as the third party claims specific performance from the unauthorised agent on the basis of Arts. 2:93(2) and 2:203(2) DCC, the unauthorised agent can claim specific performance from the third party. Cf. Koppert-Van Beek, *Handelen*, pp. 39–41, 45.

damages claim against the unauthorised agent on the basis of Art. 3:70 DCC is not possible if the third party at the time of the conclusion of the contract (or the performance of another legal act) knows (or at least should know) that the agent lacked sufficient authority. A third party who concludes a transaction with a company yet to be incorporated usually knows (or at least *should* know) that authority is lacking. Such a third party may nevertheless claim damages from the unauthorised agent on the basis of Arts. 2:93(2) and 2:203(2) DCC.[137]

5 Acting in the name of a principal yet to be named

Is it conceivable to apply Art. 3:67 DCC regarding the principal yet to be named to a legal act performed prior to the incorporation of a company which will later be named as the principal? A distinction should be made between two types of cases.

In the first type of case, the agent acts in the name of a principal yet to be named at a time that the company has not yet been incorporated. The agent mentions the company as the principal *after* it has been incorporated. In this type of case, Art. 3:67 DCC on the principal yet to be named applies. Articles 2:93 and 2:203 DCC on acting in the name of a company yet to be incorporated do not apply, because the agent never acted in the name of a company yet to be incorporated: not at the time of the performance of the legal act (at that time he acted in the name of a principal yet to be named) nor at the time the agent mentions the name of the principal (at that time the company has already been incorporated).[138]

In the second type of case, the agent also acts in the name of a principal yet to be named at a time that the company has not yet been

---

[137] Cf. Koppert-Van Beek, *Handelen*, p. 57. Moreover, if the (public or private) limited liability company does not perform its obligations arising from a legal act performed in its name prior to its incorporation *and which it subsequently has ratified*, the persons who acted in the name of the (public or private) limited liability company to be incorporated shall be jointly and severally liable for any loss suffered by a third party as a result thereof if they were aware, or could reasonably have been aware, that the (public or private) limited liability company could not perform its obligations, without prejudice to the liability of the directors in respect thereof on account of such ratification. If the (public or private) limited liability company is declared bankrupt within one year after its incorporation, such knowledge that the (public or private) limited liability company could not perform its obligations shall be presumed (Arts. 2:94(3)/ 2:204(3) DCC).

[138] Cf. Koppert-Van Beek, *Handelen*, pp. 61–2.

incorporated. However, in this second type of case, the principal mentions the name of the company as the principal *prior to* its incorporation. In this type of case, as soon as the agent mentions the company yet to be incorporated as the principal, Art. 3:67 DCC no longer applies: the agent acts in the name of a company yet to be incorporated, with the effect that the specific provisions of Art. 2:93 or Art. 2:203 DCC apply.[139]

6 Rabobank *v.* Hemmen

It follows from the above that in cases where the special provisions of Art. 2:93 or Art. 2:203 DCC apply, the general rules regarding unauthorised agency do not apply. However, the reverse is also true: if Art. 2:93 or Art. 2:203 DCC do not apply, the general rules regarding unauthorised agency can be applied. This may be illustrated by the case *Rabobank* v. *Hemmen*.[140]

The facts were as follows: W. Hof concluded in the name of Hemmen BV *i.o.* (*in oprichting*, yet to be incorporated) a credit facility with Rabobank, but Hemmen BV never was incorporated. Instead, an existing company acquired the name Hemmen BV due to an amendment of its articles of association. Hemmen BV subsequently went bankrupt. Between the trustee in bankruptcy of Hemmen BV and Rabobank the question arose whether Hemmen BV was allowed to ratify the acts which had been performed in the name of (the never incorporated) Hemmen BV *i.o.*

The Dutch Supreme Court ruled that analogous application of Art. 2:93 or Art. 2:203 DCC was, in this case,[141] not possible and that therefore the Court of Appeal should have investigated whether the general

---

[139] Cf. *ibid.*, pp. 60–2.

[140] HR 11 April 1997, NJ 1997, 583 with annotation by Ma; JOR 1997/64, with annotation by H. J. de Kluiver. See also on *Rabobank* v. *Hemmen* – extensively – P. van Schilfgaarde, 'Uitleg van rechtshandelingen' (1997) 6282 *WPNR* 587; (1997) 6283 *WPNR* 611, reprinted in *Peter van Schilfgaarde Select. Een bloemlezing uit zijn werk* (Uitgaven vanwege het Instituut voor Ondernemingsrecht, Rijksuniversiteit Groningen, nr. 35), (Deventer: Kluwer, 2000), pp. 385–408; V. van den Brink, 'Uitleg van rechtshandelingen of uitleg van gedingstukken', in H. J. van Kooten, L. Strikwerda, L. Timmerman and H. M. Wattendorff (eds.), *Hartkampvariaties. Opstellen aangeboden aan prof. mr. A. S. Hartkamp ter gelegenheid van zijn afscheid als procureur-generaal bij de Hoge Raad der Nederlanden* (Deventer: Kluwer, 2006), pp. 1–13.

[141] An analogous application of Arts. 2:93(1)/2:203(1) DCC *is* conceivable in the case of legal persons other than (public or private) limited liability companies which are finally incorporated. See HR 24 January 1997, NJ 1997, 399, with annotation by Ma (*Stichting Diva*).

rules of private law could be applied, in particular, the provisions regarding legal acts in general (Arts. 3:35 and 3:36 DCC) and the general provisions regarding consensual agency, including Art. 3:61 (2) DCC on apparent authority, 3:67 DCC on the principal yet to be named and 3:69 DCC on ratification.[142]

X Conclusion

It is submitted that the drafters of the 1992 Dutch Civil Code have succeeded in producing a modern and coherent set of rules regarding unauthorised agency. It can be derived from the many references in the Dutch parliamentary history to foreign legal systems and international (draft) conventions that the drafters have conducted comparative legal research.[143] This has no doubt enhanced the quality of their work. Despite the fact the rules regarding unauthorised agency have been enacted fairly recently, the legal literature (in its turn often inspired by comparative legal research) has not been hesitant in criticising the rules and has generally suggested a flexible attitude towards them. In addition, the Dutch Supreme Court has furthered legal development by applying the rules regarding unauthorised agency with considerable latitude. Let me provide three examples to substantiate these concluding observations.

First, according to the text of Art. 3:61(2) DCC on apparent authority, a reasonable belief of (sufficient) authority must have been created by the principal of his own doing. However, the legal literature has advocated that the third party is protected not only where the impression has been created by the principal but also where it is due to other circumstances that come within the ambit of the risks borne by the principal. The Dutch Supreme Court, in its turn, has adopted this approach in a number of its decisions, with equitable results.[144]

Second, the Dutch Supreme Court has rejected the idea that one must clearly distinguish between circumstances which could constitute

---

[142] A similar approach was already suggested by Hartkamp, 'Bekrachtiging', p. 132. Cf. De Kluiver, 'Bekrachtiging', pp. 80–1; Koppert-Van Beek, *Handelen*, pp. 55–7.

[143] See, on the influence of comparative law on Title 3 of Book 3 DCC regarding consensual agency: V. J. A. Sütö, 'De invloed van Meijers' rechtsvergelijkende expertise op zijn toelichting bij het ontwerp van volmacht 1954', in C. J. H. Jansen, M. van de Vrugt (eds.), *Recht en geschiedenis* (Nijmegen: Ars Aequi Libri, 1999), pp. 169–81. See, on the influence of comparative law on the DCC in general, V. J. A. Sütö, *Nieuw Vermogensrecht en rechtsvergelijking–reconstructie van een wetgevingsproces (1947–1961)* (Den Haag: Boom Juridische uitgevers, 2004).

[144] See IV 5(a).

grounds for apparent authority and those which could constitute (apparent) ratification, because in many cases such clear distinction cannot be made in practice and therefore the same circumstances may be taken into account in relation to both matters. This flexible, undogmatic approach is to be welcomed – dogmatic distinctions should not hinder legal practice.[145]

Third, inspired by the legal literature, the Dutch Supreme Court has accepted that, in cases in which the special provision regarding acting in the name of a company yet to be incorporated does not apply (for instance, because the company has never been incorporated), the general rules regarding unauthorised agency can be applied.[146]

It is hoped that the courts and the legal literature will continue treating the rules regarding unauthorised agency with latitude and that they will continue drawing on comparative legal research, which often points the way to legal development.

---

[145] See VII 2.   [146] See IX 6.

PART 2

The common law

6

Unauthorised agency in English law

CHENG-HAN TAN

Table of Contents

I Introduction[1]

Typically, an agency relationship arises when one party, known as the principal, authorises another, known as the agent, to act on the principal's behalf and the agent agrees to do so. The principal and agent relationship is therefore generally constituted by the mutual consent of the principal and the agent. They will be held to have consented if they have agreed to what amounts in law to such a relationship, even if they do not recognise it themselves and even if they have professed to disclaim it. The consent must, however, have been given by each of them, either expressly or by implication from their words and conduct.[2]

Where the principal and agent have given their consent to the agency relationship arising between them, the agent will have actual authority, within the scope of what has been agreed, to affect the principal's legal relations, usually by entering into a contract with a third party that will be binding on the principal. By this, commerce is facilitated, for it will often be difficult or inconvenient for a person or other entity engaged in business always to transact directly with the counterparty, particularly where the business undertaking is a large and complex one. Much day-to-day transacting will be facilitated by officers and employees of the business undertaking acting within the scope of the authority that has been conferred on them, whether expressly or by implication. By this, the law of agency in England is able to multiply the individual's legal personality in space[3] and even time,[4] the latter through the doctrine of ratification.

However, as the law of agency operates principally in the commercial realm where transactional certainty to the contracting parties is important, this has meant that it could not be limited only to cases where the agent has actual authority. If commercial transactions in the modern economy are to take place quickly and efficiently, and parties are to have reasonable faith in the enforceability of such transactions, any such limits would substantially increase the costs of transacting. Inquiries would have to be made and, in the case of corporations, formal resolutions may be required. This would significantly reduce the efficacy of allowing business undertakings to use agents. Additionally, in modern commerce

---

[1] The leading work on the law of Agency in England is F. M. B. Reynolds, *Bowstead & Reynolds on Agency*, 18th edn (London: Sweet & Maxwell, 2006).

[2] *Garnac Grain Co. Inc.* v. *HMF Faure & Fairclough Ltd* [1968] AC 1130 at 1137.

[3] P. H. Winfield, *Pollock's Principles of Contract*, 13th edn (London: Stevens & Sons, 1950), p. 45.

[4] W. Muller-Freienfels, 'Law of Agency' (1957) 6 *Am J Comp L* 165.

there is often a need to repose some degree of discretion to agents which they may exceed inadvertently, or agents could even in good faith knowingly exceed their authority. Where this occurs, the agent may be liable to the third party for misrepresentation or breach of the agent's warranty of authority. But this could be cold comfort to the third party, who will often prefer to look to the principal on the contract entered into, as this was what the third party had bargained for. Accordingly, unless there are circumstances where the law of agency will allow such contracts to be enforced, there is a danger that faith in the utility of agents will be severely undermined to the detriment of commercial convenience and the efficient operation of markets. If the law were such that there would never be any circumstances under which a principal would be bound by the unauthorised acts of its agent, a third party would always have to refer to the principal to be certain of entering into a binding transaction since a principal would be able to resile from an unauthorised contract entered into by its agent, no matter how reasonable it was objectively for the third party to have thought that the agent was properly authorised. The principal would also have less incentive to put in place procedures to ensure that its agents acted properly.[5]

At the same time, the fact that agents, who often have to negotiate and conclude contracts where circumstances are fluid, enter into unauthorised transactions does not mean that those transactions are not in the interests of their principals. Principals will often wish to have the benefit of the acts of their agents notwithstanding the lack of authority on the part of those agents. The law of agency should allow principals a means to do so provided this does not cause undue prejudice to the legitimate interests of third parties.

From this brief introduction, it may be seen that the law of agency has pragmatic and practical reasons for not ruling out the prospect that unauthorised acts by agents can have legal consequences on their principals. The utility of the law of agency would otherwise be severely diminished and any such absolute rule would also be unfair to third parties who reasonably believed the agent to be authorised and conducted their affairs on such a basis. As Steyn LJ put it, a theme that runs through the law of contract is that the reasonable expectations of honest men must be protected.[6] A similar theme enervates the law of agency,

---

[5] S. J. Stoljar, *The Law of Agency: Its History and Present Principles* (London: Sweet & Maxwell, 1961), pp. 29–30.

[6] *First Energy (UK) Ltd* v. *Hungarian International Bank Ltd* [1993] 2 Lloyd's Rep 194 at 196.

where there are many instances in which the legitimate interests of third parties and principals are protected notwithstanding the existence of unauthorised agency.

II Apparent authority

1 General

Apparent authority, or as it is sometimes also known, ostensible authority, is intended to protect the interests of third parties who reasonably believed that the agent was authorised. Where the agent was not so authorised, the principal is nevertheless bound. As its name suggests, apparent authority involves the appearance of authority, not the existence of it. Thus apparent authority can arise not only when an agent exceeds authority or the authority has been terminated, but also where a person who has never been an agent is allowed to appear as agent. Notwithstanding the absence of real authority, the agent may bind the principal where the third party has acted on the faith of such appearance of authority, usually by entering into a contract with the agent.[7] The doctrine is not an unqualified one; if there are no – or virtually no – limits on the circumstances under which an unauthorised agent can bind a principal, this will also severely undermine the law of agency, as business undertakings cannot then safely use agents to the same extent as is currently the case. The consequence will again be a significant increase in the costs of transacting. What the doctrine therefore does is to protect the interests of third parties to an extent that the law deems legitimate.[8]

2 Representation of authority

For apparent authority to be established, the principal must in some way have manifested to the third party that the agent had the power to enter into the transaction in question. The cases often speak of this manifestation as a representation by words or conduct from the principal to the

---

[7] Although the principal is bound *vis-à-vis* the third party, the agent who exceeds his or her authority may be liable to the principal for breach of duty.

[8] See also D. H. Bester, 'The Scope of an Agent's Power of Representation' (1972) 89 *SALJ* 49, 50; G. H. L. Fridman, *The Law of Agency*, 7th edn. (London: Butterworths, 1996), p. 121.

third party that the agent has authority.[9] This requirement for manifestation of authority from the principal ensures that the doctrine of apparent authority will not overreach because its application is ultimately subject to the voluntary acts of the principal itself, even if the principal may not fully appreciate the legal effect of such acts. What the principal is taken to have manifested should be determined objectively by recourse to all the surrounding circumstances and not subjectively either from the principal's or third party's point of view. The representation can be made expressly or by implication. The latter may arise where an agent is appointed to a position in which it is usual for someone in that position to have certain authority. The principal may have limited that authority but such limitation of authority may not be known to a third party dealing with the agent. Certainly, from the perspective of fairness, it can be appreciated that a principal who has in some way led the third party to believe that the agent had authority should take responsibility for the consequences of such acts.

Traditionally, the operative representation must be one of fact and not of law. However, this may require reconsideration in light of the decision of the House of Lords in *Kleinwort Benson Ltd* v. *Lincoln City Council*,[10] where recovery in restitution was permitted for money paid under a mistake of law. While *Kleinwort Benson* dealt with a quite different issue, it prompts reconsideration of all situations in which the distinction between law and fact arises.[11]

3 Representation must be made by the principal

It follows from the preceding point that a representation that the agent has authority cannot be made by the agent or some person other than the principal. The cases frequently stress that an agent cannot generally make representations as to what he is authorised to do.[12] If this were not the position, anyone with some nexus to the principal can claim to have authority to bind the principal and cause the principal to incur

---

[9] *Rama Corp. Ltd* v. *Proved Tin and General Investments Ltd* [1952] 2 QB 147 at 149–50; *Freeman & Lockyer (a firm)* v. *Buckhurst Park Properties (Mangal) Ltd* [1964] 2 QB 480 at 503–4; *Hely-Hutchinson* v. *Brayhead Ltd* [1968] 1 QB 549.

[10] [1999] 2 AC 349.   [11] Reynolds, *Bowstead and Reynolds on Agency*, 8-024.

[12] *Lanyon* v. *Blanchard* (1811) 2 Camp 597; *Attorney-General for Ceylon* v. *Silva* [1953] AC 461; *British Bank of the Middle East* v. *Sun Life Assurance Co. of Canada Ltd* [1983] 2 Lloyd's Rep 9; *Armagas Ltd* v. *Mundogas SA (The Ocean Frost)* [1986] AC 717; *Re Selectmove Ltd* [1995] 1 WLR 474.

obligations to a third party. Commercial undertakings would be forced to take extraordinary steps to attempt to inform all and sundry exactly what their employees could or could not do, often perhaps to no avail.

This is not to say that a principal cannot act in such a manner as to manifest to a third party that an agent has authority to represent what the authority of another agent is,[13] or as to the agent's own authority itself.[14] If, for example, a principal said to a third party that he was leaving an agent to negotiate a contract and that the agent would inform the third party of the parameters of the negotiations, a representation by the agent as to what he has authority to agree upon will be binding on the principal even if not in accordance with the principal's instructions to the agent. This is because such representations by the agent can be traced back to a representation of authority by the principal itself.

In this light, the decision of the Court of Appeal in *First Energy (UK) Ltd* v. *Hungarian International Bank Ltd*[15] appears to have gone too far and risks undermining well-established principles and the delicate balancing exercise posed by the need to protect third parties without unfairly binding principals to transactions that they did not authorise. In that case, the plaintiffs required credit facilities and entered into negotiations with the defendant bank. Virtually all the negotiations were with the senior manager of the bank's Manchester branch, who expressly informed the plaintiffs that he had no authority to sanction a facility nor did anybody from the bank later hold him out to have such authority. The negotiations were lengthy and reached an advanced stage to the point that a facility letter signed by a director and assistant director of the bank was sent to the plaintiffs. Although the plaintiffs countersigned the letter and returned it to the bank, it was accepted that this did not give rise to an agreement, as it was an express term of the facility letter that a contract would only come into existence if the bank signed and returned one of the copies that had been signed by the plaintiffs and the bank never did so. Notwithstanding this, the bank did enter into an *ad hoc* binding agreement in respect of a specific project that the plaintiffs wanted to undertake. Negotiations continued and the parties discussed another interim arrangement in respect of some new projects that

---

[13] *British Bank of the Middle East* v. *Sun Life Assurance Co. of Canada Ltd* [1983] 2 Lloyd's Rep 9.

[14] Reynolds, *Bowstead and Reynolds on Agency*, 8-022; *Soplex Wholesale Supplies Ltd and PS Refson & Co. Ltd* v. *Egyptian International Foreign Trade Co.* [1985] 2 Lloyd's Rep 36; *Armagas Ltd* v. *Mundogas SA* [1986] 1 AC 717 at 732, 777.

[15] [1993] 2 Lloyd's Rep 194.

the plaintiffs wanted to enter into. The senior manager sent three agreements to the plaintiffs, one in respect of each of the new projects that the plaintiffs had secured. These agreements were duly executed by the plaintiffs and returned to the bank. In the meantime, however, the bank had a change of mind and decided that it was no longer interested in the plaintiffs' business. This left the plaintiffs without financing and they commenced an action against the bank. It was held that although the senior manager of the branch was understood by the plaintiffs not to have authority to approve credit facilities and no one from the bank held him out as having any such authority, the senior manager had apparent authority to communicate to the plaintiffs that approval had been given for the credit facilities by those who had authority to make such decisions. Consequently, the bank was bound.

It is submitted that the correctness of *First Energy* is debatable.[16] Indeed, in *Habton Farms* v. *Christopher N. Nimmo*[17] the learned judge took the view that *First Energy* was a very special case on its own facts and that the Court of Appeal had not meant to override the principles set out by Robert Goff LJ in *Armagas Ltd* v. *Mundogas SA*.[18] If *First Energy* is correct, it should perhaps be limited to a banking context where bank officers are frequently required to obtain ultimate approval from their superiors and who then communicate the decision to potential borrowers. Furthermore, in *First Energy* there was a lengthy period of negotiations between the prospective borrower and the senior manager of the branch in which the senior manager was the principal means of communication for the bank's senior management.

As a matter of principle, it is possible that an agent who does not have apparent authority to enter into a transaction may have apparent authority to make representations of fact. However, in the absence of

---

[16] *First Energy* appears to have been applied in two cases, *DMA Financial Solutions Ltd* v. *Baan UK Ltd*, 2000 WL 1629568 (Ch D) and *Pharmed Medicare Private Ltd* v. *Univar Ltd* [2002] EWHC 690, where on appeal ([2002] EWCA Civ 1569) the Court of Appeal found that there was apparent authority (in the conventional sense) to contract, therefore making it unnecessary to determine the *First Energy* point. Neither case was one where the third party knew that the agent did not have the authority to enter into the transaction in question. See also *Biggs and another* v. *Sotnicks (a firm)* [2001] EWCA Civ 1356, where the Court of Appeal may have implicitly endorsed *First Energy*. *First Energy* has also been applied in Singapore in the case of *Hong Kong and Shanghai Banking Corp. Ltd* v. *Jurong Engineering Ltd* [2000] 2 SLR 54, where again there was no knowledge of any lack of authority on the part of the agent and accordingly any views as to the correctness of *First Energy* are *obiter dicta* only.
[17] 2002 WL 45310. [18] [1986] AC 717.

circumstances and facts analogous to those found in *First Energy*, if a third party knows that an agent does not have authority to enter into a transaction, it must generally follow that such an agent cannot bind his principal simply by later saying to the third party that the agent has since consulted with his principal who has now authorised the agent to enter into the transaction. If an agent could bind his principal through such a statement, the general rule that the representation must be made by the principal can be evaded all too easily. In *Armagas Ltd* v. *Mundogas SA* an argument to such effect was rejected by the Court of Appeal[19] and the House of Lords.[20] Similarly, the agent cannot, without some manifestation to such effect from the principal, have any apparent authority to communicate to the third party the principal's approval or agreement to the transaction.[21] Both approximate to the same thing and indeed the judgments in the Court of Appeal and the House of Lords in *Armagas* appear to treat as interchangeable a representation by the agent that the principal has now authorised the agent to enter into a transaction and a representation that the principal has approved the entering into of the transaction. Indeed, in the recent House of Lords decision in *Criterion Properties plc* v. *Stratford UK Properties LLC*, Lord Scott reiterated the point that apparent authority can only be relied upon by someone who does not know that the agent lacked authority.[22]

Closely related to the preceding discussion are situations where a person has authority only if certain facts are true or have occurred and the third party relies on that person's representation that such a state of affairs has indeed come to pass. In *United Bank of Kuwait* v. *Hammoud*[23] a solicitor who did not have actual authority to do so gave undertakings to third parties. In relation to one of the third parties, the solicitor represented that in the firm he was a salaried partner who would shortly be in control of funds belonging to a client and undertook to transfer those funds to the third party. Subsequently, while the solicitor was employed as an assistant solicitor in a different firm, a representation and undertaking of a similar nature was made to another third party. It was held that the firms were liable on the undertakings given, as the

---

[19] *Ibid.* at 730–5, 758–9.   [20] *Ibid.* at 779.

[21] See also American Law Institute, *Restatement of the Law, Third: Agency* (St Paul, MN: American Law Institute, 2006), § 2.03, comment *d*, where it is stated that if the agent tells the third party that a transaction is beyond the agent's authority, it is not reasonable for the third party to believe thereafter that the agent has such authority absent a credible change in circumstances.

[22] [2004] 1 WLR 1846 at 1856.   [23] [1988] 1 WLR 1051.

solicitor had apparent authority to give the undertakings. The result can be justified on the basis that an agent can have apparent authority to make representations of fact and such representations, when reasonably relied upon, can in appropriate circumstances give rise to apparent authority to bind the principal. Therefore, where a solicitor makes a representation of fact as well as giving an undertaking that is within the ordinary business of a solicitor, and this is relied upon by a third party, the firm will be bound. In *Hammoud* Lord Donaldson MR said that the banks, knowing that the solicitor was practising with established firms, were entitled to assume the truth of what he stated unless alerted to the fact that the contrary might be the case.[24]

The distinction between cases such as *Hammoud* and those where an agent effectively makes a representation as to his own authority may be a fine one but is nevertheless readily recognisable. While a representation made by an agent that the approval of the principal has since been sought and obtained is undoubtedly a representation of fact, it is ultimately a representation as to the agent's own authority. On the other hand, in relation to other representations of fact that may provide the basis upon which to find that the agent had apparent authority to bind the principal, not only must this representation of fact be one that the agent appears to have authority to make, but the underlying transaction itself must also be within the apparent authority of the agent.[25] In many cases, the two will be inextricably related. Whether the representation of fact is one that the third party is entitled to rely upon will depend on the circumstances. Many of the same rules that determine whether an agent has apparent authority to bind the principal will also apply to the issue of whether the agent had apparent authority to make the representation of fact in question. Where the necessary elements are present, the third party is entitled to act on the basis of the agent's representation of fact without further inquiry. However, where the transaction appears abnormal or there are other circumstances giving rise to suspicion, the third party should make such inquiries as ought reasonably to be made.[26] Where the agent is a professional person acting in such capacity, it may be easier to rely on representations of fact made by him. It is suggested that Lord Donaldson's remarks in *Hammoud* about solicitors' *prima facie* being

[24] *Ibid.* at 1067.
[25] *United Bank of Kuwait* v. *Hammoud* [1988] 1 WLR 1051; *Hirst* v. *Etherington* [1999] Lloyd's Rep PN 938; *JJ Coughlin Ltd* v. *Ruparelia* [2004] PNLR 4.
[26] See also II 4, below, on the issue of reliance by the third party.

persons of good character whose words are their bond and whose statements do not require the same degree of confirmation which might otherwise be appropriate in the case of statements made by others who are not members of so respected a profession, should be best understood in this broad context.[27]

4 Third party must have relied upon the representation

It is suggested that the doctrine of apparent authority exists to protect the legitimate expectations of third parties and as such the doctrine can only be invoked against a principal if the third party has in some way relied upon the representation made.[28] If the third party did not in any way rely on the representation by changing its position because of what the principal manifested, there is no basis for complaint.[29] The change of position will usually come about by the third party entering into a contract with the agent.

Accordingly, if the third party was ignorant of the representation made by the principal, no apparent authority can arise in the third party's favour.[30] In the same vein, if the third party did not know of the existence of a principal, the doctrine cannot apply. Thus apparent authority cannot arise against an undisclosed principal, since the third party deals with the agent believing that the agent is the sole contracting party. Similarly, if the third party did not believe that the agent had authority despite the appearance of authority[31] or the circumstances are such that the third party ought to have known of the lack of authority, there can be no reliance on any representation by the principal. In the past, this issue could have arisen in the context of companies if there were restrictions on the powers of agents in the company's constitutional documents of which the law regarded third parties as having constructive notice.[32] Today, the doctrine of constructive notice of the contents of a company's constitutional documents has been abolished.[33] In addition, s. 35A(1) of

---

[27] [1988] 1 WLR 1051 at 1066; and cf. *Hirst* v. *Etherington* [1999] Lloyd's Rep PN 938, where it is suggested that some of the *dicta* to this effect in *Hammoud* may go too far.

[28] *Freeman & Lockyer (a firm)* v. *Buckhurst Park Properties (Mangal) Ltd* [1964] 2 QB 480 at 503.

[29] *Ibid.* at 503; *Farquharson Bros & Co.* v. *C. King & Co.* [1902] AC 325.

[30] *Armagas Ltd* v. *Mundogas SA* [1986] AC 717 at 778.

[31] *Bloomenthal* v. *Ford* [1897] AC 156.

[32] *Mahony* v. *East Holyford Mining Co. Ltd* (1874–75) LR 7 HL 869.

[33] See Companies Act 1985, s. 711A(1).

the Companies Act 1985 provides that, in favour of a person dealing with a company in good faith, the power of the board of directors to bind the company, or authorise others to do so, shall be deemed to be free of any limitation under the company's constitution. As such, there is no longer any reason why apparent authority cannot exist simply because an agent of a company purports to enter into a transaction that is outside the scope of the company's constitution.[34]

Where an agent is acting within the usual authority of a person in his position, but the transaction appears abnormal or there are other circumstances giving rise to suspicion, the third party should make such inquiries as ought reasonably to be made to ensure that such authority as does exist is sufficient to bind the principal.[35] For if a person dealing with an agent knows or has reason to believe that the contract or transaction is contrary to the commercial interests of the agent's principal, it will be very difficult for that person to assert with any credibility that he believed the agent did have actual authority. Lack of such a belief would be fatal to a claim that the agent had apparent authority.[36]

This aside, the fact that the agent may have been acting fraudulently to benefit himself rather than his principal does not of itself mean that the principal is not bound if what the agent has done is within the scope of his apparent authority.[37] As long as the third party reasonably believed that the agent was acting properly, the third party is deserving of the law's protection.

5 Theoretical basis for apparent authority

It has been said that the theoretical underpinnings of apparent authority are shaky and in the long run may require reconsideration, and that

---

[34] Note should also be taken of s. 35(1) of the Companies Act 1985 (which will be replaced by s. 39(1) Companies Act 2006). This section states that the validity of an act done by a company shall not be called into question on the ground of lack of capacity by reason of anything in the company's memorandum. For this reason, it is suggested that the old common law rule that companies cannot ratify unauthorised acts of agents that are *ultra vires* should no longer apply as a general rule. The legislative amendments relating to the *ultra vires* doctrine were required to give effect to the First Council Directive 68/151/EEC of 9 March 1968 on coordination of safeguards which, for the protection of the interests of members and others, are required by member states of companies within the meaning of the second paragraph of Art. 58 of the Treaty, with a view to making such safeguards equivalent throughout the Community, OJ 1968 No. L65, 14 March 1968, pp. 8–12.

[35] *Hopkins* v. *TL Dallas Group Ltd* [2005] 1 BCLC 543.

[36] *Criterion Properties plc* v. *Stratford UK Properties LLC* [2004] 1 WLR 1846.

[37] *Lloyd* v. *Grace, Smith & Co.* [1912] AC 716; *Morris* v. *CW Martin & Sons Ltd* [1966] 1 QB 716.

there is much argument as to whether apparent authority should be regarded as being based on estoppel or not.[38] Lord Denning MR described estoppel as a principle of justice and of equity, and not a rule of evidence or a cause of action. It arises when a person, by his words or conduct, has led another to believe in a particular state of affairs. In such circumstances, the former will not be allowed to go back on what he has said or done when it would be unjust or inequitable for him to do so.[39] The doctrine of estoppel has developed in a number of different areas. For the purposes of this chapter, it is sufficient to state that while estoppel cannot be used as a cause of action, it may facilitate a successful claim to the extent that it prevents the other party from asserting or proving a fact that is inconsistent with the earlier words or conduct of that person.[40]

The main rival to the estoppel theory as the underlying basis for apparent authority is the objective theory of agency, which states that just as ordinary liability in contract is based on voluntary promises, a principal's liability in contract is based on the principal's voluntary representations to third parties concerning the scope of the agent's authority.[41] The estoppel view is the dominant one in England and much of the Commonwealth, while the objective theory view dominates in the United States.[42] In practical terms, it probably does not matter significantly which view is preferred. On either view, there must be some manifestation of authority moving from the principal from which either the principal is estopped or, alternatively, the principal is bound because liability should be determined objectively by what has been manifested

---

[38] Reynolds, *Bowstead and Reynolds on Agency*, 8-029.

[39] *Moorgate Mercantile Co Ltd* v. *Twitchings* [1976] QB 225 at 241.

[40] Thus, in the context of apparent authority, the third party sues on the contract entered into by the agent on behalf of his principal. The cause of action is founded on the contract and not the representation made by the principal. However, the principal is prevented from raising the agent's lack of authority as a defence and in the absence of some other reason to deny relief to the third party, the claim will succeed.

[41] W. W. Cook, 'Agency by Estoppel' (1905) *Colum L Rev* 536; W. W. Cook, 'Agency by Estoppel: A Reply' (1906) *Colum L Rev* 34; M. Conant, 'The Objective Theory of Agency: Apparent Authority and the Estoppel of Apparent Ownership' (1968) 47 *Neb L Rev* 678.

[42] See *Restatement (Third) of Agency*, § 2.03. If the objective theory rather than estoppel is taken as the basis for apparent authority, the absence of reliance on the part of the third party will not be fatal to an assertion of apparent authority. Nevertheless, since under US law a third party must reasonably believe that the agent has authority to act on behalf of the principal, establishing that the third party took an action as a result of the principal's manifestation may help to establish that the third party believed the manifestation to be true. See *Restatement (Third) of Agency*, § 2.03, comment e.

rather than what the principal subjectively intended. The only practical significance is that if estoppel is the basis for apparent authority, a principal who wishes to take the benefit of its agent's unauthorised acts must always ratify, since a cause of action cannot be founded on an estoppel. Ratification, which would be subject to limits, would not be necessary under the objective theory, since the legal consequences flow from what the parties have manifested.

The estoppel theory has, however, been criticised on two main grounds.[43] First, it is said that estoppel involves some change of position in reliance on a representation, the representation thereby preventing the representor from asserting otherwise. In the case of apparent authority, the change of position can be very small; for example, in the case of an executory contract, it has been argued that there is insufficient change of position because the contract remains unperformed and the third party may not yet have suffered any loss. The third party is neither bound nor is he estopped.[44] Secondly, it is said that the representation is permitted to be very general indeed, in that simply placing the agent in a position which carries usual authority[45] will suffice.[46] Thus, even when the third party may not be familiar with the extent of the powers of the kind of agent appointed to a particular position, such agent has apparent authority of that kind. Such persons must, of course, have believed that the manager did have the requisite authority.

It is suggested that these concerns should not overly trouble us. Unless the change of position is *de minimis*, which clearly it is not where the third party enters into a contract with the agent, there is no reason why the fact that the contract is executory should prevent an estoppel from arising. In any event, there will at least be a good many cases where the third party, by entering into the contract with the agent, has foregone another opportunity, thereby incurring a loss if the contract (though still executory) is not given effect. Owing to the need for commercial certainty, the general rule must be that if the third party has entered into the contract because of a manifestation by the principal, and it was reasonable for the third party to have done so in the circumstances, an estoppel

---

[43] Generally, see Reynolds, *Bowstead and Reynolds on Agency*, 8-029.

[44] Cook, 'Agency by Estoppel', 44–45. See also C. A. Wright, 'The American Law Institute's Restatement of Contracts and Agency' (1935) 1 *UTLJ* 17, 41–2; R. Powell, *The Law of Agency*, 2nd edn. (London: Pitman & Sons Ltd, 1961), p. 71.

[45] But which authority has been circumscribed by the principal without the knowledge of the third party.

[46] Reynolds, *Bowstead and Reynolds on Agency*, 8-029.

arises in the third party's favour.[47] Furthermore, since the principal may ratify the act of its agent within a reasonable time, the third party incurs a detriment in terms of the limits on the third party's freedom of action while the contract remains capable of ratification.

As to the fact that the representation is permitted to be very general, it has to be said that if an agent can have implied actual authority by virtue of being appointed to a particular position, there is no reason why such an act cannot amount to a sufficiently unequivocal representation which would support an estoppel. In cases of apparent authority that arise from being appointed to a particular position, the representation is a material one insofar as there is a common practice peculiar to a certain position that has been built up over a period of time. It has also been said that the doctrine of estoppel is one of the most flexible and useful in the armoury of the law and that the various types of estoppel are governed by a general principle, namely that when the parties to a transaction proceed on the basis of an underlying assumption engendered by the other, neither of them will be allowed to go back on the assumption when it would be unfair or unjust to do so.[48] Whether or not one agrees with that, it is undeniable that the doctrine is indeed a flexible one. Lord Goff has said that it is unconscionability which provides the link between them.[49] Whichever view is taken, it is suggested that there is little difficulty with regarding apparent authority as one form of estoppel unique within the law of agency.[50]

---

[47] See also American Law Institute, *Restatement of the Law, Second: Agency* (St Paul, MN: American Law Institute, 1958), § 8, comment *d*, where it is said that: 'it is not irrational to hold that merely entering into a contract is a change of position which would enable the third person to bring an action against the principal.'

[48] *Amalgamated Investment & Property Co. Ltd* v. *Texas Commerce International Bank Ltd* [1982] 2 QB 73 at 122, per Lord Denning MR; cited with apparent approval by Lord Bingham in *Johnson* v. *Gore Wood & Co. (a firm)* [2002] 2 AC 1 at 33, but see Lord Goff at 41, where he doubted if the many circumstances that are capable of giving rise to an estoppel can be accommodated within a single principle. See also *First National Bank plc* v. *Thomson* [1996] Ch 231 at 236.

[49] *Johnson* v. *Gore Wood & Co.* [2002] 2 AC 1 at 41.

[50] Admittedly though, some of the cases involving apparent authority to dispose of property create difficulties in the understanding of apparent authority as based on estoppel. Any discussion of this difficult issue is outside the scope of this chapter but a fuller discussion may be found in C.-H. Tan and H. Tjio, 'Rethinking Apparent Authority', in A. Tan and A. Sharom (eds.), *Developments in Singapore and Malaysia Law: Proceedings of the National University of Singapore – University of Malaya Centennial Law Symposia 2005* (Singapore: Marshall Cavendish, 2006), p. 50.

III Ratification

1 General

Ratification provides a means by which the principal can take the benefit of an agent's unauthorised acts. Ratification arises where the agent was initially unauthorised and the principal wishes to take the benefit of the agent's act. The principal can do so by adopting what its agent has done and by so doing will retrospectively clothe the agent with authority from the outset. The doctrine of ratification facilitates the utility of the law of agency because an agent who in the exercise of his discretion exceeds his authority can have his acts adopted if the principal wishes to affirm the agent's acts, albeit retrospectively. Aside from cases where agents have exercised their judgment in good faith in a fluid commercial environment to enter into a contract despite their lack of authority, the doctrine of ratification also provides a means to cure technical and minor defects in an agent's authority. The doctrine is thus an efficient one insofar as it reduces litigation over whether the agent has acted within authority or not. Where the third party disputes the agent's authority, the principal can put the matter right through the simple act of ratification. There is also not much harm to the third party insofar as the third party had originally given consent to the transaction. In a great many cases, the third party will not even be aware that the agent had not been clothed with authority and that ratification had taken place because there is no need to communicate the act of ratification to the third party. The third party will only be unhappy with ratification if the market has moved against it but there is no compelling reason why, as a general principle, a third party who finds itself bound to a contract because of ratification should be in a better position than any other contracting party. Similarly, the third party should not be placed in a worse position than other contracting parties because of ratification and, as such, ratification is subject to certain limits, some of which are principally intended to prevent unfairness to third parties.

Prior to any ratification, the third party is not bound by the contract entered into with the agent. Where the agent has apparent authority, however, the third party may enforce the contract against the principal. A principal who wishes to take the benefit of the contract must ratify and cannot rely on apparent authority since, under English law, the basis for apparent authority is estoppel, which cannot be used to found a cause of action. Until ratification takes place, the third party may also claim against the agent for breach of warranty of authority.[51]

2 Requirements for ratification

(a) What amounts to ratification

Ratification may be express or implied from conduct, for example taking delivery of goods ordered by an agent and making payment, or receiving the purchase money from an unauthorised sale made by an agent.[52] Although ratification is a unilateral act of the will and need not be communicated to the third party,[53] the conduct on the part of the principal must show unequivocally that the principal has affirmed the agent's acts. Often such conduct will take the form of the principal performing its obligations under the contract that the agent has entered into. On the other hand, simply re-taking possession of one's own property and exercising rights of ownership over such property may not amount to ratification.[54] In general, mere acquiescence or silence will also not amount to ratification but the circumstances may be such that acquiescence and silence can amount to ratification,[55] for example where the principal knows that it is being regarded by the third party as having accepted that the agent has not exceeded his authority and takes no step to dispute the agent's authority within a reasonable time.[56] Silence or inactivity may, in appropriate cases, also give rise to an estoppel against the principal which prevents him from saying that he has not ratified.[57]

A principal ratifying the act of its agent must ratify the act in its entirety. It is not permissible to ratify part of what the agent has done while disclaiming the rest.[58] That would cause the third party to become bound to a contract which differs from the one that was intended. In exceptional cases, however, it may be possible to ratify for one purpose

---

[51] See IV, below, on breach of warranty of authority.

[52] *Hunter v. Parker* (1840) 7 M & W 322.

[53] *Harrisons & Crossfield Ltd v. LNW Railway Co. Ltd* [1917] 2 KB 755 at 758; *Shell Co. of Australia Ltd v. NAT Shipping and Bagging Services Ltd (The Kilmun)* [1988] 2 Lloyd's Rep 1 at 11, 14.

[54] *Forman & Co. Pty Ltd v. The Liddesdale* [1900] AC 190.

[55] *De Bussche v. Alt* (1878) 8 Ch D 286 at 312–13; *Bank Melli Iran v. Barclays Bank (Dominion, Colonial and Overseas)* [1951] 2 Lloyd's Rep 367.

[56] *Suncorp Insurance & Finance v. Milano Assicurazioni SpA* [1993] 2 Lloyd's Rep 225 at 241.

[57] Reynolds, *Bowstead and Reynolds on Agency*, 2-075.

[58] *Smith v. Henniker-Major & Co.* [2003] Ch 182.

but not for another, as in *Harrisons & Crossfield Ltd* v. *LNW Railway Co. Ltd.*[59] In that case an employee of the railway company who was on sick leave presented himself in uniform and stole goods that the railway company had been asked to carry. The railway company prosecuted its employee for larceny and for this purpose adopted the employee's possession of the goods. In an action by the owner of the goods against the railway company for breach of duty as common carriers, it was held that, notwithstanding the railway company's adoption of its employee's possession of the stolen goods, there was no ratification of the contract of carriage and only a ratification of the employee's possession to the minimum extent necessary to allow the railway company to prosecute its employee for larceny.

(b) Knowledge of circumstances

For ratification to be effective, the principal must have full knowledge of the agent's unauthorised act.[60] This rule is necessary for the reasonable protection of the principal.[61] Nevertheless, it should not be taken too far. From the third party's standpoint, the third party will usually not be in a position to know the extent of the principal's knowledge of what the agent has done. It would therefore be most unsatisfactory if the principal, having ratified, could easily repudiate what it had adopted because of a lack of full knowledge on its part. Accordingly, the rule is balanced by another, namely that if the principal chooses to ratify knowing that he does not have exact knowledge of what the agent has done, the ratification is valid as the principal in such circumstances must be taken to have borne the risk of imperfect knowledge.[62] All the circumstances of the case will have to be taken into account in determining which rule applies.

(c) Agent must have purported to act on behalf of the person ratifying

For ratification to take place, the agent must have purported to act on behalf of the person ratifying. This means that the only person who can ratify the unauthorised acts is the person on whose behalf the agent has acted. Thus a principal can ratify even though the agent actually intended

---

[59] [1917] 2 KB 755.
[60] *Lewis* v. *Read* (1845) 13 M & W 834; *De Bussche* v. *Alt* (1878) 8 Ch D 286 at 313.
[61] Reynolds, *Bowstead and Reynolds on Agency*, 2-068.
[62] *Haseler* v. *Lemoyne* (1858) 23 LJCP 103.

to act for himself, although using the principal's name.[63] On the other hand, an undisclosed principal cannot ratify the unauthorised acts of its agent, since in undisclosed agency the existence of the principal is not known and the agent purports to contract in his own name.[64] This is to be contrasted with the unnamed but ascertainable principal who can ratify.[65]

While it may seem strange at first glance that the common law should allow undisclosed principals to intervene on a contract where the agent has acted within the scope of actual authority but not allow undisclosed principals to ratify, it is suggested that the position is amply justifiable. When a third party enters into an ordinary commercial contract with an agent, the third party is generally willing to treat as a party to the contract anyone on whose behalf the agent may have been authorised to contract, whether the existence of such a person is disclosed to the third party or not.[66] It has been suggested, therefore, that when the third party contracts with the agent, although the fact that the agent is acting for a principal is unknown to the third party, the latter agrees implicitly that he is contracting with the agent *and* the agent's principal, should there be one.[67] The third party therefore impliedly contracts with the agent as well as the agent's undisclosed principal from the outset. This is because, in ordinary commercial contracts, it is usually a matter of indifference to the third party whether there is an undisclosed principal or not.[68]

If the legal relationship between the undisclosed principal and the third party is to be accounted for on the basis of an implied contract, the reason why the undisclosed principal cannot ratify a contract entered into by the unauthorised agent becomes readily explicable.[69] If the agent was unauthorised, no implied contract could have arisen between the undisclosed principal and the third party at the time the agent contracted personally. The agent would be the sole contracting party and to allow ratification subsequently to take place would be inconsistent with the

---

[63] *Re Tiedemann and Ledermann Frères* [1899] 2 QB 66.

[64] *Keighley, Maxsted & Co.* v. *Durant* [1901] AC 240.

[65] *National Oilwell (UK) Ltd* v. *Davy Offshore Ltd* [1993] 2 Lloyd's Rep 582 at 592–7; see also F. M. B. Reynolds, 'Some Agency Problems in Insurance Law', in F. D. Rose (ed.), *Consensus ad Idem: Essays in the Law of Contract in Honour of Guenter Treitel* (London: Sweet & Maxwell, 1996), p. 77.

[66] *Teheran-Europe Co. Ltd* v. *ST Belton (Tractors) Ltd* [1968] 2 QB 545 at 555.

[67] C.-H. Tan, 'Undisclosed Principals and Contract' (2004) 120 *LQR* 480.

[68] *Keighley, Maxsted & Co.* v. *Durant* [1901] AC 240 at 261.

[69] See, however, *Restatement (Third) of Agency*, § 4.03, which does not limit ratification to situations of disclosed agency. This is contrary to the rule stated in *Restatement (Second) of Agency*, § 85(1).

contract entered into with the third party. This is unlike the case where the agent was authorised and the implied contract between the undisclosed principal and the third party arose at the same time as the contract between the agent and the third party. To allow ratification where the agent for the undisclosed principal was not authorised at the outset would be to effect a modification of the existing contractual relationship which would require fresh consideration.[70] In disclosed agency this problem does not arise. The agent purports to act for the principal and is clearly not a party to the contract. Fresh consideration is therefore unnecessary.[71]

(d) Principal must have been in existence at the time when the act was done

This rule is relevant largely in the context of companies where promoters of a company seek to enter into transactions on behalf of the company before it is properly incorporated. In the case of *Kelner* v. *Baxter*,[72] it was held that the company, when formed, could not ratify the transaction. The agent, insofar as he or she was acting on behalf of the company, would be personally liable for breach of warranty of authority, misrepresentation, or possibly on an implied contract, though it has been held that no liability arises where a person signs as the company.[73] The position is now governed by s. 36C of the Companies Act 1985, which provides that a contract purporting to be made by or on behalf of a non-existent company will, subject to any agreement to the contrary, be binding on the person purporting to act for the company or as agent for it, and such person is accordingly personally liable on the contract.[74] It

---

[70] English law requires a promise to be supported by consideration from the promisee. A promise unsupported by consideration is not enforceable at law. In general, consideration is usually described as the giving of something of value in return for the promise. This may be a benefit that the promisee confers on the promisor, or a detriment incurred by the promisee for the promise. The benefit or detriment must not, as a general rule, be something that the promisee is already obliged to confer or incur as the case may be. Thus, where there is an existing contractual relationship, both parties are already bound to fulfil the obligations agreed upon and any modification of the contract in favour of one of the parties must be supported by fresh consideration from that party to support the modification.

[71] Tan, 'Undisclosed Principals', p. 505.   [72] (1866) LR 2 CP 174.

[73] *Newborne* v. *Sensolid (Great Britain) Ltd* [1954] 1 QB 45.

[74] This provision was enacted to give effect to the First Council Directive 68/151/EEC of 9 March 1968 on coordination of safeguards which, for the protection of the interests of members and others, are required by member states of companies within the meaning of the second paragraph of Art. 58 of the Treaty, with a view to making such safeguards equivalent throughout the Community, OJ 1968 No. L65, 14 March 1968, pp. 8–12. It is soon to be replaced by s. 51(1) of the Companies Act 2006. See also Chapter 9, (Scotland) III 5(c)(i).

has been held that such person may also sue on the contract.[75] There is as yet no legislation in England equivalent to that found in some Commonwealth jurisdictions which allows a company when it comes into existence to ratify an act done on its behalf prior to incorporation.[76] In England ratification is not possible, and the company is required to enter into an entirely new contract.[77]

3 Effect of ratification

The effect of ratification is to clothe the agent with authority from the outset of the transaction in question. The contract entered into is therefore treated as valid from its inception and all the parties will derive rights and obligations accordingly. In general, this will mean that any breach of duty on the part of the agent will be waived by the principal since the principal has seen it fit to adopt its agent's acts. Similarly, the agent will, *prima facie*, be entitled to remuneration or indemnification in the usual manner. This, however, presupposes that the principal has ratified the agent's acts free of any constraints. By this is not meant that the principal did not ratify with full knowledge; rather the principal may have ratified with a view to preserving its commercial reputation or as a matter of business necessity to avoid losing a major customer or supplier. In such circumstances, a distinction may be drawn between the 'external' and 'internal' aspects of agency. The principal is bound by its ratification to perform the contract with the third party, but may continue to hold the agent liable for breach of duty with all the consequences that follow.[78] For a principal to effect a 'limited' ratification of this nature will require the principal to establish that, but for such constraints on the principal's freedom, it would not have ratified the agent's acts.

Rather controversially, however, in *Bolton Partners* v. *Lambert*[79] it was held that the retrospective nature of ratification prevented the third party from validly withdrawing his offer before the principal's affirmation of the agent's act. In that case, the third party had made an offer to the managing director of the principal. The managing director was not authorised to accept the offer but did so on behalf of the principal. The

---

[75] *Braymist Ltd* v. *Wise Finance Co. Ltd* [2002] Ch 273.
[76] E.g., see s. 41 of the Singapore Companies Act.
[77] S. Mayson, D. French and C. Ryan, *Mayson French and Ryan on Company Law*, 24th edn (Oxford: Oxford University Press, 2007), pp. 597–8.
[78] *Suncorp Insurance and Finance* v. *Milano Assicurazioni SpA* [1993] 2 Lloyd's Rep 225 at 235.
[79] (1889) 41 Ch D 295.

third party later purported to withdraw his offer, after which the principal ratified its managing director's acceptance. As ratification operated retrospectively and conferred authority on the agent from the outset, the purported withdrawal was held ineffective. The principal was therefore entitled to specific performance of the contract.

Bolton Partners v. *Lambert* has been severely criticised by academic commentators.[80] The retrospective effect of ratification need not have been extended to cases where the third party has withdrawn from the transaction prior to ratification. It could have been validly held in such circumstances that, upon withdrawal, nothing remains for any ratification to have any effect. In *Fleming* v. *Bank of New Zealand* the Privy Council reserved the right to reconsider it should it become necessary to do so and Lord Lindley, who was one of the judges in *Bolton Partners* and who delivered the judgment in *Fleming*, said there that *Bolton Partners* 'presents difficulties'.[81]

Bolton Partners is in fact difficult to reconcile with two earlier cases, *Kidderminster Corporation* v. *Hardwick*[82] and *Walter* v. *James*.[83] In the former, two of the three judges expressed the view that, even if the principal's act amounted to a ratification, it had come too late, as it had taken place after the withdrawal from the contract by the defendant.[84] In *Walter* v. *James*, the agent and the third party agreed to cancel the transaction and it was held that no ratification could take place thereafter. If ratification may be prevented by the agreement of the agent and the third party to undo the transaction, this must surely be on the basis that there did not exist a concluded contract until affirmation on the part of the principal. It cannot be that the purported agent had any authority to rescind the contract. If the agent was not authorised to enter into the original transaction, the agent will also generally have no authority to withdraw from it, or to assent to the termination of the transaction. As it is the absence of a valid concluded contract that must ultimately justify the result in *Walter* v. *James*, it is difficult to see how it can be easily reconciled with *Bolton Partners*.

Nevertheless, for all the reservations against *Bolton Partners*, it has stood for more than a hundred years. In *Presentaciones Musicales*

---

[80] See, e.g., E. Wambaugh, 'A Problem as to Ratification' (1895) 9 *Harv L Rev* 60; T. G. Pappas, 'Rescission by Third Party Prior to Principal's Ratification of Agent's Unauthorized Action' (1948) 2 *Vand L Rev* 100; E. Fry (ed. G. R. Northcote), *A Treatise on the Specific Performance of Contracts*, 6th edn (London: Stevens, 1921), Additional Note A.

[81] [1900] AC 577 at 587.   [82] (1873) LR 9 Exch 13.   [83] (1871) LR 6 Exch 124.

[84] (1873) LR 9 Exch 13 at 22–3, *per* Kelly CB and Pigott B.

SA v. *Secunda* Dillon LJ said that overruling *Bolton Partners* was not a course open to the Court of Appeal.[85] As such, *Bolton Partners* will be regarded as good law unless overturned by the House of Lords.

Bolton Partners does not apply where the agent enters into the contract 'subject to ratification'. Where such a phrase is used, it is clear to the third party that the agent has no authority and the agent must seek the approval of the principal. There is thus to the third party's mind clearly no contract, nor has the agent incurred any liability under any warranty of authority which would be the case where the phrase was not used. As such, a contract made subject to ratification is no more binding on the other party than an unaccepted offer which can at any time be withdrawn before acceptance.[86]

The rule in *Bolton Partners* can potentially cause great injustice to third parties. If an agent is unauthorised and there is also no apparent authority, neither the principal nor the third party will be bound at the outset. However, the third party may potentially be bound at the discretion of the principal. This can place the third party in an invidious position because the risk of market movements will fall solely on the third party, since the principal will only ratify if it makes commercial sense to do so. What is unjust to the third party is not that he will be held to what has been agreed but that the very existence of an enforceable contract is a matter which is solely within the control of the principal with the attendant loss of commercial certainty that this places on third parties. As such, if there were no limits on the ability of the principal to ratify, third parties would potentially be taking a significant risk if they contracted with an agent without being absolutely certain that the agent was properly authorised. Some of the limits to ratification have been developed by the courts to mitigate this very risk that third parties are exposed to.

4 Limits to ratification

(a) Principal must ratify in time

There are numerous statements to the effect that ratification must take place within a reasonable time and what constitutes a reasonable time

[85] [1994] Ch 271 at 280.

[86] *Watson* v. *Davies* [1931] 1 Ch 455; *Warehousing & Forwarding Co. of East Africa Ltd* v. *Jafferali & Sons Ltd* [1964] AC 1.

will depend on all the circumstances.[87] It is also often said that where a time limit is fixed for the doing of an act, ratification cannot be allowed to take place after such time because this will have the effect of lengthening the time for the doing of the act in question.[88] Thus, in *Dibbins* v. *Dibbins*,[89] it was held that no ratification could take place after the time provided for the exercise of the option.

Notwithstanding these general principles, it has been held that where proceedings have been commenced without authority, ratification of such proceedings may be effective even if ratification has taken place after the expiration of any limitation period.[90] The basis for this decision poses doctrinal difficulties. The majority justified their decision on two grounds. First, it was said that the writ filed was not a nullity. Secondly, reliance was placed on the case of *Pontin* v. *Wood*,[91] where an action had been commenced within the limitation period. However, the writ was defective because the indorsement did not sufficiently particularise the cause of action. This could be cured by further pleadings, the filing of which did not require the leave of the court. As the writ was not a nullity, the defect could be cured by the filing of a statement of claim even though the limitation period in respect of the intended cause of action had expired before the statement of claim was filed.

Neither ground is really convincing. It is difficult to see how the question of nullity is relevant to the issue of whether ratification had taken place on a timely basis. As will be discussed below, an act that is a nullity cannot be ratified. Since this is a distinct ground on which to refuse ratification, the limits on ratification that relate to time should not be conditional on whether the writ was a nullity or not since all acts that are nullities can never be ratified in any event.[92]

As for the case of *Pontin* v. *Wood*, no issue of ratification arose as it was not a case involving a writ that was filed without authority. What was in issue was whether the writ could be set aside because of a procedural defect that was not remedied within the limitation period. It is submitted that there is a world of difference between the *Pontin* and *Secunda* cases. Procedural defects are generally curable, particularly where the leave of

---

[87] *Metropolitan Asylums Board* v. *Kingham & Sons* (1890) 6 TLR 217 at 218; *Re Portuguese Consolidated Copper Mines Ltd* (1890) 45 Ch D 16.

[88] *Ainsworth* v. *Creeke* (1868) LR 4 CP 476; *Dibbins* v. *Dibbins* [1896] 2 Ch 348; *Presentaciones Musicales SA* v. *Secunda* [1994] Ch 271 at 279.

[89] [1896] 2 Ch 348.   [90] *Presentaciones Musicales SA* v. *Secunda* [1994] Ch 271.

[91] [1962] 1 QB 594.

[92] C.-H. Tan, 'The Principle in *Bird* v. *Brown* Revisited' (2001) 117 *LQR* 626, 641–3.

the court is not required. In *Secunda*, the action had not been properly commenced for lack of authority. To allow ratification after the expiry of the limitation period effectively extends the time for the claimant to authorise the commencement of proceedings. It is therefore difficult to see what the distinction is between *Secunda* and the other cases where it was held that a time limit fixed for the doing of an act could not be extended by ratification.[93]

Presentaciones Musicales v. *Secunda* has been followed in *Smith* v. *Henniker-Major & Co.*, where the Court of Appeal stated that the *Secunda* case was binding on the court to the effect that ratification of proceedings is not automatically barred after the expiration of the limitation period.[94] The crucial element is whether the ratification will cause any unfair prejudice to the third party.[95] In this regard, it is difficult to see why there would not in general be unfair prejudice to a third party if a principal was allowed to ratify an action begun without authority after the limitation period has expired. Allowing ratification in such cases effectively extends the time for the claimant to authorise the commencement of proceedings and would appear to be contrary to the policy behind the Limitation Act 1980.

One possible reason[96] for allowing ratification in such circumstances may be because proceedings that are begun without authority are nevertheless capable of leading to a valid enforceable order in favour of the claimant unless the defendant takes steps to strike out the action.[97] Since the onus is on the defendant to set aside the action, and such an objection cannot comprise part of the substantive defence but must be the subject of a distinct application to the court,[98] it is arguable that at any time prior to such an application it is open to the claimant to ratify even if the limitation period has expired. This is because, in the absence of any application to strike out the action, the matter will be heard on its merits and any order eventually made by the court cannot be challenged.

---

[93] *Ibid.*, 635–6.
[94] [2003] Ch 182 at 206. See also the decision of the Employment Appeal Tribunal in *Nottinghamshire Healthcare NHS Trust* v. *Prison Officers Association* [2003] ICR 1192.
[95] See also *Owners of the Borvigilant* v. *Owners of the Romina G* [2003] 2 Lloyd's Rep 520.
[96] See Tan, 'Principle in *Bird* v. *Brown*', pp. 639–40.
[97] Pursuant to r. 3.4 of the Civil Procedure Rules.
[98] *Russian Commercial and Industrial Bank* v. *Comptoir d'Escompte de Mulhouse* [1925] AC 112 at 130; *Richmond* v. *Branson & Son* [1914] 1 Ch 968; *Selangor United Rubber Estates Ltd* v. *Cradock* [1969] 3 All ER 965 at 975–6.

What seems clear from the cases is that there is no absolute rule that where a time limit is fixed for the doing of an act, ratification cannot be allowed to take place after such time. It has therefore been suggested that the time limits rule should be seen as part of the more general rule that ratification must take place within a reasonable time.[99] In determining what is a reasonable time, the courts are entitled to take all the circumstances into account, including whether a time limit was stipulated and whether there is ultimately any unfair prejudice to the third party. Indeed, as a general rule there will be a need to establish unfair prejudice to the third party before ratification is precluded,[100] since the presence of unfair prejudice will be an important determinant of whether ratification has taken place within a reasonable time.[101]

(b) At time of ratification, principal must be capable of lawfully doing the act which is being ratified

In the case of *Bird* v. *Brown*, it was said that the doctrine of ratification 'must be taken with the qualification, that the act of ratification must take place at a time, and under circumstances, when the ratifying party might himself have lawfully done the act which he ratifies'.[102] Thus a principal cannot ratify an act if, at the time of ratification, the principal lacks the legal capacity to authorise the act in question. A principal may also not be entitled to ratify certain acts that were lawful at the time they were entered into, but were no longer so at the time of ratification.

In addition, it is also said that ratification can never operate retrospectively to affect rights of property that have become vested in another person.[103] A principal cannot ratify an act that would have the effect of

---

[99] Tan, 'Principle in *Bird* v. *Brown*', pp. 636–9. See also *Metropolitan Asylums Board* v. *Kingham & Sons* (1890) 6 TLR 217 at 218, where Fry LJ said that ratification must take place within a reasonable time 'which cannot extend after the time at which the contract is to commence'.

[100] Reynolds, *Bowstead and Reynolds on Agency*, 2-087.

[101] Though probably not in all cases. For example, it has been said that if the third party tells the principal that the third party wishes to withdraw from the transaction, or the third party gives the principal an ultimatum to ratify within a relatively short period of time (though not unreasonably so), this will shorten what would otherwise be a reasonable time for ratification: see *Re Portuguese Consolidated Copper Mines Ltd* (1890) 45 Ch D 16. There may well be no unfair prejudice to the third party if the abridged time for ratification was not adhered to compared with what would otherwise be regarded as being a reasonable time.

[102] (1850) 4 Exch 786.

[103] See, e.g., *Presentaciones Musicales SA* v. *Secunda* [1994] Ch 271, particularly the judgment of Roch LJ at 285–6.

divesting rights of property that have arisen in favour of another since the agent's unauthorised act.[104] It may be, however, that while it is true that ratification should not operate in a manner that displaces vested property rights, this is better justified as an issue which arises out of property law rather than by any limitation on the doctrine of ratification. There is no reason why ratification cannot take place even where property rights have become vested in others since the effect of ratification may simply be to render the third party liable under the contract entered into with the unauthorised agent (assuming that ratification has taken place within a reasonable time) without displacing any property rights that have already accrued to others.

In *Owners of the Borvigilant* v. *Owners of the Romina G*[105] the Court of Appeal held that there was no absolute rule that a contract (or indeed any other act) could not be ratified if the effect of ratification would be to divest an accrued property right. The better view, according to the Court of Appeal, was that this would be the case only if to permit ratification would unfairly prejudice a third party. Perhaps a better analysis might have been to say that ratification cannot generally divest property rights that have accrued to others outside the triangular principal–agent–third party relationship but that ratification in such circumstances can nevertheless affect the rights and obligations of the parties within the triangular relationship itself. At any rate, the *Borvigilant case* was clearly not an appropriate case for the operation of the rule relating to property rights because the property right that was affected was a cause of action by the third party against the principal and not a property right accruing to someone outside the principal–agent–third party dynamic.[106] The consequence of ratification is that the third party's rights will be affected and such fact of itself cannot be a valid defence against ratification.

(c) Nullities cannot be ratified

It is a well-established principle in agency law that a nullity can never be ratified.[107] A void act is devoid of any legal effect and there is nothing to be ratified. Similarly, illegal acts cannot be ratified.[108] In this context it is

---

[104] As was the case on the facts of *Bird* v. *Brown* itself.   [105] [2003] 2 Lloyd's Rep 520.

[106] It was argued that ratification could not be valid as it would deprive the third party of a cause of action in negligence against the principal as the contract being ratified contained clauses that excluded the principal's liability.

[107] See, e.g., *Watson* v. *Davies* [1931] 1 Ch 455 at 469.

[108] See *Bedford Insurance Co. Ltd* v. *Instituto de Resseguros do Brasil* [1985] QB 966; *Brook* v. *Hook* (1871) LR 6 Exch 89.

also often said that forgeries cannot be ratified because a forgery is a nullity.[109] This, however, depends on the nature of the forgery. Strictly speaking, a forgery occurs where a signature or seal has been counter-feited.[110] However, where a person has signed a document or affixed a seal on behalf of another person without the latter's authorisation, such acts constitute forgeries also.[111] It is said that a forgery in the former category cannot be ratified insofar as the perpetrator does not intend to act on behalf of the party whose signature or seal has been counter-feited.[112] In the latter category, the forgeries may be ratified because the person who has signed the document or affixed the seal intends to do so as agent.[113]

5 Ratification by companies

Generally, where an agent acting on behalf of a company has entered into an unauthorised transaction, such act may be ratified by the direc-tors where the transaction in question is one that they are capable of entering into.[114] Where the act of the agent is beyond the powers of the directors because it is a matter that should be properly determined by the shareholders in general meeting, the matter can only be ratified by the shareholders.[115]

Previously, where companies entered into a transaction that was beyond their capacity, such an act was null and void and could not be ratified.[116] However, s. 35(1) of the Companies Act 1985 effectively abolishes the *ultra vires* rule and therefore, in principle, there should be nothing to prevent ratification of what would in the past have been regarded as an *ultra vires* transaction.[117] In fact, s. 35(3) of the 1985 Act provides expressly that 'action by the directors which but for subsection (1)

---

[109] *Brook* v. *Hook* (1871) LR 6 Exch 89.
[110] See the observations in *Northside Developments Pty Ltd* v. *Registrar-General* (1990) 170 CLR 146 at 184–5, 199–200, 207–8.
[111] *Northside Developments Pty Ltd* v. *Registrar-General* (1990) 170 CLR 146.
[112] *Brook* v. *Hook* (1871) LR 6 Exch 89 at 100.
[113] *M'Kenzie* v. *British Linen Co.* (1881) 6 App Cas 82 at 99–100.
[114] *Reuter* v. *Electric Telegraph Co.* (1856) 6 E & B 341; *Wilson* v. *West Hartlepool Railway & Harbour Co.* (1865) 2 De G J & S 475.
[115] *Spackman* v. *Evans* (1868) LR 3 HL 171.
[116] See generally, P. J. Omar, 'Crossing Time's Boundaries: A Comparative View of Legal Responses to the Pre-Incorporation Contract' (2005) *Sing JLS* 76.
[117] Section 35(1) Companies Act 1985 is soon to be replaced by s. 39(1) Companies Act 2006. See also Chapter 9 (Scotland) III 5(c)(i).

would be beyond the company's capacity may only be ratified by the company by special resolution'. It is suggested that the same should be applicable to acts performed on behalf of the company by other agents who are not directors. Where the act performed by the agent is in breach of the company's articles of association, it has been suggested that ratification must also be by way of a special resolution.[118]

IV Breach of warranty of authority

1 General

In keeping with the objective of providing reasonable protection to third parties, an unauthorised agent who enters into a contract with a third party will be liable to the third party for breach of warranty of authority if the agent had indicated to the third party, either expressly or impliedly, that the agent was authorised.[119] The liability on the part of the agent is contractual and not based on any notion of negligence. This reflects the antiquity of the law of agency and the consequent need for third parties to be protected in some form against negligent misrepresentations of authority well before negligent misstatements were recognised as being actionable at law. Indeed, as we shall see, the third party may be liable even in the absence of any fault whatsoever. This rule can be explained on the basis that, in consideration of the third party agreeing to enter into a contract with the agent's principal, the agent warrants to the third party that the agent has the requisite authority.[120] This warranty of authority can be given expressly or by implication through conduct, for example a solicitor who commences an action warrants that he has the authority to do so.[121] This is a type of collateral contract for which there is strict liability for breach.[122] If the agent did not have the authority that was warranted, the agent is in breach of the warranty of authority and it does not matter whether the agent was fraudulent, negligent or without blame

---

[118] See G. Morse, *Charlesworth's Company Law*, 17th edn. (London: Sweet & Maxwell, 2005), p. 94.

[119] *Collen* v. *Wright* (1857) 8 E & B 647.

[120] A warranty may be implied even where the transaction with the person representing himself or herself as having authority to act does not result in a contract with the principal, see Reynolds, *Bowstead and Reynolds on Agency*, 9-064.

[121] *Yonge* v. *Toynbee* [1910] 1 KB 215; *Fernee* v. *Gorlitz* [1915] 1 Ch 177.

[122] *Collen* v. *Wright* (1857) 8 E & B 647; *SEB Trygg Liv Holding* v. *Manches* [2005] All ER (D) 136.

whatsoever.[123] While this can sometimes cause hardship to the agent, for example where the agent did not know that his authority had been terminated,[124] the agent rather than the third party is in a better position to ascertain the existence of the authority, and the agent may also be entitled to be indemnified by the principal if the principal did not inform the agent of the termination of authority. Thus the absolute liability of the agent is justified even where the agent has been without fault because the third party is the more vulnerable of the two, being less able to protect itself.

What the agent warrants is that the agent has authority to enter into the contract on the principal's behalf. The agent does not warrant that the principal will be able to perform the contract. This can be significant in the context of damages. Where there has been a breach of warranty, damages should be assessed so as to put the third party in the position it would have been in if the warranty was true. Accordingly, if it can be established that the breach has not caused the third party any damage beyond what the third party would have sustained even if the warranty was true, the third party may not be entitled to substantial damages from the agent.[125] Thus where the principal was already insolvent and would not have been able to perform the contract, the third party would not have been able to recover the full extent of the third party's loss from the principal even if the principal was bound by the agent's act. This is a relevant fact in determining the amount of damages the agent will have to pay to the third party. Similarly, if the agent had apparent authority, there would be a breach of the warranty of authority since apparent authority is not real authority. However, since the third party would be able to hold the principal to the contract under the doctrine of apparent authority, the third party has not suffered any real loss from the agent's breach. The third party will therefore at best be entitled to nominal damages from the agent. The same general result holds true in cases where ratification has taken place and, indeed, it is arguable that there is not even a breach of warranty in the first place due to the retrospective nature of ratification.

---

[123] An exception arises in the case of a donee of a power of attorney. Section 5(1) of the Powers of Attorney Act 1971 states that a donee who acts in pursuance of the power at a time when it has been revoked shall not, by reason of the revocation, incur any liability if at the time he did not know that the power had been revoked.

[124] As in *Yonge* v. *Toynbee* [1910] 1 KB 215, where the agent's authority was terminated due to the supervening mental capacity of the principal.

[125] See, e.g., *Beattie* v. *Lord Ebury* (1871–72) LR 7 Ch App 777 at 805.

2 Representation must be of fact

Traditionally, for a breach of warranty of authority to arise, the representation which is made by the agent must be one of fact and not of law. If the facts are equally known to the parties, and what is relied upon by the third party is a matter as to law only, it has been held that the agent is not liable.[126] Admittedly, the distinction between a mistake of fact and one of law is sometimes not easy to draw[127] and this distinction may now require reconsideration in view of *Kleinwort Benson Ltd* v. *Lincoln City Council*.[128] It is suggested that there is no reason why representations of law should not equally be subject to an implied warranty of authority from the agent. What is important is that the agent has represented that he or she has authority and this representation has formed the basis on which the third party has entered into a transaction with the principal. It may be that, compared to representations of fact, there are likely to be more instances of representations of law that are so obviously untenable that the third party ought not to have relied upon them. If that is the case, the third party will not be able to rely on the agent's representation for the reasons set out in the next section. However, in principle it would seem more consistent with the overall policy of the law of agency to protect the legitimate expectations of third parties that representations of law are not inevitably excluded from the doctrine of breach of warranty of authority.

3 Representation must have been relied upon

The third party must have relied upon the agent's representation. If the third party knew that the agent did not have authority, there is no breach of any warranty of authority.[129] Similarly, if the third party must have known that the agent did not intend to warrant any authority that might otherwise exist, no liability may be imposed on the agent. Thus where the words that were used were words that were well understood in the trade as meaning to negative the implication of a warranty by the agent, there can be no basis for fixing the agent with a warranty that he never intended to give, and which would be wholly inconsistent with the general understanding of persons engaged in the business in which

---

[126] *Beattie* v. *Lord Ebury* (1874–75) LR 7 HL 102; *Rashdall* v. *Ford* (1866) LR 2 Eq 750.

[127] See, e.g., *Thomas Cherry and John M'Dougall* v. *Colonial Bank of Australasia* (1869) LR 3 PC 24; *Weeks* v. *Propert* (1873) LR 8 CP 427.

[128] [1999] 2 AC 349.   [129] *Halbot* v. *Lens* [1901] 1 Ch 344.

the agent was employed.[130] On the same basis, if the agent informed the third party that he could not be sure if he had been properly authorised, or if the authority that had been given was still valid, there would be no basis on which the third party could rely on any warranty of authority. Any such warranty would be excluded by the agent's express qualifications.[131]

4 Liability in tort

In addition to contractual liability, an agent may also be liable in tort if he has fraudulently represented that he has authority. Where such a representation has been made negligently, a claim for negligent misrepresentation may also be possible if the agent owes a duty of care to the third party. While there do not appear to be any English cases on this point, there are at least two Commonwealth decisions that take different approaches. The first is the New Zealand decision of *Kavanagh* v. *Continental Shelf Company (No. 46) Ltd.*[132] In that case it was held that liability in tort could be the gateway to establishing vicarious liability on the employer for the negligence of its employee and this was one reason in public policy to deny such a claim in tort.

It is debatable whether this is a good basis on which to deny a claim in negligent misrepresentation. In *Armagas Ltd* v. *Mundogas SA* Lord Keith of Kinkel said that, at the end of the day, the question was whether the circumstances under which a servant had made a fraudulent misrepresentation that had caused loss to an innocent party contracting with him were such as to make it just for the employer to bear the loss.[133] Such circumstances existed where the employer, by words or conduct, had induced the injured party to believe that the servant was acting in the lawful course of the employer's business. They did not exist where such belief, although it is present, had been brought about through misguided reliance on the servant himself, when the servant was not authorised to do what he was purporting to do, when what he was purporting to do was not within the class of acts that an employee in his position was usually authorised to do, and when the employer had done nothing to represent that he was authorised to do it. Such reasoning would appear to be equally applicable to a claim founded on negligent misrepresentation

---

[130] *Lilly, Wilson & Co.* v. *Smales, Eeles & Co.* [1892] 1 QB 456.
[131] *Yonge* v. *Toynbee* [1910] 1 KB 215 at 227.   [132] [1993] 2 NZLR 648.
[133] [1986] AC 717 at 782–3.

which would limit the ability of a third party to impose vicarious liability on a principal for a breach of warranty of authority on the part of an agent-employee.[134]

It should also be noted that in *Kavanagh* v. *Continental Shelf Company (No. 46) Ltd*[135] the court also relied on another, 'more important', policy consideration, namely the effect of the Public Bodies Contracts Act. The court said that while it would not rule finally against any claim in negligence solely on the first public policy ground, it was satisfied that weighing both policy considerations together clearly went against a duty of care in tort which carried the consequence of imposing tortious liability on the employer.

A different view was taken in the Singapore case of *Fong Maun Yee* v. *Yoong Weng Ho Robert*.[136] In that case, a solicitor had represented wrongly that he acted for the vendor of a property. In fact the vendor had not appointed him to act and the company resolution to such effect was a forgery made by the property agent to deceive the potential purchaser (and the solicitor). The Court of Appeal held that the solicitor's representation to the potential purchaser that he was acting for the vendor was both negligent in tort and a breach of his warranty of authority.

5 Unidentified principals

Agents frequently act for principals who are unnamed. This is because the identity of the principal is frequently unimportant, or the agent acts for many principals and it is cumbersome to identify all of them, or the agent may prefer not to reveal who his principals are to avoid them being approached directly by the third party. Where, however, an agent who purports to act for an unidentified principal does not in fact have a principal, there are several possibilities. The first is that the agent was all along acting for himself, in which case the agent will be personally liable.[137] A second possibility is that his liability should be based on a collateral contract that he has a principal fitting the description (if any) given.[138] The third possible solution is that the agent is liable for breach

---

[134] See also Reynolds, *Bowstead and Reynolds on Agency*, 9-061, where it is suggested that vicarious liability in torts of misrepresentation modifies to meet the contractual position.

[135] [1993] 2 NZLR 648.   [136] [1997] 2 SLR 297.

[137] *Gardiner* v. *Heading* [1928] 2 KB 284.

[138] Reynolds, *Bowstead and Reynolds on Agency*, 9-089.

of warranty of authority since the agent has represented that he has been authorised by a principal even if he has not named the principal.

V Conclusion

For the law of agency to be a useful facilitator of commercial transactions, it has to maintain a balance between the rights and obligations of the principal, the agent and the third party. This underscores why unauthorised acts by agents may not be devoid of effect. An agent who has acted in an unauthorised manner may have his or her acts adopted because the transaction is still advantageous to the principal, and there is no reason why the third party who had earlier given consent to the transaction should not be bound to it. A contrary approach would in fact encourage highly technical litigation about whether the agent has acted strictly within the agent's mandate. In addition, if ratification were not possible, principals, in order to avoid technical disputes about what an agent was authorised to do, might confer more broadly worded mandates on their agents which would then increase the likelihood of principals being bound in circumstances that were unintended. On the same basis, a third party who has relied on words and acts by the principal should not be prejudiced if the agent, contrary to what the principal has represented, turned out not to have actual authority. Where what the third party has relied on is not an act by the principal but what the agent has said or done, the third party should be entitled to claim against the agent for any loss that the third party has suffered by entering into an unauthorised transaction.

Within each of these broad doctrines, namely ratification, apparent authority and breach of warranty of authority, the law of agency continues to strive for a proper balancing of the rights and obligations of the parties to this triangular relationship. Thus the ability of the principal to ratify is not unqualified. Rather, ratification is only allowed to operate in a manner that does not cause undue prejudice to third parties. And while ratification will normally operate as a waiver of the agent's breach of duty, this will not hold true if the principal did not have sufficient freedom in deciding whether or not to ratify. In the case of apparent authority, the doctrine is bounded by the principal's acts so as to keep it within reasonable limits. As such, liability is not imposed on the principal because of representations made by the agent, unless authority to make those representations can be traced back to something the principal said or did. Similarly, if the third party must have known the truth of the matter, the third party cannot hold the principal to the principal's representation. As for breach of warranty of authority, the agent's potential liability is limited to such damages as would follow from the lack of authority so that if the principal is bound by the doctrine of apparent authority but cannot for some reason perform the contract, it is likely that only nominal damages will be awarded against the agent.

It is ultimately through a sensible and nuanced balancing of rights and obligations between the principal, the agent, and the third party that the law of agency continues to retain its vital role in commercial transactions.

The *Restatement (Third) of Agency* and the unauthorised agent in US law

DEBORAH A. DEMOTT

I Introduction

Contemporary agency law in the United States reflects the dominant influence of a relatively uniform body of common law principles, applied in a context in which statutes and regulatory rules are also significant. Common law agency principles bring intellectual coherence to a legal landscape with potentially disparate features, many stemming from the federal structure of the United States. In six states, basic principles of agency were codified to some extent in the nineteenth and early twentieth centuries, for the most part reflecting then-contemporary common law.[1] Louisiana's current codification of agency, adopted in 1997, draws to some extent on the Quebec Civil Code.[2] Moreover, contemporary applications of common law agency principles often occur in a context in which other statutory material is highly relevant, as is inevitably so when an agent or a principal owes its legal personality to a statute's recognition of a particular type of organisational form, such as a corporation or a limited partnership.

The first and second *Restatements of Agency* have long dominated as statements of the foundational elements of common law agency doctrine in the United States. In part, their influence may be explained by the fact that, after 1914, the subject attracted no comprehensive account in a treatise.[3] *Restatement (Third) of Agency*, although representing continuity with the earlier Restatements, also departs from their style, structure and substantive formulations in major ways. This chapter begins by briefly recounting the history of the first two *Restatements of Agency* as a prelude to explaining the necessity for the changes embodied

---

[1] Alabama (Ala. Code § 8-2-1 to 9) (initial codification 1923); California (Cal. Civ. Code §§ 2019 to 2022; 2026 to 2030, 2295 to 2300, 2304 to 2339, 2342 to 2345, 2349 to 2351, 2355 to 2357) (initial codification 1872); Georgia (Ga. Code §§ 10-6-1 to 10-6-6, 10-6-20 to 10-6-39, 10-6-50 to 10-6-64, 10-6-80 to 10-6-89, 10-6-100 to 10-6-102, 10-6-120 to 10-6-121) (initial codification 1863); Montana (Mont. Code Ann. §§ 28-10-101 to 28-10-105, 28-10-201 to 28-10-215, 28-10-301 to 28-10-303, 28-10-401 to 28-10-423, 28-10-510 to 28-10-503, 28-10-601 to 28-10-609, 28-10-701 to 28-10-704, 28-10-801 to 28-10-802 (initial codification 1895); North Dakota (ND Cent. Code §§ 3-01-01 to 3-01-11, 3-02-01 to 3-02-16, 3-03-01 to 3-03-09, 3-04-01 to 3-04-03, 3-05-01 to 3-05-02, 3-06-01 to 3-06-06 (initial codification 1877); South Dakota (SD Codif. Laws ch. 59-1 to 59-9, 59-2-1 to 59-2-7, 59-3-1 to 59-3-18, 59-4-1 to 59-4-2, 59-5-1 to 59-5-3, 59-6-1 to 59-6-10, 59-7-1 to 59-6-8, 59-8-1 to 59-8-2, 59-9-1 to 59-9-8 (initial codification 1877). The codifications in California, Montana, North Dakota and South Dakota are based on the Field Civil Code. That Code, less successful than its counterpart procedural code, represented a nineteenth-century project of legal rationalisation and reform. On the codification movement, see L. M. Friedman, *A History of American Law* (New York: Simon & Schuster, 1973), pp. 340–55. For additional discussion of these codifications, see American Law Institute, *Restatement of the Law, Third: Agency* (St Paul, MN: American Law Institute, 2006), Introduction.

[2] La Civ. Code, Art. 2985-3032 (successor to Civil Code of 1870).

[3] The last comprehensive treatise was the two-volume work, F. R. Mechem, *A Treatise on the Law of Agency, Including Not Only a Discussion of the General Subject, but also Special Chapters on Attorneys, Auctioneers, Brokers and Factors*, 2 vols, 2nd edn (Chicago: Callaghan, 1914).

in *Restatement (Third)*. The chapter then analyses how *Restatement (Third)* addresses aspects of the problem of the unauthorised agent, examining each basis on which an agent's action may be attributed to the principal as well as the legal consequences that may follow for an agent who takes unauthorised action.

II. The *Restatements of Agency*

Agency was among the group of subjects initially chosen by the American Law Institute for treatment in *Restatements*, just as nineteenth- and early twentieth-century codifiers of the common law included the subject in codes. The first *Restatement of Agency*, begun in 1923 with Professor Floyd R. Mechem of the University of Chicago law faculty as Reporter, was completed in 1933. Professor Warren A. Seavey of Harvard Law School's faculty became Reporter in 1928 following Professor Mechem's death.[4] Professor Seavey also served as Reporter for *Restatement (Second) of Agency*, completed in 1957.[5] Undeniably, the first two *Restatements of Agency* proved useful and influential, articulating a basic vocabulary of concepts and justifications for ascribing responsibility for actions taken by representatives acting on behalf of others.

Nonetheless, by 1995, despite the frequency with which courts continued to cite it, *Restatement (Second)* was showing its age. Its dated quality stemmed to some extent from the simple consequence of ongoing legal development over almost forty years. For example, in *Restatement (Second)*, it is basic doctrine that a principal's loss of capacity terminates an agent's actual and apparent authority to take action on the principal's behalf, doing so regardless of any prior manifestation to the contrary made by the principal while competent.[6] By 1995, the widespread adoption of statutes permitting the creation of durable powers of attorney suggested that it was neither necessary nor desirable to treat as automatically void actions taken by a principal on behalf of a principal who

---

[4] This may explain why Professor Seavey is sometimes misidentified as the initial Reporter for Agency. See N. Duxbury, *Patterns of American Jurisprudence* (Oxford: Clarendon Press, 1995), p. 24; L. Kalman, *Legal Realism at Yale* (Chapel Hill, NC: University of North Carolina Press, 1986), p. 14.

[5] On Professor Seavey's life and times, see D. B. King and W. A. Seavey, *A Harvard Law School Professor: Warren A. Seavey's Life and the World of Legal Education* (Buffalo, NY: W.S. Hein, 2005).

[6] American Law Institute, *Restatement of the Law, Second: Agency* (St Paul, MN: American Law Institute, 1958), §§ 120, 122(1) (consequences of principal's loss of capacity equated to consequences of principal's death).

has lost capacity when such actions are consistent with prior expressions of intention by the principal that the agent continue to be authorised to act. *Restatement (Second)*'s position seemed at odds with general recognition that the law, in response to evident social needs, should enable a competent principal to appoint a representative with authority to deal on the principal's behalf when the principal herself is not able to do so personally.[7]

Moreover, *Restatement (Second)* had general characteristics that fundamentally distanced it from current thinking and preoccupations and perhaps help explain the paucity of academic scholarship on agency in the United States over the last few decades. Three qualities in particular situate it in an earlier era of legal scholarship: (1) its style and structure; (2) the assumption it made about the nature of legal subjects; and (3) the assumption it made about the relationship between statutes and the common law. Each of these qualities merits brief discussion as a preface to the choices made in *Restatement (Third)*.

1 Style and structure

Restatement (Second), like the first *Restatement of Agency*, exemplifies qualities that G. Edward White identifies in legal treatises written in the United States between 1880 and 1910: 'massive analytical syntheses' that went beyond descriptive compendia of existing rules to impose intellectual order through a classificatory scheme.[8] 'Massive' fairly describes *Restatement Second*'s girth. It occupies two stout volumes, plus a separate *Appendix* containing Reporter's Notes and annotations to the first *Restatement*. Much of its girth stems from its style, which is characterised by precise articulation of often small variations on central points, totaling 528 separately enumerated points of black letter, many with lettered offshoots. Repetition occurs frequently because each point is replayed for transactions in which a principal is undisclosed, in contrast to transactions in which the third party has notice that the agent deals on behalf of

---

[7] See *Restatement (Third)*, § 3.08 (termination of agent's actual authority due to principal's loss of capacity is effective only when agent or third party has notice that principal has lost capacity; principal may through a written instrument make an agent's actual authority effective upon a principal's loss of capacity or confer it irrevocably regardless of such loss) and § 3.11(2) (agent's apparent authority ends 'when it is no longer reasonable for the third party with whom the agent deals to believe that the agent continues to act with actual authority').

[8] G. E. White, *Tort Law in America: An Intellectual History*, expanded edn (Oxford: Oxford University Press, 2004), p. 34.

a principal. More importantly, in the structure of *Restatement (Second)*, like that of the first *Restatement*, classification and precise articulation of doctrine do much of the work while underlying rationales and explanations may go unarticulated. This gives the work as a whole a dogmatic cast that is jarring to contemporary readers.

2 Assumed nature of legal subjects

The paradigmatic legal subject in the first two *Restatements* is an individual person and only rarely a partnership, corporation or other legal or commercial entity. This assumption has the effect of distancing the *Restatements* from the world in which most of us live and work, the world that generates most contemporary disputes that implicate agency doctrines one way or another. Contemporary agency disputes, that is, often require the application of agency doctrines to resolve disputes between an organisation and a third party (which may also be an organisation) when the organisation has dealt with the third party through an agent, whether or not an employee and whether or not the agent is an individual person.

However, although basic agency ideas apply in such contexts, their analysis may be more complex. For example, an organisational principal may make manifestations in ways that an individual typically would not. An organisation may confer a title on an agent – for example, vice-president for marketing – that, reasonably understood by third parties, signifies that the principal assents to being bound by actions taken by the agent that are typically within the authority of holders of a comparable title. Moreover, when a principal is an organisation, an agent's duties of loyalty and performance are owed to the organisation, not the agent's superior in the organisation although the agent's ties to the superior may be more immediate than the more abstract affinities tying the agent to the organisation.

3 Relationships among statutes and the common law

Relatedly, *Restatement (Second)* assumed the proper subject of law for *Restatement* purposes to be the common law, unblemished by statutory meddling.[9] Among its other consequences, this assumption had the

---

[9] See *Restatement (Second)*, Scope Note, p. 2 ('[n]o statements are made as to rules resulting from legislative change, except where substantially similar legislation has been adopted

effect of excluding consideration of the mutual influence that statutes and the common law may have on each other, including the possibility that statutes may be a basis on which common law doctrines should draw in some instances.[10] The assumption also precluded discussion of the relevance of common law doctrines in the context of contemporary administrative regulation.[11]

The assumed nature of legal subjects in the prior *Restatements* is necessarily tied to their treatment of statutory material. Thus, the introductory Scope Note to *Restatement (Second)* states that: '[t]he Restatement of this subject does not deal with special applications of the principles of agency to persons or combinations of persons concerning whom special rules exist.'[12]

Nonetheless, in resolving questions raised by statutes of all sorts, courts often turn to common law agency doctrines and draw implications from *Restatement* formulations. This is so even when the question involves just the sort of legal person excluded from the universe of *Restatement (Second)*! For example, in *Meyer* v. *Holley*, a private action under the federal Fair Housing Act, the United States Supreme Court held that vicarious liability for an employee's violation of the Act extended to the corporation that employed him but not to the corporation's president.[13] Why? The statute itself does not explicitly impose liability on a superior agent within an organisation and 'ordinary... vicarious liability rules' do not impose such liability.[14] Thus, common law agency doctrine appears to exert a form of gravitational pull on judicial reasoning, a phenomenon that a contemporary treatment of agency should not ignore.

by, or proposed to, all the states ...'). And even then, the common law remained the *Restatement* rule. See, e.g., *ibid.*, § 175, comment *d* (noting that 'statutes have frequently changed the rule' stated on the power of an agent entrusted with a chattel to bind the principal beyond the scope of the agent's actual authority).

[10] For much fuller elaboration of this and related points, see D. A. DeMott, 'Statutory Ingredients in Common Law Change: Issues in the Development of Agency Doctrine', in S. Worthington (ed.), *Commercial Law and Commercial Practice* (Oxford: Hart, 2003), p. 57.

[11] For a relatively recent example, see S. Pulliam and G. Zuckerman, 'SEC Examines Rebates Paid to Large Funds', *Wall Street Journal*, 6 January 2005, pp. C1, C4 (describing enquiry into practice in which managers of mutual and hedge funds personally retain rebates paid by brokerage funds that execute securities trades on behalf of funds). The duties of loyalty that any agent owes a principal are helpful starting points in identifying why such practices may be troublesome. See *Restatement (Third)*, §§ 8.01–8.06.

[12] *Restatement (Second)*, Scope Note, p. 2.   [13] 537 US 280 (2003).   [14] *Ibid.* at 285.

4 *Signal characteristics of* Restatement (Third)

(a) In general

Restatement (Third) is much more than an updated version of *Restatement (Second)*. *Restatement (Third)* focuses much more on addressing how discrete doctrines may fit together, how tensions among doctrines may be resolved, and how doctrines might be justified. Structurally, *Restatement (Third)* makes many fewer black-letter assertions of points of legal doctrine (seventy-five), while expanding articulated explanations and rationales. *Restatement (Third)* does not restrict its formulations to individual actors as prototypical legal subjects. Encompassing the implications of agency within organisational settings required an enriched vocabulary, including terms such as 'superior' and 'subordinate' co-agents of the same principal.[15] *Restatement (Third)* frequently discusses relationships among common law doctrines and statutory and regulatory materials.

In working on *Restatement (Third)*, it proved helpful to step back from the abundance of doctrinal formulations in *Restatement (Second)* to broader intellectual terrain. Given the large number of reported agency cases in the United States in the last few decades, it was important to proceed in two steps: (1) to identify a range of prototypical situations to be resolved through doctrine; and (2) to identify a set of bases on which to justify the attribution of responsibility to a principal for an agent's actions; and to do both prior to focusing on doctrinal formulations in detail. This approach made it possible to identify the distinct contribution made by a doctrine and to consider whether its consequences were justifiable. As discussed in section III 6 of this chapter, the doctrine of inherent agency power appeared in this light to have usefully done little distinct work in recent cases and, consequently, is not used in *Restatement (Third)*.

(b) The significance of manifestations

In this process, it also became evident that the concept of 'manifestation' had pervasive significance and required more formal and consistent

---

[15] See *Restatement (Third)*, § 1.04(9). A subordinate co-agent is not a subagent of the subordinate's superior. Co-agents share a common principal, such as an organisation, while a subagent has two principals. See *ibid.*, comment *i*. These are the appointing agent and that agent's principal. See *ibid.*, § 3.15, comment *b*. An appointing agent is responsible to that agent's principal for the subagent's conduct. When an agent is itself a corporation or other legal person, its officers and employees who are designated to work on the principal's behalf are subagents of an organisational principal: *ibid.*

treatment than that provided by *Restatement (Second)*. For example, an agent's actual authority is grounded in the agent's reasonable interpretation of a manifestation made to the agent by the principal.[16] An agent acts with apparent authority when a third party reasonably believes the agent to be authorised and the belief is traceable to a manifestation made by the principal.[17] A manifestation consists of conduct by a person, 'observable by others, that expresses meaning'.[18] *Restatement (Third)*, § 1.03 states that a person may manifest assent or intention 'through written or spoken words or other conduct', which eliminates any suggestion that only through an individualised or explicit representation or communication may a principal make a manifestation to a person.[19]

Thus, a principal may manifest assent to an agent's right to engage in conduct by placing the agent in a particular position with defined responsibilities, or by placing an agent in an industry or a setting in which it is customary for an agent to have authority of a specific scope. Absent notice to third parties to the contrary, placing an agent in such a position constitutes a manifestation by the principal that the principal assents to be bound by actions by the agent that fall within that scope. It should not be necessary for a third party who interacts with the agent, believing the principal's manifestation to be true, to establish a communication made directly by the principal to the third party. This is because the principal's manifestation constitutes expressive action, taken by the principal, in a context in which actors external to the principal should be able to take the principal's action seriously. On the other hand, when a third party has reason to know that an agent's actual authority is subject to limits, it is not reasonable for the third party to take action based on a belief that the agent is authorised, however beguiling the agent may prove to be.

The commentary accompanying § 1.03 recognises that manifestations by principals concerning agents do not occur in vacuums and that the meaning a third party may reasonably ascribe to a manifestation depends on the context in which it is made.[20] For example, prior dealings between a principal and a third party may shape how the third party understands

---

[16] *Restatement (Third)*, §§ 2.01, 2.02, 3.01.   [17] *Ibid.*, §§ 2.03, 3.03.
[18] *Ibid.*, § 1.03, comment *b*.
[19] For an earlier recognition that 'manifestation' might carry broader as well as narrower meanings, see S. A. Fishman, 'Inherent Agency Power – Should Enterprise Liability Apply to Agents' Unauthorized Contracts?' (1987) 19 *Rutgers LJ* 1, 41.
[20] *Restatement (Third)*, § 1.03, comment *e*.

the principal's manifestations, as may the context associated with an industry. Likewise, an agent's interpretation of manifestations made by the principal occurs in a context defined by their prior dealings, among other circumstances.

III Bases for attribution

This section explores the application of *Restatement (Third)* to the problem of the unauthorised agent, in particular the bases on which a transaction entered into by an unauthorised agent may bind the principal. The section begins with a brief discussion of the nature of actual authority as a preface to examining the practical and theoretical importance of other bases for attribution.

1 Actual authority

An agent acts with actual authority 'when, at the time of taking action that has legal consequences for the principal, the agent reasonably believes, in accordance with the principal's manifestations to the agent, that the principal wishes the agent so to act'.[21] The focal point for determining whether an agent acted with actual authority is the time the agent takes or determines to take action. Thus, the agent's interpretation of the principal's manifestations must be reasonable as of that time. Developments known to the agent that occur subsequently to the principal's initial manifestation may be relevant to assessing the reasonableness of the agent's interpretation at the time the agent takes action.

Moreover, manifestations of assent by the principal made prior to the time the agent acts are subject to subsequent manifestations by the principal that limit or vary the initial manifestation of assent. A principal's power to limit or vary a prior manifestation of assent operates independently of rights that any contract between principal and agent may create in the agent. Thus, a principal may vary or even terminate an agent's actual authority although doing so breaches a contract with the agent. For example, in *Government Guaranty Fund* v. *Hyatt Corp.*, the court held that the owner of a resort hotel had power to revoke authority granted to the hotel's manager for a ten-year term, although by so revoking authority the owner breached the terms of the management

---

[21] *Ibid.*, § 2.01.

contract.[22] Although the manager had a right to seek money damages, it had no specifically enforceable right to continue managing the hotel.

The nature of actual authority creates significant obstacles for third parties when a principal asserts after the fact of a transaction that the agent lacked authority to commit the principal. The circumstances requisite to establishing actual authority are often not transparent to parties external to the principal's organisation or the principal's relationship with an externally positioned agent, turning as they do on an agent's reasonable interpretation of manifestations made to the agent by the principal. Moreover, even when a principal has given an agent an explicit statement of authority in an instrument that the agent may display to third parties, the agent's actual authority is, as noted above, always vulnerable to subsequent manifestations to the contrary that the principal makes to the agent.

The opacity of actual authority from the perspective of a third party helps explain the large number of cases in which third parties succeed in claims against principals on some basis other than actual authority. To be sure, in some cases it is unquestionable that the agent acted without actual authority. In many others, although it is likely that the agent acted consistently with a reasonable interpretation of manifestations made by the principal to the agent, proof will elude the third party with whom the agent dealt.

2 Apparent authority

Restatement (Third) defines apparent authority as 'the power held by an agent or other actor to affect a principal's legal relations with third parties when a third party reasonably believes that the actor has authority to act on behalf of the principal and that belief is traceable to the principal's manifestations'.[23] Apparent authority is the basis on which principals are subjected to liability in a large number of litigated cases. The robustness of apparent authority turns on the manifold ways in which a principal may make a manifestation concerning an agent's authority, coupled with a third party's ability to establish the requites of apparent authority from a perspective external to the relationship

---

[22] 95 F 3d 291 (3rd Cir. 1996); accord, *2660 Woodley Road Joint Venture* v. *ITT Sheraton Corp.* 1998 WL 1469541 (D. Del. 1998); *Pacific Landmark Hotel Ltd* v. *Marriott Hotels Inc.* 23 Cal. Rptr 2d 555 (Ct. App. 1994).

[23] *Restatement (Third)*, § 2.03.

between principal and agent. Apparent authority reinforces or backstops actual authority by reducing the opportunity a principal may otherwise have to speculate at the expense of third parties by initially clothing an agent with externally visible trappings of authority, then later claiming the agent's authority to have been subject to undisclosed limitations when the transaction to which the agent has committed the principal turns out to be disadvantageous from the principal's standpoint.[24] Apparent authority is a robust doctrine because it is not necessary for a third party to establish that an attempt to speculate at the third party's expense led the principal to deny that the agent acted with actual authority. Indeed, apparent authority may be operative, although no collusion occurred between agent and principal and although the agent's motives appear to have been entirely self-serving.

When an agent acting with apparent authority commits a principal to a contract, *Restatement (Third)*, like *Restatement (Second)*, equates the consequences for the principal to those that follow when an agent acts with actual authority.[25] This stems from the long tradition embodied in the *Restatements* of crisp demarcation between apparent authority and estoppel as distinct bases for attribution.[26] Thus, the principal (but not the agent, unless the agent and the third party so agree) becomes a party to the contract and may assert contractual rights against the third party, which also becomes a party to the transaction.[27] It is not necessary for the principal separately to establish ratification of the agent's action.[28] Likewise, the third party's remedies against the principal are not limited to reliance losses.[29]

---

[24] *Ibid.*, comment *c*.

[25] *Ibid.*, §§ 6.01, 6.02; *Restatement (Second)*, § 159 ('[a] disclosed or partially disclosed principal is subject to liability upon contracts made by an agent acting within his apparent authority if made in proper form and with the understanding that the apparent principal is a party. The rules as to the liability of a principal for authorized acts, are applicable to unauthorized acts which are apparently authorized.').

[26] *Restatement (Third)*, § 2.03, comment *c*; *Restatement (Second)*, § 8, comment *d* and § 8B, comment *a* (characterising estoppel as 'fundamentally a doctrine in the law of torts').

[27] *Restatement (Third)*, §§ 6.01, 6.02; *Restatement (Second)*, § 292.

[28] Thus, *Restatement (Third)* limits ratification to action taken by an agent or other actor without actual or apparent authority. *Restatement (Third)*, § 4.01(1). This is consistent with the position taken by *Restatement (Second)*, § 82 (defining ratification as 'the affirmance by a person of a prior act which did not bind him but which was done or professedly done on his account, whereby the act, as to some or all persons, is given effect as if originally authorized by him').

[29] See *Linkage Corp.* v. *Trustees of Boston University* 679 NE 2d 191 (Mass. 1997); *State* v. *Delacruz* 977 SW 2d 95 (Mo. Ct App. 1998).

It is often said that a third party who proceeds against a principal on the basis of apparent authority must show 'reliance'. What 'reliance' requires in this context is rarely articulated. Moreover, when an agent acts with apparent authority, the party who suffers injury as a consequence may not be the party to whom the principal made a manifestation about the agent's authority. In such cases, the injured party is a 'fourth party', injured as a result of action taken by a third party when the third party's action is traceable to the principal's manifestation concerning the agent's authority. The United States Supreme Court recognised this application of apparent authority in *American Society of Mechanical Engineers, Inc.* v. *Hydrolevel Corp.*[30] In *Hydrolevel*, an officer of an organisation that set and promulgated safety standards for heating equipment also manufactured a component used in commercial heating equipment. Having received an enquiry from a building owner about the safety of a component manufactured by a competitor, the officer replied on organisational stationery that the organisation assessed the competitor's component as unsafe, an untrue assertion that led the building owner to purchase a component manufactured by the officer's business. The Court, finding that the building owner reasonably believed that the organisation had authorised the officer's response to the building owner's enquiry, held that the officer had acted with apparent authority. In the competitor's antitrust suit against the standard-setting organisation, the Court held that the officer's actions were attributable to the organisation because the officer had acted with apparent authority.[31] Along the same lines, *Restatement (Third)* recognises that a principal may be subject to vicarious liability for a tort committed by an agent in dealing with a third party when action taken by the agent with apparent authority constitutes the tort or enables the agent to conceal its commission.[32]

---

[30] 456 US 556 (1982).

[31] Defamatory statements made by agents may also generate fourth party victims when an agent acts with apparent authority. The victim of a defamatory statement may not be the audience for the statement; an agent acts with apparent authority in making such a statement when it is reasonable for the audience to believe that the agent has authority to make it that is traceable to a manifestation of the principal. On apparent authority and defamatory statements made by agents acting with apparent authority, see *Restatement (Third)*, § 7.08, comment *d*; *American Society of Mechanical Engineers Inc.* v. *Hydrolevel Corp.* 456 US 556 (1982) at 566.

[32] *Restatement (Third)*, § 7.08.

3 Estoppel

Although *Restatement (Third)* incorporates a capacious treatment of the concept of manifestation, it also recognises that circumstances may warrant imposition of liability on a principal when it is not possible to establish a manifestation made by the principal. The doctrinal basis is estoppel. This subsection focuses on the operation of estoppel when a principal is disclosed or unidentified; subsection 4 examines the application of estoppel to undisclosed principals.[33]

As stated in *Restatement (Third)*, § 2.05, although a person has made no manifestation that an actor has authority as an agent and is not otherwise subject to liability stemming from a transaction purportedly done on the person's behalf, the person may be subject to liability to 'a third party who justifiably is induced to make a detrimental change in position because the transaction is believed to be on the person's account'.[34] To establish the person's liability, a third party who changed position must establish either that '(1) the person intentionally or carelessly caused' the third party to believe the actor acted with authority; or that '(2) having notice of such belief and that it might induce others to change their positions, the person did not take reasonable steps to notify them of the facts'.[35] In contrast with the consequences of an agent's action taken with apparent authority, estoppel does not create rights in the person estopped.[36]

The most memorable cases applying this doctrine against disclosed principals involve roguish impostors who acquire an agent's trappings, allegedly as a consequence of the defendant's failure to use due care. For example, in *Luken v. Buckeye Parking Corp.*, a customer of a public parking lot surrendered his car to an impostor who masqueraded as a lot attendant and gave the customer an official-looking ticket for his car, stating that he was the owner's agent.[37] The impostor subsequently destroyed the car in a collision. The court held that the trial raised

---

[33] A principal is disclosed when the third party with whom an agent deals has notice that the agent is acting for a principal and has notice of the principal's identity. A principal is unidentified when the third party has notice that an agent is acting on behalf of a principal but does not have notice of the principal's identity. A principal is undisclosed when the third party has no notice that the agent is acting on behalf of any principal. *Ibid.*, § 1.04(2). *Restatement (Second)* used the terminology of 'partially disclosed' principal while criticising it as less accurate than 'unidentified' principal. See *Restatement (Second)*, § 4(2), comment *g*.

[34] *Restatement (Third)*, § 2.05.   [35] *Ibid.*

[36] *Ibid.*; *Restatement (Second)*, § 8B, comment *b*.   [37] 68 NE 2d 217 (Ohio Ct App. 1945).

questions within the jury's province because acts and omissions on the part of the parking lot owner may have led a reasonably prudent person to believe the impostor to be the owner's agent. Similarly, in *Hoddeson* v. *Koos Bros.*, the plaintiff surrendered cash to purchase items of furniture to a nicely suited impostor who appeared to her to be a member of a furniture store's sales force and who promised that the furniture would be delivered to her residence in due course.[38] No furniture ever arrived. The court held that the store's failure to exercise reasonable surveillance over its sales floor and force breached a duty owed to the customer. The reasonableness of the customer's belief in the impostor's position and authority may be more questionable in *Hoddeson* because the customer received no receipt from the purported salesman analogous to the ticket received by the car owner in *Luken*.

The underlying principle of accountability in certain situations in which a principal's conduct falls short of a manifestation reaches beyond settings in which a business enterprise has dealings with members of the retail public to other contexts in which a person owes others a duty of care concerning how indicia or other trappings of agency may be used.[39] In *MacAndrews & Forbes Co.* v. *United States*, a shipper of fox skins on board a steam ship sued to recover their value when the skins were not delivered to their consignee at the port of delivery.[40] The ship's broker, on behalf of the cargo owner, gave a bill of lading for the skins to a customs broker and wrote a letter to the ship's delivery clerk directing that the skins be delivered to 'our truckmen'. The trucker's representative took the letter to the public garage where it housed its trucks and placed the letter, 'as was its practice, in the desk drawer of the office of the garage, where their truckmen would go to find it'.[41] Instead, the letter appears to have been purloined from the unlocked drawer by an impostor who presented it to the ship's clerk and carried off the fox skins. The court held that the cargo owner's loss was more fairly characterised as the consequence of its agent's negligence in enabling the faux-trucker to deceive the ship's delivery clerk, as opposed to the decision of the ship's

---

[38]   135 A 2d 702 (NJ Super. Ct 1957).

[39]   For a suggestion otherwise, limited to the authority of *Luken* and *Hoddeson*, see *Raclaw* v. *Fay, Conmy & Co.*, 668 NE 2d 114 (Ill. App. Ct 1996) (accounting firm, defendant in case, allowed actor who claimed to be its agent to use its address, office and telephone number to market investment products; dispositive that firm did not market investment products to general public and that plaintiffs neither visited its office not investigated whether it actually marketed the investment products).

[40]   23 F 2d 667 (3rd Cir. 1928).   [41]   *Ibid.* at 667.

clerk to release the cargo to the impostor. The clerk had no duty to enquire further when presented with 'such an appearance of integrity as would naturally procure the goods',[42] because imposing such a duty would be impracticable in the bustle when a ship offloads cargo to persons who appear authorised to receive it.

Estoppel as defined in *Restatement (Third)* requires a causal link between the defendant's carelessness and the plaintiff's change in position, as well as requiring that the change of position be justifiable. In contrast to the illustrative cases discussed above, these criteria may be pressed a bit harder on the more complex facts of a recent Australian case, *Pacific Carriers Ltd* v. *BNP Paribas*.[43] The actor in question in *Pacific Carriers* was not an impostor, but the manager of a bank's documentary credit department who lacked authority to bind the bank to a guarantee or indemnity. However, the manager stamped two letters of indemnity with the stamp used to authenticate letters of credit. The stamped letters of indemnity, presented by a shipper to a carrier that delivered cargo in reliance on the letters, carried no indication that the manager's authority to affix the authenticating stamp extended only to letters of credit and not to letters of indemnity. The signatures on the letters themselves were illegible. The court found that the presence of the stamp on the letters was likely more significant to the carrier than the signatures and that the bank, having situated the departmental manager in a position to sign and stamp the documents, was accountable for the consequences of imposing no internal check on the final form in which documents left the bank.

The analysis in *Pacific Carriers* is consistent with the elements of *Restatement (Third)*, § 2.05 but the context is more complex than the illustrative US cases. The causal link in *Pacific Carriers* between the carrier's decision to deliver the cargo and the lack of more robust control measures within the bank is not as straightforward as the link in *MacAndrews & Forbes* between the ship's clerk's release of the fox skins and the carelessness that led to the impostor's possession of delivery instructions. That the indemnity letters in *Pacific Carriers* were signed illegibly introduces the possibility that the carrier's representatives also failed to use appropriate care in determining whether to release the cargo.[44] However, in the specific transactional context, it may be that the bank's failure to impose tighter

---

[42] *Ibid.* at 668.   [43] (2004) 218 CLR 451 (Australia)

[44] For critical assessments of *Pacific Carriers*, see F. M. B. Reynolds, 'Apparent Authority and Illegible Signatures' (2005) 121 *LQR* 55; P. Watts, 'The Creep of Negligence into Agency Law in Australia' (2005) 26 *Aust Bar Rev* 185.

internal controls is more significant, just as the *MacAndrews & Forbes* court concluded that the ship's clerk could not reasonably be expected to make further inquiry in fraught circumstances.[45] If so, then the carrier's change in position could be characterised as 'justified' for purposes of the establishing a justifiable change in position under *Restatement (Third)*, § 2.05.[46]

4 Undisclosed principals

A principal is undisclosed when the third party with whom an agent deals has no notice that the agent acts on behalf of any principal.[47] The situation, which may be more accurately characterised as one of 'undisclosed agency', by definition is not one in which apparent authority would be operative.

Like *Restatement (Second)*, *Restatement (Third)* recognises the possibility that an undisclosed principal may be bound by an agent's unauthorised action. *Restatement (Third)* identifies two distinct bases for grounding an undisclosed principal's liability. First, the principal may ratify the agent's action,[48] a possibility explored in subsection 6. Second, in a relatively small number of instances the principal may be estopped to deny that the agent acted with authority. As stated in *Restatement (Third)*, § 2.06, an undisclosed principal is subject to an estoppel doctrine

---

[45] For example, the court observes (218 CLR 451 at 468):

> Commercial documents, such as the letters of indemnity in the present case, are commonly relied upon, and intended to be relied upon, by third parties who act upon an assumption of authenticity created or reinforced by their mode of execution, and by the fact and circumstances of their delivery. Within a commercial enterprise, such as a bank, there will normally be internal lines of authority, and procedures, designed to ensure that, when documents issue to third parties, appearances are reliable. Such an enterprise might induce or assist an assumption, not only by the representation conveyed by its organizational structure, and lines of communication with third parties, but also by a failure to establish appropriate internal procedures designed to protect itself, and people who deal with it in good faith, from unauthorized conduct.

[46] The commentary to § 2.04 characterises this element as requiring reasonable belief in the actor's authority on the part of the third party who changes position. See *Restatement (Third)*, § 2.04, comment d (estoppel 'protects third parties who reasonably believe an actor to be authorized as an agent when the belief cannot be shown to follow directly or indirectly from the principal's own manifestations').

[47] *Restatement (Third)*, § 1.04(2)(b).

[48] See *Restatement (Third)*, § 4.03. This is contrary to the position stated in *Restatement (Second)*, § 85(1), limiting ratification to situations in which an actor purported to act as an agent.

comparable to that applicable to disclosed and unidentified principals under § 2.05. Thus, when an undisclosed principal has caused or is aware of a third party's belief about an agent that will lead the third party justifiably to change position, the principal is subject to liability to the third party if the principal does not take reasonable steps to notify the third party of the facts. Additionally, under § 2.06 a principal may not rely on instructions given an agent that limit or narrow the scope of the agent's authority to 'less than the authority a third party would reasonably believe the agent to have under the same circumstances if the principal had been disclosed'.[49] The intention is to encompass situations in which a third party would not have reason to enquire further into the scope of the agent's authority if the third party knew the agent acted on behalf of a principal.[50] Like the doctrine of apparent authority, the availability of estoppel against an undisclosed principal backstops the doctrine of actual authority in circumstances when the principal might otherwise be enabled to speculate at the expense of third parties with whom the agent deals.

5 Ratification

(a) In general

In *Restatement (Third)*, as in *Restatement (Second)*, ratification is a basis on which the legal consequences of an agent's action may be attributed to the principal when the agent acted without either actual or apparent authority.[51] The breadth with which the doctrine of apparent authority operates in contemporary cases helps explain the relatively small number of cases in which ratification is the sole basis on which a principal is subject

---

[49] *Restatement (Third)*, § 2.06. In *Restatement (Second)*, an undisclosed principal was subject to liability on transactions when an agent lacked actual authority under two different doctrines. First, if the agent was a general agent authorised to conduct transactions, the principal was subject to liability 'for acts done on his account, if usual or necessary in such transactions, although forbidden by the principal to do them': *Restatement (Second)*, § 194. A 'general' agent was one appointed 'to conduct a series of transactions over a period of time' who could 'properly be regarded as part of the principal's organization in much the same way as a servant is normally part of the master's business enterprise': *ibid.*, § 161, comment *a*. Second, when an undisclosed principal entrusted an agent with 'the management of his business', the principal was subject to liability to third parties 'with whom the agent enters into transactions usual in such business and on the principal's account, although contrary to the directions of the principal': *ibid.*, § 195.

[50] *Ibid.*, comment *c*.   [51] *Restatement (Third)*, § 4.01(1); *Restatement (Second)*, § 82.

to liability in the wake of a transaction entered into by an agent who lacked actual authority. Ratification often serves the function of clarifying situations in which it is ambiguous or unclear whether an agent acted with actual authority.[52]

A principal ratifies an agent's action by making a manifestation of assent or other conduct indicative of assent that the agent's action shall affect the principal's legal relations.[53] A principal's conduct, if unaccompanied by an explicit expression of assent to be bound, effects ratification when it is justifiable only on the assumption that the principal has chosen to be bound by the legal consequences of the agent's action.[54] The efficacy of ratification does not turn on whether the principal communicates assent to the agent or to third parties whose legal position will be affected by the ratification. Ratification has an immediate effect on legal relations as between principal, agent, and the relevant third parties, recasting them as they would have been had the agent acted with actual authority.[55] However, ratification is ineffective as against rights or other interests acquired by persons not parties to the transaction in question that were acquired in the subject matter prior to the ratification.[56]

Subject to this limitation, one might think of a principal's power to ratify as an option held by the principal to elect to be bound by an agent's prior act that the principal may exercise with the benefit of hindsight. The option-like characteristic of a principal's power to ratify also helps explains why a ratification must encompass the entirety of an act or other single transaction that would not otherwise be attributable to the principal.[57] Were the principal able to choose among the aspects of a single transaction or act or among their legal consequences, embracing some and rejecting others, the principal would be empowered to obtain the benefits of an agent's action without bearing its liabilities. The principal would also be empowered to speculate at the expense of the agent, choosing to ratify a transaction to bind a third party while reserving the possibility of asserting a claim against the agent for loss suffered from an unauthorised transaction if the transaction eventually proves disadvantageous to the principal.[58]

A principal is not bound by a ratification if the principal, at the time of manifesting assent to an agent's action, lacked knowledge of material facts and was unaware of such lack of knowledge.[59] The burden of

---

[52] *Restatement (Third)*, § 4.01, comment *b*.   [53] *Ibid.*, § 4.01(2)(b).
[54] *Ibid.*, Comment *d*.   [55] *Ibid.*, § 4.02(1) and comment *b*.   [56] *Ibid.*, § 4.02(2)(c).
[57] *Ibid.*, § 4.07.   [58] *Ibid.*, § 4.02, comment *b*.   [59] *Ibid.*, § 4.06.

establishing the principal's knowledge falls to the party who claims that a ratification occurred, an allocation that is consistent with allocating the burden of establishing the existence of a relationship of agency to the party who claims a particular relationship to be one of agency.[60]

Restatement (Third), § 4.03 permits a person to ratify an act 'if the actor acted or purported to act as an agent on the person's behalf'.[61] Thus, a person may elect to become bound by the action of one who was not an agent at all at the time of the action, such as the roguish impostors discussed in subsection C. Under § 4.03, an undisclosed principal may ratify the unauthorised action of an agent. In contrast, *Restatement (Second)* restricted the power to ratify to disclosed and unidentified principals by conditioning the power on whether the actor 'purported' to act as an agent.[62] So to restrict the power to ratify was unwarranted and inconsistent with the result reached in relatively recent cases.[63] The restriction was unnecessary to prevent a stranger to a transaction from claiming its benefits because an undisclosed principal is not a 'stranger' to the agent with whom the third party dealt. The restriction was also unnecessary to protect the third party to the transaction; although ratification has the effect of adding a party (the previously undisclosed principal) as a party to the transaction, the result is no different from the consequences that stem from recognising that an undisclosed principal may acquire rights and become subject to liabilities through an agent's actions. The third party loses no claims for breach of warranty of authority that the third party would otherwise have against the agent because no such warranties are made by an agent for an undisclosed principal. Finally, from the standpoint of the principal, ratification reflects a choice made by the principal. Denying the choice to one category of principals – those who were undisclosed when the agent acted – is neither necessary nor desirable.

(b) Entities yet to be formed

A person, including a company or other entity, cannot be a principal in an agency relationship unless the person has legal capacity at the time.[64]

---

[60] *Ibid.*, § 1.02, comment *b.*   [61] *Ibid.*, § 4.03.   [62] See *Restatement (Second)*, § 85(1).

[63] See *Coyle* v. *Smith* 300 So. 2d 738 (Fla. Ct App. 1974); *Acuri* v. *Figliotti* 398 NYS 2d 923 (Dist. Ct. 1977); *Young & Rubicam Inc.* v. *Ticket Holding Marketing Inc.* 1989 WL 4210 (ND Ill. 1989).

[64] At least at the time the relationship is created. *Restatement (Third)*, § 3.08(2) recognises that an individual may through a written instrument make an agent's actual authority irrevocable effective upon the principal's loss of capacity or confer it irrevocably regardless of the principal's loss of capacity.

Capacity presupposes existence, with the consequence that an entity yet to be formed becomes a party to contracts purportedly made on its behalf only by taking action once its legal existence is established. Under *Restatement (Third)*, § 4.04, a person lacks capacity to ratify an act if the person does not exist at the time of the act. Thus, when an entity chooses to become a party to a contract made on its behalf prior to its existence, the entity is adopting the contract, not ratifying the act of the actor who purported to act on the unformed entity's behalf.

Adoption is not the full equivalent of either novation or ratification. Unlike a novation, an adoption does not by itself release obligors from liabilities created by the original transaction. Thus, a person who purports to act on behalf of an entity yet to be formed becomes and remains subject to liability on a transaction entered into on its behalf absent agreement otherwise with the other party to the transaction. Moreover, in contrast to ratification, adoption by an entity does not operate retroactively. The time of adoption may become the relevant time for certain purposes, such as when duties of performance under the contract are to be rendered.[65]

6 Inherent agency power

Restatement (Second), in an innovation from the first *Restatement*, identified an additional basis on which the legal consequences of an agent's action might be attributed to the principal. *Restatement (Second)* characterised this basis as 'inherent agency power', defining it as 'the power of an agent which is derived not from authority, apparent authority or estoppel, but solely from the agency relation and exists for the protection of persons harmed by or dealing with a servant or other agent'.[66] The situations in which inherent agency power applied distinctively fell into two very different categories. First, and most frequently, inherent agency power was 'the power of a servant to subject his employer to liability for faulty conduct in performing his master's business'.[67] Second, inherent agency power was the basis on which an agent might bind a principal in a transaction for which the agent lacked actual authority when the agent's

---

[65] See *McArthur v. Times Printing Co.* 51 NW 216, 217 (Minn. 1892) (oral employment contract not within provision of Statute of Frauds applicable to contracts not to be performed within one year of their making; contract for term of eighteen months, made on behalf of corporation-yet-to-be formed, adopted by corporation thirteen months after contract made).

[66] *Restatement (Second)*, § 8A.   [67] *Ibid.*, comment *b*.

departure from authorised action was only a matter of slippage from the scope of authorised action on the part of a general agent;[68] when the agent, acting solely in the agent's own interests, entered into a transaction that would bind the principal were the agent's motives proper; and when the agent, authorised to dispose of goods owned by the principal, departed from the authorised disposal method.

An initial difficulty with inherent agency power is that it appears motivated by an attempt to bridge legal consequences stemming from very different bodies of primary law. That is, the rationales and policy justifications for imposing tort liability differ from rationales and policy justifications applicable in transactional settings. As a category-spanning bridge, inherent agency power seemed more like an artefact of an abstract scheme of classification than a normative doctrine articulating elements requisite to the imposition of liability.[69] A further difficulty stemmed from the possibility that an agent's unauthorised action might, if seen as an instance of inherent agency power, subject a principal to liability on a transaction when the third party with whom the agent dealt had notice that the agent lacked authority. To be sure, more specific formulations in *Restatement (Second)* appear alert to the need to foreclose this risk,[70] but inherent agency power as a freestanding doctrine always had the potential to range more widely and to provoke the imposition of liability when unwarranted by the circumstances.

Restatement (Third) jettisons inherent agency power as a basis on which to subject a principal to liability. Its ability to do so stems in part from a recognition that the bridging function assigned to inherent agency power was too heroic to be useful. Thus, the circumstances under which a principal is subject to vicarious liability for torts committed by an employee

---

[68] Specifically, when 'a general agent does something similar to what he is authorized to do, but in violation of orders': *Ibid.*

[69] See G. McMeel, 'Philosophical Foundations of the Law of Agency' (2000) 116 *LQR* 387 (characterising inherent agency power as an example of an 'ontological' as opposed to a 'normative' theory of agency law).

[70] See *Restatement (Second)*, § 161 (liability of disclosed or partially disclosed principal for acts done on principal's account by a general agent 'which usually accompany or are incidental to transactions which the agent is authorize to conduct … although forbidden by the principal' only when 'the other party reasonably believes that the agent is authorized to do them and has no notice that he is not so authorized') and § 165 (liability of a disclosed or partially disclosed principal 'upon a contract purported to be made on his behalf by an agent authorized to make it for the principal's benefit, although the agent acts for his own or other improper purposes' subject to qualifier 'unless the other party has notice that the agent is not acting for the principal's benefit').

or other agent are articulated and justified on their own terms. The circumstances under which unauthorised transactions entered into by an agent should generate legal consequences for the principal are articulated using the previously described normative vocabulary of apparent authority, estoppel and ratification. No gap in liability should result that would require or justify resort to inherent agency power.

In one rare recent instance in which the outcome reached by the court turns explicitly on inherent agency power, the result is problematic because it operates in favour of a third party that proceeded with a transaction on notice that the agent lacked actual authority to bind the principal. In *Menard Inc.* v. *Dage/MTI*, the third party dealt with a corporation through its president.[71] Although the third party knew that the president had required specific authorisation from the board of directors to commit the corporation to prior comparable transactions, it entered into a real estate transaction although the president lacked such authorisation and although the third party had no notice of any circumstance suggesting that the corporation had augmented the scope of its president's authority. A majority of the court acknowledged that the president lacked either actual or apparent authority to bind the corporation to the transaction but nonetheless subjected the corporation to liability on the basis of the president's inherent agency power.[72]

Effectively, the court's analysis in *Menard* allocates to a principal an ongoing burden of informing third parties with whom an agent deals that the principal has not removed restrictions on the agent's authority already known to the third party. But so to charge the principal is in sharp tension with a well-settled agency doctrine and the widely shared intuitions that underlie it. It is well established that an agent's apparent authority may survive or linger after the termination of actual authority because a third party may reasonably believe that the agent is authorised to take action and the belief is traceable to a manifestation made by the principal.[73] The underlying intuition is that one may reasonably assume

---

[71] 726 NE 2d 1206 (Ind. 2000).

[72] For a trenchant critique of *Menard* and inherent agency power more generally, see J. D. Ingram, 'Inherent Agency Powers: A Mistaken Concept Which Should Be Discarded' (2004) 29 *Okla City U L Rev* 583. Inherent agency power is not without defenders: see M. P. Ward, 'A Restatement or a Redefinition: Elimination of Inherent Agency Power in the Tentative Draft of the Restatement (Third) of Agency' (2002) 59 *Wash & Lee LR* 1585.

[73] See *Restatement (Third)*, § 3.11(2) (apparent authority 'ends when it is no longer reasonable for the third party with whom the agent deals to believe that the agent continues to act with actual authority').

an agent's actual authority to be an ongoing or continuing circumstance until placed on notice of circumstances to the contrary. It is difficult to see why comparable reasoning should not apply to restrictions on an agent's authority known to a third party.

IV Liabilities of the unauthorised agent

An agent's unauthorised action may subject the agent to liability to the principal or to the third party with whom the agent dealt. Liability to the principal results when the agent acts without actual authority but the principal is nonetheless bound by the agent's action, typically because the agent acted with apparent authority. The agent's liability to the principal is extinguished if and when the principal ratifies the agent's action. An agent is subject to liability to the third party with whom the agent dealt when the principal is not bound by the agent's action on any basis, including apparent authority contemporaneous with the action or subsequent ratification by the principal.

Even if an agent acts with actual authority in a transaction with a third party, unless the agent and the third party agree otherwise, the agent becomes a party to the contract, and thus subject to liability to the third party, if the agent does not disclose the identity of the principal on whose behalf the agent deals. This is so even when the principal is unidentified because the third party knows that the agent acts on behalf of some principal but does not have notice of the principal's identity.[74] The rationale is that, although notice that an agent represents some principal enables the third party to negotiate with the agent for additional protection or for the agent's primary liability on the contract, only with notice of the principal's identity will the third party be enabled to assess the relative value of the agent's liability relative to that of the principal.

1 Lack of actual authority

An agent owes the principal duties to act only within the scope of the agent's actual authority and to comply with lawful instructions received from the principal or persons designated by the principal.[75] A breach of either duty subjects the agent to liability for loss caused the principal.[76]

Additionally, taking action beyond the scope of actual authority may trigger duties of disclosure to the principal. An agent has a duty to use

---

[74] *Ibid.*, § 6.02.   [75] *Ibid.*, § 8.09.   [76] *Ibid.*, comment *b*.

reasonable effort to disclose to the principal all facts that are material to the agent's duties to the principal when the agent knows, has reason to know, or should know that the principal would wish to have the facts, subject to any manifestation by the principal to the contrary.[77] The facts that an agent has a duty to disclose may include information material to alternate arrangements that the principal may wish to make in light of the agent's unauthorised action. In *Merrill Lynch, Pierce, Fenner & Smith Inc. v. Cheng*, as a consequence of a computer malfunction a securities broker overbought his customer's account in options, contrary to the customer's express instructions.[78] The broker, after telling the customer about the unauthorised purchase and the subsequent decline in the options' price, then informed the customer that his choices consisted of either selling the options or providing more cash to cover the debit in the customer's account in the hope of a rise in the options' price. The court held that the broker breached his duty to his customer by failing to inform him that, alternatively, the customer had the right to reject the unauthorised purchase.

2 *Principal is not bound by agent's action*

A person who purports to make a contract, conveyance or representation on behalf of another may explicitly represent to a third party that the principal has authorised the action. Such an explicit representation creates an express warranty that the agent (or purported agent) acts with actual authority. Additionally, an agent (or purported agent) impliedly warrants that a contract, conveyance or representation purportedly made on behalf of another is made with authority. If the agent or purported agent lacks power to bind, the agent or purported agent is subject to liability for damages caused by breach of the implied warranty, including loss of the benefit expected from performance by the principal, unless the third party knows that the actor lacks actual authority or the actor makes a manifestation to the third party that no warranty is given.[79] However, if performance by the principal would not have benefited the third party – most typically because of intervening insolvency on the part of the principal – the third party's recovery may be limited to out-of-pocket losses.[80]

---

[77] *Ibid.*, § 8.11 (1). An agent's duty to make such disclosure to the principal is subject to any superior duty of confidentiality that the agent owes to another person: *ibid.*, § 8.11(2).
[78] 901 F 2d 1124 (DC Cir. 1990). [79] *Restatement (Third)*, § 6.10. [80] *Ibid.*, comment *b*.

The implied warranty doctrine allocates to agents responsibility for assuring an accurate match between actual authority and actions taken purportedly on a principal's behalf.[81] Of course, an agent who breaches the implied warranty of authority does not become a party to the transaction; enabling an agent or purported agent to acquire rights to performance from the third party would conflict with the third party's most basic expectation of receiving performance from, and rendering performance to, the principal purportedly represented by the agent.

The content of the implied warranty of authority – that action is taken with actual authority – does not precisely match the elements of liability for breach. An agent or purported agent is not subject to liability for breach of the implied warranty of authority if the principal is bound on some other basis, such as apparent authority or ratification by the principal. This may reduce the likelihood that a third party who incurs costs in establishing that a principal is bound will seek to recover its costs from an agent or purported agent, arguably leaving the third party in a worse position than had the principal rendered performance without contesting the agent's authority.[82]

Most cases, like the rule stated in *Restatement (Third)*, § 6.10, do not characterise the third party's claim for breach of warranty as equivalent to a tort claim based on misrepresentation and thus do not limit the third party's recovery to damage or loss suffered, excluding the benefit of the bargain had the principal been bound by the agent's action. Enabling the third party to recover expectation damages better recognises the underlying function of the doctrine, which is safeguarding the third party's expectation that the agent or purported agent's action will be effective to bind the principal and oblige the principal to render performance to the third party. When the principal is not bound, the third party loses the benefit anticipated through the principal's performance. Indeed, limiting the third party's recovery to out-of-pocket loss may tempt some agents (and purported agents) to take the risk of breaching the implied warranty in the hope that either the principal will ratify the agent's unauthorised action or the third party will not suffer provable out-of-pocket losses.

V Conclusion

Drafting *Restatement (Third) of Agency* provided an ongoing opportunity to consider how best to articulate the common-law doctrines that

---

[81] *Ibid.*, comment *b*.   [82] *Ibid.*, comment *b*.

underlie the varied institutions and practices based on ascribing legal consequences from one person's actions to another person. It proved possible to take into account the role of statutes of all sorts and of organisations in relation to common-law doctrines. It also proved possible to consider the distinct contribution made by each doctrine and the underlying rationales at work throughout common-law agency doctrine in the United States.

Notwithstanding their dated qualities, the prior *Restatements* articulated basic concepts and doctrines in an accessible manner and, as it happened, attracted no competing or alternative scholarly account. Stripped of doctrinal subtleties, agency deploys a relatively small number of congruent basic principles that work in well-understood ways and that carry relatively predictable consequences. Some agency doctrines – such as apparent authority – are dependent in their application on specific factual context, inevitably requiring close calls in some cases. But that does not vitiate the underlying coherence of agency doctrine as a whole. *Restatement (Third)*'s contribution may be to make more evident this underlying coherence and thereby to enhance common-law agency's ongoing salience as a source of coherence in a complex legal world.

Unauthorised agency, the American *Restatements* and other common law countries

FRANCIS REYNOLDS

Table of contents

I Introduction

The American *Restatements of the Law* consist of statements of general principles of law for the area concerned, accompanied by a technical commentary which provides explanation and development of those principles, and further notes by the Reporter on the particular topic raised, giving indications of case-law in the area (which often contains conflicting lines of decision one of which may have been chosen) and references to relevant secondary literature. Of necessity, they may well in areas of controversy adopt particular formulations of principle rather than others: that is to say, they may contain creative choices of principle by the Reporter, approved by the Institute. In their format they are codes, or quasi-codes, for particular legal topics, accompanied by two levels of commentary. With the possibility of minor exceptions in very small dependent territories, they have however no legislative force. No court in the United States need adhere to the principles chosen. Rather, they are put forward by a prestigious but private organisation, the American Law Institute, as offering authoritative but optional guidance in the area of law restated. They carry considerable weight in the United States, but they do not in general bind any court charged with giving a decision.

The differences of style between the new *Restatement (Third) of Agency*[1] and its predecessor, *Restatement (Second) of Agency*[2] of 1958, are explained by Professor Deborah DeMott, the Reporter for *Restatement (Third)*, in the previous chapter.[3] In general the new *Restatement (Third)* is far less detailed in its formulated (or 'black letter', so called from their appearing in bold type to distinguish them from the commentary) rules than *Restatement (Second)* (for which the Reporter was Professor Warren Seavey of the Harvard Law School). Fewer principles are stated, and those stated are at a greater degree of generality; there is also more emphasis on the problems of corporations and unincorporated bodies ('organisational principals') than hitherto; and in the commentary and Reporter's notes there are more references to statutes (which, like judicial decisions, vary from state to state, but can be a pointer to accepted or desirable legal policy). All this creates a greater need for the filling out of the propositions by the Reporter's notes, and these are far more substantial and systematic than in *Restatement (Second) of Agency*. As with its predecessors in their times, *Restatement (Third) of Agency* is a distinguished document which will provide lucid and authoritative guidance for many over the coming years.

Such an authoritative document is bound also to carry weight in other common law countries (of which the principal for our purposes here may be said to be England, Ireland, Australia, Canada and New Zealand, but there are others such as Singapore[4] and Hong Kong and, of course, the countries of the Indian subcontinent and many territories in the African continent). All of these share the generalised common law notions of agency which emerge so clearly from Professor DeMott's chapter. Citations to the *Restatements* in courts outside the United States have, however, been rare, and are likely to continue to be so. It is important to bear in mind that in all those common law countries, although the law is also developed largely from judicial decisions, the scene as regards the precedents from which the law is built up is quite different from that in the United States. The *Restatements* can offer guidance to judges and practising lawyers in a country containing more than fifty separate jurisdictions and no single court charged with resolving differences

---

[1] American Law Institute, *Restatement of the Law, Third: Agency* (St Paul, MN: American Law Institute, 2006).
[2] American Law Institute, *Restatement of the Law, Second: Agency* (St Paul, MN: American Law Institute, 1958).
[3] See Chapter 7 (US).
[4] This is emphasised by the fact that the chapter on English law in this book is actually written by a Singaporean lawyer and academic.

between them in the area of private law. Among these jurisdictions there is a huge accumulation of case law which can never be fully assimilated or reconciled. The other common law countries are either single jurisdictions, or federations with power of final decision in private as well as public law matters vested in a supreme tribunal such as the House of Lords (in the United Kingdom), the High Court of Australia or the Supreme Court of Canada. In these countries there may often be different lines of decision, but to nothing like the same extent; and for any particular question there may well be a decision or authoritative judgment, or both. This, unless a successful argument is advanced to reinterpret or change it, may give 'the' answer to a particular question. If the case is not conclusive on the point, it may be necessary to consider and reconcile other cases in a way that might prove irritating (or even futile) to a person drafting a codification or quasi-codification which, like the *Restatements*, starts on the basis that there are bound to be differing lines of authority, and that choices have to be made.[5]

The purpose of this chapter is to suggest certain differences of approach among other common law countries which may follow from these factors, in the context of the three main topics to which this book is addressed.

II Apparent authority

It is plain that all legal systems have difficulty in providing a complete explanation of the cases in which an agent who is not authorised, but appears to be so, binds, and perhaps entitles, his principal – a result that all legal systems need to achieve to some degree. The traditional common law explanation bases the result on estoppel, that the principal is in appropriate circumstances estopped (prevented) from denying the agent's authority. It seems (perhaps surprisingly, in view of the specifically common law nature of the doctrine) that this justification is used also in South Africa,[6] a mixed jurisdiction, though it is not in another, Scotland.[7] Under this reasoning it is the conduct of the principal – though often conduct of a very general nature – which justifies his being liable. But the estoppel reasoning only justifies his liability: he cannot sue unless he ratifies, and a ratification is subject to the

---

[5] For an example see the group of cases referred to in n. 37, below.
[6] See Chapter 10 (South Africa), II 1.   [7] See Chapter 9 (Scotland), II 1.

normal restrictions that prevent unfair ratification in common law countries.[8]

This explanation can be said to leave insufficient scope in practice for paying attention to the reasonableness of the third party's belief, and the extent to which further enquiries by the third party might or might not have been officious[9] (a problem for which recent French law appears to have developed a technique for emphasising and solving).[10] But the estoppel explanation has also been somewhat unsatisfactory as regards theory. Classical expositions of the common law notion of estoppel[11] have stricter requirements in stronger terms than seem appropriate to the sort of facts involved in most apparent authority situations. It is traditionally said that for estoppel there must be a clear and unequivocal representation or statement made to another, intended to be acted on or given with knowledge that it is likely to be acted or relied on, and in fact acted or relied on by the representee. In the situation of apparent authority, where the supposed representation is as to authority of an agent, although such requirements are sometimes demonstrably complied with, they are often not. The so-called 'representation' may not be addressed to anyone specifically, there certainly may not be an intention that it be acted on (though the fact that it may be requires to have been anticipatable), and action in reliance, other than by entering into a transaction, may not be easy to demonstrate. Very often all the principal has done is put someone in a role which would normally carry authority. All these different and sometimes mutually inconsistent points are duly taken in particular judgments within the huge panoply of American decisions, as well as in England and elsewhere.

It must be in reaction to such problems that Restatement (Third) of Agency (hereinafter 'the Restatement') articulately takes a different line, by basing the principal's legal position in apparent authority situations on the objective interpretation which common law uses to determine whether words or acts have contractual (or other) effect.[12] The authority is still attributed to the principal's conduct: it must be the case that the

---

[8] See on ratification III, below.

[9] A point taken in *Waugh* v. *HB Clifford & Sons Ltd* [1982] Ch 374, where the question was as to the authority of a solicitor in litigation.

[10] See Chapter 2 (France), II.

[11] See the leading case of *Low* v. *Bouverie* [1891] 3 Ch 82; also a useful formulation by a highly respected Australian judge, Dixon J, in *Thompson* v. *Palmer* (1933) 49 CLR 507 at 547.

[12] For an English exposition of the objective approach, see *The Hannah Blumenthal* [1983] 1 AC 854 at 915–16.

third party 'reasonably believes the actor has authority … and that belief is traceable to the principal's manifestations.[13] The word 'manifestation' is selected, and used (in several of the propositions formulated) to indicate the conduct of the principal which generates authority: it is more objective in thrust than the word 'representation', which English courts and books tend to use and which carries overtones of the estoppel formulation. This objective (or even, because it moves from 'representation' to 'manifestation', 'super-objective') formulation enables *Restatement (Third)* more clearly than its predecessor to differentiate from it cases where what might be called 'true' estoppel, in its authentic form, is applied in an agency situation.[14] It also enables the (outside the United States at least, welcome) disappearance of 'inherent agency power', a curious and enigmatic concept invented by Seavey and directed to explaining certain difficult cases which do not yield to normal conceptual analysis, which has (so far as I know) never made any impression outside the United States.[15]

In England (to which I shall henceforth confine myself: there could well be differences, albeit probably comparatively slight, in some of the other common law countries, and I obviously cannot claim expertise over the differing nuances), the terminology of estoppel cannot be abandoned unless a different formulation is adopted in a decision of the supreme tribunal, at present[16] the House of Lords. This is because the estoppel justification is clearly stated in an authoritative judgment of an authoritative judge, Lord Justice Diplock, in 1964;[17] and this explanation has been followed since, indeed very recently.[18] No English judge below appellate level could depart from it, and a middle tier appellate court (the Court of Appeal) would require considerable argument before doing so. No English book would be justified in taking a different line unless it was specifically advocating change. The most that can be done is to point out that the traditional requirements appear in rather a weak form, a form

---

[13] See *Restatement (Third)*, § 2.03, comment *c*.

[14] See Chapter 7 (US), III 2, III 3.   [15] See Chapter 7 (US) III 6.

[16] It is shortly to be re-formed and redesignated as a Supreme Court.

[17] *Freeman & Lockyer* v. *Buckhurst Park Properties (Mangal) Ltd* [1964] 2 QB 480 at 503. 'Each form of estoppel has its own elements, although some are common to others. The similarities warrant their recognition as a form of estoppel but the differences make each a distinct form with its own history and requirements': The Hon Mr Justice K. R. Handley, *Estoppel by Conduct and Election* (London: Sweet & Maxwell, 2006), p. 20.

[18] *Lloyd's Bank plc.* v. *Independent Insurance Co. Ltd* [2000] QB 110 at 121–2; *AMB Generali Holding AG* v. *SEB Trygg Liv Holding Aktiebolag* [2006] EWCA Civ 1237, [2006] 1 Lloyd's Rep 318 at [31].

which could be said to be applicable in the agency context only.[19] It can also be pointed out that, in some countries, particularly Australia, the view has been taken that estoppel doctrine should only be interpreted as carrying sufficient consequences to satisfy the particular equities of the situation. This, if applied to agency cases, could mean that the reasoning might sometimes only justify damages for reliance loss, or negative interest, rather than full expectation loss on a contract, or positive interest.[20] Such a result would not be convenient, and has not so far as I know been put forward in this context; though I note that something like it might be an arguable point in at least one other legal system.[21]

There is, however, a possible drawback to the alternative approach adopted by the *Restatement*. On this approach, I would assume that the principal is said to be liable on an unauthorised contract because he has given an appearance of assent to it by means of his agent, who appeared to be authorised to communicate such assent. There is not much difficulty with that. But when the third party enters into the transaction with the agent, the third party likewise gives an appearance of assent to a person apparently authorised to receive it, and since the assent is actually genuine as well, there is even less difficulty in seeing a bilaterally binding contract formed on the basis of objective criteria. The logical consequence is that not only can the third party sue the principal: the principal can sue the third party without any recourse to the notion of ratification, which would be required under the estoppel explanation, weak or strong. From this surprising result, Seavey in *Restatement (Second)* did not shrink;[22] and it is likewise adopted by Professor DeMott in *Restatement (Third)*.[23]

The practical difference is not great, but does exist. If the estoppel plus ratification explanation is adopted, where the third party discovers that the act was unauthorised, he can repudiate the transaction for that reason alone: the principal can ratify, but subject to controls on unfair operation of the ratification concept,[24] which would probably not permit it in such a situation. But on what I have ventured to call the 'super-objective'

---

[19] I discuss this point in F. M. B. Reynolds, *Bowstead and Reynolds on Agency*, 18th edn (London: Sweet & Maxwell, 2006), 8-026, 8-029.

[20] See G. E. Dal Pont, *The Law of Agency* (Chatsworth, NSW: Butterworths Australia, 2nd edn (2008), §§ 20.12, 20.13. In England the point usually arises in connection with land: see S. Gardner, 'The Remedial Discretion in Proprietary Estoppel – Again' (2006) 120 LQR 492–512.

[21] See Chapter 4 (Germany), III, IV.   [22] *Restatement (Second)*, § 8, comment *d*.

[23] See § 2.03 and Reporter's notes.   [24] See III, below.

explanation, there is a contract from the time of formation and the principal can simply enforce it against the repudiating third party.

The Reporter's Notes to *Restatement (Third)* cite only one actual decision in support of such a proposition.[25] In it a woman sought to discontinue an insurance policy. The person with whom she communicated had no actual authority to receive the discontinuance notification, though he appeared to be authorised and hence had apparent authority. She was killed in an air accident the next day. The question arose as to whether she was insured at the time. Her representatives argued that she had been because the notice of discontinuance had not been given to a person authorised to receive it. This argument was rejected. *Restatement (Second)* was cited to the effect that she could have relied on the doctrine of apparent authority against the company: hence the company could assert the discontinuance against her (or her estate). The court cited a comment from *Restatement (Second)*: 'the principal becomes immediately a contracting party with both *rights* and *liabilities* to [*sic*] the third person' (emphasis added).[26]

The application of agency reasoning to this situation is not straightforward, but it seems possible to suggest a different way of resolving the dispute. One might say that she had given notification of discontinuance to a person apparently authorised to receive it: hence it was she who was relying on the authority of the agent to create a legal effect on her policy, which, the notification being validly given, had been created. On this basis reliance on *Restatement (Second)* was unnecessary.

The logic of what I have ventured above to call the 'super-objective interpretation' approach seems superior, but the explanation that the third party can enforce because the principal cannot deny authority, but the principal can only do so against the third party subject to the rules as to ratification, may sometimes give fairer results.

III Ratification

The theory that apparent authority enables the principal to sue as well as be sued must mean that the role for ratification under the *Restatement* is reduced. If the third party discovers that the agent was not authorised to contract, he can rely on the doctrine of apparent authority to enforce the

---

[25] *Equitable Variable Life Insurance Co.* v. *Wood* 362 SE 2d 741 (Va., 1987), cited in Reporter's notes to § 2.03, notes to comment *e*.
[26] *Ibid.*

contract: and provided that this doctrine is applicable, the principal can enforce it against the third party also. The logical result is that if the third party, on learning of the lack of authority, seeks or purports to withdraw from the contract, he cannot validly do so because he is already bound to it. The rules of ratification, however, would probably (subject in English law to problems discussed below) allow this; and outside this particular context *Restatement (Third)* certainly would, as I shall note in the next paragraph. In such a situation, there would often be some uncertainty as to whether the contract is in fact binding under the doctrine of apparent authority, and this can obviously be a disputable issue that might have to go to judicial resolution. The principal may, of course, concede the agent's apparent authority; but it is not clear that this will work for all cases. Be that as it may, under the *Restatement*, therefore, the doctrine of ratification must presumably be limited to situations where the third party's belief in apparent authority is unrealistic, and to cases where the third party knows at the time of contracting that the agent has no authority – a situation where, as also appears below, it is not clear that all other common law jurisdictions would admit the relevance of ratification at all.

Passing from this topic, *Restatement (Third)*, starting from the point that ratification is of its nature retrospective, contains a specific provision preventing a ratification that would have 'adverse and inequitable' effects on the rights of third parties.[27] Recent English cases use a similar technique.[28] The *Restatement*, however, goes further in giving three specific but non-exclusive indications of where this is likely to be so, of which the first is 'any manifestation of intention to withdraw from the transaction made by the third party'. This sounds reasonable enough,[29] but anyone dealing with this question outside the United States, or at least in England, would have to overcome a specific nineteenth-century Court of Appeal decision[30] giving a retrospective effect to ratification in (what appear to be) such circumstances.

---

[27] *Restatement (Third)*, § 4.05.

[28] See *Smith* v. *Henniker-Major & Co.* [2003] EWCA Civ 762, [2003] Ch 182 (where the rule is said to be a 'judgmental application of principle, not … an exercise of judicial discretion, though in practice the two are closely akin'); *The Borvigilant* [2003] EWCA Civ 935, [2003] 2 Lloyd's Rep 520.

[29] Subject to a slight doubt as to whether 'manifestation of intention to withdraw' differs from an actual operative withdrawal.

[30] It is slightly misleading to say, as does comment *c*, that English cases have 'long declined to permit the third party to withdraw': it is this one case that is the sticking-point. Compare *Watson* v. *Davies* [1931] 1 Ch 455, n. 37 below.

In *Bolton Partners Ltd* v. *Lambert*[31] Mr Lambert offered to buy from the vendor company a lease of a sugar factory subject to various conditions, and the acting managing director of the company wrote to him saying that the directors accepted his offer. In fact what had happened was the company's works committee had resolved that the offer should be accepted, and a letter written accordingly, and that the company's solicitor should be instructed to prepare the appropriate documents. It was accepted that neither the acting managing director nor the works committee had actual or (it seems) apparent authority to accept the offer or to bind the company by a sale of its property. When the draft agreement was sent to Mr Lambert, he objected to certain terms and subsequently withdrew his offer on the ground of alleged misrepresentations made to him as to the value of the property. The directors then authorised the issue of a writ, and subsequently confirmed the minutes of the works committee.

The initial dispute was as to whether the parties had entered into a binding contract at all. The view was put for Mr Lambert that they had not done so, by reason of the conditional nature of his purported acceptance to the vendor's offer. This was rejected by the court (and the question of the alleged misrepresentations was not pursued). It was in no way suggested that Mr Lambert was aware of the works committee's lack of authority at the time when he purported to withdraw from the contract, or that this knowledge justified him in doing so. Probably most lawyers would agree that if the third party discovers the lack of authority, he can withdraw on that basis alone: there is no transaction at that time, though it should be noted that there may well have been a possibility of arguing apparent authority, and if there was none, then the agent would be liable for breach of warranty of authority, discussed below. But in this case the third party, Mr Lambert, was alleging, not that there had been no authority, but that no contract had been formed at all, an interpretation which was rejected by the court.

On the basis of there being a valid contract, he was then by his actions in breach of it, unless it could be said that ratification after withdrawal was ineffective despite the 'withdrawal' being on a ground not related to authority. It may well be possible to argue that although the reason for withdrawal from the transaction which Mr Lambert gave was invalid, there existed at that time a valid reason (lack of authority), and that this justified the same argument as that above, that at the time of withdrawal

[31] (1889) 41 Ch D 295.

there was no transaction, and that this should not be curable by a ratification. It is established in English law that a party may give an invalid reason for terminating a contract, and later rely on a valid reason if it existed, whether known to him or not, at the time of the termination.[32] Perhaps the decision could yield to such an analysis. But the case is often misunderstood,[33] and the matter is not as straightforward as it might appear on first impression. Whatever the right answer, if an issue as to ratification after withdrawal arose in such a stark form, *Bolton v. Lambert* would have to be analysed.[34]

There is a second possible difference, though perhaps largely theoretical, from the English law as to ratification. The *Restatement* appears to be based on an assumption that the ratification rules can be operative even though the third party knew at the time of contracting that the agent had no authority.[35] A similar unstated assumption appears in the discussion of ratification in the Principles of European Contract Law and the UNIDROIT Principles of International Commercial Contracts of 2004.[36] Codifications of this type can take a quasi-legislative role. But as a matter of common law principle, if the third party knows that the agent has no authority, the most he can be doing is making an offer to the agent's principal, which may (or may not) be intended to be irrevocable; or if it is the agent who makes the offer to him, he is indicating that he will accept when the principal's offer is made. If, before anything further occurs, the principal accepts or confirms the offer, a contract may come into existence: the word 'ratification' may indeed be used, and the original transaction may even be said to have been 'subject to ratification'. But, at common law, promises not to revoke offers and statement of intention to accept are not binding without consideration: so unless

---

[32] *Boston Deep Sea Fishing & Ice Co.* v. *Ansell* (1888) 39 Ch D 339 (an employment case). (In fact in the present case two justifications were offered, both invalid.)

[33] E.g. by H. Kötz (trans. T. Weir), *European Contract Law I* (Oxford: Clarendon Press, 1997), p. 234.

[34] As it was in *Watson* v. *Davies* [1931] 1 Ch 455, n. 37 below. It had been attacked three years after it was decided, in the leading English work on specific performance: see E. Fry, *A Treatise on the Specific Performance of Contracts*, 3rd edn (London: Stevens, 1892), Additional Note A. No doubt the standing of the writer, who became Lord Justice Fry, means that even his extra-judicial utterances could be invoked in argument. But the case was said comparatively recently to be binding at Court of Appeal level in England, in *Presentaciones Musicales SA* v. *Secunda* [1994] Ch 271 at 280. Tribunals such as the High Court of Australia and the Supreme Court of Canada would have a freer hand.

[35] This approach was taken by Seavey in *Restatement (Second)*, Appendix, Reporter's note to § 85.

[36] *Principles of European Contract Law*, Art. 3:207; *UNIDROIT Principles*, Art. 2.2.9.

consideration (i.e. some feature making the transaction non-gratuitous) can be found, the third party may withdraw. There is simply nothing to ratify.[37] It may be said that this result is equally well secured by the *Restatement* principle already referred to, that there can be no ratification after a withdrawal by the third party. But whereas an acceptance, or an offer as the case may be, has to be communicated to the other party to be effective, this is not so of ratification, and this could in a particular situation cause a difference. In general, technical rules such as this, and that preventing ratification in part, or references to change of circumstances, seem likely to make an analysis of this situation under the rubric of ratification less convenient.

It should be noted, finally in this context, that it is in fact much more likely that it is the third party that seeks to hold the principal to a ratification rather than the reverse. Litigation in which claimants argue actual, apparent authority and ratification is common,[38] particularly in view of the fact that ratification need not be communicated. Situations where a principal unfairly seeks to thrust a ratification upon the third party who has become justifiably disillusioned about the contract must actually be fairly rare.

Although the doctrine of the undisclosed principal is not within the scope of this book, many civil lawyers know that in the common law an agent authorised by a principal can by contract bind and entitle his principal even though the agent in dealing does not state that he has a principal. The *Restatement*, unlike its predecessor, permits such a person to ratify: that is to say it applies the doctrine even though the agent was not authorised at the time of dealing. In England this is contrary to a decision of the House of Lords[39] which is most unlikely to be reconsidered – though a case could be made for not applying such a rule where the intermediary already has a pre-existing agency relationship with the principal.

---

[37] See *Watson v. Davies* [1931] 1 Ch 455, a case very similar to *Bolton v. Lambert*, n. 31, above, but decided to contrary effect, where Maugham J says: 'In a case where the agent for one party to a negotiation informs the other that he cannot enter into a contract binding his principal except subject to his approval, there is in truth no contract or contractual relation until the approval has been obtained … an acceptance by an agent subject in express terms to ratification by his principal is legally a nullity until ratification.' Compare *Re Portuguese Consolidated Copper Mines* (1890) 45 Ch D 16, where there was no repudiation at all and ratification was effective.

[38] For recent examples, see *The Borvigilant*, see n. 28, above; *AMB Generali Holding AG v. SEB Trygg Liv Holding Aktiebolag*, see n. 18 above.

[39] *Keigyhley, Maxsted & Co v. Durant* [1901] AC 240.

IV The *falsus procurator*

The basis of the liability of a *falsus procurator* given in the *Restatement* is, so far as I know, accepted throughout the common law world. The unauthorised agent is liable on, in common law terms, an implied collateral contract whereby (unless the circumstances clearly indicate otherwise) he guarantees that he has authority (his lack of care being irrelevant); and his liability is for the benefits anticipated by the claimant third party from the transaction and not merely for reliance loss (negative interest). Although not all civil lawyers would accept these two features (which were during the nineteenth century themselves both controversial in England), they are accepted in the Principles of European Contract Law[40] and the UNIDROIT Principles of International Commercial Contracts.[41] This device for securing the liability of the *falsus procurator* in England evolved in the mid-nineteenth century, and the case establishing it[42] proved a pathfinding precedent for the imposition of liability for statements and other indications causing financial loss at a time when tort liability was inadequately developed for the purpose. It is of interest to note that the decision was fairly soon after followed in England by corrective legislation protecting donees of powers of attorney whose authority had unknown to them been revoked, and those who dealt with them.[43]

A leading case in England made an agent whose principal had, unknown to him, become mentally incapable, liable under this head; and the same reasoning would apply in respect of a principal who had died. The *Restatement* avoids this consequence by providing elsewhere[44] that death and mental incapacity do not revoke authority until the occurrence of either becomes known to the agent; hence the warranty would not be broken. But this may not be accepted everywhere: the technical notion that loss of capacity or death simply removes a principal, and that a valid act cannot be done in the name of a dead (or mentally incapacitated) person, remains for solution in other common law countries.

A significant feature that should be noted in conjunction with the liability of the *falsus procurator* is that, under the *Restatement*, the agent of a (disclosed but) unidentified principal is actually *prima facie* a party

---

[40] Art. 3:204(2).   [41] Art. 2.2.6(1).   [42] *Collen* v. *Wright* (1857) 7 E & B 647.
[43] Powers of Attorney Act 1859, re-enacted in various forms subsequently.
[44] *Restatement (Third)*, §§ 3.07, 3.08.

to the main contract together with the principal, quite apart from his collateral guarantee of authority.[45] This provides a different route to the agent's liability, and such reasoning appears to be thought relevant also in Belgian law.[46] English courts accept the possibility that the agent can be a party to the main contract, but reject its application as an actual prima facie rule.[47]

Going further than the *Restatement*, extension of the reasoning applicable to secure the liability of a *falsus procurator* is considered in many English cases. It is long established that the agent does not warrant or promise that his principal will perform the contract, or is solvent. He does, however, warrant that he has a principal who has capacity. It has recently been decided that the duty may be owed to others than the initial third party.[48] In the case of solicitors issuing legal process, it has recently been decided that the promise is that the solicitor has a client who has authorised the proceedings, but not that the client has the name by which he appears in the proceedings.[49] Decisions in this area have the function of working out the boundaries of a strict liability under common law which might otherwise be dangerously wide, in that it might extend to other forms of misrepresentation.

---

[45] *Restatement (Third)*, § 6.02, following *Restatement (Second)*, § 321.

[46] Chapter 3 (Belgium), VI.

[47] See *Vlassopoulos Ltd* v. *Ney Shipping Co. Ltd (The Santa Carina)* [1977] 1 Lloyd's Rep 478.

[48] *Penn* v. *Bristol & West Building Society* [1997] 1 WLR 1356 (warranty by solicitor of vendor of land given not only to purchaser but also to financial institution lending money on the security of the land).

[49] *AMB Generali Holding AG* v. *SEB Trygg Liv Holding Aktiebolag*, see n. 18, above.

PART 3

Mixed legal systems

Unauthorised agency in Scots law

LAURA MACGREGOR

I Introduction

In the Introduction to this book, Scots and South African law were
described as 'mixed' legal systems: the product of civilian foundations
overlaid by later common law influence. Agency law in Scotland reflects
this 'mixed' nature. The first major source of Scots agency law is the body
of work produced by the Scottish institutional writers, whose works are
considered to be an actual source of law. The most notable of those
writers, James Dalrymple, Viscount Stair, writing in the latter half of the
seventeenth century, analysed the law of mandate in his *Institutions*.[1]

---

[1] I, 10, 12.

Throughout his title he makes frequent reference to Roman law, principally the Digest and Institutes. It is not surprising, therefore, that some of the solutions found there have a distinctly civilian flavour. Another institutional writer, George Joseph Bell, who produced the first edition of his book on what we would now call commercial law between 1800 and 1804,[2] developed those early principles of mandate into a body of law which more clearly resembles modern agency law. In his works he makes extensive use of English case-law. Case-law, both Scots and English, is the second main source of agency law in Scotland. Indeed, the influence of English case-law has grown so that, today, English precedents are discussed as much if not more than Scottish ones in the Scottish courts.

The resultant 'mixture' poses a challenge to those seeking to analyse Scots agency law. The most significant problem is that there may be no answer to the question, what is the law? There is as yet no textbook devoted solely to Scots agency law, although there are single agency chapters in more general works.[3] As a result, a large percentage of a chapter such as this one must be devoted to the task of finding the law. This chapter therefore differs from the others in this book, not only from the civilian ones where the main point of reference is a code, but also from the common law chapters where a higher volume of case-law and scholarship has created a more fully developed body of law.

In view of the problems in 'finding the law', there are those who advocate complete assimilation with English agency law. The advantages and disadvantages of this course of action cannot be fully analysed here. The high usage of English case-law in Scottish courts makes it at least a possibility. There are, however, many factors pointing against such assimilation, particularly 'structural' differences existing between the two legal systems. Scots law possesses no doctrine of consideration, and this means that English agency concepts and precedents motivated by the requirements of consideration are likely to be inappropriate in Scotland. Linked to this is the more open attitude of Scots law to privity of contract, reflected in the presence of both an enforceable unilateral promise and a common law third party right. As is argued later in this chapter,[4] in a tri-partite situation such as agency, these concepts are

---

[2] The title of the first edition was *Treatise on the Law of Bankruptcy*. The title *Commentaries on the Law of Scotland* was used in later editions.
[3] The most recent analysis is L. Macgregor, 'Agency and Mandate', in *The Laws of Scotland: Stair Memorial Encyclopaedia*, Reissue (Edinburgh: Butterworths, 2002).
[4] See part III, particularly III 5(c)(i).

assets the potential of which has not yet been fully explored. Another significant issue pointing against assimilation is the fact that the range of English estoppels is not applicable in Scotland, where a more unitary native concept, personal bar, exists. Finally on this point, with the moves towards the development of a European contract law, and the emergence of a Draft Common Frame of Reference,[5] now would be an unusual time to assimilate with English law.

II Apparent authority

1 General

In Scottish cases on apparent authority reference is often made to the concept as developed in an English case, *Freeman & Lockyer* v. *Buckhurst Park Properties (Mangal) Ltd*, where Lord Diplock defined the concept as follows:[6]

> a legal relationship between the principal and the contractor created by a representation, made by the principal to the contractor, intended to be and in fact acted on by the contractor, that the agent has authority to enter on behalf of the principal into a contract of a kind within the scope of the 'apparent' authority, so as to render the principal liable to perform any obligations imposed on him by such a contract.[7]

Apparent authority is, in general, a concept which developed relatively recently. Stoljar noted that the principles of agency as a whole were not fully formulated until the turn of the nineteenth century,[8] and Atiyah traced the development of apparent authority through the nineteenth century.[9] Although there are Scottish cases from the eighteenth and early nineteenth centuries containing reasoning similar to that

---

[5] The Draft Common Frame of Reference ('DCFR') is intended to act as a '"toolbox" or handbook for the EU legislator, to be used when revising existing and preparing new legislation in the area of contract law', see European Parliament resolution of 12 December 2007 on European Contract Law, B6-0513/2007. It is not intended to be binding in nature. The DCFR was delivered to the Commission on 28 December 2007.

[6] See most recently *Ben Cleuch Estates Ltd* v. *Scottish Enterprise* [2006] CSOH 35 at 127, per Lord Reed, where he adopts the opinion of Lord Cullen in the unreported case of *Capital Land Holdings Ltd* v. *Secretary of State for the Environment* (28 July 1995, unreported).

[7] [1964] 2 QB 480 at 503.

[8] See S. J. Stoljar, *The Law of Agency* (London: Sweet & Maxwell, 1961), pp. 3 and 14.

[9] P. S. Atiyah, *The Rise and Fall of Freedom of Contract* (Oxford: Clarendon Press, 1979), p. 496 *et seq.*

found in modern apparent authority cases, they are true examples of mandate (gratuitous) and not agency (non-gratuitous). They involve representation of a 'paterfamilias' by his wife,[10] a family member[11] or servants[12] and are probably not relevant to modern commercial relationships.

There are also relevant Scottish cases from the nineteenth century, although the solutions applied there were not referred to as either 'ostensible' or 'apparent' authority.[13] Instead, use is made of a more general private law concept: homologation.[14] This concept, more fully analysed in the section of this chapter on ratification,[15] can be defined as knowledge and acquiescence by the principal of a course of conduct by the agent. Homologation was most notably used by the Second Division of the Inner House of the Court of Session in *International Sponge Importers* v. *Watt and Sons*.[16] Although this case eventually proceeded to the House of Lords, their Lordships did not share the Scottish court's view of the importance of homologation. Homologation has recently been identified as a forerunner and component part of the modern idea of personal bar (Scotland's version of estoppel), which is explored below.[17]

English precedents are routinely cited in modern Scottish cases. Apparent authority is closely related to estoppel. Thus, in a leading Scottish case, Lord Rodger explained that apparent authority is 'in both

---

[10] Gloag contrasts Scots law on this point with English law, see W. M. Gloag, *The Law of Contract: A Treatise on the Principles of Contract in the Law of Scotland*, 2nd edn. (Edinburgh: W. Green, 1929), p. 147, n. 6, where he refers to *Debenham* v. *Mellon* (1880) 6 App Cas 24.

[11] *Knox* v. *Hay* (1813) Hume 351; *Ferguson & Lillie* v. *Stephen* (1864) 2 M 804.

[12] *Oliver* v. *Grieve* (1792) Hume 319; *Inches* v. *Elder* (1793) Hume 322; *Dewar* v. *Nairne* (1804) Hume 340; *Mortimer* v. *Hamilton* (1868) 7M 158.

[13] Aside from the mandate cases discussed at n. 11 and n. 12 above, notable examples from the late eighteenth and the twentieth centuries include *The North of Scotland Banking Company* v. *Behn, Möller, & Co.* (1881) 8R 423; *Thomas Hayman & Sons* v. *The American Cotton Oil Co.* (1907) 45 SLR 207; *British Bata Shoe Co.* v. *Double M Shah Ltd* 1980 SC 311; *Dornier GmbH* v. *Cannon* 1991 SC 310; *Bank of Scotland* v. *Brunswick Developments (1987) Ltd (No. 2)* 1998 SLT 439. Only in the more recent ones is it possible to see usage of the terms 'apparent authority' and 'ostensible authority'.

[14] *Swinburne and Company* v. *The Western Bank of Scotland* (1856) 18 D 1025; *Finlayson* v. *The Braidbar Quarry Co* (1864) 2 M 1297 at 1303, per Lord Benholme; *Colvin* v. *Dixon* (1867) 5 M 603 at 609–610, per Lord Curriehill.

[15] See part III below.

[16] 1911 SC (HL) 57 at 68, per Lord Ardwall and at 61, per Lord Low.

[17] E. C. Reid, 'Personal Bar: Case-law in Search of Principle' (2003) *EdinLR* 340 at 341 and see II 2 below.

systems ... built on the doctrine which is known as estoppel in English law and personal bar in Scots law'.[18] Personal bar is, however, an elusive concept, which is only beginning to be analysed in the work of Elspeth Reid and John Blackie.[19] The analytical framework for personal bar used in this chapter is that suggested by Reid and Blackie.

2 Doctrinal basis

Gloag stated in the context of his discussion of apparent authority, that: 'any general theory is difficult to find or apply.'[20] Reid and Blackie's analysis of personal bar may assist in answering this question. They indicate that personal bar 'penalises inconsistent conduct'.[21] This may suggest an underlying purpose of protection of the reasonable expectations of the third party.

Bearing in mind the purpose of third party protection, and the fact that it is a form of personal bar, the result is that the third party is *entitled* and not *obliged* to make use of apparent authority. It is difficult to envisage circumstances in which a principal could 'force' the third party to adhere to a 'contract' formed by an unauthorised agent. This could only occur if the third party, himself, were personally barred. This might occur where the third party first gave the principal the impression that he was content to be bound and then sought to deny that impression. However, an important requirement of personal bar, 'unfairness', is lacking. It is the principal, and not the agent, who created the misleading impression of authority. It therefore seems unlikely that the third party could be personally barred, and thus unlikely that he could be forced to adhere to the 'contract'.

---

[18] 1998 SLT 439 at 443–4, per Lord President Rodger. It should be noted that, in England, there is much argument as to whether apparent authority should be regarded as based on estoppel or not. The main difficulties with the estoppel approach are: (1) the representation giving rise to the estoppel is, in this area, permitted to be very general; and (2) the detriment incurred by the representee may be small. Arguably, apparent authority has become a doctrine in its own right, see F. M. B. Reynolds, *Bowstead and Reynolds on Agency*, 18th edn. (London: Sweet & Maxwell, 2006), 8-029.

[19] Reid, *Case-law*, and E. C. Reid, 'Acquiescence in the Air: *William Grant* v. *Glen Catrine Bonded Ware*' (2001) JR 191 at 193; E. C. Reid and J. W. G. Blackie, *Personal Bar* (Edinburgh: W. Green, 2006). Before the publication of this work, the only alternative was J. Rankine, *A Treatise on the Law of Personal Bar in Scotland* (Edinburgh: W. Green, 1921), which is a guide to case-law rather than a reasoned analysis of the area.

[20] Gloag, *Contract*, p. 147.   [21] Reid and Blackie, *Personal Bar*, para. 2-01.

3 Scope

The scope of apparent authority in Scots law is extensive. It may arise in connection with the agent's acts in general, and is not limited to the unauthorised conclusion of contracts on the principal's behalf.[22] It operates not only where the agent exceeds his authority, but also where he has no authority whatsoever,[23] and can arise whether the principal is an individual or a legal person such as a company.[24] Its most common field of application lies in cases where the principal has either terminated or limited the agent's authority and has failed to notify third parties that he has done so, and the agent continues to act in spite of the withdrawal or limitation.[25] In such situations, the principal is obliged to notify third parties of the withdrawal or limitation, and such notification should be direct where a course of dealing exists, but can be by advertisement where no such course exists.[26] This type of situation occurs, for example, where a partnership fails to notify third parties that an individual partner has left the partnership.[27]

Apparent authority may also arise in situations where an event such as the death, mental incapacity or bankruptcy of the principal has terminated the principal/agent relationship. In such cases, the third party or the agent or even both may be unaware that the agent's authority has terminated. Although this issue is one which would undoubtedly have been more significant in the last century when communication networks were undeveloped, it nevertheless remains a relevant issue. This view is supported by the presence of rules within PECL governing this type of situation.[28]

---

[22] The explanations of this concept found in Gloag, *Contract*, pp. 147–9 and J. J. Gow, *The Mercantile and Industrial Law of Scotland* (Edinburgh: W. Green, 1964), pp. 517–20 refer to agents' acts in general and are not limited to the conclusion of contracts.

[23] Reid and Blackie, *Personal Bar*, para. 13-04, relying on English authority, *Freeman and Lockyer* v. *Buckhurst Park Properties (Mangal) Ltd* [1964] QB 480.

[24] Many of the leadings cases concern representation of non-legal persons, for example, *British Bata Shoe Co.* v. *Double M Shah Ltd* 1980 SC 311.

[25] See Lord Coulsfield *et al.* (eds.), *Gloag and Henderson's The Law of Scotland*, 12th edn. (Edinburgh: W. Green, 2007), para. 19.23; F. Davidson and L. Macgregor, *Commercial Law in Scotland*, 2nd edn (Edinburgh: W. Green, 2008), para 2.4.2.3. See also Gloag, *Contract*, p. 147, where he cites G. J. Bell, *Principles of the Law of Scotland* (Edinburgh: W. Blackwood, 1899), s. 288 and *North of Scotland Banking Company* v. *Behn, Möller, & Co* (1881) 8R 423.

[26] See, generally, Macgregor, 'Agency and Mandate' para. 81.

[27] The Partnership Act 1890, s. 36 is, in effect, this principle in statutory form.

[28] Art. 3:209 PECL.

Relatively early authority can be found in Scots law which analyses the effect of the principal's death, mental incapacity or bankruptcy on the agent's ability to contract. The sources are the works of the institutional writers, Stair and Erskine, and one rather remarkable case: *Pollok* v. *Paterson*,[29] decided by a bench of five judges in the Second Division in 1811. In their general discussion of the contract of mandate[30] the institutional writers note the general rule that the relationship of mandate terminates on the death of either party[31] before citing two exceptions. First, the mandatar/agent is entitled to complete any partially performed transactions notwithstanding the death of the mandant/principal. Secondly, an exception *'bonae fidei'* exists, which permits the mandatar to carry out transactions where he is unaware of the mandant's death, whether or not those transactions have commenced at the time of death or not.[32] The judges in *Pollok* v. *Paterson*[33] take matters a step further by extending the reasoning to situations of mental incapacity and sequestration. Lord Meadowbank explained why the particular event which terminated the agency relationship did not act to terminate the agent's authority: 'Once given, the mandate continues *sua natura*, and does not require a continuation of mental exertion or approbation.'[34] He confirmed that third parties dealing with the mandatary are protected, provided that they have acted in good faith.[35] Roman and civilian authorities were discussed in the case, and clearly had an impact on the outcome.[36]

---

[29] 10 Dec (1811) FC 369. The case concerned the mental incapacity and eventual sequestration of the principal.

[30] Macgregor, 'Agency and Mandate', paras. 18–28; J. Erskine, *An Institute of the Law of Scotland*, J. B. Nicholson (ed.), 8th edn. (Edinburgh: Butterworths/Law Society of Scotland, 1871, reprinted 1989), III, III, 41.

[31] '[F]or this contract arising from a singular affection or friendship betwixt both, the removal of either resolves that tie'; 1st Viscount Stair (James Dalrymple), *Institutions of the Law of Scotland*, D. M. Walker (ed.), 6th edn. (Glasgow and Edinburgh: University Presses of Glasgow and Edinburgh, 1981), 1.12.6.

[32] Erskine and Stair cite Inst 3.26.10 in support of the exceptions. Erskine additionally cites D 14.3.17.2-3.

[33] 10 Dec (1811) FC 369.   [34] 10 Dec (1811) FC 369 at 376.

[35] 10 Dec (1811) FC 369 at 377.

[36] At 377, per Lord Meadowbank and at 382, per Lord Justice-Clerk Boyle. Both indicate that they are relying on Roman sources but are not specific as to which ones. They are probably referring to the same passage of the Digest relied on by Erskine, namely D 14.3.17.2-3. Counsel for the pursuer cited the discussion of this passage by both Pothier and Voet, see R. J. Pothier, *Treatise on the Law of Obligations* (London: A. Strahan, 1806) para. 448 on D.14.3.17.2-3 and Voet. Lib. 17.1. 15. lib. 14. 3. 3.

Cases post-dating the works of the institutional writers support the proposition that the agent's authority continues in situations of mental incapacity[37] or death.[38] Bankruptcy is, however, a rather more complex area. Although *Pollok* v. *Paterson* suggests that the agent's authority may continue beyond the bankruptcy of the principal, one would imagine that this rule would be superseded by modern bankruptcy legislation. It seems unlikely that the agent's authority would survive in the face of the vesting of the insolvent party's goods in the trustee in bankruptcy. Nevertheless, it is notable that the PECL do indeed enable the agent to remain authorised until the third party knows or ought to know that the principal is insolvent.[39] The old Scots rule may therefore still be appropriate.

4 Effect

As already noted, personal bar prevents the principal from pleading the agent's lack of authority in any issue with the third party. Being, in essence, procedural in nature, it is unlikely that it has any stronger, 'constitutive' effect which would act to 'create' a contract where none otherwise existed.[40] This issue could be an important one. Logically, it should follow that specific implement is not available where there is, in fact, no contract. There appears to be no authority to confirm that this is indeed the case. The position in English law seems to be similarly unclear. Certainly, the principal there has no right to sue the third party without first ratifying the agent's actings, and this would tend to support the conclusion that no contract exists.[41] However, Powell, with whom Fridman agrees, suggested that the law 'presumes' a contract to exist,[42]

---

[37] *Pollok* v. *Paterson* 10 Dec (1811) FC 369; *Wink* v. *Mortimer* (1894) 11 D 995.

[38] *Campbell* v. *Anderson* [1829] 3 W & S 384, in an extremely short speech in the House of Lords, the Lord Chancellor, John Singleton Copley, at 187, described the case as a 'question of bona fides'.

[39] Art. 3:209(1)(d) PECL.

[40] See Rankine, *Personal Bar*, p. 1, where he describes the doctrine as a 'parcel of the law of evidence'; Reid also notes that it 'suppresses rights rather than creates them': see 'Case-law', p. 345.

[41] Reynolds, *Agency*, 8-031. Although raising an action of specific performance would probably amount to implied ratification by the principal, see M. J. Bonell, 'Agency', in A. Hartkamp, M. Hesselink, E. Hondius *et al.*, (eds.), *Towards a European Civil Code* (Nijmegen/The Hague: Ars Aequi Libri/Kluwer Law International, 2004), p. 387.

[42] R. Powell, *Law of Agency*, 2nd edn (London: Pitman, 1961), p. 70 and G. H. L. Fridman, *The Law of Agency*, 7th edn (London: Butterworths, 1996), p. 121.

and Reynolds may agree.[43] It is unfortunate that this point remains unclear, particularly in view of the fact that specific implement is, at least in theory, the innocent party's primary remedy for breach of contract in Scots law.[44]

Consideration must also be given to the situations of 'fourth parties' or those who derive title from third parties. Those involved in sale of goods contracts are protected by legislation applying throughout the UK. This protects *bona fide* third parties purchasing from mercantile agents in possession of goods without title to the same,[45] or purchasing from a mercantile agents generally.[46]

5 Requirements

The requirements of a Scottish case of apparent authority are set out below, drawing on Reid and Blackie's recent analysis of personal bar:

(a) inconsistent conduct of the principal;
(b) indicators of unfairness: the third party reasonably believed that the principal would not deny the agent's authority;
(c) the third party's reasonable belief has caused him to act or to omit to act; and
(d) prejudice to the third party.

(a) Inconsistent conduct of the principal

In common with other forms of estoppel-based reasoning, the conduct of the principal is the essence of personal bar.[47] Whereas common law

---

[43] Reynolds, *Agency*, 8-031, where he at least describes it as 'a contract'. See also P. Feltham, D. Hochberg and T. Leech, in S. Bower, *The Law Relating to Estoppel by Representation*, 4th edn (London: Butterworths, 2004), para. V.6.1.

[44] See L. Macgregor, 'Specific Implement in Scots Law', in J. Smits, D. Haas and G. Hesen (eds.), *Specific Performance in Contract Law: National and Other Perspectives* (Antwerp and London: Intersentia, 2008).

[45] Sale of Goods Act 1979, s. 24, seller in possession after sale, s. 25, buyer in possession after sale.

[46] Factors (Scotland) Act 1890, s. 1, applying Factors Act 1889 to Scotland.

[47] Cases in which the central importance of the principal's conduct are emphasised include *British Bata Shoe Co* v. *Double M Shah Ltd* 1980 SC 311 at 316–318, per Lord Jauncey; *Thomas Hayman & Sons* v. *The American Cotton Oil Co* (1907) 45 SLR 207 at 212, per the Lord Justice-Clerk J. H. A. Macdonald; *Dornier GmbH* v. *Cannon* 1991 SC 310 at 314, per Lord President Hope; *Bank of Scotland* v. *Brunswick Developments (1987) Ltd (No. 2)* 1998 SLT 439 at 444, per Lord President Rodger.

systems use 'representation' for this purpose,[48] Reid and Blackie use 'inconsistency'. This they break down into four parts.[49]

The first requirement stipulates that: 'To the obligant's knowledge, the rightholder has behaved in a way which was inconsistent with the exercise of the right.'[50] Applied to the apparent authority context, this dictates that the principal, to the third party's knowledge, has behaved in a manner inconsistent with the exercise of his right to plead the agent's lack of authority in an action raised by the third party. Generally, in personal bar, silence may amount to 'conduct'[51] and this is consistent with *dicta* in Scottish apparent authority cases. Indeed, it has been suggested that apparent authority is more likely to involve conduct of a passive rather than an active nature.[52] Passive behaviour is also involved in the standard 'textbook' example, where the principal withdraws or limits the agent's authority but fails to notify business associates that he has done so.

An example of passive conduct in an apparent authority context occurred in the Scottish House of Lords case, *International Sponge Importers* v. *Watt and Sons*.[53] In this case the agent was a travelling agent who sold sponges on behalf of the principal. Payment for goods was made by cheque in the name of the principal, sent directly by the customer to the principal. The agent began to accept payment either by cheque made out in his own name or in cash, and eventually absconded with the principal's funds. It was held that the principal could not recover such sums from the customer, having failed to object to the new method of payment used by the agent. As a case on apparent authority, it is rather unhelpful, however. Evidence of the principal's acquiescence was extremely weak: he may only have been aware of one incidence of unauthorised behaviour, and even that instance is doubtful because his other employees were also involved in the fraud. Nevertheless, the case certainly suggests that the courts do not rigidly

---

[48] See, e.g., English or South African law, but notably not the *Restatement (Third)*, which uses a wider notion of 'manifestation': see *Restatement (Third) of Agency* (2006), §1.03.

[49] Reid and Blackie, *Personal Bar*, paras. 2-04–2-39.

[50] *Ibid.*, paras. 2-07–2-27.   [51] *Ibid.*, para. 2-22.

[52] See Lord Diplock in *Freeman & Lockyer* v. *Buckhurst Park Properties (Mangal) Ltd* [1964] 2 QB 480 at 503, approved by Lord President Hope in *Dornier GmbH* v. *Cannon* 1991 SC 310 at 314 and by Lord Macfadyen in *John Davidson (Pipes) Ltd* v. *First Engineering Ltd* 2001 SCLR 73 at 78.

[53] *International Sponge Importers* v. *Watt and Sons* 1911 SC (HL) 57.

apply the requirement of acquiescence or conduct on the part of the principal, and this may act to the benefit of the third party.

Proceeding with Blackie and Reid's remaining three requirements of 'inconsistency', the second stipulates that: 'At the time of so behaving, the rightholder knew about the right.'[54] Applied to apparent authority this becomes: the principal, at the time of the relevant conduct, was aware of the agent's lack of authority. The third requirement stipulates that: 'Nonetheless the rightholder now seeks to exercise the right.'[55] This becomes: the principal attempts, in the context of an action raised by the third party, to plead the agent's lack of authority. Finally, the fourth requirement stipulates that: 'Its exercise will affect the obligant.'[56] If the principal asserts the agent's lack of authority, the third party would indeed be affected because he would not have a contract with the principal.

There is no evidence in Scots law of a development occurring in England, of a move away from the principal's conduct as the sole factor leading to liability. As Reynolds has noted, this marks the move away from estoppel-type reasoning towards a concept based on 'the objective analysis applicable to the formation of contracts'.[57] Lord Steyn has explored a similar theme, both in judgments[58] and in articles,[59] most famously in *First Energy (UK) Ltd* v. *Hungarian International Bank Ltd*.[60] As an English Court of Appeal case, this case would be persuasive rather than binding on a Scottish court in a later case.

(b) Indicators of unfairness: the third party reasonably believed that the principal would not deny the agent's authority

The conduct of the third party is also relevant in an apparent authority case. Reid and Blackie's framework utilises 'indicators of unfairness', not all of which are relevant in each case: '[U]nfairness depends upon context.'[61] Two of the indicators worth noting for their relevance in this context are: (1) 'the obligant reasonably believed that the right would not

---

[54] Reid and Blackie, *Personal Bar*, paras. 2-28–2-37.

[55] *Ibid.*, para. 2-38.   [56] *Ibid.*, para. 2-39.

[57] Reynolds, *Agency*, 8-029, although he ultimately concludes that an estoppel justification should be retained. For strong support for a broader rationale, see I. Brown, 'The Agent's Apparent Authority: Paradigm or Paradox?' (1995) *JBL* 360.

[58] *Darlington Borough Council* v. *Wiltshier Northern Ltd* [1995] 3 All ER 895 at 903–4.

[59] J. Steyn, 'Contract Law: Fulfilling the Reasonable Expectations of Honest Men' (1997) 113 *LQR* 433; 'Written Contracts: To What Extent May Evidence Control Language?' (1988) 41 *CLP* 23.

[60] [1993] 2 Lloyd's Rep 194.   [61] Reid and Blackie, *Personal Bar*, para. 2-40.

be exercised';[62] and (2) 'as a result of that belief the obligant acted, or omitted to act, in a way which was proportionate'.[63] Applied to an apparent authority situation these become: the third party reasonably believed that the principal would not deny the agent's authority, and this reasonable belief has caused the third party to act or to omit to act.

Scottish apparent authority cases certainly suggest that the third party's belief must be reasonable. More specifically, the circumstances of the transaction may be so highly unusual as to give rise to a duty of inquiry on the part of the third party.[64] Should he fail to perform this duty, apparent authority will not arise. This has recently been affirmed in several Scottish cases,[65] including one before the First Division of the Inner House of the Court of Session.[66] It is also clear that the further the transaction strays from the normal course of business, the more likely it is that the courts will find that apparent authority is not present.[67] Thus, where an agent offered a price to a third party which was below market value, indicating that he was 'hard up' and 'badly wanting money', not surprisingly, it was held that apparent authority did not exist.[68] So also where the third party was asked to send cheques to an employee of the principal with the name of the payee left blank, which were later returned after payment with the individual employee's name completed, apparent authority was again held to be lacking.[69]

(c) The third party's reasonable belief has caused him to act or to omit to act

In Scots law the third party must actually have believed in the existence of authority, and a causal nexus must exist between the principal's conduct

---

[62] *Ibid.*, paras. 2-47–2-50.   [63] *Ibid.*, paras. 2-51–2-54.

[64] *City of Glasgow Bank* v. *Moore* (1881) 19 SLR 86 at 93, per Lord President Inglis; *Paterson Bros* v. *Gladstone* (1891) 18R 403 at 406, per Lord President Inglis; *Thomas Hayman & Sons* v. *The American Cotton Oil Co* (1907) 45 SLR 207; Gloag, *Contract*, pp. 151–2.

[65] *British Bata Shoe Co Ltd* v. *Double M Shah Ltd* 1980 SC 311 at 318, per Lord Jauncey, relying on Scottish authority cited by Gloag, *Contract*, pp. 151–2 and also F. M. B. Reynolds and B. J. Davenport, *Bowstead on Agency*, 14th edn (London: Sweet & Maxwell, 1976), pp. 253–4.

[66] *Dornier GmbH* v. *Cannon* 1991 SC 310 at 315, per Lord President Hope.

[67] See, e.g., *Colvin* v. *Dixon* (1867) 5M 603; *Hamilton* v. *Dixon* (1873) 1R 72; *Walker* v. *Smith* (1906) 8F 619; *Dornier GmbH* v. *Cannon* 1991 SC 310 at 315, per Lord President Hope.

[68] *Thomas Hayman & Sons* v. *The American Cotton Oil Co* (1907) 45 SLR 207.

[69] *British Bata Shoe Ltd* v. *Double M Shah Ltd* 1980 SC 311.

and that belief. This is illustrated in cases where an absence of an actual belief proves fatal to a case.[70]

(d) Prejudice to the third party

Reid and Blackie's fourth indicator suggest that the third party must suffer a loss: 'the exercise of the right would cause prejudice to the obligant which would not have occurred but for the inconsistent conduct.'[71] Thus, were the principal to deny the agent's authority, prejudice would be caused to the third party which would not have occurred but for the principal's inconsistent conduct. According to Reid, prejudice is easily established: 'Prejudice is almost always present, or B [the obligant] would not trouble to oppose A [the rightholder].'[72] Prejudice in itself is, however, insufficient. A further causal nexus must be present, linking the principal's inconsistent conduct with the prejudice which would be suffered if the principal were permitted to act in this way.[73] To explain the type of prejudice required, Reid quotes the following influential statement from Dixon J in, *Grundt* v. *Great Boulder Pty Gold Mines Ltd*: 'the real detriment or harm from which the law seeks to give protection is that which would flow from the change of position if the assumption were deserted that led to it.'[74] The prejudice to the third party in an apparent authority case is clear. His expected contract does not exist. The causal nexus is present: the prejudice would not have occurred but for the principal's inconsistent conduct.

6 Conclusion

The Scottish concept of apparent authority emerges as a relatively flexible idea. The requirement of conduct on the part of the principal is not rigidly applied. It is fulfilled where the principal's conduct involves little more than silence, or the simple appointment of the agent to a particular post. This flexible attitude is to be welcomed, given that it enlarges the class of third

---

[70] *Smith* v. *North British Railway Co* (1850) 12 D 795; *North of Scotland Banking Company* v. *Behn, Möller & Co* (1881) 8R 423; *City of Glasgow Bank* v. *Moore* (1881) 19 SLR 86; *Main & Co* v. *Young* (1907) 23 Sh Ct Rep 295. See also Reid and Blackie, *Personal Bar*, paras. 2-51–2-54.

[71] Reid and Blackie, *Personal Bar*, paras. 2-55–2-59.

[72] Reid, 'Case-law', p. 359.   [73] *Ibid.*

[74] [1937] 59 CLR 641 at 674, cited with approval by Lord Rodger in *William Grant* v. *Glen Catrine Bonded Warehouse* 2001 SC 901 at 921, and see Feltham, Hochberg and Leech, *The Law Relating to Estoppel by Representation*, para. V.5.9.

parties who are protected. Fortunately, this trend is likely to continue in view of the wide formulation of 'inconsistent conduct' found in Reid and Blackie's recent analysis of personal bar.

III Ratification

1 Doctrinal basis

A 'full' definition of ratification in the context of agency appears at a relatively late stage in Scots law, in a footnote inserted by the editor of the seventh edition of Bell's *Commentaries*.[75] Reference is made there to two passages from the Digest[76] and the works of Pothier,[77] as follows:

> An agency may be confirmed and established, and its powers extended, or it may even be entirely created, by subsequent adoption and ratification on the part of the principal, according to the rule, *Omnis ratihabitio retro-trahitur et mandato priori aequiparatur.*[78]

The 'dual function' of ratification should be noted: in Scots law, as in Roman law,[79] it operates not only to validate an unauthorised action, but also to create the agency relationship itself.[80] What is notable is that the cases cited in support of this statement are almost entirely English.[81]

---

[75] G. J. Bell, *Commentaries on the Law of Scotland and on the Principles of Mercantile Jurisprudence*, 7th edn. (Edinburgh: T. & T. Clark, 1870), I, 510, n. 5. The word 'ratifyit' does, however, appear in an earlier source, J. Balfour, *Balfour's Prackticks* (Edinburgh: Gregg Associates for the Stair Society, 1754, reprinted 1962–63), p. 164.

[76] Dig 50.17.60 Ulpian: 'He is always understood to direct something to be done who does not prevent another from intervening in his behalf. If, however, anyone who did not consent should ratify a transaction, he will be liable to an action on mandate.' See also Dig 46.3.12.4 Ulpian: 'But even if I pay someone who is not a genuine agent, but the principal ratifies the payment, a release will take place; for ratification is equivalent to mandate.'

[77] Pothier, *Law of Obligations*: 'If I contract myself in the name of a person who had not given me an authority, his ratification will in like manner make him be considered as having contracted by himself by my ministry; for ratification is equivalent to an authority, *ratihabitio mandata comparator.*'

[78] Bell, *Commentaries*, I, 512, n. 5 (continued from 510).

[79] See Dig 46.3.12.4, quoted in n. 76, above.

[80] Where ratification creates the agency relationship, the agent must have purported to act on the principal's behalf; see Macgregor, 'Agency and Mandate', para. 61; J. J. Gow, *The Mercantile and Industrial Law of Scotland* (Edinburgh: W. Green, 1964), pp. 517 and 520; Lord Coulsfield *et al.* (eds.), Gloag and Henderson, *The Law of Scotland*, 12th edn. (Edinburgh: W. Green, 2007), para. 19.25.

[81] There is only one Scots one: *Western Bank* v. *Addie* (1865) 3 M 899, *revsd* (1867) 5M (HL) 80.

Ratification is not, however, an English import. Prior to 1870, a different concept, homologation, carried out a similar function.[82]

Homologation is a difficult concept to define. Its meaning is dependent to some extent on context and has also changed over time.[83] A particular meaning noted by Reid and Blackie seems appropriate in an agency context: 'a party could not deny that which he or she had already approved.'[84]

Analysis by the most influential institutional writer, Stair, reflects the dual nature of homologation. First, he noted its use as a defence, where the defender pleads the pursuer's knowledge or approbation of the defender's right, either expressly or through conduct.[85] Secondly, he analyses it in the context of his discussion of the consent required to conclude contracts or constitute unilateral promises, where proof by writ was not required.[86] Mandate is one of the contracts falling within this class. The principal's consent is a key issue:

> this consent may be either expressed by word, writ or fact, by doing deeds importing consent, which therefore is called homologation whereof acceptance of any right is a special kind and it takes place in many cases, but it cannot take place unless it be proven or presumed that the homologator knew the right.[87]

Stair's definition is probably the most helpful, highlighting the importance of the homologator's (in an agency context, the principal's) consent. A related issue is the principal's knowledge. Full consent cannot, of course, be provided unless the principal is aware of all the relevant facts.

Later definitions of homologation are wider, depicting the concept as a tool to 'cure' defective contracts. It is, for example, described in Bell's *Commentaries* as follows:

> that assent or approbation of a deed, conveyance, settlement, or contract, which is inferred from circumstances; supplying, in the case of the obliger

---

[82] See Bell, *Commentaries*, I, 139–141. It is this passage on homologation, and not Bell's discussion of agency, to which Trayner refers when discussing the meaning of the maxim *omnis ratihabitio retrotrahitur et mandato priori aequiparatur*. For usage in case-law, see, e.g., *Salvesan & Co. v Rederi Aktiebolaget Norstjernan* 1903 10 SLT 543, per Lord Moncrieff at 545, *affd* (HL) (1903) 6 F 101.

[83] Reid and Blackie, *Personal Bar*, paras. 1-11–1-15.

[84] *Ibid.*, para. 1-11.

[85] *Institutions* IV, x1, 29, see discussion in Reid and Blackie, *Personal Bar*, para. 1-12.

[86] *Institutions* I, X, 11.

[87] *Institutions* I, X, 11. See also Erskine, *Institute*, III, III, 47.

or granter, the want of legal evidence of consent, and establishing as a recognised engagement a contract defectively entered into.[88]

Some of the definitions focus on the deed, contract or 'engagement' which the agent has sought to conclude. This approach can be contrasted with modern English definitions in which ratification appears as an expression of the principal's consent to the agent's *act*.[89] This difference of focus is probably not important: the ultimate effect is the same. In modern Scots law, ratification can apply to acts other than the conclusion of contracts by the agent.

Where ratification operates to create the principal/agent relationship, the consent of the agent is, of course, required in addition to that of the principal. Perhaps the agent's consent lies, as Fridman has suggested, in the agent's actings on behalf of the principal.[90]

As has been illustrated above, the doctrinal basis of ratification in Scots law is not particularly clear, although it certainly seems to have strong links to the more general concept of homologation. The central factor appears to be the consent of the principal, usually to the 'engagement' which the agent has concluded on his behalf. Stair's contribution is the most useful, highlighting the key role of consent, provided through words or actions.

2 Scope

As noted above, ratification in Scots law may operate both where the agent has insufficient authority and also where the agent is completely unauthorised. It applies to acts in general, and not simply to

---

[88] I, 140. See also Bell, *Principles of the Law of Scotland*, s. 27: 'Homologation … is an act "of the obligor or his legal representative" approbatory of a preceding engagement, which in itself is defective or informal "or unauthorised," either confirming it or adopting it as binding.' For other relevant definitions, see Reid and Blackie, *Personal Bar*, p. 8, referring to the works of the seventeenth-century writer, J. N. Dirleton, *Some Doubts and Questions, in the Law, Especially of Scotland* (Edinburgh: George Mosman, published posthumously, 1698), 7. s.v. 'Approbatio'. See also Lord Moncreiff in *Gardner* v. *Gardner* (1830) 9S 138 at 140, quoted by T. B. Smith, *Short Commentary on the Law of Scotland* (Edinburgh: W. Green, 1962), p. 293.

[89] Reynolds rationalises ratification as the retrospective adoption of a transaction which is entered into by another, classing it as a notion *sui generis*. Reynolds, *Agency*, 2-050.

[90] Fridman, *The Law of Agency*, pp. 109–10. Ratification as the creation of the contract in Scots law, based firmly on consent, is in marked contrast to Powell's views: 'It is absurd to say that A's unilateral act on P's behalf, and P's subsequent unilateral ratification of that act, constitute any such agreement.', pp. 109–10 and p. 120.

the unauthorised conclusion of contracts. It may operate where the principal is either an individual, or a legal person, for example, a company.

A significant problem which affects the scope of the concept is the doubt that surrounds the type of transactions that may be ratified. Gloag explained:

> The plea of homologation imports that the court is asked to hold that a party has expressly or impliedly recognised the validity of an obligation which he has the right to challenge … *But it implies the existence of a real, though, voidable obligation*; it is not applicable to the semblance of an obligation which can be shewn to be completely void.[91]

Applied to an agency context, this explanation is problematic. As a general rule, the agent acting without authority is unable to conclude a valid obligation on behalf of the principal. One could conclude from that that no obligation whatsoever is created by an unauthorised agent, i.e. that any contract created by the unauthorised agent is void. And yet, clearly, ratification may indeed operate to cure acts carried out by agents. That does not square with Gloag's assertion that a 'real' obligation exists from the outset. Indeed, his use of 'voidable' is, it is suggested, incorrect. Voidable obligations are valid unless and until reduced at the option of an innocent party who has, for example, been subject to a misrepresentation. That is not an accurate description of this situation.

Gloag's attitude to this question is nevertheless consistent with that of the institutional writers Stair, Erskine and Bell. Erskine distinguished between those obligations which are inherently null and those which, although legal nullities, are productive of a 'natural' obligation.[92] Only the latter could be homologated. Erskine's examples of the latter class include acts by persons lacking capacity and deeds which have not been signed in accordance with formal requirements.[93] These formulations are difficult to apply to a modern commercial context. Ratification is, of course, not now limited to acts by those lacking capacity or the curing of

---

[91] *Contract*, p. 544 (emphasis added). See also Smith, *Short Commentary*, p. 293.

[92] Erskine, *Institute*, III, III, 47. Like Stair, Erskine was influenced by the theory of natural law, and saw no real difference between moral and legal obligations; see A. J. Mackenzie Stuart, 'Contract and Quasi-contract', in D. M. Walker (ed.), *An Introduction to Scottish Legal History* (Edinburgh: W. Green, 1992), p. 253.

[93] Erskine, *Institute*, III, III, 47. Bell too indicated that homologation could only operate where the deed was 'objectionable, but not absolutely null': Bell, *Commentaries*, I, 140, although suggesting that the limitation applied only where the person homologating is not an original party to the deed.

defective deeds. It has a much wider ambit. Indeed, Erskine's examples potentially cause more problems. An incapax could not, according to the modern law, ratify, lacking capacity at the time the agent enters into the contract on his behalf.[94] Whilst a dividing line clearly exists between those acts possessing a residual validity and which can be ratified and those which are void and cannot, the location of this line is not clear. It is perhaps not surprising that English law has also struggled with this problem.[95] Unfortunately, as is explored below, the problem has a significant practical impact.

3 Position of the third party and other directly interested persons prior to ratification

(a) Ability of the third party to 'withdraw' unilaterally prior to ratification

This issue has received little attention in Scots law. The leading English case of *Bolton Partners* v. *Lambert*[96] has not been fully analysed by a Scottish court.[97] In that case an agent who was not authorised to do so purported to accept an offer tendered by a third party. The third party then purported to withdraw from that 'contract'. Following the attempted withdrawal, the principal ratified the agent's unauthorised acceptance. The court held that the principal and third party were bound by a valid contract, notwithstanding the fact that the third party's withdrawal pre-dated the act of ratification. The retrospective effect of ratification bound the third party from the moment at which the agent purported to act on the principal's behalf. This case has been criticised, usually on the basis that the third party was prevented from withdrawing from what was not, at the point of the purported withdrawal, a valid contract.[98]

The status of this case as an authority is, not surprisingly, controversial. Although its binding nature was accepted by the Court of Appeal in *Presentaciones Musicales SA* v. *Secunda*,[99] it was severely criticised by the

---

[94] III 5(c)(i).   [95] Reynolds, *Agency*, 2-052 and 2-056.   [96] [1889] 41 Ch D 295.

[97] See the more detailed analyses of this case in Chapter 6 (English law), III 3 and Chapter 8 (Unauthorised agency, the American *Restatement* and other common law countries), III.

[98] See, e.g., Fridman, *The Law of Agency*, p. 100.

[99] [1994] Ch 271 at 280 (Dillon LJ: overruling *Bolton* was 'not a course open to this court').

Privy Council in *Fleming* v. *Bank of New Zealand*.[100] It has been referred
to in only two Scottish cases.[101] In those cases, none of the judges was
prepared either to accept or reject the English approach.[102] The issue
remains undecided in Scotland.

There are arguments for and against the third party's right of withdrawal in this situation. He is undoubtedly left in a situation of uncertainty pending the principal's decision whether or not to ratify, and this
is clearly a matter for concern.[103] However, the third party can be
accused of 'snatching' at the opportunity to withdraw from a contract
which the passage of time has rendered unattractive. It should be recalled
that the third party, unaware of the agent's lack of authority, considered
himself bound in a contract with the principal from the very outset.
Concerns over the third party's uncertainty can be addressed in other
ways, for example, by imposing a time limit on the principal to ratify
within a reasonable time. Presently, this is not a specific requirement in
Scots law, although one would imagine that a court might impose such a
time limit, either as part of a general duty to act reasonably or as part of
the nascent duty of good faith in contract in Scots law.[104] The principal is
subject to a duty to ratify within a reasonable time in English law,
although the principles appear to be relatively under-developed in that
system.[105]

There has been a failure to develop Scots rules on the third party's
right to withdraw in the *Bolton* v. *Lambert* situation. Scots lawyers will
look with interest at the other chapters of this book on this issue. It is,
however, probably not possible to formulate a solution without first
resolving the more significant problem of the parties' obligations

---

[100] [1900] AC 577 at 587.

[101] *Licenses Insurance Corporation & Guarantee Fund* v. *Shearer and others* 1906 14 SLT
345; *Goodall* v. *Bilsland* 1909 SC 1152.

[102] See, in particular, the comments of Lord Salvesan in *Goodall* v. *Bilsland* 1909 SC 1152 at
1183.

[103] Although Reynolds has suggested the following limitation to the principal's power to
ratify, namely that he must ratify within a time which is reasonable in all the circumstances, see *Agency* 2-087.

[104] On the duty of good faith, see *Smith* v. *Bank of Scotland* 1997 SC (HL) 111 and
H. MacQueen, 'Good Faith', in H. MacQueen and R. Zimmermann (eds.), *European
Contract Law: Scots and South African Perspectives* (Edinburgh: Edinburgh University
Press, 2006), pp. 43–73.

[105] Reynolds, *Agency*, 2-087, although this requirement appears to have received little
attention in the cases, with the exception of *Metropolitan Asylums Board Managers* v.
Kingham & Sons (1890) 6 TLR 217 at 218, per Fry LJ.

pre-ratification and, in particular, the type of obligation created by an unauthorised agent at that time.[106]

(b) Partial ratification

Ratification may not be partial. Ratification of any part of the agent's contract implies ratification of the whole.[107]

4 Effect of ratification

(a) Retroactive effect

Perhaps the most important issue concerning ratification is its retrospective effect. Effective ratification means that the agent is treated as though he had been fully authorised from the moment when he purported to enter into the contract on the principal's behalf. The implications of this principle are far-reaching, and are explored in the sections which follow.

(b) The position of 'fourth parties'

Fourth parties can be adversely affected by ratification too (this term referring to any party other than the principal, agent or third party). Although protection of fourth parties is clearly required, the difficulty lies in the manner in which it could be achieved. Erskine suggests that such parties are completely unaffected by the homologation of another.[108] In a similar vein, Bell indicates that homologation cannot affect a party entitled to rely on a real right.[109] These views, which have

---

[106] One finds little assistance in the case itself – Lindley LJ suggested that the agent's act was not a complete nullity, *Bolton Partners* v. *Lambert* (1889) 41 Ch D 295 at 309; see Reynolds, *Agency*, 2-085 in the context of a discussion of contracts where the agent purports to conclude subject to ratification; Fridman, *The Law of Agency*, pp. 99–100; C.-H. Tan, 'The Principle in *Bird v Brown Revisited*' (2001) 117 *LQR* 626 at 641.

[107] Gloag, *Contract*, p. 147, where he cites Bell, *Commentaries*, I, 513 and S. M. Leake, *Principles of the Law of Contracts*, 6th edn (London: Stevens & Sons, 1911), p. 325. Bell suggests that the issue may depend on whether or not the deed is divisible into parts. If it is not, then homologation of part is homologation of the whole, but if it is, then 'the homologation of one of the separate parts will not confirm the whole': Bell, *Commentaries*, I, 139.

[108] Erskine, *Institute*, III, III, 49. Rather confusingly, such parties are often referred to as 'third parties', as can be seen in this source.

[109] Bell, *Commentaries*, I, 141. Although he cites *Liddel* v. *Dick's Creditors* (1744) M 5721 in support of this view, he suggests in n. 7, p. 141 that Lord Kilkerran's *dictum*, 'that it was never found in any case that homologation was good in a competition', was a little too broad. Gow too appears to recognise this exception in his discussion of the case *Keighley Maxsted & Co* v. *Durrant* [1901] AC 240 in *The Mercantile and Industrial Law of Scotland*, at 520.

not been developed in case-law, could form the basis of a modern protective rule. Alternatively, other legal bases could be used, such as the general equitable jurisdiction possessed by a Scottish court allowing it to refuse access to a remedy.[110] Another alternative is the as yet undeveloped duty of good faith in Scots law.[111] Whatever basis is used, it seems unlikely that a Scots court would fail to apply the protection which is clearly required. At the moment, the uncertainty in Scots law can be contrasted with the position in English law and under PECL where protections exist.[112]

(c) Acts which can no longer be validly carried out at the time of ratification

In the Scottish case of *Goodall* v. *Bilsland*,[113] an agent was authorised to object to the renewal of a licence before a licensing court. When he was unsuccessful, he appealed to the Licensing Appeal Court, but without first obtaining the principal's authority to do so. Although the principal purported to ratify the agent's actions at a later stage, it was held that ratification was ineffective because it occurred outside the time limit within which appeals must be raised. Although this case suggests that a rule indeed exists requiring ratification within an applicable time limit, the scope and justification of that rule are far from clear.[114] For example, it is not known which type of acts it applies to (contracts, other juristic acts), nor is it clear whether it applies to all time limits or only those of a sufficient degree of importance. To Reynolds, this is an example of the general exception prohibiting ratification where it would unfairly prejudice (what has been described above as) a fourth

---

[110] The operation of this general power can be seen in cases where the court awards damages rather than specific implement, although in that context the power is used extremely sparingly in exceptional circumstances; see Macgregor, 'Specific Implement in Scots Law'.

[111] See n. 104 above.

[112] Art. 3:207(2) PECL; Reynolds, *Agency*, 2-087. This exception had been discussed in previous editions of this book, and was recently confirmed in two English cases: *Smith* v. *Henniker-Major & Co* [2003] EWCA Civ 762, [2003] Ch 182, per Robert Walker LJ at [71] and *The Borvigilant* [2003] EWCA Civ 935, [2003] 2 Lloyd's Rep 520, per Clarke LJ at [70].

[113] *Goodall* v. *Bilsland* [1909] SC 1152.

[114] *Goodall* appears to contradict an earlier Scottish case, *Licenses Insurance Corporation & Guarantee Fund* v. *Shearer and others* 1906 14 SLT 345. However, the reasoning of the Second Division seems to rest more on a desire not to disturb arbitration proceedings rather than the ability of a principal to ratify outwith a time limit. On the latter issue, Lord Kyllachy expressly reserved his opinion, describing it (at 348) as 'a question of some difficulty'.

party.[115] According to Reynolds, not every time limit is relevant – ratification is only excluded where it is essential to the validity of an act that it should be done within a certain time.[116]

This confusion is compounded because of the existence of cases, both Scottish and English, which appear to flout the time-limit exception. In *Presentaciones Musicales SA* v. *Secunda*[117] the Court of Appeal held ratification to be effective where it appeared to take place after the expiry of a limitation period. The Court held that the agent's initially unauthorised action of issuing a writ could be ratified outside the limitation period.[118] Another puzzling case is the Scottish House of Lords case, *Alexander Ward & Co Ltd* v. *Samyang Navigation Co. Ltd*,[119] in which an action for debt was raised in the name of a company at a time when no directors were in office. The court held liquidators entitled to ratify the raising of the action. The root of the problem is, again, the failure to identify the nature of the nullity affecting the agent's initial act.

5 Act of ratification: requirements

By the late nineteenth century Bell was able to suggest the following prerequisites of homologation,[120] all of which are familiar as prerequisites of the modern concept of ratification, namely:

1. the principal's assent must be clear and indisputable;[121]
2. the contract (or conveyance or settlement) must be fully known to the person homologating;[122]
3. it [i.e. the homologating act] must be an act that can be fairly ascribed to no other purpose than that of giving sanction to the deed or contract in question.

Modern case-law has expanded upon those conditions. In this section, the issues of time limits and form are considered first in subsections

---

[115] Reynolds, *Agency*, 2-087.

[116] *Ibid.*, 2-089. Reynolds presents this qualification concerning time limits as the main exception to the full retroactive effect of ratification.

[117] [1994] 2 All ER 737.

[118] The court made a specific finding that the initial act of the agent was not a nullity: see *Presentaciones Musicales SA* v. *Secunda* [1994] Ch 271, per Dillon LJ at 279–280, where he relies on *Pontin* v. *Wood* [1962] 1 QB 594.

[119] 1975 SC (HL) 26.   [120] Bell, *Commentaries*, I, 140.

[121] Erskine, *Institute*, III, III, 47.

[122] See Stair, *Institutions*, I, X, 11 and in Erskine, *Institute*, III, III, 47.

(a) and (b). Following that, the requirements applying to the principal are considered in subsection (c). These are that the principal must:

(i) be in existence and have legal capacity (i.e. be a competent principal) at the time the act was carried out by the agent;
(ii) be susceptible of ascertainment at that time;
(iii) have been made aware of all the material facts.

The single condition applying to the agent, that he must make clear to the third party his capacity as agent for a disclosed and identified or identifiable principal, is considered in subsection (d).

(a) Time limit

As noted above, English authority exists[123] suggesting that the principal must ratify within a reasonable time. Although no authority can be found confirming that this is the position in Scotland, the courts are likely to apply such a rule for the reasons discussed above.[124]

(b) No particular form required

Ratification may be implied[125] in addition to express and this is perhaps not surprising given that the agency relationship itself may arise as an implication from conduct.[126] Where the original deed is subject to a specific requirement, e.g. a contract relating to land which must be constituted in writing, it is likely that ratification would require to adopt a similar form.

Whether an inference of ratification may be made where the 'conduct' on the part of the principal amounts to silence only is a complex question. Gloag answers it in the affirmative subject to the provisos that the relationship of principal and agent already exists and the principal has knowledge of what the agent has done.[127] In certain of the cases cited by Gloag, the inference of ratification is not surprising, the principal having received goods or services and not paid for the same.[128] One case not

[123] Reynolds, *Agency*, 2-087.   [124] See III 4(a), above.
[125] *Lombe* v. *Scott* (1779) 9 M 5627; *Pierson* v. *Balfour* 1 Dec (1812) FC; *Woodrow & Son* v. *Wright* (1861) 24 D 31, especially at 36, per Lord Denholme; *Ballantine* v. *Stevenson* (1881) 8 R 959; and Gloag, *Contract*, p. 146.
[126] *Barnetson* v. *Petersen Bros* (1902) 5 F 86; *Morrison* v. *Statter* (1885) 12R 1152.
[127] Gloag, *Contract*, p. 146, citing *Pierson* v. *Balfour* 1 Dec (1812) FC; *Lombe* v. *Scott* (1779) 9 M 5627; *Ballantine* v. *Stevenson* (1881) 8 R 959.
[128] *Brown* v. *Dickson* (1711) M 6018; *Barnetson* v. *Petersen* (1902) 5 F 86.

cited by Gloag seems to suggest that the principal is subject to a positive duty to return such goods to avoid the inference of ratification.[129] Delay by the principal may also strengthen the inference.[130] However, there are other cases in which the inference is not made because, taking a 'common sense' approach, the facts simply do not amount to consent on the part of the principal.[131]

In the overall assessment of the circumstances which may amount to ratification, the principal's knowledge of the agent's actions is a key issue.[132] This issue has been analysed by the institutional writers again in the context of homologation, where they suggest a high standard: according to Bell, 'full' knowledge of the circumstances on the part of the principal is required.[133] This requirement continued to be emphasised in more modern works, reference often being made to the English case, *Forman v. The Liddesdale*.[134] In that case an agent had instructed repairs to a ship which were not within the scope of the agent's authority. When the ship came back into the principal's possession and was sold by him, no inference of ratification of the repairs was made, the principal having had no choice but to accept delivery of the ship.

Where silence is involved, Reynolds notes that 'ratification merges almost imperceptibly into estoppel'.[135] There may be a similarly close connection between ratification and personal bar in Scots law. The individual factual issues emphasised in the cases, knowledge on the part of the principal and inconsistent conduct by him, could be constitutive of personal bar. However, it is probably more accurate to rationalise this area, as argued above, as the attribution of the principal's consent: the idea which is central to the concept of homologation.

---

[129] *Lindsay & Allan* v. *Campbell* (1800) Morison's Dict, Mandate, Appendix, Pt I, 2. See also *Moir* v. *Clark's Trustees* 1936 SLT (Sh Ct) 40.

[130] *Ballantine* v. *Stevenson* (1881) 8 R 959.

[131] See, e.g., *Woodrow & Son* v. *Wright* (1861) 24 D 31 or *Arnot* v. *Stevenson* (1698) M 6017.

[132] See the useful analysis provided by Sheriff Brown in *Moir* v. *Clark's Trustees* 1936 SLT (Sh Ct) 40 at 44.

[133] Bell, *Commentaries*, I, 140. See also Stair, I, X, 11; Erskine, *Institute*, III, 48; Bell, *Principles* s. 27; Gloag, *Contract*, p. 146.

[134] *Forman & Co Pty Ltd* v. *The Liddesdale* [1900] AC 190.

[135] Reynolds, *Agency*, 2-075, although see Waller J in *Suncorp Insurance and Finance* v. *Milano Assicurazioni SpA* [1993] 2 Lloyd's Rep 225 at 234 and Fridman, *The Law of Agency*, p. 105.

(c) Requirements applying to the principal

(i) The principal must be in existence and possess the requisite legal capacity at the time the act was carried out by the agent

The principal must not only be in existence at the time when the agent purported to enter the contract on his behalf, but must also have legal capacity at that time.[136] Both requirements arise because of the retrospective effect of ratification.

Many of the cases illustrative of the requirement of 'existence' involve promoters who enter into contracts on behalf of companies which have not yet been incorporated.[137] Statutory rules now exist imposing personal liability on a promoter in this situation.[138]

The requirement relating to capacity was, at one time, highly relevant in a company law context. Previously, contracts entered into by directors or other agents for the company which were outside the company's objects clause could not be ratified by the shareholders.[139] In such circumstances, neither the third party nor the company would be bound. Under existing law, matters are more complex. It is crucial to draw a distinction between contracts which are entered into between third parties and the company in circumstances where: (i) the directors or the company have exceeded or abused the company's constitutional powers; and (ii) the directors have exceeded or abused their own constitutional powers. With regard to the capacity of the company, i.e. (i), it is now provided that the company has the capacity to enter into a contract or that such capacity can be assumed.[140] As a result, as regards third parties and the company, the contract is binding. However, internally, where the directors have abused

---

[136] *Boston Deep Sea Fishing and Ice Co. Ltd* v. *Farnham* [1957] 3 All ER 204, although see the Scottish House of Lords case, *Alexander Ward & Co.* v. *Samyang Navigation Co. Ltd* 1975 SC (HL) 26, in which the House held that ratification by liquidators of a company was effective where an action for debt had been raised at a time when no directors were in office.

[137] *Tinnevelly Sugar Refining Co.* v. *Mirrlees, Watson and Yaryan Co Ltd* (1894) 21 R 1009; *Kelner* v. *Baxter* (1866) LR 2 CP 174; *Cumming* v. *Quartzag Ltd* 1980 SC 276.

[138] Companies Act 1985 (c. 6), s. 36C(1): 'A contract which purports to be made by or on behalf of a company at a time when the company has not been formed has effect, subject to any agreement to the contrary, as one made with the person purporting to act for the company or as agent for it, and he is personally liable on the contract accordingly.' This section will be replaced by the coming into force of s. 51(1) Companies Act 2006 (in more or less identical terms).

[139] For an illustration, see *Ashbury Railway Carriage and Iron Co. Ltd* v. *Riche* (1875) LR 7 HL 653.

[140] Companies Act 1985, s. 35(1). This section will be replaced by the coming into force of s. 39(1) Companies Act 2006 (which is in more or less identical terms).

the powers of the company, the actions of the director may only be ratified by the company by special resolution.[141] Moreover, any relief from liability incurred by the director may be authorised by special resolution.[142]

Insofar as a third party deals with a company in good faith, the power of the directors to bind the company (i.e. (ii) above) is deemed to be free of any limitation under the company's constitution. This will include limitations imposed by the objects clause.[143] In such circumstances the company and the third party will be bound by the contract where the directors have exceeded their powers. Internally, the shareholders may ratify the director's abuse of his constitutional powers by ordinary resolution.[144] Where a director exceeds or abuses his powers, he will also be in breach of his statutory duty to observe the company's constitution.[145] An ordinary resolution of the shareholders may also absolve the director of such a breach.[146] Where an ordinary resolution is passed, the court must refuse an aggrieved shareholder leave to raise derivative proceedings against a director, in terms of which the shareholder could argue that the director's breach of the constitution (i) has caused the company loss or (ii) has resulted in a gain in the hands of the director which should be restored to the company.[147]

(ii) Principal must be ascertained

Whilst the principal need not be actually named in the contract, according to the Scottish writer Trotter, he 'must have been so designated as to be ascertainable with reasonable certainty'.[148] Both Trotter and Lord McLaren, the editor of Bell's *Principles*, cite a leading English case on this point, *Watson v. Swann*,[149] where Wiles J explained the policy underlying this rule:

---

[141] Companies Act 1985, s. 35(3). Whether and how the shareholders are to ratify the actions of a director where they have exceeded or abused the company's powers is not dealt with in the Companies Act 2006, so the law remains unclear. A special resolution is a resolution of the shareholders passed by a majority of not less than 75 per cent (Companies Act 2006, s. 283(1)).

[142] Companies Act 1985, s. 35(3).

[143] Companies Act 1985, s. 35A(1). This section will be replaced by the coming into force of s. 40(1) Companies Act 2006 (which is in more or less identical terms).

[144] *Bamford* v. *Bamford* [1970] Ch 212. An ordinary resolution is a resolution of the shareholders passed by simple majority, i.e. 51 per cent (Companies Act 2006, s. 282(1)).

[145] Companies Act 2006, s. 171(a).   [146] Companies Act 2006, s. 239(1).

[147] Companies Act 2006, s. 268(1)(c)(ii).

[148] W. F. Trotter, *The Law of Contract in Scotland* (Edinburgh: W. Hodge, 1913), p. 370. According to Gloag, *Contract*, p. 143, he must be 'identified as the representative of an interest on behalf of which the contract was made'.

[149] [1862] 11 CB (NS) 757, see Trotter, *The Law of Contract in Scotland*, and Lord McLaren in Bell, *Commentaries*, I, 512, n. 5.

> The law obviously requires that the person for whom the agent professes to act must be a person capable of being ascertained at the time. It is not necessary that he should be named; but there must be such a description of him as shall amount to a reasonable designation of the person intended to be bound by the contract ... A stranger who had given him no orders to effect a policy for him clearly cannot by any supposed ratification assume the benefit of the contract.[150]

This general policy also justifies the exclusion of ratification by undisclosed and unnamed principals. In this way, third parties are prevented from being placed in a situation of uncertainty. This limitation is potentially significant – the body of case-law on these situations suggest that these methods of acting are common. The exclusion is perhaps tempered by the fact that the requirement of identification is not strictly applied. In *Lyell v. Kennedy*[151] an agent continued to collect rents payable to a deceased principal, professing to do so on behalf of the heir, whoever he might be. Thus, identification as a member of a class appears to be sufficient.

The relatively lax approach to ascertainment in Scots law is of interest given the criticism which this limitation has received in English law. Reynolds, in particular, has suggested that if the third party is willing to contract on the basis of not knowing the identity of the principal, then ratification ought to be possible.[152] It is indeed difficult to argue against this view. If the law recognises that agents may act on behalf of such principals, it ought to do so in all respects, including the ability to ratify.

(iii) Principal must be aware of all the material facts

This requirement was explored above in the context of the method of ratification. Because ratification is an expression of the principal's consent, it can only exist where the principal is aware of all the facts.

(iv) The agent must contract as an agent for a disclosed and identified or identifiable principal

This requirement is, in a sense, requirement (c)(ii) above observed from the agent's perspective: part (c)(ii) focused on the principal's position, and the ability of a third party to ascertain the identity of that principal. This part c(iv) focuses on the manner in which the agent acts, and what

---

[150] [1862] 11 CB (NS) 757 at 771, per Willes J .
[151] [1889] 14 App Cas 437.   [152] Reynolds, *Agency*, 2-065.

that communicates to the third party about the relationship between principal and agent.

Much of the discussion centres around the English House of Lords case, *Keighley Maxsted* v. *Durant*.[153] The agent, although authorised to buy corn at a specific price, was unable to find it at that price. He bought at a higher price, intending the purchase to be a joint speculation on his own behalf and that of the principal. The principal purported to ratify the agent's actions. When the agent failed to take delivery of the goods, the sellers sued the principal. Ratification was held to be ineffective. The approach of the House of Lords is explained by what is, by now, a famous quotation from Lord Mcnaughten that 'civil obligations are not to be created by, or founded upon, undisclosed intentions'.[154]

Expressions of this rule appear to have at their foundation the protection of the third party. To permit ratification here might involve 'unfair surprise'. This view is supported by the fact that even if the agent secretly intends the transaction to be for his own benefit, provided that he purported to act on the principal's behalf, the principal is entitled to ratify.[155] The third party's perception is paramount. However, the application of this policy to the facts of *Keighley Maxsted* failed to protect the third party, who found himself unable to implement the contract. Arguably, the case is not an example of ratification by an undisclosed principal, but rather a case of ratification where the agent has exceeded his authority.[156]

Although *Keighley Maxsted* is cited by Scottish writers as the leading authority,[157] two other Scottish cases directly contradict it, one of which, *Lockhart* v. *Moodie & Co*[158] is on similar facts.[159] In that case A and B had entered into a joint venture for the purchase of yarn. A authorised B to buy the yarn at a maximum price but B purchased at a higher price. The purchase was made in B's own name, and B did not disclose the existence of A to the seller. The case is, therefore, an example of acting for an undisclosed principal. B became bankrupt, and the seller brought an

---

[153] [1901] AC 240.   [154] Lord Macnaughten at 247.
[155] *Re Tiedemann and Ledermann Frères* [1899] 2 QB 66.   [156] Reynolds, *Agency*, 2-061.
[157] Gloag, *Contract*, p. 143; Gow, *The Mercantile and Industrial Law of Scotland*, p. 520.
[158] [1877] 4 R 859.
[159] The other case is *Barnetson* v. *Petersen* (1902) 5 F 86, in which the owner of a ship was held liable to pay for the services of a ship-broker, employed by charterers. Although it appears to contradict *Keighley Maxsted*, it probably concerns a disclosed but unnamed principal rather than an undisclosed principal. *Keighley Maxsted* was not cited to the court. For another example of ratification/homologation, see *Reid's Trustees* v. *Watson's Trustees* (1896) 23 R 636.

action against A for the sums due. The First Division held A liable, but only to the extent of the approved price. The ratio of the case, is, however, difficult to identify, nor is there any real discussion of ratification. Lord Deas focused almost entirely on the partnership angle of the case. By contrast, Lord President Inglis, in a very short judgment, focused on the effect which the agent's actions in excess of his mandate had on the contractual relationships. In his view, the agent bound his principal only for the authorised price.[160] The First Division's approach in *Lockhart* was undoubtedly pragmatic and fair, and the case exists as a precedent which could be applied to permit ratification by an unnamed or undisclosed principal. This course of action would have the benefit of consistency with PECL.[161]

6 Conclusion

Ratification emerges as an area dogged by theoretical uncertainties. Its overall rationale is not clear, although it is suggested here that it is an expression of the principal's consent to a transaction or 'engagement' with the third party. Where it arises as an inference from silence, it may be an application of the concept of personal bar. Its requirements are strict, and possibly overly so, particularly where ratification by an undisclosed or unnamed principal is prohibited. Scots law could develop a fairer rule by rejecting the much-criticised *Keighley Maxsted* v. *Durrant*[162] and developing the Scottish case *Lockhart* v. *Moodie & Co.*[163]

As has been illustrated above, the most serious difficulty lies in the failure to define the type of obligation created by the unauthorised agent at the moment he purports to enter into a contract on the principal's behalf. A dividing line appears to exist between those acts which cannot be ratified and those which possess a 'core' validity and are therefore ratifiable. The content of these classes is not clear.

---

[160] (1877) 4 R 859 at 866.

[161] See 3:207 on ratification and 3:203 on unidentified principals. The commentary to 3:207 indicates that a principal may ratify even though he was not in existence nor identifiable at the time the agent entered into the contract. 3:203 also contains a very wide undisclosed principal doctrine. Agents may act for undisclosed principals provided that they disclose the identity of the principal within a reasonable time after a request by the third party.

[162] [1901] AC 240.   [163] (1877) 4 R 859.

Finally, there is a need to develop a general principle excluding ratification where it would have an unfairly prejudicial effect on fourth parties. The groundwork is already present in the works of the institutional writers. One hopes that the development of a Scottish-based solution is possible.

IV Liability of the *falsus procurator*

1 General

The third party who finds that he is not bound in a contract with the principal, as he expected to be, suffers a loss which is actionable against the unauthorised agent. Although actions are clearly available to him in either delict or contract, there appear to be very few reported Scottish cases.[164] In one of those actions based on contract which eventually proceeded to the House of Lords, the Inner House of the Scottish Court of Session noted that they had not been referred to Scottish case-law and approved the following general description of the action, drawn from English case-law:[165]

> Where a person by asserting that he has the authority of the principal induces another person to enter into any transaction which he would not have entered into but for that assertion, and the assertion turns out to be untrue to the injury of the person to whom it is made, it must be taken that the person making it undertook that it was true, and he is liable personally for the damage that has occurred.[166]

2 Doctrinal basis

Although it is clear that the action is a contractual one, the very small amount of case-law which exists makes it difficult to state the principles with certainty. Perhaps the most interesting aspect is the relevance of the agent's knowledge at the time of purporting to enter the contract on the

---

[164] *Rederi Aktiebolaget Nordstjernan* v. *Salvesan & Co.* 1902 10 SLT 44; 1903 10 SLT 543, (1903) 6 F (HL) 101; *Anderson* v. *Croall & Sons* (1903) 6 F 153; *Irving* v. *Burns* 1915 SC 260.

[165] *Rederi Aktiebolaget Nordstjernan* v. *Salvesan & Co* 1903 10 SLT 543, per Lord Moncreiff at 545; also approved at the House of Lords stage of the same case; see (1903) 6 F 101, per Lord Chancellor Halsbury at 101.

[166] *Firbanks Exrs* v. *Humphreys* (1886) 18 QBD 54, per Lord Esher, and *Collen* v. *Wright* (1857) 7 E & B 301, per Mr Justice Willes; *affd* 8 E & B 647.

principal's behalf. The action is not limited to cases in which the agent is fraudulent or negligent. It is also available where the agent behaves innocently, unaware of his lack of authority. Where the agent is fully aware of his lack of authority, a delictual action would be available, involving proof of fraud on the part of the agent.[167] Although there appear to be no relevant cases, there seems no reason to doubt that in Scots law, as in English law, an action is available where the agent's conduct is negligent rather than fraudulent.[168]

Gloag summarises the legal basis of the action as follows (referring to the agent): 'by what amounts to a legal fiction, it will be implied that he contracts that he has authority, and he will therefore be liable in damages for breach of that contract if it turns out that he has none.'[169] Although the wording is ambiguous, here Gloag envisages the formation of an actual contract between agent and third party, and this is supported by his reference to Pothier.[170] However, Gloag later indicated that this is an example of a wider principle 'applicable to all cases where A, by representing as a matter of fact that he possesses a certain authority, has induced B to act to his prejudice.'[171]

The leading, almost the only, reported case on the contractual action is *Anderson v. Croall & Sons*,[172] in which an auctioneer purported to sell a horse at what was known as a 'Race Meeting'. In terms of the rules of the meet, certain of the horses were sold by the auctioneer at the end of the race. The auctioneer mistakenly believed that the horse in question was to be sold because of circumstances which were mainly the fault of the principal's employee. The auctioneer was held liable, but it is unclear on what basis. The mistake, and the auctioneer's failure to take reasonable

---

[167] See Gloag, *Contract*, p. 154, relying on J. Story, *Commentaries on the Law of Agency*, 9th edn by C. P. Greenough (Boston, MA: Little Brown, 1882), s. 264 as authority.

[168] On the basis of the English case of *Hedley Byrne & Co. Ltd v. Heller & Partners Ltd* [1964] AC 465. It should be noted that misrepresentation has a common law basis in Scots law, in contrast to English law, where the basis is statutory (Misrepresentation Act 1967).

[169] Gloag, *Contract*, p. 155.

[170] Referring to the case where the unauthorised agent indicates that the principal will ratify, Pothier states: 'if I promise that he shall ratify it, this promise is an agreement which I make in my own name with the person with whom I contract, and by which I am in my own obliged to obtain such ratification; and in default of obtaining it, I am obliged to answer for his damages.' Pothier, *Treatise on the Law of Obligations*, s. 75. Gloag also refers to English authority and Bell, *Commentaries*, I, 543, note where the editor too discusses English case law.

[171] Gloag, *Contract*, p. 155, referring to *Sheffield Corporation v. Barclay* [1905] AC 392, per Lord Chancellor Halsbury at 397.

[172] (1903) 6 F 153.

care to prevent the mistake, are emphasised in the judgment.[173] Although the agent's good faith has been suggested as a basis, there is certainly no reference to this basis in the case itself.[174]

What then can be proposed as a legal basis for this action? Gloag's proposal, that where A, by representing as a matter of fact that he possesses a certain authority, has induced B to act to his prejudice, is an accurate description of the facts. However, it seems unsatisfactory to use the legal fiction of an implied contract. Neither party intended to enter into a contract. Use could be made here of the Scottish unilateral promise or *pollicitatio*. Following this line of reasoning, one could say that the agent makes a separate and enforceable promise to the third party either that he is already fully authorised, or, if not, that he will obtain the requisite authority. In accordance with the general rules on promise, there is no requirement of acceptance on the part of the third party. The third party's action is one of breach of promise for which he could obtain damages, in essence the pure expectation of a contract with the principal.

Scots law may simply have unquestioningly followed English law on this issue. In doing so it has failed to take into account the fact that the English analysis is motivated by the doctrine of consideration, a concept which is not part of Scots law. English law cannot without difficulty recognise a unilateral warranty. A contract must be employed and consideration identified. Here, consideration is provided by the third party either in his promise to enter into an (invalid) contract with the principal or his act of entering into a contract with another party.[175] A promissory solution seems to be much less cumbersome, and more reflective of the realities of the situation, bearing in mind that agent and third party do not intend to enter into a contract.

3 Scope

Although no authority can be cited for these propositions, there seems no reason to doubt that the action is available either where the agent enters into unauthorised contracts or where the agent carries out other juridical acts on the principal's behalf. Similarly, there is no reason to doubt that it

---

[173] (1903) 6 F 153, per the Lord Justice-Clerk J. H. A. MacDonald and Lord Trayner at 158.

[174] See Viscount Dunedin, J. Wark and A. C. Black (eds.), *Encyclopaedia of the Laws of Scotland* (Edinburgh: W. Green & Son Ltd, 1913), vol. 1, para. 530.

[175] *Penn* v. *Bristol and West Building Society* [1997] 3 All ER 470, per Waller LJ at 474–7.

is available whether the parties are individuals or legal persons such as companies.

4 Effect

As stated above, the current legal basis of this action appears to be an implied contract between agent and third party, in terms of which a warranty is given that the agent is authorised. This contract is, of course, separate from the contract which the agent purports to conclude on the principal's behalf.

The third party's remedy for breach of warranty is damages, calculated by reference to the loss which the third party suffers in not having the expected contract.[176] The third party must be placed in the position he would have been in had the warranty been true. Thus, the measure has been described as 'the difference between the profit which would have been made on the abortive contract, and the best terms which could be obtained in the market when the misrepresentation was discovered'.[177] Normal rules of ascertainment of damages will apply, for example, no damages will be payable where the third party suffers no loss, the contract which the agent purportedly formed being with an insolvent principal.[178] Where the action is delictual in nature, damages would seek to compensate the third party's reliance losses, rather than his contractual expectations.

Even though specific implement is, at least in theory, the primary remedy for breach of contract in Scots law, it is unlikely to be available in this context. The contract between agent and third party is, of course, a legal fiction. To enforce it against the agent might involve requiring the agent to achieve the impossible, by procuring the grant of the requisite authority from his principal. Impossibility is, of course, one of the grounds upon which specific implement may be refused by a court.[179]

---

[176] (1903) 6 F 153, per Lord Moncrieff at 159; *Rederi Aktiebolaget Nordstjernan* v. *Salvesan & Co.* 1903 10 SLT 543, per Lord Moncreiff at 546–7; affd (HL) (1905) 7 F 101. See also Gow, *The Mercantile and Industrial Law of Scotland*, p. 529.

[177] *Rederi Aktiebolaget Nordstjernan* v. *Salvesan & Co.* 1903 10 SLT 543, per Lord Moncreiff at 547.

[178] *Irving* v. *Burns* 1915 SC 260.

[179] See *Purie* v. *Lord Couper* (1662) Mor 16583; *Nisbet* v. *Lord Balmerino* (1673) Mor 459; *Plato* v. *Newman* 1950 SLT (Notes) 29, analysed in Macgregor, 'Specific implement in Scots Law'.

5 Requirements

(a) Conduct of the agent

As noted above, given that this action is contractual in nature, there is no requirement of fault on the part of the agent. He may be liable for breach of warranty even where he honestly believed that he was authorised. The warranty itself is usually implied rather than express – the agent in transacting with the third party impliedly warrants that he possesses sufficient authority. The agent may, of course, provide an express warranty.

(b) Inducement

Actual inducement is required: the warranty must induce the third party to believe that the agent is authorised to make the particular contract, and that he is indeed bound by a contract. Thus, a third party who is already aware of the agent's lack of authority has not been induced and cannot use this action.[180]

(c) Conduct of the third party

There is no evidence in case-law of the third party being placed under a duty to act reasonably in the context of this action. However, there are similarities between this action and the action for misrepresentation. Where the latter is at issue, the misrepresentation must be such as would induce the reasonable man to enter into the contract. It is likely that a similar reasonableness requirement would apply here.[181] The third party's conduct is thus relevant as part of the overall analysis of causation. There are similarities here with apparent authority, where the standard of reasonable behaviour was also applied to the third party in the context of the assessment of causation.[182]

(d) No similar action for principal

At one time it was not clear whether a similar action was available to the principal against the agent.[183] The House of Lords eventually confirmed that the appropriate action for the principal where he suffers loss as a

---

[180] Bell, *Commentaries*, I, 542, note; Gloag, *Contract*, 156; *RBS* v. *Skinner* 1931 SLT 382.
[181] See W. W. McBryde, *The Law of Contract in Scotland*, 3rd edn (Edinburgh: W. Green, 2007), para. 15-68
[182] II 5(c).
[183] *Rederi Aktiebolaget Nordstjernan* v. *Salvesan & Co.* 1902 10 SLT 44; 1903 10 SLT 543.

result of his agent's misrepresentation of the extent of his authority is an action for breach of duty.[184]

V Acting in the name of a principal yet to be named

Although Scots law recognises the agent's ability to act for a disclosed but unnamed principal, the legal principles are subject to doubt. Where the agent acts in this way, either the principal or the agent may be bound in a contract with the third party. There appear to be two competing theories as to how one ascertains which party is bound. It may depend upon whose 'credit' or financial reputation the third party relies on at the moment of formation of the contract. If he relies on the agent's reputation, he is bound to the agent and if he relies on the unnamed principal's, then he is bound to the principal.[185] An alternative analysis relies on the doctrine of 'election': if the third party elects to sue the agent, then the contract lies between third party and agent, and *mutatis mutandis* the principal.[186] It is suggested that the former is the more satisfactory theory. The latter leaves the question of identification of the contractual ties to a late stage, i.e. only when the third party decides to sue.[187]

Given the paucity of case-law on disclosed but unnamed agency, it is difficult to state the rules which apply where that agent is, additionally, unauthorised. Where the agent is unauthorised, and the third party is relying on the credit of the principal, it is unlikely that a contract could be formed. The normal rule of unauthorised agency would apply. Where, however, the third party relies on the agent's credit, there would seem to be no reason to deny the existence of a contractual tie between agent and third party. The third party looks primarily to the agent to perform, so the existence or otherwise of his authority seems to be an unimportant issue.

The above situation should be distinguished from that in which the agent acts for a non-existent principal, where the general rule is that the agent is personally bound in a contract with the third party.[188] The most common practical consequence of this rule lies in the field of company

---

[184] *Rederi Aktiebolaget Nordstjernan v. Salvesan & Co.* (HL) (1905) 7 F 101.
[185] Macgregor, 'Agency and Mandate', para. 138, and see, e.g., *Lamont, Nisbet & Co.* v. *Hamilton* 1907 SC 628 at 635, per Lord President Dunedin.
[186] Macgregor, 'Agency and Mandate', para. 139, and see, e.g., *Ferrier v. Dods* (1865) 3 M 561.
[187] Macgregor, 'Agency and Mandate', para. 140.   [188] *Ibid.*, para. 165.

law, as analysed immediately below. This rule would also apply in a case where the principal is an unincorporated association.[189]

VI Acting in the name of a company yet to be incorporated

As noted above,[190] the retrospective effect of ratification binds the principal from the moment at which the agent purported to enter into a contract on his behalf. This being the case, the principal must be in existence at the time the agent purported to act. This rule is applied to the company law context unchanged. As a result, promoters acting for as yet unincorporated companies become personally bound by contracts which they purport to conclude on the non-existent company's behalf.[191] The same statutory provisions apply in both Scotland and England. The contract entered into by the agent cannot be ratified. The company, should it wish to take advantage of that contract, must enter into a new contract on similar terms.[192]

There seems no doubt that this result is commercially impractical.[193] It is not surprising to note, therefore, that attempts have been made to utilise the Scottish common law third party right, or *jus quaesitum tertio*, as a solution to this problem. Similar attempts have been made in South African law with regard to the *stipulatio alteri*, although with more success compared to Scotland.[194] The unincorporated company, so the argument goes, is a *tertius* who can obtain a benefit from the contract entered into by the promoter with the third party. There is no require-ment of acceptance on the part of the *tertius* in Scots law, and so the fact that it is not in existence at the moment of conclusion of that contract is not problematic. This argument failed in the only Scottish case in which it was raised, although on unsound grounds, namely that there was, in fact, no contract between promoter and third party.[195] Nevertheless, a more significant problem, not aired in the case itself, exists: the Scottish

---

[189] *McMeekin v. Easton* (1889) 16 R 363.   [190] III 4(a).

[191] Companies Act 1985, s. 36C; Companies Act 2006, s. 51(1).

[192] S. Mayson, D. French and C. Ryan, *Mayson, French and Ryan on Company Law*, 24th edn (Oxford: Oxford University Press, 2007–8), p. 598.

[193] See also Reynolds, *Agency*, 2-062, where the results are described as 'inconvenient'.

[194] Chapter 10 (South Africa) III 2(c), although the law in South Africa is now on a statutory footing, see s. 35 South African Companies Act.

[195] *Cumming v. Quartzag Ltd* 1980 SC 276 and see comment by H. MacQueen, 'Promoter's Contracts, Agency and the *Jus Quaesitum Tertio*' 1982 *SLT* 257 and in 'Obligations', *The Laws of Scotland: Stair Memorial Encyclopaedia* (Edinburgh: Butterworths/Law Society of Scotland, 1987–96), vol. XV, paras. 834 and 840.

concept can only operate to confer benefits, not burdens. To apply this
concept to promoters of pre-incorporation contracts is, of course, to
confer burdens in addition to benefits on the company as *tertius*.[196] As
MacQueen has pointed out, South African law was able to avoid this
particular problem because of its requirement of acceptance on the part
of the *tertius*.[197] One is drawn to agree with MacQueen, that the only
solution to this problem in Scots law is legislative reform.[198]

VII Conclusion

Scots agency law faces significant challenges. As this chapter has illustrated, the principles are often to be found in ancient sources: either the
works of the institutional writers or cases which may no longer be
relevant due to their age. Some of the concepts appearing in these sources
can only be applied with difficulty in a modern context, homologation
being a prime example. Nor can Scots lawyers rely on a large amount of
case-law to develop new legal bases. There is, however, cause for optimism. Personal bar is a key concept in an agency context, particularly in
apparent authority. Previously shrouded in mystery, it has now been
fully explored in a recent book by Reid and Blackie.[199] Their excellent
analysis is available for use by the Scottish courts. Another significant
factor is the dynamic academic environment which currently exists in
Scotland. This environment has made possible comparative works on
Scots and South African law.[200] Solutions from another mixed legal
system such as South Africa may be attractive to Scots lawyers.

   Of the three concepts which form the focus of this project, in a Scottish
context, apparent authority is the area requiring the least development.
The requirement of the principal's conduct has not been applied strictly
by the courts. Its flexibility is beneficial, helping to achieve the goal of
third party protection. This trend is set to continue, given the wide ambit
of 'inconsistent conduct' in Reid and Blackie's formulation.[201]

---

[196] See MacQueen, 'Obligations', para. 834.   [197] See *Ibid.*, para. 834.
[198] See *Ibid.*, para. 834.   [199] Reid and Blackie, *Personal Bar.*
[200] K. Reid and R. Zimmermann (eds.), *A History of Private Law in Scotland* (Oxford:
Oxford University Press, 2000); R. Zimmermann, D. Visser and K. G. C. Reid (eds.),
Mixed Legal Systems in Comparative Perspective (Oxford: Oxford University Press,
2004); and H. MacQueen and R. Zimmermann (eds.), *European Contract Law: Scots
and South African Perspectives* (Edinburgh: Edinburgh University Press, 2006).
[201] See II 5(a) above.

Ratification suffers from the most significant problems. The failure clearly to analyse the nature of the obligation created by the unauthorised agent at the moment he purports to enter into a contract on the principal's behalf is a real difficulty. Only once this issue has been resolved can related questions be tackled, principally the third party's right to withdraw, but also the general exception prohibiting ratification where it would prejudice the rights of fourth parties. The question of time limits is also subject to an unacceptable degree of doubt.

Breach of warranty of authority emerges as a concept which has benefited from almost no analysis, either in case-law or scholarship. Although this is indeed unfortunate, it does appear to be the least important of the three concepts in practice.

What this chapter has also highlighted is that Scots law fails to make the most of existing attributes. Its open attitude to privity of contract could be a significant advantage, permitting the use of innovative solutions. An example is the potential use of unilateral promise as a legal basis for breach of warranty of authority. As has been argued here, another concept which could also prove fruitful is the nascent idea of good faith in contract.[202] In the current academic climate, there is no reason to doubt that Scots lawyers will make good use of scholarship, comparative and otherwise, in order to overcome the challenges it currently faces.

---

[202] See n. 104.

Unauthorised agency in South African law

DAVID YUILL

Table of contents

I Introduction[1]

The South African law of agency has been described as a combination of 'the Roman-Dutch law of mandate and the modern Anglo-American principles of commercial agency'[2] and it is an area of South African law where the mixed nature of the South African legal system is especially evident. English law, in particular, has had a very strong influence on the development of the South African law of agency. Much of the reason for this lies in the fact that the particular brand of Roman-Dutch law that was imported into South Africa on the sailing ships of the Dutch East India Company and which forms the basis of the South African common law, did not have a particularly well-developed set of rules relating to agency, or at least agency as it is understood in its modern sense.[3] With the British occupation of the Cape, and subsequently the rest of South Africa, English law filtered into many aspects of the South African legal system, and agency was one such area. The comprehensive set of rules

---

[1] Literature: B. P. Wanda (original text by J. C. de Wet), 'Agency and Representation', in W. A. Joubert et al. (ed.), *The Law of South Africa*, 2nd edn, 34 vols. (Durban: LexisNexis Butterworths, 2003), vol. 1, pp. 167–223; D. J. Joubert, *Die Suid-Afrikaanse Verteenwoordigingsreg* (Cape Town: Juta, 1979); A. J. Kerr, *The Law of Agency*, 4th edn (Durban: Butterworths, 2006); J. E. R. de Villiers and J. C. Macintosh, *The Law of Agency in South Africa*, 3rd edn by J. M. Silke (Cape Town, Juta, 1981).

[2] D. J. Joubert, 'Agency and *Stipulatio Alteri*', in R. Zimmerman and D. Visser (eds.), *Southern Cross: Civil Law and Common Law in South Africa* (Oxford: Clarendon, 1996), p. 341.

[3] *Ibid.*, pp. 335–6; H. R. Hahlo and E. Kahn, *The Union of South Africa: The Development of its Laws and Constitution* (London: Stevens, 1960), p. 695. While Roman-Dutch law of the sixteenth and seventeenth centuries did have a detailed set of rules on the contract of mandate, which regulated the relationship between principal and agent, the concept of direct representation, i.e. the agent directly binding the principal to a third party, had only recently been recognised and thus the Roman-Dutch theory in this regard was poorly developed.

and wealth of case-law to be found in the English law of agency provided a welcome resource for South African judges faced with a paucity of Roman-Dutch authority on the subject, and one that they chose to draw on frequently.[4]

Thus, regular reference to English decisions and authorities (and to a lesser extent American and other authorities) can be found in South African case-law and textbooks on agency.[5] The substantial influence that English law has had on the South African law of agency is evident in this chapter – the doctrine of estoppel and the rules relating to ostensible authority, the implied warranty of authority and the rule in *Kelner v. Baxter* are all imports from English law, and much of the terminology that is used is that of English law. That is not to say, however, that the English law of agency has been taken over wholesale. Roman-Dutch principles still play a role and even those principles that have been imported directly from English law have developed a distinctly South African flavour. In recent years, the reliance on English and other outside sources has waned as a wealth of local jurisprudence has been developed on the subject.

What then of unauthorised agency, the subject of this work? As in other jurisdictions, the general rule in South African law is that a person who purports to act on behalf of another, cannot create any obligations nor incur any liability for the other unless he has been given authority to do so. South African law recognises two exceptions to this rule – ostensible authority and ratification. In certain situations, an agent who acts without authority can also be held personally liable. These three possibilities will now be examined in greater detail below.

---

[4] De Villiers and Macintosh, *Agency*, p. 11; B. Beinart, 'The English Legal Contribution in South Africa: The Interaction of Civil and Common Law' (1981) *Acta Juridica* 7 at 47. See also R. W. Lee, *An Introduction to Roman-Dutch Law*, 5th edn (Oxford: Clarendon, 1953), p. 310, where it is stated that 'the English law of agency has been substantially adopted and followed'.

[5] Joubert, 'Agency and *Stipulatio Alteri*', pp. 340–1. English works that are regularly cited include F. M. B. Reynolds, *Bowstead and Reynolds on Agency*, 18th edn (London: Sweet & Maxwell, 2006) and G. Spencer Bower, *The Law Relating to Estoppel by Representation*, 4th edn, by P. Feltham, D. Hochberg and T. Leech (London: Butterworths, 2004), while American authorities such as J. Story, *Commentaries on the Law of Agency as a Branch of Commercial and Maritime Jurisprudence*, 9th edn by C. P. Greenough (Boston: Little Brown, 1882) and the *Restatement of the Law, Second: Agency* (St Paul, MN: American Law Institute, 1958) are also often referred to. Pothier is regularly quoted by Kerr in his textbook on the South African law of agency.

II Ostensible authority[6]

1 Introduction

In the absence of actual authority, South African law recognises that a principal[7] can nevertheless be held liable should he create the appearance that a person has the authority to act on his behalf, and the third party acts on the basis of that appearance to his detriment. The term used to describe this legal phenomenon is 'ostensible' or 'apparent' authority. The terminology is that of English law and, as in English law, ostensible authority is dealt with as a form of estoppel by representation.[8] Thus, the principal is held liable, not because he has given any kind of authority for the acts purportedly carried out on his behalf, but because he is estopped from denying that he did not give actual authority for those acts.

Despite some resistance by Roman-Dutch purists, the generally accepted view is that the legal principles relating to the doctrine of estoppel by representation were received into South Africa from English law.[9] Although the South African principles relating to ostensible authority (as a form of estoppel by representation) therefore largely reflect those of English law, they are not identical in every respect:

> Like any other immigrant that has been here for some time, the original 'Englishness' has to certain extent faded in favour of a more South African appearance. But the immigrant's background remains and our Courts have not overlooked it in adopting it into the South African legal milieu.[10]

---

[6] See, in general, P. J. Rabie, 'Estoppel', in W. A. Joubert *et al.* (eds.), *The Law of South Africa*, 1st reissue, 34 vols. (Durban: Butterworths, 1993 onwards), vol. 9, §§ 283–308; J. P. Sonnekus, *Rabie's The Law of Estoppel in South Africa*, 2nd edn (Durban: Butterworths, 2000); Wanda, 'Agency and Representation', §§ 210–12; De Villiers and Macintosh, *Agency*, pp. 440–52; Joubert, *Verteenwordigingsreg*, pp. 109–27; Kerr, *Agency*, pp. 94–109.

[7] For ease of reference the parties involved in a typical situation of unauthorised agency, namely the unauthorised agent, the person for whom the 'agent' purports to act and the third party/ies with whom the 'agent' deals, will be referred to respectively as the 'agent', the 'principal' and the 'third party'.

[8] See, however, D. H. Bester, 'Scope of an Agent's Power of Representation', (1972) 89 *SALJ* 49, who expresses the view that basing the liability of the principal for the unauthorised acts of his agent in estoppel is not always satisfactory, and argues for the recognition of an extra category of liability, in terms of which the principal is held liable, for reasons of policy, 'merely because the person who acted was his agent'.

[9] For a summary of the reception of estoppel in South African law, see R. Zimmermann, 'Good Faith and Equity', in R. Zimmerman and D. Visser (eds.), *Southern Cross: Civil Law and Common Law in South Africa* (Oxford, Clarendon: 1996), pp. 221–7. See also Rabie, 'Estoppel', paras. 284–7.

[10] *Sonday* v. *Surrey Estate Modern Meat Market (Pty) Ltd* 1983 (2) SA 521 (C) at 527A–B.

In the most recent case on the matter, the Supreme Court of Appeal has set out the following requirements for holding a principal liable on the basis of ostensible authority:[11]

1. a representation by words or conduct, made by the principal and not the agent, that the agent had the authority to act as he did;
2. a representation in such a form that the principal should reasonably have expected that outsiders would act on the strength of it;
3. reliance by the third party on such representation;
4. the reasonableness of such reliance; and
5. prejudice to the third party as a consequence thereof.

Each of these requirements will be examined and discussed in greater detail below.

2 Representation by the principal

In order to satisfy the first of the requirements listed above, there must not only be a representation which creates the appearance of authority, but the representation must be made either by the principal himself, or else by someone authorised or permitted to make such representation on his behalf. Generally speaking, representations made by the agent himself as to his own authority cannot incur any liability for the principal.[12]

The representation may be made expressly (either verbally or in writing) or tacitly by means of conduct. Conduct in the form of inaction or silence can also constitute a representation, although in order for it to do so, the silence or inaction must have occurred in circumstances which gave rise to a duty on the principal to speak or act. It has been held that such a duty arises 'when a person … should reasonably have expected, in the light of his/her relationship with the other party concerned and of all the other relevant facts, that his/her failure to speak or act could mislead and cause prejudice to the other party'.[13] Thus, for example, it was held that a liquor store owner had a duty to tell his suppliers that he had sold his business to a third

---

[11] *Glofinco v. Absa Bank Ltd t/a United Bank* 2002 (6) SA 470 (SCA) at 479.

[12] *Rosebank Television & Appliance Co. (Pty) Ltd v. Orbit Sales Corporation (Pty) Ltd* 1969 (1) SA 300 (T) at 303D; *Hosken Employee Benefits (Pty) Ltd v. Slabe* 1992 (4) SA 183 (W) at 191A; *Glofinco v. Absa Bank Ltd t/a United Bank* 2002 (6) SA 470 (SCA) at 480.

[13] *Jones and others v. Trust Bank of Africa Ltd and others* 1993 (4) SA 415 (C) at 425B–C.

party, and his failure to do so constituted a misrepresentation capable of founding an estoppel.[14]

It has also been recognised that the appointment of an agent to a particular position may also constitute a representation to the outside world that the agent has the authority to perform the acts usually associated with such position.[15] As has been noted, however, a representation of this nature is subject to the implicit limitation that an agent will not have the authority to carry out acts that fall outside the normal scope of his position.[16] The question of what constitutes the normal authority of someone appointed to a particular position has not always proved easy to answer in practice, as is demonstrated by two recent decisions in the South African courts regarding the ostensible authority of a bank manager.

NBS Bank Ltd v. *Cape Produce Co. (Pty) Ltd*[17] was one of a string of cases arising from a large-scale fraud committed by the manager of a branch of a well-respected South African financial institution. The manager in question, a certain Assante, had, through various brokers, persuaded a number of investors to deposit money with the appellant bank by offering attractive interest rates in excess of the going rate at the time. Assante was not acting on behalf of the bank at all, however, but was involved with a fraudulent scheme of his own. The essence of the fraud was that the deposits received from the unwary investors were deposited in an account in favour of a firm of attorneys, his partners-in-crime, from where they were channelled on to certain third parties. Eventually, the whole scheme collapsed, leaving a number of the investors, including the respondent, substantially out of pocket. There was obviously no question of Assante having actual or implied authority to do what he did – the crux of the case was therefore whether or not Assante had ostensible authority. The court noted that the usual business of a bank such as the appellant included the acceptance and repayment of deposits, and such business was carried out through its branches. In appointing Assante as a branch manager, the appellant was therefore representing to the outside world that Assante had authority to accept deposits on its behalf

---

[14] *Stellenbosch Farmers' Winery Ltd* v. *Vlachos t/a The Liquor Den* 2001 (3) SA 599 (SCA) at 604B.
[15] *South African Eagle Insurance Co. Ltd* v. *NBS Bank Ltd* 2002 (1) SA 560 (SCA) at 573H–574B; *Reed NO* v. *Sager's Motors (Pvt) Ltd* 1970 (1) SA 521 (RA) at 524H–525A; *South Africa Broadcasting Corporation* v. *Coop and others* 2006 (2) SA 217 at 236H–237A.
[16] *Glofinco* v. *Absa Bank Ltd t/a United Bank* 2002 (6) SA 470 (SCA) at 481C–D and H–I.
[17] 2002 (1) SA 396 (SCA). See also *South African Eagle Insurance Co. Ltd* v. *NBS Bank Ltd* 2002 (1) SA 560 (SCA) and *African Life Assurance Co. Ltd* v. *NBS Bank Ltd* 2001 (1) SA 432 (W), which arose out of the same fraud.

and agree on the terms thereof with outsiders. The fact that Assante's authority was subject to certain internal limitations which he exceeded was held not to be relevant – in accordance with the general rule of South African law, outsiders are not bound by any private limitations placed on an agent's authority unless they are aware of them or unless they are brought to their notice.[18]

An interesting comparison can be made with the case of *Glofinco v. Absa Bank Ltd t/a United Bank*,[19] which also involved one of South Africa's seemingly plentiful supply of fraudulent bank managers. In this case, however, the bank manager's acts were held not to fall within the normal scope of her authority. The facts were as follows: a branch manager of the respondent, one Horne, had undertaken, purportedly on behalf of the bank, to stand surety for a series of post-dated cheques provided to the appellant by a third party who was a client of the bank. Certain of the cheques were subsequently dishonoured, and the appellant looked to the respondent bank for satisfaction. Although, on the face of it, the guaranteeing of cheques would seem to fall squarely within the normal scope of activity of a bank manager, there were a number of factors which made the transaction a highly unusual one. The most obvious red flag was the fact that, if the bank was sufficiently satisfied as to its client's creditworthiness to stand surety for its client's cheques, why did they not lend the client the money themselves and earn the interest, instead of allowing it to obtain funds at an exorbitant cost from the appellant? The court therefore held that the bank had not, in appointing Horne as a manager, represented that she had authority to undertake an unusual transaction of this nature, which was so patently inimical to the bank's interests. In the minority decision, however, Nugent JA noted that 'the question to be asked in each case … is not whether the principal would ordinarily have concluded the disputed contract, but rather whether the contract is of a kind that falls within the scope of the plaintiff's ordinary business'.[20] In his view, the guaranteeing of a cheque did fall within the ostensible authority of a bank manager such as Horne, and the fact that in this particular case it was not commercially sensible for the bank to do so, was not the concern of an innocent third party. It is submitted that the minority approach to determining whether or not a representation has been made is

---

[18] *Haddad v. Livestock Products Central Co-op. Ltd* 1961 2 SA 362 (W) at 367E; *Dicks v. SA Mutual Fire & General Insurance Co. Ltd* 1963 (4) SA 501 (N).
[19] 2002 (6) SA 470 (SCA).   [20] *Ibid.* at 493F–G.

preferable. The fact that a particular transaction may not make commercial sense is rather a factor that should be taken into account in determining whether or not the third party's reliance on the representation was reasonable.

In respect of companies, it has been noted that the appointment by a company of someone as a director, manager or company secretary does not in and of itself constitute an automatic representation that such person has the authority to represent the company.[21] There must, therefore, be some further representation of authority which is relied on by the third party. In the case of the appointment of someone as a managing director, however, such appointment is generally considered to constitute a representation that such person has authority to represent the company in such areas as traditionally fall within the scope of a managing director's powers.[22] This is because a managing director, generally speaking, usually has much more wide-ranging powers to represent the company than an ordinary director.

3 Representation that could reasonably have been expected to be acted on

The fact that a principal makes a representation regarding the authority of his agent is not in and of itself sufficient – South African law further requires that the representation is of such a nature that the principal could reasonably have expected it to be acted on.[23] The test is an objective one – i.e. the representation must be one that a reasonable man in the position of the principal would have expected that third parties would be misled thereby. Although this would appear to be similar to a test for negligence, and although fault is required for a successful reliance on

---

[21] *Rosebank Television & Appliance Co. (Pty) Ltd* v. *Orbit Sales Corp. (Pty) Ltd* 1969 (1) SA 300 (T) at 303A; *Hosken Employee Benefits (Pty) Ltd* v. *Slabe* 1992 (4) SA 183 at 190C–F; M. S. Blackman *et al.*, 'Companies', in W. A. Joubert *et al.* (eds.), *The Law of South Africa*, 1st re-issue (Durban: Butterworths, 1993 onwards), vol. 4(1), para. 35.

[22] Blackman, 'Companies', para. 35. *Big Dutchman (SA) (Pty) Ltd* v. *Barclays National Bank Ltd* 1979 (3) SA 267 (W).

[23] *Monzali* v. *Smith* 1929 AD 382 at 386: 'A Court of law would not hold a person bound by consequences which he could not reasonably expect and are therefore not the natural result of his conduct'; see also *Quinn & Co. Ltd* v. *Witwatersrand Military Institute* 1953 (1) SA 155 (T) at 159E–F; *Connock's (SA) Motor Co. Ltd* v. *Sentraal Westelike Kooperatiewe Mpy Bpk* 1964 (2) SA 47 (T) at 51A; *NBS Bank Ltd* v. *Cape Produce Co (Pty) Ltd and others* 2002 (1) SA 396 at 412D.

estoppel in other areas of South African law,[24] it has been specifically stated that fault on the part of the principal is not a requirement for a claim based on ostensible authority.[25]

As was noted by Trollip J in the case of *Connock's (SA) Motor Co. Ltd v. Sentraal Westelike Ko-op*,[26] this approach differs somewhat from that of English law, where the primary focus is on the reasonableness of the third party's reliance on the representation. South African law, however, considers matters from the point of view of both representor and representee. Trollip J explained this as follows:

> to have regard only to the position of the representee in applying the objective test could in certain circumstances bear unjustly or unduly harshly on a representor, especially if he as innocent or blameless, and because the foundation of estoppel is still equity, our courts have evolved a different approach.[27]

One of the factors which the court indicated should be taken into account in this regard is the representor's awareness or ignorance of any facts that would give his conduct the particular significance attached to by the representee.

In the *Connock's Motors* case, the court was dealing specifically with a representation made by unintentional conduct, and it noted *obiter* that different considerations may possibly apply to express representations, or those made by conduct with the intention that they be acted upon. In this regard it has been held that express representations must be precise and unambiguous in order to be actionable.[28] Rabie questions the merit of this requirement, however, and submits that the test used for tacit representations should apply equally to express representations.[29] There does not appear to be any good reason why an express representation

---

[24] Fault on the part of the owner of an asset is required before he can be estopped from vindicating his property from a third party: *Oakland Nominees (Pty) Ltd* v. *Gelria Mining Investment Co. (Pty) Ltd* 1976 (1) SA 441 (A) at 452E–G; *Jones and others* v. *Trust Bank of Africa Ltd and others* 1993 (4) SA 415 (C) 424 H–J.

[25] *Glofinco* v. *ABSA Bank Ltd (t/a United Bank)* 2001 (2) SA 1048 (W) at 1061I–J; Wanda, 'Agency and Representation', § 211.

[26] 1964 (2) SA 47 (T). See also *Glofinco* v. *ABSA Bank Ltd (t/a United Bank)* 2001 (2) SA 1048 (W) at 1060G–1061C.

[27] 1964 (2) SA 47 (T) at 50D–E.

[28] *Hartogh* v. *National Bank* 1907 TS 1092 at 1104; *Southern Life Association Ltd* v. *Beyleveld NO* 1989 (1) SA 496 (A) at 503I.

[29] Sonnekus, *The Law of Estoppel in South Africa*, p. 37.

which is reasonably capable of misleading another, should not be capable of creating an appearance of ostensible authority, simply because it is not sufficiently precise or unequivocal. In many instances it may be the very ambiguity of the representation that makes it reasonably capable of misleading. It is hoped, therefore, that Rabie's suggestion is followed.

It has also been contended by certain authorities that a representation capable of founding an estoppel must have been made with the intention that it be acted upon,[30] but this contention appears to have been rejected.[31]

4 Reliance by the third party on the representation

A third party who wishes to succeed with a claim based on ostensible authority, must not only show that there was a representation of authority by the principal, but that he was aware of such representation[32] and relied on it in acting to his detriment. In other words, a causal link must be shown between the representation and the third party's actions. The test of legal causation that has been primarily favoured by the South African courts in the area of ostensible authority and in estoppel in general is the 'proximate' or 'real' cause test, which, as the name suggests, requires that the representation must be the primary or most direct cause of the third party acting to his detriment.[33] This test has not always proved easy to apply in practice, however, particularly in situations where more than one causative element is present.[34]

---

[30] De Villiers and Macintosh, *Agency*, p. 444. *Harriman* v. *Kahn* 1950 (2) SA 200 (N) at 203; *Hauptfleisch* v. *Caledon Divisional Council* 1963 (4) SA 53 (C) at 57A–C.

[31] *NBS Bank Ltd* v. *Cape Produce Co. (Pty) Ltd and others* 2002 (1) SA 396 (SCA) at 412A; Wanda, 'Agency and Representation', § 211; Rabie, *The Law of Estoppel in South Africa*, pp. 48–49.

[32] *Dicks* v. *SA Mutual Fire & General Insurance Co.* 1963 (4) SA 501 (N) at 508F: 'where the party setting up estoppel had no knowledge of the representation there can clearly be no causal connection between such representation and the alteration of his position to his detriment.'

[33] *Weedon* v. *Bawa* 1959 (4) SA 735 (D) at 741H; *Grosvenor Motors (Potchefstroom) Ltd* v. *Douglas* 1956 (3) SA 420 (A) at 426A; *Saambou-Nasionale Bouvereniging* v. *Friedman* 1979 (3) SA 978 (A) at 1005F; *Big Dutchman (SA) (Pty) Ltd* v. *Barclays National Bank Ltd* 1979 (3) SA 267 (W) at 283C.

[34] The difficulties of applying the proximate cause test in such situations are demonstrated by comparing the decisions of *Grosvenor Motors (Potchefstroom) Ltd* v. *Douglas* 1956 (3) SA 420 (A) and *Kajee* v. *HM Gough (Edms) Bpk* 1971 (3) SA 99 (N), where different results were reached on largely similar facts.

In *Stellenbosch Farmers' Winery Ltd* v. *Vlachos t/a The Liquor Den*,[35] a recent Supreme Court of Appeal decision, the respondent had sold his liquor business to a third party, without informing the appellant that he had done so. As a result, the appellant unwittingly continued to supply liquor to the third party, in the erroneous belief that the respondent was still running the business. When the appellant became suspicious and contacted the business directly, the new owner fraudulently misrepresented himself as the respondent. On this basis, the appellant continued to supply the business with liquor, until such time as the new owner absconded, whilst still owing a large sum of money to the appellant. The appellant sought to claim this money from the respondent, claiming he was estopped from denying the debt was his. The court found that although there had been a duty to speak on the respondent, and that his failure to do so amounted to a misrepresentation capable of founding an estoppel, the fraudulent misrepresentation by the third party was the primary cause of the appellant acting to its detriment.

Despite concurring with the decision, Marais JA, in a separate judgment, questioned the usefulness of words such as 'proximate' and 'real' in situations where more than one causal element exists, each of which is a contributing factor in creating of an incorrect impression in the mind of a third party. There is some merit in this contention. If, as in the *Stellenbosch Farmers'* case, one is dealing with two misrepresentations, each of which is made with fault and each of which played an important role in misleading an innocent third party, it does seem a somewhat artificial exercise to attempt to determine which of the two was more 'proximate'.[36]

An alternative approach was suggested in the cases of *Autolec* v. *Du Plessis*[37] and *Credit Corporation* v. *Botha*,[38] where it was held that it was not necessary for the representation to be *the* inducing cause of the third party to act to his detriment; it was sufficient that it was *an* inducing cause. This broader approach has some academic support,[39] but did not enjoy widespread approval in the courts.[40]

It appears, however, that the courts may be moving away from reliance on a single test for causation. In a number of other fields of South African

---

[35] 2001 (3) SA 599 (SCA).   [36] *Ibid.* at 612B–E.   [37] 1965 (2) SA 243 (O) at 248D–G.
[38] 1968 (4) SA 837 (N) at 850F–851A.
[39] Kerr, *Agency*, p. 133; A. J. Kerr, 'Causation in Estoppel by Misrepresentation' (1977) 94 *SALJ* 270; Joubert, *Verteenwordigingsreg*, p. 113.
[40] See *Barclays Bank International Ltd* v. *African Diamond Exporters (Pty) Ltd* 1977 (1) SA 298 (W).

law, the trend in recent years has been to utilise a more flexible test for determining legal causation.[41] This test has been described as 'one in which factors such as reasonable forseeability, directness, the absence or presence of a *novus actus interveniens*, legal policy, reasonability, fairness and justice all play their part'.[42] In the *Stellenbosch Farmers' Winery* case it was suggested *obiter* that there was no good reason why this approach should not be applied in the field of estoppel. It is to be hoped that this suggestion will be followed. The more flexible test will surely prove a more useful and adaptable tool in addressing the perennially problematic issue of legal causation than the 'proximate cause' test.

5 Reasonableness of the reliance

As in English and American law, a third party who claims that he relied on a principal's representation of authority is required to demonstrate that his reliance was reasonable.[43] Objectively speaking, if the representation is of such a nature that it could have been reasonably expected to mislead, then it would normally stand to reason that it would be reasonable for the third party to rely on it. However, the subjective position of the third party is also taken into account. Obviously, if the third party is aware that the agent with whom he interacts does not have the necessary authority, there can be no question of reasonable reliance.[44] Similarly, if a third party has his suspicions about the agent's authority, he must first allay such suspicions before proceeding. If he fails to do so, then he proceeds at his own risk– he cannot allege that he reasonably relied on a representation if he 'consciously abstained from doing something which in the ordinary course of business he would have done because he was afraid of finding out the truth'.[45] It is furthermore not sufficient that his suspicions are quelled by assurances of the agent himself.[46]

---

[41] S v. *Mokgheti en Andere* 1990 (1) SA 32 (A) (criminal law); *International Shipping Company (Pty) Ltd* v. *Bentley* 1990 (1) SA 680 (A) (delict).

[42] *Standard Chartered Bank of Canada* v. *Nedperm Bank Ltd* 1994 (4) SA 747 (A) at 765A–B.

[43] Sonnekus, *The Law of Estoppel in South Africa*, pp. 53–5; *Quinn & Co. Ltd* v. *Witwatersrand Military Institute* 1953 (1) SA 155 (T); *Monzali* v. *Smith* 1929 AD 382 at 389.

[44] *Standard Bank of SA Ltd* v. *Oneanate Investments (Pty) Ltd* 1995 4 SA 510 (C); *Hauptfleisch* v. *Caledon Divisional Council* 1963 (4) SA 53 (C) at 57C–D. In the case of a company, the knowledge of the lack of authority may also be imputed – that is knowledge of the company's employees or agents that can be attributed to it.

[45] *Hartogh* v. *National Bank Ltd* 1907 TH 207 at 212.

[46] *African Life Assurance Co Ltd* v. *NBS Bank Ltd* 2001 (1) SA 432 at 451F; *Wolpert* v. *Uitzigt Properties (Pty) Ltd and others* 1961 (2) SA 257 (W) at 366H–267A; *Glofinco* v. *ABSA Bank Ltd (t/a United Bank) and others* 2001 (2) SA 1048 (W) at 1066H.

In the *Glofinco* case,[47] the bench was sharply divided on the issue of the reasonableness of the appellant's reliance on the respondent bank's representation. The majority held that the reliance of Braude, a director of the appellant, on the bank's alleged representation that Horne had authority to bind the bank had not been reasonable. Having pointed out the number of unusual factors about the transaction, the court noted that Braude was no financial 'neophyte', and by his own admission had had concerns about the transaction. He had gone so far as to question Horne as to her credentials and the bank's reasons for entering into the transaction, but had accepted her answers without further verification. As such, the court held that he had relied on assurances from the purported agent herself as to her own authority, rather than representations from her principal, the bank, and as such they thus found that no ostensible authority existed.

The minority, however, took a different view. They pointed out that one should not underestimate the capacity that the 'trappings of trustworthiness' have for allaying suspicion, or lose sight of the fact that Braude was dealing with a senior bank manager, whom he had no reason to distrust. As was noted rather pointedly by Nugent JA: 'I do not think it is unreasonable for a member of the public, when dealing with the affairs of a bank, to trust the word of a bank manager, which is what Braude did. What is surprising is only that a bank should submit that it was.'[48]

The *Glofinco* decision raises interesting questions as to the extent to which third parties should be expected to question the authority of representatives of institutions with which they transact. Of the two conflicting approaches, it is submitted that the minority view is preferable. Too heavy a burden should not be placed on the man on the street to have to satisfy himself as to the authority of every appointed official with whom he deals, unless obvious grounds for suspicion exist. As was pointed out with reference to the *Glofinco* decision, 'the public can't be expected to question the mandate of every bank manager if business activities are to continue to thrive'.[49]

---

[47] *Glofinco v. Absa Bank Ltd t/a United Bank* 2002 (6) SA 470 (SCA) at 496, the facts of which are set out in II 2 above.

[48] *Ibid.* at 496.

[49] J. C. Sonnekus, 'Skynverwekking en 'n Verdeelde Appelhof' (2003) 14 *Stellenbosch L Rev* 29 at 50.

6 Prejudice to the third party

The final requirement for a claim based on ostensible authority is that the third party must show not only that he relied on the representation of authority made to him, but that in doing so he altered his position to his prejudice.[50] It is not necessary for the third party to show that he suffered prejudice at the time that he altered his position; what must be proved is that he will be prejudiced if the principal is allowed to deny his representation of authority.[51]

There is not a great deal of clarity on the exact nature and degree of prejudice that is required. In general, the South African courts have tended to interpret the concept of prejudice (in the context of estoppel) very widely, so much so that some commentators have gone so far as to suggest that a mere alteration of position by the third party, such as, for example, by entering into a contract with an unauthorised agent, may be sufficient to satisfy the requirement of prejudice.[52] This view is not borne out by the cases, however, and it appears that the South African courts still require some form of actual prejudice, albeit in the very broad sense of the word.[53]

In his authoritative work on the South African law of estoppel, Rabie, after a comprehensive examination of the case law, concludes that the prejudice suffered by the third party must be of a patrimonial nature.[54] The latest case on the matter has confirmed his views.[55] It is clear, however, that the concept of patrimonial prejudice is not interpreted restrictively by the courts. It is apparent from a number of decisions that a third party does not necessarily need to show that he *will* suffer actual financial loss; the possibility that he *may* suffer loss or that his patrimony may in some way be diminished is sufficient to constitute prejudice.[56]

---

[50] *Hosken Employee Benefits (Pty) Ltd* v. *Slabe* 1992 (4) SA 183 at 190J; *NBS Bank Ltd* v. *Cape Produce Co. (Pty) Ltd and others* 2002 (1) SA 396 at 412D–E.

[51] De Villiers and Macintosh, *Agency*, p. 449; Rabie, 'Estoppel', § 460; *Jonker* v. *Boland Bank Pks Bpk* 2000 (1) SA 542 (O) at 549G–H.

[52] Bester, 'Scope of Agent's Power', 56; Kerr, *Agency*, p. 139; *Peri-Urban Areas Health Board* v. *Breet NO and another* 1958 (3) SA 783 (T) at 790E–F. See also J. van der Walt, 'Wat word van die nadeelvereiste by bedrog en estoppel?' (1973) *THRHR* 386.

[53] *Jonker* v. *Boland Bank Pks Bpk* 2000 (1) SA 542 (O) at 547G–548G; Joubert, *Verteenwordigingsreg*, p. 115; *Hosken Employee Benefits (Pty) Ltd* v. *Slabe* 1992 (4) SA 183 at 191C–D.

[54] Sonnekus, *The Law of Estoppel in South Africa*, pp. 59–65.

[55] *Jonker* v. *Boland Bank Pks Bpk* 2000 (1) SA 542 (O) at 548B–G.

[56] *Autolec Ltd* v. *Du Plessis* 1965 (2) SA 243 (O) at 250H: 'Although the change of position must involve the practical or business affairs of the representee and not merely affect him philosophically or in his religious or other sentimental values the detriment is not

Thus, for example, an insurance company which had failed to repudiate liability under an insurance policy within a reasonable time was estopped from doing so, as the insured party, in acting on the belief that the insurer had accepted liability, had failed to take steps to deal properly with a claim instituted against it by a third party.[57] The court held that this constituted sufficient prejudice for the claim based on estoppel to succeed, even thought there was no guarantee that the third party's claim would be successful.

The question has also been raised as to whether in South African law a third party who is successful in a claim based on estoppel may recover more than he has in fact been prejudiced by. Although this is yet to be conclusively answered, there is strong support for the view that the relief that a third party may obtain should not exceed the extent of his loss.[58] As has been noted, this accords with the position in American law, but not that of English law.[59]

7 Ostensible authority and companies

A third party who wishes to hold a company liable in South African law on the basis of ostensible authority faces certain complications. The first of these is the hurdle created by the so-called 'doctrine of constructive notice'. The basis of this doctrine is that every person who deals with a company is deemed to have full knowledge of the provisions of the company's public documentation, in particular its memorandum and articles.[60] If, therefore, it would be clear from reading the company's public documentation that the person or persons purporting to represent the company do not have the authority to do so, then a third party is deemed to have knowledge of this, regardless of whether or not he actually does, and is thus not entitled to claim that an appearance of authority has been created.

The operation of the doctrine of constructive notice is qualified, however, by what is known as the '*Turquand* rule', a rule imported

---

limited to direct, instantaneous and palpable loss of money, but also includes less gross and easily calculable detriment.'

[57] *Resisto Dairy (Pty) Ltd* v. *Auto Protection Insurance Co. Ltd* 1963 (1) SA 632 (A).

[58] *Jonker* v. *Boland Bank Pks Bpk* 2000 (1) SA 542 (O); *Durban Superannuation Fund* v. *Campbell* 1949 (3) SA 1057 (D) at 1069; Rabie, *The Law of Estoppel in South Africa*, pp. 71–2.

[59] Sonnekus, *The Law of Estoppel in South Africa*, pp. 69–71.

[60] H. S. Cilliers and M. L. Benade, *Corporate Law*, 3rd edn (Durban: LexisNexis Butterworths, 2000), p. 190; Blackman, 'Companies', § 181.

from English law.[61] The rule provides that any person dealing with the company in good faith is entitled to assume that any internal procedures that may be referred to in the memorandum and articles or other company documentation have been complied with. In the context of ostensible authority, this therefore means that if the memorandum and articles provide that certain persons will have authority to represent the company in certain transactions provided that certain formalities are complied with, then the third party will be entitled to assume that those formalities have been complied with. Thus, for example, if a director of a company is authorised by its articles to purchase property for the company provided that such purchase has been approved by a general meeting of the shareholders, then a third party wishing to sell property to the company and dealing with such director, is entitled to presume that the required shareholder approval has been given. The application of the *Turquand* rule is subject to the limitation that a third party must act in good faith, and cannot be aware that the necessary internal formalities have not been complied with. It also does not apply if the circumstances were such that the reasonable man would have been put on his guard and would have made further enquiries.[62]

The question has been raised whether the *Turquand* rule can apply if the internal formalities have been imposed by the Companies Act itself. There has been some debate on this matter. In the most recent case dealing with the issue, *Farren* v. *Sun Service SA Photo Trip Management (Pty) Ltd*,[63] it was held that the *Turquand* rule could not prevail over the provisions of a section of the Companies Act, nor would a claim for estoppel be upheld if to do so would achieve a result contrary to the intention of the legislature.[64]

In respect of transactions which are *ultra vires* the company, i.e. transactions which fall outside the capacity of the company, as specified in the objects clause in its memorandum, the position previously was that a third party could never succeed with a claim based on ostensible authority, as he

---

[61] *Royal British Bank* v. *Turquand* (1856) 6 E & B 327; 119 ER 886.

[62] Blackman, 'Companies', § 180; *Big Dutchman (SA) (Pty) Ltd* v. *Barclays National Bank Ltd* 1979 (3) SA 267 (W) 280; *Hosken Employee Benefits (Pty) Ltd* v. *Slabe* 1992 (4) SA 183 at 190C–F.

[63] 2004 (2) SA 146.

[64] See, however, *Levy* v. *Zalrut Investments (Pty) Ltd* 1986 (4) SA 479 (W) at 487–488 where it was remarked *obiter* that an estoppel can be raised in such circumstances if it will not frustrate any public policy considerations behind the legislation (a conclusion which the judge in *Farren* v. *Sun Service SA Photo Trip Management (Pty) Ltd* 2004 (2) SA 146 specifically refutes (at 156H–157D)).

would always be deemed to have constructive notice that the act was *ultra vires*, and therefore could not be authorised. This has been changed somewhat by the introduction of s. 36 of the Companies Act,[65] which provides that no act of a company shall be void solely because the company lacked the capacity to carry out such act, or because the directors of the company lacked authority to act for that reason alone. In respect of any transaction which falls under this section, the company is therefore bound regardless of whether or not the third party had actual or constructive knowledge of the fact that the act was *ultra vires*. It must be noted, however, that the section applies only to acts which are unauthorised because they are *ultra vires*. If the agent lacks authority for any additional reason, i.e. because there is a failure to comply with a provision of the articles, then s. 36 does not apply, and if the third party has actual or constructive knowledge of this additional defect in authority, then they will not be able to claim that an appearance of authority has been created.

III Ratification[66]

1 Introduction

South African law also recognises that the acts of an agent who does not have authority or who acts in excess of the authority granted to him, may nevertheless become binding on his principal if the principal chooses to ratify them after the fact. The result is that such acts become valid

---

[65] No. 61 of 1973. For an instructive commentary on the interaction between this section and the principles of agency, see J. S. A. Fourie, 'Volmagbeperkings en Ultra Vires Handelinge – Aspekte can Artikel 36 van die Maatskappywet in Oenskou' (1990) 1 *Stellenbosch L Rev* 388–99. See also, by the same author, 'Die wisselwerking tussen Suid-Afrikaanse maatskappyeregleerstukke' (1988) 51 *THRHR* 218–27 at 224. It should be noted that a complete overhaul of South African company law is imminent, and there is an advanced draft of a new Companies Bill which is expected to become law in 2010. Section 20 of the current draft of the Bill includes provisions equivalent to s. 36 of the current Act, but also provides, *inter alia*, that shareholders may ratify, by special resolution, any *ultra vires* actions of the company and (in what appears to be a statutory implementation of the *Turquand* rule) specifies that any third party dealing with a company in good faith is entitled to presume that the company has complied with all the requirements of the Act, its memorandum of incorporation and any rules of the company unless the person knew or reasonably ought to have known of any failure by the company to comply with any such requirement.

[66] See, in general, Wanda, 'Agency and Representation', §§ 200–9; De Villiers and Macintosh, *Agency*, pp. 282–305; Joubert, *Verteenwordigingsreg*, pp. 141–67; Kerr, *Agency*, pp. 80–94; S. R. van Jaarsveld, *Die Leerstuk van Ratifikasie in die Suid-Afrikaanse Verteenwordigingsreg* (Cape Town: HAUM, 1974).

retrospectively, as if the necessary authority had existed at the time that the act was carried out. The South African doctrine of ratification has been described as a combination of Roman, Roman-Dutch and English rules on the subject.[67] The idea that authority could be granted *ex post facto* was recognised in both Roman and Roman-Dutch law,[68] but the Roman-Dutch principles relating to ratification were not as comprehensive as their English law counterparts, and so it was English law that was once again turned to to fill any gaps. Although the South African doctrine of ratification has therefore developed in a somewhat piecemeal manner, it has nevertheless developed a comprehensive set of rules which, on the whole, are effective in practice.

2 Requirements

(a) Intention

Various requirements for a valid ratification can be identified from an examination of the South African case-law and textbooks on agency. The first of these is that the person ratifying must have the intention to affirm the unauthorised acts carried out on his behalf.[69] In determining the principal's intention, South African law has adopted an essentially objective approach.[70] The question that is asked is whether an intention to ratify is the only reasonable inference from the principal's words or actions. An intention to ratify is not in and of itself sufficient, however – South African law further requires, as in English law, that such intention 'must be expressed either with full knowledge of all the material circumstances, or with the object of confirming the agent's action in all events, whatever the circumstances may be'.[71] Thus, when ratifying, the principal must therefore be in possession of such facts are as necessary for him to make an informed decision as to what he is ratifying;[72] alternatively,

---

[67] *Ibid.*, p. 185.
[68] Joubert, 'Agency and *Stipulatio Alteri*', p. 348; De Villiers and Macintosh, *Agency*, p. 282.
[69] *Reid* v. *Warner* 1907 TS 961 at 971; *Wilmot Motors (Pty) Ltd* v. *Tucker's Fresh Meat Supply Ltd* 1969 (4) SA 474 (T) at 477.
[70] Joubert, *Verteenwordigingsreg*, p. 160; Van Jaarsveld, *Ratifikasie*, pp. 233, 236.
[71] *Reid* v. *Warner* 1907 TS 961 at 971–2; *Lazarus* v. *Gorfinkel* 1988 (4) SA 123 (C) at 136E–F.
[72] H. Grotius, Opinion No. 73, *Consultatien, Advysen en Advertissementen, gegeven en geschreven bij verscheiden treffelijke rechts-geleerden in Holland* (Rotterdam: Isaak Naerus, 1662–83), Vol: III, p. 27. See further De Villers and MacKintosh, *Agency*, p. 296 as to what constitutes 'material circumstances'.

he must demonstrate an intention to ratify his agent's acts regardless of the consequences, with full knowledge that he may not have all the necessary information at his disposal.

A party who wishes to prove the latter bears a heavy burden of proof: effectively, he must show that the principal was aware of his right to be fully informed and then opted to waive it before ratifying.[73] An example of the latter occurred in the case of *Mort* v. *Henry Shields-Chiat*,[74] where a *curator ad litem* who had been appointed for a mentally incapable litigant ratified the unauthorised acts carried out by the litigant's attorney without apprising himself of all the details relating to the attorney's mandate. The court held that the ratification was valid, and the litigant was bound by the terms of the original mandate given to the attorney.

(b) Agent must act in the name of the principal

A second requirement for a valid ratification in South African law is that the agent must make it clear at the time the transaction is entered into that he is acting on behalf of a principal, and not for his own account.[75] An important consequence of this requirement is that only the principal on whose behalf the agent professes to be acting may ratify the act. The fact that he may have the intention of acting on behalf of another is not sufficient – this intention must be expressed to the third party with whom he deals. It is not necessary that the principal be named – he must, however, be at least objectively identifiable.[76]

The South African courts have also indicated that they will consider the substance of the transaction rather than the form: an agent who professes to act on behalf of another must have a genuine intention to do so. If he is in fact acting in his own name, ratification by the professed principal will not be allowed.[77]

---

[73] *Ibid.*; Van Jaarsveld, *Ratifikasie*, p. 234; *Osry* v. *Hirsch, Loubser & Co.* 1922 CPD 537; *Laws* v. *Rutherford* 1924 AD 261.

[74] 2001 (1) SA 464 (C).

[75] J. Voet, *Commentarius ad Pandectas* (Cape Town: J. C. Juta, 1879), 17, 1, 9; *Keystone Trading Co.* v. *Die Verenigde Maatskappij* 1926 TPA 218; *Jagersfontein Garage & Transport Co.* v. *Secretary, State Advances Office* 1939 OPD 37 at 41; *Lazarus* v. *Gorfinkel* 1988 (4) SA 123 (C) at 136C–D.

[76] Van Jaarsveld, *Ratifikasie*, p. 214; De Villers and Macintosh, *Agency*, p. 291. See also Joubert, *Verteenwordigingsreg*, p. 143.

[77] *Caterers Ltd* v. *Bell and Anders* 1915 AD 698 at 710; *Lazarus* v. *Gorfinkel* 1988 (4) SA 123 (C) at 136C–D.

(c) The principal must be in existence

A requirement that has caused certain difficulties in practice (primarily in the context of contracts concluded on behalf of companies not yet incorporated) is the requirement that the principal who purports to ratify must have existed at the time that the transaction was concluded.[78] As far as companies are concerned, the South African legislature thus chose to regulate the matter by statute, and s. 35 of the South African Companies Act[79] now provides that a contract concluded by a person professing to act as an agent for a company yet to be incorporated can be validly ratified by the company after its incorporation, provided that the formalities of the section are satisfied.[80]

Even prior to the legislative intervention, however, the prohibition against acting on behalf of a non-existent principal is less of an issue in South Africa than perhaps in certain other jurisdictions. This was due to the Roman-Dutch institution of *stipulatio alteri* (contract for the benefit of a third party), which allows two parties to agree to confer a benefit on a third party who is not party to the agreement. Upon accepting the benefit, the third party then becomes a party to the agreement. Because the original parties act as principals and not as agents, there is no question of ratification, and it is not necessary that the principal be in existence at the time the contract is concluded. It has been held that the

---

[78] *McCullough* v. *Fernwood Estate Ltd* 1920 AD 204 at 207; *Sentrale Kunsmis Korporasie (Edms) Bpk* v. *NKP Kunsmisverspreiders (Edms) Bpk* 1970 (3) SA 367 (A) at 390; *Swart* v. *Mbutsi Development (Pty) Ltd* 1975 (1) SA 544 (T) at 550C.

[79] No. 61 of 1973. This section is the successor to s. 71 of the Companies Act 46 of 1926. A similar procedure is provided for close corporations in terms of s. 53 of the Close Corporations Act 69 of 1984.

[80] As regards the application of s. 35 in general, see P. M. Meskin, J. A. Kunst and K. E. Schmidt (eds.), *Henochsberg on the Companies Act*, 5th edn, 2 vols. (looseleaf) (Durban: Butterworths, 1994), vol. 1, pp. 60–4. A failure to comply with the requirements of s. 35 cannot be remedied by estoppel: *Trust Bank of Africa Ltd* v. *Appletime Engineering (Pty) Ltd and others* 1981 (1) SA 374 (D) at 377F–G. As noted in footnote 65 above, a new South African Companies Act is likely to be introduced by 2010. Section 21 of the current draft of the new Companies Bill deals with pre-incorporation contracts, and differs substantially from s. 35 of the current Act. Although it permits a person to enter into an agreement on behalf of a still-to-be-formed company and allows for the company to become a party thereto upon its incorporation and ratification of the contract, it *inter alia*, requires the company formally to ratify or reject the agreement within three months of its incorporation (failing which the company will automatically be assumed to have ratified the contract and become a party thereto) and provides that in the event of the company not being incorporated, or the company rejecting any part of the agreement, the persons concluding such agreement on behalf of the company will be jointly and severally liable for any liabilities arising out of such agreement.

introduction of s. 35 has not affected the right of parties to conclude a pre-incorporation contract by means of a *stipulatio alteri*, and parties who do so need not comply with the formalities of s. 35.[81] It may also be used for other situations involving a non-existent principal, for example, a parent contracting on behalf of an unborn child.

(d) Capacity

In accordance with the general rules of contract, it is required that a principal who wishes to ratify must have legal capacity at the time of ratification. Those with no legal capacity, such as the mentally ill or infants, cannot ratify. Those with limited capacity, such as minors, can ratify with assistance from their guardians, and can ratify unassisted acts which only have benefits for themselves.[82]

A more contentious issue is whether the principal must have legal capacity at the time the act was carried out in his name. Although it has been suggested that this is not necessary,[83] most South African authorities are of the opinion that if the principal had no capacity at the time the act was carried out, then it is not possible for him to ratify later if he regains capacity.[84] Unauthorised acts carried out on behalf of a minor, however, may be ratified by the minor himself when he attains majority.[85]

(e) Act must be capable of ratification

There are certain juristic acts which cannot be ratified in South African law. Acts for which certain legal formalities are prescribed at the time of their conclusion, fall into this category.[86] An example of this is s. 2(1) of the Alienation of Land Act,[87] which requires that an agent involved in the purchase or sale of immovable property must act with written authority from his principal – such authority cannot be given *ex post*

---

[81] *Ex parte Vickerman and others* 1935 CPD 429; *Martian Entertainments* v. *Berger* 1949 (4) SA 583 (OK). This also applies in respect of close corporations: see *Build-A-Brick BK en 'n ander* v. *Eskom* 1996 (1) SA 115 (O).

[82] Wanda, 'Agency and Representation', § 202.

[83] *Ibid.*, § 202, where it is argued that although ratification has retrospective effect, the act itself is not antedated, and accordingly legal capacity at the time of ratification should be all that is required.

[84] Van Jaarsveld, *Ratifikasie*, p. 219; Kerr, *Agency*, p. 100; Joubert, *Verteenwordigingsreg*, p. 155.

[85] *Mort NO* v. *Henry Shields-Chiat* 2001 (1) SA 464 (C) at 470.

[86] *Neugarten and others* v. *Standard Bank of South Africa Ltd* 1989 (1) SA 797 (A).

[87] No. 68 of 1981.

facto.[88] Acts which are absolute nullities, due to the fact that they are prohibited by statute or common law, can also not be ratified.[89] This includes *ultra vires* acts carried out on behalf of a company, which will be discussed in greater detail below.

(f) Transaction must be ratified as a whole

It has been specified in a number of South African cases that an unauthorised transaction can only be ratified as a whole – a principal cannot choose to ratify those parts of a transaction which are favourable to him and repudiate those which are not.[90] On this basis, it was held in *Bouygues Offshore Another* v. *Owner of the MT TIGR and another*[91] that a principal who had ratified the conclusion of a contract on his behalf by his agent, could not escape liability for misrepresentations made by his agent by claiming that he had not ratified them. It is possible, however, for a principal to ratify certain transactions within a series of separate transactions, and repudiate others.[92]

3 The manner of ratification

South African law recognises that ratification may be effected either expressly or tacitly. It is seen as a unilateral juristic act, and the person who ratifies does not need the consent of his agent or any third party to do so. In respect of an express ratification, it has been held that the ratification, whether oral or written, must be communicated to either the agent or the third party: if communicated to an outside party, with no intention that it be communicated to the agent or third party, it will not have any effect *inter partes*.[93] Tacit ratification is less easily inferred. The

---

[88] Pre-incorporation contracts concluded in terms of s. 35 of the Companies Act 1973 are specifically excluded from this provision: s. 2(2) of the Alienation of Land Act 1981. See also *Gaybelle Investment (Pty) Ltd* v. *Hermer* 1951 (1) SA 486 (W) at 488.

[89] *Cape Dairy and General Livestock Auctioneers* v. *Sim* 1924 AD 167 at 170. *Neugarten and others* v. *Standard Bank of South Africa Ltd* 1989 (1) SA 797 (A) 808H–809A.

[90] *Theron* v. *Leon* 1928 TPD 719 at 723; *Jagersfontein Garage & Transport Co.* v. *Secretary, State Advances Office* 1939 OPD 37 at 46.

[91] 1995 (4) SA 49 (C) at 72C–E.

[92] *Broderick Motors Distributors (Pty) Ltd* v. *Beyers* 1968 (2) SA 1 (O) at 5.

[93] *Reid* v. *Warner* 1907 TS 961 at 974. See, however, Wanda, 'Agency and Representation', § 201, where it is suggested that any expression of ratification addressed solely to the agent will not be sufficient – it must be brought to the attention of the third party for it to be binding on the third party. See also *Jagersfontein Garage & Transport Co.* v. *Secretary, State Advances Office* 1939 OPD 37 at 41.

general rule is that it will only be considered to have taken place when the principal's conduct is of such a nature that the only reasonable interpretation is that he intended to ratify the act.[94] This has been held, in certain circumstances, to include inaction or acquiescence on the part of the principal. In *Wilmot Motors (Pty) Ltd* v. *Tucker's Fresh Meat Supply Ltd*,[95] it was stated that 'where there is a failure to repudiate a contract in circumstances which call for a repudiation, the reasonable inference is that the person concerned intended to acquiesce in the contract'. Circumstances which call for repudiation would include those where there is a special relationship between the principal and the unauthorised agent (such as an already existing agency relationship, or a parent/child relationship) and the principal has been made aware of the unauthorised act carried out purportedly on his behalf.

Thus, in *Dreyer* v. *Sonop Bpk*,[96] a father who had failed to repudiate liability for a school blazer purchased by his son while at boarding school, despite being sent an account and a series of monthly reminders, was held to have ratified his son's conduct. In *Wilmot's* case, the principal's failure to repudiate an account for repairs to a motor car which had been initiated by one of its employees, after having paid for an earlier account, was held to amount to ratification by acquiescence. In the absence of such a relationship, however, a failure to repudiate will not easily be assumed to give rise to an inference of ratification.[97] Thus, in *Alli* v. *De Lira*,[98] it was held that no such obligation existed when a person received a letter of demand from someone with whom he had no prior dealings, and thus no intention to ratify could be inferred from his failure to reply to such letter.

4 Time period for ratification

The general rule in South African law is that ratification must take place within a reasonable time, failing which the third party will be entitled to object to the validity thereof.[99] No set guidelines as to what constitutes a

---

[94] De Villiers and Macintosh, *Agency*, p. 298; Kerr, *Agency*, pp. 87–8; Van Jaarsveld, *Ratifikasie*, p. 236.

[95] 1969 (4) SA 474 (T) at 477H.   [96] 1951 (2) SA 392 (O).

[97] D. J. Joubert, 'The Law of Agency' (1975) *Annual Survey of South African Law* 95.

[98] 1973 (4) SA 635 (T).

[99] *Peak Lode Mining Co (Pty) Ltd* v. *Union Govt* 1932 TPD 48 at 52; *Sentrale Kunsmis Korporasie (Edms) Bpk* v. *NKP Kunsmisverspreiders (Edms) Bpk* 1970 (3) SA 367 (A) at 398H. Van Jaarsveld, *Ratifikasie*, p. 240; Kerr, *Agency*, p. 89.

reasonable time have been laid down by the South African judiciary, and it has been stated that each case will have to be determined on its own merits.[100] An important requirement, however, is that the act must still be capable of ratification at the time that ratification takes place. If the third party has withdrawn from the transaction, or if the transaction is no longer capable of being performed in the original manner (for example, if the subject matter of the transaction has been destroyed), then ratification cannot take place.

In the event that an agent acting without authority performs an act which is required to be performed within a certain fixed period, then the third party is not obliged to recognise a ratification of the act which is done after the period has expired.[101] Thus, for example, the ratification of an application for a date of appeal made by an attorney without authority after the time in which such application could be made was held to be invalid.[102] Similarly, it has been held that a landlord could not ratify a notice of termination of lease after the date on which such notice could validly have been given.[103]

In the event that both parties are aware of the agent's lack of authority, they may also agree on a specific time period in which the principal may ratify, in which case the third party will be contractually obliged to wait the agreed-upon time before withdrawing.

5 Legal position during the interim period

The legal position prior to the ratification of an agent's unauthorised act is a matter of some debate in South African law. There is general consensus that, prior to ratification of an unauthorised transaction, the transaction can have no legal effect between the principal and third party, and neither party can acquire rights nor incur obligations therefrom.[104] This is in accordance with the basic principles of the South African law of

---

[100] *Legg & Co.* v. *Premier Tobacco Co.* 1926 AD 132.

[101] *Finbro Furnishers (Pty) Ltd* v. *Peiner* 1935 CPD 378 at 380.

[102] *Ibid.* See, however, the discussion of *Smith* v. *Kwanonqubela Town Council* 1999 (4) SA 947 below.

[103] *Sheik Abdool* v. *Juma Musjid Trust* 1929 NPD 75. See also *Uitenhage Municipality* v. *Uys* 1974 (3) SA 800 (E); *Donaldson Investments (Pty) Ltd* v. *Anglo-Tvl Collieries Ltd* 1979 (1) SA 959 (W).

[104] Van Jaarsveld, *Ratifikasie*, pp. 202–9; Wanda, 'Agency and Representation', § 205; De Villers and Macintosh, *Agency*, p. 305; *Jagersfontein Garage & Transport Co.* v. *Secretary, State Advances Office* 1939 OPD 37 at 46: 'For it is clear, that prior to ratification the juristic act cannot exist as such; it is born from ratification.'

agency. There are opposing views, however, as to under what circumstances the third party may withdraw prior to ratification, and it is not a matter which has yet come before the South African courts. Certain authorities have suggested that he can do so only with the consent of the agent.[105] Unless, however, the agent and third party have come to a separate agreement to allow the principal a time period in which to ratify, it is difficult to see on what basis this view can be supported. As the principal does not have any rights from the transaction prior to ratification, and cannot prevent the third party from withdrawing, how can the agent, with whom the third party did not intend to contract, acquire such a right from a transaction which has no legal effect? It is submitted that the view that the third party can withdraw unilaterally at any time prior to ratification is to be preferred.[106]

As noted above, it is also possible in South African law to conclude a contract for the benefit of a third party. If the 'agent' and third party opt to use this mechanism, then a contractual relationship will exist between them, and the third party's right to withdraw will be governed by the terms thereof.

6 Effect of ratification

The effect of ratification is that the unauthorised act is conferred with retrospective validity, as if the necessary authority had existed at the time the act was carried out.[107] This is subject to the exception, however, that ratification will not operate retrospectively to the prejudice of any vested rights acquired by outsiders prior to ratification.[108] Such right need not be limited to a proprietary right – any subjective right that may have vested in an outsider should be protected by this exception.[109] In *Smith* v. *Kwanonqubela Town Council*,[110] the Supreme Court of Appeal discussed the question of whether the act of an agent in initiating litigation without the necessary authority could be ratified after the agent's lack of *locus*

---

[105] De Villiers and Macintosh, *Agency*, p. 293; Joubert, *Verteenwordigingsreg*, p. 151.

[106] H. Grotius, *De Jure Belli Ac Pacis Libri Tres*, Vol. 2, Book 1 (trans. F. W. Kelsey) (Oxford: Clarendon Press, 1925), pp. 2, 11, 18; Van Jaarsveld, *Ratifikasie*, pp. 202–9; Wanda, 'Agency and Representation', § 205; J. C. de Wet and A. H. van Wyk, *Die Suid-Afrikaanse Kontrakteg en Handelsreg*, 5th edn, 2 vols. (Durban: Butterworths, 1992), p. 112.

[107] Voet, *Commentarius ad Pandectas*, pp. 3, 5, 14; Van Jaarsveld, *Ratifikasie*, p. 249; Joubert, *Verteenwordigingsreg*, p. 162; De Villiers and Macintosh, *Agency*, p. 302.

[108] *Smith* v. *Kwanonqubela Town Council* 1999 (4) SA 947 at 954A–B; *Jagersfontein Garage & Transport Co.* v. *Secretary, State Advances Office* 1939 OPD 37 at 46–47.

[109] Van Jaarsveld, *Ratifikasie*, p. 251; Joubert, *Verteenwordiginingsreg*, p. 167.

[110] 1999 (4) SA 947.

standi was objected to. The court held that a party to litigation did not have a right to prevent the other party from remedying a legal defect, and thus no substantive rights of the party in question were affected by the ratification.[111] The court did indicate, however, that the situation may be different if the litigation were required to be initiated within a fixed time, as with an appeal.[112]

In the case of *Peak Lode Mining Co. (Pty) Ltd* v. *Union Govt*,[113] it was held that s. 71 of the old Companies Act[114] (the predecessor to s. 35 of the current Act) does not operate with retrospective effect. Thus, the appellant company which had ratified (in accordance with s. 71) a contract in terms of which certain mineral claims had been purchased on its behalf prior to its incorporation, was held to be liable for transfer duty on such claims only from the date that it had ratified the agreement, and not from the date that the contract was concluded on its behalf. This decision has been justifiably criticised by a number of academics.[115] Not only is it not in accordance with the general principles of ratification, but it is also in conflict with the express wording of the provision, which states that the contract can be ratified 'as if [the company] had been duly formed, incorporated and registered at the time the contract was made'. Criticism notwithstanding, the *Peak Lode* decision still currently represents the position in South African law. It has been suggested, however, that this may well be re-considered should the matter again come before the South African courts.[116]

The ratification by the principal of his agent's acts does not deprive him of any claim he may have against his agent for acting without the necessary authority, or exceeding the authority given to him. In the case of *Mine Workers' Union* v. *Brodrick*[117] it was held that the ratification by the principal of an unauthorised act carried out by his employee did not prevent him from holding such employee liable for breach of mandate and dismissing him.

---

[111] *Ibid.* at 954B–E.
[112] *Ibid.* at 953C–G. See also *Finbro Furnishers (Pty) Ltd* v. *Peimer* 1935 CPD 378.
[113] 1932 TPD 48.   [114] No. 46 of 1926.
[115] R. Jooste, 'When do Pre-Incorporation Contracts have Retrospective Effect?' (1989) 106 *SALJ* 507–16; Wanda, 'Agency and Representation', § 207; Joubert, *Verteenwordigingsreg*, p. 154; Van Jaarsveld, *Ratifikasie*, p. 219.
[116] Jooste, 'Pre-Incorporation Contracts', p. 510. See also Meskin, Kunst and Schmidt (eds.), *Henochsberg*, p. 64.
[117] 1948 (4) SA 958 (A).

7 Ratification by companies

(a) Ultra vires acts

Originally, the position in South African law was that any *ultra vires* transaction carried out on behalf of a company was considered to be void *ab initio*, and not capable of ratification, even by unanimous consent of the shareholders.[118] As far as the third party is concerned, the position has been changed somewhat by the introduction of s. 36 of the Companies Act,[119] which, as noted above, provides that no act of a company shall be void solely because the company lacked the capacity to carry out such act, or because the directors of the company lacked authority to act for that reason alone. Any transaction which therefore falls under this section will thus no longer be invalid and the question of ratification therefore does not arise. It must be noted, however, that the section does not apply to *ultra vires* acts which are invalid for any additional reasons, for example because they do not comply with a provision in the company's articles. In this case, the common law rule still applies, and the act cannot be ratified.[120]

(b) Intra vires

Whether or not an unauthorised act which is *intra vires* the company can be ratified depends upon the reason for the lack of authority. Generally speaking, a company can ratify any acts which are within its capacity – the persons or organs of the company who must ratify are those who would have had the power to authorise the transaction in the first place.[121] If, however, the reason for the lack of authority is as a result of a breach of the provisions of the articles of the company, then the situation is more problematic. Because the articles are considered to be a contract between the members and the company,[122] it is not possible for the members to act contrary to their provisions, and as authority cannot be granted for an act which would contravene the articles, thus, logically speaking, ratification is not possible. It has been suggested that the best way of solving the problem in such situations is to amend the articles by special resolution to remedy the problem, and then enter into the transaction afresh.[123]

---

[118] Van Jaarsveld, *Ratifikasie*, p. 215; Fourie, 'Die wisselwerking', p. 224.
[119] No. 61 of 1973. See, however, footnote 65 above.
[120] See, in general, Fourie, 'Die wisselwerking', pp. 224–6.
[121] Blackman, 'Companies', § 180.
[122] Section 65(2) of the Companies Act 61 of 1973, confirming the common law position.
[123] Fourie, 'Die wisselwerking', p. 226.

IV Personal liability of the unauthorised agent

1 Introduction

The question as to what extent an agent who acts without authority may incur liability is a contentious one in South African law. Although it is generally accepted that the unauthorised agent may, in certain situations, be held personally liable by the third party, the extent of his liability, and the legal basis therefor, is still the subject of considerable academic and judicial debate. In certain cases, the South African courts have turned to English law for solutions, with varying degrees of success. It is undoubtedly an area of the South African law of agency which is not yet completely settled.

2 The implied warranty of authority

(a) Background

Up until the early years of the twentieth century, the approach adopted by the South African judiciary in situations of unauthorised agency was that followed by the Roman-Dutch common law – namely that the unauthorised agent could be held personally liable on the contract concluded with the third party in place of his supposed principal.[124] This approach was emphatically rejected in the landmark decision of *Blower* v. *Van Norden*.[125] Chief Justice Innes held that this rule was 'inconsistent with the modern views of agency as recognised in our courts', and by holding the agent personally liable had created 'a new contract which neither of the parties contemplated'.[126] The correctness of this reasoning has been described as 'unassailable',[127] and justifiably so. He further noted that application of the rule would, in certain cases, have inequitable results: should the agent be a wealthy man, and the principal a man of straw, the third party would be able to recover more from the former than he would have been able to from the latter.

In place of the rejected Roman-Dutch doctrine, the learned justice instead opted to import a concept which had recently found favour in

---

[124] See *Blower* v. *Van Noorden* 1909 TS 890 at 897–9, 902–6 for a summary of the Roman-Dutch authorities and South African case-law in this regard. See also Wanda, 'Agency and Representation', § 214.

[125] *Ibid.*   [126] *Ibid.* at 899.

[127] See Wanda, 'Agency and Representation', § 214; De Wet and Van Wyk, *Suid-Afrikaanse Kontrakisreg*, 114.

English law – the implied warranty of authority.[128] This new addition to the South African law of agency was described as follows:

> What takes place is this: the agent in effect represents to the other contracting party that he has authority to bind his principal; and within the limits of that authority he consents to the terms of the agreement on his principal's behalf. There is a representation by the agent personally, and a contract by him in his capacity as agent. The representation is in respect of a matter which is peculiarly within his knowledge, and of which the other party knows nothing at all. But the latter enters into the contract on the faith of that representation, and the agent intends that he shall do so; it forms the basis of the whole agreement. Under the circumstances, we are surely justified in implying, on the part of the agent, a personal undertaking that his principal shall be bound by the contract, and that, if not, he will place the other party in as good a position as if the principal were bound.[129]

This decision has subsequently been confirmed in a number of other cases,[130] and despite some academic debate as to the true legal nature of the warranty and a judicial suggestion that the matter is still open for discussion,[131] must still be considered to represent the position in South African law as it stands at present. Although it has been suggested that Innes CJ was referring to an actual warranty, tacitly agreed on between the parties,[132] the generally accepted construction is that of a fictitious warranty implied by a rule of law. The liability of the agent is thus quasi-contractual.[133]

(b) Requirements

What then are the requirements for such a warranty to be implied? As is clear from the above quotation, it is not only important that an agent makes a representation of authority, but that it is the agent's representation that causes the third party to enter into the agreement.[134] In *Blower's*

---

[128] Reynolds, *Bowstead on Agency*, Art. 112, pp. 457–8.
[129] *Blower* v. *Van Noorden* 1909 TS 890 at 906.
[130] *Nebendahl* v. *Schroeder* 1937 SWA 48; *Calder-Potts* v. *McMillan* 1956 (3) SA 360 (E); *Indrieri* v. *Du Preez* 1989 (2) SA 721 (C).
[131] *Claude Neon Lights (SA) Ltd* v. *Daniel* 1976 (4) SA 403 (AD) at 409D–G and see IV 6, below.
[132] Joubert, 'Agency and *Stipulatio Alteri*', p. 351.   [133] Kerr, *Agency*, p. 246.
[134] See *Claude Neon Lights (SA) Ltd* v. *Daniel* 1976 (4) SA 403 (A) at 409, where the necessity for a causal link between the agent's representation of authority and the conclusion of the contract was emphasised.

case the agent (Van Noorden) and third party (Blower) jointly but mistakenly interpreted a telegram from Van Noorden's principal to mean that the requisite authority had been given to sell the principal's farm to Blower, when in fact it had not. Despite the fact that Van Noorden signed the agreement as agent, it was held that this representation did not induce Blower to enter into the agreement: it was Blower's own erroneous interpretation (jointly made with Van Noorden) of the telegram received by Van Noorden that caused him to believe that Van Noorden had the necessary authority. Accordingly, no warranty of authority was implied. In *Nebendahl v. Schroeder*[135] the court reached the same conclusion on analogous facts, and it appears that when the third party possesses the same degree of knowledge as the agent, and is therefore as well placed as the agent to assess whether or not the necessary authority exists, then no warranty of authority will be implied.

Fault on the part of the agent is not required.[136] It has been questioned, however, whether strict liability is fair in such situations: should the *bona fide* agent who unwittingly represents that he has authority which he does not, be held accountable to the same degree as the agent who is negligent or even fraudulent? This question will be considered more fully below.[137]

A further important requirement is proof of the agent's lack of authority, the burden of which lies with the third party. In the case of *Knox v. Davis*,[138] the agent and principal gave contradictory statements regarding whether or not the necessary authority had been given. The court found that the third party had not proven the agent's lack of authority to their satisfaction, and accordingly the agent could not be held liable for a breach of warranty of authority. In *Germie Motors (Pty) Ltd v. Ericsen*[139] the defendant, acting as an agent, had sold a stolen car to the plaintiff. He expressly warranted to the plaintiff that he had the necessary authority from his principal, which he did. However, because his principal had had fraudulent intent, the court found that the mandate given to the agent was illegal and void, and accordingly held that the defendant did not have the authority which he warranted. The decision was reversed on appeal, however[140] – the court found that the mandate given to the defendant by the principal was, in and of itself, inherently

---

[135] 1937 SWA 48.
[136] Joubert, *Verteenwoordigingsreg*, p. 80; Kerr, *Agency*, p. 248.
[137] See IV 6, below.   [138] 1933 EDL 109.   [139] 1985 (2) SA 389 (C).
[140] *Ericsen v. Germie Motors (Pty) Ltd* 1986 (4) SA 67 (A).

lawful, and the fact that the principal had had nefarious intentions did not change this fact. Accordingly, the defendant was held to have the requisite authority, and was not liable for a breach of his warranty of authority.

(c) Damages

In the event that an agent is held liable for a breach of an implied warranty of authority, he is obliged to place the aggrieved third party in the position he would have been in should the warranted authority have existed: i.e. as if a valid contract had been concluded between him and the intended principal. This does not mean that he can be required to deliver specific performance of the original agreement, but only that he make good the loss suffered by the third party as a result of the principal not being bound. The third party cannot recover more from the agent than he would have been able to from the principal. Consideration therefore has to be given to the patrimonial position of the purported principal, and his ability to perform in terms of the original contract. Should the principal be insolvent or impoverished, the damages that the third party will be able to recover from the agent will be limited.[141] The terms of the original contract also have to be taken into account. If, for example, the principal's performance would have been subject to the fulfilment of any conditions, the third party would have to show that these conditions would have been fulfilled in order to claim damages from the agent. This was the case in *Calder-Potts* v. *McMillan*,[142] where the defendant, claiming to act as the authorised agent of a particular company, purported to sell two of the company's trading stations to the plaintiff. He did not have the necessary authority and the company subsequently repudiated the sale. The sale was subject to government approval, however, and as the plaintiff had failed to allege in his claim that such approval would have been granted, the defendant successfully resisted the claim.

In the event that the third party has unsuccessfully litigated against the principal, he may also be entitled to claim the reasonable costs of such litigation from the unauthorised agent.[143]

---

[141] *Langford* v. *Moore and others* (1900) 17 SC 10; *Blower* v. *Van Noorden* 1909 TS 890 at 903–5; *Ex Parte De Villers and another NNO: In Re Carbon Developments* 1992 (2) SA 95 at 144.
[142] 1956 (3) SA 360 (E).   [143] Kerr, *Agency*, p. 249.

3 Contractual liability

An unauthorised agent may also incur liability if he explicitly or tacitly warrants to the third party that he has the necessary authority from his purported principal.[144] Such warranty is considered to be a separate agreement between the agent and the third party, and the agent's liability accordingly arises not from the original contract, but from the breach of such warranty.

Similarly, an agent who admits his lack of authority, but guarantees that his principal will ratify the act can be held contractually accountable for breach of this guarantee in the event that ratification is not forthcoming. The key difference between such a guarantee and the warranty of authority is that in the case of the latter, the unauthorised agent will be liable for breach of warranty as soon as the agreement is concluded. In the case of the former, however, the agent will only be liable, if and when his principal does not ratify. In the event that a time for ratification is not agreed on, then a reasonable time should be allowed.[145]

The damages payable by the agent for a breach of warranty or undertaking to secure ratification will be those agreed on between the parties. In the event that no provision is made therefor, then damages will be calculated in the same manner as with the implied warranty of authority.[146]

4 Delictual liability

An alternative option for the third party is a claim in delict, based on the agent's misrepresentation of authority. The general delictual requirements apply to such a claim. Thus, the third party must show that there was a misrepresentation by the agent, that it was made unlawfully and with fault, and that it was the proximate cause of the loss suffered by him.[147]

The degree of fault required for such a claim has long been a contentious issue. While it has been generally accepted that a fraudulent

---

[144] As was the case in *Germie Motors (Pty) Ltd* v. *Ericsen* 1985 (2) SA 389 (C); Wanda 'Agency and Representation', § 216.

[145] See III 4, above as to what constitutes a reasonable time.

[146] Wanda, 'Agency and Representation', § 216.

[147] *Bayer South Africa (Pty) Ltd* v. *Frost* 1991 (4) SA 559 at 568B–C. See also, in general, J. Neethling, J. M. Potgieter and P. J. Visser, *The Law of Delict*, 5th edn (Durban: LexisNexis Butterworths, 2006), pp. 274–81.

misrepresentation can found a claim in delict,[148] the South African courts were, for many years, loath to recognise a claim based on negligent misrepresentation,[149] particularly misrepresentations made in the contractual context. This changed, however, with the case of *Administrateur, Natal* v. *Trust Bank van Afrika Bpk*,[150] in which the Appellate Division confirmed that South African law does recognise an action in delict for negligent misrepresentations which cause pure economic loss. Unfortunately, the court specifically left open the question of delictual liability in cases of negligent misrepresentations made in a contractual context. The matter was finally clarified in *Bayer South Africa (Pty) Ltd* v. *Frost*,[151] where delictual liability based on a negligent misrepresentation which induced a contract was expressly recognised.

The question of unlawfulness is determined by considering whether there is a legal duty on the agent not to make such a misrepresentation. In most cases, the fact that the representation is made in a contractual context, and concerns something that is usually exclusively within the agent's knowledge and is material to the third party's decision to enter the contract, will indicate the existence of such a legal duty.

If the third party is successful with his claim, the agent is required to make good the loss suffered by him as a result of the misrepresentation. This differs from the contractual measure of damages in that the third party is restored to the financial position he was in prior to the misrepresentation occurring, as opposed to being placed in the position he would have been had the principal been bound.

5 The non-existent principal

In situations where an agent's lack of authority is due to the fact that his principal did not exist, or lacked the capacity to act, a different set of rules has been applied. The South African courts were originally inclined to follow the 'rule' supposedly laid down in the English case of *Kelner* v. *Baxter and others*,[152] that an agent who entered into a contract on behalf of a non-existent principal could be held personally liable on the contract.[153] A number of commentators have rejected the contention that

---

[148] *Trotman and another* v. *Edwick* 1951 (1) SA 443 (A) at 449.
[149] *Hamman* v. *Moolman* 1968 (4) SA 340 A.   [150] 1979 (3) SA 824 (A).
[151] 1991 (4) SA 559.   [152] (1867) LR 2 CP 174.
[153] See Wanda, 'Agency and Representation', § 185.

Kelner v. *Baxter* is authority for such a rule, and its application has been criticised.[154]

In more recent years, the South African courts have followed suit. In *Nordis Construction Co. (Pty) Ltd* v. *Theron, Burke and Isaac*,[155] the plaintiff, a construction company, concluded an agreement with the defendant, a firm of engineers, to carry out certain construction work for a particular company, on whose behalf the defendants claimed to be acting. Both parties erroneously believed that the company existed, when in fact it had not yet been incorporated. When the company was subsequently incorporated, it failed to ratify the agreement. The plaintiff sought to hold the defendant personally liable on the contract on the basis of the principles set out in *Kelner* v. *Baxter*. Leon J held that the case before him was distinguishable from *Kelner* on the grounds that neither party was aware of the principal's non-existence, whereas in *Kelner* the parties contracted in full awareness of that fact. Accordingly, in *Kelner's* case, it had been possible, as a matter of construction (albeit somewhat strained construction), to find that the parties had intended that the agents would be personally liable, particularly as the contract would be a nullity otherwise. In the case at hand, however, both parties believed that the defendant was acting on behalf of an existing principal, who would be a party to the agreement. The judge therefore felt that 'to hold the defendant personally liable upon such a contract would be to make a new contract for the parties which neither of them ever intended',[156] and the plaintiff's action accordingly failed. This decision was approved in *Terblanche* v. *Nothnagel*,[157] which confirmed that an agent of a non-existent principal could only be held personally liable on the contract if it was clear that this was the intention of the parties. In both the *Terblanche* and *Nordis* cases, the parties did not know that the principle was non-existent. It has been argued that the rule should apply equally, however, in situations where the parties are aware that the principal does not exist – the parties may not be aware, for example, that it is legally impossible to contract on behalf of a non-existent principal.[158] It is submitted that this viewpoint is correct – the intention of the parties,

---

[154] *Ibid.* at § 185, where it is stated that the 'rule in *Kelner* v. *Baxter* is not acceptable'; J. T. R. Gibson, *South African Mercantile and Company Law*, 8th edn (Cape Town: Juta, 2000), pp. 209–10; See also Reynolds, *Bowstead and Reynolds on Agency*, 2-062, where the results are described as 'inconvenient'.

[155] 1972 (2) SA 535 (D).   [156] *Ibid.* at 545H.

[157] 1975 (4) SA 405 (C). See also *Akromed Products (Pty) Ltd* v. *Suliman* 1994 (1) SA 673 (T).

[158] Wanda, 'Agency and Representation', § 185.

as with all contracts, should be paramount. The fact that both parties are aware of the principal's non-existence is only a factor that may indicate that the parties intended the agent to be personally liable.

What then of the implied warranty of authority in such situations? In the case of *Indrieri* v. *Du Preez*,[159] the defendant signed an acknowledgement of debt in favour of the plaintiff as an agent for a company which, unbeknown to both parties, had already been de-registered. The plaintiff originally sought to hold the defendant liable on one of two grounds – either personally liable on the acknowledgement of debt itself, in accordance with principles laid down in *Kelner* v. *Baxter*, or alternatively, for breach of warranty of authority. In light of the decisions in the *Nordis* and *Terblanche* cases, however, the plaintiff opted not to pursue his first claim, a decision which the judge confirmed to be the correct one. As to the claim for breach of warranty of authority, the judge, while affirming the decision in *Blower* v. *Van Norden*, pointed out that the third party can receive no more in damages from the unauthorised agent then he would have been able to get from the principal, and in the case of a non-existent principal 'it is axiomatic that a non-existent company cannot pay anything at all'.[160] Counsel for the plaintiff suggested that, for the purposes of giving effect to the warrant of authority, the court should make use of the fiction that the principal did in fact exist and was capable of meeting its obligations. The judge rejected this argument on two grounds – first, because it would have the effect of making the agent liable on the contract as if he were the principal and secondly because it would have the anomalous result that the liability of an agent who innocently concluded a contract on behalf of a non-existent principal would exceed that of an agent successfully sued in delict for having fraudulently done so. The plaintiff's claim for breach of warranty of authority therefore did not succeed. The judge did note, however, that any party who found himself in similar circumstances would not necessarily be without a remedy. He could not foresee many situations in which an agent who represented that he had the authority of a non-existent principal was not either negligent or fraudulent, and accordingly the aggrieved party may still have an action in delict on the basis of the agent's misrepresentation.[161] *In casu*, however, this was not the claim that the defendant had to meet.

---

[159] 1989 (2) SA 721 (C).   [160] *Ibid.* at 727E.

[161] See *Kantey & Temper (Pty) Ltd and anor* v. *Van Zyl No* 2007 (1) SA 610, where it was held on the particular facts of the case that the appellants (who, in concluding a contract with a company which subsequently went into liquidation, were purportedly acting on

It therefore appears that the implied warranty of authority is of little use in such situations. The only damages that the third party may be able to claim are the costs of any fruitless litigation against the principal. An action in delict is the most appropriate remedy for the third party in cases of this nature, provided he can prove fault. As pointed out in the *Indrieri* case, however, there cannot be very many situations where the agent acting for a non-existent principal, cannot be said to be fraudulent or negligent. An agent may still be held accountable, of course, if he has given an actual warranty of authority, or an undertaking to secure ratification. He may, however, face a similar problem in proving his damages, unless they have been agreed on and quantified in advance.[162]

6 The implied warranty of authority – has the final word been spoken?[163]

Despite its long-standing acceptance by the South African courts, the implied warranty of authority has a number of detractors within the South African academic community, who have argued that the true legal basis for the unauthorised agent's liability in such situations should be based in delict.[164] One of the chief critics of the implied warranty has been one of South Africa's pre-eminent jurists, J. C. de Wet, who expressed the view that it is 'misleading to speak of an "implied warranty" when the "warranty" is not based on tacit consensus but on a misrepresentation and that in the absence of consensus the real basis of liability can only be misrepresentation'.[165] The argument is a persuasive one – the language

behalf of a consortium which was never formed) had a legal duty to inform the other contracting party of their principal's existence, and were held to be negligent in failing to do so, resulting in them being held liable in delict for losses suffered by the other contracting party.

[162] See footnote 80 above, however, regarding s. 21 of the proposed new Companies Act, which provides that persons concluding an agreement on behalf of a non-existent company which is not subsequently incorporated can be held jointly and severally liable for any liabilities arising out of such agreement. It does not appear that there would need to be any fault on the part of such person before he or she can be held liable under this proposed new section.

[163] For a useful summary of the legal basis of the implied warranty of authority, see De Villiers and Macintosh, *Agency*, p. 584, n. 95.

[164] See, *inter alia*, Van Jaarsveld, *Ratifikasie*, pp. 224–6, N. J. van der Merwe, 'Wanbeskouings oor Wanvoorstelling' (1964) *THRHR* 194 at 199 *et seq.*; J. R. Harker, 'The Liability of an Agent for Breach of Warranty of Authority' (1985) 102 *SALJ* 596–603 at 602.

[165] De Wet and Van Wyk, *Die Suid-Afrikaanse Kontraktereg*, pp. 115–18.

of *Blower* v. *Van Norden* and much of the subsequent case-law is more reminiscent of liability based on misrepresentation than liability based on consensual warranty, and from a theoretical point of view it would undoubtedly be more satisfactory to base the action in delict.

Those who have supported keeping the action based in quasi-contract, however, have expressed certain concerns about going down the delictual route. One of the primary concerns was whether any damages would be recoverable in cases of negligent misrepresentation.[166] In light of the decisions in *Administrateur, Natal* v. *Trust Bank van Afrika Bpk*[167] and *Bayer South Africa (Pty) Ltd* v. *Frost*,[168] this is no longer a factor. Another concern raised is the fact that the agent will escape liability if fault on his part cannot be proved. This begs the question, however, whether it is fair to place the innocent agent on an equal footing liability-wise with the negligent or fraudulent agent. Even those who are in favour of the implied warranty of authority have expressed some concern with this idea. Kerr suggests that in cases where the agent innocently misrepresents his authority, the third party should only be allowed to claim restitutional damages. Joubert also recognises that strict liability may operate unfairly in certain situations, and gives the example of the English case of *Yonge* v. *Toynbee*,[169] where an agent was held liable for a breach of his warranty of authority due to the fact that his principal had, unbeknown to him, become insane subsequent to granting the agent authority, but prior to the agent acting on his behalf. This would perhaps suggest that an action based in delict, which requires fault on the part of the agent, may prove a more equitable solution.[170]

An additional argument in favour of an action based in delict is that a delictual measure of damages, which would compensate the third party for the actual loss that he has suffered, may be more beneficial to such third party than placing him in the situation he would have been in should the principal have been bound. The case of the non-existent principal is good example of this, as was illustrated above. Similarly too, in situations where the principal is poor or insolvent, the action based on the implied warranty of authority may provide the third party with little reward. Consider the case of *Calder-Potts* v. *McMillan*,[171]

---

[166] Kerr, *Agency*, pp. 250–251; D. J. Joubert, 'Die Waarborg van Volmagsbestaan' (1969) 32 *THRHR* 109–25 at 119.
[167] 1979 (3) SA 824 (A).   [168] 1991 (4) SA 559.   [169] [1910] 1 KB 215.
[170] Van Jaarsveld, *Ratifikasie*, pp. 225–6 cf. Kerr, *Agency*, pp. 250–1.
[171] 1956 (3) SA 360 (E).

where the plaintiff's failure to prove that the contract would have become unconditional meant that his claim based on implied warranty of authority failed. Should he have claimed in delict from the defendant, however, he would have been able to receive back the money he spent on buying farms that he had already spent in anticipation of the contract coming into effect.

It is of interest to note that there has been a similar debate in English law.[172] It has also been suggested that the third party should, in certain situations, have an election as to whether to hold the third party personally liable on the contract or to claim damages from him,[173] which reflects the approach adopted by German law.[174] In light of the weighty objections put forward by the court in *Blower's* case against holding the agent personally liable on the contract, however, this suggestion is unlikely to hold much water with the South African courts.

Academic criticism notwithstanding, the decision in *Blower* v. *Van Norden* has not yet been overturned and must still be considered to reflect the position of South African law at present. The Appellate Division has noted *obiter*, however, that the true basis of the claim is yet to be decided by our courts, and has indicated that it is open to argument in this regard.[175] For the reasons suggested above, it is hoped that (in the absence of any actual warranty of authority or undertaking to secure ratification by the agent) consideration may be given to basing the agent's liability in situations of unauthorised agency in delict.

V Conclusion

Despite the limitations of the Roman-Dutch law of agency, South African law has over time developed a practical and effective set of rules to deal with the various problems that arise in the field of unauthorised agency. Often, this has been done with the help of imports from English law or other jurisdictions, although certain foreign imports have proved more successful than others. The doctrine of ostensible authority, for example, despite some initial resistance to its adoption, has generally been incorporated successfully into the South African legal system. Other rules,

---

[172] See Reynolds, *Bowstead and Reynolds on Agency*, Art. 112, pp. 458–9.
[173] J. S. McLennan, 'Some Thoughts on Remedies for an Agent's Breach of Warranty of Authority' (1987) 104 *SALJ* 321–4.
[174] See § 179 BGB; Joubert, 'Die Waarborg', p. 116. See on § 179 BGB: Chapter 4 (Germany), VI.
[175] *Claude Neon Lights (SA) Ltd* v. *Daniel* 1976 (4) SA 403 (AD) at 409D–G.

such as the rule in *Kelner* v. *Baxter*, have been criticised and ultimately rejected. In certain situations, Roman-Dutch law has provided the answer. Thus, for example, the *stipulatio alteri* has proved a useful mechanism to sidestep the rule against contracting on behalf of a non-existent principal. In other cases, legislative intervention has helped remedy the problem, such as the introduction of s. 35 of the Companies Act.

There are a number of areas, however, where the South African law of agency is still a work in progress, as has been pointed out in this chapter. In the field of ratification, for example, there is as of yet no clarity as to in what circumstances a third party may withdraw prior to ratification of an agent's unauthorised act by his principal. Certain of the requirements for a successful claim based on ostensible authority are still a matter of some debate, such as the nature and extent of prejudice that is required, or the appropriate test to be used to prove legal causation. The true legal basis for the personal liability of the unauthorised agent is another area where the law is not yet settled. Despite its long-standing acceptance by the South African courts, the implied warranty of authority has not received unqualified academic approval, and has demonstrated certain limitations in practice. As suggested, a possible alternative is to base the liability of the agent in delict, although this approach is yet to find favour with the courts.

In these areas, as well as other areas mentioned in the text, it will no doubt be useful to consider the approaches adopted by other legal systems. The mixed nature of South African law means that it can look to both civil and common law systems for answers and it has shown in the past that is not afraid to learn from other systems where necessary. It is hoped that this approach is to be followed in future.

PART 4

International 'codes'

Unauthorised agency in the Principles
of European Contract Law

DANNY BUSCH

Table of contents

I Introduction

This chapter concentrates on the rules with respect to unauthorised agency provided by the Principles of European Contract Law.[1] These principles devote an entire chapter to agency (Chapter 3: Authority of

---

[1] Referred to below as 'PECL'. See for the text of the PECL, including comments and comparative footnotes: O. Lando and H. Beale (eds.), *Principles of European Contract Law. Part I: Performance, Non-performance and Remedies* (Dordrecht/London/Boston: Martinus Nijhoff Publishers, 1995); O. Lando and H. Beale (eds.), *Principles of European Contract Law. Parts I and II* (The Hague/London/Boston: Kluwer Law International, 2000); O. Lando, E. Clive, A. Prüm, R. Zimmermann (eds.), *Principles of European Contract Law. Part III* (The Hague: Kluwer Law International, 2003). The text of the PECL is also available at http://frontpage.cbs.dk/law/commission_on_european_contract_law/Skabelon/pecl_engelsk. htm. See generally on the PECL: A. S. Hartkamp, 'Principles of Contract Law', in A. Hartkamp, M. Hesselink, E. Hondius *et al.* (eds.), *Towards a European Civil Code*, 3rd edn (Nijmegen/ The Hague: Ars Aequi Libri/Kluwer Law International, 2004), pp. 125–43; R. Zimmermann, 'The Principles of European Contract Law. Contemporary Manifestation of the Old, and Possible Foundation for a New, European Scholarship of Private Law', in F. Faust and G. Thüsing (eds.), *Beyond Borders: Perspectives on International and Comparative Law,*

Agents). The PECL are of a non-binding nature and aim to establish rules of general contract law within the European Union.[2]

The PECL provide the general rule that where an agent acts without (sufficient) authority, his acts do not bind the principal. This general rule is exempted in cases where the doctrine of apparent authority applies or where the principal subsequently ratifies the unauthorised act. In addition, the PECL provide that the third party may hold an unauthorised agent (the *falsus procurator*) liable for the damage which the third party has suffered as a consequence of the agent's lack of authority.

In this chapter, in part II, I first examine the scope of the PECL. In part III I examine the distinction made between direct and indirect agency. In part IV I devote some attention to the general effect of unauthorised agency. I then turn to the main exceptions to the general effect of unauthorised agency: apparent authority (V) and ratification (VI). Part VII follows with some remarks about the liability of the *falsus procurator* and part VIII with a treatment of the interrelationship between apparent authority, ratification and the liability of the *falsus procurator*. Part IX elaborates on a special case which can be associated with unauthorised agency, namely acting in the name of a principal yet to be named. Part X ends this chapter with some concluding observations.

II Scope

The agency provisions in the PECL directly apply only to representation in the conclusion of contracts (Art. 3:301 (1) PECL).[3] However, pursuant to the linking provision of Art. 1:107 PECL (Application of the Principles by Way of Analogy), these provisions can in principle be applied to legal acts other than the conclusion of contracts.[4]

Symposium in Honour of Hein Kötz (Köln: Carl Heymanns Verlag, 2006), pp. 111–47 (both with further references).

[2] On the purposes of the PECL, see Art. 1:101 PECL (Application of the Principles): '(1) These Principles are intended to be applied as general rules of contract law in the European Union. (2) These Principles will apply when the parties have agreed to incorporate them into their contract or that their contract is to be governed by them. (3) These Principles may be applied when the parties: (a) have agreed that their contract is to be governed by "general principles of law", the "lex mercatoria" or the like; or (b) have not chosen any system or rules of law to govern their contract. (4) These Principles may provide a solution to the issue raised where the system or rules of law applicable do not do so.'

[3] Art. 3:301(1) PECL reads as follows: 'This Chapter governs the authority of an agent or other intermediary to bind its principal in relation to a contract with a third party.'

[4] Art. 1:107 PECL (Application of the Principles by Way of Analogy): 'These Principles apply with appropriate modifications to agreements to modify or end a contract, to unilateral promises and other statements and conduct indicating intention.'

Furthermore, the PECL are limited to agency created by the exercise of the will of the principal (consensual agency). The PECL explicitly provide that they do not govern an agent's authority bestowed by law or the authority of an agent appointed by a public or judicial authority (Art. 3:101 (2) PECL).[5]

References to the creation of agency through the 'will' of the principal should not, however, be taken to indicate that the PECL are irrelevant as regards representation with respect to company law. This is not the case, although the position is undoubtedly complex. Comment B to Art. 3:101 PECL (Scope of the Chapter) provides that, although the powers of representation conferred upon company directors by statute are not covered, if a company grants authority to act on its behalf to an employee other than a director, the PECL do apply.[6] Moreover, it seems that the PECL apply to representation of companies yet to be incorporated. This is evident from comment B to Art. 3:207 PECL (Ratification by Principal) which uses the example of an agent who acts in the name of a company not yet created to illustrate that in such cases the principal is bound as a result of ratification as from the moment at which it came into existence. However, Comment B makes it clear that special rules of the applicable company law with respect to pre-incorporation contracts take precedence over the terms of PECL.[7]

Finally, the PECL consider only the 'external' aspects of agency. In other words, they focus on the relationship between the principal or agent and the third party rather than the 'internal' relationship between the principal and agent (Art. 3:101 (3) PECL).[8]

III Direct and indirect agency

The PECL follow the traditional civil law distinction between direct and indirect agency (Art. 3:102 PECL).[9]

---

[5] Art. 3:101(2) PECL reads as follows: 'This Chapter does not govern an agent's authority bestowed by law or the authority of an agent appointed by a public or judicial authority.'

[6] Lando and Beale, *Principles of European Contract Law. Parts I and II*, pp. 197–8.

[7] *Ibid.*, p. 214.

[8] Art. 3:101(3) PECL reads as follows: 'This Chapter does not govern the internal relationship between the agent or intermediary and its principal.' However, an exception occurs where the internal relationship affects the power of representation of the agent. For example, certain grounds for terminating the power of representation of the agent are based on the relationship between the principal and the agent. See Art. 3:209 PECL, on which see V 3 below.

[9] Art. 3:102 PECL (Categories of Representation) reads as follows: '(1) Where an agent acts in the name of a principal, the rules on direct representation apply (Section 2). It is irrelevant whether the principal's identity is revealed at the time the agent acts or is to be

Direct agency is dealt with in Section 2 (Direct Representation) of Chapter 3 (Authority of Agents) of the PECL. Direct agency occurs where the agent enters into contracts in the name of the principal and possesses the necessary authority to do so. The effect of this is that the acts bind the principal and the third party directly to each other and the agent himself is not bound to the third party (Art. 3:202 in conjunction with Art. 3:201 PECL).[10]

Indirect agency is dealt with in Section 3 (Indirect Representation) of Chapter 3 (Authority of Agents) of the PECL. Indirect agency occurs where the intermediary (designated as such in the PECL to distinguish him from a direct representative[11]) contracts in his own name but on behalf of the principal with a third party. As the intermediary contracts in his own name, the contract is concluded between the third party and the intermediary. The principal is not a party to this contract (Arts. 3:102(2) and 3:301(1) PECL).[12] However, since it cannot be denied that the principal is closely involved in an economic sense in the contract between the third party and the intermediary (since the intermediary acts on behalf of the principal), the third party and the principal can sue one another directly if a 'fault' occurs in the course of the legal relationship between the principal, the agent and the third

revealed later. (2) Where an intermediary acts on instructions and on behalf of, but not in the name of, a principal, or where the third party neither knows nor has reason to know that the intermediary acts as an agent, the rules on indirect representation apply (Section 3).' Cf. Lando and Beale, *Principles of European Contract Law. Parts I and II*, pp. 199–200; D. Busch, *Indirect Representation in European Contract Law* (The Hague: Kluwer Law International, 2005), p. 211.

[10] Art. 3:202 PECL (Agent Acting in Exercise of its Authority): 'Where an agent is acting within its authority as defined by Article 3:201, its acts bind the principal and the third party directly to each other. The agent itself is not bound to the third party.' Art. 3:201 PECL (Express, Implied and Apparent Authority) reads as follows: '(1) The principal's grant of authority to an agent to act in its name may be express or may be implied from the circumstances. (2) The agent has authority to perform all acts necessary in the circumstances to achieve the purposes for which the authority was granted. (3) A person is to be treated as having granted authority to an apparent agent if the person's statements or conduct induce the third party reasonably and in good faith to believe that the apparent agent has been granted authority for the act performed by it.' Cf. H. L. E. Verhagen, 'Comment on Arts. 3:201 and 3:202 PECL', in D. Busch, E. Hondius, H. van Kooten, *et al.* (eds.), *The Principles of European Contract Law and Dutch Law. A Commentary* (The Hague / London / New York / Nijmegen: Ars Aequi Libri / Kluwer Law International, 2002), pp. 141–50; Busch, *Indirect Representation*, pp. 211–13 (with further references).

[11] Lando and Beale, *Principles of European Contract Law. Parts I and II*, p. 220.

[12] See, for the text of Art. 3:102(2) PECL, n. 9 above. Art. 3:301(1) PECL reads as follows: '(1) Where an intermediary acts: (a) on instructions and on behalf, but not in the name, of a principal, or (b) on instructions from a principal but the third party does not know and has no reason to know this, the intermediary and the third party are bound to each other.'

party, for instance due to the bankruptcy of the agent (Arts. 3:301(2), 302–304 PECL).[13]

IV Unauthorised agency

In the PECL, the concepts of unauthorised agency, apparent authority and ratification are dealt with in Section 2 (Direct Representation) of Chapter 3 (Authority of Agents). In the PECL these concepts are therefore only associated with direct agency and not with indirect agency. Notwithstanding the fact that it is arguable that these concepts should nevertheless apply to (certain cases of) indirect agency,[14] the focus of this chapter is on direct rather than indirect agency. In the remainder of this chapter 'direct agency' is simply referred to as 'agency'.

The general effect of unauthorised agency is explicitly provided in Art. 3:204(1) PECL:

> Where a person acting as agent acts without or outside the scope of its authority, its acts are not binding upon the principal and the third party.

---

[13] Art. 3:301(2) PECL reads as follows: '(2) The principal and the third party are bound to each other only under the conditions set out in Articles 3:302 to 3:304.' Art. 3:302 PECL (Intermediary's Insolvency or Fundamental Non-performance to Principal): 'If the intermediary becomes insolvent, or if it commits a fundamental non-performance towards the principal, or if prior to the time for performance it is clear that there will be a fundamental non-performance: (a) on the principal's demand, the intermediary shall communicate the name and address of the third party to the principal; and (b) the principal may exercise against the third party the rights acquired on the principal's behalf by the intermediary, subject to any defences which the third party may set up against the intermediary.' Art. 3:303 PECL (Intermediary's Insolvency or Fundamental Non-performance to Third Party) reads as follows: 'If the intermediary becomes insolvent, or if it commits a fundamental non-performance towards the third party, or if prior to the time for performance it is clear that there will be a fundamental non-performance: (a) on the third party's demand, the intermediary shall communicate the name and address of the principal to the third party; and (b) the third party may exercise against the principal the rights which the third party has against the intermediary, subject to any defences which the intermediary may set up against the third party and those which the principal may set up against the intermediary.' Art. 3:304 PECL (Requirement of Notice) reads as follows: 'The rights under Articles 3:302 and 3:303 may be exercised only if notice of intention to exercise them is given to the intermediary and to the third party or principal, respectively. Upon receipt of the notice, the third party or the principal is no longer entitled to render performance to the intermediary.' See, on indirect representation in the PECL: Busch, *Indirect Representation*, pp. 213–22, 225–85.

[14] See, on 'unauthorised indirect representation', 'apparent authority for indirect representation' and 'ratification of unauthorised indirect representation', Busch, *Indirect Representation*, pp. 232–7.

This means that neither the principal nor the third party is bound or entitled under the contract concluded by the unauthorised agent. This rule protects the autonomy of the principal because it prevents him from being bound and entitled against his will.

V Apparent authority

1 General

The PECL contain an exception to the general rule that neither the principal nor the third party is bound or entitled in cases of unauthorised agency if the doctrine of apparent authority applies; i.e. if the third party reasonably believes that the agent was authorised to conclude the contract concerned and where such beliefs can be traced back to acts or conduct of the principal or to other factors which lie within the principal's sphere of risk.

In the PECL, in cases of apparent authority the principal is to be treated as having granted authority. This means that one is asked to assume that full authority exists and thus that a valid contract is concluded by the unauthorised agent. This implies the following. (1) If third party T successfully invokes apparent authority, principal P and T are both bound and entitled under the contract concluded by unauthorised agent A. (2) If in a case of apparent authority P is willing to uphold the unauthorised act, T cannot choose not to rely on the appearance of authority. In such a case, P and T are therefore both bound and entitled as well. In view of this, apparent authority in the PECL is based on the protection of reasonable beliefs. Not only the reasonable belief of the third party that the agent was duly authorised is protected, but also the reasonable belief of the principal that the third party was willing to conclude a contract with him.[15]

2 Legal basis

Article 3:201(3) PECL deals with apparent authority. It reads as follows:

---

[15] Comment D to Art. 3:201 PECL (Express, Implied and Apparent Authority) is therefore incomplete, because it only refers to the protection of the reasonable belief of the third party: '[Art. 3:201(3) PECL on apparent authority] is provided in order to protect the third party, provided that he has relied, and was entitled to rely, upon the impression that the principal had in fact granted authority.'

A person is to be treated as having granted authority to an apparent agent
if the person's statements or conduct induce the third party reasonably
and in good faith to believe that the apparent agent has been granted
authority for the act performed by it.

3 Scope

It follows from the overall scope of Chapter 3 (Authority of Agents)[16]
that Art. 3:201(3) PECL on apparent authority directly applies only to
apparent consensual agency in the conclusion of contracts.

However, pursuant to the linking provision of Art. 1:107 PECL
(Application of the Principles by Way of Analogy), *inter alia* Art. 3:201
(3) PECL on apparent authority can in principle be applied to apparent
authority with respect to legal acts other than the conclusion of contracts.[17]

Furthermore, the limitation to apparent consensual agency does not
mean that Art. 3:201(3) PECL on apparent authority is irrelevant in
relation to company law. Comment B to Art. 3:101 PECL (Scope of the
Chapter) provides that, although the powers of representation conferred
upon company directors by statute are not covered, if a company grants
authority to act in its name to an employee other than a director, the
PECL do apply.[18] In view of this, it seems that if a company *appears* to
have granted authority to act in its name to an employee other than a
director, Art. 3:201(3) PECL on apparent authority can be applied.

Article 3:209 PECL deals with apparent authority in the special case
that an agent continues to conclude contracts in the name of his principal
despite the fact that his authority has already ended.[19] Article 3:209 DCC

---

[16] See II, above.

[17] Cf. II, above. See for the text of Art. 1:107 PECL (Application of the Principles by Way of
Analogy) n. 4, above.

[18] Cf. II above. Lando and Beale, *Principles of European Contract Law. Parts I and II*,
pp. 197–8.

[19] Art. 3:209 PECL (Duration of Authority) reads as follows: '(1) An agent's authority
continues until the third party knows or ought to know that: (a) the agent's authority has
been brought to an end by the principal, the agent, or both; or (b) the acts for which the
authority had been granted have been completed, or the time for which it had been
granted has expired; or (c) the agent has become insolvent or, where a natural person,
has died or become incapacitated; or (d) the principal has become insolvent. (2) The
third party is considered to know that the agent's authority has been brought to an end
under paragraph (1) (a) above if this has been communicated or publicised in the same
manner in which the authority was originally communicated or publicised. (3) However,
the agent remains authorised for a reasonable time to perform those acts which are
necessary to protect the interests of the principal or its successors.'

is a *lex specialis* in relation to the general provision on apparent authority (Art. 3:201(3) PECL).

Article 3:209 (1) PECL provides that an agent's authority continues until the third party knows or ought to know that: (a) the agent's authority has been brought to an end by the principal, the agent, or both; or (b) the acts for which the authority had been granted have been completed, or the time for which it had been granted has expired; or (c) the agent has become insolvent or, where a natural person, has died or become incapacitated; or (d) the principal has become insolvent. According to Comment C to Art. 3:209 PECL (Duration of Authority):

> This rule is a reflection of the principle underlying Arts 3:102 and 3:202 PECL,[20] that for the agent's authority to be effective *vis-à-vis* the third party, the third party must know or have reason to know that the agent has acted as such. The same principle applies in the converse situation, so that the agent's authority must be considered as continuing until the third party obtains actual or constructive knowledge that it has come to an end. The agent's express or implied authority, although extinguished for one reason or other, remains existent *vis-à-vis* the third party as an apparent authority.[21]

Article 3:209(2) PECL deals with a specific case of 'constructive knowledge' of a revocation of authority. It makes clear that the third party is considered to know that the agent's authority has been brought to an end by the principal, the agent, or both (Art. 3:209(1)(a) PECL) if this has been communicated or publicised in the same manner in which the authority was originally communicated or publicised. This rule is of particular importance if the grant of authority has been publicised, for example by notice in a newspaper.[22]

Finally, Art. 3:209(3) PECL provides that the agent remains authorised for a reasonable time to perform those acts which are necessary to protect the interests of the principal or his successors. Comment E to Art. 3:209 (Duration of Authority) PECL makes it clear that there is no necessity if another agent has been granted authority immediately upon extinction or if the principal himself (or his successor) is in a position to undertake all necessary and urgent acts.[23]

---

[20] See for the text of Arts 3:102 (Categories of Representation) and 3:202 (Agent Acting in Exercise of its Authority) PECL n. 9 and n. 10, respectively.
[21] Lando and Beale, *Principles of European Contract Law. Parts I and II*, p. 217.
[22] *Ibid.*   [23] *Ibid.*

4 Effect

In the PECL in cases of apparent authority 'a person is to be treated as having granted authority' (Art. 3:201(3) PECL). This means that one is asked to assume that full authority exists and thus that a valid contract is concluded by the unauthorised agent. As previously explained (V 1), this implies the following. (1) If third party T successfully invokes apparent authority, principal P and T are both bound and entitled under the contract concluded by unauthorised agent A. (2) If in a case of apparent authority P is willing to uphold the unauthorised act, T cannot choose not to rely on the appearance of authority. In such a case, P and T are therefore both bound and entitled.

5 Requirements

Article 3:201(3) PECL sets out the requirements which have to be met in order successfully to invoke the doctrine of apparent authority:

(a) statements or conduct by the principal;
(b) the third party could reasonably believe that the agent had sufficient authority; and
(c) the third party has presumed the existence of sufficient authority.

These three requirements will now be discussed in more detail.

(a) Statements or conduct of the principal, supplemented by risk principle

The PECL have – at least formally – adopted the classical 'of the principal's own doing' principle, pursuant to which the apparent authority must somehow be traced back to an act or conduct of the principal. After all, Art. 3:201(3) PECL on apparent authority refers to the principal's 'statements or conduct'.

However, the example provided by Comment D to Art. 3:201 PECL makes it clear that, according to the PECL, the third party should be protected not only where the impression has been created by the principal's act or conduct, but also where it is due to other circumstances that come within the ambit of the risks borne by the principal (the 'risk principle'):

> A jeweller's shop has instructed its employee not to accept personal cheques from a customer. The employee disregards the instruction. The jeweller is

bound by virtue of the employee's apparent authority to accept cheques since payment by personal cheque in jewellers' shops is general practice.[24]

Although this example may look like an instance of implied usual authority (which is a type of actual and not apparent authority), it is clearly not intended to be so, being located in the section on apparent authority. In using this example, it appears that the drafters of the PECL intended to extend apparent authority by adopting the risk principle.

(b) The third party could reasonably believe that the agent had sufficient authority

It follows from the text of Art. 3:201(3) PECL on apparent authority that it is required that the third party could 'reasonably' believe that the agent had (sufficient) authority. In other words, as Comment D to Art. 3:201 PECL phrases it, it is required that the third party 'was entitled to rely ... upon the impression that the principal had in fact granted authority'.[25]

(c) The third party has presumed the existence of sufficient authority

It also follows from the text of Art. 3:201(3) PECL on apparent authority that it is not only required that the third party could reasonably believe that the agent had (sufficient) authority, but also that the third party acted 'in good faith'. This means, in the words of Comment D to Art. 3:201 PECL, that it is required that the third party 'has relied ... upon the impression that the principal had in fact granted authority'.[26]

(d) No detriment required

Art. 3:201(3) PECL on apparent authority does not require the reliance of the third party to be detrimental.

VI Ratification

1 General

As previously explained,[27] if an unauthorised agent concludes a contract in the name of the principal, the general rule is that neither

---

[24] Lando and Beale, *Principles of European Contract Law. Parts I and II*, p. 203.
[25] *Ibid.*   [26] *Ibid.*   [27] See IV.

the principal nor the third party is bound or entitled (Art. 3:204(1) PECL).[28] Although the comments to the PECL do not provide any information about this issue, this general rule protects the autonomy of the principal because it prevents him from being bound and entitled against his will. However, the principal's autonomy is not violated if he has no objection to the contract concluded by his unauthorised agent and thus it seems practical that he should have the possibility of ratifying it.

A situation of apparent ratification is conceivable under the PECL. Article 2:102 PECL (Intention), provides that 'the intention of a party to be legally bound by contract is to be determined from the party's statements or conduct as they were *reasonably*[29] understood by the other party'. Pursuant to the linking provision of Art. 1:107 PECL (Application of the Principles by Way of Analogy), this provision may, *inter alia*, be applied to the act of ratification.[30] In view of this, there can be a ratification in a situation where the principal did not intend to ratify, but where the third party reasonably believed that there was a valid ratification. It is not entirely clear whether the third party is only *entitled* and not *obliged* to treat such appearance of ratification as constituting a valid ratification. In any event, in cases where it is clear that the principal wishes to uphold the ratification, it will often be contrary to good faith and fair dealing (Art. 1:201 PECL)[31] for the third party to take the position that the principal did not, in fact, intend to ratify.

2 Legal basis

Ratification is dealt with in Art. 3:207 PECL, which reads as follows:

1. Where a person acting as an agent acts without authority or outside its authority, the principal may ratify the agent's acts.
2. Upon ratification, the agent's acts are considered as having been authorised, without prejudice to the rights of other persons.

---

[28] See, for the text of Art. 3:204(1) PECL, IV, above. [29] Emphasis added.
[30] See, for the text of Art. 1:107 PECL (Application of the Principles by Way of Analogy), n. 4, above.
[31] Art. 1:201 PECL reads as follows: '(1) Each party must act in accordance with good faith and fair dealing. (2) The parties may not exclude or limit this duty.'

3 Scope

It follows from the overall scope of Chapter 3 (Authority of Agents)[32] that Art. 3:207 PECL on ratification directly applies only in the context of consensual agency in the conclusion of contracts.

However, pursuant to the linking provision of Art. 1:107 PECL (Application of the Principles by Way of Analogy), *inter alia* Art. 3:207 PECL on ratification can in principle be applied to ratification with respect to legal acts other than the conclusion of contracts.[33]

Furthermore, the limitation to ratification in the context of consensual agency does not mean that Art. 3:207 PECL on ratification is irrelevant in relation to company law. This is evident from comment B to Art. 3:207 PECL on ratification, which uses the example of an agent who acts in the name of a company not yet created to illustrate that in such cases the principal is bound as a result of ratification as from the moment at which it came into existence. However, Comment B makes it clear that special rules of the applicable company law with respect to pre-incorporation contracts take precedence over the terms of the PECL.[34]

4 Position of the third party prior to ratification

Article 3:208 PECL (Third Party's Right with Respect to Confirmation of Authority) addresses the position of the third party prior to ratification. It reads as follows:

> Where the statements or conduct of the principal gave the third party reason to believe that an act performed by the agent was authorised, but the third party is in doubt about the authorisation, it may send a written confirmation to the principal or request ratification from it. If the principal does not object or answer the request without delay, the agent's act is treated as having been authorised.

The ratification of an act of the agent which is not covered by the principal's authority, lies in the principal's discretion. Article 3:208 PECL, by contrast, intends to provide the third party with a means to force the principal to clarify the agent's authority.[35]

---

[32] See II above.

[33] Cf. II above. See, for the text of Art. 1:107 PECL (Application of the Principles by Way of Analogy), n. 4, above.

[34] Lando and Beale, *Principles of European Contract Law. Parts I and II*, p. 214.

[35] *Ibid.*, p. 215.

According to Comment B to Art. 3:208 PECL, such a burden may only be laid upon the principal for good reason. This condition consists of three elements which are set out in the first sentence of the article. (1) The principal's statements or conduct must have given the third party reason to believe in the principal's authorisation. The third party's belief must be reasonable and bona fide. (2) The third party must be in doubt about the authorisation. Again, this doubt must be reasonable and bona fide. (3) The third party must send a written confirmation of the act undertaken by the agent to the principal or he must request ratification from the principal.[36]

As described in Comment C to Art. 3:208 PECL, the receipt of the letter of confirmation, or the request for ratification in the circumstances described in Art. 3:208 PECL, imposes a burden upon the principal. If the principal does not agree, he must indicate his objection to the third party without delay. If he does not do so or objects too late, his silence or delay is regarded as a confirmation of his having authorised the agent to undertake the act in question.[37]

5 Effect of ratification

(a) Retroactive effect

The effect of ratification is stated in Art. 3:207(2) PECL: the agent's acts are regarded as having bound, from the beginning, the principal and the third party. The principal takes over the benefits as well as the burdens produced by the agent's acts.[38]

(b) Rights granted to fourth parties prior to ratification are respected

Article 3:207(2) PECL also provides that a ratification is 'without prejudice to the rights of other persons' (i.e. persons other than the principal, the agent and the third party: in short, 'fourth parties'). The question of the rights which fourth parties may have acquired is outside the scope of the PECL.[39]

6 The act of ratification: requirements

There are few requirements to which the act of ratification is subject in the PECL.

---

[36] *Ibid.*, p. 214.   [37] *Ibid.*   [38] *Ibid.*   [39] *Ibid.*

(a) No specific time limit

Ratification is not subject to a specific time limit. It should, however, be noted that the right of ratification is subject to the general prescriptive period of three years (Art. 14:201 PECL).[40] In addition, there is of course the mechanism of Art. 3:208 PECL (Third Party's Right with Respect to Confirmation of Authority) discussed in VI 4, above.

(b) No particular form required

Comment A to Art. 3:207 PECL states that 'ratification may be made by express declaration', but that it 'may also be implied from acts of the principal which unambiguously demonstrate its intention to adopt the contract made by the agent'.[41] Comment A to Art. 3:207 PECL provides the following example:[42]

> In the name of her principal P, a merchant, agent A has contracted with T, also a merchant, for the purchase of the most recent model of computer for EUR 22,500 although her authority was limited to EUR 20,000, which T did not know. After learning what A has done, P sends instructions about delivery of the machine. This implies ratification of A's act.

(c) Act of ratification may be expressed *vis-à-vis* the third party or the agent

It is clear from Comment A to Art. 3:207 PECL that ratification should not necessarily be addressed to the third party, but can also be addressed to the agent.[43] An approach in which the ratification must not necessarily come to the attention of the third party in order to be effective is problematic from a practical point of view, because how would the third party know that ratification has taken place?

VII Liability of the *falsus procurator*

1 General

If neither the doctrine of apparent authority nor the doctrine of ratification applies, neither the principal nor the third party is bound or entitled under the contract concluded by the unauthorised agent. In such cases,

---

[40] Art. 14:201 (General Period) PECL reads as follows: 'The general period of prescription is three years.'
[41] Lando and Beale, *Principles of European Contract Law. Parts I and II*, p. 213.
[42] *Ibid.*, pp. 213–14.   [43] *Ibid.*, p. 213.

the third party can generally hold the unauthorised agent (the *falsus procurator*) liable for the damage which he has suffered as a consequence of the agent's lack of authority. This rule is exempted if the third party (1) knew or (2) could not have been unaware of the agent's lack of authority. It can therefore be said that the doctrine of the liability of the *falsus procurator* aims to protect the reasonable beliefs of the third party.

It is evident from Comment C to Art. 3:204 PECL (Agent Acting Without or Outside its Authority) that in the PECL the liability of the *falsus procurator* is based on an implied warranty of authority (i.e. on a legal act).[44]

2 Legal basis

Article 3:204(2) PECL on the liability of the *falsus procurator* reads as follows:

> Failing ratification by the principal according to Article 3:207, the agent is liable to pay the third party such damages as will place the third party in the same position as if the agent had acted with authority. This does not apply if the third party knew or could not have been unaware of the agent's lack of authority.

3 Scope

It follows from the overall scope of Chapter 3 (Authority of Agents)[45] that Art. 3:204(2) PECL on the liability of the *falsus procurator* directly applies only in the context of consensual agency in the conclusion of contracts.

However, pursuant to the linking provision of Art. 1:107 PECL (Application of the Principles by Way of Analogy), *inter alia*, Art. 3:204(2) PECL can in principle be applied to the liability of the *falsus procurator* in the context of unauthorised legal acts other than the conclusion of contracts.[46]

Furthermore, the limitation to consensual agency does not mean that Art. 3:204(2) PECL on the liability of the *falsus procurator* is irrelevant in relation to company law. Comment B to Art. 3:101 PECL (Scope of the Chapter) provides that, although the powers of representation conferred upon company directors by statute are not covered, if a company grants

---

[44] *Ibid.*, p. 208. [45] See II, above. [46] Cf. II, above.

authority to act in its name to an employee other than a director, the PECL do apply.[47] In view of this, it seems that if an employee other than a director acts in the name of the relevant company with insufficient authority, Art. 3:204(2) PECL on the liability of the *falsus procurator* can be applied.

4 Effect

The effect of Art. 3:204(2) on the liability of the *falsus procurator* is not that the unauthorised agent himself becomes bound by the contract which he has purported to conclude in the name of the principal. The unauthorised agent is merely liable towards the third party for expectation damages. This means that the agent is liable to pay the third party such damages as will place the third party in the same position as if the agent had acted with authority. Comment C to Art. 3:204 PECL makes it clear that if the agent proves that the principal could not have performed the contract, nor have paid compensation (for instance because the principal is insolvent) the agent need not even pay damages.[48]

5 Requirements

There are only a few requirements to which the liability of the unauthorised agent is subject.

(a) Bad faith of the unauthorised agent not required

In the PECL it is not required that the false agent is in some way at fault. Even in cases that the false agent did not know and could not reasonably know that he had insufficient authority he can be held liable.

(b) Good faith of the third party required

In the PECL the third party cannot claim damages if the third party knew or could not have been unaware of the agent's lack of authority (Art. 3:204(2), second sentence, PECL).

(c) Damage

Obviously, in order for the unauthorised agent to be liable, the third party must have suffered damage as a consequence of the agent's lack of authority.

---

[47] Cf. II, above. Lando and Beale, *Principles of European Contract Law. Parts I and II*, pp. 197–8.
[48] *Ibid.*, p. 208.

VIII The interrelationship between apparent authority, ratification and the liability of the *falsus procurator*

1 General

Now that we have at some length discussed apparent authority, ratification, and the liability of the *falsus procurator*, I will turn to considering the relationship between the three doctrines. Are they mutually exclusive or is it conceivable that they coincide in certain cases?

2 Apparent authority and ratification

In the PECL, it seems that apparent authority and (apparent) ratification may coincide. It seems that circumstances taking place *after* the conclusion of the contract are not only relevant as to the question of whether there is (apparent) ratification or not, but also as to whether there is apparent authority or not. This means that sometimes a third party will be able to invoke both apparent authority and (apparent) ratification on the same facts. The PECL have adopted the general rule that, in interpreting a contract, regard should *inter alia* be had to 'the conduct of the parties, even *subsequent*[49] to the conclusion of the contract' (Art. 5:102(b) PECL). In line with this provision, it seems that as regards the doctrine of apparent authority later circumstances should also be taken into account. If that is accepted, the doctrines of apparent authority and (apparent) ratification may coincide. This is a welcome approach, because in practice a clear distinction cannot always be drawn.

3 Apparent authority and liability of the falsus procurator

In the PECL the doctrine of apparent authority and the liability of the *falsus procurator* are mutually exclusive. Either there is a valid contract because third party T successfully invokes the doctrine of apparent authority, in which case T cannot successfully sue agent A for damages on the basis of Art. 3:204(2) PECL on the liability of the false agent, or vice versa.

The PECL provide that in cases of apparent authority the principal is to be treated as having granted authority (Art. 3:201(2) PECL). As previously explained,[50] this means that one is asked to assume that

---

[49] Emphasis added.   [50] See V 1.

full authority exists and thus that a valid contract is concluded by the unauthorised agent. It follows that not only the principal is bound and entitled under the contract, but also the third party. As a consequence, if in a case of apparent authority principal P is willing to uphold the unauthorised act, third party T cannot choose not to rely on the appearance of authority and instead turn to agent A on the basis of Art. 3:204(2) PECL regarding the liability of the false agent.

4 Ratification and liability of the falsus procurator

After ratification the agent will generally be freed from his liability pursuant to Art. 3:204(2) PECL regarding liability of the false agent. The reason for this is that as a consequence of the retroactive effect of ratification, the third party will not normally have suffered any damage.

This is different in (at least) the following case. Art. 3:207(2) PECL provides that a ratification is 'without prejudice to the rights of other persons' (i.e., persons other than the principal, the agent and the third party; in short, 'fourth parties'). Therefore, if the third party suffers damage as a consequence of this, A remains liable on the basis of Art. 2:204(2) PECL. One example (which I have already provided in the chapter on the Netherlands[51]) is as follows. Unauthorised agent A grants a right of pledge to T1 on a claim belonging to principal P. Thereafter, P grants a right of pledge on the same claim to T2 and subsequently ratifies the grant of pledge to T1. The right of pledge of T2 takes priority above the right of pledge of T1. If T1 suffers any loss because his right of pledge ranks second instead of first, A can be held liable on the basis of Art. 3:204(2) PECL.

IX Acting in the name of a principal yet to be named

Article 3:203 PECL contains a special provision for circumstances in which a person enters into a contract (with or without authority) in the name of a principal whose identity is to be revealed at a later time. If the agent or pseudo-agent fails to reveal this identity within a reasonable time, he himself is bound by the contract with the third party.

Where the identity of the principal is to be revealed later and the agent does not disclose the identity of the principal within a reasonable time, a situation *may* exist in which the agent still does not have a principal

---

[51] Chapter 5 (The Netherlands), VII 4.

at the time when the contract is concluded. In such cases there is unauthorised agency. Exceptionally, in such cases of unauthorised agency, the third party can regard the agent as his contractual counterparty. This does not constitute a serious breach of the principle of autonomy. The third party is prepared to contract with a principal whose identity is not known to him at the time of the conclusion of the contract and is therefore evidently unconcerned about the identity of his contractual counterparty. There can, therefore, be no objection that the agent is the counterparty in such cases.[52]

X Conclusions

This chapter concentrated on the rules with respect to unauthorised agency provided by the PECL.

In part II it was explained that the agency provisions in the PECL directly apply only to consensual agency in the conclusion of contracts, but that they may be applied by way of analogy to other cases as well.

In part III it was set out that the PECL follow the traditional civil law distinction between direct and indirect agency.

In part IV it became clear that in cases of unauthorised agency neither the principal nor the third party is bound or entitled under the contract concluded by the unauthorised agent.

In part V I turned to the first main exception to the general effect of unauthorised agency: apparent authority. It turned out, *inter alia*, that in the PECL the doctrine of apparent authority not only applies where the third party reasonably believes that the agent was authorised to conclude the contract concerned where such beliefs can be traced back to acts or conduct of the principal, but also if such beliefs can be traced back to other factors which lie within the principal's sphere of risk.

In part VI I turned to the second main exception to the general effect of unauthorised agency: ratification. It became clear, *inter alia*, that the third party prior to ratification by the principal in certain cases has the right to request from the principal a confirmation of authority. If the principal does not object or answer the request without delay, the agent's act is treated as having been authorised. It was also set out that ratification in the PECL has retroactive effect, however without prejudice to rights of 'fourth persons'.

---

[52] See Busch, *Indirect Representation*, pp. 21, 240.

Part VII examined the liability of the *falsus procurator*. In the PECL, the third party can generally hold the unauthorised agent liable for the damage which he has suffered as a consequence of the agent's lack of authority. This rule is exempted if the third party (1) knew or (2) could not have been unaware of the agent's lack of authority.

Part VIII dealt with the interrelationship between apparent authority, ratification and the liability of the *falsus procurator*. It was concluded that apparent authority and (apparent) ratification may sometimes coincide and that apparent authority and the liability of the *falsus procurator* are mutually exclusive. It was also concluded that, after ratification, the agent will generally be freed from his liability, because, as a consequence of the retroactive effect, the third party will not normally have suffered any damage.

Finally, part IX elaborated on acting in the name of a principal yet to be named. It was concluded that where the identity of the principal is to be revealed later and the agent does not disclose the identity of the principal within a reasonable time, a situation *may* exist in which the agent still does not have a principal at the time when the contract is concluded. In such cases there is unauthorised agency. Exceptionally, in such cases of unauthorised agency, the third party can regard the agent as his contractual counterparty.

Unauthorised agency in the UNIDROIT Principles of International Commercial Contracts 2004

DANNY BUSCH

Table of contents

I Introduction

This chapter is devoted to the rules with respect to unauthorised agency provided by the UNIDROIT Principles of International Commercial Contracts 2004.[1] These principles devote an entire section to agency

[1] Variously referred to below as 'UNIDROIT Principles' or 'UP'. See for the UP with commentary: *UNIDROIT Principles of International Commercial Contracts 2004* (Rome: International Institute for the Unification of Private Law, 2004), pp. 75–6. The full text of the UP with commentary is also available at www.unidroit.org/english/ principles/contracts/principles2004/integralversionprinciples2004-e.pdf. On the UP see the many publications listed on www.unilex.info. Please note that there is a previous initiative of UNIDROIT concerned with the harmonisation of agency law, namely the Geneva Convention on Agency in the International Sale of Goods, which dates from 1983 (the 'UNIDROIT Agency Convention'). The UNIDROIT Agency Convention has not yet entered into force, since the requirement of a minimum of ten ratifications (see Art. 33) has still not been fulfilled. The rules on authorised agency in the UNIDROIT Agency Convention are largely identical to those provided by the UNIDROIT Principles. See

(see Chapter 2: Formation and Authority of Agents, Section 2: Authority of Agents). The UNIDROIT Principles are of a non-binding nature and aim to establish rules of general contract law at a universal level.[2]

The UNIDROIT Principles provide the general rule that where an agent acts without (sufficient) authority, his acts do not bind the principal. This general rule is exempted in cases where the doctrine of apparent authority applies or where the principal subsequently ratifies the unauthorised act. In addition, the UNIDROIT Principles provide that the third party may hold an unauthorised agent (the *falsus procurator*) liable for the damage which the third party has suffered as a consequence of the agent's lack of authority.

In this chapter, in part II, I first examine the scope of the UP. In part III I examine the concept of agency used in the UNIDROIT Principles. In part IV I devote some attention to the general effect of unauthorised agency. Afterwards, I then turn to the main exceptions to the general effect of unauthorised agency: apparent authority (V) and ratification (VI). Part VII follows with some remarks about the liability of the *falsus procurator* and part VIII with a treatment of the interrelationship between apparent authority, ratification and the liability of the *falsus procurator*. Part IX ends this chapter with some concluding observations.

II Scope

The agency provisions in the UNIDROIT Principles apply only to agency in the conclusion of contracts (Art. 2.2.1(1) UP).[3]

---

further on the UNIDROIT Agency Convention D. Busch, *Indirect Representation in European Contract Law* (The Hague: Kluwer Law International, 2005), pp. 175–95, with many further references, to which should be added M. J. Bonell, 'Agency', in A. Hartkamp, M. Hesselink, E. Hondius, C. Joustra, E. du Perron and M. Veldman (eds.), *Towards a European Civil Code*, 3rd edn (Nijmegen/The Hague: Ars Aequi Libri/Kluwer Law International, 2004), pp. 381–97.

[2] On the purposes of the UP, see the Preamble of the UP: 'These Principles set forth general rules for international commercial contracts. They shall be applied when the parties have agreed that their contract be governed by them. They may be applied when the parties have agreed that their contract be governed by general principles of law, the lex mercatoria or the like. They may be applied when the parties have not chosen any law to govern their contract. They may be used to interpret or supplement international uniform law instruments. They may be used to interpret or supplement domestic law. They may serve as a model for national and international legislators.'

[3] Art. 2.2.1(1) UP reads as follows: 'This Section governs the authority of a person ("the agent") to affect the legal relations of another person ("the principal") by or with respect to a contract with a third party, whether the agent acts in its own name or in that of the principal.'

Furthermore, the UNIDROIT Principles are limited to agency created by the exercise of the will of the principal (consensual agency). The UNIDROIT Principles explicitly provide that they do not govern an agent's authority conferred by law or the authority of an agent appointed by a public or judicial authority (Art. 2.2.1(3) UP).[4]

References to the creation of agency through the 'will' of the principal should not, however, be taken to indicate that the UNIDROIT Principles are irrelevant as regards representation with respect to company law. This is not the case, although the position is undoubtedly complex.

Comment 5 to Art. 2.2.1 UP (Scope of the Section) states that if, under the special rules governing the authority of its bodies or officers, a corporation is prevented from invoking a limitation to their authority against third parties, that corporation may not rely on Art. 2.2.5(1) UP[5] on unauthorised agency to claim that it is not bound by an act of its bodies or officers that falls outside the scope of their authority. On the other hand (as Comment 5 continues), as long as the general rules laid down in the agency section do not conflict with the special rules on the authority of bodies, officers or partners, they may well be applied in lieu of the latter. Thus, for instance, a third party seeking to demonstrate that the contract he has concluded with an officer of a corporation binds that corporation may invoke either the special rules governing the authority of that corporation's bodies or officers, or, as the case may be, the general rules on apparent authority laid down in Art. 2.2.5(2) UP.[6]

Finally, the UNIDROIT Principles consider only the 'external' aspects of agency. In other words, they focus on the relationship between the principal or agent and the third party rather than the 'internal' relationship between the principal and agent (Art. 2.2.1(2) UP).[7]

---

[4] Art. 2.2.1(3) UP reads as follows: 'It does not govern an agent's authority conferred by law or the authority of an agent appointed by a public or judicial authority.'

[5] Art. 2.2.5(1) UP reads as follows: 'Where an agent acts without authority or exceeds its authority, its acts do not affect the legal relations between the principal and the third party.'

[6] Art. 2.2.5(2) UP reads as follows: 'However, where the principal causes the third party reasonably to believe that the agent has authority to act on behalf of the principal and that the agent is acting within the scope of that authority, the principal may not invoke against the third party the lack of authority of the agent.' See for Comment 5 to Art. 2.2.1 UP: *UNIDROIT Principles*, pp. 75–6.

[7] Art. 2.2.1(2) UP reads as follows: 'It governs only the relations between the principal or the agent on the one hand, and the third party on the other.' Comment 1 to Art. 2.2.1 UP makes it clear that even those provisions which describe issues affecting both the internal and the external relations (see, e.g., Arts 2.2.2 and 2.2.10 UP on the establishment and

III Disclosed and undisclosed agency

The UNIDROIT Principles are not based on the civil law distinction between direct and indirect representation but instead apply a uniform concept of agency, very much like that in common law jurisdictions. Article 2.2.1(1) UP states that its section on agency 'governs the authority of a person ("the agent") to affect the legal relations of another person ("the principal") by or with respect to a contract with a third party, whether the agent acts in its own name or in that of the principal.' However, a distinction is made at a later point between two different types of agency, namely disclosed and undisclosed agency.

Disclosed agency is dealt with in Art. 2.2.3 UP (Agency Disclosed). Disclosed agency occurs where (1) an agent acts within the scope of his authority and (2) the third party knew or ought to have known that the agent was acting as an agent. The effect of this is that the acts of the agent shall directly affect the legal relations between the principal and the third party and no legal relation is created between the agent and the third party (Art. 2.2.3(1) UP). However, the acts of the agent shall affect only the relations between the agent and the third party, where the agent with the consent of the principal undertakes to become the party to the contract (Art. 2.2.3(2) UP). According to Comment 4 to Art. 2.2.3 UP this is the case, in particular, where a principal, who wants to remain anonymous, instructs the agent to act as a 'commission agent', i.e. to deal with the third party in his own name without establishing any direct relation between the principal and the third party.[8] The cases described in Art. 2.2.3(1) UP would in civil law countries amount to direct agency, whereas the cases described in Art. 2.2.3(2) UP would in civil law countries amount to indirect agency.

Undisclosed agency is dealt with in Art. 2.2.4 UP (Agency Undisclosed). Undisclosed agency occurs where (1) an agent acts within the scope of his authority and (2) the third party neither knew nor ought to have known that the agent was acting as an agent. The effect of this is that the acts of the agent shall affect only the relations between the agent and the

---

termination of the agent's authority, Art. 2.2.7 UP on conflict of interests and Art. 2.2.8 UP on sub-agency), consider those issues only with respect to their effects on the third party. The rights and duties as between principal and agent are governed by their agreement and the applicable law which, with respect to specific types of agency relationships, such as those concerning 'commercial agents', may provide mandatory rules for the protection of the agent. See *UNIDROIT Principles*, p. 74.

[8] *UNIDROIT Principles*, p. 80.

third party (Art. 2.2.4(1) UP). However, where such an agent, when contracting with the third party on behalf of a business, represents himself to be the owner of that business, the third party, upon discovery of the real owner of the business, may exercise also against the latter the rights he has against the agent (Art. 2.2.4(2) UP). The cases described in Art. 2.2.4 UP would in civil law countries often amount to indirect agency.

IV Unauthorised agency

In the UNIDROIT Principles, the concepts of unauthorised agency, apparent authority and ratification are in principle associated with agency in general and not just with what in civil law countries would be named direct agency. Notwithstanding the fact that these concepts therefore also apply to (a certain case of) what in civil law countries would be termed indirect agency, the focus of this chapter is on the type of agency which in civil law countries would be termed direct agency. In the remainder of this chapter this type of agency is simply referred to as 'agency'.

The general effect of unauthorised agency is explicitly provided in Art. 2.2.5(1) UP: 'Where an agent acts without authority or exceeds its authority, its acts do not affect the legal relations between the principal and the third party.' This means that neither the principal nor the third party is bound or entitled under the contract concluded by the unauthorised agent. This rule protects the autonomy of the principal because it prevents him from being bound and entitled against his will. Comment 1 to Art. 2.2.5(1) UP provides the following illustration.

> Principal B authorises agent A to buy on its behalf a specific quantity of grain but without exceeding a certain price. A enters into a contract with seller C for the purchase of a greater quantity of grain and at a higher price than that authorised by B. On account of A's lack of authority, the contract between A and C does not bind B, nor does it become effective between A and C.

V Apparent authority

1 General

The UNIDROIT Principles contain an exception to the general rule that neither the principal nor the third party is bound or entitled in cases of unauthorised agency if the doctrine of apparent authority applies, i.e. if the third party reasonably believes that the agent was authorised to conclude the contract concerned and where such beliefs can be traced back to acts or conduct of the principal or to other factors which lie within the principal's sphere of risk.

In the UNIDROIT Principles, in cases of apparent authority the principal may not invoke against the third party the lack of authority of the agent. Comment 2 to Art. 2.2.5 UP makes it clear that apparent authority is an application of the general principle of good faith (Art. 1.7 UP), as well as part of the express prohibition against inconsistent behaviour (Art. 1.8 UP, a provision which did not appear in the 1994 edition of the UP).[9] The references to good faith and the prevention of inconsistent behaviour suggest an underlying purpose of protection of the reasonable expectations of the third party. It is consistent with this protective aim that the third party is *entitled* to invoke apparent authority but not *obliged* to do so.[10]

2 Legal basis

Article 2.2.5(2) UP deals with apparent authority. It reads as follows:

> [W]here the principal causes the third party reasonably to believe that the agent has authority to act on behalf of the principal and that the agent is acting within the scope of that authority, the principal may not invoke against the third party the lack of authority of the agent.

3 Scope

It follows from the overall scope of Section 2 (Authority of Agents) of Chapter 2 (Formation and Authority of Agents)[11] that Art. 2.2.5(2) UP

---

[9] Art 1.7 UP (Good Faith and Fair Dealing) reads as follows: '(1) Each party must act in accordance with good faith and fair dealing in international trade. (2) The parties may not exclude or limit this duty.' Art 1.8 UP (Inconsistent Behaviour) reads as follows: 'A party cannot act inconsistently with an understanding it has caused the other party to have and upon which that other party reasonably has acted in reliance to its detriment.' See for Comment 2 to Art. 2.2.5 UP: *UNIDROIT Principles*, p. 83.

[10] Cf. F. M. B. Reynolds, 'Authority of agents' (2005) *ICC International Court of Arbitration Bulletin*, Special Supplement, UNIDROIT Principles: New Developments and Applications, p. 9 at 13.

[11] See II, above.

on apparent authority applies to apparent consensual agency in the conclusion of contracts.

The limitation to apparent consensual agency does not mean that Art. 2.2.5(2) UP on apparent authority is irrelevant in relation to company law. Comment 5 to Art. 2.2.1 UP (Scope of the Section) provides the following example of how apparent authority can operate in relation to representation of companies:

> A, Managing Director of Ruritanian company B, has been given the authority by the Board of Directors of the company to carry out all transactions falling within the company's ordinary course of business except the hiring and dismissal of employees. A hires C as the new accountant of B's branch in foreign country X. B refuses to be bound by this appointment on account of A's lack of authority to hire employees. C may overcome B's objection by invoking Section 35A of the Ruritanian Companies Act stating that '[i]n favour of a person dealing with a company in good faith, the power of the board of directors to bind the company, or authorise others to do so, shall be deemed to be free of any limitation under the company's constitution'. Yet C, who as a national of a foreign country X may not be familiar with that special provision of the Ruritanian Companies Act, may equally rely on the general rule on apparent authority laid down in Art. 2.2.5(2) UP and claim that, in view of A's position as Managing Director of B, it was reasonable for C to believe that A had the authority to hire employees.[12]

Article 2.2.10 UP (Termination of Authority) deals with apparent authority in the special case that an agent continues to conclude contracts on behalf of the principal despite the fact that his authority has already ended.[13] Article 2.2.10 UP is a *lex specialis* in relation to the general provision on apparent authority (Art. 2.2.5(2) UP). Comment 4 to Art. 2.2.10 UP provides that it also applies, with appropriate modifications, to subsequent restrictions of an agent's authority.[14]

Article 2.2.10(1) UP provides that even if the agent's authority has been terminated for one reason or another, the agent's acts continue to affect the legal relationship between the principal and the third party as long as the third party is neither aware nor ought to know that the agent

---

[12] *UNIDROIT Principles*, p. 76.

[13] Art. 2.2.10 UP reads as follows: '(1) Termination of authority is not effective in relation to the third party unless the third party knew or ought to have known of it. (2) Notwithstanding the termination of its authority, an agent remains authorised to perform the acts that are necessary to prevent harm to the principal's interests.'

[14] *UNIDROIT Principles*, p. 93.

no longer has authority. Obviously the situation is clear whenever either the principal or the agent gives the third party notice of the termination. In the absence of such notice it will depend on the circumstances of the case whether the third party ought to have known of the termination.[15]

After termination of the agent's authority, the circumstances of the case may make it necessary for the agent to perform additional acts in order to prevent the principal's interests from being harmed.[16] Therefore, Art. 2.2.10(2) UP provides that, notwithstanding the termination of his authority, an agent remains authorised to perform the acts that are necessary to prevent harm to the principal's interests.

4 Effect

If unauthorised agent A concludes a contract with third party T and T successfully invokes the doctrine of apparent authority, principal P may not invoke against T the lack of authority of A. This implies the following: (1) T can sue P on the contract concluded by A, notwithstanding the fact that A was unauthorised; (2) P, however, has no right to sue T, unless he ratifies the unauthorised act.[17]

In view of the fact that the doctrine of apparent authority exists for the benefit of T, it seems that T is *entitled* to invoke it but not *obliged* to do so if he does not wish to do so.[18]

5 Requirements

Article 2.2.5(2) UP sets out the requirements which have to be met in order successfully to invoke the doctrine of apparent authority:

(a) declaration or conduct by the principal; and
(b) the third party reasonably believed that the agent had sufficient authority.

These two requirements will now be discussed in more detail.

(a) Declaration or conduct of the principal, supplemented by risk principle

The UNIDROIT Principles have – at least formally – adopted the classical 'of the principal's own doing' principle, pursuant to which the apparent authority must somehow be traced back to an act or conduct of

---

[15] *Ibid.*, pp. 92–3. [16] *Ibid.*, p. 93. [17] See VIII(2). [18] See V1.

the principal. The UNIDROIT Principles state that the principal should 'cause' the apparent authority (Art. 2.2.5(2) UP).

However, the fact that Comment 2 to Art. 2.2.5 UP provides that the position occupied by the apparent agent in the organisation's hierarchy and the type of transaction involved can constitute apparent authority, makes it clear that, according to the UNIDROIT Principles, the third party should be protected not only where the impression has been created by the principal's act or conduct, but also where it is due to other circumstances that come within the ambit of the risks borne by the principal (the 'risk principle'). This is confirmed by an example given in Comment 2 to Art. 2.2.5 UP:

> A, a manager of one company B's branch offices, though lacking actual authority to do so, engages construction company C to redecorate the branch's premises. In view of the fact that a branch manager normally would have the authority to enter into such a contract, B is bound by the contract with C since it was reasonable for C to believe that A had the actual authority to enter into the contract.[19]

(b) The third party reasonably believed that the agent had sufficient authority

It follows from the text of Art. 2.2.5(2) UP on apparent authority that it can only be successfully invoked if the third party reasonably believed that the agent had (sufficient) authority. Comment 2 to Art. 2.2.5 UP makes it clear that whether or not the third party's belief was reasonable will depend on the circumstances of the case.[20]

(c) No detriment required

The UNIDROIT Principles do not require the reliance of the third party to be detrimental. This seems somewhat surprising, because according to Comment 2 to Art. 2.2.5 UP (Agent Acting Without or Exceeding its Authority) the doctrine of apparent authority is not only an application of the general principle of good faith (Art. 1.7 UP), but also of the prohibition of inconsistent behaviour (Art. 1.8 UP).[21] The latter provision requires detrimental reliance, but this requirement does not reappear in Art. 2.2.5(2) UP on apparent authority. In any event, it is submitted that a detriment should not be required because it is the reasonable belief of the third party in itself which deserves protection.

---

[19] *UNIDROIT Principles*, p. 84.   [20] *Ibid.*
[21] See, for the text of Arts 1.7 UP and 1.8 UP, n. 9 above.

VI Ratification

1 General

As previously explained,[22] where an agent acts without authority or exceeds his authority, his acts do not affect the legal relations between the principal and the third party (Art. 2.2.5(1) UP).[23] Although the comments to the UNIDROIT Principles do not provide any information about this issue, this general rule protects the autonomy of the principal because it prevents the principal from being bound and entitled against his will. However, the principal's autonomy is not violated if he has no objection to the contract concluded by his unauthorised agent and thus it seems practical that the principal should have the possibility of ratifying it. According to Comment 1 to Art. 2.2.9 UP ratification is to be qualified as a subsequent authorisation of the agent.[24]

A situation of apparent ratification is conceivable under the UNIDROIT Principles. This follows from Art. 1.8 UP (Inconsistent Behaviour), stating that: 'a party cannot act inconsistently with an understanding it has caused the other party to have and upon which that other party reasonably has acted in reliance to its detriment.' In view of this, there can be a ratification in the case that the principal did not intend to ratify, but where the third party reasonably believed that there was a valid ratification. Strictly speaking, the UP require a detriment. However, a detriment should not be required because the reasonable belief of the third party that the principal intended to ratify in itself deserves protection. The prevention of inconsistent behaviour suggests an underlying purpose of protection of the reasonable expectations of the third party. It is consistent with this protective aim that the third party is *entitled* to invoke apparent ratification but not *obliged* to do so.

2 Legal basis

The possibility of ratification is expressed in Art. 2.2.9(1) UP:

> An act by an agent that acts without authority or exceeds its authority may be ratified by the principal. On ratification the act produces the same effects as if it had initially been carried out with authority.

---

[22] See IV.   [23] See, for the text of Art. 2.2.5(1) UP, IV, above.
[24] *UNIDROIT Principles*, p. 90.

3 Scope

It follows from the overall scope of Section 2 (Authority of Agents) of Chapter 2 (Formation and Authority of Agents)[25] that Art. 2.2.9 UP on ratification applies in the context of consensual agency in the conclusion of contracts.

The limitation to consensual agency does not mean that Art. 2.2.9 UP on ratification is irrelevant in relation to company law. As we have seen in Comment 5 to Art. 2.2.1 UP (Scope of the Section),[26] apparent authority can operate in relation to representation of companies. In view of this, it seems that there can be no objection to an application of ratification in relation to representation of companies in appropriate cases either.

4 Position of the third party prior to ratification

(a) The third party in good faith may withdraw unilaterally prior to ratification

Pursuant to Art. 2.2.9(3) UP, the third party in good faith may withdraw unilaterally prior to ratification by the principal.[27] According to Comment 4 to Art. 2.2.9 UP on ratification, the reason for granting the innocent third party such a right is to avoid that the principal is the only one in a position to speculate and to decide whether or not to ratify depending on market developments.[28]

(b) Reasonable time for ratification

The principal may in principle ratify at any time. According to Comment 3 to Art. 2.2.9 UP on ratification, the reason for this is that normally the third party does not even know that he has contracted with an agent who did not have authority or who exceeded his authority. However (as Comment 3 continues), even if the third party knows from the outset, or subsequently becomes aware, that the agent was a false agent, he will have a legitimate interest not to be left in doubt indefinitely as to the ultimate fate of the contract concluded with the false agent. Accordingly,

---

[25] See II, above.   [26] See II and V 3, above.

[27] Art. 2.2.9(3) UP reads as follows: 'If, at the time of the agent's act, the third party neither knew nor ought to have known of the lack of authority, it may, at any time before ratification, by notice to the principal indicate its refusal to become bound by a ratification.'

[28] *UNIDROIT Principles*, p. 91.

Art. 2.2.9(2), first sentence, UP grants the third party the right to set a reasonable time limit within which the principal must ratify if he intends to do so. Comment 3 to Art. 2.2.9 UP on ratification makes it clear that in such cases ratification must be notified to the third party. If the principal does not ratify within that period of time he can no longer do so (Art. 2.2.9(2), second sentence, UP).[29]

(c) Third party may refuse partial ratification

Article 2.2.9(1), second sentence, UP provides that on ratification the agent's acts produce the same effects as if they had been carried out with authority from the outset.[30] According to Comment 2 to Art. 2.2.9 UP on ratification, it follows that the third party may refuse partial ratification of the agent's acts by the principal, because this would amount to a proposal by the principal to modify the contract that the third party has concluded with the agent.[31] However, it may be argued that in certain circumstances T may be *obliged* to accept a partial or conditional ratification because of his duty to mitigate damage (Art. 7.4.8 UP).[32] This seems a fair approach because even if the third party accepts a partial or conditional ratification, the *falsus procurator* remains liable on the basis of Art. 2.2.6 UP to the extent that T – notwithstanding a partial or conditional ratification by P – has suffered damage as a consequence of the unauthorised agency.

5 Effect of ratification

(a) Retroactive effect

Article 2.2.9(1) UP provides that 'on ratification the act produces the same effects as if it had initially been carried out with authority'. Thus, ratification has retroactive effect.

---

[29] Art. 2.2.9(2) UP reads as follows: 'The third party may by notice to the principal specify a reasonable period of time for ratification. If the principal does not ratify within that period of time it can no longer do so.' See, for Comment 3 to Art. 2.2.9 UP, *UNIDROIT Principles*, p. 91.

[30] See, for the text of Art. 2.2.9(1) UP, VI 2 above.   [31] *UNIDROIT Principles*, p. 91.

[32] Art. 7.4.8 UP (Mitigation of Harm) reads as follows: '(1) The non-performing party is not liable for harm suffered by the aggrieved party to the extent that the harm could have been reduced by the latter party's taking reasonable steps. (2) The aggrieved party is entitled to recover any expenses reasonably incurred in attempting to reduce the harm.'

(b) Are rights granted to fourth parties prior to ratification respected?

The UNIDROIT Principles take the position that the effect of ratification on persons other than the principal, the agent and the third party ('fourth parties') is outside its scope. Comment 5 to Art. 2.2.9 UP, states that:

> [Art. 2.2.9 UP] deals only with the effects of ratification on the three parties directly involved in the agency relationship, i.e.: the principal, the agent and the third party. In accordance with the scope of this Section as defined in Art. 2.2.1, the rights of other third persons are not affected. For instance, if the same goods have been sold first by the false agent to C, and subsequently by the principal to another person D, the conflict between C and D as a result of the principal's subsequent ratification of the first sale will have to be solved by the applicable law.[33]

6 The act of ratification: requirements

There are few requirements to which the act of ratification is subject in the UNIDROIT Principles.

(a) No specific time limit

Ratification is not subject to a specific time limit. The right of ratification, however, is subject to the general limitation periods provided by Art. 10.2 UP.[34] This means that the general limitation period for ratification is three years, beginning on the day after the day the principal knows or ought to know of the unauthorised act. In any event, the maximum limitation period is ten years beginning on the day after the day the unauthorised act was performed. In addition, there are of course the mechanisms of Arts. 2.2.9(3) (third party in good faith may withdraw unilaterally prior to ratification) and 2.2.9(2) UP (reasonable period for ratification) discussed in VI 4(a) and (b), above.

---

[33] *UNIDROIT Principles*, p. 91–2.

[34] Art. 10.2 UP reads as follows: '(1) The general limitation period is three years beginning on the day after the day the obligee knows or ought to know the facts as a result of which the obligee's right can be exercised. (2) In any event, the maximum limitation period is ten years beginning on the day after the day the right can be exercised.'

(b) No particular form required

Comment 1 to Art. 2.2.9 UP provides that ratification is not subject to any requirement as to form. As it is a unilateral manifestation of intent, it may be either express or implied from words or conduct.[35]

(c) Must the act of ratification have been expressed
vis-à-vis the third party?

Comment 1 to Art. 2.2.9 UP states that ratification, though normally communicated to the agent, to the third party, or to both, need not be communicated to anyone, provided that it is manifested in some way and can therefore be ascertained by probative material.[36] An approach in which the ratification must not necessarily come to the attention of the third party in order to be effective is problematic from a practical point of view, because how would the third party know that ratification has taken place? Therefore, it does not come as a surprise that in the UNIDROIT Principles this approach cannot completely be preserved. As mentioned before (VI 4(b)), in relation to the case that the third party sets the principal a reasonable time for ratification (Art. 2.2.9 (2) UP), Comment 3 to Art. 2.2.9 UP remarks that 'it goes without saying that in such a case ratification must be notified to the third party'.[37]

VII Liability of the *falsus procurator*

1 General

If neither the doctrine of apparent authority nor the doctrine of ratification applies, neither the principal nor the third party is bound or entitled under the contract concluded by the unauthorised agent. In such cases, the third party can generally hold the unauthorised agent (the *falsus procurator*) liable for the damage which he has suffered as a consequence of the agent's lack of authority. This rule is exempted if the third party (1) knew or (2) ought to have known that the agent had no authority or was exceeding his authority. It can therefore be said that the doctrine of the liability of the *falsus procurator* aims to protect the reasonable beliefs of the third party.

It is not clear whether the liability of the *falsus procurator* is based on an implied warranty of authority (i.e. on a legal act) or derives directly from the UNIDROIT Principles.

---

[35] *UNIDROIT Principles*, p. 90.   [36] *Ibid.*
[37] *UNIDROIT Principles*, p. 91. Cf. Reynolds, 'Authority of agents', p. 12.

2 Legal basis

Article 2.2.6 UP on the liability of the *falsus procurator* reads as follows:

(1) An agent that acts without authority or exceeds its authority is, failing ratification by the principal, liable for damages that will place the third party in the same position as if the agent had acted with authority and not exceeded its authority.

(2) However, the agent is not liable if the third party knew or ought to have known that the agent had no authority or was exceeding its authority.

3 Scope

It follows from the overall scope of Section 2 (Authority of Agents) of Chapter 2 (Formation and Authority of Agents)[38] that Art. 2.2.6 UP on the liability of the *falsus procurator* applies in the context of consensual agency in the conclusion of contracts.

The limitation to consensual agency does not mean that Art. 2.2.6 UP on the liability of the *falsus procurator* is irrelevant in relation to company law. As we have seen in Comment 5 to Art. 2.2.1 UP (Scope of the Section),[39] apparent authority can operate in relation to representation of companies. In view of this, it seems that there can be no objection to an application of liability of the false agent in relation to representation of companies in appropriate cases either.

4 Effect

The effect of Art. 2.2.6 UP on the liability of the *falsus procurator* is not that the unauthorised agent himself becomes bound by the contract which he has purported to conclude in the name of the principal. The unauthorised agent is merely liable to the third party for expectation damages. This means that the third party should be placed in the same financial position as if a valid contract had been concluded with the principal. Or, as Comment 1 to Art. 2.2.6 UP formulates it: 'the liability of the false agent is not limited to the so-called reliance or negative interest, but extends to the so-called expectation or positive interest. In other words, the third party may recover the profit that would have

[38] See II, above.   [39] See II and V 3, above.

resulted if the contract concluded with the false agent had been a valid one.'[40] Comment 1 to Art. 2.2.6 UP provides the following example:[41]

> Agent A, without being authorised by principal B, enters into a contract with third party C for the sale of a cargo of oil belonging to B. Failing B's ratification of the contract, C may recover from A the difference between the contract price and the current market price.

5 Requirements

There are only a few requirements to which the liability of the unauthorised agent is subject.

(a) Bad faith of the unauthorised agent not required

The UNIDROIT Principles do not require that the false agent is in some way at fault. Even in cases where the false agent did not know and could not reasonably know that he had insufficient authority, he can be held liable.

(b) Good faith of the third party required

In the UNIDROIT Principles the third party cannot claim damages if he knew or ought to have known that the agent did not have authority or was exceeding his authority (Art. 2.2.6(2) UP).

(c) Damage

Naturally, in order for the unauthorised agent to be liable, the third party must have suffered damage as a consequence of the agent's lack of authority.

VIII The interrelationship between apparent authority, ratification and the liability of the *falsus procurator*

1 General

Now that we have at some length discussed apparent authority, ratification and liability of the *falsus procurator*, I now turn to considering the relationship between the three doctrines. Are they mutually exclusive or is it conceivable that they coincide in certain cases?

---

[40] *UNIDROIT Principles*, p. 85.   [41] *Ibid.*

2 Apparent authority and ratification

In the UNIDROIT Principles, it seems that apparent authority and (apparent) ratification may coincide. It seems that circumstances taking place *after* the conclusion of the contract are not only relevant as to the question of whether there is (apparent) ratification or not, but also as to whether there is apparent authority or not. This means that sometimes a third party will be able to invoke both apparent authority and (apparent) ratification on the same facts. The UNIDROIT Principles have adopted the general rule that, in interpreting a contract, regard should be had among other things to 'the conduct of the parties *subsequent*[42] to the conclusion of the contract' (Art. 4.3(c) UP). In line with this provision it seems that, as regards the doctrine of apparent authority, later circumstances should also be taken into account. If that is accepted, the doctrines of apparent authority and (apparent) ratification may coincide. This is a welcome approach, because in practice a clear distinction cannot always be drawn.

In the case of the UNIDROIT Principles, the doctrines of apparent authority and (apparent) ratification may also coincide in a different manner. In the UNIDROIT Principles, apparent authority only works *against* the principal, as a consequence of which the only way for the principal to obtain an action against the third party is to (impliedly) ratify the agent's unauthorised act.[43]

3 Apparent authority and liability of the falsus procurator

In the UNIDROIT Principles the doctrine of apparent authority and the liability of the *falsus procurator* are mutually exclusive. Either there is a valid contract because third party T successfully invokes the doctrine of apparent authority, in which case T cannot successfully sue agent A for damages on the basis of the relevant provision, or vice versa.

Now that in the UNIDROIT Principles the doctrine of apparent authority exists for the benefit of the third party, it seems that the third party is *entitled* and not *obliged* to invoke it if he does not wish to do so.[44] Therefore, third party T seems entitled *not* to invoke the doctrine of apparent authority and instead turn to agent A on the basis of Art. 2.2.6 UP regarding the liability of the false agent (this may, for instance, be beneficial for T in case P has gone bankrupt).

---

[42] Emphasis added.   [43] See also V 4, above.   [44] See V 1, above.

4 *Ratification and liability of the* falsus procurator

As we have seen, in the UNIDROIT Principles the third party in good faith may withdraw unilaterally prior to a ratification (Art. 2.2.9(3) UP).[45] If third party T withdraws before ratification takes place, agent A remains liable in damages on the basis of Art. 2.2.6 UP regarding the liability of the false agent.

After ratification A will generally be freed from his liability pursuant to Art. 2.2.6 UP regarding the liability of the false agent. The reason for this is that as a consequence of the retroactive effect of ratification, T will not normally have suffered any damage. This may be different in (at least) the following situation, however.

Comment 2 to Art. 2.2.9 UP makes it clear that T may refuse partial ratification of A's acts by P. If T refuses, A obviously remains liable. However, it may be argued that in certain circumstances T may be *obliged* to accept a partial or conditional ratification because of his duty to mitigate damage (Art. 7.4.8 UP). This seems a fair approach because even if the third party accepts a partial or conditional ratification, the *falsus procurator* remains liable on the basis of Art. 2.2.6 UP to the extent that T – notwithstanding a partial or conditional ratification by P – has suffered loss as a consequence of the unauthorised agency.[46]

IX Conclusions

This chapter concentrated on the rules with respect to unauthorised agency provided by the UNIDROIT Principles.

In part II it was explained that the agency provisions in the UNIDROIT Principles apply directly only to consensual agency in the conclusion of contracts, but that they may be applied to other cases as well.

In part III it was set out that the UNIDROIT Principles apply a uniform concept of agency, very much like in common law jurisdictions, and that it further distinguishes between disclosed and undisclosed agency.

In part IV it became clear that, in cases of unauthorised agency, neither the principal nor the third party is bound or entitled under the contract concluded by the unauthorised agent.

---

[45] See VI 4(a), above.
[46] See, for Comment 2 to Art. 2.2.9 UP, *UNIDROIT Principles*, p. 91. See, for the text of Art. 7.4.8 UP (Mitigation of Harm), n. 32, above. See also VI 4(c), above.

In part V I turned to the first main exception to the general effect of unauthorised agency: apparent authority. It turned out, among other things, that in the UNIDROIT Principles the doctrine of apparent authority not only applies where the third party reasonably believes that the agent was authorised to conclude the contract concerned where such beliefs can be traced back to acts or conduct of the principal, but also if such beliefs can be traced back to other factors which lie within the principal's sphere of risk.

In part VI I turned to the second main exception to the general effect of unauthorised agency: ratification. It became clear, among other things, that the third party in good faith may withdraw unilaterally prior to ratification. It was also set out that the third party may, by notice to the principal, specify a reasonable period of time for ratification and that – if the principal does not ratify within that period of time – he can no longer do so. It was also set out that ratification in the UNIDROIT Principles has retroactive effect.

Part VII examined the liability of the *falsus procurator*. In the UNIDROIT Principles, the third party can generally hold the unauthorised agent liable for the damage which he has suffered as a consequence of the agent's lack of authority. This rule is exempted if the third party (1) knew or (2) ought to have known that the agent had no authority or was exceeding his authority.

Part VIII dealt with the interrelationship between apparent authority, ratification and the liability of the *falsus procurator*. It was concluded that apparent authority and (apparent) ratification may sometimes coincide and that apparent authority and the liability of the *falsus procurator* are mutually exclusive. It was also concluded that, after ratification, the agent will generally be freed from his liability, because as a consequence of the retroactive effect the third party will not normally have suffered any damage.

PART 5

Conclusions

Comparative law evaluation

DANNY BUSCH AND LAURA MACGREGOR

Table of contents

I Introduction

In this chapter we come to the heart of the matter, namely identifying common approaches, or the 'common core' of the rules on unauthorised agency. In addition, as set out in the introductory chapter, we highlight the areas where the common core is deficient. To the extent that the common core is lacking, we suggest which approach is preferable.

In part II we devote some attention to the nature and general effect of unauthorised agency. Afterwards, we turn to the main exceptions to the general effect of unauthorised agency: apparent authority (III) and ratification (IV). In part V a treatment of the liability of the *falsus procurator* is provided. Part VI contains a treatment of the interrelationship between apparent authority, ratification and the liability of the *falsus procurator*. Parts VII and VIII each elaborate on special cases which can be associated with unauthorised agency, namely, acting in the name of a principal yet to be named and acting in the name of a company yet to be incorporated.

II Unauthorised agency

In the legal systems studied, unauthorised agency arises in a wide variety of cases.[1] It arises when the agent concludes a contract in the name of the principal, but has no authority at all, when he exceeds his authority or when the agent's authority has ended at the time of the conclusion of the contract.[2] The chapter on Dutch law discussed the possibility of applying the rules on unauthorised agency where the agent's authority has been nullified with retroactive effect (effect *ex tunc*), for instance because it was granted due to an error or under threat.[3] Although this possibility is not mentioned in the other chapters, it is likely that this problem is treated in the same way in those other legal systems.

The general rule in all the legal systems studied is the same: neither the principal nor the third party is bound or entitled under a contract (or other legal act) concluded by an unauthorised agent.[4] This rule protects the autonomy of the principal because it prevents him from being bound or entitled against his will. However, the interests of the third party must also be considered. As we have seen in the previous chapters, and as is elaborated on later in this chapter, in all the legal systems studied the doctrine of apparent authority in particular performs the function of

---

[1] In at least some of the legal systems studied the concept may even apply in (certain cases of) indirect agency. However, as explained in the Introduction, the focus of this book is on direct rather than indirect agency. In this comparative law evaluation we will therefore not discuss the possibility of applying the concept of unauthorised agency to (certain cases of) indirect agency.

[2] Thus explicitly: Chapter 2 (France), I, II 1 (Art. 2005 CC); Chapter 3 (Belgium), II 2, III 2 (Arts. 2005 and 2009 BCC); Chapter 4 (Germany), I, III 1 (§ 169 BGB, §§ 170 and 171 BGB, § 172 BGB, § 56 HGB, 15(1) and (3) HGB); Chapter 5 (the Netherlands), III, IV 3 (Art. 3:76 DCC); Chapter 6 (England), II 1; Chapter 9 (Scotland), II 3; Chapter 10 (South Africa), III 1; Chapter 11 (PECL), IV (Art. 3:204(1) PECL), V 3 (3:209 PECL); Chapter 12 (UP), IV (Art. 2.2.5(1) UP), V 3 (Art. 2.2.10 UP).

[3] Chapter 5 (the Netherlands), III.

[4] See explicitly: Chapter 2 (France), I; Chapter 3 (Belgium), II 2; Chapter 4 (Germany), II; Chapter 5, (the Netherlands) III; Chapter 6 (England), I; Chapter 9 (Scotland), I; Chapter 11 (PECL), IV (Art. 3:204(1) PECL); Chapter 12 (UP), IV (Art. 2.2.5(1) UP).

redressing the balance between the legitimate interests of the principal and those of the third party. This it does by providing the third party with the ability to sue the principal despite the fact that the agent was unauthorised.

The question of the exact legal nature of the unauthorised legal act prior to ratification has in most chapters not been addressed, possibly because the question has not (yet) received much attention. It has, however, been addressed in the chapters on Dutch law and German law. In Dutch law the unauthorised legal act is usually termed 'invalid',[5] whereas in German law it is described as 'floating' (*schwebende Unwirksamkeit*). The unauthorised legal act is neither void nor unenforceable nor is it completely valid, rather it is 'floating'.[6] The Dutch qualification of the unauthorised legal act as 'invalid' fails in our view to make it sufficiently clear that the principal is able to ratify the unauthorised legal act. 'Voidable' would be similarly incorrect, because it suggests that the unauthorised legal act is valid unless and until avoided, such as is the case with certain defects of consent.[7] The German solution is, in our view, attractive in its recognition that the relationship between principal and third party prior to ratification is one which cannot be placed within existing categorisations of void, voidable and invalid contracts.

III Apparent authority

1 General

A theme which unites the various differing concepts of apparent authority is the giving of validity to appearances, and protection of those who rely, in good faith, on such appearances.

Thus, in French law *mandat apparent* is part of the more general application of the wider doctrine of *l'apparence* 'whereby the French courts will attach legal consequences to a person's erroneous perception of reality'.[8] A similar approach can be found in Belgian law, where apparent authority is based on the doctrine of appearances (*schijnleer* or *vertrouwensleer*).[9] In taking this approach, the French and Belgian legal systems moved away from what had previously been the position, where liability required fault on the part of the principal and was based

---

[5] Chapter 5 (the Netherlands), III.   [6] Chapter 4 (Germany), V 1.
[7] Cf. Chapter 9 (Scotland), III 3.   [8] Chapter 2 (France), II 1.
[9] Chapter 3 (Belgium), III 2.

on tort.[10] In the Netherlands the doctrine of apparent authority is – as in France and Belgium – based on the protection of reasonable beliefs.[11] The *Restatement (Third) of Agency* and the PECL follow a similar approach.[12] The same holds true for Germany, where *Anscheinsvollmacht*, *Duldungsvollmacht* and (other) cases of constructive notice are often said to be based on the somewhat similar concept of liability for reliance (*Vertrauenshaftung*).[13]

The idea of an estoppel, which lies at the root of the doctrine of apparent authority in England and South Africa, is similar in nature: the principal is prevented from deviating from the apparent legal position which he has been intimately involved in creating.[14] In Scotland a comparable concept (personal bar) serves as the doctrinal basis.[15] In the UNIDROIT Principles apparent authority is (*inter alia*) based on the prohibition of inconsistent behaviour, a concept which is also very close to estoppel.[16] The principal's conduct – in particular the extent to which he contributed to the apparent situation – is clearly at the centre of the concepts of estoppel, personal bar and inconsistent behaviour and is considered in more detail below. However, the behaviour of the third party too is highly relevant – standards of behaviour are applied to him as part of the exercise of determining on whom the loss ought to fall.

2 Scope

The scope of application of the doctrine of apparent authority is extensive in many respects. It generally operates both in cases where the agent exceeds his authority, and where he has no authority whatsoever.[17] In Belgian law at least, and probably also in the other systems, it can operate

---

[10] Chapter 3 (Belgium), III 2; Chapter 4 (France), II 1 (Art. 1382 CC).

[11] Chapter 5 (the Netherlands), IV 1.

[12] Chapter 7 (US), III 2; Chapter 11 (PECL), V 1. It should be noted that in the *Restatement (Third) of Agency*, alongside the doctrine of apparent authority, the doctrine of estoppel is used as a separate basis of attribution of unauthorised acts to the principal. See Chapter 7 (US), III 3 (*Restatement (Third) of Agency* § 2.05).

[13] Chapter 4 (Germany), III, Introduction, III 4(c), IV 1.

[14] Chapter 6 (England), II 5; Chapter 10 (South Africa), II 1.

[15] Chapter 9 (Scotland), II 2.

[16] Chapter 12 (UP), V 1. It should, however, be noted that apparent authority in the UP is not only based on the prohibition against inconsistent behaviour (Art. 1.8 UP), but also based on the general principle of good faith (Art. 1.7 UP).

[17] Thus explicitly: Chapter 2 (France), I; Chapter 3 (Belgium), III 3; Chapter 6 (England), II 1; Chapter 9 (Scotland) II 3.

where the contract of agency between principal and agent is affected by nullity.[18] Furthermore, in most of the systems studied, the doctrine of apparent authority not only operates in the context of the unauthorised conclusion of contracts, but also (sometimes by way of analogy) to other unauthorised legal acts.[19] In addition, in some of the systems studied the doctrine extends beyond the context of consensual unauthorised agency (e.g. in the context of authority pursuant to a statutory provision or judicial order or in the context of representation by a body of a legal person).[20] Finally, at least in the Netherlands, the doctrine can even apply to unauthorised legal acts performed outside the area of patrimonial law, in areas such as family law, procedural law and public law.[21]

Many of the legal systems analysed in this book contain special provisions which seek to achieve an equitable solution where the agent's authority has terminated and yet the agent is unaware of this fact, for example, because of the death, mental incapacity or bankruptcy of the principal or merely because the principal revoked the authority granted to his agent.

Some systems contain detailed provisions for the effects of termination of authority towards the third party. For example, Dutch law provides that the third party who has *actual* knowledge of either the

---

[18] Chapter 3 (Belgium), III 3.

[19] Thus explicitly *Restatement (Third) of Agency*, § 2.03, where apparent authority is defined as 'the power held by an agent or other actor to affect a principal's *legal relations* with third parties when a third party reasonably believes the actor has authority to act on behalf of the principal and that belief is traceable to the principal's manifestations' (emphasis added). See Chapter 7 (US), III 2. The Dutch doctrine of apparent authority likewise applies to unauthorised agency with respect to legal acts in general. See explicitly the text of Art. 3:61(2) DCC on apparent authority: 'Where a *legal act* has been performed in the name of another person, the third party who, on the basis of a declaration or conduct of that other person, has assumed and in the given circumstances could reasonably assume the existence of sufficient authority, may not have invoked against him the inaccuracy of this assumption.' (emphasis added). See Chapter 5 (the Netherlands), IV 2. Similarly, German law, where *Duldungsvollmacht*, *Anscheinsvollmacht* and (other) cases of constructive notice can all be applied with respect to legal acts in general. See Chapter 4 (Germany), III, IV (where reference is made to the agent's actions). See also Chapter 9 (Scotland) II 3; Chapter 11 (PECL), V 3 (Art. 3:201(3) PECL read in conjunction with Art. 1:107 PECL).

[20] Chapter 5 (the Netherlands), IV 3. See also Chapter 3 (Belgium), III 3, where it is commented that apparent authority can also be applied when the principal is a legal person. See further Chapter 9 (Scotland) II 3. In South African law, apparent authority can sometimes operate in the context of legal persons as well, see Chapter 10 (South Africa), II 7. Similarly, in the PECL and the UNIDROIT Principles the doctrine of ratification can sometimes be applied in the context of legal persons. See Chapter 11 (PECL), V 3; Chapter 12 (UP), V 3.

[21] Chapter 5 (the Netherlands), IV 3 (Art. 3:61(2) DCC read in conjunction with Art. 3:79 DCC).

termination itself or the terminating event will not be able to consider the agent as remaining authorised. It is furthermore provided that the agent's lack of authority cannot be invoked by the principal where the third party has no actual knowledge of the termination itself or the terminating event. However, in four situations the Dutch legislature considered it appropriate for the principal to be able to invoke the termination of the agent's authority against the third party even though the third party had no actual knowledge of the termination itself or the terminating event. The first situation concerns cases where the third party is deemed to have received a communication with respect to the termination, although the communication actually failed to reach him. The first situation also concerns cases where the termination has been made public, but where the third party did not notice the publication of the termination of the agent's authority. The second situation concerns the case where the death of the principal is generally known (e.g. the death of a famous person whose death has been extensively publicised and/or broadcast). The third situation concerns cases where the appointment or employment that gave rise to the agent's authority has been terminated in a fashion apparent to third parties. Finally, the fourth situation concerns the case where the third party exclusively relied on the agent's statement that he was so authorised. In such cases, the termination of this authority may always be invoked by the principal against the third party.[22] A similarly detailed approach is also adopted in German law and the PECL.[23]

In this context it is worth noting that French and Belgian law both devote statutory provisions to this situation, protecting the third party in good faith against a revocation of authority by the principal.[24] In Belgian law the legal doctrine and case-law have developed the general doctrine of apparent authority[25] from these statutory provisions. Similarly, Scots law contains relatively early authority on the termination of authority because of the principal's death, mental incapacity or bankruptcy. Possibly this is a reflection of a shared civilian background.[26]

---

[22] Chapter 5 (the Netherlands), IV 3 (Art. 3:76(1) DCC).

[23] Chapter 4 (Germany), III 1 (§ 169 BGB (authority ends as a consequence of the termination of the underlying contract), § 170 and § 171 BGB (declaration or notice of the authority to the third party), § 172 BGB (authority in writing)); Chapter 11 (PECL), V 3 (Art. 3:209 PECL (Duration of Authority)).

[24] Chapter 2 (France), II 1 (Art. 2005 CC); Chapter 3 (Belgium), III 2 (Arts. 2005 and 2009 BCC).

[25] Chapter 3 (Belgium), III 2.

[26] Chapter 9 (Scotland), II 3 (*Pollock* v. *Paterson* 10 Dec (1811) FC 369, per Lord Meadowbank at 377).

Other systems follow a more general approach, such as the UNIDROIT Principles, which simply provide that termination of authority is not effective in relation to the third party unless the third party knew or ought to have known of it and that, notwithstanding the termination of its authority, an agent remains authorised to perform the acts that are necessary to prevent harm to the principal's interests.[27]

We favour the general approach in the UNIDROIT Principles. It provides the courts with a certain degree of discretion as to whether a third party ought to have known of the termination of the authority of the agent. It seems misconceived to seek to enumerate every factual circumstance in which the agent's authority has been terminated, unbeknown to him. A broad discretion is therefore necessary. In our view, this type of discretion is required to enable the court to make 'tailor-made' decisions.

3 Effect

The legal systems studied adopt the same approach by allowing the third party to sue the principal, notwithstanding the fact that the agent was not (sufficiently) authorised. The exact nature of such entitlement differs, however. The systems studied also diverge in that not all of them entitle the principal to sue the third party on the basis of apparent authority, and, if they do, not in all circumstances. Broadly speaking, there are three different approaches.

The least far-reaching approach can be found in those systems which use an estoppel (or a similar concept, such as personal bar or the prohibition against inconsistent behaviour) to explain apparent authority. Thus, in England, Scotland, South Africa and the UNIDROIT Principles, apparent authority only operates in order to prevent certain conduct on the part of the principal, namely, the denial that the agent was authorised. Thus, the third party can hold the principal liable, not because the principal has given any kind of authority to his agent for the acts purportedly carried out on his behalf, but because he is estopped from denying that he did not in fact give actual authority for those acts. In other words, the principal cannot deny that a valid contract has been concluded with the third party. From this it follows that the third party can claim damages from the principal on a contractual basis, i.e. the third party can claim expectation damages (rather than reliance damages). Specific performance, however,

---

[27] Chapter 12 (UP), V 3 (Art. 2.2.10 UP (Termination of Authority)).

is rare in common law systems and therefore unlikely to be available in this context. The position is slightly different in Scotland, where specific implement is, at least in theory, the primary remedy. However, given that the Scottish version of apparent authority is a type of personal bar, there is no contract which the third party can seek to enforce. The position is probably also different in the UNIDROIT Principles, which in general acknowledge the right to performance.[28] Furthermore, it follows from the very nature of estoppel (and the similar concepts of personal bar and inconsistent behaviour) that it can only serve as a basis for a right of the third party to sue the principal and not the other way around. The principal cannot invoke the doctrine of apparent authority and can therefore only sue the third party after he has (impliedly) ratified the unauthorised act.[29]

The most far-reaching approach can be found in the *Restatement (Third) of Agency* and the PECL. In those legal systems, both the third party and the principal can invoke apparent authority. In these systems apparent authority is merely an application of the objective theory of contract. Consequently, an act which is unauthorised but which reasonably appears to be authorised is simply considered a valid act. In view of this, the third party and the principal receive as much protection as they would have had if they had been bound and entitled under a valid contract. Consequently, both principal and third party can invoke apparent authority. If one of them invokes the doctrine, principal and third party are both bound and entitled under the unauthorised contract. This means that both principal and third party are entitled to contractual damages, i.e. expectation rather than reliance damages. In addition (in any event in the PECL), the principal and the third party are entitled to specific performance, which is – at least in theory – the primary contractual remedy in civil law jurisdictions.[30]

An intermediate position can be found in Belgium and the Netherlands. In both these systems, only the third party (and not the

---

[28] See Chapter 7, Section 2 (Right to performance) of the UNIDROIT Principles.

[29] Chapter 6 (England), II 5; Chapter 9 (Scotland), II 4; Chapter 10 (South Africa), II 1; Chapter 12 (UP), V 4.

[30] Chapter 7 (US), III 2; Chapter 11 (PECL), V 4. It should be noted that although in the *Restatement (Third) of Agency* (and in the *Restatement (Second) of Agency*) apparent authority is not based on estoppel but on the objective theory of contract, estoppel is – alongside apparent authority – accepted as a basis of attribution of the unauthorised legal act. See Chapter 7 (US), III 3 (*Restatement (Third) of Agency* § 2.05). See, for the point that the PECL in general acknowledge the right to performance, Section 1 (Right to Performance) of Chapter 9 (Particular Remedies for Non-Performance) of the PECL.

principal) can invoke apparent authority. In both systems, the third party is *entitled* and not *obliged* to invoke it, although in the Netherlands in practice he may be bound by the requirements of reasonableness and fairness to concede this stance where it is clear that the principal wishes to uphold the unauthorised legal act. However, if the third party successfully invokes apparent authority, neither the principal nor the third party can deny that a valid contract exists and consequently both the principal and the third party are bound and entitled under the contract concluded by the unauthorised agent. This means that, as soon as the third party successfully invokes the doctrine, the principal can additionally sue the third party. Both principal and third party are entitled to expectation damages. Furthermore, because specific performance is, at least in theory, the primary remedy in these systems, both principal and third party will be entitled to specific performance.[31]

In practical terms, it is probably not particularly significant which of the above three approaches is applied. In the objective approach the principal can sue the third party on the basis of apparent authority. In the estoppel approach the principal cannot sue the third party on that basis, nor can he do so in the intermediate approach to the extent that the

---

[31] Chapter 3 (Belgium), III 5; Chapter 5 (the Netherlands), IV 4. It should be noted that the situation in Germany is more complex and at least partially subject to much debate. A distinction must be made between cases of constructive authority (prolongation of an authority which has already ended, the authority of employees in stores and warehouses and *Duldungsvollmacht*) on the one hand, and 'true' apparent authority (*Anscheinsvollmacht*) on the other. The cases of constructive authority are generally (but not always) regarded as cases in which the legal fiction applies that the agent was authorised, although in reality he was not. See Chapter 4 (Germany), III. It can be inferred from this that, in terms of a legal fiction, a valid contract is concluded between the principal and the third party, allowing them to sue one another claiming not only expectation damages (rather than reliance damages) but also specific performance. The exact legal nature of cases of 'true' apparent authority is subject to much debate. The prevailing view is that it should be equated with constructive authority. According to the authors of the chapter on German law (and although this is not the prevailing view in Germany), it should be regarded as a device which merely protects the reliance of the third party and gives him a claim for damages for the reliance interest (rather than expectation damages) and does not grant him a right of specific performance. See Chapter 4 (Germany), IV 1 and VII. In other words, according to the authors of the chapter on German law, in cases of 'true' apparent authority, it is likely that no legal fiction applies, dictating that the agent was authorised where in reality he was not. In these authors' view, the situation is therefore not assimilated with a valid contract and hence it is likely that the principal does not have the right to sue the third party in such cases. The position in France is also not entirely clear. The third party can sue the principal on the basis of *mandat apparent*, but it is not clear whether the principal can sue the third party on that basis. See Chapter 2 (France), II and n. 13.

third party has not already invoked apparent authority. However, if in the estoppel approach and the intermediate approach the principal nevertheless sues the third party, this is likely to amount to an implied ratification. Furthermore, a claim for specific performance will be more difficult to justify in the estoppel approach than in the objective or intermediate approach. However, also in civil law countries where the objective or intermediate approach applies, claims are in practice usually settled by payment of damages.

4 Requirements

(a) Words or conduct of the principal, and extensions beyond that basis

The legal systems studied display a similar tension between the desire to impose liability on the principal only where the erroneous impression of authority was created through his actions and a recognition that liability must extend wider in order to achieve the ultimate goal of third party protection.

In most of the systems studied, the starting point is indeed the identification of words or conduct on the part of the principal which caused the impression of authority. This approach is taken in Dutch law, English law, German law, South African law, the PECL and the UNIDROIT Principles.[32] In English law and South African law, words or conduct of the principal are classified as a 'representation' of authority.[33] Other systems have a slightly wider approach, Scotland relying on 'inconsistent conduct'[34] and the Restatement (Third) of Agency on 'manifestations'[35] on the part of the principal, which the author of the US chapter notes can be made by the principal in 'manifold ways'.[36] However, even in those systems where the starting point is words or conduct on the part of the principal, liability extends wider, including situations in which the principal has remained silent or passive notwithstanding the fact that circumstances impose a duty on him to act in order to dispel the

---

[32] Chapter 4 (Germany), IV 1; Chapter 5 (the Netherlands), IV 5(a) (Art. 3:61(2) DCC); Chapter 6 (England), II 3; Chapter 10 (South Africa), II 2; Chapter 11 (PECL), V 5 (a) (Art. 3:201(3) PECL); Chapter 12 (UP), V 5(a) (Art. 2.2.5(2) UP).

[33] Chapter 6 (England), II 3; Chapter 10 (South Africa), II 2.

[34] Chapter 10 (Scotland), II 5(a).

[35] Chapter 7 (US), III 2 (Restatement (Third) of Agency § 2.03).

[36] Chapter 7 (US), III 2.

erroneous impression of authority.[37] In particular, while liability may not be imposed on a principal for a single unauthorised transaction, repeat transactions may lead to a finding that he has tolerated the course of dealing.[38]

However, liability extends even further in most of the legal systems studied. In Dutch law, English law, German law, Scots law, South African law, the PECL and the UNIDROIT Principles, the 'representation' commonly takes the form of the appointment of the agent to a position in which it is usual to have certain authority.[39] Limitations of authority unknown to third parties, in that case, will not be effective. Provisions imposing liability on the principal where he has left goods with agents working in warehouses or stores, 'factors' or 'mercantile agents' in common law parlance, are no more than examples of this type of liability.[40]

Liability also extends further in the *Restatement (Third) of Agency*, where, through the operation of an estoppel, a third party may be protected where the transaction is believed to be for the principal's account. Liability is imposed where the third party can establish either: (1) that 'the person intentionally or carelessly caused' the third party to believe the actor acted with authority; or (2) that 'having notice of such belief and that it might induce others to change their positions, the person did not take reasonable steps to notify them of the facts'.[41]

---

[37] See, e.g., Chapter 5 (the Netherlands), IV 5(a) (HR 1 March 1968, NJ 1968, 246 (*Molukse Evangelische Kerk* v. *Clijnk*)); Chapter 9 (Scotland), II 5(a) (*International Sponge Importers* v. *Watt and Sons* 1911 SC (HL) 57); Chapter 10 (South Africa), II 2 (*Jones and others* v. *Trust Bank of Africa Ltd and others* 1993 (4) SA 415 (C) at 425B–C).

[38] See Chapter 9 (Scotland), II 5(a) (*International Sponge Importers* v. *Watt and Sons* 1911 SC (HL) 57). See also the German concept of *Duldungsvollmacht*, applicable where the principal knowingly tolerated the course of action, as opposed to *Anscheinsvollmacht* which is appropriate where there is no knowledge of the unauthorised agent's acts. See Chapter 4 (Germany), III 4(a) and (b).

[39] Chapter 4 (Germany), III 2 (§ 54(3) and § 56 HGB (the authority of employees in stores and warehouses)); Chapter 5 (the Netherlands), IV 5(a) (HR 27 November 1992, NJ 1993, 287, with annotation by PvS (*Felix* v. *Aruba*); HR 9 October 1998, 1999, NJ 581 (*Hartman* v. *Bakker*); HR 24 April 1992, NJ 1993, 190, with annotation by HJS (*Kuyt* v. *MEAS*)); Chapter 6 (England), II 2; Chapter 9 (Scotland) II 5(a); Chapter 10 (South Africa), II 2 (*South African Eagle Insurance Co. Ltd.* v. *NBS Bank Ltd* 2002 (1) SA 560 (SCA) at 573H–574B; *Reed NO* v. *Sager's Motors (Pvt) Ltd* 1970 (1) SA 521 (RA) at 524H–525A); Chapter 11 (PECL), V 5(a); Chapter 12 (UP), V 5(a).

[40] See Chapter 4 (Germany), III 2 (§ 54 (3) and § 56 HGB. See, for English law, the Factors Act 1889, s. 2, applied to Scotland by the Factors (Scotland) Act 1890, s. 1. It is notable that in the UK and Germany the third party is only protected by this legislation where he has acted in good faith.

[41] Chapter 7 (US), III 3 (*Restatement (Third) of Agency* § 2.05).

It should be noted that South African law applies a unique requirement here: the representation itself must have been of such a nature
that the principal could reasonably have expected it to be acted on.[42] This
additional objective requirement, not found in Scots or English law,
has a protective effect towards the principal. As was noted in one of the
leading cases:

> to have regard only to the position of the representee in applying the
> objective test could in certain circumstances bear unjustly or unduly harshly
> on a representor, especially if he is innocent or blameless, and because the
> foundation of estoppel is still equity, our courts have evolved a different
> approach.[43]

The requirement seems slightly unusual, given the trend in almost all of
the systems to increase rather than decrease liability on the principal's part.

In contrast to the position in the systems commented on above, in
some of the civil law systems studied the starting position is more
objective. In these systems the focus is not on the principal's words or
conduct, but rather on the appearance of the agent's authority in the
circumstances. In both the Belgian and French legal systems, historically,
liability was tort-based, dependent on the principal's fault.[44] As is nar-
rated in the chapter on French law, fault began to be very widely defined
before being abandoned.[45] In the modern approach, the focus has shifted
to the legitimacy of the third party's belief in the agent's authority in the
circumstances.[46] So too in Belgian law, what is required in a modern
context is the appearance of sufficient authority to represent.[47] However,
even in these systems the analysis is not entirely objective. After animated debate in legal doctrine, the Belgian Court of Cassation finally
decided that the appearance of authority must be 'imputable' to the
principal.[48] Imputability was later defined. It means that the principal

---

[42] Chapter 10 (South Africa), II 3 (*Monzali* v. *Smith* 1929 AD 382).

[43] Chapter 10 (South Africa), II 3 (*Connock's Motor Co* v. *Sentraal Westelike Ko-op* 1964 (2)
SA 47 (T) at 50D–E, per Trollip J). Although it appears that this requirement only applies
where the representation is implied, the author of the chapter on South African law
argues in favour of its application to cases of express representation also, see Chapter 10
(South Africa), II 3.

[44] Chapter 2 (France), II 1; Chapter 3 (Belgium), III 2.   [45] Chapter 2 (France), II 1.

[46] Chapter 2 (France), II 1 (*Cass Ass Plén 13-12-1962, Banque Canadienne Nationale, D*
1963, J 277, note J Calais-Auloy).

[47] Chapter 3 (Belgium), III 4(b).

[48] Chapter 3 (Belgium), III 4(d) (Cass. 20 January 2000, *RW* 2001–02 (summary), 501, obs.
(mistake *RW* 2001–02, 792), *TBH* 2000, 483, obs. P.-A. Foriers and *RGDC* 2001, 407).

had 'voluntarily contributed by his conduct, even faultless, to create an appearance or had tacitly permitted the appearance to exist'.[49] So too in French law, the principal's fault is not entirely irrelevant, some arguing that it can be taken into account if it has created or contributed to the erroneous belief of the third party.[50]

Dutch law contains possibly the most overt recognition of the tension between the subjective and objective approaches. In the Netherlands, liability is based on the principal's conduct: the third party's reasonable belief must have been created by the principal 'of his own doing', i.e. by way of his declaration or conduct.[51] This is supplemented by the 'risk principle', however, an idea which had its source in Dutch academic literature, but has been applied in recent Dutch case law.[52] The risk principle permits Dutch courts to impose liability on the principal where the impression of authority has been created not by the principal's conduct as such, but by other circumstances that come within the ambit of the risks borne by the principal.[53] The task thus becomes more discretionary, involving an assessment of who ought to bear the risk of giving the impression of authority. In the PECL and UNIDROIT Principles the 'of the principal's own doing' principle is similarly supplemented by the risk principle.[54]

At first glance there appears to be a difference of approach between English law, German law, Scots law and South African law on the one hand, where liability is more firmly linked to the principal's actions, and Belgian law, Dutch law, French law, the PECL and the UNIDROIT Principles on the other hand, where the focus falls on the whole circumstances of the case. However, it is unlikely that there is any real difference of approach. Each legal system attempts to carry out a type of uneasy compromise. No legal system appears to have rejected the connection with the principal's conduct entirely. The courts benefit from some discretion in their selection of the circumstances which they consider to be relevant. In essence, the exercise involves the 'manipulation' of such circumstances in order to decide on whom the loss ought to fall. Liability

---

[49]   Chapter 3 (Belgium), III 4(d) (Cass. 25 June 2004, *RGDC* 2004, 457).

[50]   Chapter 2 (France), II 2(a) (i) (under the heading 'circumstances relating to the principal').

[51]   Chapter 5 (the Netherlands), IV 5(a) (under the heading 'declaration or conduct of the principal').

[52]   Most notably in HR 27 November 1992, *NJ* 1993, 287, with annotation by PvS (*Felix* v. *Aruba*). See Chapter 5 (the Netherlands), IV 5(a) (under the heading 'risk principle').

[53]   See Chapter 5 (the Netherlands), IV 5(a) (under the heading 'risk principle').

[54]   Chapter 11 (PECL), V 5(a) (Comment D to Art. 3:201 PECL); Chapter 12 (UP), V 5(a) (Comment 2 to Art. 2.2.5 UP).

is more likely to fall on the principal as the party with more control over the situation, compared to the third party.

There are factors which support the use of the whole circumstances in the exercise of attributing liability. It avoids the strained expansion of the 'of the principal's own doing' idea which is taking place in certain jurisdictions. More and more factors are being classed, unconvincingly, as 'conduct' of the principal.[55] By placing the focus on all the circumstances of the case and thus expanding liability beyond 'conduct', the courts are able to focus on issues lying within the principal's responsibility. To this extent it is a less artificial method of imposing liability. It makes explicit factors which were already implicit in classical apparent authority reasoning, and provides those factors with a clearer legal basis. As a more nuanced approach, it enables the courts to reach solutions which can be 'tailor-made' to the case. In this way, particularly in the systems which adhere more firmly to the 'of the principal's own doing' approach, the courts can redress the balance which, in those systems, is likely to be weighted towards protection of the principal.

There are, however, arguments against this more expansive approach. It may result in a large, and perhaps unmanageable, increase in the principal's liability. Whether this is likely to occur is difficult to assess. It may well be that the end result would not be markedly different from the current approach, in which the 'of the principal's own doing' idea is artificially extended. Like any discretionary concept, its success depends on the manner in which it is applied by the courts. It is unlikely that the discretion could be limited by specifying all potentially relevant issues: the courts would be asked to apply a relatively open discretion, guided by factors highlighted as significant in existing case-law. Certainly the Dutch experience suggests that the discretion is workable. It may even act as an incentive for the principal to ensure that his agents act within the confines of their authority in the future.

(b) Third party could reasonably presume the existence of sufficient authority

Although the principal's actions form the main focus of enquiry for liability in apparent authority, the third party's actions are also relevant. In certain of the systems studied, the duties imposed on the third party

---

[55] See, e.g., *First Energy (UK) Ltd* v. *Hungarian International Bank Ltd* [1993] 2 Lloyd's Rep 194 at 201, per Steyn LJ (on which see Chapter 6 (England), II 3); *Pacific Carriers Ltd* v. *BNP Paribas* (2004) 208 ALR 213 at 226 (a decision of the full court).

could be described as 'overt' ones. The essential question here is whether the third party acted reasonably in presuming the existence of sufficient authority.

In Dutch law it is necessary that the third party in the given circumstances could reasonably assume the existence of sufficient authority.[56] This issue is judged against the background of the principles of reasonableness and fairness.[57] Depending on the circumstances of the case reasonableness and fairness can result in a duty to investigate whether the agent possesses sufficient authority.[58] In the PECL it is, according to the Comments, likewise required that the third party 'was entitled to rely ... upon the impression that the principal had in fact granted authority', although this requirement is not elaborated on further in the Comments.[59] In the UNIDROIT Principles it is similarly required that the third party reasonably believed that the agent had (sufficient) authority. The Comments make it clear that whether or not the third party's belief was reasonable will depend on the circumstances of the case.[60] In German law this is not stipulated as a separate requirement, but it seems unlikely that a court would allow a third party successfully to invoke apparent authority where the belief of the third party was *not* reasonable.

In the Belgian and French systems, this idea has its basis in good faith.[61] In both systems, a number of factual issues have been identified as relevant to the assessment of the legitimacy of the third party's belief, for example, the third party's status, education and employment details, including the type of responsibility involved in his employment.[62] The author of the chapter on French law notes that non-professionals are more likely to find that their belief is excused compared to professionals.[63] It is likely that the

---

[56] Chapter 5 (the Netherlands), IV 5(b). The German test is similar, the point of reference being a reasonable person in the shoes of the third party who would have reasonably inferred that the agent was acting with authority, see Chapter 4 (Germany), IV 1.

[57] *Redelijkheid en billijkheid* (Arts. 6:2 and 3:11 DCC). See Chapter 5 (the Netherlands), IV 5(b).

[58] Chapter 5 (the Netherlands), IV 5(b) (HR 24 April 1992, NJ 1993, 190, with annotation by HJS (*Kuyt* v. *MEAS*)).

[59] Chapter 11 (PECL), V 5(b) (Comment D to Art. 3:201 PECL).

[60] Chapter 12 (UP), V 5(b) (Comment 2 to Art. 2.2.5 UP).

[61] Chapter 2 (France), II 2(a)(i) (under the heading 'circumstances relating to the victim of the apparent authority'); Chapter 3 (Belgium), III 4(c).

[62] Chapter 2 (France), II 2(a)(i) (under the heading 'circumstances relating to the victim of the apparent authority'); Chapter 3 (Belgium), III 4(c).

[63] Chapter 2 (France), II 2(a)(i) (under the heading 'circumstances relating to the victim of the apparent authority').

same factual issues would be relevant in cases decided by the courts in common law countries and in mixed legal systems.[64]

The treatment of this issue in England, Scotland, South Africa and in the *Restatement (Third) of Agency* is slightly different. In those systems the focus lies on the third party's reliance on the representation.[65] Reliance is, of course, a component part of estoppel and so its appearance here is not surprising, given that apparent authority is, in the common law systems based on, or at least closely related to, the law of estoppel.[66] Nevertheless, the concept of 'reliance' is a difficult one which suffers from a lack of analysis.[67] For example, there is often a failure clearly to distinguish between the reasonableness of the reliance (the issue considered in this section) and actual reliance (the issue considered immediately below). This is true of English law,[68] less so of Scots law,[69] but not true of South African law, where the distinction is clearly made.[70] This problem may arise as a result of the manner in which common law systems use case-law to expand such ideas. For example, there is no real difference of treatment of cases in which it is clear that the third party knew that the agent was not authorised, and in which actual causation is lacking, and cases in which the third party only suspected that the agent was not authorised, in which the third party is unsuccessful because he failed to investigate his suspicions, and thus failed to meet the standard of reasonable behaviour. The legal systems studied probably reach the same results on similar facts. This proposition is supported by the fact that, in

---

[64] See, e.g., the leading South African case of *Glofinco v. Absa Bank Ltd t/a United Bank* 2002 (6) SA 470 (SCA) at 496, in which it was noted that the third party was no financial 'neophyte', and by his own admission had had concerns about the transaction. See Chapter 10 (South Africa), II 5.

[65] Chapter 6 (England), II 4; Chapter 7 (US), III 2; Chapter 9 (Scotland), II 5(b); Chapter 10 (South Africa), II 5.

[66] Chapter 6 (England), II 5 (estoppel); Chapter 9 (Scotland), II 2 (personal bar); Chapter 10 (South Africa), II 1. It should, however, be noted that apparent authority is, in the *Restatement (Third) of Agency* and the *Restatement (Second) on Agency*, strictly speaking not based on estoppel. The author of the US chapter remarks that there is a 'crisp demarcation between apparent authority and estoppel as distinct bases for attribution'. See Chapter 7 (US), III 2.

[67] The author of the US chapter notes that '[w]hat "reliance" requires in this context is rarely articulated'. See Chapter 7 (US), III 2.

[68] See Chapter 6 (England), II 4 (where these issues are considered together in the same section).

[69] See Chapter 9 (Scotland), II 5(b) and (c) (where these issues are considered in separate sections).

[70] See Chapter 10 (South Africa), II 4, 5 (where these issues are considered in separate sections).

many of the systems studied, unusual circumstances may combine in order to impose a duty of inquiry.[71] It is also perhaps not surprising that the standard of behaviour required of the third party is more clearly articulated in systems possessing more developed ideas of good faith, such as the Dutch and French systems, in contrast to the common law ones, where such ideas remain in a state of infancy.

(c) Third party has presumed the existence of sufficient authority

In most systems actual causation must be proved.[72] In the common law systems and the mixed legal systems studied, this involves asking whether the third party did, in fact, rely on the principal's representation.[73] In those systems, as is the case in some of the civil law systems, this issue is illustrated by cases in which the third party is defeated because it is proved that he was actually aware that the agent was not authorised.[74] In the PECL it is likewise required that the third party has actually relied upon the impression that the principal had in fact granted authority.[75] In the UNIDROIT Principles, however, the only requirement is that the third party reasonably believed that the agent was authorised: there is no

---

[71] Chapter 3 (Belgium) III 4(c) (Brussels 29 September 2004, *Bank Fin R* 2005, 340, obs. H. van Acker; Brussels 23 October 2003, *Rev not b* 2004, 260); Chapter 5 (the Netherlands), IV 5(b) (HR 24 April 1992, NJ 1993, 190, with annotation by HJS (*Kuyt* v. *MEAS*)); Chapter 6 (England), II 4 (*Hopkins* v. *TL Dallas Group Ltd* [2005] 1 BCLC 543); Chapter 9 (Scotland), II 5(b) (*Dornier GmbH* v. *Cannon* 1991 SC 310 at 315, per Lord President Hope).

[72] See, e.g., Belgian law, in which this is the subjective part of the subjective and objective enquiry required in order to establish the legitimacy of the third party's belief: the third party must not have been aware that the appearance does not correspond with reality. See Chapter 3 (Belgium), III 4(c). In German law the inference of the third party must be 'directly caused' by the principal's words and/or actions. See Chapter 4 (Germany), IV 1.

[73] Chapter 6 (England), II 4 (see in particular *Freeman & Lockyer* v. *Buckhurst Park Properties (Mangal) Ltd* [1964] 2 QB 480 at 503); Chapter 9 (Scotland), II 5(c); Chapter 10 (South Africa), II 4.

[74] Chapter 2 (France), II 2(a)(i) (under the heading 'circumstances relating to the victim of the apparent authority') (*CA Bastia 20-12-1985 SARL d'Etudes et de Réalisations Immobilières Sériomo*; *Ass Le Cyste et Ass diocésaine du diocese d'Ajaccio* v. *Consorts Orazzi*, D 1987, 363); Chapter 9 (Scotland), II 5 (c) (*Smith* v. *North British Railway Co.* [1850] 12 D 795; *North of Scotland Banking Company* v. *Behn, Möller & Co* (1881) 8R 423; *City of Glasgow Bank* v. *Moore* (1881) 19 SLR 86; *Main & Co.* v. *Young* (1907) 23 Sh Ct Rep 295); Chapter 10 (South Africa), II 5 (*Standard Bank of SA Ltd* v. *Oneanate Investments (Pty) Ltd* 1995 4 SA 510 (C); *Hauptfleisch* v. *Caledon Divisional Council* 1963 (4) SA 53 (C) at 57C–D).

[75] Chapter 11 (PECL), V 5(c) (Comment D to Art. 3:201 PECL).

separate condition that the third party actually believed that the agent was authorised.[76]

The approach of Dutch law is notable: the third party who has already proved that he acted reasonably in presuming the existence of authority need not fulfil the further causal requirement, unless the principal succeeds in shifting the burden of proof.[77] This is, we would suggest, a reasonable and well-balanced approach.

(d) Loss

The importance of the third party's reliance on the principal's represen-tation is noted above. This is, of course, relevant in systems in which apparent authority is a form of estoppel by representation (England and South Africa) or personal bar (Scotland). It is also relevant in the German system in which *Duldungsvollmacht* and *Anscheinsvollmacht* (types of apparent authority) are often (but not by all the legal authors) regarded as a device protecting the third party's reliance. Given the underlying basis of estoppel and personal bar (namely detrimental reliance), it is not surprising to note that loss too is an important issue in those systems.[78]

By contrast, loss as a concept receives little attention in Belgium, France, the Netherlands and in the PECL.[79] This may be because it is so obvious that it goes without saying. In other words, it is assumed that the third party is able to prove a relevant loss, otherwise his case would fail at the first hurdle.

Looking at the analyses of loss appearing in the chapters on English, Scots and South African law, it is clear that it has suffered from a some-what troubled history. The root of the problem appears to be the rela-tionship between apparent authority and estoppel. Apparent authority cases fit the estoppel by representation model only with difficulty, parti-cularly because the loss suffered by the third party is considered to be small in comparison to other estoppel by representation cases.[80] For

---

[76] Chapter 12 (UP), V 5.

[77] Chapter 5 (the Netherlands), IV 5(c) (HR 26 September 2003, NJ 2004, 460, with annotation by JBMV under NJ 2004, 461; JOR 2004/32, with annotation by SCJJK (*Regiopolitie Gelderland-Zuid* v. *Hovax*)).

[78] Chapter 4 (Germany), III 4(c) (*Duldungsvollmacht*), IV 1 (*Anscheinsvollmacht*); Chapter 6 (England), II 5; Chapter 9 (Scotland), II 5 (d); Chapter 10 (South Africa), II 6.

[79] Chapter 2 (France) (loss is not treated as a separate requirement); Chapter 3 (Belgium), III 4(e) (according to the modern view a separate condition of damage is not necessary); Chapter 5 (the Netherlands), V 5 (b) (loss is not treated as a separate requirement); Chapter 11 (PECL), V 5 (d) (no detriment required).

[80] See in particular Chapter 6 (England), II 5.

example, in English law, the third party's change of position in entering into a contract with the principal is identified as the relevant loss.[81] However, there is evidence in these cases of 'broad views' being taken by the judiciary. In both Scots and South African law, although the third party must prove that he has suffered prejudice through an alteration to his position, prejudice itself is interpreted very broadly.[82]

Taking all of these issues into account, it seems that not much will be lost if the requirement of a detriment were removed in those systems which explain apparent authority on the basis of estoppel or personal bar. It is interesting to note that in the UNIDROIT Principles apparent authority is not only based on the general principle of good faith, but also on the prohibition of inconsistent behaviour, which is a concept very close to estoppel. Indeed, the provision on inconsistent behaviour in the UNIDROIT Principles requires detrimental reliance. However, this requirement does not re-appear in the provision on apparent authority.[83] In other words, in the UNIDROIT Principles it is possible to explain apparent authority (at least in part) as a concept very close to an estoppel (prohibition of inconsistent behaviour) without at the same time requiring detrimental reliance. This approach could be used as an example for legal reform in England, Scotland and South Africa.

IV Ratification

1 General

Each of the systems studied exhibits a similar attitude towards the ability of the principal to ratify the contract. As a general rule, the unauthorised agent fails to form a contract between principal and third party.[84] Ratification may therefore be available as a method allowing the principal to give effect to what would otherwise be a non-binding contract.

---

[81] Chapter 6 (England), II 5.

[82] Chapter 9 (Scotland), II 5(d); Chapter 10 (South Africa), II 6. Indeed, a dictum of Dixon J in *Grundt* v. *Great Boulder Pty Gold Mines Ltd* (1937) 59 CLR 541 at 674, has proved influential in both Scottish and South African cases and commentary, see Chapter 9 (Scotland), II 5(d).

[83] Chapter 12 (UP), V 5(c) (contrast Art. 1.8 UP on the prohibition of inconsistent behaviour with Art. 2.2.5(2) UP on apparent authority).

[84] See explicitly: Chapter 2 (France), I; Chapter 3 (Belgium), II 2; Chapter 4 (Germany), II; Chapter 5, (the Netherlands) III; Chapter 6 (England), I; Chapter 9 (Scotland), I; Chapter 11 (PECL), IV (Art. 3:204(1) PECL; Chapter 12 (UP), IV (Art. 2.2.5(1) UP).

In many systems ratification is rationalised as the unilateral legal act of the principal.[85] The nature of that act is an expression of the principal's consent to the transaction which the agent purported to conclude on the principal's behalf.[86] Many of the systems exhibit the same bi-partite analysis to this question seeking, first, full knowledge on the part of the principal of all the circumstances[87] and, secondly, the willingness or intention to ratify.[88] Those two steps are, of course, linked given that the principal cannot truly consent unless he is aware of the full facts.[89]

In all the systems studied ratification may be not only express but also implied, arising as an inference from the principal's conduct.[90] This objective approach is a practical one, allowing all parties to proceed on the basis of appearances. The need for this approach is probably most pressing in commercial transactions, and it is not surprising to note a class of commercial cases in German law in which mere passivity has been held to amount to ratification in circumstances where business parties would ordinarily expect an explicit objection from the principal

---

[85] Thus explicitly: Chapter 2 (France), III 1; Chapter 3 (Belgium), IV 4(a); Chapter 4 (Germany), V 2 (where the act of ratification is referred to as 'the declaration of ratification'); Chapter 5 (the Netherlands), V 1 (Arts 3:33 and 3:35 DCC); Chapter 6 (England), III 2(a); Chapter 7 (US) III 5(a) (*Restatement (Third) of Agency*, § 4.01(2)); Chapter 9 (Scotland) III 2; Chapter 10 (South Africa), III 3.

[86] Thus explicitly: Chapter 2 (France), III 1; Chapter 3 (Belgium), IV 1; Chapter 4 (Germany), V 2(a); Chapter 5 (the Netherlands), V 1 (see in particular Art. 3:33 DCC); Chapter 6 (England) III 2(a); Chapter 7 (US), III 5(a) (*Restatement (Third) of Agency*, § 4.01 (2)); Chapter 9 (Scotland), III 1; Chapter 10 (South Africa), III 2(a); Chapter 11 (PECL), VI 6(b); Chapter 12 (UP), VI 6(b).

[87] Thus explicitly: Chapter 2 (France), III 1; Chapter 6 (England), III 2(b) (*Lewis v. Read* (1845) 13 M & W 834; *De Bussche v. Alt* (1878) 8 Ch D 286 at 313); Chapter 7 (US), III 5(a) (*Restatement (Third) of Agency*, § 4.06); Chapter 9 (Scotland) III 5(c) (iii); Chapter 10 (South Africa), III 2(a) (*Reid v. Warner* 1907 TS 961 at 971–2; *Lazarus v. Gorfinkel* 1988 (4) SA 123 (C) at 136E–F).

[88] Thus explicitly: Chapter 2 (France), III 1; Chapter 3 (Belgium), IV 1; Chapter 4 (Germany), V 2(a); Chapter 5 (the Netherlands), V 1 (see in particular Art. 3:33 DCC); Chapter 6 (England) III 2(a); Chapter 7 (US), III 5(a) (*Restatement (Third) of Agency*, § 4.01(2)); Chapter 9 (Scotland), III 1; Chapter 10 (South Africa), III 2(a); Chapter 11 (PECL), VI 6(b); Chapter 12 (UP), VI 6(b).

[89] Thus explicitly: Chapter 2 (France), III 1 (*Veuve Taconet v. Mage, Cass. Civ 30-12-1935*, D 1936, 81).

[90] Chapter 2 (France), III 1 (Art 1998 (2) CC); Chapter 3 (Belgium), IV 1 (Art. 1998(2) BCC); Chapter 4 (Germany), V 2(a); Chapter 5 (the Netherlands), V 1 (Arts. 3:33 and 3:35 DCC); Chapter 6 (England), III 2(a); Chapter 7 (US), III 5(a) (*Restatement (Third) of Agency*, § 4.01 (2) (b) and Comment (d)); Chapter 9 (Scotland), III 5 (b); Chapter 10 (South Africa), III 3; Chapter 11 (PECL), VI 6(b); Chapter 12 (UP), VI 6(b).

where he did not authorise the transaction.[91] The principal's performance of the contract with the third party may provide the necessary
'conduct' in order to constitute ratification, although re-taking possession of his goods may not.[92] South African law takes a stricter approach
than the other systems, providing that tacit ratification is only possible
where ratification is the only reasonable interpretation of the principal's
conduct.[93] This is another interesting example of a rule applied by South
African law in order to protect the principal, which is not present in any
of the other systems studied.

Taking this issue to its most extreme level, each legal system must
tackle the circumstances in which silence alone on the part of the
principal may constitute consent and therefore ratification. It is usually
insufficient,[94] although the circumstances may give rise to a duty on the
part of the principal to act, and if he fails in this he may be found to have
ratified.[95] Because inaction rather than action on the principal's part
is involved, the proviso of full knowledge on the part of the principal is
more important than ever.[96]

2 Scope

In most of the systems studied the ambit of ratification is wide. It covers
both cases in which the agent has acted beyond his existing authority and
those in which he has no authority at all.[97] However, there is confusion as

---

[91] Chapter 4 (Germany), V 2(a) (RGZ 103, 95, 98).

[92] Chapter 6 (England), III 2(a) (*Forman & Co. Pty Ltd* v. *The Liddesdale* [1900] AC 190).

[93] Chapter 10 (South Africa), III 3.

[94] Chapter 2 (France), III 1 (*Veuve Taconet* v. *Mage, Cass Civ 30-12-1935,* D 1936, 81).

[95] See in particular: Chapter 2 (France), III 1 (*George Blanche* v. *Boutonnet et autres, Cass Req 9-6-1931,* S 1931, 1, 312; *de la Châteigneraie* v. *Commune de Marsillargues, Cass Req 4-6-1872,* S 1872, 1, 295); Chapter 4 (Germany), V 2(a) (RGZ 103, 95, 98); Chapter 5 (the Netherlands), V 6 (b) (HR 13 January 1989, NJ 1989, 320 (*Gemeente Vianen* v. *Niemans Onroerend Goed BV*)); Chapter 6 (England), III 2(a) (*Suncorp Insurance & Finance* v. *Milano Assicurazioni SpA* [1993] 2 Lloyd's Rep 225 at 241); Chapter 9 (Scotland), III 5(b) (*Lindsay & Allen* v. *Campbell* (1800) Morison's Dict, Mandate, Appendix, Pt I, 2; *Moir* v. *Clark's Trustees* 1936 SLT (Sh Ct) 40); Chapter 10 (South Africa), III 3 (*Wilmot Motors (Pty) Ltd* v. *Tucker's Fresh Meat Supply Ltd,* 1969 (4) SA 474 (T) at 477 H).

[96] See in particular: Chapter 2 (France), III 1 (*Lerestif des Tertres* v. *Thomas, Cass Civ,* D 1863, 457).

[97] Thus explicitly: Chapter 2 (France), III, introduction; Chapter 3 (Belgium), IV 2 (in Belgian and French law this has been achieved as a result of an expansive interpretation of art 1998(2) of both the Belgian and the French Civil Codes, which, read literally, only apply to cases of breach of authority); Chapter 7 (US), III 5(a); Chapter 9 (Scotland), III 2; Chapter 11 (PECL), VI 2 (Art. 3:207(1) PECL); Chapter 12 (UP), VI 2 (Art. 2.2.9 (1) UP).

to the type of acts which can be successfully ratified, particularly in the common law systems and the mixed legal systems. All of those systems identify a class of acts which, as absolute nullities, cannot be ratified. The content of this class, however, is difficult to identify. What is clear is that ratification of an illegal act is not permitted in the mixed legal systems and in English law.[98] By contrast, in the other systems there is little doubt as to the type of acts that are ratifiable.

The scope of the doctrine of ratification is wide in other respects. In Belgian law at least, and probably also in other systems, it can operate where the contract of agency between principal and agent is affected by nullity.[99] Furthermore, in most of the systems studied, the doctrine of ratification not only operates in the context of the unauthorised conclusion of contracts, but also (sometimes by way of analogy) to at least certain other unauthorised legal acts.[100] In addition, in some of the systems studied, the doctrine extends beyond the context of consensual unauthorised agency (e.g. in the context of authority pursuant to a statutory provision or judicial order or in the context of representation by a body of a legal person).[101] Finally, at least in the Netherlands, the doctrine can even apply to legal acts performed outside

---

[98] Chapter 6 (England), III 4(b), III 4(c); Chapter 9 (Scotland), III 2; Chapter (South Africa), III 2(e).

[99] Chapter 3 (Belgium), IV 2.

[100] Chapter 2 (France), III, introduction; Chapter 3 (Belgium), IV 2 (see Art. 1998(2) of both the Belgian and French Civil Code); Chapter 4 (Germany), V 4 (ratification may operate beyond the conclusion of unauthorised contracts, for instance in connection with certain unilateral transactions); Chapter 5 (the Netherlands), V 2 (ratification applies to unauthorised agency with respect to legal acts in general, see explicitly the text of Art. 3:69(1) DCC on ratification: 'A *legal act* entered into by a person acting, without the authority to do so, as agent in the name of another, may be ratified by the latter and the legal act will then have the same effect as if it had been performed pursuant to a sufficient authority.' (emphasis added)); Chapter 7 (US), III 5(a) (ratification is according to the author of the US chapter 'a basis on which the legal consequences of an agent's *action* may be attributed to the principal when the agent acted without either actual or apparent authority' (emphasis added) (*Restatement (Third) of Agency*, § 4.01(1); *Restatement (Second) of Agency*, § 82)); Chapter 9 (Scotland) III 2; Chapter 11 (PECL), V 3 (Art. 3:207 PECL, read in conjunction with Art. 1:107 PECL).

[101] Thus explicitly Chapter 5 (the Netherlands), V 3 (Art. 3:78 DCC, read in conjunction with Art. 3:78 DCC). See also Chapter 6 (England), III 5 (where it is remarked that companies may ratify unauthorised acts). Compare also Chapter 4 (Germany), VIII 2(a); Chapter 9 (Scotland) III 2; Chapter 10 (South Africa), III 7(b); Chapter 11 (PECL), VI 3; Chapter 12 (UP), VI 3 (in German law, Scots law, South African law, the PECL and the UNIDROIT Principles, the doctrine of ratification can sometimes be applied in the context of legal persons).

the area of patrimonial law, in areas such as family law, procedural law and public law.[102]

3 Position of third party and other directly interested persons prior to ratification

As already stated in II, above, each legal system provides that the unauthorised agent fails to form a contract between principal and third party. Beyond this rather bald statement, analysis of the legal position prior to ratification is scant. As noted directly above, the common law and mixed legal systems exhibit a failure to distinguish between types of acts which are potentially ratifiable and those which are so fundamentally flawed that they cannot be ratified. As already mentioned in II above, the situation prior to ratification is analysed most clearly in German law, where the principle of *schwebende Unwirksamkeit* is applied. To quote from the chapter on German law: 'It stipulates that the contract is neither void nor enforceable, rather it is "floating" and awaiting either ratification or refusal by the principal or revocation by the third party.'[103] As mentioned in II, above, this solution is attractive in its recognition that the relationship between principal and third party prior to ratification is one which cannot be placed within existing categorisations of void, voidable and invalid contracts.

(a) Third party may withdraw prior to ratification

The ability of the third party to withdraw from the transaction prior to ratification by the principal emerges as possibly the most contentious issue in ratification. The English case of *Bolton Partners Ltd* v. *Lambert*[104] upholds the retroactive effect of ratification to its full extent, rendering the third party unable to withdraw even where the withdrawal pre-dates ratification by the principal. In this case the third party was treated as bound from the moment the agent purported to enter into the transaction. Although the case is undoubtedly controversial, it remains good law.[105] It is notable that exceptions have developed which go some way towards limiting its effect, in particular by ruling out ratification where it would

---

[102] Chapter 5 (the Netherlands), V 3 (Art. 3:69 DCC read in conjunction with 3:79 DCC).
[103] Chapter 4 (Germany), V 1.
[104] (1889) 41 Ch D 295, discussed in Chapter 2 (England), III 3; Chapter 8 (US compared with other Common Law countries), III.
[105] Chapter 6 (England), III 3.

unfairly prejudice the interests of the third party.[106] The matter has not, as yet, come before the Scottish or South African courts.[107] South African commentators are clearly split on the issue, the author of the chapter on South Africa favouring the third party's unlimited right to withdraw.[108]

The Dutch and German civil codes both provide the third party with a limited right to withdraw. The third party, in both systems, must make some form of declaration prior to ratification. In Dutch law this declaration takes the form of an indication from the third party that he considers the act to be invalid for want of authority. German law is less specific on the exact nature of the declaration. In both systems the third party cannot do so if, at the time of conclusion of the contract, he either knew or ought to have known that a want of authority existed.[109] Similarly, in the UNIDROIT Principles, the third party in good faith may withdraw unilaterally prior to ratification.[110] The *Restatement (Third) of Agency* also provides the third party with a right to withdraw prior to ratification. However, unlike the position in Dutch law, German law and in the UNIDROIT Principles, the *Restatement (Third) of Agency* does not appear to contain the restriction that the third cannot do so if he knew or ought to have known of the lack of authority.[111]

---

[106] Chapter 6 (England), III 4(a) (*Owners of the Borvigilant* v. *Owners of the Romina G* [2003] 2 Lloyd's Rep 520).

[107] Chapter 9 (Scotland), III 3(a); Chapter 10 (South Africa), III 5. In the chapters on Belgian and French law (Chapters 2 and 3), this question has not been addressed, probably because it has not yet come before the Belgian and French courts nor been discussed in the academic literature.

[108] Chapter 10 (South Africa), III 5.

[109] Chapter 4 (Germany), V 3 (§ 178 BGB); Chapter 5 (the Netherlands), V 4(a) (Art. 3:69(3) DCC). With respect to Dutch law it should be remembered here that the words 'at the time of his acting' in Art. 3:69(3) DCC denote the fact that one must distinguish between legal acts in which the third party is actively involved and legal acts in which the third party is only involved in a passive sense. There is, for example, no 'acting' on the side of the third party if the unauthorised agent terminates or nullifies a contract: the role of the third party is merely a passive one. In such cases, the third party may *also* reject the legal act concerned if he, at the time of the termination or nullification, understood or should have understood that no sufficient authority had been granted. By contrast, if the involvement of the third party is an active one – in particular in the case of the conclusion of a contract – the third party may *only* reject the contract if he at the time of the conclusion of the contract did not understand and under the circumstances could not have understood that insufficient authority had been granted. See Chapter 5 (the Netherlands), V 4(a).

[110] Chapter 12 (UP), VI 4(a) (Art. 2.2.9(3) UP).

[111] See *Restatement (Third) of Agency* § 4.05: 'A ratification of a transaction is not effective unless it precedes the occurrence of circumstances that would cause the ratification to have adverse and inequitable effects on the rights of third parties. These circumstances

The rule that the third party may withdraw unilaterally prior to ratification has been criticised by, for example, Reynolds, who argues that it enables the third party 'to play the market'.[112] However, in line with what has been suggested in the chapter on Dutch law, it may be argued that if the third party rejects the unauthorised act merely because he wishes to conclude a more favourable contract elsewhere, this rejection is null and void. It is also possible that the third party would lose the power to reject because it is contrary to good faith and fair dealing. The third party's ability to withdraw may, in principle, be supported by the argument that, in practice, a party is often unable to obtain certainty as to his legal position. The third party may withdraw unilaterally prior to ratification only where he is in good faith, and this limitation takes sufficient account of the principal's interests.[113]

A similar rule is not found in the PECL, although the terms of Art. 3:208 PECL are relevant to this issue. This Article provides the third party with a (very limited) means to obtain certainty as to his position. This provision is dealt with in (b) immediately below.

(b) Additional protections for third parties and other directly interested persons

Dutch law, German law and the UNIDROIT Principles are notable in their attempts to extend the protections of a third party potentially affected by ratification. All three systems contain provisions which seek to enable the third party to clarify his legal position.

In German law this takes the form of the clarification procedure. In terms of this procedure the third party may demand a declaration from the principal confirming whether or not he ratifies the contract. This demand sets a two-week period for clarification, the failure of the principal to respond timeously constituting a deemed refusal of ratification. A declaration of ratification which comes too late remains without effect.[114]

---

include: (1) any manifestation of intention to withdraw from the transaction made by the third party; (2) any material change in circumstances that would make it inequitable to bind the third party, unless the third party chooses to be bound; and (3) a specific time that determines whether a third party is deprived of a right or subjected to a liability.' This section corresponds in substance to *Restatement (Second) of Agency*, §§ 88, 89, 90 and 95, Comment *b*.

[112] F. M. B. Reynolds, 'Authority of Agents' (2005) *ICC International Court of Arbitration Bulletin*, Special Supplement, UNIDROIT Principles: New Developments and Applications, 9 at 13.

[113] Chapter 5 (the Netherlands), V 4(a).

[114] Chapter 4 (Germany), V 3 (§ 177(2) BGB).

Dutch law allows directly interested persons such as the third party to determine a reasonable period for ratification. Failure to ratify within this period leads to the loss of the power to ratify. Although the strict wording of the provision tends to suggest that it only protects the third party where it is clear that there is unauthorised representation, it is argued in the chapter on Dutch law that the provisions can be applied where it is unclear whether unauthorised agency exists.[115] The UNIDROIT Principles similarly provide that 'the third party may by notice to the principal specify a reasonable period of time for ratification' and that 'if the principal does not ratify within that period of time it can no longer do so'.[116]

The approach in the PECL is very different from the approach adopted in Dutch law, German law and the UNIDROIT Principles. According to the PECL, where statements or conduct of the principal gave the third party reason to believe that an act performed by the agent was authorised, but the third party is in doubt about the authorisation, it may send a written confirmation to the principal or request ratification from it. If the principal does not object or answer the request without delay, the agent's act is treated as having been authorised. The fact that Art. 3:208 PECL only applies in cases where statements or conduct of the principal gave the third party reason to believe that the agent's act was authorised, but the third party is in doubt about the authorisation, justifies the fact that the principal is bound where he fails to answer the request for ratification (or confirmation).[117]

The approach adopted in the PECL is not as attractive as the solution adopted by Dutch law, German law and the UNIDROIT Principles. The third party, too, should be able to obtain certainty outside the scope of cases where statements or conduct of the principal gave the third party reason to believe that an act performed by the agent was authorised, but the third party is in doubt about the authorisation.

It should finally be noted that Dutch law also provides the third party with certainty if there is doubt as to whether the agent has sufficient authority: a party may reject a declaration made by an agent as invalid if he has forthwith asked the agent for proof of his authority and if he does

---

[115] Chapter 5 (the Netherlands), V 4 (b) (Art. 3:69(4) DCC).

[116] Chapter 12 (UP), VI 4(b) (Art. 2.9(2) UP).

[117] In a similar vein: H. L. E. Verhagen, 'Comment on Art 3:207 PECL', in: D. Busch, E. Hondius, H. van Kooten, *et al.* (eds.), *The Principles of European Contract Law and Dutch Law. A Commentary* (The Hague/London/New York/Nijmegen: Ars Aequi Libri/ Kluwer Law International, 2002), p. 166.

not receive without delay proof in writing of the agent's authority or confirmation thereof by the principal. However, proof of the agent's authority cannot be required if: (1) the principal has informed the third party of the agent's authority; (2) it has been made public in a manner determined by law or by usage; or (3) if it results from an appointment known to the third party.[118] The adoption of such additional rules should, in our view, be welcomed.

(c) Partial ratification

In most of the legal systems studied, partial or conditional ratification is not possible.[119] Comment 2 to Art. 2.2.9 UP makes it clear that the third party may refuse partial ratification of the agent's acts by the principal, given that it would amount to a proposal by the principal to modify the contract that the third party has concluded with the agent.[120] It is submitted that this is the correct approach, although there may be room for exceptions. For example, it has been argued that the third party should sometimes be obliged to accept a partial ratification because of a duty to mitigate loss.[121]

4 Effect of ratification

(a) Retroactive effect

In all the systems studied, ratification has retroactive effect. The legal act performed by the unauthorised agent has the same effect as if it had been performed by an authorised agent. The principal is therefore bound by the contract which the unauthorised agent purported to conclude on his behalf from the moment at which the agent purported to do so.[122]

---

[118] Chapter 5 (the Netherlands), V 4(d) (Art. 3:71 DCC).

[119] Chapter 5 (the Netherlands), V 4(c) (Art. 3:69(4), second sentence, DCC); Chapter 6 (England), III 2(a) (*Smith* v. *Henniker-Major & Co* [2003] Ch 182, although note the possibly exceptional case, *Harrisons & Crossfield Ltd* v. *LNW Railway Co. Ltd* [1917] 2 KB 755, in which ratification was permitted for one purpose but not for another); Chapter 7 (US), III 5(a) (*Restatement (Third) of Agency* § 4.07); Chapter 9 (Scotland), III 3(b); Chapter 10 (South Africa), III 2(f) (*Theron* v. *Leon* 1928 TPD 719 at 723; *Jagersfontein Garage & Transport Co* v. *Secretary, State Advances Office* 1939 OPD 37 at 46); Chapter 12 (UP), VI 4(c) (Comment 2 to Art. 2.2.9 UP).

[120] See Chapter 12 (UP), VI 4(c) (Comment 2 to Art. 2.2.9 UP).

[121] Chapter 5 (the Netherlands), V 4(c); Chapter 12 (UP), VI 4(c) (Art. 7.4.8 UP).

[122] Chapter 2 (France), III 2(b); Chapter 3 (Belgium), IV 3(a); Chapter 3 (Germany), V 2(b) (§ 184 (1); Chapter 5 (the Netherlands), V 5(a) (3:69 (1) DCC); Chapter 6 (England), III 3; Chapter 7 (US), III 5(a) (*Restatement (Third) of Agency*, § 4.02(1) and Comment(b));

Ratification affects not only the 'external' but also the 'internal' agency relationship. The consequences for the agent under his contract with the principal must also, therefore, be considered. Ratification, as an expression of the principal's consent to the unauthorised transaction, seems to imply that the principal cannot pursue the agent for breach of duty. Nevertheless, some legal systems allow the principal to ratify subject to the right to pursue the agent for breach of duty.[123] For English and South African law this represents a rare example of the separation of the internal and external aspects of agency.

(b) Rights granted to fourth parties prior to ratification

Consideration must be given to the rights of persons who are not parties to the transaction in question, sometimes known as fourth parties. In nearly all the systems studied, ratification is ineffective towards such parties who have acquired rights prior to ratification.[124] This rule is particularly useful in a commercial setting because it furthers legal certainty.

(c) Position of acts which themselves could not have been effectively carried out at the time of ratification

The systems studied display differing attitudes to the position of acts which themselves could not have been effectively carried out at the time of ratification. Roughly speaking, there are three approaches.

Chapter 9 (Scotland), III 4(a); Chapter 10 (South Africa), III 6; Chapter 11 (PECL), VI 5(a) (Art. 3:207(2) PECL); Chapter 12 (UP), VI 5(a) (Art. 2.2.9(1), second sentence, UP).

[123] Chapter 2 (France), III 2(a) (*Cass Civ 9-5-1853*, DP 1853, I, 293); Chapter 6 (England), III 3 (*Suncorp Insurance and Finance* v. *Milano Assicurazioni SpA* [1993] 2 Lloyd's Rep 225 at 235); Chapter 10 (South Africa), III 6 (*Mine Workers' Union* v. *Brodrick* 1948 4 SA 958 (A)).

[124] Chapter 2 (France), III 2(b); Chapter 3 (Belgium), IV 3(b) (Cass 6 February 1953, *Pas* 1953, I, 436 and *RPS* 1953, 224, concl H de Termicourt, obs. PD); Chapter 5 (the Netherlands), V 5(b) (Art. 3:69(5) DCC); Chapter 6 (England), III 4(b) (where it is argued that 'ratification cannot generally divest property rights that have accrued to others outside the triangular principal-agent-third party relationship but that ratification in such circumstances can nevertheless affect the rights and obligations of the parties within the triangular relationship itself'); Chapter 7 (US), III 5(a) (*Restatement (Third) of Agency*, § 4.02(2)(c)); Chapter 9 (Scotland), III 4(b) (where it is argued that the Scottish court would be unlikely to allow ratification to have a detrimental effect on fourth parties); Chapter 10 (South Africa), III 6 (*Smith* v. *Kwanonqubela Town Council* 1999 (4) SA 947 at 954A–B; *Jagersfontein Garage & Transport Co.* v. *Secretary, State Advances Office* 1939 OPD 37 at 46–47); Chapter 11 (PECL), VI 5(b) (Art. 3:207(2) PECL). The UNIDROIT Principles, however, take the position that the effect of ratification on persons other than the principal, the agent and the third party is outside their scope. See Chapter 12 (UP), VI 5(b).

First, there are systems where it is, in principle, accepted that ratification has the desired effect if at the time of ratification the relevant legal act can no longer be performed validly. That is the position in Dutch law. Thus, the principal may ratify an appeal by an unauthorised agent if, at the time of ratification, the term for appeal has already expired. It is interesting to note that this possibility was accepted, amongst other things, because (1) rights of 'fourth parties' (i.e. parties other than the principal, the agent and the third party) are sufficiently protected by Art. 3:69(5) DCC (which provides that rights granted by the principal to 'fourth parties' before ratification are respected, see directly above); and (2) the third party may, in principle, prevent ratification by rejecting the legal act concerned prior to ratification (Art. 3:69(3) DCC, see IV 3(a), above).[125]

Second, there are systems where ratification in principle does not have the desired effect if at the time of ratification the relevant legal act can no longer be validly performed. That is the approach in French law, as becomes apparent from a French court decision dating from 1934.[126] The third party made an offer to an agent to buy goods, stipulating that this offer had to be accepted within a certain time frame. The agent had no authority to accept, but nevertheless did so within the agreed time limit. The principal attempted to ratify but the ratification came after the term of the offer had lapsed. The court held that ratification was not valid since the consent of the third party had lapsed. The same approach is adopted in Belgium. For example, in procedural law, the principal cannot ratify the act of the unauthorised agent who raises an appeal if, at the time of ratification, the term for appeal has already expired.[127]

Third, there are systems where the answer to this question very much depends on the circumstances of the case. This may be illustrated by reference to English law. As the author of this chapter points out, under English law a principal may not be entitled to ratify certain acts that were lawful at the time they were entered into, but were no longer so at the time of ratification.[128] However, at the same time, ratification of unauthorised legal proceedings is not automatically barred after the expiration of the limitation period.[129] Perhaps, as the author of the chapter on English law

---

[125] Chapter 5 (the Netherlands), V 5(c).
[126] Chapter 2 (France), III 1, *in fine* (*Civ* 18-4-1934, Gaz Pal 1934, 1, 970).
[127] Chapter 3 (Belgium), IV 3(c) (Comm. Gent 11 December 1987, *TRV* 1988, 376; State Council 29 May 1990, *Arr RvSt* 1990, no 35201).
[128] Chapter 6 (England), III 4(b).
[129] Chapter 6 (England), III 4(a) (*Smith* v. *Henniker-Major & Co.* [2003] Ch 182 at 206).

suggests, 'the crucial element is whether the ratification will cause unfair prejudice to the third party'.[130] In Scotland and South Africa the answer to this question also appears to depend on the circumstances.[131]

5 Act of ratification: requirements

(a) Within a particular time

The legal systems studied employ different approaches as to whether a time limit applies to ratification. There are roughly three approaches. First, there are systems in which the act of ratification is subject only to a general limitation period.[132] Second, there are systems where the act of ratification must always take place within a reasonable time. In English law, for example, it has been suggested that in determining what constitutes a reasonable time, the courts are entitled to take all the circumstances into account, including whether a time limit exists for the act to be ratified and whether there is ultimately any unfair prejudice to the third party.[133] Third, in Belgian law, ratification is not subject to any general or specific time limit. This statement must, however, be qualified in that in Belgium ratification, in principle, does not have the desired effect if at the time of ratification the relevant legal act can no longer be validly performed. This means that valid ratification must take place before that time, and a long period of silence on the part of the principal may be considered an implied ratification.[134]

The variety of approaches displayed by the different legal systems studied is somewhat surprising. We would suggest that ratification

---

[130] Chapter 6 (England), III 4(a).

[131] Chapter 9 (Scotland), III 5(c); Chapter 10 (South Africa), III 4 and III 6 (contrast, in particular, *Finbro Furnishers (Pty) Ltd* v. *Peiner* 1935 CPD 378 at 380 and *Smith* v. *Kwanonqubela Town Council* 1999 (4) SA 947 at 954 B–E).

[132] Chapter 5 (the Netherlands), V 6(a) (Art. 3:306 DCC: 'Unless otherwise provided for by law, rights of action are prescribed on the expiry of twenty years'), but see V 4(b) (Art. 3:69(4) DCC: a directly interested person (e.g. the third party) can set a reasonable time for ratification; if the principal does not ratify within that time, he can no longer do so); Chapter 11 (PECL), VI 6(a) (Art. 14:201 PECL: 'The general prescription period is three years'); Chapter 12 (UP), VI 6(a) (Art. 10.2 UP: '(1) The general limitation period is three years beginning on the day after the day the obligee knows or ought to know the facts as a result of which the obligee's right can be exercised. (2) In any event, the maximum limitation period is ten years beginning on the day after the day the right can be exercised.').

[133] Chapter 6 (England), III 4 (a). A similar approach is adopted in South African law, see Chapter 10 (South Africa), III 4 and 6, also Chapter 9 (Scotland), III 5(a).

[134] Chapter 3 (Belgium), IV 3(c), IV 4(b).

should take place within a reasonable time, taking into account all the circumstances of the case. By allowing the parties to achieve certainty as quickly as possible, this approach accords with commercial convenience. One must recall the fact that the principal, in contrast to the third party, is the one party who is in possession of all of the relevant facts. Bearing this context in mind, the time limit imposes on the principal only a minor degree of inconvenience.

(b) No particular form required

In none of the systems studied are formal steps required in order to constitute ratification.[135] The only exception to this position occurs where the initial act of the agent was subject to formalities. In that case the act of ratification must similarly comply with such formalities.[136]

(c) Communication of act of ratification

Surprisingly, the different legal systems studied take varying approaches to the issue of communication of the ratification to the third party. Nor is it possible to see a pattern amongst the civil law countries, the common law countries and the mixed legal systems. Only in Dutch law is communication to the third party an absolute requirement.[137] German law, South African law and the PECL permit ratification either to the third party or to the agent.[138] Communication to the third party is not a requirement in either French or English law.[139] This approach is justified by the author of the chapter on French law by pointing out that the third party already consented to the act when he contracted with the agent.[140] According to the *Restatement (Third) of Agency* and the UNIDROIT

---

[135] Chapter 2 (France), III 1 (Art. 1998(2) CC); Chapter 3 (Belgium), IV 4(c); Chapter 4 (Germany), V 2(a) (§ 182 (2) BGB); Chapter 5 (the Netherlands), V 6(b) (Art. 3:37 DCC); Chapter 6 (England), III 2(a); Chapter 7 (US), III 5(a) (*Restatement (Third) of Agency*, § 4.01(2)(b), Comment (*d*)); Chapter 9 (Scotland), III 5(b); Chapter 10 (South Africa), III 3; Chapter 11 (PECL), VI 6(b); Chapter 12 (UP), VI 6(b).

[136] Chapter 2 (France), III 1 (*Civ 13-12-1875*, DP 1875, 1, 97); Chapter 3 (Belgium), IV 4(c) (Brussels 23 December 1999, *JT* 2000, 310); Chapter 5 (the Netherlands), V 6(b) (Art. 3:69(2) DCC); Chapter 9 (Scotland) III 6(b).

[137] Chapter 5 (the Netherlands), V 6(c) (Art. 3:37(3) DCC).

[138] Chapter 4 (Germany), V 2, introduction; Chapter 10 (South Africa), III 3 (although the author of this chapter notes disagreement on this issue); Chapter 11 (PECL), VI 6(c) (Comment A to Art. 3:207 PECL).

[139] Chapter 2 (France), III 1, *in fine*; Chapter 6 (England), III 2(a) (*Harrisons & Crossfeld Ltd* v. *LNW Railway Co. Ltd* [1917] 2 KB 755 at 758; *Shell Co. of Australia Ltd* v. *NAT Shipping and Bagging Services Ltd (The Kilmun)* [1988] 2 Lloyd's Rep 1 at 11, 14).

[140] Chapter 2 (France), III 1, *in fine*.

Principles, ratification need not be communicated to anyone.[141] In *Restatement (Third) of Agency* ratification takes the form of a manifestation, not dependent for its validity on communication to the third party or agent.[142]

It has already been suggested in the chapters on the PECL and the UNIDROIT Principles that an approach in which ratification need not necessarily come to the attention of the third party in order to be effective is problematic from a practical point of view. It is obviously unsatisfactory for the third party to be unaware of whether ratification has actually taken place.[143] Therefore, it is not surprising that, in the UNIDROIT Principles and in German law, this position cannot be maintained. As far as the UNIDROIT Principles are concerned, where the third party sets the principal a reasonable time for ratification (Art. 2.2.9(2) UP), the explanatory notes remark that 'it goes without saying that in such a case ratification must be notified to the third party'.[144] Similarly, in the chapter on German law it is remarked that a declaration to the agent is weaker than the declaration to the third party. This is because the former may be nullified under § 177(2) DCC if the third party begins the process of clarification.[145]

(d) The existence and capacity of the principal

Most systems provide that the principal must be in existence and possess legal capacity where ratification operates, although they differ on whether these requirements must apply at the time of performance of the unauthorised legal act, or at the time of ratification, or at both of these times.

In French, Belgian, Dutch and English law the principal must have legal capacity at the time of ratification.[146] In English law, the *Restatement (Third) of Agency* and in Scots law the principal must be in existence and have legal capacity at the time of the unauthorised act

---

[141] Chapter 7 (US), III 5(a) (*Restatement (Third) of Agency*, § 4.01(2) and Comment (*b*)); Chapter 12 (UP), VI 5(c) (Comment 1 to Art. 2.2.9 UP).

[142] Chapter 7 (US), III 5(a) (*Restatement (Third) of Agency*, § 4.01(2) and Comment (*b*)).

[143] Chapter 11 (PECL),VI 6(c); Chapter 12 (UP), VI 6(c). Cf. Reynolds, 'Authority of Agents', p. 12.

[144] Chapter 12 (UP), VI 6(c) (Comment 3 to Art. 2.2.9 UP). See on Art. 2.2.9(2) UP: Chapter 12 (UP), VI 4(b) and this chapter, IV 3(b).

[145] Chapter 4 (Germany), V 2, introduction. See on § 177(2) BGB: Chapter 4 (Germany), V 3 and this chapter, IV 3(b).

[146] Chapter 2 (France), III 1, *in fine*; Chapter 3 (Belgium), IV 4(d); Chapter 5 (the Netherlands), V 6(d); Chapter 6 (England), III 4(b).

itself.[147] In South Africa, a principal must in any event possess legal capacity at the time of ratification. Furthermore, and although it has been suggested that this is not necessary, most South African authorities suggest that if the principal had no capacity at the time the act was carried out, it is not possible for him to ratify later if he regains capacity. In other words, according to most South African authorities the principal must not only possess legal capacity at the time of ratification, but also at the time of the unauthorised act itself. However, unauthorised acts carried out on behalf of a minor may be ratified by the minor himself when he attains majority.[148]

The issue of capacity is most relevant in the context of company law. The legal systems studied display differing attitudes to pre-incorporation contracts, or contracts entered into on behalf of companies not yet in existence. In some legal systems, such contracts are not valid and cannot be ratified.[149] Other solutions must be found in these legal systems, such as, for example, adoption of the contract as occurs in the US.[150] In England, the parties must enter into an entirely new contract.[151] The mixed legal systems, Scotland and South Africa, have, as is described in the relevant chapters, applied native common law concepts of third party rights in contract to solve this particular problem, successfully in South Africa but unsuccessfully in Scotland.[152] In Belgian and Dutch law, too, ratification is possible in such circumstances.[153] The PECL similarly permit ratification in such circumstances, but note that the special rules of the applicable company law with respect to pre-incorporation contracts take precedence over the terms of the PECL.[154] In Germany, § 177 BGB on ratification is applied by way of analogy to the case of companies not yet incorporated. However, from a practical point of view

---

[147] For English law, see *Kelner* v. *Baxter* (1866) LR 2 CP 174; Chapter 7 (US), III 5(b) (*Restatement (Third) of Agency*, § 4.04); Chapter 9 (Scotland), III 6(c)(i).

[148] Chapter 10 (South Africa), III 2(d).

[149] Chapter 6 (England), III 2(d); Chapter 7 (US), III 5(b) (*Restatement (Third) of Agency*, § 4.04); Chapter 9 (Scotland), III 5(c)(i).

[150] Chapter 7 (US), III 5(b) (adoption – unlike ratification – does not operate retroactively). In France the technique of adoption is also used, see Chapter 2 (France), V.

[151] Chapter 6 (England), III 2(d).

[152] Chapter 9 (Scotland), V; Chapter 10 (South Africa), III 2(c), although it is no longer necessary to use the *stipulatio alteri* as a solution following the enactment of s. 35 South African Companies Act.

[153] Chapter 3 (Belgium), VII (Art. 60 of the Company Code); Chapter 5 (the Netherlands), IX 3 (Arts 2:93(1) and 2:203(1) DCC).

[154] Chapter 11 (PECL), VI 3 (Comment B to Art. 3:207 PECL).

the most common case of a non-existent principal is dealt with under the special rules of company law. For example, according to a judge-made rule, a GmbH (private limited liability company) coming into existence automatically becomes the debtor, in which case there is no room for ratification.[155]

This divergence of approach seems unsatisfactory. There seems to us to be no good reason why the principal should not be able to ratify if at the time the unauthorised legal act was done he did not have the legal capacity to do so or was not yet in existence. The relevant time is the time of ratification. This is because the principal is, at this time, able to express his will. If at that time the principal is willing to ratify, he should in principle be able to do so. We reject the German judge-made rule that a GmbH coming into existence automatically becomes the debtor. There seems to be no good reason why in that particular case an exception should be made to the rule that the principal of an unauthorised agent is in principle only bound and entitled if he ratifies the unauthorised legal act.

The issue of capacity is also relevant to situations in which directors purport to enter into contracts which are outside the terms of the company's objects clause. Both the South African and UK Companies Acts contain provisions protecting third parties from acts of the directors which are outside the power of the company.[156] The provisions do not have the effect of permitting ratification in every case, and are subject to limitations.

(e) Acting in the name of the principal

As explained in the Introduction, this book considers unauthorised agency in the context of direct rather than indirect agency. Cases in which the agent acts in his own name are therefore not considered. However, the ability of an undisclosed principal to ratify a contract made by an unauthorised agent is a difficult one which has been much discussed in the systems which recognise the concept of the undisclosed principal. An analysis of ratification would be incomplete without at least noting the position in these countries.

---

[155] Chapter 4 (Germany), VIII 2(a), where the German position is dealt with in further detail.

[156] Chapter 6 (England), III 5 and Chapter 9 (Scotland) III 5(c)(i) (see s. 35(1) and (3) of the Companies Act, which apply in the same manner throughout the whole of the UK, soon to be replaced by s. 39(1) Companies Act 2006); Chapter 10 (South Africa), III 7(a) (South African Companies Act s 36).

The general position in English and South African law is that ratification by an undisclosed principal is not possible.[157] The author of the chapter on English law provides an interesting discussion of the policy reasons for this stance. In summary, the concept of the undisclosed principal rests on an implied contract between the third party and the principal. No such contract may be implied where the agent acts without authority. Ratification is therefore not possible.[158] This can be contrasted with the position under *Restatement (Third) of Agency* which permits ratification by undisclosed principals.[159] The author of the chapter on US law provides compelling arguments in favour of such ratification, the most pressing of which is the fact that '... the result is no different than the consequences that stem from recognising that an undisclosed principal may acquire rights and become subject to liabilities through an agent's actions'.[160] The controversy surrounding this issue is also reflected in the fact that, although native Scottish authorities point in favour of ratification, some have expressed the view that the Scottish courts would follow the leading English case, *Keighley, Maxted & Co.* v. *Durant.*[161]

A full analysis of the policy reasons for and against ratification by an undisclosed principal is not possible in this context. However, it can be noted here that the difficulties experienced stem from the failure to identify the contractual relationships which arise in a situation of an undisclosed principal. In England it has been argued that where an agent acts for an undisclosed principal, a contract is formed from the outset between the principal and the third party.[162] By contrast, in Scotland, it has been argued that the contract is formed between the agent and the

---

[157] Chapter 6 (England), III 2(c) (*Keighley, Maxsted & Co.* v. *Durant* [1901] AC 240 at 261); Chapter 10 (South Africa), III 2(b) (that undisclosed principals cannot ratify follows from the requirement in South Africa that the agent must act in the name of the principal at the time of the conclusion of the contract, which is in the case of undisclosed principals by definition not the case).

[158] Chapter 6 (England), III 2(c).

[159] Chapter 7 (US), III 5(a) (*Restatement (Third) of Agency*, § 4.03, a reversal of the position under *Restatement (Second) of Agency*, § 85(1)). The same approach is followed in the UNIDROIT Principles, where the provision on ratification (Art. 2.2.9 UP) applies to agency in general, whether disclosed (Art. 2.2.3 UP) or undisclosed (2.2.4 UP). Cf. Chapter 12 (UP), III, IV.

[160] Chapter 7 (US), III 5(a).

[161] [1901] AC 240. See Chapter 9 (Scotland), III 5(c)(iv), where it is noted that one of the leading authors on Scots law, W. M. Gloag, made this argument.

[162] By the author of the English chapter in 'Undisclosed Principals and Contract' (2004) 120 *LQR* 480.

third party.[163] Until a proper rationale for this concept has been formulated, a convincing answer to the question of ratification in this context is unlikely to be found.

V Liability of the *falsus procurator*

1 General

In each of the systems studied, if neither the doctrine of apparent authority nor the doctrine of ratification applies, the principal and the third party will not be bound by the contract (or other legal act) concluded by the unauthorised agent. In such cases, the third party can generally hold the unauthorised agent (the *falsus procurator*) liable for the damage which he has suffered as a consequence of the agent's lack of authority.[164]

It is important to note at the outset that the general approach of each of the legal systems studied is that the agent acting outside the scope of his authority or without any authority does not become a contracting party in the contract which the third party purported to conclude with the principal.[165] This is the case even in German law, where the third party has a right to choose between damages or specific performance as against the agent. In the words of the author of the chapter on German law: 'specific performance does not mean there was a valid contract between the agent and third party. The agent does not become a party to the contract but only to a relationship established by law, which carries with it certain consequences.'[166] In other words, in each of the legal systems studied, the false agent does not simply 'step into the shoes' of the principal.

In Dutch law, English law, German law, South African law, the *Restatement (Third) of Agency* and the PECL, liability can be based on

---

[163] L. Macgregor, 'Agency and Mandate', in *The Laws of Scotland: Stair Memorial Encyclopaedia*, Reissue (Edinburgh: Butterworths, 2002), para. 149.

[164] Chapter 2 (France), IV; Chapter 3 (Belgium), V 4; Chapter 4 (Germany), VI 2(b); Chapter 5 (the Netherlands), VI 4; Chapter 6 (England), IV 1; Chapter 7 (US), IV 2; Chapter 9 (Scotland), IV 4; Chapter 10 (South Africa), IV 2(c); Chapter 11 (PECL), VII 4; Chapter 12 (UP), VII 4.

[165] Chapter 2 (France), IV; Chapter 3 (Belgium), V 4; Chapter 4 (Germany), VI 2(a); Chapter 5 (the Netherlands), VI 4; Chapter 6 (England), IV 1; Chapter 7 (US), IV 2; Chapter 9 (Scotland), IV 4; Chapter 10 (South Africa), IV 2(c); Chapter 11 (PECL), VII 4; Chapter 12 (UP), VII 4.

[166] Chapter 4 (Germany), VI 2(a).

breach of a contractual warranty of authority which results in payment
of damages on an expectation basis. Such damages seek to put the third
party in the position he would have been in had the warranty been true.
This warranty may be either express or implied, breach of either involving an expectation measure of damages. Where the warranty is
express, the agent explicitly or tacitly warrants to the third party that
he is authorised, possibly as part of a separate agent/third party agreement. Express warranties are likely to be rare, and the more difficult
situation is where the warranty is implied and therefore, in fact, fictitious. In the context of such an action, fault on the side of the agent is
irrelevant.[167]

However, contractual actions take a different form in France and
Belgium. Here the agent sometimes provides an express guarantee that
the principal will ratify. If such ratification is not forthcoming the agent
may be liable.[168] A significant difference of approach is immediately
noticeable. In the legal systems which utilise such a guarantee, the agent
providing the guarantee discloses to the third party that he is not
authorised. In the systems which make use, instead, of an implied or
express warranty of authority, there is no disclosure of a lack of authority;
indeed, the agent takes the risk that he may lack authority.

In most systems liability can also be based on tort. In England,
Scotland and South Africa, this is the case where the agent either fraudulently or negligently misrepresented that he was authorised.[169] While
examples of the former are relatively easy to find in English law, there
appear to be no examples of the latter in either English or Scots law. The
existence of conflicting Commonwealth decisions is, however, noted in
the chapter on English law.[170] South Africa has recognised an action
applicable where the agent acts negligently.[171] Dutch law, too, contains
an action in tort, which can be applied where the agent knew or

---

[167] Chapter 4 (Germany), VI, introduction; Chapter 5 (the Netherlands), VI 1, VI 5(a);
Chapter 6 (England), IV 1; Chapter 7 (US), IV 2 (*Restatement (Third) of Agency*, § 6.10);
Chapter 9 (Scotland), IV 2; Chapter 10 (South Africa), IV 2(a), IV 2(b); Chapter 11
(PECL), VII 1.

[168] Chapter 2 (France), IV; Chapter 3 (Belgium), VIII. See Art. 1997 CC and Art. 1997 BCC,
both *in fine* (*promesse de porte-fort*).

[169] Chapter 6 (England), IV 4; Chapter 9 (Scotland), IV 2; Chapter 10 (South Africa), IV 4.

[170] Chapter 6 (England), IV 4 (*Kavanagh v. Continental Shelf Company (No. 46) Ltd* [1993]
2 NZLR 648 (New Zealand); *Fong Maun Yee v. Yoong Weng Ho Robert* [1997] 2 SLR 297
(Singapore)).

[171] Chapter 10 (South Africa), IV 4 (*Bayer South Africa (Pty) Ltd v. Frost* 1991 (4) SA 559).

ought to have known of his lack of authority.[172] Nevertheless, it must be said that the tort actions play a much less prominent role in England, Scotland, South Africa and the Netherlands, the contractual action being the dominant one. The preference for a contractual action may be explained by the lower measure of damages applicable in tort actions, i.e. on a reliance rather than an expectation basis.[173] In addition, the preference for a contractual action may be explained by the fact that in tort some degree of fault on the part of the agent must be established, whereas in contract the liability is strict. In French and Belgian law it appears that an action against the agent will usually be based on tort, requiring proof of fault by the third party.[174] As explained above, a contractual action will sometimes be available in France and Belgium, but only in the rare case that the agent guarantees that the principal will ratify.

It should also be noted that the task of identifying a legal basis for the breach of warranty of authority has clearly been a difficult one. In English law the warranty is given in the context of a collateral contract: the agent offers to warrant his authority to the third party. The agent's offer is accepted by the third party through conduct, when that third party enters into a contract with the principal. The dictates of consideration must be met, and are indeed met in the act by the third party of entering into a contract with the principal.[175] The Scottish concept has developed by reference to English law, but with the important difference that consideration is not a requirement in Scots law. This raises the possibility that the Scottish version might be better analysed using *pollicitatio*, the enforceable unilateral promise.[176] The South African position is complex and possibly as yet unresolved. The implied warranty given by the agent

---

[172] Chapter 5 (the Netherlands), VI 3 (Art. 6:162 DCC on *onrechtmatige daad*, see HR 31 January 1997, NJ 1998, 704 (*Reisbureau De Globe* v. *Provincie Groningen*)).

[173] However, in the case that the transaction with the principal would have been loss-making, reliance damages will be preferable.

[174] Chapter 2 (France), IV; Chapter 3 (Belgium), V 2. At first glance, the claim appears to be contractual in nature, basing liability on a breach of a warranty duty. However, Art. 1997 CC and Art. 1997 BCC (on which provisions liability of the false agent is based *a contrario* in France and Belgium) are generally said to be a specific application of the general tort provision of Art. 1382 CC and Art. 1382 BCC. It should, however, be noted that a minority of legal authors in Belgium considers the claim to be contractual in nature.

[175] Chapter 6 (England), IV 1; F. M. B. Reynolds, *Bowstead & Reynolds on Agency*, 18th edn (London: Sweet & Maxwell, 2006), 9-062.

[176] Chapter 9 (Scotland), IV 2, *in fine*.

is a personal undertaking that the principal will be bound by the contract. As a fictitious warranty implied as a result of a rule of law, arguably the South African system is the most logical in describing the agent's liability as quasi-contractual, rather than contractual.[177] In Dutch law, liability is described as being based on breach of warranty of authority. Like English law, Scots law and South African law, Dutch law has struggled to identify a legal basis for this warranty. Debate in the Dutch Parliament suggested that the warranty should be rationalised as the unilateral act of the agent.[178] In French law, in cases in which it is possible to base liability on a 'guarantee' given by the agent that the principal will ratify, the legal basis of the action is clearly a promise.[179]

2 Scope

The scope of application of the liability of the *falsus procurator* is extensive in many respects. It generally operates both in cases where the agent exceeds his authority and where he has no authority whatsoever.[180] Furthermore, in most of the systems studied, the liability of the *falsus procurator* not only operates in the context of the unauthorised conclusion of contracts, but also (sometimes by way of analogy) to other unauthorised legal acts.[181] In addition, in some of the systems studied the doctrine extends beyond the context of consensual unauthorised agency (e.g. in the context of authority pursuant to a statutory provision or judicial order or in the context of representation by a body of a legal

---

[177] Chapter 10 (South Africa), IV 2(a).   [178] Chapter 5 (the Netherlands), VI 1.

[179] Chapter 2 (France), IV.

[180] Thus explicitly: Chapter 2 (France), IV; Chapter 3 (Belgium), V 3; Chapter 12 (UP), VII 2 (Art. 2.2.6(2) UP).

[181] See Chapter 3 (Belgium), V 1 (where reference is made to legal acts in general); Chapter 4 (Germany), VI 5 (the liability of the *falsus procurator* may also arise in relation to certain unilateral transactions (§ 180, second sentence, BGB and § 179 BGB); Chapter 5 (the Netherlands), VI 2 (Art. 3:70 DCC on the liability of the *falsus procurator* specifically provides the following: 'He who *acts* as agent warrants to the third party the existence and the extent of his authority, unless the third party knows or should have known that sufficient authority is lacking, or unless the third party has fully communicated the content of his authority to the third party' (emphasis added)); Chapter 7 (US), IV 2 (where it is stated that 'an agent (or purported agent) impliedly warrants that *a contract, conveyance, or representation* purportedly made on behalf of another is made with authority' (emphasis added)); Chapter 9 (Scotland) IV 2; Chapter 11 (PECL), VII 3 (Art. 3:204(2) PECL read in conjunction with 1:107 PECL).

person).[182] Finally, at least in the Netherlands, the doctrine can even apply to legal acts performed outside the area of patrimonial law, such as in the context of family law, procedural law and public law.[183]

3 Effect

In all the systems studied, the general effect of the liability of the *falsus procurator* is that the false agent is liable to the third party in damages, typically expectation damages. Accordingly, the third party must be placed in the financial position he would have been in had the agent been sufficiently authorised.[184] An exception to this general approach can be found in German law, where an unauthorised agent acting in good faith can only be held liable for the reliance interest.[185]

As was noted in V 1 above, in the legal systems studied, the unauthorised agent himself does not become bound and entitled under the contract which he has purported to conclude in the name of the principal. As is noted in the chapter on South African law, originally the Roman-Dutch rule held the agent liable, and this rule applied until the early years of the twentieth century.[186] The German legal system alone appears to permit this possibility. As already stated in V 1 above, it gives to the third party the option to require either specific performance or damages from the agent, and the former option is perhaps an echo of the same Roman-Dutch rule.

---

[182] Thus explicitly: Chapter 5 (the Netherlands), VI 3 (Art. 3:70 DCC in conjunction with 3:78 DCC). In Germany, the PECL and the UNIDROIT Principles the liability of the *falsus procurator* sometimes applies in the context of legal persons as well. See Chapter 4 (Germany), VIII 2(b); Chapter 9 (Scotland) IV 3; Chapter 11 (PECL), VII 3; Chapter 12 (UP), VII 3.

[183] Chapter 5 (the Netherlands), VI 3 (Art. 3:70 DCC read in conjunction with 3:79 DCC).

[184] Chapter 4 (Germany), VI 2(b); Chapter 5 (the Netherlands), VI 4; Chapter 6 (England), IV 1; Chapter 7 (US), IV 2, *in fine* (*Restatement (Third) of Agency*, § 6.10); Chapter 9 (Scotland), IV 4; Chapter 10 (South Africa), IV 2(c); Chapter 11 (PECL), VII 4 (Art. 3:204 (2) PECL); Chapter 12 (UP), VII 4 (Art. 2.2.6(1) UP). In Belgium the situation is not entirely clear. As is set out in the chapter on Belgian law, according to the general rules on tort law a victim can only claim reliance damages. However, in connection with pre-contractual liability part of the case-law is moving towards a recognition of liability for expectation damages. In line with this development the author of the Belgian chapter argues that Belgian law should also be able to accept that the unauthorised agent is liable to pay expectation damages to the third party, if there was a legitimate belief of the third party that the agent had been sufficiently authorised. See Chapter 3 (Belgium), V 4. The position in French law is not clear either. See Chapter 2 (France), IV, n. 184.

[185] Chapter 4 (Germany), VI 3 (§ 179(2) BGB).   [186] Chapter 10 (South Africa), IV 2(a).

However, even German law does not go as far as stipulating that an actual contract binds the agent and the third party. Although the agent has the same rights as he would have had under an actual contract, specific performance, if granted, relates not to a contract but to a relationship established by law.[187]

Given the importance of specific performance in civil law systems generally, it is not surprising to note that this remedy is at least potentially available to third parties in this type of situation in other civil law countries as well.[188] The theoretical and practical difficulties inherent in its use were noted by two of the contributors.[189] Although opinion is divided in Belgium, some argue that the third party may request that the judge award compensation *in natura*.[190]

Specific performance has quite a different character in common law systems and South African law. The remedy is a discretionary one in England, available in limited circumstances where damages would not be an appropriate remedy.[191] The absence of reference to this remedy in the chapters on common law jurisdictions and in the chapter on South African law is therefore not surprising. On this question, Scotland must be aligned with civil law countries given that it is, in that country, at least in theory, the primary remedy. The author of the Scottish chapter has been unable to trace any single case in which a third party has sought specific implement against an unauthorised agent.[192]

4 Requirements

(a) Relevance of bad faith of the unauthorised agent

There are roughly two different approaches to the question of the relevance of bad faith of the unauthorised agent. On the one hand, there are systems where, in order for the unauthorised agent to be liable to the third party, the agent need not be at fault. This means that, in cases where the unauthorised agent did not know and could not reasonably

---

[187] Chapter 4 (Germany), VI 2(a) (§ 179(1) BGB).
[188] Chapter 2 (France), IV; Chapter 3 (Belgium), V 4; Chapter 5 (the Netherlands), VI 4.
[189] Chapter 3 (Belgium), V 4; Chapter 5 (the Netherlands), VI 4.
[190] Chapter 3 (Belgium), V 4.
[191] See E. Peel, *Treitel: The Law of Contract*, 12th edn (London: Sweet & Maxwell, 2007), para. 21-016.
[192] Chapter 9 (Scotland), IV 4.

know that he had insufficient authority, he can be held liable. This is the approach adopted by systems where the liability of the false agent is (primarily) based on a contractual warranty of authority. Most of the systems studied take this approach.[193] To give an example, in one of the leading cases in English law, an agent remained liable even though he was unaware of the termination of his agency relationship because of his principal's incapacity.[194] The potential unfairness of this approach was noted in the chapters on English and South African law, but was justified by the fact that the agent is the party who is best placed to verify his authority. On the other hand, there are systems where the false agent must be at fault. This is the approach taken in the systems where the liability of the false agent is (primarily) based on tort.[195]

It should be noted that in at least two of the systems studied where the strict approach applies, this is tempered somewhat. First, in German law, an agent who is unaware of his lack of authority is bound to pay reliance rather than expectation damages, subject to a cap or ceiling of the third party's expectation interest.[196] Second, in Dutch law the agent is not liable where he did not know nor ought to have known of the termination of authority.[197]

Taking all of these issues into account, we favour the strict approach for the reason stated in the chapters on English and South African law, namely that the agent as compared with the third party is the party best placed to verify his authority.

(b) Good faith of the third party and causal issues

In most of the systems studied, the conduct of the third party is relevant to the assessment of the unauthorised agent's liability to the third party. In Dutch law, German law, the PECL and the UNIDROIT Principles the same rule applies: no damages are available where the third party knows

---

[193] Chapter 4 (Germany), VI, introduction (§ 179(1) BGB); Chapter 5 (the Netherlands), VI 5(a) (Art. 3:70 DCC); Chapter 6 (England), IV 1; Chapter 7 (US), IV 2 (*Restatement (Third) of Agency*, § 6.10); Chapter 9 (Scotland), IV 5(a); Chapter 10 (South Africa), IV 2(b); Chapter 11 (PECL), VII 5(a); Chapter 12 (UP), VII 5(a). It should be noted that in most of these systems liability can also be based on tort, in which case fault on the side of the agent is required. See V 1, above.

[194] Chapter 6 (England), IV 1 (*Yonge* v. *Toynbee* [1910] 1 KB 215).

[195] Chapter 2 (France), IV; Chapter 3 (Belgium), V 2. It should be noted that in French law liability of the false agent can sometimes be based on contract. See V 1, above.

[196] Chapter 4 (Germany), VI 3.

[197] Chapter 5 (the Netherlands), VI 5(a) (Art. 3:76(2) DCC).

or ought to have known that authority was lacking.[198] In the *Restatement (Third) of Agency* a similar approach is taken.[199]

In English law, Scots law and South African law, the same results are achieved in a different manner. The issue is often decided as part of the causal analysis. The agent's breach of warranty must be relied upon and must cause, or induce, the third party's loss. Actual knowledge of lack of authority leads to the lack of a causal nexus between misrepresentation and loss. Like most other systems studied, English law, Scots law and South African law go further to apply to the third party a duty of reasonable behaviour – he is not entitled to be wilfully blind as to the lack of authority.[200] This approach could be criticised, however, given that the warranty is implied rather than explicit.

Similar results are probably also achieved in Belgium. The author of the Belgian chapter argues that when the third party knows or ought to have known that authority was lacking, one may conclude that the agent did not commit a tort because he was not at fault and is therefore not liable towards the third party for damages. However, according to the author of the Belgian chapter, one may also conclude that the conduct of the third party, knowing the lack of authority, constitutes a fault of the third party, resulting in a partial breach of the causal nexus and in a share of the liability between the agent and the third party.[201]

In French law the behaviour of the third party is also highly relevant. In a similar manner as is the case in English law, Scots law, South African law and Belgian law, the issue is often decided as part of the causal analysis. When the third party *knows* that the agent is acting in breach of his authority and yet does not obtain a personal commitment from the agent, the third party will have no action against the agent. This is so

---

[198] Chapter 4 (Germany), VI 4 (§ 179(3), first sentence, BGB); Chapter 5 (the Netherlands), VI 5(b) (Art. 3:70 DCC). The same rule probably applies if the third party claims damages on the basis of the general tort provision of Art. 6:162 DCC. This is slightly different if the agent continues to act in the name of the principal despite the fact that his authority has already ended in the circumstances described in Art. 3:76(1) DCC (*inter alia* where the termination has been made public). In the cases described there, the third party can also claim damages from the unauthorised agent if it can be argued that the third party should have known that the authority has ended, as long as he has no actual knowledge (and as long as the agent knew or should have known that his authority had ended) (Art. 3:76(2) DCC). In other words, the third party in such cases has no duty to investigate; Chapter 11 (PECL), VII 5(b) (Art. 3:204(2), second sentence, PECL); Chapter 12 (UP), VII 5(b) (Art. 2.2.6 (2) UP).

[199] Chapter 7 (US), IV 2 (*Restatement (Third) of Agency*, § 6.10).

[200] Chapter 6 (England), IV 3 (e.g. *Halbot* v. *Lens* [1901] 1 Ch 344); Chapter 9 (Scotland), IV 5(b); Chapter 10 (South African), IV 2(b) (e.g. *Nebendahl* v. *Schroeder*, 1937 SWA 48).

[201] Chapter 3 (Belgium), V 2.

because the third party bears the risk of contracting with an agent while being aware of his lack of authority. The acceptance by the third party of the risk that the agent does not have the requisite authority breaks the chain of causation. Furthermore, the agent will not be liable if the third party is negligent by being *unaware* of the agent's limitation of power. In the latter situation, according to the author of the chapter on French law, it has been suggested that a share of liability should be possible.[202]

The general position in each of the legal systems on the third party's behaviour appears to be very similar. An issue which is in some countries resolved by an application of a duty of good faith, is in other countries resolved as part of the causal analysis.

(c) Damage, causation, burden of proof

In all the systems studied, for the unauthorised agent to be liable, the third party must have suffered damage as a consequence of the agent's lack of authority. Several authors mention the example of the insolvency of the principal, in which case no liability arises or, if it does, it is limited to out-of-pocket losses.[203]

Dutch law deserves specific mention here. The Dutch Supreme Court has ruled that the false agent is required to prove that the contract would *not* have been duly performed had the agent been duly authorised.[204] It is submitted that this is a fair approach. The agent will usually be in a better position to establish this fact.

VI The interrelationship between apparent authority, ratification and the liability of the *falsus procurator*

1 General

Now that we have examined apparent authority, ratification and the liability of the *falsus procurator* separately, we can turn to the interrelationship between the three doctrines.

---

[202] Chapter 2 (France), IV.

[203] Chapter 4 (Germany), VI 1 (OLG Hamm MDR 1993, 515); Chapter 6 (England), IV 1; Chapter 7 (US), IV 2 (*Restatement (Third) of Agency*, § 6.10, Comment (*b*)); Chapter 9 (Scotland), IV 4 (*Irving* v. *Burns* 1915 SC 260); Chapter 10 (South Africa), IV 2(c) (*Langford* v. *Moore and others* (1900) 17 SC 10; *Blower* v. *Van Noorden* 1909 TS 890 at 903–5; *Ex Parte De Villers & another NNO: In Re Carbon Developments* 1992 (2) SA 95 at 144).

[204] Chapter 5 (the Netherlands), VI 5(c) (HR 20 February 2004, NJ 2004, 254 (*Vreeswijk* v. *Van Heeckeren van Kill*); HR 8 October 2004, NJ 2006, 478, with annotation by Jac Hijma (*Arnold van de Kamp Makelaardij BV* v. *F. van der Veer Beleggingen BV*)).

2 Apparent authority and ratification

As we have seen in a number of the legal systems studied, apparent authority is based on an estoppel or similar concept. In these legal systems, apparent authority only works *against* the principal, meaning that the principal can only obtain an action against the third party by (impliedly) ratifying the agent's unauthorised act.[205] This approach can be contrasted with the legal systems in which the principal can (sometimes) sue the third party on the basis of apparent authority, often because it is based on the objective theory of contract.[206] In such legal systems, the principal need not resort to ratification in order to sue the third party. The doctrine of ratification therefore plays a more modest role than in the legal systems in which apparent authority is based on a form of estoppel. In our view, this difference of approach is of little practical relevance. In both approaches the principal can sue the third party, either on the basis of apparent authority or on the basis of (implied) ratification.

Interesting perspectives on the interrelationship between apparent authority and ratification are also provided by the chapter on Dutch law. In the Netherlands it follows from *Kuijpers* v. *Wijnveen*[207] that it is not only in relation to ratification that the court is allowed to take into account circumstances which took place *after* the conclusion of the contract, but also in relation to apparent authority (e.g. not reacting to a confirmation of an order). Thus, a third party will sometimes be able to invoke both doctrines on the basis of the same facts. In this sense, both doctrines may coincide in Dutch law.[208] In the PECL and the UNIDROIT Principles, it seems that apparent authority and (apparent) ratification may coincide in a similar manner. The PECL have adopted the general rule that in interpreting a contract regard should be had,

---

[205] Chapter 6 (England), II 5; Chapter 9 (Scotland), II 4; Chapter 10 (South Africa), II 1; Chapter 12 (UP), V 4, VIII 2. See also this chapter, III 3.

[206] Chapter 7 (US), III 2; Chapter 11 (PECL), V 4 (in all the aforementioned legal systems the objective theory of contract approach is followed, allowing the principal to sue the third party on the basis of apparent authority). See also: Chapter 3 (Belgium), III 5; Chapter 5 (the Netherlands), IV 4 (in Belgium and the Netherlands an intermediate position is taken, with characteristics of both the estoppel approach and the objective theory of contract approach: only the third party can invoke apparent authority, but as soon as the third party sues the principal on that basis, the principal may sue the third party as well). Compare also Chapter 4 (Germany), IV 1 and VII (sometimes the objective theory of contract is applied and sometimes the estoppel approach). See also this chapter, III 3.

[207] HR 12 January 2001, NJ 2001, 157.   [208] Chapter 5 (the Netherlands), VII 2.

amongst other issues, to 'the conduct of the parties, even *subsequent*[209] to the conclusion of the contract' (Art. 5:102(b) PECL). Similarly, the UNIDROIT Principles have adopted the general rule that in interpreting a contract regard should be had amongst other things to 'the conduct of the parties *subsequent*[210] to the conclusion of the contract' (Art. 4.3(c) UP). In line with these provisions it appears that, as regards the doctrine of apparent authority, later circumstances should also be taken into account. If that is accepted, the doctrines of apparent authority and (apparent) ratification may coincide in both international instruments.[211] The position is entirely different in England and Scotland. In these legal systems it is not possible to use the subsequent acts of contracting parties to interpret the meaning of a contract.[212] In view of this, it seems that apparent authority and (apparent) ratification cannot in those legal systems coincide in a similar manner as in Dutch law, the PECL and the UNIDROIT Principles. We welcome an approach which permits the court to take into account circumstances which took place *after* the conclusion of the contract. This is because, in practice, a clear distinction between apparent authority and (apparent) ratification cannot always be drawn.

3 Apparent authority and liability of the falsus procurator

In all the systems studied, apparent authority and the liability of the *falsus procurator* are mutually exclusive. Either the third party sues the principal on the basis of apparent authority, in which case the third party cannot successfully sue the false agent for damages on the basis of the liability of the *falsus procurator*, or *vice versa*.

In order to understand the exact interrelationship between apparent authority and the liability of the *falsus procurator*, a distinction should be drawn between systems in which apparent authority is based on the objective theory of contract and systems in which apparent authority is

---

[209] Emphasis added.   [210] Emphasis added.
[211] Chapter 11 (PECL), VIII 2; Chapter 12 (UP), VIII 2.
[212] For Scots law, see W. M. Gloag, *The Law of Contract, a Treatise on the Principles of Contract in the Law of Scotland*, 2nd edn (Edinburgh: W. Green, 1929), p. 375; W. W. McBryde, *The Law of Contract in Scotland*, 3rd edn (Edinburgh: W. Green, 2007) para. 8–14, although the Scottish Law Commission has noted that this rule is often breached, see *Report on Interpretation in Private Law* (Scot Law Com no. 160) (1997), n. 55 to para. 2.27. For English law, see Peel, *Treitel: The Law of Contract*, para. 6-002; and *James Miller & Partners v. Whitworth Street Estates (Manchester) Ltd* [1970] AC 583 and *Wickman Ltd v. Schuler AG* [1974] AC 325.

based on notions which produce a weaker effect.[213] In the former, there is a valid contract between principal P and third party T from the outset. This means that if P is willing to uphold the contract, T cannot choose not to rely on the appearance of authority and instead turn to false agent A on the basis of the liability of the *falsus procurator*.[214] In the latter, T is generally entitled *not* to invoke apparent authority and instead turn to A.[215] However, in Dutch legal doctrine it has been argued that this should be different where it is clear that P indicates that he wishes to uphold the unauthorised legal act, because in such cases it will often be contrary to reasonableness and fairness for T to take the position that P did not, in fact, grant A (sufficient) authority.[216] Moreover, if P indicates that he is willing to uphold the contract, this is likely to amount to an implied ratification, with the effect that A will generally be freed from his liability against T. Given that this is the case, in practical terms it is probably not particularly significant whether apparent authority is based on the objective approach or on a notion which produces a weaker effect.

4 Ratification and liability of the falsus procurator

In the legal systems studied where this is permitted, if third party T withdraws from the transaction before ratification takes place, agent A remains liable.[217]

In the legal systems studied, *after* a ratification A will generally be freed from his liability towards T. The reason is that, as a consequence of the retroactive effect of ratification, T will not normally have suffered any

---

[213] On this distinction, see this chapter, III 3, above.

[214] Chapter 7 (US), IV; Chapter 11 (PECL), VIII 3. See also German law, where in certain cases of constructive notice (a type of apparent authority) the legal fiction applies that the agent was sufficiently authorised. The consequence of this is that the liability of the *falsus procurator* on the basis of § 179 BGB is excluded. With respect to 'true' apparent authority (*Anscheinsvollmacht*) the prevailing view (although not the view of the authors of the chapter on German law) is that it is to be regarded as a case of constructive authority as well, with the effect that the third party in such a situation cannot turn to the unauthorised agent on the basis of § 179 BGB either. Chapter 4 (Germany), IV and VII.

[215] Thus explicitly: Chapter 2 (France), IV, *in fine*; Chapter 5 (the Netherlands), IV 4, VII 3; Chapter 11 (UP), V 4, VIII 3. See also German law, where in a specific case of constructive notice (a type of apparent authority) the third party has an option not to rely on apparent authority and instead turn to the unauthorised agent on the basis of § 179 BGB. See Chapter 4 (Germany), VII. Compare also Chapter 3 (Belgium), III 5.

[216] Chapter 5 (the Netherlands), IV 4, VII 3.

[217] Chapter 4 (Germany), VI 1, VII; Chapter 5 (the Netherlands), VII 4; Chapter 12 (UP), VIII 4.

damage.[218] However, in at least some of the legal systems studied, there are exceptions to this rule where good grounds exist.

Nearly all of the legal systems studied contain a similar exception to the effect that, if the principal has granted rights to 'fourth parties' (i.e. parties other than the principal, the agent and the third party) prior to ratification, these rights are respected.[219] Therefore, if T suffers damage as a consequence, A remains liable towards T. For example, an unauthorised agent A grants a right of pledge to third party T1 over a claim belonging to principal P. Thereafter, P grants a right of pledge over the same claim to third party T2 and subsequently ratifies the grant of pledge to T1. The right of pledge of T2 takes priority above the right of pledge of T1. If T1 suffers any damage because his right of pledge ranks second instead of first, A can be held liable.[220]

Secondly, partial or conditional ratification is almost invariably not possible.[221] However, as previously mentioned,[222] it is sometimes argued that in certain circumstances T may be *obliged* to accept a partial or

---

[218] Thus explicitly: Chapter 3 (Belgium), IV 3(a); Chapter 4 (Germany), VII; Chapter 5 (the Netherlands), VII 4; Chapter 6 (England), III 1; Chapter 7 (US), IV; Chapter 11 (PECL), VIII 4; Chapter 12 (UP), VIII 4.

[219] Chapter 2 (France), III 2(b); Chapter 3 (Belgium), IV 3(b) (Cass. 6 February 1953, *Pas* 1953, I, 436 and *RPS* 1953, 224, concl. H. de Termicourt, obs. PD); Chapter 5 (the Netherlands), V 5(b) (Art. 3:69(5) DCC); Chapter 6 (England), III 4(b) (where it is argued that 'ratification cannot generally divest property rights that have accrued to others outside the triangular principal-agent-third party relationship but that ratification in such circumstances can nevertheless affect the rights and obligations of the parties within the triangular relationship itself'); Chapter 7 (US), III 5(a) (*Restatement (Third) of Agency*, § 4.02(2)(c)); Chapter 9 (Scotland), III 5 (b) (where it is argued that the Scottish court would be unlikely to allow ratification to have a detrimental effect on 'fourth parties'); Chapter 10 (South Africa), III 6 (*Smith* v. *Kwanonqubela Town Council* 1999 (4) SA 947 at 954A–B; *Jagersfontein Garage & Transport Co.* v. *Secretary, State Advances Office* 1939 OPD 37 at 46–47); Chapter 11 (PECL), VI 5(b) (Art. 3:207(2) PECL). The UNIDROIT Principles, however, take the position that the effect of ratification on persons other than the principal, the agent and the third party is outside their scope. See Chapter 12 (UP), VI 5(b) (Comment 5 to Art. 2.2.9 UP).

[220] Thus explicitly: Chapter 5 (the Netherlands), VII 4; Chapter 11 (PECL), VIII 4.

[221] Thus explicitly: Chapter 5 (the Netherlands), V 4(c) (Art. 3:69(4), second sentence, DCC); Chapter 6 (England), III 2(a) (*Smith* v. *Henniker-Major & Co.* [2003] Ch 182, although note the possibly exceptional case, *Harrison & Crossfield Ltd* v. *LNW Railway Co. Ltd* [1917] 2 KB 755, in which ratification was permitted for one purpose but not for another); Chapter 7 (US), III 5(a), third paragraph (*Restatement (Third) of Agency*, § 4.07); Chapter 9 (Scotland), III 4(b); Chapter 10 (South Africa), III 2(f) (*Bouygues Offshore and another* v. *Owner of the MT TIGR and another*, 1995 (4) SA 49 (C) at 72C–E); Chapter 12 (UP), VI 4(c) (Comment 2 to Art. 2.2.9 UP).

[222] See this chapter, IV 3(c) above.

conditional ratification because of his duty to mitigate damage. This seems a fair approach because even if the third party accepts a partial or conditional ratification, the *falsus procurator* remains liable to the extent that the third party – notwithstanding a partial or conditional ratification by the principal – has suffered damage as a consequence of the unauthorised agency.[223]

Thirdly, the unauthorised agent may occasionally be held liable even after the principal has ratified to the extent that the need for ratification has delayed the performance of the contract.[224]

VII Acting in the name of a principal yet to be named

Nearly all of the legal systems studied contain specific rules applying to agents contracting for unnamed or unidentified principals. If the agent does not in fact have a principal, there is a special type of unauthorised agency. In most of the legal systems studied, the agent becomes personally bound and entitled under the contract which he has purported to conclude on behalf of an unnamed principal, often if he has not disclosed the identity of his principal within a certain time frame.[225] Exceptionally, in such cases of unauthorised agency, the third party can regard the agent as his contractual counterparty. This, we would suggest, does not constitute a serious breach of the principle of autonomy. The third party is

---

[223] Chapter 5 (the Netherlands), VII 4; Chapter 12 (UP), VIII 4.

[224] Chapter 4 (Germany), VII. In that case, however, the liability of the false agent is not covered by § 179 BGB on the liability of the *falsus procurator*, but by the general rules of pre-contractual liability (§§ 280 in 311(2) BGB).

[225] Chapter 2 (France), VI (*déclaration de command/convention de prête-nom*); Chapter 3 (Belgium), VI 4 (*commandverklaring* or *déclaration de command*); Chapter 5 (the Netherlands), VIII (Art. 3:67 DCC); Chapter 7 (US), IV (*Restatement (Third) of Agency*, § 6.02); Chapter 11 (PECL), IX (Art. 3:203 PECL). In German law, § 179 BGB (contracts) and § 180 (unilateral legal transactions) BGB on the liability of the *falsus procurator* are (at least according to the prevailing view) applied by way of analogy to the case that the agent acts in the name of a principal to be named where in fact there is no principal. This means that the third party can as a general rule either claim expectation damages or specific performance from the false agent. See Chapter 4 (Germany), VIII 1. In English law the situation is not clear. According to the author of the chapter on England, there are several possibilities in such cases. The first is that the agent was acting for himself all along in which case the agent will be personally liable. A second possibility is that his liability should be based on a collateral contract that he has a principal fitting the description (if any) given. The third possible solution is that the agent is liable for breach of warranty of authority since the agent has represented that he has been authorised by a principal even if he has not named the principal. See Chapter 6 (England), IV 5; Chapter 9 (Scotland) IV.

prepared to contract with a principal whose identity is unknown to him at the time of the conclusion of the contract and is therefore evidently unconcerned about the identity of his contractual counterparty. There can be no objection, therefore, to the rule that the agent is the counter-party in such cases.[226]

VIII Acting in the name of a company yet to be incorporated

1 General

Article 7 of the First Directive for the Harmonisation of Company Law[227] obliged the member states of the European Union to introduce rules for the protection of third parties in the case of performance of legal acts (such as the conclusion of contracts) in the name of a company prior to its incorporation. It is interesting to see, however, that this directive has been implemented in different ways in the European countries studied in this book.

2 Apparent authority

When a party acts in the name of a 'company yet to be incorporated', the third party generally knows or ought to have known that the principal does not yet exist and that the agent is therefore unauthorised. This means that in most cases there cannot be an appearance of authority. In view of this, when an agent concludes a contract (or performs another legal act) in the name of a company yet to be incorporated, the third party will usually not be able successfully to invoke (an analogous application of) apparent authority.[228]

3 Ratification

As previously discussed,[229] the legal systems studied display differing attitudes to pre-incorporation contracts, or contracts entered into on

---

[226] See also Chapter 5 (the Netherlands), VIII; Chapter 11 (PECL), IX.
[227] First Council Directive 68/151/EEC of 9 March 1968 on coordination of safeguards which, for the protection of the interests of members and others, are required by member states of companies within the meaning of the second paragraph of Art. 58 of the Treaty, with a view to making such safeguards equivalent throughout the Community, OJ 1968 No. L65, 14 March 1968, pp. 8–12.
[228] Thus explicitly: Chapter 5 (the Netherlands), IX 2.
[229] See this chapter, IV 5(d), above.

behalf of companies not yet in existence. In some legal systems, such contracts are not valid and cannot be ratified.[230] Other solutions must be found in these legal systems, such as, for example, adoption of the contract as occurs in the US.[231] In England, the parties must enter into an entirely new contract.[232] The mixed legal systems, Scotland and South Africa, have, as is described in the relevant chapters, applied native common law concepts of third party rights in contract to solve this particular problem, successfully in South Africa but unsuccessfully in Scotland.[233] In Belgian and Dutch law, too, ratification is possible in such circumstances.[234] The PECL similarly permit ratification in such circumstances, but note that the special rules of the applicable company law with respect to pre-incorporation contracts take precedence over the terms of the PECL.[235] In Germany, § 177 BGB on ratification is applied by way of analogy to the case of companies not yet incorporated. However, from a practical point of view, the most common case of a non-existent principal is dealt with under the special rules of company law. For example, according to a judge-made rule a GmbH (limited liability company) coming into existence automatically becomes the debtor, in which case there is no room for ratification[236]

As previously discussed,[237] there seems to be no good reason why the principal should not be able to ratify where the company was not yet in existence at the time the unauthorised legal act was done. The relevant time is the time of ratification when the principal is able to express his will. If at that time he was willing to ratify, he should in principle be able to do so. We reject the German judge-made rule that a GmbH coming into existence automatically becomes the debtor. There seems to be no good reason why in that particular case an exception should be made to

---

[230] Chapter 6 (England), III 2(d); Chapter 7 (US), III 5(b) (*Restatement (Third) of Agency*, § 4.04); Chapter 9 (Scotland), III 6(c)(i).

[231] Chapter 7 (US), III 5(b) (adoption – unlike ratification – does not operate retroactively). In France the technique of adoption is also used, see Chapter 2 (France), V.

[232] Chapter 6 (England), III 2(d).

[233] Chapter 9 (Scotland), V; Chapter 10 (South Africa), III 2(c), although it is no longer necessary to use the *stipulatio alteri* as a solution following the enactment of s. 35 South African Companies Act. See also s. 21 of the South African draft Companies Bill, commented on in more detail in Chapter 10 (South Africa), footnotes 65 and 80.

[234] Chapter 3 (Belgium), VII (Art. 60 of the Company Code); Chapter 5 (the Netherlands), IX 3 (Arts 2:93(1) and 2:203(1) DCC).

[235] Chapter 11 (PECL), VI 3 (Comment B to Art. 3:207 PECL).

[236] Chapter 4 (Germany), VIII 2(a), where the German position is dealt with in further detail.

[237] See this chapter, IV 5(d) above.

the rule that the principal of an unauthorised agent is in principle only bound and entitled if he ratifies the unauthorised legal act.

4 Liability of the falsus procurator

Applying the general concept of an implied warranty of authority poses difficulties in the context of liability of a person acting in the name of a 'company yet to be incorporated'. In such cases, the third party usually knows, or at least ought to have known, that he is dealing with an unauthorised agent, because he knows that the principal is not yet in existence. In Dutch law, German law, the PECL and the UNIDROIT Principles, this usually means that the third party cannot claim damages from the false agent, because the third party knows or at least ought to have known that authority was lacking.[238] A similar problem arises in French law (the agent will not be liable if the third party's ignorance of the limitation of power is due to his own fault) and in the *Restatement (Third) of Agency* (no damages are available if the third party knows that the false agent lacks actual authority).[239] In English law, Scots law and South African law, the agent's breach of warranty must be relied upon and must cause, or induce, the third party's loss. Actual knowledge of lack of authority leads to the lack of a causal nexus between misrepresentation and loss.[240] Such a third party can therefore not usually claim damages from the unauthorised agent on the basis of an implied warranty of authority. In addition, in South African law (quite apart from whether the third party usually knows or ought to know that authority is lacking) it was ruled in *Indrieri* v. *Du Preez* that the third party can receive no more damages from the unauthorised agent than he would have been able to receive from the principal. It was further stated: 'it is axiomatic that a non-existent company cannot pay anything at all'.[241]

It is not surprising, therefore, that, in at least some of the legal systems studied, there are special provisions on the liability of persons acting in

---

[238] Chapter 4 (Germany), VI 4 (§ 179(3), first sentence, BGB); Chapter 5 (the Netherlands), VI 5(b), IX 4 (Art. 3:70 DCC); Chapter 11 (PECL), VII 5(b) (Art. 3:204(2), second sentence, PECL); Chapter 12 (UP), VII 5(b) (Art. 2.2.6(2) UP).

[239] Chapter 2 (France), IV; Chapter 7 (US), IV 2 (*Restatement (Third) of Agency* § 6.10).

[240] Chapter 6 (England), IV 3 (e.g. *Halbot* v. *Lens* [1901] 1 Ch 344); Chapter 9 (Scotland), IV 5(b); Chapter 10 (South Africa), IV 2(b) (e.g. *Nebendahl* v. *Schroeder*, 1937 SWA 48).

[241] 1989 (2) SA 721 (C) at 727 E. See Chapter 10 (South Africa), IV 5.

the name of a company yet to be incorporated.[242] A common 'theme'
which can be discerned is that the agent is liable, albeit that liability is
achieved in different ways. In the Netherlands, for example, those who
perform a legal act in the name of a company yet to be incorporated,
unless the contrary is expressly stipulated in respect of such legal act, will
be bound jointly and severally thereby until the public or private limited
liability company concerned has ratified such legal act after its incorporation.[243] The position in Belgian law[244] and in German law is quite
similar. In German law, in the case of public and private limited liability
companies and associations, all persons acting in the name of the future
company are liable. In practice, this liability only takes place where the
incorporation of the company fails later on. Where the company comes
into existence it assumes the obligations created by the acts of the agent,
and thereby relieves the agent of his liability.[245] In the chapter on South
African law, it is pointed out that in the case of the liability of an agent
acting on behalf of a company yet to be incorporated an action in delict is
the most appropriate remedy for the third party, provided that the third
party can prove fault. In that system, too, the agent may be held accountable if he has given an actual warranty of authority, or an undertaking to
secure ratification. It may be difficult to prove damage, however, unless
the loss has been agreed and quantified in advance.[246]

---

[242] It should be noted that the question as to the liability of the *falsus procurator* in cases of
companies yet to be incorporated has not been addressed in all of the chapters.

[243] Chapter 5 (the Netherlands), IX 4.

[244] Chapter 3 (Belgium), VII (Art. 60 of the Company Code).

[245] Chapter 4 (Germany), VIII 2(b) (§ 41(1), second sentence, *Aktiengesetz*, § 11(2) *GmbH-
Gesetz*, § 54, second sentence, BGB).

[246] Chapter 10 (South Africa), IV 5.

14

Comparative conclusions

DANNY BUSCH AND LAURA MACGREGOR

Table of contents

I General

In all the legal systems studied the general effect of unauthorised agency is that the principal and third party are neither bound nor entitled under a contract (or other legal act) concluded without (sufficient) authority. This rule protects the autonomy of the principal because it prevents him from being bound and entitled against his will.

1 Apparent authority

However, the interests of the principal are obviously not the only interests involved. In particular, one must take account of the interests of the third party. In the legal systems studied, the doctrine of apparent authority in particular fulfils the function of achieving a balance between the legitimate interests of the principal and those of the third party. Apparent authority allows the third party to sue the principal notwithstanding the fact that the agent was unauthorised.

The various concepts of apparent authority found in the legal systems contain a high degree of similarity. A common characteristic is the giving of validity to appearances, and the protection of the third party who relies, in good faith, on such appearances. Another common factor is the visible tension between the desire to impose liability on the principal only where the erroneous impression of authority was created by him, through his actions, and a recognition that liability must extend wider in order to achieve the ultimate goal of third party protection. As yet, no legal system appears to have rejected the connection with the principal's conduct entirely. At the same time, more and more factors are being classed, perhaps unconvincingly, as 'conduct' of the principal.

In our view, a wide approach to apparent authority is welcome because it takes into account not only the principal's conduct but also all the other circumstances of the case. This allows the courts to focus on a number of issues which may lie within the principal's sphere of responsibility. To this extent it is a less artificial method of imposing liability. It makes explicit factors which were already implicit in classical apparent authority reasoning, and provides those factors with a clearer legal basis. It is a more nuanced approach, enabling the courts to reach solutions which can be 'tailor-made' to each case. In this way the courts can redress the balance in those systems which adhere more firmly to the 'of the principal's own doing approach'.

There are, of course, disadvantages in a wider approach. It could lead to large, and perhaps unmanageable, increases in the principal's liability. Whether this is likely to occur is difficult to tell. The end result may indeed not differ markedly from the current approach, where the 'of the principal's own doing' idea is artificially extended. Like any discretionary concept, its success depends on the manner in which it is applied by the courts. The discretion would require to be an 'open' one: it is unlikely that it could be defined by reference to all potentially relevant issues. Experience from case-law could also inform the approach. Lessons could be learned from the French approach, which is, as is illustrated in Chapter 2, a particularly 'factual' one. The courts in that legal system pay careful attention to the characteristics of both principal and agent and the information reasonably available to both. Certainly, the Dutch experience suggests that a discretionary approach is workable. It may even act as an incentive for the principal to ensure that his agent acts within the confines of his authority in the future.

2 Ratification

Each of the legal systems contains a similar concept of ratification. As explained above, the general effect of unauthorised agency is that the principal and third party are neither bound nor entitled under a contract (or other legal act) concluded without (sufficient) authority. This rule protects the principal's autonomy. However, his autonomy is not violated where he has no objection to the contract (or other legal act) concluded by his unauthorised agent. To permit him to ratify is therefore a practical solution. In all the systems studied, ratification has retroactive effect: after ratification, the unauthorised contract (or other legal act) is as effective as it would have been had it been performed by an authorised agent.

However, in this context, too, the interests of the principal are not the only ones involved. Regard must be had to the interests of the third party and parties other than the principal, the agent and the third party, sometimes referred to as 'fourth parties'.

As far as the interests of the third party are concerned, his ability to withdraw from the transaction prior to ratification by the principal is probably the most contentious issue. The influential English case of *Bolton Partners Ltd* v. *Lambert*[1] upholds the retrospective effect of ratification to its full extent, rendering the third party unable to withdraw where his purported withdrawal is followed by ratification. In *Bolton*, the third party was treated as bound by a contract with the principal from the moment the agent purported to enter into the transaction. Although the case is undoubtedly controversial, it remains good law. In contrast to the position in English law, the Dutch and German Civil Codes both provide the third party in good faith with a right to withdraw from the transaction prior to ratification. However, the difference in approach between English law on the one hand and German and Dutch law on the other may not be as wide as it first appears. In English law, as in some of the other legal systems studied, exceptions have developed which go some way towards limiting the strict effect of this approach, in particular by preventing ratification in circumstances where it would unfairly prejudice the interests of the third party. Clearly, what is required is another delicate balance between the interests of the principal and those of the third party.

The solution to the problem of the third party's right to withdraw ought to be informed by relevant policy factors. To allow the third party to withdraw potentially allows him to 'play the market'. However, this may not be an accurate description of the situation. If the third party rejects the unauthorised act merely because he wishes to conclude a more favourable contract elsewhere, the rejection may be null and void. He could be prevented from this course of action on the basis that it would be contrary to good faith and fair dealing. We would suggest that the best

---

[1] (1889) 41 Ch D 295.

solution is to provide the third party with a limited right to withdraw. In making this decision we are motivated by the fact that the third party, through no fault of his own, is placed in a position of uncertainty. His right must, however, be limited: he must act in good faith. This proviso ensures that the interests of the principal are sufficiently protected.

Looking beyond the immediate actors in the agency situation, the legal systems studied display a consistent attitude to fourth parties. Nearly all of them contain protective rules providing that ratification is ineffective where fourth parties have acquired rights prior to ratification.

The comparative analysis has also shed light on some significant problems inherent in ratification. Of particular note is the inability of Scots and English law properly to analyse the legal situation prior to ratification, and, in particular, the type of obligation concluded by the unauthorised agent. Certain acts by the agent clearly possess a sufficient degree of validity to allow ratification to operate. However, in both systems, a class of acts exists which is so fundamentally flawed that ratification may not operate. The dividing line between the classes and the content of each one is far from clear. Lessons could be learned from German law where an attempt has been made to analyse the pre-ratification situation using the concept of a 'floating contract' or *schwebende Unwirksamkeit*. Until this significant problem has been tackled, neither system is likely to achieve workable solutions to several problematic issues, such as the third party's ability to withdraw or the relevance of time limits applying to the legal act in question.

3 Liability of the falsus procurator

In each of the systems studied, where the third party cannot make use of the doctrine of apparent authority and the principal does not choose to ratify, the principal and the third party will not be bound by the contract (or other legal act) concluded by the unauthorised agent. In such cases, the third party can generally hold the unauthorised agent liable for the losses which he has suffered as a consequence of the agent's lack of authority, typically for expectation damages. This means that the third party is placed in the financial position which he would have been in had the agent been sufficiently authorised. This action is an important weapon in the third party's armoury.

This is not to say, however, that the interests of the unauthorised agent are entirely ignored. Indeed, it is possible to find measures in each of the legal systems having a protective effect towards him. In the systems where the agent's liability is based on tort, he can only be held liable if he was at fault in some way. In those where his liability is based on an express or implied warranty of authority, he can be liable without fault on his part. However, in at least two of the systems studied where the stricter approach applies, it is tempered in some way.

The first system is German law, where an agent who is unaware of his lack of authority is bound to pay reliance rather than expectation damages, subject to a cap or ceiling of the third party's expectation interest. Secondly, in Dutch law, the agent is not liable where he neither knew nor ought to have known of the termination of his authority.

It is suggested that the strict approach is the most appropriate one to apply here, perhaps tempered by a rule similar to the Dutch one which protects the agent's position in circumstances where it would be difficult or impossible for him to become aware of the termination of his authority. A strict approach is appropriate as a reflection of the fact that the agent is the party best-placed to verify his authority. As is the case in the context of apparent authority and ratification, the third party is the party who suffers from an 'information asymmetry'. He does not possess the information necessary to verify the extent of the agent's authority. This being the case, it is appropriate for him to be able to recover his full losses from the agent, not simply his reliance expenditure.

It is perhaps worth noting, finally, the limited role played by this concept in some of the legal systems studied, particularly the Scots and English ones. For reasons which are not absolutely clear, there is very little case-law on breach of warranty of authority. It may be because agents tend to have a weaker financial covenant than principals and thus constitute a less attractive target for the third party. The case-law which does exist indicates that the third party is more likely to opt for the contractual and not the delictual route, perhaps drawn by the more attractive measure of damages.

II Mixed legal systems

In the Introduction to this book, the principal aim of the project was identified as the search for a 'common core' within European agency law. We sought to identify this common core (if any) and to assess the same, presenting our view of the 'best' solution. A further, ancillary aim was also identified which related to the presence within the project of two mixed legal systems. The particular aim, explored more fully in the Introduction, can be summarised in two points here: first, we wanted to see whether Scots and South African law could learn from one another, drawing on their shared structural nature (civilian foundations overlaid with strong common law influence); and secondly, we wanted to see whether there was evidence that the law in those systems is, in effect, a choice of the 'best' elements of the common law and the civil law. In this section we set out some of our conclusions relating to the mixed legal systems.

Before analysing the substantive conclusions, it is perhaps instructive to repeat a question posed in the Introduction – can Scots and South African law be described as 'mixed' in nature in the specific context of agency law? In both systems, the common law influence has been dominant. In both legal systems, extensive use has been made, at one time or another, of English case-law. In Scots law at least, this continues to be the case. Is there evidence in either system of the continuing relevance of the civilian background? In the Introduction it was suggested that at least one of the ways in which civilian influence can apply is through the use of general private law concepts, such as personal bar/estoppel or ratification. With the conclusion of this project, the extent of the impact of these concepts can be measured. As has been illustrated in the Scottish chapter in particular, personal bar has been developed in a manner which increases third party protection, particularly through the use of a wide unitary notion of 'inconsistent conduct'.[2] It is perhaps no accident that the recently published book in which this expansive concept has been explored draws extensively on South African law.[3]

Looking beyond general private law concepts, with the conclusion of the project, we can identify agency-specific examples of ongoing civilian influence. It was suggested in the Introduction that the most significant advantage which could be drawn from civilian roots was the more relaxed attitude to privity of contract. In the tri-partite agency situation, a third party right in contract is likely to be a useful tool. This prediction has proved to be an accurate one. One particular example is the use of the *stipulatio alteri* in South African law to circumvent the prohibition on ratification by non-existent principals.[4] As can be seen in the other national chapters, each legal system has struggled with this difficult issue.

---

[2] Chapter 9 (Scotland) II 5(a).
[3] E. C. Reid and J. G. Blackie, *Personal Bar* (Edinburgh: W. Green, 2006), which makes extensive use of both South African case-law and scholarship, particularly J. C. Sonnekus Rabie's, *The Law of Estoppel in South Africa*, 2nd edn (Durban: Butterworths, 2000).
[4] See the explanation provided in Chapter 10 (South Africa) III 2(c).

The South African solution allows the agent and the party normally described as the third party in agency to conclude a contract as *principals*. The remaining party, i.e. the party who would normally be described as the principal in agency, becomes the *tertius*. The contracting parties can intend to benefit the *tertius*. When he comes into existence, and accepts that benefit, he becomes a party to that agreement. The advantages of this analysis are clear. Because of his status as *tertius* rather than principal it makes no difference that he is not in existence when the original contract between agent and third party is concluded. Indeed, the issue of ratification need never arise. This solution has been used to good effect in the context of pre-incorporation contracts in company law. It is true that this particular issue is governed by statute in South African law.[5] However, the *stipulatio alteri* route remains possible. Parties who would prefer not to fulfil the requirements of s. 35 can choose this alternative route. Section 21 of the new South African Companies Bill will, once enacted, bring change to this area. Section 21 provides that a promoter can enter into a contract on behalf of an unincorporated company. That company can become a party to the contract upon its incorporation and ratification of the contract. The company must formally ratify or reject the contract within three months of incorporation. Failure to do so means that the company is automatically considered to have ratified. Where the company is not incorporated or it rejects part of the agreement, the promotor is jointly and severally liable under the agreement with the company.

Scots law has been less successful in the use of its third party right, the *jus quaesitum tertio*. The attempt to use this concept in the context of pre-incorporation contracts failed in the only Scottish case in which it was raised, *Cumming* v. *Quartzag Ltd*.[6] As explained in the Scottish chapter, it failed on unsound grounds, namely that no contract in fact existed between promoter and third party. Nevertheless, as MacQueen has pointed out, the Scottish concept can confer only benefits, not burdens.[7] To apply this concept to pre-incorporation contracts would be to confer both burdens and benefits on the company as *tertius*. This being the case, *jus quaesitum tertio* cannot provide a solution to this problem. South African

---

[5] Section 35, South African Companies Act.

[6] *Cumming* v. *Quartzag Ltd* 1980 SC 276 and see generally the explanation contained in Chapter 9 (Scotland) VI.

[7] See H. MacQueen, 'Promoter's Contracts, Agency and the *Jus Quaesitum Tertio*' 1982 *SLT* 257 and H. MacQueen, 'Obligations', in Sir T. B. Smith *et al.* (eds.), *The Laws of Scotland: Stair Memorial Encyclopaedia* (Edinburgh: Butterworths/Law Society of Scotland, 1987–96), vol. XV, paras. 834 and 840.

law avoided this particular problem through its requirement of acceptance on the part of the *tertius*. By contrast, in Scots law, the *tertius* need not accept the benefit conferred by the contracting parties.[8]

Several conclusions can be drawn from the shared experience involving third party rights. Importantly, it highlights the fact that workable solutions to agency problems can be achieved using tools lying beyond the law of agency. The actors need not always wear the mantels of principal, agent and third party. Alternative solutions although possible, must be subject to certain provisos. Examples include: (1) the expectations of the actors involved in an agency situation, which are created by the law of agency, must not be overturned; (2) each party must act in good faith; and (3) no party can be unfairly prejudiced. The use of third party rights as a solution in the context of pre-incorporation contracts seems particularly appropriate. Each of the three parties shares a common goal, and consents to the overall contractual arrangement. Unfortunately, because of structural difficulties, Scots law cannot benefit from the South Africa experience here. Statutory intervention is the only solution.

There is little evidence of the more relaxed attitude to privity being employed to good effect beyond the context of pre-incorporation contracts. Both of the mixed legal systems could therefore be accused of failing to make use of this important attribute, a legacy of the civilian past. A potential role for its use has been suggested in the Scottish chapter in the context of the *falsus procurator*.[9] As is illustrated in the other national chapters, there have been difficulties in providing this concept with a convincing legal basis. Clearly, the third party ought to have an action against the unauthorised agent who has caused him to suffer loss, but the legal basis of such action is less clear. Certain of the legal systems, such as Scots and English law, base the action on an implied warranty by the agent to the third party. In English law, the requirement of consideration excludes the possibility of a gratuitous warranty. This being the case, English law implies a contract between agent and third party. The warranty is given as part of that fictitious contract. Consideration is provided by the third party when he promises the agent that he will enter into a contract with the principal. Scots law has, it seems, rather unquestioningly followed this English solution, even though the requirement of consideration is not part of Scots law.

As explored in the Scottish chapter, there is another solution. Scots law could make use of its enforceable unilateral promise, or *pollicitatio*.

---

[8] See MacQueen, 'Obligations', para. 834.   [9] Chapter 9 (Scotland) IV 2.

Following this reasoning, the agent promises to the third party either that he is already properly authorised, or, if not already authorised, that he will obtain the requisite authority. This being a unilateral promise, there is no need for acceptance by the third party. If the agent fails to obtain the requisite authority, he stands in breach of promise. The third party then has a claim against him for damages for breach of promise. This solution seems to reflect more accurately the practical context. The third party usually assumes that the agent is fully authorised. It also avoids the use of a legal fiction. It is, of course, similar to the concept of the *promesse de porte-fort* explored in the French and Belgian chapters.[10] Experience in those countries certainly suggests that a promissory solution is workable. There may indeed be other contexts in which it could be used. The benefits of the relaxed attitude to privity have yet to be fully explored.

Moving to consider the second question, it will undoubtedly surprise no one that there is little evidence that Scots and South African law present models of what, to quote Lévy-Ullman, 'will be, some day ... the law of the civilised nations'.[11] In particular, Scots law could more accurately be described as being in an undeveloped state. At times South African law is equally open to criticism. Although that system has clearly benefited from a larger body of case-law and analysis, at times the solutions adopted are odd ones, which would not form part of a 'model' agency law. One example is the extra requirement applied in apparent authority cases that the representation is only effective if the principal, in making it, could reasonably have expected it to be acted upon.[12] This extra requirement operates in the principal's favour, adding a further hurdle for the third party to cross in order to reach his goal of compensation. Viewed against the backdrop of the other chapters of this book, which uniformly display progress towards increased third party protection, this certainly seems an unusual development.

Looking to the future, it remains to be seen whether full use can be made of the mixed nature of Scots law. Experience from the past suggests that the works of the institutional writers can provide a route to the use

---

[10] Chapter 2 (France) IV; Chapter 3 (Belgium) VIII. In fact, Gloag, the leading author on Scots contract law, writing in 1929, seems tacitly to recognise this possibility, supporting his explanation of breach of warranty of authority with a reference to the relevant section of Pothier, see W. M. Gloag, *The Law of Contract, a Treatise on the Principles of Contract in the Law of Scotland*, 2nd edn (Edinburgh: W. Green, 1929), p. 155, n. 3, where he refers to R. J. Pothier, *Treatise on the Law of Obligations* (London: A. Strahan, 1806), s. 75.

[11] H. Lévy-Ullman (trans. F. P. Walton), 'The Law of Scotland,' 1925 *JR* 370 at 390.

[12] Chapter 10 (South Africa) II 3.

of civilian concepts. A notable example is *Pollok* v. *Paterson*,[13] decided in 1811. In this case, the bench of five judges drew on the works of those writers and thus, indirectly, on relevant passages from the Digest to resolve problems caused where an agent's authority terminates without his knowledge.[14] The similarities between the solution adopted in that case and the current provision in PECL are striking.[15] Whether a modern court would prove as innovative in its use of older sources is less certain. The works of the institutional writers are approached, understandably, with caution because of their age. Additionally, achieving consistency between Scots and English law is a significant issue, and, to some, perhaps even an overriding one.

The future may be 'brighter' for South African law in comparison with Scots law. The judiciary there has, thus far, proved more willing to develop agency law in a more innovative way. Those judges are, of course, not subject to the same pressures as their Scottish counterparts to achieve consistency with English law. Importantly, South African law has an agency textbook, whereas Scots law does not. An example of innovation in the South African courts is the development of limitations to the concept of the undisclosed principal.[16] As is suggested in the Scottish chapter, there is cause for optimism in the vibrant academic environment which currently exists. It should be emphasised, however, that these arguments should not be interpreted as suggesting that an English solution is, necessarily, a 'bad' one. On the contrary, English law is currently 'blazing a trail' towards the development of a rational exception excluding ratification where it would have an unfairly prejudicial effect on the interests of third parties.[17] What is being suggested here is that a legal system faced with a *lacuna* in the law should develop solutions which 'fit' well within the underlying structure of that legal system. Solutions from other mixed legal systems can act as 'transplants' likely to thrive in new and similar surroundings.

---

[13] 10 Dec (1811) FC 369. The case concerned the mental incapacity and eventual sequestration of the principal.

[14] See the explanation in Chapter 9 (Scotland) II 3.

[15] Art 3:209(1)(d) PECL.

[16] See the discussion of the case of *Cullinan* v. *Noordkaaplandse Aartappelkernmoerkwekers Koöperasie Beperk* 1972 (1) SA 761, discussed in L. Macgregor, 'Agency', in H. MacQueen and R. Zimmermann (eds.), *European Contract Law: Scots and South African Perspectives* (Edinburgh: Edinburgh University Press, 2006) p. 123 at p. 137 *et seq.*

[17] See Chapter 6 (England) III 4, and, in particular, *Owners of the Borvigilant* v. *Owners of the Romina G* [2003] 2 Lloyd's Rep 520.

BIBLIOGRAPHY

Chapter 1 (Introduction)

Busch, D., 'Indirect Representation and the Lando Principles: An Analysis of Some Problem Areas from the Perspective of English Law' (1999) 7 *ERPL* 319–48
    Indirect Representation in European Contract Law (The Hague: Kluwer Law International, 2005)

Collier, J., 'Actual and Ostensible Authority of an Agent: A Straightforward Question and Answer' (1984) 43 *CLJ* 26–7

du Plessis, J., 'The Promises and Pitfalls of Mixed Legal Systems: The South African and Scottish Experiences' (1998) *Stell LR* 338–50
    'Comparative Law and the Study of Mixed Legal Systems', in M. Reimann and R. Zimmermann (eds.), *The Oxford Handbook of Comparative Law* (Oxford: Oxford University Press, 2006)

Kokkini-Iatridou, D. *et al.*, *Een inleiding tot het rechtsvergelijkende onderzoek* (Deventer: Kluwer, 1988)

Lévy-Ullman, H. (trans. F. P. Walton), 'The Law of Scotland' (1925) *JR* 370–91

MacQueen, H. L., 'Scots and English Law: The Case of Contract' (1998) *CLP* 204–29

McMeel, G., 'The Philosophical Foundations of the Law of Agency' (2000) 116 *LQR* 387–411

Oderkerk, A. E., *De preliminaire fase van het rechtsvergelijkend onderzoek* (Nijmegen: Ars Aequi Libri, 1999)

Reid, K. G. C., 'The Idea of Mixed Legal Systems' (2003) 78 *Tul LR* 5–40

Smits, J. M., *The Contribution of Mixed Legal Systems to European Private Law* (Antwerp: Intersentia, 2001)
    The Making of European Private Law: Towards a Ius Commune Europaeum as a Mixed Legal System (trans. N. Kornet) (Antwerp: Intersentia, 2002)

Tan, C.-H., 'Undisclosed Principals and Contract' (2004) 120 *LQR* 480–509

Verhagen, H. L. E., 'Agency and representation', in J. M. Smits, *Elgar Encyclopaedia of Comparative Law* (Cheltenham/Northampton: Edward Elgar, 2006), pp. 33–56

Whitty, N. R., 'The Civilian Tradition and Debates on Scots Law' (1996) *TSAR* 227–39 and 442–57

Wilson, W. A., 'The Importance of Analysis', in D. Carey Miller and D. W. Meyers (eds.), *Comparative and Historical Essays in Scots Law: A Tribute to Professor Sir Thomas Smith* (Edinburgh: Butterworths and Law Society of Scotland, 1992)

Zimmermann, R., Visser, D. and Reid, K. G. C., *Mixed Legal Systems in Comparative Perspective* (Oxford: Oxford University Press, 2004)

Zweigert, K. and Kötz, H., *Introduction to Comparative Law* (trans. T. Weir), 3rd edn (Oxford: Oxford University Press, 1998)

Chapter 2 (France)

Bell, J., Boyron, S. and Whittaker, S., *Principles of French Law*, 2nd edn (Oxford: Oxford University Press, 2008)

Bénabent, A., *Droit civil: Les contrats spéciaux civils et commerciaux*, 5th edn (Paris: Montchrestien, 2001)

Boudot, M., 'Apparence' (2003) *Répertoire de droit civil*, 1–19

Bouloc, *RTD Comm* 1994, p. 548, No 12

Bradgate, R. and White, F., *Commercial Law*, 8th edn (Blackstone: London, 2001)

Calais-Auloy, J., *D* 1963, J 277–9

　　D 1966, J 449–50

Capitant, H. (ed.), *Les Grands Arrêts de la Jurisprudence Civile*, 10th edn (Paris: Dalloz, 1997)

Chen, C. W., *Apparence et représentation en droit positif français* (Paris: LGDJ, 2000)

Cornu, G., *RTD Civ* 1963, 573–4

　　RTD Civ 1969, 804–6

　　RTD Civ 1977, 570–72

Cozian, M., Viandier, A. and Barbaux-Deboissy, F., *Droit des sociétés*, 17th edn (Paris: Litec, 2004)

Danis-Fatôme, A., *Apparence et contrat* (Paris: LGDJ, 2004)

De Quenaudon, R., 'Le mandat', *Jurisc Dalloz*, fascicule 20

Didier, P. and Lequette, Y. *De la représentation en droit privé* (Paris: LGDJ, 2000)

Esmein, P., *JCP* 1963, II, 13104

Flattet, G., *Les contrats pour le compte d'autrui: essai critique sur les contrats conclus par un intermédiaire en droit français* (Toulouse: F. Boisseau, 1950)

Guestin, J., *Traité de droit civil: Introduction générale* (Paris: LGDJ, 1994)

Huet, J., *Traité de droit civil: les principaux contrats spéciaux*, 2nd edn. (Paris: LGDJ, 2001)

　　Droit civil: Les contrats spéciaux civils et commerciaux, 5th edn (Paris: Montchrestien, 2001)

Izorche, M. L., 'A propos du contrat sans représentation' (1999) *D Chron* 369–74

Le Gall, J., *French Company Law* (London: Oyez Publishing, 1974)

Le Tourneau, Ph., 'Mandat' (2000) *Répertoire de droit civil* 26–52

Malaurie, P., Aynès, L. and Gautier, P. Y., *Cours de droit civil: Les Contrats spéciaux*, 14th edn (Paris: Cujas, 2002)

Monéger J., 'Baux commerciaux et théorie de l'apparence' (1993) I *Juris-Classeur périodique: édition notariale et immobilière* 103–9

Storck, M., *Essai sur le mécanisme de la représentation dans les actes juridiques, LGDJ, Bibl. dr. Privé, t.* 172, 1982

Vidal, D., *Droit des sociétés*, 4th edn (Paris: LGDJ, 2003)

Chapter 3 (Belgium)

Baudry-Lacantinerie G., *Traité théorique et pratique de droit civil*, XIX (Paris: Larose and Tenin, 1908)

Boonen, H., 'De rechtsschijn', *RW* 1950–51

Cauffman, C., 'The Principles of European Contract Law', *TPR* 2001

Demogue, R., *Traité des obligations en général*, vol. I (Paris: Librairie Arthur Rousseau, 1923)

De Page, H., *Traité élémentaire de droit civil belge* (Brussels: Bruylant, 1945–1975)

De Page, H. and Meinertzhagen-Limpens, A., *Traité élémentaire de droit civile belge*, vol. IV, *Les Principaux Contrats* (Brussels: Bruylant, 1997)

Depuyt, D., 'Artikel 848 Ger.W.', in P. Depuydt, J. Laenens, D. Lindemans, and S. Raes, *Gerechtelijk recht. Commentaar van rechtspraak en rechtsleer* (Antwerp: Kluwer Rechtswetenschappen, 2005), p. 137

De Quenaudon, R., in *Juris-classeurs civils*, v° *art. 1991 à 2002 C.C.*, fasc. 20, 2002, no. 12

Dirix, E., *Obligatoire verhoudingen tussen contractanten en derden*, (Antwerp: Kluwer, 1984)

Dirix, E., Tilleman, B. and Van Orshoven, P., *De Valks juridisch woordenboek* (Antwerp: Intersentia, 2001)

Dumont, M.-P., *L'opération de commission* (Paris: Litec, 2000)

Foriers, P-A., 'L'apparence, source autonome d'obligations, ou application du principe général de l'exécution de bonne foi', *JT* 1989, 543

'Le droit commun des intermédiaires commerciaux: courtiers, commissionnaires, agents', in B. Glansdorff (ed.), *Les intermédiaires commerciaux* (Brussels, Editions du Jeune Barreau de Bruxelles, 1990), p. 79

'Aspects de la représentation en matière contractuelle', in *Les Obligations Contractuelles* (Brussels: Jeune Barreau Edn, 2000)

Foriers, P.-A. and Glansdorff, F., *Contrats spéciaux*, vols. I and III (Brussels: Brussels University Press, 2000)

Foriers, P.-A. and Jafferali, R., 'Le mandat (1991 à 2004)', in F. Glansdorff, *Actualités de quelques contrats spéciaux* (Brussels: Bruylant, 2005), pp. 91–2

Gilcart, S., *La société en formation, Une étude du mécanisme sui generis de l'article 60 du Code des sociétés* (Mechelen: Wolters Kluwer Belgium, 2004)

Herbots, J. H., Stijns, S., Degroote, E., Lauwers, W. and Samoy, I., 'Overzicht van rechtspraak (1995–1998): Bijzondere Overeenkomsten', *TPR* 2002, 57

Kluyskens, A., *Beginselen van burgerlijk recht*, vol. IV, *De contracten* (Antwerp: Standaard, 1952)

Kruithof, R., 'La théorie de l'apparence dans une nouvelle phase', *RCJB* 1991, 68–73 'Overzicht van rechtspraak', *TPR* 1994, 225–7

Kruithof, R., Bocken, H., De Ly, F. and De Temmerman, B., 'Overzicht van rechtspraak (1981–1992). Verbintenissen', *TPR* 1994, 171

Lambrecht, B. and Samoy, I., 'Schijn van berusting en ontkentenis van proceshandeling' (obs. to Brussels 10 June 2002), *P&B* 2002, 307–12

Laurent, F., *Principes de droit civil français*, 33 parts (Brussels: Bruylant, 1878)

Limpens, L., *La vente en droit belge* (Brussels: Bruylant, 1960)

Limpens, L., Paulus, C. and Ras, H. E., *Preadviezen, De zaakwaarneming naar Belgisch recht en naar Nederlands recht* (Zwolle: Tjeenk Willink, 1968)

Paulus, C., *Zaakwaarneming*, in *APR* (Brussels: Larcier, 1970)

Paulus, C. and Boes, R., 'Lastgeving', in *Algemene Praktische Rechtsverzameling* (Gent: Story-Scientia, 1978)

Petel, P., *Le contrat de mandat* (Paris: Dalloz, 1994)

Sagaert, V., 'Zaakwaarneming', in E. Dirix and A. van Oevelen (eds.), *Bijzondere overeenkomsten, Commentaar met overzicht van rechtspraak en rechtsleer* (Deurne: Kluwer, 2003)

Samoy, I., *Middellijke vertegenwoordiging. Vertegenwoordiging herbekeken vanuit het optreden* in *eigen naam voor andermans rekening* (Antwerp and Oxford: Intersentia, 2005)

'De gevolgen van gesimuleerde rechtshandelingen', in J. Smits and S. Stijns (eds.), *Inhoud en werking van de overeenkomst naar Belgisch en Nederlands recht*, (Antwerpen-Groningen: Intersentia, 2005), pp. 268–9

Stijns, S., 'Het algemeen regime van de verbintenis', in S. Stijns and H. Vandenberghe (eds.), *Verbintenissenrecht, Themis* (Bruges: Die Keure, 2000–01), p. 18 *Leerboek verbintenissenrecht* (Bruges: Die Keure, 2005)

Stijns, S. and Vandenberghe, H. (eds.), *Verbintenissenrecht, Themis* (Bruges: Die Keure, 2000–01)

Stijns, S. and Samoy, I., 'La confiance légitime en droit privé des contrats', in E. Dirix and Y.-H. Leleu (eds.), *Rapports belges au congrès de l'académie internationale de droit comparé à Utrecht* (Brussels: Bruylant, 2006), pp. 277–8

Stijns, S. and Callens, P., 'Over tijdelijke vennootschappen en (schijn-)vertegenwoordiging', *TRV* 1989, 73

Stijns, S., Van Gerven, D. and Wery, P., 'Chronique de jurisprudence (1985–1995). Les obligations: les sources', *JT* 1996, 696

Storck, M., in *Juris-classeurs civils*, v° art. 1119 C.civ., fasc. 7–1, 1992, no. 76

Tilleman, B., 'Lastgeving', in *Algemene Praktische Rechtsverzameling* (Deurne: Kluwer, 1997), pp 143, 151

'Sterkmaking', in *Ad amicissimum amici scripsimus, Vriendenboek Raf Verstegen* (Bruges: Die Keure, 2004) p. 292

'Volmacht en sterkmaking bij oprichting van vennootschappen', in A. Benoit-Moury, O. Caprasse, N. Thirion and B. Tilleman (eds.), *De oprichting van vennootschappen en de opstartfase van de ondernemingen* (Brussels: Die Keure, 2003), p. 332

Van Gerven, W., *Bewindsbevoegdheid* (Brussels: Bruylant, 1962)

'Algemeen deel', in *Beginselen van Belgisch Privaatrecht*, I, (Antwerp: Story-Scientia, 1987), p. 227

Van Gerven, W., and Covemaeker, S., *Verbintenissenrecht* (Leuven: Acco, 2006)

Van Liempt, F., 'Hoever reikt het mandaat ad litem van een advocaat in het kader van een gerechtelijke vereffening-verdeling?', in W. Pintens and J. Du Mongh, (eds.), *Patrimonium 2006* (Antwerp: Intersentia, 2006), pp. 373–4

Van Oevelen, A., 'De juridische grondslag en de toepassingsvoorwaarden van de verbondenheid van de lastgever bij een schijnmandaat', *RW* 1989–90, 1429–30

Van Ommeslaghe, P., 'L'apparence comme source autonome d'obligation et le droit belge' (1983) *Rev Dr Int Comp* 154

Van Quickenborne, M., 'Le fondement de l'inopposabilité des contre-lettres', *RCJB* 1975, 268

Verbruggen, C., 'La théorie de l'apparence: quelques acquis et beaucoup d'incertitudes', in *Mélanges offerts à Pierre Van Ommeslaghe* (Brussels: Bruylant, 2000)

Verougstraete, I., 'Wil en vertrouwen bij het totstandkomen van overeenkomsten', *TPR* 1990, 1193

Wéry, P., *L'exécution forcée en nature des obligations contractuelles non pécuniaires* (Brussels: Kluwer, 1993)

'Droit des contrats, Le mandat', in *Répertoire Notarial* (Brussels: Larcier, 2000)

Chapter 4 (Germany)

Baumbach, A., and Hopt, K J., *Handelsgesetzbuch: HGB*, 33rd edn, (München: Beck-Verlag, 2008)

Bork, R., *Allgemeiner Teil des Bürgerlichen Gesetzbuchs*, 2nd edn (Tübingen: Mohr Siebeck-Verlag, 2006)

Canaris, C.-W., *Die Vertrauenshaftung im deutschen Privatrecht* (München: Beck-Verlag, 1971)

Flume, W., *Allgemeiner Teil des Bürgerlichen Rechts – Das Rechtsgeschäft*, vol. II (Berlin: Springer Verlag, 1965)

Krebs, P., C. Schmidt (ed.), *Münchener Kommentar zum Handelsgesetzbuch*, vol. 1, 2nd edn (München: Beck-Verlag, 2005)

Laband, P., 'Die Stellvertretung bei dem Abschluß von Rechtsgeschäften nach dem allgemeinen Deutschen Handelsgesetzbuch' (1866) 10 *ZHR*, 183

Larenz, K. and Wolf, M., *Allgemeiner Teil des Bürgerlichen Rechts*, 9th edn (München: Beck-Verlag, 2007)

Leipold, D., *BGB I: Einführung und allgemeiner Teil: ein Lehrbuch mit Fällen und Kontrollfragen*, 4th edn (Tübingen: Mohr Siebeck-Verlag, 2007)

Lobinger, T., *Rechtsgeschäftliche Verpflichtung und autonome Bindung* (Tübingen: Mohr Siebeck-Verlag, 1999)

Löwisch, M. and Neumann, D., *Allgemeiner Teil des BGB*, 7th edn (München: Beck-Verlag, 2004)

Lutter, M., P. Hommelhoff and W. Bayer *GmbH-Gesetz: Kommentar*, 16th edn (Köln: Otto Schmidt-Verlag, 2004)

Pentz, A., in W. Bayer (ed.), *Münchener Kommentar zum Aktiengesetz*, vol. I, 2nd edn (München: Beck-Verlag/Verlag Franz Vahlen, 2000)

Schilken, E., in J. von Staudingers Kommentar zum Bürgerlichen Gesetzbuch mit Einführungsgesetz und Nebengesetzen, 1st book – Allgemeiner Teil §§ 164–240, 15th edn (Berlin: Sellier – de Gruyter, 2004)

Schmidt-Kessel, M., in H. Prütting, G. Wegen and G. Weinreich, G., *BGB: Kommentar*, 2nd edn (Neuwied: Luchterhand-Verlag, 2007)

Schmidt-Kessel, M., *Handelsrecht – Unternehmensrecht*, in M. Schulze and R. Zuleeg, *Europarecht* (Baden-Baden: Nomos-Verlag, 2006)

Schramm, K.-H., in F. J. Säcker (ed.), *Münchener Kommentar zum Bürgerlichen Gesetzbuch*, vol. I §§ 1–240, 5th edn (München: Beck-Verlag, 2006)

Chapter 5 (The Netherlands)

van den Brink, V., 'Uitleg van rechtshandelingen of uitleg van gedingstukken', in H. J. Van Kooten, L. Strikwerda, L. Timmerman and H. M. Wattendorff (eds.), *Hartkampvariaties. Opstellen aangeboden aan prof. mr. A. S. Hartkamp ter gelegenheid van zijn afscheid als procureur-generaal bij de Hoge Raad der Nederlanden* (Deventer: Kluwer, 2006), pp. 1–13

Busch, D., *Indirect Representation in European Contract Law* (The Hague: Kluwer Law International, 2005)

'Uitleg van overeenkomsten' (2002) *NTBR* 410–13

Ernes, A. L. H., 'Schijn van volmacht op grond van functie?' (1999) 6346 *WPNR* 143–147

Onbevoegde vertegenwoordiging (Deventer: Kluwer, 2000)

'De positie van de tussenpersoon jegens een derde: instaan voor bestaan en omvang van een volmacht' (2005) *NTHR* 73–80

'Aanstellingsvolmacht, schijn van volmachtverlening en "usual authority"' (2004) *NTBR* 167–72

Florijn, E. O. H. P., *Ontstaan en ontwikkeling van het nieuwe Burgerlijk Wetboek*, (Maastricht: Universitaire Pers Maastricht, 1994)

Gepken-Jager, E. E. G., *Vertegenwoordiging bij NV en BV: Een rechtsvergelijkend onderzoek naar de uitvoering van artikel 9 eerste EG-richtlijn inzake het vennootschapsrecht* (Uitgave vanwege het Instituut voor Ondernemingsrecht Rijksuniversiteit Groningen no. 34) (Deventer: Kluwer, 2000)

Van der Grinten, W. C. L., *Lastgeving* (Monografieën Nieuw BW: B-serie; 81) (Deventer: Kluwer, 1999)

Haanappel, P. P. C., Mackaay E., *New Netherlands Civil Code: Patrimonial Law (Property, Obligations and Special Contracts)*, (Deventer/Boston: Kluwer Law and Taxation Publishers, 1990)

New Netherlands Civil Code: Patrimonial Law (Property, Obligations and Special Contracts) (The Hague/London/New York: Kluwer Law International, 1999) (CD-ROM edition)

Hartkamp, A. S., 'Bekrachtiging van nietige rechtshandelingen in het nieuwe burgerlijk wetboek', in P. Abas, N. J. P. Giltay Veth, Y. Scholten and G. J. Wolffensperger (eds.), *Non sine causa: opstellen aangeboden aan Prof. Mr. G. J. Scholten ter gelegenheid van zijn afscheid als hoogleraar aan de Universiteit van Amsterdam* (Zwolle: Tjeenk Willink, 1979), pp. 115–134

Hartkamp, A. S. and Sieburgh, C. H., *Mr. C. Asser's Handleiding tot de beoefening van het Nederlands burgerlijk recht, Verbintenissenrecht, Algemene leer der overeenkomsten*, 12th edn (Deventer: *Kluwer* 2005)

Hijma, J., van Dam, C. C., van Schendel, W. A. M. and W. L. Valk, *Rechtshandeling en Overeenkomst* (Studiereeks Burgerlijk Recht deel 3), 5th edn (Deventer: Kluwer, 2007)

de Kluiver, H. J., 'Bekrachtiging van rechtshandelingen en besluiten. Over Art. 3:58 BW als vangnet en trampoline', in S. C. J. J. Kortmann, N. E. D. Faber and J. A. M. Strens-Meulemeester (eds.), *Vertegenwoordiging en tussenpersoon* (Serie Onderneming en Recht deel 17) (Deventer: Tjeenk Willink, 1999), pp. 69–88

Koppert-Van Beek, M. S., *Handelen namens een op te richten vennootschap* (Deventer: Kluwer, 2003)

Kortmann, S. C. J. J., *Mr. C. Asser's Handleiding tot de beoefening van het Nederlands burgerlijk recht, Vertegenwoordiging en rechtspersoon, De vertegenwoordiging*, 8th edn (Deventer: Kluwer, 2004)

Maeijer, J. M. M., *Mr. C. Asser's Handleiding tot de beoefening van het Nederlands burgerlijk recht, Vertegenwoordiging en rechtspersoon, De rechtspersoon*, 8th edn (Deventer: Tjeenk Willink, 1997)

Nieskens-Isphording, B. W. M., van der Putt-Lauwers, A. E. M., *Derdenbescherming* (Monografieën Nieuw BW. A-serie; 22), 3rd edn (Deventer: Kluwer, 2002)

du Perron, C. E., *Overeenkomst en derden* (Deventer: Kluwer, 1999)

Reehuis, W. H. M. and E. E. Slob (eds.), *Invoering Boeken 3, 5 en 6, Parlementaire Geschiedenis van het nieuwe Burgerlijk Wetboek, Boek 3, Vermogensrecht in het algemeen* (Deventer: Kluwer, 1990)

van Schaick, A. C., *Volmacht (Monografieën Nieuw BW. B-serie; 5)* (Deventer: Kluwer, 1999)

van Schilfgaarde, P., 'Uitleg van rechtshandelingen' (1997) 6282 *WPNR*, 587–592;
(1997) 6283 *WPNR*, 611–615, reprinted in *Peter van Schilfgaarde Select.
Een bloemlezing uit zijn werk* (Uitgaven vanwege het Instituut voor
Ondernemingsrecht, Rijksuniversiteit Groningen, nr. 35) (Deventer: Kluwer,
2000), pp. 385–408
'Vertegenwoordiging' (1974) 5280 *WPNR*, 669–676; (1974) 5281 *WPNR*, 693–700;
reprinted in *Peter van Schilfgaarde Select. Een bloemlezing uit zijn werk*
(Uitgaven vanwege het Instituut voor Ondernemingsrecht, Rijksuniversiteit
Groningen, nr. 35) (Deventer Kluwer, 2000), pp. 39–70
Schoordijk, H. C. F., *Vermogensrecht in het algemeen naar Boek 3 van het nieuwe
BW (titel 1t/m 5, titel 11)* (Deventer: Kluwer, 1986)
Het handelen ten behoeve van de vennootschap in oprichting (Ars Notariatus
nr. 47) (Amsterdam: Stichting tot Bevordering der Notariële Wetenschap,
1990)
'Het leerstuk van de opgewekte schijn van volmacht en de Engels-
Amerikaansrechtelijke leer van de "apparent authority"', in *Honderd jaar
rechtsleven. De Nederlandse Juristen-Vereniging 1870-1970*, (Zwolle: Tjeenk
Willink, 1970), pp. 1–24; reprinted in Van Dunné, J M, Nieuwenhuis,
J H, Vranken, J B M (eds), *Verspreid werk van Prof. Mr. H. C. F. Schoordijk*,
(Deventer: Kluwer 1991), pp. 197–221
Sütö, V. J. A., 'De invloed van Meijers' rechtsvergelijkende expertise op zijn toelichting
bij het ontwerp van volmacht 1954', in C. J. H. Jansen and M. van de Vrugt
(eds.), *Recht en geschiedenis* (Nijmegen Ars Aequi Libri, 1999), pp. 169–81
*Nieuw Vermogensrecht en rechtsvergelijking–reconstructie van een wetgeving-
sproces (1947-1961)* (Den Haag: Boom Juridische uitgevers, 2004)
Tjong Tjin Tai, T. F. E., 'Driemaal schijnvolmacht' (2001) *NbBW* 70–3
Vranken, J. B. M., *Mededelings-, informatie- en onderzoeksplichten in het verbintenissenrecht* (Zwolle: Tjeenk Willink, 1989)
van Zeben, C. J., J. W. Du Pon and M. M. Olthof (eds.), *Parlementaire Geschiedenis
van het nieuwe Burgerlijk Wetboek, Boek 3, Vermogensrecht in het algemeen*
(Deventer: Kluwer, 1981)
Zwitser, R., 'De aansprakelijkheid van de onbevoegde vertegenwoordiger naar
Burgerlijk recht en Handelsrecht' (1999) *NTBR* 199–208

Chapter 6 (England)

American Law Institute, *Restatement of the Law, Second: Agency* (St Paul, MN:
American Law Institute, 1958)
American Law Institute, *Restatement of the Law, Third: Agency* (St Paul, MN:
American Law Institute, 2006)
Bester, D. H., 'The Scope of an Agent's Power of Representation' (1972) 89 *SALJ* 49–70
Brown, I. 'The Agent's Apparent Authority: Paradigm or Paradox?' (1995) *JBL* 360–372

Conant, M., 'The Objective Theory of Agency: Apparent Authority and the Estoppel of Apparent Ownership' (1968) 47 *Neb L Rev* 678–704

Cook, W. W., 'Agency by Estoppel' (1905) 5 *Colum L Rev* 536–47

'Agency by Estoppel: A Reply' (1906) *Colum L Rev* 34–44

Fridman, G. H. L., *The Law of Agency*, 7th edn (London: Butterworths, 1996)

Fry, E. (ed. G. R. Northcote), *A Treatise on the Specific Performance of Contracts*, 3rd edn (London: Stevens, 1892)

A Treatise on the Specific Performance of Contracts, 6th edn (London: Stevens, 1921)

Mayson, S., French, D. and Ryan, C., *Mayson, French and Ryan on Company Law*, 24th edn (Oxford: Oxford University Press, 2007)

Morse, G., *Charlesworth's Company Law*, 17th edn (London: Sweet & Maxwell, 2005)

Müller-Freienfels, W., 'Law of Agency' (1957) 6 *Am J Comp L* 165–188

Omar, P. J., 'Crossing Time's Boundaries: A Comparative View of Legal Responses to the Pre-Incorporation Contract' (2005) *Sing JLS* 76–92

Pappas, T. G., 'Rescission by Third Party Prior to Principal's Ratification of Agent's Unauthorized Action' (1948) 2 *Vand L Rev* 100–108

Powell, R., *The Law of Agency*, 2nd edn (London: Pitman & Sons Ltd, 1961)

Reynolds, F. M. B., *Bowstead and Reynolds on Agency* 15th edn (London: Sweet & Maxwell, 1985)

'Some Agency Problems in Insurance Law', in F. D. Rose (ed.), *Consensus ad Idem: Essays in the Law of Contract in Honour of Guenter Treitel* (London: Sweet & Maxwell, 1996), pp. 77–95

Bowstead and Reynolds on Agency, 18th edn (London: Sweet & Maxwell, 2006)

Stoljar, S. J., *The Law of Agency: Its History and Present Principles* (London: Sweet & Maxwell, 1961)

Tan, C.-H., 'The Principle in *Bird* v. *Brown* Revisited' (2001) 117 *LQR* 626–644

'Undisclosed Principals and Contract' (2004) 120 *LQR* 480–509

Tan, C.-H. and Tjio, H., 'Rethinking Apparent Authority', in A. Tan and A. Sharom (eds.), *Developments in Singapore and Malaysian Law: Proceedings of the National University of Singapore – University of Malaya Centennial Symposia 2005* (Singapore: Marshall Cavendish, 2006), pp. 50–88.

Wambaugh, E., 'A Problem as to Ratification' (1895) 9 *Harv L Rev* 60–71

Wright, C. A., 'The American Law Institute's Restatement of Contracts and Agency' (1935) 1 *UTLJ* 17–52

Winfield, P. H., *Pollock's Principles of Contract*, 13th edn (London: Stevens & Sons, 1950)

Chapter 7 (The United States)

American Law Institute, *Restatement of the Law, Second: Agency* (St Paul, MN: American Law Institute, 1958)

American Law Institute, *Restatement of the Law, Third: Agency* (St Paul, MN: American Law Institute, 2006)

DeMott, D. A., 'Statutory Ingredients in Common Law Change: Issues in the Development of Agency Doctrine', in S. Worthington (ed.), *Commercial Law and Commercial Practice* (Oxford: Hart, 2003), pp. 57–83

Duxbury, N., *Patterns of American Jurisprudence* (Oxford: Clarendon Press, 1995)

Fishman, S. A., 'Inherent Agency Power – Should Enterprise Liability Apply to Agents' Unauthorised Contracts?' (1987) 19 *Rutgers LJ* 1–57

Friedman, L. M., *A History of American Law* (New York: Simon & Schuster, 1973)

Ingram, J. D., 'Inherent Agency Powers: A Mistaken Concept Which Should Be Discarded' (2004) 29 *Okla City U L Rev* 583–95

Kalman, L., *Legal Realism at Yale* (Chapel Hill, NC: University of North Carolina Press, 1986)

King, D. B., and Seavey, W. A., *A Harvard Law School Professor: Warren A. Seavey's Life and the World of Legal Education* (Buffalo, NY: W. S. Hein, 2005)

McMeel, G., 'Philosophical Foundations of the Law of Agency' (2000) 116 *LQR* 387–411

Mechem, F. R., *A Treatise on the Law of Agency, Including Not Only a Discussion of the General Subject, But Also Special Chapters on Attorneys, Auctioneers, Brokers and Factors*, 2 vols, 2nd edn (Chicago: Callaghan, 1914)

Pulliam, S. and Zuckerman, G., 'SEC Examines Rebates Paid to Large Funds', *Wall Street Journal*, 6 January 2005, pp. C1, C4

Reynolds, F. M. B., 'Apparent Authority And Illegible Signatures', (2005) 121 *LQR* 55–6

Story, J., *Commentaries on the Law of Agency as a Branch of Commercial and Maritime Jurisprudence*, 9th edn, by C. P. Greenough (Boston: Little Brown, 1882)

Ward, M. P., 'A Restatement or a Redefinition: Elimination of Inherent Agency Power in the Tentative Draft of the Restatement (Third) of Agency' (2002) 59 *Wash & Lee LR* 1585–633

Watts, P., 'The Creep of Negligence into Agency Law in Australia', (2005) 26 *Aust Bar Rev* 185–92

White, G. E., *Tort Law in America: An Intellectual History*, expanded edn (Oxford: Oxford University Press, 2004)

Winfield, P. H., *Pollock's Principles of Contract*, 13th edn (London: Stevens & Sons, 1950)

Chapter 8 (American *Restatements* and other common law countries)

American Law Institute, *Restatement of the Law, Second: Agency* (St Paul, MN: American Law Institute, 1958)

American Law Institute, *Restatement of the Law, Third: Agency* (St Paul, MN: American Law Institute, 2006)

Dal Pont, G. E., *The Law of Agency* 2nd edn (Chatsworth, NSW: Butterworths, Australia, 2008)

Fry, E., *A Treatise on the Specific Performance of Contracts*, 3rd edn (London, Stevens: 1892)

Gardner, S., 'The Remedial Discretion in Proprietary Estoppel – Again' (2006) 120 *LQR* 492–512

Haudley, K. R., *Estoppel by Conduct and Election* (London: Sweet & Maxwell, 2006)

Kötz, H. (trans. T. Weir), *European Contract Law I* (Oxford: Clarendon Press, 1997)

Reynolds, F. M. B., *Bowstead & Reynolds on Agency*, 18th edn (London: Sweet & Maxwell, 2006)

Chapter 9 (Scotland)

Atiyah, P. S., *The Rise and Fall of Freedom of Contract* (Oxford: Clarendon Press, 1979)

Balfour, J., *Balfour's Prackticks* (Edinburgh: Gregg Associates for the Stair Society, 1754, reprinted 1962–63)

Bell, G. J., *Principles of the Law of Scotland*, 10th edn, by W. Guthrie (Edinburgh: W. Blackwood, 1899; reprinted 1989)

 Commentaries on the Law of Scotland and on the Principles of Mercantile Jurisprudence, 7th edn, by J. McLaren (Edinburgh: T. & T. Clark, 1870; reprinted 1990)

Bonell, M. J., 'Agency' in: Hartkamp, A., Hesselink, M., Hondius, E. *et al.* (eds.) *Towards a European Civil Code*, 3rd edn (Nijmegen/The Hague: Ars Aequi Libri/Kluwer Law International, 2004), pp. 381–97

Brown, I., 'The Agent's Apparent Authority: Paradigm or Paradox?' (1995) *JBL* 360–72

Coulsfield, Lord *et al.*, (eds.), *Gloag and Henderson's The Law of Scotland*, 12th edn (Edinburgh: W. Green, 2007)

Davidson, F., and Macgregor, L., *Commercial Law in Scotland*, 2nd edn (Edinburgh: W. Green, 2008)

Dirleton, J. N., *Some Doubts and Questions, in the Law, Especially of Scotland* (Edinburgh: George Mosman, published posthumously, 1698)

Dunedin, Viscount, Wark, J. L. and Black, A. C. (eds.), *Encyclopaedia of the Laws of Scotland*, 1st edn (Edinburgh: W. Green & Sons Ltd, 1913) vol. I

Erskine, J., *An Institute of the Law of Scotland*, J. B. Nicholson (ed.), 8th edn (Edinburgh: Butterworths/Law Society of Scotland, 1871; reprinted 1989)

Feltham, P., and Hochberg, D. and Leech, T., in S. Bower, *The Law Relating to Estoppel by Representation*, 4th edn (London, Butterworths, 2004)

Fridman, G. H. L., *The Law of Agency*, 7th edn (London: Butterworths, 1996)

Gloag, W. M., *The Law of Contract, a Treatise on the Principles of Contract in the Law of Scotland*, 2nd edn (Edinburgh: W. Green, 1929)

Gow, J. J., *The Mercantile and Industrial Law of Scotland* (Edinburgh: W. Green, 1964)

Leake, S. M., *Principles of the Law of Contracts*, 6th edn (London: Stevens & Sons, 1911)

Macgregor, L., 'Agency and Mandate', in *The Laws of Scotland: Stair Memorial Encyclopaedia*, Reissue (Edinburgh: Butterworths, 2002)

'Specific Implement in Scots law', in J. Smits, D. Haas and G. Hesen (eds), *Specific Performance in Contract Law: National and Other Perspectives* (Antwerp and London: Intersentia, 2008) pp. 67–91

Mackenzie Stuart, A. J., 'Contract and Quasi-contract' in, D. M. Walker (ed.), *An Introduction to Scottish Legal History* (Edinburgh: W. Green, 1992), pp. 241–64

MacQueen, H. L., 'Promoter's Contracts, Agency and the *Jus Quaesitum Tertio*' 1982 *SLT* 257–61

'Obligations' in Sir T. B. Smith *et al.* (eds.), *The Laws of Scotland: Stair Memorial Encyclopaedia* (Edinburgh: Butterworths/Law Society of Scotland, 1987–96), vol. XV

'Good Faith', in H. MacQueen and R. Zimmermann (eds.), *European Contract Law: Scots and South African Perspectives* (Edinburgh: Edinburgh University Press, 2006), pp. 43–73

MacQueen, H. and Zimmermann, R. (eds.), *European Contract Law: Scots and South African Perspectives* (Edinburgh: Edinburgh University Press, 2006)

Mayson, S., French, D. and Ryan, C., *Mayson, French and Ryan on Company Law*, 24th edn, (Oxford: Oxford University Press, 2007–8)

McBryde, W. W., *The Law of Contract in Scotland*, 3rd edn (Edinburgh: W. Green, 2007)

Pothier, R. J., *Treatise on the Law of Obligations* (London: A. Strahan, 1806)

Powell, R., *Law of Agency*, 2nd edn (London: Pitman, 1961)

Rankine, J., *A Treatise on the Law of Personal Bar in Scotland: Collated with the English law of Estoppel in Pais* (Edinburgh: W. Green, 1921)

Reid, E. C., 'Acquiescence in the Air: *William Grant* v. *Glen Catrine Bonded Ware*' (2001) *JR* 191–9

'Personal Bar: Case-law in Search of Principle' (2003) *EdinLR* 340–66

Reid, E. C., and Blackie, J. W. G., *Personal Bar* (Edinburgh: W. Green, 2006)

Reid, K., and Zimmermann, R. (eds.), *A History of Private Law in Scotland* (Oxford: Oxford University Press, 2000)

Reynolds, F. M. B., *Bowstead and Reynolds on Agency*, 18th edn (London: Sweet & Maxwell, 2006)

Reynolds, F. M. B. and Davenport B. J., *Bowstead on Agency*, 14th edn (London: Sweet & Maxwell, 1976)

Smith, T. B., *Short Commentary on the Law of Scotland* (Edinburgh: W. Green, 1962)

Smith, Sir T. B., *et al.* (eds.), *The Laws of Scotland: Stair Memorial Encyclopaedia* (Edinburgh: Butterworths / Law Society of Scotland, 1987–96)

Stair, 1st Viscount (James Dalrymple), *Institutions of the Law of Scotland*, D. M., Walker (ed.), 6th edn (Glasgow and Edinburgh: The University Presses of Glasgow and Edinburgh, 1981)

Steyn, J., 'Written Contracts: To What Extent May Evidence Control Language?' (1988) 41 *CLP* 23–32

'Contract Law: Fulfilling the Reasonable Expectations of Honest Men' (1997) 113 *LQR* 433–42

Stoljar, S. J., *The Law of Agency* (London: Sweet & Maxwell, 1961)

Story, J., *Commentaries on the Law of Agency as a branch of commercial and maritime jurisprudence*, 9th edn by C. P. Greenough (Boston, MA: Little Brown, 1882)

Tan, C.-H., 'The Principle in *Bird v Brown* Revisited' (2001) 117 *LQR* 626–44

Trotter, W. F., *The Law of Contract in Scotland* (Edinburgh: W. Hodge, 1913)

Voet, J., *Commentarius ad Pandectas: in quo, praeter romani juris principia ac controversias illustriores, jus etiam hodiernam, et praecipuae fori quaestiones excutiuntur. Editio sexta* (The Hague: Hagea comitum, 1731) 2 v

Zimmermann, R., Visser, D. and Reid, K. G. C. (eds.), *Mixed Legal Systems in Comparative Perspective* (Oxford: Oxford University Press, 2004)

Chapter 10 (South Africa)

American Law Institute, *Restatement of the Law, Second: Agency* (St Paul, MN: American Law Institute, 1958)

Beinart, B., 'The English Legal Contribution in South Africa: The Interaction of Civil and Common Law' (1981) *Acta Juridica* 7

Bester, D. H., 'Scope of an Agent's Power of Representation' (1972) 89 *SALJ* 49

Blackman, M. S. *et al.*, 'Companies', in W. A. Joubert *et al.* (eds.), *The Law of South Africa*, 1st re-issue (Durban: Butterworths, 1993 onwards), vol. 4(1)

Cilliers, H. S. and Benade, M. L., *Corporate Law*, 3rd edn (Durban: LexisNexis Butterworths, 2000)

De Villiers, J. E. R. and Macintosh, J. C., *The Law of Agency in South Africa*, 3rd edn, by J. M. Silke (Cape Town, Juta, 1981)

De Wet, J. C. and Van Wyk, A. H., *Die Suid-Afrikaanse Kontraktereg en Handelsreg*, 5th edn, 2 vols. (Durban: Butterworths, 1992)

Fourie, J. S. A., 'Die wisselwerking tussen Suid-Afrikaanse maatskappyeregleerstukke' (1988) 51 *THRHR* 218–27

'Volmagbeperkings en Ultra Vires Handelinge – Aspekte can Artikel 36 van die Maatskappywet in Oenskou' (1990) 1 *Stellenbosch L Rev* 388–99

Gibson, J. T. R., *South African Mercantile and Company Law*, 8th edn (Cape Town: Juta, 2003)

Grotius, H, *De Jure Belli Ac Pacis Libri Tres*, vol. 2, Book 1 (trans. F. W. Kelsey) (Oxford: Clarendon Press, 1925)

Opinion No. 73, *Consultatien, Advysen en Advertissementen, gegeven en geschreven bij verscheiden treffelijke rechts-geleerden in Holland*, (Rotterdam: Isaak Naerus, 1662–83), vol. III

Hahlo, H. R. and Kahn, E., *The Union of South Africa: The Development of its Laws and Constitution* (London: Stevens, 1960)

Harker, J. R., 'The Liability of an Agent for Breach of Warranty of Authority' (1985) 102 *SALJ* 596–603

Joubert, D. J., 'Die Waarborg van Volmagsbestaan' (1969) 32 *THRHR* 109–25
Die Suid-Afrikaanse Verteenwoordigingsreg (Cape Town: Juta, 1979)
'Agency and *Stipulatio Alteri*', in R. Zimmerman and D. Visser (eds.), *Southern Cross: Civil Law and Common Law in South Africa* (Oxford: Clarendon, 1996), pp. 335–57

Jooste, R., 'The Law of Agency' (1975) *Annual Survey of South African Law* 95
'When do Pre-Incorporation Contracts have Retrospective Effect?' (1989) 106 *SALJ* 507–16

Kerr, A. J., *An Introduction to Roman Dutch Law*, 5th edn (Oxford: Clarendon, 1953)
'Causation in Estoppel by Misrepresentation' (1977) 94 *SALJ* 270
The Law of Agency, 4th edn (Durban: Butterworths, 2006)

Meskin, P. M., Kunst, J. A. and Schmidt, K. E. (eds.), *Henochsberg on the Companies Act*, 5th edn, 2 vols. (looseleaf) (Durban: Butterworths, 1994)

Mc Lennan, J. S., 'Some Thoughts on Remedies for an Agent's Breach of Warranty of Authority' (1987) 104 *SALJ* 321

Neethling, J., Potgieter, J. M., and Visser, P. J., *The Law of Delict*, 5th edn (Durban: LexisNexis Butterworths, 2006)

Pothier, R. J., (trans. B. G. Rogers and B. X. de Wet), *Treatise on the Contract of Mandate* (Johannesburg: Lex Patria, 1979)

Rabie, P. J., 'Estoppel', in W. A. Joubert *et al.* (eds.), *The Law of South Africa*, 1st re-issue, 34 vols. (Durban: Butterworths, 1993 onwards), vol. 9, pp. 266–83

Reynolds, F. M. B., *Bowstead on Agency*, 15th edn (London: Sweet & Maxwell, 1985)
Bowstead and Reynolds on Agency, 18th edn (London: Sweet & Maxwell, 2006)

Sonnekus J. C., *Rabie's The Law of Estoppel in South Africa*, 2nd edn (Durban: Butterworths, 2000)
'Skynverwekking en 'n Verdeelde Appelhof' (2003) 14 *Stellenbosch L Rev* 29

Spencer Bower, G., *The Law Relating to Estoppel by Representation*, 4th edn, by P. Feltham, D. Hochberg and T. Leech (London: Butterworths, 2004)

Story, J., *Commentaries on the Law of Agency as a Branch of Commercial and Maritime Jurspindence*, 9th edn. by C. P. Greenough (Boston: Little Brown, 1882)

van der Merwe, N. J., 'Wanbeskouings oor Wanvoorstelling' (1964) *THRHR* 194–202 van der Walt, J., 'Wat word van die nadeelvereiste by bedrog en estoppel?' (1973) *THRHR* 386-95

van Jaarsveld, S. R., *Die Leerstuk van Ratifikasie in die Suid-Afrikaanse Verteenwordigingsreg* (Cape Town: HAUM, 1974)

Voet, J., *Commontarius ad Pandectas* (Cape Town: J. C. Juta, 1879)

Wanda, B. P. (original text by J. C. de Wet), 'Agency and Representation', in W. A. Joubert *et al.* (eds.), *The Law of South Africa*, 2nd edn, 34 vols. (Durban: LexisNexis Butterworths, 2003), vol. 1, pp. 167–223

Zimmermann, R., 'Good Faith and Equity', in R. Zimmerman and D. Visser (eds.), *Southern Cross: Civil Law and Common Law in South Africa* (Oxford: Clarendon, 1996), pp. 221–7

Chapter 11 (The principles of European contract law)

Busch, D., *Indirect Representation in European Contract Law* (The Hague: Kluwer Law International, 2005)

Hartkamp, A. S., 'Principles of Contract Law', in A. Hartkamp, M. Hesselink, E. Hondius, *et al.* (eds.) *Towards a European Civil Code*, 3rd edn, (Nijmegen/ The Hague: Ars Aequi Libri/Kluwer Law International, 2004), pp. 125–43

Lando, O. and Beale, H. (eds.) *Principles of European Contract Law. Part I: Performance, Non-performance and Remedies*, (Dordrecht/London/Boston: Martinus Nijhoff Publishers, 1995)

(eds.), *Principles of European Contract Law. Parts I and II*, (The Hague/ London/Boston: Kluwer Law International, 2000)

Lando, O., Clive, E., Prüm, A. and Zimmermann, R. (eds.), *Principles of European Contract Law. Part III* (The Hague: Kluwer Law International, 2003)

Verhagen, H. L. E., 'Comment on Arts. 3:201 and 3:202 PECL', in D. Busch, E. Hondius, H. van Kooten, *et al.* (eds), *The Principles of European Contract Law and Dutch Law. A Commentary* (The Hague/London/New York/ Nijmegen: Ars Aequi Libri/Kluwer Law International, 2002), pp. 141–50

Zimmermann, R., 'The Principles of European Contract Law. Contemporary Manifestation of the Old, and Possible Foundation for a New, European Scholarship of Private Law', in F. Faust and G. Thüsing (eds.), *Beyond Borders: Perspectives on International and Comparative Law, Symposium in Honour of Hein Kötz* (Köln: Carl Heymanns Verlag, 2006), pp. 111–47

Chapter 12 (UNIDROIT Principles of international commercial contracts)

Bonell, M. J., 'Agency', in A. Hartkamp, M. Hesselink, E. Hondius *et al.* (eds.), *Towards a European Civil Code*, 3rd edn (Nijmegen/The Hague: Ars Aequi Libri/Kluwer Law International, 2004), pp. 381–97

Busch, D., *Indirect Representation in European Contract Law* (The Hague: Kluwer Law International, 2005)

Reynolds, F. M. B., 'Authority of agents' (2005) *ICC International Court of Arbitration Bulletin*, Special Supplement, UNIDROIT Principles: New Developments and Applications, pp. 9–16

Chapter 13 (Comparative law evaluation)

Gloag, W. M., *The Law of Contract, a Treatise on the Principles of Contract in the Law of Scotland*, 3rd edn (Edinburgh: W. Green, 1929)

Macgregor, L., 'Agency and Mandate', in *The Laws of Scotland: Stair Memorial Encyclopaedia*, Reissue (Edinburgh: Butterworths, 2002)

McBryde, W. W., *The Law of Contract in Scotland*, 3rd edn (Edinburgh: W. Green, 2007)

Peel, E., *Treitel: The Law of Contract*, 12th edn (London: Sweet & Maxwell, 2007)

Reynolds, F. M. B., 'Authority of Agents' (2005) *ICC International Court of Arbitration Bulletin*, Special Supplement, UNIDROIT Principles: New Developments and Applications, 9–16

Bowstead & Reynolds on Agency, 18th edn (London: Sweet & Maxwell, 2006)

Tan, C.-H., 'Undisclosed Principals and Contract' (2004) 120 *LQR* 480–509

Verhagen, H. L. E., 'Comment on Art. 3:207 PECL', in D. Busch, E. Hondius, H. van Kooten, *et al.* (eds.), *The Principles of European Contract Law and Dutch Law. A Commentary* (The Hague/London/New York/Nijmegen: Ars Aequi Libri/Kluwer Law International, 2002), pp. 163–6

Chapter 14 (Comparative conclusions)

Gloag, W. M., *The Law of Contract, a Treatise on the Principles of Contract in the Law of Scotland*, 2nd edn (Edinburg: W. Green, 1929)

Lévy-Ullman, H. (trans. F. P. Walton), 'The Law of Scotland' 1925 *JR* 370–91

Macgregor, L., 'Agency', in H. MacQueen and R. Zimmermann, (eds.), *European Contract Law: Scots and South African Perspectives* (Edinburgh: Edinburgh University Press, 2006) pp. 123–50

MacQueen, H., 'Promoter's Contracts, Agency and the *Jus Quaesitum Tertio*' 1982 *SLT* 257–61

'Obligations', in Sir T. B. Smith *et al.* (eds.), *The Laws of Scotland: Stair Memorial Encyclopaedia* (Edinburgh: Butterworths/Law Society of Scotland, 1987–96), vol. XV

Pothier, R. J., *Treatise on the Law of Obligations* (London: A. Strahan, 1806)

Reid, E. C. and Blackie, J. G., *Personal Bar* (Edinburgh: W Green, 2006)

Sonnekus, J. C., *Rabie's The Law of Estoppel in South Africa*, 2nd edn (Durban: Butterworths, 2000)

INDEX